Criminology

McGraw-Hill Series in Criminology and Criminal Justice

Binder and Geis: Methods of Research in Criminology and Criminal Justice

Bonn: Criminology

Callison: Introduction to Community-Based Corrections

De Forest, Gaensslen, and Lee: Forensic Science: An Introduction to Criminalistics

Klockars: Thinking about Police: Contemporary Readings

Nettler: Explaining Crime

Walker: The Police in America: An Introduction

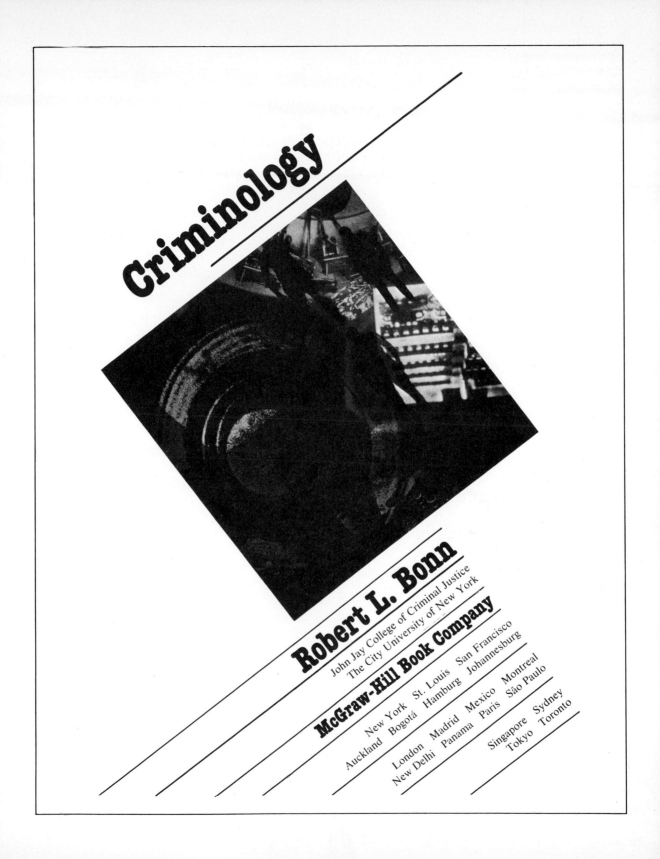

Criminology

Robert L. Bonn
John Jay College of Criminal Justice
The City University of New York

McGraw-Hill Book Company

New York   St. Louis   San Francisco
Auckland   Bogotá   Hamburg   Johannesburg
London   Madrid   Mexico   Montreal
New Delhi   Panama   Paris   São Paulo
Singapore   Sydney
Tokyo   Toronto

Criminology

234567890DOCDOC8987654

ISBN 0-07-006457-1

*See Acknowledgments on pages 503-504. Copyrights included on this
page by reference.*

This book was set in Times Roman by Santype-Byrd.
The editors were Christina Mediate, Allan Forsyth, and Susan Gamer;
the designer was Jo Jones;
the production supervisor was Diane Renda.
The photo editors were Linda Gutierrez and Kenneth Mallor;
cover photograph by H. Armstrong Roberts, Inc.
The drawings were done by Fine Line Illustrations, Inc.
R. R. Donnelley & Sons Company was printer and binder.

Library of Congress Cataloging in Publication Data

Bonn, Robert (Robert L.)
    Criminology.

    (McGraw-Hill series in criminology and criminal
justice)
    Includes bibliographical references and indexes.
    1. Crime and criminals. I. Title. II. Series.
HV6025.B66 1984   364   83-13565
ISBN 0-07-006457-1

Credits for Part-Opening Photographs
One   CHARLES GATEWOOD
Two   ARTHUR TRESS/PHOTO RESEARCHERS
Three LEONARD FREED/MAGNUM
Four   CHARLES GATEWOOD

To Ethel, Timothy, and Eti

Contents

Part Four   The Criminal Justice System

List of Boxes

Preface

Crime is an intriguing and complex subject. Virtually everyone has been victimized by crime. Virtually everyone has committed a criminal act at some point in his or her life. Crime encompasses a broad range of antisocial activities: murder, rape, robbery, assault, burglary, larceny, motor vehicle theft, marketing of defective products, some forms of price fixing, stealing from employers, some deviant sexual activities, some forms of substance abuse, some kinds of gambling, networks that organize criminal activity, and certain activities seen as threatening to the political or social order. Our response to crime is often emotional: fear, anger, outrage, and disgust are typical. Yet crime is also a source of endless fascination. It makes news every day, and it also provides the setting for much fictional entertainment. Crime, in fact, receives constant coverage by television, radio, newspapers, magazines, and books.

This book is about criminology, the academic discipline which employs scientific methodology to study crime. Criminology asks how much crime there is, what major forms it can assume, why it exists, and how the criminal justice system responds to it. In providing insight into crime, criminology deals with five key topics: *criminal acts, criminal offenders, victims of crime,* the *social contexts* within which crime occurs, and the *criminal justice system*.

COVERAGE

In writing this book, I have attempted to provide a comprehensive, balanced, clearly written work that does justice to the subject of crime and the discipline of criminology. Thus, the book includes analyses of theories of crime, data on crime, and the criminal justice system. My intent is to enable readers to appreciate the complexity and subtlety of the problem of crime while leaving them free to examine theoretical perspectives and to select the viewpoints that appear most reasonable to them. In this spirit, both "mainstream" and "conflict" perspectives are presented in detail at various points; and both "street crime" and middle- or upper-class crime are examined in depth.

ORGANIZATION

Part One of this book is a general introduction to criminology. The book opens with a chapter dealing with the definition of crime and criminology (Chapter 1), a chapter which draws on the recent historical research to discuss crime in the United States generally (Chapter 2), and a chapter on crime statistics (Chapter 3).

The first four of the five key criminological topics are the organizational basis for Parts Two and Three. In Part Two, one chapter is devoted to criminological work that has taken the *criminal act* as its focal point; two chapters are devoted to *criminal offenders*; one chapter is devoted to *victims*, and one to *social contexts*. Approaching criminology in this manner results in some overlap and duplication; certain criminological theories appear in more than one chapter. However, this approach provides clarity because it organizes criminology in terms of the topics discussed by criminologists. Moreover, this topical approach serves as an organizing structure for the chapters on types of crime in Part Three. Thus, for each of the seven major types of crime in American society, I discuss the criminal act, the criminal offender, the victim, and the social context.

The fifth criminological topic, the *criminal justice system*, is handled in Part Four. This topic has received extensive attention in recent years. My approach is to give equal weight to the three main parts of the system by devoting one chapter to the police, another to the courts, and a third to corrections. In each of these chapters, I identify three perspectives that can be used to understand the structure and operation of that part of the system.

Part Four closes with a chapter on alternatives to the criminal justice system (Chapter 19). This final chapter, an optimistic one, reflects my conviction that although the complete elimination of crime is an unrealistic goal, significant steps can be taken to reduce or curb crime. Chapter 19 describes some possible first steps, following the analytical scheme of Parts Two and Three: redefining criminal acts, rehabilitating criminal offenders, helping victims of crime, and restructuring social contexts of crime.

Finally, there is an instructor's manual which provides suggestions for classroom instruction and a test bank of multiple-choice and essay questions. The manual can be obtained from the McGraw-Hill Book Company. A student study guide is also available, for self-paced study or for classroom use.

SOME PERSONAL NOTES

This book has its roots in my experience of teaching criminology at the John Jay College of Criminal Justice (The City University of New York) over the past ten years. My students come from diverse backgrounds. Some are police, court, and correctional officers; others are aspiring to these positions. Still others are college students who are interested in learning about crime. Quite a few have been victimized by crime; some have been arrested, convicted, and imprisoned for crimes they have committed. Whatever their background, their reactions to criminological thinking have encouraged me at many points to rethink, reevaluate, and explain afresh what criminology is all about.

A number of people have aided and supported me in various ways in the writing of this book. First, there were my colleagues at John Jay. Israel Gerver, Richard Korn, Robert Lin, and the late Arthur Niederhoffer provided helpful reviews and suggestions about the manuscript in its early stages. Charles Lindner made constructive comments about the chapter on criminal courts. Special thanks must go to Alexander Smith, whose support and encouragement throughout the entire project were invaluable. Finally, the cooperation of the library staff combined with the strong criminal justice library resources at John Jay greatly facilitated my work.

Second, the book has also benefited from the comments and criticisms of outside reviewers; in particular, Ronald A. Farrell, Robert F. Meier, Peter L. Sissons, Victoria L. Swigert, and an anonymous reviewer. Each outside reviewer provided important critical input at various points in the development of the book. Without doubt, their comments made the book richer and clearer, although the final responsibility for the contents of the book is mine alone.

Finally, the editorial staff at McGraw-Hill deserves to be acknowledged for kindly advice and support, with special thanks to Allan Forsyth, Christina Mediate, Susan Gamer, and Eric Munson. Their guidance in steering the manuscript through its sequence of developmental stages has been most appreciated.

Robert L. Bonn

Criminology

PART ONE

Criminology and the Issue of Crime

1

Crime and Criminology

Chapter Contents

THE CONCEPT OF CRIME
Legal Definition
  Assumptions about human
    action
  Criminal acts
  Other issues
Social Nature

THE DISCIPLINE OF
CRIMINOLOGY
Scientific Methodology
Key Topics
A Societal Perspective
  American society
  Types of crime
  The approach of this book
SUMMARY
NOTES

Crime is a major social problem in the United States. It assumes a number of forms and stimulates a variety of reactions. Violent street crimes, for example, evoke fear in many people. Incredible though it may seem, nearly one of every two Americans is afraid to walk alone at night within a mile of home.[1] Those who do venture out often take weapons of self-defense: whistles, Mace, handguns, etc. Some have undertaken training in karate or other self-defense arts. Some rely on German shepherds or other pets, trained to attack. One study pessimistically concluded, "The fear of crime is slowly paralyzing American society."[2] Chief Justice Warren E. Burger has asked, "Must we be hostages within the borders of our own self-styled, enlightened, civilized country?"[3]

Some forms of crime evoke considerable worry. One of every four Americans worries "a lot" about someone breaking into his or her home. One of every two worries "a lot" about someone selling heroin to youngsters in the neighborhood. Similarly, many Americans worry about being cheated by corporations or being subject to illegal behavior on the part of government officials. (See Figure 1.) Responding to these worries, they guard property with alarm systems and

FIGURE 1.
Fear of victimization. (SOURCE: Nicolette Parisi, Michael R. Gottfredson, Michael J. Hindelang, and Timothy J. Flanagan, *Sourcebook of Criminal Justice Statistics—1978,* U. S. Department of Justice, Bureau of Justice Statistics, Government Printing Office, Washington, D. C., 1979, p. 289.)

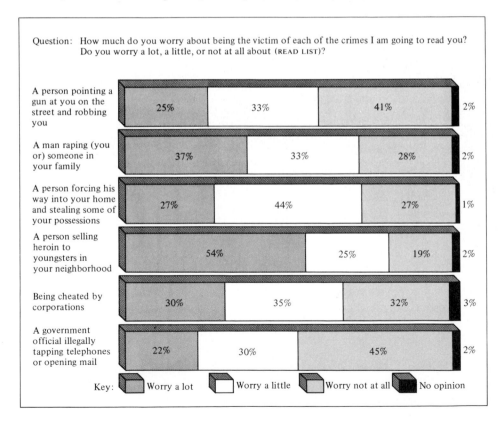

Crime takes many forms; it may be as obvious as a street mugging in broad daylight, or as subtle as the illegal pollution of the air we breathe.   (WIDE WORLD PHOTOS)

dogs, caution youngsters about their associations, create consumer protection bureaus, and form watchdog agencies.

Still other forms of crime raise concerns about the quality of life in our society. Spray-painted graffiti confront many city dwellers. Vandalism costs millions of dollars each year. Arson inhibits neighborhood development. Theft by employees reduces business profits. Gambling, prostitution, and narcotics have a dual impact: they siphon money from legitimate social activities and, at the same time, enrich the entity known as "organized crime." Dealing with these forms of crime may involve specialized police arson squads, lie-detector tests for employees, and periodic crackdowns on vice and organized crime.

Finally, there are forms of crime which threaten to undermine the integrity of American social institutions. Unsafe products, contaminated air and water, various illegal and unethical business practices, and "rip-offs" of consumers have so penetrated our consciousness that business is no longer trusted. A decade of political scandals—including Watergate, Koreagate, and Abscam, to cite only the major ones—has left us cynical or at least very disturbed about American political life. We have only begun to think about how to develop defenses against these types of crime.

In that they evoke fear, worry, concern, and threat, the various forms of crime absorb a great deal of our collective energy and attention. Selected crimes are reported as news in the papers, on television, and on radio. More serious analyses are presented in articles and books dealing with various aspects and problems of crime. Politicians running for office propose to do something about crime. Legislatures pass laws. Police, prosecutors, defense attorneys, judges, and corrections personnel are all employed by agencies in a criminal justice system established to respond to crime. Last but by no means least, writers fictionalize crime. They make it exciting, comic, and sometimes romantic. Books, movies, and television thrive on the mystery and response generated by crime.

This book will go further than the fear, worry, concern, and toleration that so often characterize the reaction to crime. It will attempt to develop a reasoned understanding of crime. To do this, it will examine the full range of topics which occupy criminological attention: topics such as the history of crime, the compilation of criminal justice statistics, criminological theories about crime, the major types of crime, and the operations of the criminal justice system. This opening chapter begins by looking at the concept of crime and the discipline of criminology.

THE CONCEPT OF CRIME

At the outset, we need to recognize that crime is a complex concept. First, we need to consider its definition in legal terms; second, its social nature.

Legal Definition

The basic legal definition of crime was advanced by Paul Tappan, a lawyer-sociologist:

> Crime is an intentional act or omission in violation of criminal law (statutory and case law), committed without defense or justification, and sanctioned by the state as a felony or misdemeanor.[4]

In a similar vein, concerning the people who are criminals, Tappan argued:

> In studying the offender there can be no presumption that arrested, indicted or prosecuted persons are criminals unless they also be held guilty beyond a reasonable doubt of a particular offense.[5]

Clear though Tappan's legalistic definition may be, it involves a number of assumptions about human action, raises considerations of which acts are or should be in the criminal law, and poses certain other problems for criminological inquiry.

Assumptions about human action

The key assumption underlying the legal definition of crime is that criminal acts are committed by reasonable persons, i.e., people who are able to use judgment to control their behavior.[6] The assumption of the "reasonable person" is embedded in common law, the legal tradition upon which the legal systems of the United States are based. The assumption has a number of important ramifications.

For one, if an act is to be regarded as a crime, it must be intended, and the intention must be specifically linked to the act. For example, intending to steal jewels from a jewelry store without actually doing so is not a crime. Similarly, finding that one has jewelry in his or her pocket upon leaving a jewelry store is not a crime if the jewels accidentally fell into the pocket. For a crime to occur, it is necessary that there be both intention and action, linked together.

The "reasonable person" assumption also allows for otherwise criminal acts to be justified by law. The justification of self-defense in case of bodily attack is used to excuse the injury or death that may be inflicted on an assailant. Similarly, the government excuses its own application of force from criminal sanction; in particular, a homicide committed by a police officer in the line of duty may be deemed justifiable and therefore noncriminal. As we shall see later, the limits of justifiable force by police in today's society are being hotly debated (see Chapter 16).

Finally, the "reasonable person" assumption includes the idea that people have the capacity to commit crimes. This implies that they must be deemed "able" before they can be blamed for committing crimes. Capacity is the most general part of the "reasonable person" assumption. It involves the concepts of duress, age, and sanity.

Duress recognizes that one person can be forced by another to commit a criminal act: for example, one person can force another to murder a third person.

In order to have capacity, a person must also be of sufficient *age* to commit a criminal act. Thus, criminal acts cannot be committed by children under age 7. For instance, if a small child were to shoot a parent with a gun, it would be presumed that he or she could not have had the intent to commit the otherwise criminal act. Between 7 and 21, the question of age and capacity has many more "ifs, ands, and buts." For the most part, common law assumes that the "legal infant," someone between the ages of 7 and 14, lacks the capacity for legal responsibility, although this assumption can be dropped or modified for serious crimes. Between the ages of 14 and 21, the common law assumes that a person has the capacity for legal responsibility, although this assumption can also be modified for certain acts. Over 21, it is assumed that people generally have the capacity for criminal acts.

It should be noted that there is no uniform, national guideline for age and criminal capacity. The legal limits and public policies employed vary from state to state: for example, in New York State, the Designated Felony Acts Law of 1978 reduced to 13 the minimum age at which persons could be held fully accountable for murder, assault, rape, and robbery. On the other hand, all states also have acts called "status offenses," which are not criminal and which apply specifically to persons under a certain age, usually 16 or 18. Examples are habitual truancy, incorrigibility, immoral or indecent conduct, and running away. For committing such acts, one can be declared a "delinquent" if under age. However, the same acts are noncriminal if committed by someone who is over the critical age.

The third criterion of capacity is *sanity*. Sanity is very problematic. Most generally, people who are subject to "defects of the mind" are considered incapable of committing a crime. In the extreme cases of senility, idiocy, and incapacitating psychosis, the lack of capacity appears clear. However, capacity has never been clearly defined in the law, and definitions used by lawyers often differ from those employed by psychologists. Most states still refer to the McNaughton rule, developed from a case originally tried in 1843:

> Every man is to be presumed to be sane, and . . . to establish a defense on the ground of insanity, it must be clearly proved that, at the time of the committing of the act, the party accused was labouring under such a defect of reason, from disease of the mind, as not to know the nature and quality of the act he was doing; or if he did know it, that he did not know he was doing what was wrong.[7]

Since 1954, some jurisdictions have attempted to develop the concept of insanity further through application of the Durham rule. Under this rule, "an accused is not criminally reponsible if his unlawful act was the product of mental disease or mental defect."[8] Moreover, the criminal act itself can be evidence of mental sickness, especially in cases involving bizarre crimes. As with the McNaughton rule, the definitions of mental incapacity implicit in the Durham rule have not been fully elaborated. A key reason is that we do not know the precise nature of "mental disease" or "mental defect." In such cases, mental capacity is determined after the act has been committed; and some criminal acts are in effect deemed noncriminal because they are committed by people suffering from mental disease or defect.

Criminal acts

The legal definition of crime also implies that the acts legally designated as crimes are the most socially harmful ones. However, in recent years this implication has been sharply questioned by some criminologists who argue that many socially harmful acts do not appear in the criminal law and by others who call attention to criminal acts that do not appear to involve a great deal of social harm. Let's review these arguments.

Although it covers a wide range of acts, the criminal law does not include certain acts which cause social harm. The United States government itself has violated basic human rights, as when it forcibly took lands guaranteed by treaty to Indian tribes, and when it evacuated and interned Japanese-Americans during World War II. Corporations have been able to perpetuate racial and sexual discrimination, engage in certain monopolistic practices, market faulty products, and employ unfair labor practices under laws which often provide for civil or administrative rather than criminal penalties. Moreover, there may also be crimes committed by officials as they enforce the law. (These issues will be discussed further in Chapter 4.)

At the same time that the criminal law excludes some acts causing social harm, it includes acts seen by many as comparatively less serious. A few common examples are gambling, public drunkenness, homosexual acts between consenting adults, and use of marijuana. Actually, laws against such acts—said by some to reflect our Puritan legacy—make up the largest part of the various state and local criminal codes.[9]

The social reaction to less serious acts is often arbitrary and subject to change. For this reason, they are often designated as *mala prohibita*—acts which are wrong mainly because they are prohibited by the state. They contrast to *mala in se*—acts which are thought to be wrong by most people in most societies, e.g., murder, robbery, assault, and incest. Whereas *mala prohibita* are often committed without much sense of wrong, *mala in se* often arouse a great sense of wrong and injury.

The relative nature of *mala prohibita* offenses is well illustrated by a variation on an old story. Three people are walking down Fifth Avenue in New York City—one carrying 1 pint of whisky, the second $100 in gold, and the third 2 ounces of marijuana. Whether or not any of these people is a lawbreaker depends upon the year. Before 1919, none of the three would have been committing a criminal act. From 1919 to 1933, the person with the pint of whisky was committing a crime. From 1934 to 1970, it was the person with the $100 in gold. From 1938 to the present, the possession of the 2 ounces of marijuana incurred criminal status—although the current climate of acceptance of marijuana use may portend legal changes. In short, at different times during the past 60 years, each of these acts was defined as a crime directed against society for which the government maintained the right to take action against the individual citizen. At other times, the same act was perfectly legal.

Other issues

Tappan's legal definition of crime has also been questioned on several other grounds. One is that if we accept the idea that criminal acts must be intentional, not justified by law, and committed by someone who is capable, there may be a great disparity between the total number of criminal acts and the number of persons held responsible for them. To begin with, most people who violate the law are not caught. Of those who are caught, the conditions for illegal behavior may exempt many from conviction and punishment even though they committed acts that were crimes. At the same time, many people are processed through the courts and punished in the absence of laws or under laws that are not "legal" or appropriate; such people may well not be criminals. Finally, in a complex society in which not only individuals but also formal organizations and the government are major actors, some acts may in fact be crimes but may be so complicated that they are impossible to prove in a court of law.[10]

Recognizing the limitations of the assumptions about human action, the acts designated as crimes, and the other issues just noted, criminologists of the past decade have moved toward conceptions of crime that go beyond criminal law and conceptions of criminals that include a much larger group than those who are tried and convicted in court. Some criminologists, for example, have held that the criminal law is by no means an objective indicator of the acts that should be crimes, since it represents the outcome of a struggle between the economic ruling class and those subject to its rule.[11] A few have sought to have criminologists study all violations of human rights, whether or not they are officially proscribed. Such an approach would expand the scope of criminological inquiry to include imperialism, war, racism, sexism, and poverty as forms of crime.[12] Other criminologists have sought a more precise estimate of the amount of crime by asking some respondents to report the crimes they have committed (whether or not they were arrested, indicted, or prosecuted; see Chapter 3) and other respondents to report victimizations they have experienced (whether or not these were reported to police; again, see Chapter 3).

In short, there are few who would restrict the scope of criminology only to those acts defined by the law as crime and to those offenders arrested, indicted, or prosecuted as criminals. To understand criminology today, we shall find it necessary to take a broad view of crime. As we shall see in Chapter 4, which acts should be in the criminal law is itself a key question for discussion. As we shall see in Chapters 5 and 6, modern positivist criminology raises the question whether an analysis of criminals can be limited to examining characteristics of those who are arrested, indicted, or convicted of crime. As we shall see in Chapter 8, critical criminologists have posed the question whether the actions of control agencies are the key influence on crime rates.

Social Nature

The complexity of crime can be further appreciated by calling attention to the social nature of particular criminal acts. In speaking about crime, it is useful to bear in mind that crime is only a small part of the totality of interactions that occur in society. Generally, people interact. They do things with one another: work together, play together, buy and sell from each other, beg for money, argue, take bets, engage in sexual relationships, etc. In a society, the number of interactions on a given day is almost uncountable. Out of the totality, relatively few involve harm; and relatively few are criminal.

Calling an act a "crime" is a response to an act. In this response the offended person transforms what he or she feels is an injury into a public harm by calling the police. In other words, crime involves, first, a feeling of hurt. We say: "I was ripped off." "I got burned." "I was violated." "I was victimized." Second, it involves bringing a private act to public attention; we "blow the whistle."[13] Typically, this means calling the police and asking them to arrest the person we accuse of being the offender.

In making an originally private act public, calling the police or some other social agency sets into motion the complex social machinery known as the "criminal justice system." The alleged offender may be arrested or simply spoken to and released. The incident may be investigated. The alleged offender may be prosecuted, tried, and possibly convicted. Following that, he or she may be then punished or treated.

As the private act is made public, the original parties assume roles in the criminal justice system. The doer of the act becomes the suspect, the defendant, and perhaps eventually the convicted offender; the injured party becomes the victim. Another party on the scene may become a witness. The act itself becomes

The social drama of the system of justice often goes on for months or years and requires all the actors to do a lot of patient waiting. (BRUCE ROBERTS/PHOTO RESEARCHERS)

redefined as a crime, an offense against society. The parties are then thrown into the social drama of criminal justice, one which has its own players, action, and script. Interesting to note, this reactive, publicizing drama may go on for months or even years—very much in contrast to the original act, which often occurred in minutes or even seconds. It may also involve considerable expense.

Thinking about the social side of the criminal act once again alerts us to the limitations of a strictly legal definition of crime. For a variety of reasons, many harmful acts in violation of the criminal law are not officially treated as crimes, because they are not brought to public attention (see Chapters 9 and 10). For some types of crime—e.g., corporate crime (Chapter 11), crimes against corporations (Chapter 12), and organized crime (Chapter 14), victims in many cases do not perceive that they have been victimized or do not make their victimization public. Finally, there are cases in which the sense of being victimized does not coincide with the legal definition of victimization; e.g., some loss of property may be the result of unintentional misplacement rather than intentional theft (see Chapter 3).

THE DISCIPLINE OF CRIMINOLOGY

Criminology is the academic discipline which employs a *scientific methodology* to describe and explain five *key topics*: criminal acts, criminal offenders, the victims of crime, the social contexts within which crime occurs, and the criminal justice system. It also requires us to look at crime from a *societal perspective*.

Scientific Methodology

In its scientific methodology, criminology is similar to other social and, for that matter, natural sciences. Thus, a science of criminology assumes that there is an underlying order or pattern to crime, one that is sufficiently regular so that generalizations can be made. Moreover, the underlying order makes it possible to analyze cause-and-effect relationships which explain why something happens and to predict that it will happen again under similar conditions. As we shall see, the attempt to explain and predict crime, criminal propensities, and victimization characterizes much criminological work.

In the spirit of science, criminology admits no sacred cows. Any question that can be answered by logical, systematic methods is an appropriate subject for inquiry. Furthermore, there are no absolute answers; old "truths" are constantly being challenged. Thus, for example, in extensive work in the late 1800s, Cesare Lombroso—called the "father" of criminology—gathered evidence claiming to show that criminals were born with characteristics similar to those of "savages" (low cranial capacity, retreating forehead, tufted and crispy hair, etc.; see Chapter 5). His work was subsequently refuted by Charles Goring, who in 1913—after examining over 3000 English convicts—concluded that Lombroso's comparison of criminals to savages was unwarranted, although he did find that people convicted of crime show certain characteristics of "defective physique" and "defective mental capacity" (see Chapter 5). Finally, skeptical of the results of this earlier line of research, critical criminologists have pursued scientific studies of the lawmaking and law enforcement process by which some offenders come to be labeled as criminals (see Chapters 6 and 17).

To be sure, criminology does differ from other social and natural sciences. To begin with, criminologists can rarely, if ever, use the controlled experiment so effectively employed by laboratory scientists. Instead, criminologists rely on personal interviews, mailed surveys, or data collected by government agencies. Second, most criminal acts are committed in secret, making it necessary to qualify many generalizations by pointing out that they apply only to crimes officially known to governmental agencies or, in some cases, to private police agencies. (For further discussion of this point, see Chapter 3.) Finally, criminology is a borrowing science. Few ideas or interpretations of facts have emerged directly from criminology. Rather, much significant criminology has emerged from the work of scholars established in areas as diverse as genetics, anatomy, clinical psychology, geography, and even climatology. At present, criminology is heavily influenced although by no means dominated by sociologists.

Nevertheless, despite its differences from other social and natural sciences, criminology is scientific in that it seeks to explain and predict crimes, criminal propensities, and risk of victimization. As it turns out, some facts and generalizations are quite well established, although others remain contested. The key to the science of criminology is the willingness to submit ideas and opinions to empirical test. It is this willingness which will enable the discipline of criminology to achieve a reasoned understanding of crime that will go beyond the emotions of fear, worry, concern, and toleration.

Key Topics

Using scientific methodology, present-day criminology seeks to explore five key topics: (1) criminal acts, (2) criminal offenders, (3) the victims of crime, (4) the social contexts within which crime occurs, and (5) the criminal justice system. Elaboration of these topics will take us into rather diverse areas of social thought.

The study of *criminal acts* asks how and why particular acts come to be defined as crimes, demands that we appreciate the political nature of crime, and takes us into the sociology of law (see Chapter 4).

The study of *criminal offenders* raises the question whether there are certain physical, psychological, or social characteristics that are unique to offenders. This question has been raised by scholars in various academic disciplines, especially biology, psychology, and sociology (see Chapters 5 and 6).

The study of the *victims of crime* asks how and why certain people become victimized by crime. It takes us into victimology, a large subject of which only one part deals with victims of crime (see Chapter 7).

The study of *social contexts of crime* raises questions concerning the relationship between crime rates and various factors—social, economic, geographic, and other. It draws on the work of sociologists, economists, historians, and geographers (see Chapter 8).

The fifth topic, the *criminal justice system*, is one to which criminologists have devoted increased attention in the 1970s and 1980s. It raises questions concerning the manner in which the police, criminal courts, and correctional agencies operate. A variety of issues are addressed. Concerning police, we shall consider discretion, corruption, and conflict with the community (Chapter 16). Concerning criminal courts, we shall address case attrition, plea bargaining, and current sentencing practices (Chapter 17). Concerning corrections, we shall want to examine the internal dynamics of prisons, the inequality of imprisonment, and the purpose of corrections (Chapter 18). Analysis of the criminal justice system draws on an understanding of the way large-scale bureaucratic organizations operate.

A Societal Perspective

Having considered the concept of crime and the discipline of criminology, we now need to examine what we mean by a "societal perspective" on crime in American society.

There are three parts to a societal perspective on crime: (1) the basic characteristics of American society that are a backdrop for the study of crime; (2) the diverse types of crime in the United States today; and (3) the approach of this text, which relates the scientific methodology and key topics of criminology to the major types of crime as well as to issues confronting the criminal justice system.

American society

As a backdrop to the study of crime in the United States, it is useful to state some general observations about American society. We can begin by noting that the United States is a postindustrial society that has produced great material wealth. Although its per capita income is no longer the very highest in the world, it continues to be substantially higher than that of most other countries. There is great material abundance. Of 63.5 million housing units, nearly two-thirds are occupied by their owners. Americans own more than 114 million cars, an average of slightly over 2 per family. Very few live without running water, electricity, and innumerable appliances designed to make life more convenient. Leisure-time industries are highly developed, and many people have substantial leisure activities. Americans consume more energy per person than any other people on the face of the earth.

Linked to this material wealth is a dynamic technology that has enabled the American economy to show continual growth and expansion. Earlier in the century, that technology enabled the United States to produce steel and automobiles at an unprecedented rate. Now, to cite only a few examples, it produces a sophisticated computer technology for processing massive amounts of word and number information, a medical technology for the practice of "miracle medicine," and a "space-age technology" that has made it possible to send humans to the moon.

The dynamism of the economy has meant the continual promise of new opportunity for workers. The number of workers employed has continually expanded. As new frontiers of technology have been developed, new types of careers have opened. No longer does the majority of the labor force work in primary industry, in which raw materials are extracted from the earth. Nor does the majority of the labor force work in secondary industry, in which raw materials are converted into goods. Rather, the majority of workers are in tertiary industry, in which activities are predominately service-oriented. In such a society, more people work with their heads than with their hands. The choice of occupations is great: the federal government's *Dictionary of Occupations* lists over 20,000 occupational titles. For this reason, we have one of the most highly educated labor forces in the world: 80 percent of Americans complete high school, and 40 percent of those completing high school go on to college. Young people are continually encouraged not to "drop out" from their education but to pursue "the many opportunities that are available."

American society is democratic. On one level, this means that Americans can vote for their leaders; here too, voting rights have been expanded continually to include as many people as possible. On another level, there is an attempt to leave individuals free from governmental restraint. Americans can live wherever they wish without having to register with the local police. They can practice the religion they like. They can voice and publish controversial opinions. In other words, speech, press, religion, and right to assemble are all "free." At the same time, a constitution contains provisions that protect people against unreasonable searches of their homes, against being held to answer for a serious crime unless on presentment of an indictment, against cruel and unusual punishments, against slavery and involuntary servitude, etc. In the attempt to guarantee individual rights, many Americans continually seek to control the excessive or arbitrary use of governmental power or force.

One might well wonder why crime is a problem in a society that is characterized by great material wealth, technological advances, promise of new opportunities, and freedom to live without governmental restraint. In such a society, why should so many want to steal the property of others? Why should some want to injure others? As we shall see, the answers to these questions are by no means simple; indeed, they will demand our attention throughout this book. As a beginning, let's consider an alternative overview of American society.

The alternative overview would begin by observing that the considerable material wealth and abundance is quite unequally distributed. In fact, material abundance is very concentrated. The richest one-fifth of the population owns no less than 76 percent of the nation's total wealth, while the poorest one-fifth owns only 0.002 percent—that is, one five-hundredth. Similarly, among American families, the highest fifth receives 41 percent of the total national income while the bottom fifth receives only 5 percent. Moreover, the further "up the ladder" one goes, the greater the concentration of wealth and income. Specifically, the richest 5 percent owns 50 percent of the total wealth. The top 1 percent, consisting of those living on inherited capital investments or holding high executive positions in corporations (or both), has enormous wealth and income. In particular, of all individuals and families, the top 1 percent owns more than half of the total market value of all privately owned stock and receives nearly half of the total dividend income from stocks.[14]

The social cost of this concentration of wealth is substantial poverty. About one-fifth of Americans can be classified as "poor" according to the federal government's criterion of $5500 per year income for a nonfarm family of four. To be poor in the United States is to have virtually no material wealth; in fact, the poorest one-fifth of the population, as mentioned above, owns only one five-hundredth of the total national wealth and earns only 5 percent of the total national income. Moreover, there is an enormous psychological cost of being poor. It is not easy to be poor in the midst of plenty. The American value system—with its emphasis on individual responsibility—leads the poor person to blame himself or herself for being poor.[15]

Underlying poverty in the United States is a weighty heritage of racial discrimination and prejudice. Thirty-one percent of the black population, nearly one out of every three black people, can be classified as poor. The comparable figure for whites is only 9 percent. Official unemployment rates for blacks are roughly double those for whites; unofficially, the disparity is even greater. Although "reverse discrimination" quotas are being utilized to open opportunities for black people, there is a long way to go before conditions are equalized. Moreover, despite the efforts, very few blacks are corporate or government leaders.

Discrimination and prejudice have also operated in various forms against the diverse ethnic groups that make up the population of the United States. As each successive group has arrived, it has been relegated to unskilled, poorly paid jobs. There has also been a pattern of rivalry and jealousy among ethnic groups. At present, the ethnic scene is further complicated by the fact that many of the most recent immigrants have entered the country illegally. We do not really know how

Wealth and poverty are seldom far apart in American society; these two places are within 10 miles of each other. (ABOVE: ROBERTA HERSHENSON/PHOTO RESEARCHERS; BELOW: WIDE WORLD)

numerous they are, to say nothing of what their status is in American society, or under what conditions they are living and working.

Another major aspect of an alternative description of American society is its organizational complexity. In the past 100 years, large, formal bureaucratic organizations have taken over one sector after another of American society.[16] Large corporations, multinational in scope, dominate the productive part of our economy. Big government with its sprawling bureaucracies intervenes, or attempts to intervene, in many areas of our business and personal lives. Labor organizations, professional associations, and trade associations are organized to express their viewpoints and to guarantee that their particular interests are served.

It is in presenting the alternative description of American society that we can begin to identify broad social factors related to the problem of crime. The theme of economic and social inequality is one which arises over and over again in the analysis of crime. While prisons overflow with minorities and poor people, crimes of the powerful and well-off far exceed those of the minorities and poor in both the amount of money they involve and the social damage they incur. Moreover, there are some basic inequities in the very manner in which crimes of the powerful and crimes of the poor are defined (see Chapter 4) as well as in the way the actors in the criminal justice system respond to criminal acts (see Chapters 16 to 18).

Types of crime

The organizational complexity of American society has added some unique dimensions to crime. For one, it has made possible two completely new types of crime: corporate crime, in which organizations, especially corporations, are perpetrators of crime; and crimes against organizations, in which organizations are victims. For another, it has made possible increases in the scale of crime: in an organizationally complex society, collusion between large organizations can assume immense proportions. Abuses of power made possible by big government can readily subvert democratic institutions.

It is the possibilities of organizational involvement in crime that underlie the typology of major crime which will be used in Part Three of this book. In all, seven major types of crime will be identified: (1) person-to-person, violent; (2) person-to-person, property; (3) corporate crime; (4) crimes against organizations; (5) crimes against the social order; (6) organized crime; and (7) political crime. Only the first two types involve people directly as offenders and victims, whether of violent crimes such as murder, rape, robbery, and assault (see Chapter 9) or of property crimes such as burglary, larceny, and motor vehicle theft in which it is an individual person who suffers the loss (see Chapter 10).

Each of the other types of crime involves organizations or society either as the offender or as the victim. In corporate crime—which may involve homicide, collusion between companies, or theft from consumers on a large scale—an organized entity is the criminal offender (see Chapter 11). In crimes against organizations—often taking the forms of theft by employees, shoplifting, or other types of larceny—the organization, especially the corporation, is the victim of crime (see Chapter 12). Crimes against the social order involve acts deemed offensive to society; supposed victims are often willing participants (see Chapter 13). In organized crime, offenders are involved in a well-developed, highly organized type of criminal collusion (see Chapter 14). Finally, political crime consists of acts which are deemed to threaten the political system (see Chapter 15).

In the public perception of crime, reflected in the discussion at the outset of this chapter, one often gets the feeling that person-to-person violence and theft are the core of the problem of crime. While it is undeniable that interpersonal violence and theft are serious crimes, we shall see that the types of crime involving organizations and society as offenders or victims are equally important. For this reason, each distinctive type of crime will be considered in a separate chapter.

The approach of this book

It is now possible to set forth the basic elements of the approach to criminology taken in this book. First of all, criminology should take a broad view of crime, one that takes legality into account but does not restrict its scope simply to the acts defined as crimes or to the offenders arrested for, indicted for, or convicted of crimes. Second, it should employ a scientific methodology to explore the key topics of crime: criminal acts, criminal offenders, the victims of crimes, the social contexts within which crimes occur, and the criminal justice system. Third, it should appreciate the complexities of American society as they relate to types and patterns of crime; in particular, it must analyze the various forms that crime can assume in an organizationally complex society.

SUMMARY

This introduction and overview began by noting that crime is a major social problem which evokes a variety of emotional reactions, including fear, worry, concern, and threat. In contrast to these emotional reactions, criminology proposes to develop a reasoned understanding of the problem of crime. To begin the process of reasoned understanding, we examined the concept of crime and the discipline of criminology.

Crime is a complex concept, one which has both a legal definition and a social nature. Legally, it is an intentional act or omission in violation of criminal law, committed without defense or justification, and prohibited by the state as a felony or misdemeanor. From a legalistic perspective, criminals are those who have been found guilty in court beyond a reasonable doubt. Since a strictly legal definition of crime would give criminology a very narrow scope, many criminologists would argue for a broad definition of crime. This broad definition includes a view of the law itself as problematic and takes into account the crimes to which people admit as well as the victimizations they experience, even though these events have not been officially reported to the police or processed through the criminal justice system. Indeed, in the particular instance, crime can be seen as a social process by which private acts between two parties are made into public matters.

The discipline of criminology involves use of scientific methodology, the study of five key topics, and assumption of a societal perspective. Although different in some respects from other social and natural sciences, criminology relies on a scientific methodology and draws upon a variety of scholarly perspectives in its study of criminal acts, criminal offenders, the victims of crime, the social contexts within which crime occurs, and the criminal justice system.

When we take a societal perspective, crime is seen in terms of the complexity of American society—a society characterized on the one hand by great material wealth, technological advances, the promise of new opportunities, and freedom from governmental restraint; and on the other hand by unequal distribution of wealth, a heritage of racial discrimination and prejudice, and organizational complexity. Organizational complexity in particular has made new types of crime possible and increased the scale of crime. Taking individuals, organizations, and society into account as offenders and victims results in seven major types of crime in the United States today: person-to-person, violent; person-to-person, property; corporate crime; crimes against organizations; crimes against the social order; organized crime; and political crime.

This text studies criminology in the broad sense outlined above: *seeing* crime in both legal and social terms; *employing* scientific methodology; *exploring* the five key topics (acts, offenders, victims, social contexts, and the criminal justice system); and *understanding* the complexities of American society as they relate to types and patterns of crime and to the responses to crime.

NOTES

1 Timothy J. Flanagan, David J. van Alstyne, and Michael R. Gottfredson, eds., *Sourcebook of Criminal Justice Statistics—1981*, U.S. Department of Justice, Bureau of Justice Statistics, Government Printing Office, Washington, D.C., 1982, p. 181.

2 Research and Forecasts, Inc., *The Figgie Report on Fear of Crime: America Afraid*, A-T-O, Willoughby, Ohio, 1980.

3 Address before the American Bar Association, Houston, Texas, February 8, 1981. Quoted in *The New York Times*, February 9, 1981.

4 Paul W. Tappan, *Crime, Justice, and Correction*, McGraw-Hill, New York, 1960, p. 10.

5 Paul W. Tappan, "Who Is the Criminal?" *American Sociological Review*, vol. 12, February 1947, pp. 96–102. Tappan's legalistic definition of crime has stimulated a great deal of criminological debate (see: Chapter 4 of the present text).

6 For another discussion of the issues considered in this section, see: Gwynn Nettler, *Explaining Crime*, 3d ed., McGraw-Hill, New York, 1984, chap. 2.

7 A. S. Goldstein, *The Insanity Defense*, Yale University Press, New Haven, Conn. 1967, p. 45.

8 *Durham v. United States*, 214 F. 2d 862, 1954. See: Lloyd L. Weinreb, *Criminal Law: Cases, Comment, Questions*, 3d ed., Foundation Press, Mineola, N.Y., 1980, pp. 465–474.

9 Alexander B. Smith and Harriet Pollack, *Criminal Justice: An Overview*, 2d ed., Holt, Rinehart and Winston, New York, 1980, chap. 2.

10 Concerning these other issues, see: Richard R. Korn and Lloyd W. McCorkle, *Criminology and Penology*, Holt, Rinehart and Winston, New York, 1965, p. 46.

11 William Chambliss and Robert Seidman, *Law, Order, and Power*, 2d ed., Addison-Wesley, Reading, Mass., 1982.

12 Herman Schwendinger and Julia Schwendinger, "Defenders of Order or Guardians of Human Rights?" *Issues in Criminology*, vol. 5, no. 2, Summer 1970, pp. 123–157.

13 Howard S. Becker, *Outsiders: Studies in the Sociology of Deviance*, Free Press, New York, 1973.

14 See: Daniel W. Rossides, *The American Class System*, Houghton Mifflin, Boston, 1976.

15 William Ryan, *Blaming the Victim*, Random House, New York, 1976.

16 Kenneth E. Boulding, *The Organizational Revolution: A Study in the Ethics of Economic Organization*, Quadrangle, Chicago, Ill., 1968.

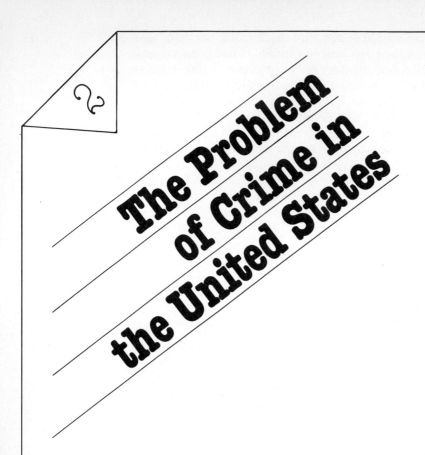

The Problem of Crime in the United States

To appreciate the forms and extent of crime in today's society, it is necessary to take a look at some of its historical roots. Crime is hardly new to the United States. The Puritans found it to be a problem. Urban centers have long experienced high crime rates. The American frontier produced very colorful outlaws. At the same time, violence has also played an important role in American life. The emergence of crime as a social problem has been influenced by American law and by the ways in which Americans have viewed offenders and victims. All these themes need to be discussed as we explore crime in the United States from a historical perspective.

Looking at crime historically is somewhat new to American criminology. Except for a few older classic works, it is only in the past decade or so that the history of crime has come to be a field of study in its own right. Today, however, we find historians and sociologists, as well as writers from a variety of other disciplines, opening up new lines of inquiry by exploring major historical trends in crime and societal reaction to it. This chapter draws heavily upon their insights.[1]

THE HISTORY OF CRIME IN AMERICA: AN OVERVIEW

Early Days

The first person in America to be tried, convicted, and hanged for murder was among the 102 pilgrims who arrived on the *Mayflower* in 1620.[2] By the middle 1630s, the Puritan colony of Plymouth, Massachusetts, established by the Pilgrims found crime to be a social problem. Concern about crime came as commerce expanded, the population increased, and Plymouth experienced increasing amounts of assault, arson, breaking and entering, embezzlement, fighting and brawling, manslaughter, theft, receiving stolen goods, pocket picking, robbery, and confidence games.

In a detailed study of crime in the Massachusetts Bay Colony, Erikson identified three "crime waves." The first was tied to the Antimonian theological controversy (1636–1638); the second to the influx of Quakers, which began in 1656; and the third to the Salem witchcraft hysteria, which first appeared in 1692. As Erikson went on to note, each of these crime waves followed a period of unsettling historical change during which the unique New England way of life appeared threatened. From this veiwpoint, the crime waves represented a clash over the proper limits or boundaries of behavior between "new deviants" (newly immigrated groups such as the Quakers) and the older agents of social control.[3]

The American colonies of the 1700s saw influxes of foreign groups, sizable population growth, and the expansion of urban centers. These developments were accompanied by increases in street crime and the commercialization of vice, especially in the important cities of Philadelphia, New York, Boston, and Charleston. By the mid-1700s, crime had become a major concern in New York, which subsequently developed the reputation for being the least safe city in the colonies. As one writer recently put it:

> With every dark corner crowded with thieves and bawds, with low dens down on the wharves handing out grog, with drunken sailors and soldiers prowling the streets at night, . . . women could not venture out after dark, . . . men were set upon by thieves, robbed and beaten.[4]

In the 1800s new forms of crime and vice emerged as the older cities continued to grow and new ones were developed. By the 1840s, criminal gangs, criminal districts, and vice areas had become established in the older urban centers. After the Civil War, New York entered the "flesh age": houses of prostitution, dance halls, concert saloons, and gambling casinos operated openly throughout the city. This open operation was linked to regular payments to corrupt police and political overlords. The political machines thrived on the extension of police protection to virtually every form of vice and crime.

Frontier Days

Nor was crime limited to the cities. The first known American crime syndicate arose in the 1760s in the back country of the Carolinas and featured theft and transportation of horses, slaves, and merchandise. During the period before the Civil War, counterfeiting and horse thievery were problems of nationwide scope. On the frontier, the colorful professional outlaw or "social bandit" emerged in the latter 1800s. Not only did such outlaws quickly become an important part of the social scene, but to this day the exploits of people like Jesse James, Billy the Kid, the Daltons, and the Younger brothers continue to delight our imagination. Although officially condemned, professional outlaws and their gangs received

Jesse James at 17. In spite of the violence of their crimes, frontier bandits like the James brothers have become romantic symbols of the old west. (BETTMAN ARCHIVE)

much public support as they robbed trains and banks operated by large, often unpopular, corporate interests.[5]

However colorful they may have been, the professional outlaws of the western frontier form a short chapter in the American experience with crime. They faded away as America moved into the twentieth century. For one thing, the frontier itself disappeared. Social development moved toward the cities. For another, the combined efforts of vigilantes, the railroads, the Texas Rangers, and the Pinkerton National Detective Agency served to control much of the predatory and criminal behavior of the outlaws.

On another type of frontier, there was the behavior of the capitalistic entrepreneurs of the 1800s, who established the large, well-known national corporations. A close look at how these corporations were established shows that many business pioneers engaged in criminal activities under the guise of conducting legitimate business activities. The Astor fortune, one of America's first, was made in part through getting Indians drunk and then swindling them out of their furs and land.[6] Cornelius Vanderbilt, "the foremost mercantile pirate and blackmailer of his day," accumulated over $100 million through control of railroads by first charging incredibly low rates in order to bankrupt competitors and then, after having obtained a monopoly, charging exorbitant rates. At the same time, he bribed local, regional, and national politicians to obtain land for roadbeds.[7] Watered-down stock issues, arson, bribery, fraud, and illegal rebates were among the outright criminal practices used by the early capitalists, later dubbed the "robber barons."[8] Indeed, in his study of the 70 largest corporations of the late 1940s, Edwin Sutherland found that 30 were illegal in their origin or began illegal activities immediately after they were formed.[9]

Twentieth Century

In the twentieth century, American crime has taken on a distinctly urban focus. For one thing, the cities continued to change rapidly as millions of new immigrants arrived, some from foreign countries and others from rural areas of the United States. Although reform movements had managed to reduce vice, criminal behavior, and some of the more blatant forms of political corruption, cities remained focal points for crime. In fact, the professional criminal underworld was comparatively untouched by the many crusades against crime.

In the crowded slums created by the waves of immigration during the early decades of the twentieth century, it was the "gangster" who became the key figure of American crime:

> He was a man with a gun, acquiring by personal merit what was denied to him by complex orderings of a stratified society. And the duel with the law was the morality play *par excellence*: the gangster with whom rides our own illicit desires, and the prosecutor, representing final judgment and the force of the law.[10]

However, gangsters had another side. They were also "racketeer" business entrepreneurs seeking to organize criminal activity in order to obtain continuing profit. Gambling, bootlegging of liquor, prostitution, and other types of vice became big business which, although risky, served as a means for talented members of the recently arrived immigrant groups to "get ahead" in a society that was not always hospitable to them. Thus, crime became "one of the queer ladders of social mobility in American life."[11]

Prohibition, the most ambitious attempt to control the manufacture, distribution, and use of alcoholic beverages, which lasted from 1920 to 1933, provided the mechanism for crime to become fully organized or "syndicated." The liquor trade and a variety of related criminal activities proved so lucrative that the Prohibition period was marked by repeated crime wars over the centralization and control of crime organizations. Contract murder using professional assassins was so profitable that an organization, Murder Incorporated, made its services available to other crime syndicates. Organized or syndicated crime remains an important part of crime in the United States.

In short, the roots of crime lie deep in our past. Recognized as a social problem as early as the 1630s, crime has assumed a variety of forms. Street crimes, criminal gangs, criminal districts and vice areas marked the older urban centers. The frontier saw the social bandit. Many business pioneers engaged in outright criminal activities. In the twentieth century the gangster emerged from the crowded slum. For some, crime has served as a ladder of mobility. Some have found it immensely profitable to organize or syndicate criminal activities.

THE HISTORY OF VIOLENCE IN AMERICA: AN OVERVIEW

In addition to its long experience with crime, American society has also known much violence. Although you might think that violence is a part of crime, a second look suggests otherwise. Much violence is never reacted to as if it were criminal. In fact, it may be socially permitted either as social protest or (in many cases) to put down social protest. Whichever way, the United States has witnessed a great amount of violence. As one historian has put it, "We have resorted so often to violence that we have long since become a trigger-happy people."[12] Since violence is so extensive, it deserves a separate discussion.

In that violence can be seen as an act which involves killing or injuring people or significantly damaging property, it might seem unusual to consider violence separately from crime. However, in this country violence has been used against religious dissenters, Indians, indentured servants, and slaves. The United States was born in the violence of revolution. At the same time, all citizens were given a constitutional right to bear arms. Dueling, lynching, blood feuds, and riots have all been part of American life. In fact, some of the violence that has characterized American society has occurred in the reaction to crime, whether officially in law enforcement or unofficially in vigilante movements.

There are two major forms of American violence: intergroup violence, which sets one group against another; and interpersonal violence, which involves individuals. Both forms appear to lack cohesion: the targets, issues, people, and places involved and affected differ greatly. Both appear to be associated with a remarkable mass amnesia: most of our violent past has been completely forgotten or left for historians to uncover at a later time.[13]

From the outset, mob violence was part of the public life of this country. Indeed, before the American Revolution, the Sons of Liberty and other patriots formed organized mobs to resist the British. "Tarring and feathering" was an American custom developed to root out Tories who sympathized with the British. Later, the years preceding the Civil War were ones of mounting violence both in the north and in the south. The development of modern urban police systems was a direct response to the eighty major urban riots of the period 1830–1865.[14]

Another side of mob violence is lynching or "the practice or custom by which persons are punished for real or alleged crimes without due process of law."[15] Lynching was first used in frontier areas to inflict corporal punishment. Later, it was used in many sections of the country, but especially against southern blacks. In fact, between 1882 and 1927 more than 4950 lynchings were recorded. In all but a few of the years between 1882 and 1903, the number of lynchings exceeded the number of lawful executions for capital crimes.[16] Now very rare, this distinctively American "institution" was always in direct violation of the constitutionally guaranteed right to a fair trial.

More systematic in their organization were the numerous vigilante groups which attempted to "create and enforce laws of their own making in the supposed absence of adequate law enforcement."[17] Again, there was an early association with the frontier; and as vigilantism developed, it tended to be strong in those

Although this cross burning by the Ku Klux Klan took place in 1982, the same scene could have been observed in 1882. Such violence by vigilante groups, common in our history, obscures the relation between violence and crime.   (WIDE WORLD PHOTOS)

areas where law enforcement was weak. Vigilante movements often drew their leaders from the top levels of society. Nevertheless, in some cases the movement went to extremes. In the western states it tended toward "instant" vigilantism in which mobs proceeded directly to lynching, thereby increasing the general level of publicly acceptable violence. Although most of the movements remained "constructive" in that they disbanded after their purposes were accomplished, others generated strong opposition, civil conflict, and subsequent anarchy. In east Texas one vigilante movement precipitated what some would call a minor war that lasted from 1840 to 1844.

Aside from the violence brought about by groups taking the law into their own hands, the United States has experienced many types of violent confrontations between diverse groups.[18] Political violence, economic violence, racial and ethnic violence, religious violence, antiradical violence, and police violence are all part of our heritage. Yet it is noteworthy that a great deal of American violence has been initiated on a "conservative" basis, that is, by established groups who felt themselves threatened by "outsiders" such as abolitionists, Catholics, radicals, workers, blacks, Asians, and other ethnic, racial, or ideological minorities.[19]

Violence also plays an important role in our politics. Although there is no "tradition" of political assassination, no fewer than four presidents were slain in the 100 years between 1865 and 1965 (Lincoln, Garfield, McKinley, and Kennedy). Assassination has also taken its toll of black civil rights leaders such as Martin Luther King, Medgar Evers, and Malcolm X. Curiously, other high political officials such as vice presidents, Supreme Court justices, and cabinet officers appear to be immune to it.[20]

Interpersonal Violence

Interpersonal violence in the United States has also taken some unique directions. One is the family blood feuds which appear to have been triggered by the animosities generated by the Civil War and allowed to continue in areas where there was no effective system of law and order. Among the more famous, the Hatfield-Coy feud lasted from 1873 to 1888, and the very bitter Sutton-Taylor feud in Texas lasted from 1869 to 1877.

Another form of interpersonal violence is dueling. Dueling between "gentlemen" was common before the Civil War and involved many well-known Americans, including Alexander Hamilton and Andrew Jackson. However, the easy availability of guns also made possible the "street duel" and "shoot-out," which subsequently became popular first in the south and later in the west.[21]

Interpersonal violence can also be seen in the high rates of violent crime, especially homicide. Compared with other countries, especially the industrialized European societies, the United States has long experienced high rates of homicide (see the section "Homicide" later in this chapter). Although many would regard the current rate—close to 10 homicides per 100,000 population per year—with alarm, it is comparable with that of the 1930s. Moreover, a separate calculation of homicides based on unofficial statistics showed that seven out of the ten years of the 1890s had homicide rates of more than 10 per 100,000. Some American cities of that period had rates several times as high.[22]

In conclusion, although American society has seen much violence in many forms, it seems not to be regarded as out of place. Perhaps this is because it is often initiated by established groups who feel threatened. Almost invariably, it has pitched citizens against citizens rather than citizens against the state. As a result, violence has been "deflected" from the symbols of national power, and we have experienced the remarkable combination of extraordinary domestic violence and a high degree of political stability.[23]

Perhaps it is even more ironic that most group violence has never been defined or reacted to as if it were criminal. This is especially true of the actions of lynch mobs and vigilante groups, many of whose members came from the "respectable" elements of American society. However, it is also true of other mob violence where prosecutions, especially against the representatives of the established social interests, were minimal. The net result is a separation in our thinking about crime and violence. Crime is seen as if it were private or interpersonal, while violence is often not treated as if it were criminal. In particular, violence in public confrontations between groups somehow does not "count" as crime.

AMERICAN CRIMES

This discussion of crime and violence in the United States has, so far, overlooked two key questions: *how* and *why* acts are defined as criminal. As was noted in Chapter 1, acts defined as criminal in one time and place may not be criminal at other times and places. Hence, we need to turn our attention to American crimes and ask what is unique about them.

It is important to recognize (see Chapter 1) that an act is criminal because it is specifically prohibited by public law and the state can take action against and penalize the offender for having committed it. In applying this definition to crime in American society, two questions are raised: (1) What is the form of the American state? (2) Which acts are prohibited by criminal law?

The American State

To define the state as a social institution, sociologists usually follow the definition set forth by Max Weber, the famous German sociologist:

> . . . a human community that (successfully) claims the *monopoly of the legitimate use of physical force* within a given territory.[24]

It follows that the criminal law is an important instrument of the state in that it specifies the social situations in which the use of force is illegal. In addition, the legal use of force is for the most part restricted to the armed forces, the national guard, and police departments.

Decentralization of the American state

Historically, the state in American society has been a weak institution. To begin with, there is not *one state* but 50 states, a federal "state," and many more local governmental units which sometimes operate as "states." Criminal law specifying how force may be utilized is, for the most part, set forth in state codes. Since these codes reflect local situations, there are points of difference both among the various state codes and in their enforcement. Certain acts defined as crimes in one state may be defined differently in other states. As the federal "state" has grown, the federal government has also developed its own code of criminal offenses—for example, kidnapping and bank robbery are federal crimes. Yet this code may conflict with state criminal codes at various points. In day-to-day operations the lack of cooperation among federal, state, and local agencies can be so great that law enforcement efforts are impeded in many instances.

The decentralization of the state is evident in the administration of the criminal law. In contrast to the English common law, which left the prosecution of criminal offenses to private persons, the American system featured the role of the public prosecutor. Variously called the "district attorney," "corporation counsel," "solicitor," "state's attorney," "county attorney," or "city attorney," the public prosecutor enjoys immense power in the American system because it is he or she who decides whether or not to prosecute criminal cases. The prosecutor has remained an immensely independent figure in the criminal justice system. States do not provide central supervision over local public prosecutors. In some states this independence is reinforced by local popular election of prosecutors.[25]

Another aspect of decentralization is evident in the widespread lynchings and vigilante movements discussed earlier. In these social movements, which functioned well into the 1900s, "popular justice" was so strong that unauthorized use of force was not only possible but also socially acceptable. Such movements can be seen as the product of a localism in which popular prejudices were allowed to override legal rights guaranteed by the Constitution. Indeed, in its original form the Constitution contained no limits on state criminal procedure. Not until the adoption of the Fourteenth Amendment in 1868 were there provisions that states could not deprive a person of life, limb, or property without due process of law and that states could not deny equal protection under the law. Not until the 1920s was there a case in which the Supreme Court set aside a state conviction on the ground that the defendant had not been accorded due process.

Finally, the strength of local influences in criminal justice is reflected in the brief history of the Law Enforcement Assistance Administration (LEAA). Created through the Omnibus Crime Control and Safe Streets Act of 1968, LEAA was historically significant in that it was the first federal agency charged with reducing crime and delinquency in the entire United States. Nevertheless, LEAA had to operate by channeling federal financial aid to state and local governments. In the mid-1970s it received grants running into billions of dollars which were disbursed to state and local agencies. Although critics may have argued that LEAA was "a coordinated system of legal repression for the advanced capitalist society,"[26] criminal justice remained basically a local government activity.[27] By 1980, LEAA's budget has been severely cut and its operations drastically curtailed. There are today still more than 15,000 federal, state, and local law enforcement agencies beset by a variety of communication problems and bureaucratic rivalries. Although some steps toward coordination and consolidation have been taken, the criminal justice arm of the "state" has remained a patchwork of independent, semiautonomous agencies.

Other characteristics of the American state

Aside from decentralization, the American state and its criminal justice apparatus are unique in that (1) their history is short, (2) change has been continuous, and (3) civil rights and liberties designed to curtail the power of state agencies have been extended to individuals.

Concerning history, the United States is a young country. Although much was borrowed from the Anglo-Saxon common-law tradition, new law had to be developed. Corporate law, in particular, did not grow until the late 1800s. In the early years the legislatures took the lead in the development of law; after 1875 the initiative moved to the courts.[28]

The need for continual change in criminal law and criminal justice agencies was evident in both the substance of the law and the manner in which it was administered. With changed social conditions, technological development, and development of new organizational forms, the criminal law has seen the emergence of many new crimes while older ones have become obsolete. At the same time, the volume of criminal court case loads increased markedly, especially in the emergent urban centers. Between 1871 and 1895, for instance, the volume of cases handled by federal criminal courts tripled. After 1910, there was much growth in the volume of cases docketed in both federal and state courts.[29]

Finally, the American system provides for some checks upon the arbitrary use of the power of the state. The basic liberties specified in the Bill of Rights include bearing arms, not being subject to unreasonable search and seizure, and speedy and public trial with presentment or indictment of a grand jury. As a result, the state does not monopolize all legitimate use of force, is not able to use police power arbitrarily, and is not always able to determine the outcomes of prosecutions for criminal offenses. In other words, our individual freedom involves a trade-off in that it demands restrictions on the power of the state.

In American society, then, the state appears to defy some of the characteristics suggested by Weber's definition. Historically weak, the United States has not one state but 50 states in addition to a federal government or what one might call a "federal state." Local influences have proved to be of immense importance, especially for criminal justice institutions. A comparatively short history, a continual need for change, and checks upon arbitrary use of state power have all kept the American state from becoming a monolithic or dominant institution. On the other hand, law has developed rapidly since the late 1800s. New crimes have emerged in response to changes in technology and social conditions. The sheer volume of cases docketed in criminal court increased markedly in the twentieth century.

American Criminal Law

Having looked at the nature of the American state and having considered the criminal law at several points, we can turn now to a more detailed discussion of the substance of American criminal law.

A society's criminal law reflects its norms (i.e., its manners and morals) as well as its power structure. Acts become defined as crime when there is a sense that a wrong has been committed, when someone or something is conceived of as a victim, and when someone in a position of legislative or judicial authority enacts or enforces a rule. Some criminal laws are well established in that there is relative agreement that the acts involved ought to be prohibited. However, other criminal laws change in response to changes in norms, shifts of power, and new social conditions.

American criminal law is the product of a variety of social norms enacted or enforced by different groups and different state governments in American society. Our first laws concerned the person-to-person crimes of homicide, assault, robbery, and burglary which were "imported" from England when our country was founded. These crimes had emerged in the British common law when the king or the "state" took over the right of private or family revenge in the 1100s. Many of the laws concerning private property also are of English origin—especially those from the 1700s, when England emerged as an industrial society. Generally speaking, there is considerable public agreement that acts against the person and against private property ought to be regarded as crimes.[30]

However, some criminal laws, such as those regulating personal moral behavior and business practices, reflect norms about which there is substantial disagreement. In these laws, inconsistencies may abound. In his article "Crime as an American Way of Life," Daniel Bell has pointed out one major inconsistency in laws that reflects uniquely American norms. As he puts it:

> Americans have had an extraordinary talent for compromise in politics and extremism in morality. The most shameless political deals (and "steals") have been rationalized as expedient and realistically necessary. Yet in no other country have there been such spectacular attempts to curb human appetites and brand them as illicit, and nowhere else such glaring failures. From the start America was at one and the same time a frontier community where "everything goes," and the fair country of the Blue Laws.[31]

Following from such inconsistencies, it might be observed that some acts which appear to be crimes are never made illegal and that others, while illegal, may be rarely enforced. At the same time, still other acts which appear relatively harmless are illegal and regularly enforced. Let's look at a few examples.

There are several areas of antisocial behavior which appear comparatively untouched by criminal law. We have already considered the tolerance of violence, especially that directed toward "outsider groups." In addition to the tolerance of corrupt politics mentioned in the quotation from Bell, there is also much tolerance of business acquisitiveness that is expressed as corporate crime. Organized crime, although it thrives on violation of laws enforcing various forms of public morality, has in some respects been left remarkably unhindered in its operations. The relative tolerance and underenforcement of the law concerning these forms of crime point up what is perhaps the most blatant double standard in American criminal law: acts of the powerful and wealthy, which can involve immense cost and do much social damage, often evoke relatively little societal reaction; but acts of the poor and powerless are far more likely to be defined as crimes, prosecuted, and penalized even though the amount of injury and property loss involves far less economic and social cost.

The laws designed to enforce public morality in areas such as sexual behavior, gambling, and substance use have had an erratic and uneven history. At times, enormous efforts have been devoted to their enforcement. At other times, the same activities have been allowed to operate with impunity or even legally. Perhaps the sharpest example is Prohibition. In this instance a moralistic philosophy was turned into a law, ambitiously designed to regulate "the manufacture, sale, or transportation of intoxicating liquors within, the importation thereof into or the exportation thereof from the United States." The law reached the unusual legal status of an amendment to the Constitution of the United States. Although the use of alcohol was then and still could be regarded as a social problem, raising it to the status of a criminal offense proved singularly unsuccessful. As it turned out, the unenforceability of this law and the subsequent widespread lack of public support led to its repeal 13 years later through the Twenty-First Amendment.[32]

Other laws designed to enforce public morality in areas such as sexual behavior, gambling, and substance use have become part of the criminal code in many states. Reflecting the decentralization that characterizes American society, the variation by state is striking. Nevada is unique in that it permits legalized prostitution at the option of counties. It also has legalized casino gambling, although it does not legalize the lottery or numbers. Connecticut has legalized a lottery, numbers, and various other types of betting but not casino gambling. Penalties for cultivation, sale, and possession of marijuana and hashish differ considerably from state to state. Concerning alcohol, a few states have remained "dry" since Prohibition; several have rejected the Uniform Alcoholism and Intoxication Act.[33]

Over and above the variations among states, public reception of the laws designed to regulate private moral behavior has been very uneven, especially among ethnic groups by whom some of the behaviors regulated by the laws are regarded as socially acceptable. (One case in point is playing the numbers in black and hispanic communities.) Unlike Prohibition, these other laws intended to regulate public morality have generally remained on the books even if they are enforced erratically at times. Some observers have argued that these laws are part of a power play in which upper-class Americans use the pretext of containing these specific forms of behavior as a means of rigorously policing the general behavior of more recently arrived immigrant groups.[34]

Despite the incredible amount of social energy and resources that have been put into enforcement of laws related to sexual behavior, gambling, and substance use, their utility and effectiveness are still very questionable. Many of the "crimes" regulated by these laws are "victimless" in that the supposed victim is actually a willing participant in the act.[35] Some are not regarded as wrong in various states. Some are not seen as wrong by significant groups in the population. For reasons such as these, it is questionable whether behaviors of this type can or should be regulated by criminal law. A number of observers have been led to the conclusion that there is an "overreach" of the criminal law and a need for decriminalization of many offenses.[36]

To summarize briefly, as a creation of the state, American criminal law reflects both the norms and the power structure of American society. Some parts of the criminal law are well established, having been carried over from English common law. Other parts are comparatively unsettled in that they embody norms about which there is substantial disagreement among various subgroups in American society. Moreover, given the decentralized state in American society, there is considerable variation in criminal law from state to state. Laws designed to enforce public morality are particularly problematic. Varying not only from state to state but also from group to group within a state, they may even change rapidly over time. Today, there are some observers who would question whether or not public morality related to sexual behavior, gambling, and substance abuse can or should be regulated by criminal law.

OFFENDERS AND VICTIMS: PERCEPTIONS AND DATA

Once acts are placed into criminal law, specific criminal incidents have two key actors: offender and victim. In our consideration of the general problem of crime in the United States, it is also important to examine American thinking about offenders and victims. As we shall see, the perception of offenders suffers from some unwarranted preconceptions and biases, while victims have long been the forgotten people of criminal justice.

Offenders

Crime and "outsiders"

Usually "outsiders," most often the poor and powerless, are blamed for crime, arrested as offenders, and put into prison. Although we saw earlier that the Puritans blamed the Quakers very early in American history, it was during the Jacksonian period of the 1830s that this particular form of thinking became well established. This period saw the impact of massive social changes, such as movement to the cities, immigration, and population increases, and in addition a change from a society in which status hierarchies were relatively fixed to one in which people were expected to be upwardly mobile. To informed Americans of the time, these social changes were of grave concern: "Would the poor now corrupt the society? Would criminals roam out of control? Would chaos be so acute as to drive Americans mad?"[37] From their point of view, the answers lay in reform, not of institutions but of individuals, especially those who were of the "criminal class" or "corrupted by vice." They felt that underneath it all lay moral weakness and that the vices which "caused" poverty also "caused" crime.[38]

The link between vice, poverty, and crime was carried one step further in the thinking of the reformers of the post-Civil War period. They argued that the typical offender was a member of the "dangerous classes," who had to be "straightened out" for his or her own good. In particular, privileged groups viewed those below them as "dangerous"; danger and criminality were virtually identical concepts.[39] By 1872, one of the leading professionals in corrections put it as follows:

> An immense proportion of our ignorant and criminal class are foreign born; and of the dangerous classes here, a very large part, though native born, are of foreign parentage.[40]

> In the poorer quarters of our great cities may be found huddled together the Italian bandit and the bloodthirsty Spaniard, the bad man from Sicily, the Hungarian, Croatian and the Pole, the Chinaman and the Negro, the Cockney Englishman, the Russian and the Jew with all the centuries of hereditary hate back of them.[41]

In only one sense were the reformers correct. Prison populations did come from "outsider" groups and from those of low economic and social status. Even today this is so. A review of the census of prisoners in the United States shows that they tend to have low income, high unemployment, few occupational skills, and low education—in other words, all the attributes associated with poverty in the United States. In addition, minorities and blacks are greatly "overrepresented" in prison populations. Although the correspondence is not exact, offenders who are arrested show characteristics quite similar to those who are convicted and imprisoned.[42]

Crime and wealth

However, what the reformers and many "informed" Americans overlooked was the intimate relationship between crime and wealth in American society. At the same time that reformers were discussing how to "correct the evil ways" of the members of the "dangerous classes," for many middle- and upper-class Americans crime was the "highroad to wealth."[43] Ironically, some of these people could trace their origins to poverty or to the "dangerous classes." Whether their wealth was attained through racketeering or through the more socially acceptable business acquisitiveness that crossed the line to fraud, bribery, or commercial deception, it became clear that crime committed in a socially acceptable manner could be extremely profitable. Indeed, offenders of this type would not be regarded as offenders. In many cases the law would be written or interpreted in such a way that it was impossible for them even to be arrested.

For the middle- or upper-class offender committing the right kind of crime, crime functioned as a "queer" ladder of social mobility. For talented youngsters of the lower social classes, it provided an opportunity to climb out of poverty. Payoffs went to the racketeers who could effectively organize crime, to the businesspeople who could get around the law, and to the politicians who knew how to take a bribe without being caught. Once earned, money brought status and social respectability. Few people asked how it was earned.[44]

Overlooking crimes of the wealthy and powerful while focusing on the crimes of the poor has remained a feature of the American perspective on crime. Even today, mention of the word "offender" conjures up an image of a young person, male, who is likely to be black. Rarely are the crimes of the wealthy and powerful objects of public attention or law enforcement efforts.

Crime and social class: Self-report studies

The fact is that offenders come from all walks of life. Virtually everyone violates a law at some point in his or her life, even though only a fraction of the potential candidates are ever arrested, convicted, or imprisoned. These conclusions are supported by self-report studies of criminal behavior which involve criminologists' surveys of groups of people to find out the extent of their involvement in crime and delinquency. Although self-report surveys have usually been taken on limited samples and youthful populations, their findings suggest that crime is far more general than is suggested by official statistics.

In general, self-report surveys show that the amount of unreported crime and delinquency is tremendous.[45] Virtually every American has committed a criminal offense at some time, but at least nine out of ten criminal or delinquent acts remain unknown to or ignored by those in authority.[46] In one study where the official records of chargeable offenses were checked to see how often the names of self-confessed offenders appeared, the proportion was only 1 percent. Even for serious offenses such as felonious theft, motor vehicle theft, breaking and entering, and armed robbery, the findings show that numerous violations remain unreported to police and do not result in court action.[47]

The picture of the offender derived from self-report surveys contrasts considerably with that of the offender who is typically arrested, convicted, and imprisoned. For example, one self-report survey queried nearly 2000 people in New Jersey, Iowa, and Oregon as to whether certain acts had been or would be committed, such as: taking something that does not belong to you (worth about $5 and worth about $50), gambling illegally, cheating on income tax, physically harming somebody on purpose, and smoking marijuana.[48] In a detailed analysis that measured social class by income, occupation, and education, interviewers found few significant differences among those of lower and higher status. In those instances where the differences were related to status, the acts had been committed more often by those of higher status; for example, smoking marijuana was reported more often by high-status than by low-status respondents. In addition, high-status respondents were more likely to say they would commit the acts if the situation permitted it.

Studies such as these lead criminologists to question the seemingly obvious relationship between crime and social class. One recent review of more than 35 studies found little or no relationship between social class and criminality, especially in the studies completed during the 1970s.[49] These studies rely heavily upon data from self-report surveys. To explain the disparity between the pictures of self-reported and arrested offenders, the comments of Steven Box and Julienne Ford are especially useful:

> Both working and middle class persons find themselves in circumstances which are likely to result in their committing criminal acts. . . . Working class offenders (along with other underprivileged offenders) are much more at risk of being officially treated as criminals: they are more likely to be suspected, apprehended, tried and imprisoned.[50]

We can persist in the belief that the criminal offender is generally lower-class only if we ignore both the historical patterns of crime in the United States and the recently emerged research findings on self-reported delinquent and criminal behavior.

Perhaps the most curious part of the picture of crime is that the victims who bear the brunt of crime have long been its forgotten people. Actually, ignoring the victim is not uniquely American. It began centuries ago in the Middle Ages, when the state assumed the right of private or family revenge. Even the injured person's right to restitution became converted under criminal law into a fine that went to the state.[51] So complete was the neglect of the victim that until the mid-1960s there were neither any studies of victims nor any attempts to collect comprehensive data about them. In its survey of what was known as of 1965, the President's Commission on Crime wrote:

> One of the most neglected subjects in the study of crime is its victims: the persons, households, and businesses that bear the brunt of crime in the United States. Both the part the victim can play in the criminal act and the part he could have played in preventing it are often overlooked.[52]

Disregard of victims in general contrasts markedly with the experience of the individual victim. Most people are totally unprepared for the reality of victimization, which is an experience of considerable depth and emotional reaction.[53] Undeniably, many experiences of victimization touch us intimately in that they violate our personal or social self. Violent crimes inflicted on the person, forced sexual encounters, and loss of personal belongings forcibly taken from us are experiences not easily forgotten.

In that property is an extension of self, we are also "victimized" through loss of property that we own. Burglary is an act against our household or business. Motor vehicle theft involves our cars. Larcenies usually involve smaller items such as thefts from motor vehicles, thefts of bicycles, and personal thefts of wallets and pocketbooks. Perhaps even more subtle are the smaller losses we don't always see, such as the overcharges by corporations based on subtle interpretations of rules, the defective products we buy but cannot return, and the increased prices we pay because the cost of crime has been added onto a product. Although systems of insurance may cushion some losses, the possibility of theft remains a distinct part of our everyday life.

Numbers of victims

One important aspect of the "rediscovery" of the crime victim dates from 1965, when the President's Commission on Crime turned its attention to *how much* victimization actually occurs. It had long been recognized that large numbers of crimes went unreported to the police. The question was: How many? The research efforts were most comprehensive. The key study sponsored by the Commission was conducted by the National Opinion Research Center, a large social science organization specializing in public opinion surveys.[54] It used a representative national sample of no less than 10,000 households. Of the households surveyed, slightly less than 20 percent reported that at least one person in the household had been criminally victimized in some way during the previous year. Overall, the study found that about twice as much crime was reported to interviewers as was reported to police authorities.

TABLE 1. Numbers of Crimes Reported to LEAA Survey Interviewers Compared with Numbers Reported in Uniform Crime Reports (UCR), Selected Years[a]

Year	LEAA survey	UCR	Ratio: LEAA survey to UCR
1973	37,295,866	8,666,200	4.3 to 1
1974	39,693,366	10,192,000	3.9 to 1
1975	40,462,561	11,256,600	3.6 to 1
1976	41,171,937	11,304,800	3.6 to 1
1977	42,086,186	10,935,800	3.8 to 1
1978	42,165,814	11,141,300	3.8 to 1
1979	43,010,459	12,152,700	3.5 to 1

[a] Totals include personal, household and business victimizations.

SOURCES: Figures calculated from data presented in the *Uniform Crime Reports* for the years shown; and Timothy J. Flanagan, David T. van Alstyne, and Michael R. Gottfredson, *Sourcebook of Criminal Justice Statistics—1981*, U.S. Department of Justice, Bureau of Justice Statistics, Government Printing Office, Washington, D.C., 1982, p. 233. Business victimizations were estimated for the years 1977, 1978, and 1979 by averaging the business victimization for the four preceeding years.

The pathbreaking work of the President's Commission on Crime has led to ambitious attempts to survey crime victims. The most comprehensive are the surveys of victims conducted since 1972 by the Law Enforcement Assistance Administration (LEAA) and Bureau of the Census. These surveys use a national panel of occupants of 65,000 randomly selected households who are questioned every six months in rotation to produce quarterly estimates of the crime rate for the United States as a whole. The interviews focus on rape, robbery, assault, burglary, and theft.[55]

Like the National Opinion Research Center, LEAA found far more criminal victimizations reported to survey interviewers than to police. Table 1 shows a comparison for the years 1973 to 1979. Although the ratio of LEAA figures to UCR figures appears to have gotten smaller over this time period, victimizations counted by LEAA still outnumber those reported to the police and included in the Uniform Crime Reports (UCR) by more than three to one.

Although the LEAA surveys report far more crime than the UCR figures, it should be mentioned that these two sources of data show somewhat contrasting trends. The smaller increases shown in recent years of the victim surveys suggest that the historically high crime rates of the 1970s may be leveling off somewhat. This trend has led some observers to project "a bit of hope for the immediate future" in an otherwise "grim picture of crime in America."[56] On the other hand, the UCR figures show a pattern of continuing increases in numbers of reported crimes. One result is a slight decline in the ratio between crimes reported to LEAA surveys and those reported to police (see Table 1).

Victimology

Although there are reservations about victim surveys, it should be said that victimology has become a new concern of criminologists. In the past decade a number of books have appeared; and there is now a journal, *Victimology*, devoted to the subject. Given the historical neglect of the victim, this concern is long overdue. In surveying the forms of crime in American society, we will have occasion to call attention to the different ways—some subtle, others quite obvious—in which virtually everyone is victimized at one time or another.

CRIME AND AMERICAN SOCIETY

Having reviewed the history of crime and violence in America, the nature of crime, and viewpoints on offenders and victims, we must now consider the larger setting of crime in the United States. Offenders and victims do not act in a vacuum. Rather, a social situation brings them into contact with each other. Certain social situations appear to generate high crime rates or to have unique types of crime associated with them. Thus, in this final section of the chapter, we will take into account certain characteristics of American society itself.

To gain a perspective on how certain features of American society contribute to the problem of crime, it is useful first to ask how crime and violence in American society compare with crime and violence in other societies. Following that, we will examine the particular social situations that appear to be associated with high—or at any rate relatively high—crime rates.

Some Comparisons and Trends

Is the United States an unusually criminal or violent society? Is it more or less violent today than in the past? These are important questions, ones that can be answered only by means of comparisons. Unfortunately, even comparisons yield no definitive answer, because the definitions of crime and violence differ greatly in other societies and change continually in response to new social conditions. However, some major points do stand out, and data permitting an examination of trends in homicide and comparisons with other countries are available.

Domestic violence

Domestic violence seems to accompany social change in all countries. In comparison with other countries, the United States is somewhere in the middle with regard to the total amount of violence experienced. It does have "the bloodiest and most violent labor history of any industrial nation in the world,"[57] and its racial relations have remained bitter. There have also been distinctly American forms of violence—lynching, vigilantism, family feuding, and widespread dueling—which have endured in a society that is very permissive about gun ownership for all social groups. At the same time, it can also be said that

> nothing in the experience of the United States or any other democratic state can compare with the wholesale violence wreaked by the totalitarian powers upon their people. All the violence of all kinds committed on American soil from the first settlements to the most recent clash between demonstrators and police could be tucked away in a small corner among the casualties of Stalin's terror, which are estimated at about twenty million, or among the six million or more Jewish victims of the Nazis' genocidal mania. Even the civil violence of recent years, which is surely one of our most tumultuous periods, pales before the contemporary experience of Algeria, Nigeria, Indonesia, or Venezuela.[58]

Perhaps more significant than the total amount of violence is—as we saw in the discussion of the history of violence—its dispersion among diverse groups and places, its deflection away from central governmental authority, and its denial in the sense of being quickly forgotten.

Homicide

A somewhat different perspective emerges if we compare homicide rates in different countries. It is evident that the United States today has a homicide rate which is far higher than that of other technologically advanced, industrialized societies for which statistics are available (see Table 2). At the same time, the rate

TABLE 2. Homicide Rates[a] per 100,000 Population for Selected Nations (Year for Which Rates Apply Is Given in Parentheses)

Country	Rate
Mexico	43.4 (1975)
Chile	40.5 (1976)
Guatamala	28.4 (1977)
Columbia	22.3 (1969)
Northern Ireland	17.6 (1977)
Venezuela	12.2 (1977)
United States	11.3 (1976)
Sweden	8.3 (1978)
Israel	7.4 (1978)
Cuba	7.2 (1971)
Equador	7.1 (1976)
Poland	6.8 (1978)
Canada	6.5 (1977)
Finland	6.3 (1975)
France	5.3 (1977)
Costa Rica	4.5 (1978)
United Kingdom	3.9 (1977)
West Germany	3.4 (1978)
Denmark	3.0 (1978)
Ireland	2.8 (1976)
Australia	2.8 (1977)
New Zealand	2.7 (1976)
Austria	2.5 (1978)
Japan	2.5 (1978)
Belgium	2.4 (1976)
Czechoslovakia	2.4 (1977)
Netherlands	1.7 (1978)
Italy	1.6 (1972)
Norway	1.3 (1977)
Greece	1.0 (1978)
Spain	0.6 (1976)

[a] These rates also include "other external causes" and may therefore be slightly inflated. E.g., the rate of 11.3 for the United States in 1976 is in excess of the rate reported in the Uniform Crime Reports for that year (8.8).

SOURCE: United Nations, *Demographic Yearbook, 1979,* New York, 1980, pp. 434–448.

is lower than that of third world countries such as Chile, Columbia, Guatamala, Mexico, and the Philippines. It should also be noted that many countries, most notably the Soviet Union, do not publish homicide statistics.

Comparison of homicide rates in the United States with those of Canada and the United Kingdom is especially revealing. Despite its similar background of pioneers and a "melting pot" society, Canada has a homicide rate less than one-third that of the United States. The whole of the United Kingdom, with a population of 54 million, has fewer homicides per year than Manhattan, with a population of 1.7 million. Philadelphia and Toronto each have populations of about 2 million; but Philadelphia had 430 murders in 1973 while Toronto had only 45. The differences are even more extreme when we consider homicides committed with guns. Unique among industrialized countries in its permissiveness about gun ownership, the United States has a "gun murder" rate almost 200 times greater than that of Japan or the Netherlands, 100 times greater than that of England or West Germany, and 20 times greater than that of Canada, Australia, or Italy.[59]

Other person-to-person crime

Because crimes other than homicide are defined and counted so differently in different societies, international comparisons of crime rates are very difficult to make. However, the question whether the United States has more crime today than in the past is one to which some thought has been given. There is, to begin with, the public perception of crime, from which it can be argued that "there has always been too much crime. Virtually every generation since the founding of the Nation and before has felt itself threatened by the spectre of rising crime and violence."[60]

In the twentieth century the increased use of crime statistics has made Americans more aware of trends in crime. Beginning in 1900, nationwide homicide statistics began to be collected. In 1933, a national data-gathering effort—uniform crime reporting—centralized the collection of data, especially for its Part I index offenses: homicide, assault, forcible rape, robbery, burglary, larceny, and motor vehicle theft. More recently, the victim surveys of the mid-1960s and panel surveys of the 1970s have uncovered extensive amounts of crime that have remained unreported in the uniform crime reporting system.

The Uniform Crime Reports (UCR) convey the impression that crime in the United States is at an all-time high. Figures 2 and 3 show the rates of reported crimes—those for which someone, most often the victim, has notified the police. (Crime reporting will be discussed further in Chapter 3.) As is evident from Figures 2 and 3, all seven index crimes have shown enormous increases since 1960, with property crimes literally going off the chart.

However, some recent research demands that we take a closer look at the currently high rate of reported crime. Take homicide, for example. The homicide rate was very high in the 1930s and peaked at 9.7 per 100,000 in 1933. It then dipped for several decades, began to rise in the mid-1960s, and now hovers around its 1933 peak. Each of the remaining crime index offenses is at or near its all-time high. But, taking a longer-range perspective, we can note that the urban centers of the middle 1800s showed rates of crime comparable to those of recent years.[61]

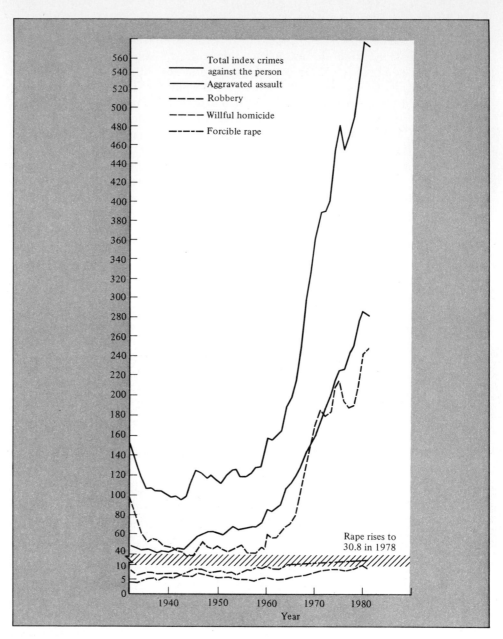

FIGURE 2.
Trends in index crimes, 1933–1981; reported crimes against the person.
(SOURCES FOR FIGURE 2 AND FIGURE 3:   1. For pre-1960 data, President's
Commission on Law Enforcement and Administration of Justice, *The Challenge
of Crime in a Free Society*, Government Printing Office, Washington, D. C.,
1967, p. 102.   2. For post-1960 data, Nicolette Parisi, Michael R. Gottfredson,
Michael J. Hindelang, and Timothy J. Flanagan, *Sourcebook of Criminal
Justice Statistics—1978*, U. S. Department of Justice, Bureau of
Justice Statistics, Government Printing Office, Washington, D. C., 1979, p. 443;
and *Uniform Crime Reports*.)

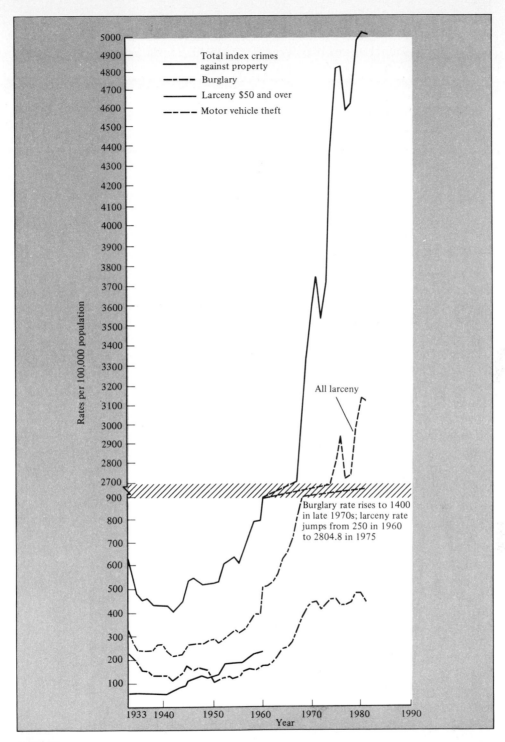

FIGURE 3.
Trends in index crimes, 1933–1981; reported crimes against property.

Moreover, a separate calculation of homicides based on unofficial statistics showed that (as was noted earlier in this chapter) seven out of the ten years of the 1890s had homicide rates of 10 or more per 100,000, considerably in excess of the present "peak."[62]

In short, it would appear that America has experienced rates of violence and homicide that are substantially higher than those of other industrialized nations. Moreover, officially reported crime rates have shown dramatic increases in recent years. At the same time, historical research shows that the presently high rates are not without precedent. All this suggests that we should consider whether there are certain broad social factors, characteristics, or trends in American society that are related to the high crime rates. In other words, we need to examine the way in which American society creates conditions that generate crime.

Social Factors and Crime Rates

The relationship of social factors to crime rates has been a concern of sociologists who have studied crime. At this point, it will be useful to take a look at their work and to identify a few of the broader social trends related to crime. In later chapters, as we examine the research findings of sociologists, we shall consider these trends as well as other social factors far more systematically as part of what we may call the "social context" of crime.

Calling attention to social factors and crime rates implies once again that crime is a social phenomenon and that criminal situations are produced by society. We have already seen that American values influence what acts are defined as crime; that crime has served for many offenders as an avenue of mobility, although most offenders have been pictured as part of the "dangerous classes"; and that victims have long been ignored. Now we need to consider how social change in general and two specific kinds of social change—urbanization and the growth of formal organizations—influence crime rates.

Social change and crime

In the most general sense, crime rates are very much related to social change. In considering social change, it is important to recognize that American society has experienced continuous, almost relentless change throughout its history. Born in revolution, fighting a bloody civil war 70 years later, expanding westward during the entire 1800s, and experiencing industrialization, urbanization, and continual immigration throughout its history, the United States has rarely stood still. Long traditions and settled lifestyles have not characterized its social life.

Such continous social change is important for crime because periods of rapid change are often associated with unique forms of crime or particularly high crime rates. As we have seen, the frontier produced the outlaw, the slum produced the gangster, emergent big business produced the robber baron, and Prohibition produced the racketeer. Social change generates high crime rates when it throws individuals, groups, or both into positions where they are willing and able to exploit and victimize others. For example, the shift from agricultural to industrial society in the post-Civil War period allowed some people to become extremely wealthy by using fraudulent means to exploit others. At the same time, landless people, unwilling or unable to work, were often attracted to criminal pursuits.

The importance of social change in general will become clear if we examine two specific social trends as they relate to crime: urbanization and the growth of formal organizations. While it may appear at first sight that neither has much to do with crime, a systematic look suggests that both are definitely related to it. Let us consider urbanization first and then consider the growth of formal organizations.

Urbanization

Crime has long had a distinctly urban focus. As we have seen, unsafe streets, freely operating vice, and corrupt public officials have been part of the city since colonial times. Whether measured officially or by victim surveys, crime rates are considerably higher in urban areas than in rural areas. Robbery is a characteristically urban crime. In fact, of all the robberies that occur nationwide, over half take place in the 32 largest cities—although these cities have only 15 percent of the population. Even though the depopulation of some large cities during the 1970s led to a drop in urban crime, the cities continue to have a share of crime far greater than their share of the population.[63]

There are, of course, many reasons why crime has an urban focus. In cities, people of different classes and racial or ethnic groups meet one another as strangers. Moreover, they are able to remain anonymous, comparatively untouched by the bonds of family, kinship, and community involvement that would otherwise restrain their behavior.[64] Finally, the city affords immense opportunities to commit crime. Not only are more people able to meet each other as offenders and victims, but more property and money are available to be stolen.

The urban locus of crime means that one of the reasons behind the comparatively high and increasing crime rate of the United States is urban growth. Since colonial times, cities in the United States have grown relentlessly. Their populations numbered in the thousands during the 1700s, the hundreds of thousands during the 1800s, and the millions during the 1900s. Today, there are 38 cities of more than 1 million. Moreover, the balance between rural and urban population has shifted as the cities have grown. In 1800, only 6 percent of Americans lived in areas classified as cities. By 1920, it was 50 percent; by 1950, 65 percent. Today, it is well over 70 percent.

The cities have also been much affected by the dramatic population changes experienced in the United States. Quoting numbers about size of cities obscures the immense changes forced by the waves of immigrants to America, especially in the latter 1800s and early 1900s. Not only were the city populations larger, but they also contained substantially larger proportions of newcomers. Cities of this period developed extensive slum areas characterized by poverty, high crime, poor health, low living standards, and transiency. Most often, newcomers moved into urban slums. As they became established, they often left the slums, allowing still newer groups to take their place. This process of continual change has meant that urban populations have been anything but stable.

Crowded, anonymous cities offer many opportunities for crime. (JAN LUKAS/
EDITORIAL PHOTOCOLOR ARCHIVES)

Growth of formal organizations

Powerful though it may be, urbanization is not the only social trend that is related
to crime. A second, the growth of formal organizations, is also related to crime,
although in an entirely different manner. To examine this trend, we need to
consider what is meant by the growth of formal organizations and the unique
forms of crime which have been made possible by such organizations.

   The organizational changes that dramatically shaped the forms of American
crime took place in the post-Civil War period. These changes—characterized by
Kenneth Boulding as a "revolution"—have meant the emergence of special-

purpose, large-scale, bureaucratic-type organizations in literally every area of American life.[65] Perhaps the most conspicuous form is the national (now multinational) corporation. Large corporations like American Telegraph and Telephone, International Business Machines, and General Motors employ more people, serve more customers, and command more resources than most states and many countries do. Other areas of social life are also dominated by bureaucracies. The federal government is one of the world's largest bureaucracies; its arms reach into literally every area of social activity in the country. Many labor unions, religious groups, hospitals, and schools have also come to function as large-scale, special-purpose bureaucratic organizations.

These organizational changes have dramatically influenced the forms and scope of crime in the United States. They directly paved the way for completely new forms of crime: crimes in which the organization is the offender, especially "corporate crime"; and crimes in which it is the victim, "crimes against organizations." The importance of these two major forms of crime (to be discussed at length in Chapters 11 and 12) becomes apparent when we realize that losses and personal injuries resulting from corporate crime and crimes against corporations far exceed those incurred from person-to-person crimes.

It must also be noted that one aspect of the push toward bureaucratic organization is a centralization of power and wealth in the United States. This centralization has led to the emergence of a "power elite" with enormous wealth and influence.[66] Its growth has been so rapid that there are few rules which effectively govern its actions. The result is a moral uneasiness or "structural immorality":

> A society that is in its higher circles and on its middle levels widely believed to be a network of smart rackets does not produce men with an inner moral sense; a society that is merely expedient does not produce men of conscience. A society that narrows the meaning of 'success' to the big money and in its terms condemns failure as the chief vice, raising money to the plane of absolute value, will produce the sharp operator and the shady deal. Blessed are the cynical, for only they have what it takes to succeed.[67]

The rapid development of organizational society has left many with the sense that something is wrong somewhere. Crime thrives where there is law without a supporting morality or sense of right and wrong and where the environment is an impersonal one that separates offender from victim.

SUMMARY

This chapter has taken a very broad view of the problem of crime in the United States. Looking first at the history of crime, we saw that crime and vice appeared very early, especially in urban centers. The frontier saw the outlaw, the slum the gangster, the multinational corporation the robber baron, and Prohibition the racketeer. Violence, too, has been prevalent, although it has tended to lack cohesion, to set a variety of groups and individuals against each other, and to be quickly forgotten.

Turning our attention from history to other aspects of the problem of crime, we saw that the American state has been a comparatively weak, decentralized institution and that American criminal law appears to lack rhyme and reason at a number of points, especially in the areas of sexual behavior, gambling, and substance abuse. Offenders who are arrested, convicted, and imprisoned have typically come from "outsider" groups and from people of low economic and social status. At the same time, crime has been a "highroad to wealth" for certain people. Some recent studies suggest that all groups are involved in criminal activity. Victims have been comparatively neglected; only recently have there been studies of victims and concern with victimology.

In comparison with other societies, the United States is somewhere in the middle with regard to the total amount of violence experienced. The United States is less violent than totalitarian societies and third world countries in the throes of social change; but it has experienced more violence and has recorded dramatically higher homicide rates than other technologically advanced industrial societies. Since 1960, officially reported rates of all major person-to-person crimes have increased sharply. In interpreting these comparisons and trends, social factors are very important. The broadest of these factors is the rate of general social change; but crime rates and forms of crime are also related to urbanization and to the growth of formal organizations.

This chapter has taken a wide perspective and presented a great deal of material. That will prove to be valuable: many of the themes advanced here will be expanded in Part Three, as we examine the seven major forms of crime in American society today. Moreover, the groundwork has also been laid for an analytical approach to these major forms in terms of the act, the offender, the victim, and the social context.

However, before we delve further into criminology, we need to examine how systematic knowledge about crime is generated. That is, we need to consider crime statistics—the topic of Chapter 3.

NOTES

[1] For a review of historical criminology, see Michael S. Hindus, "The History of Crime: Not Robbed of Its Potential, But Still on Probation," in Sheldon L. Messinger and Egon Bittner, eds., *Criminology Review Yearbook*, Sage, Beverly Hills, Calif., 1979, pp. 217–241.

[2] The discussion on the following pages is indebted to James A. Inciardi, *Reflections on Crime: An Introduction to Criminology and Criminal Justice*, Holt, Rinehart and Winston, New York, 1978, chap. 2. See also: Hugh David Graham and Ted Robert Gurr, eds., *Violence in America: Historical and Comparative Perspectives*, Sage, Beverly Hills, Calif., 1979.

[3] Kai T. Erikson, *Wayward Puritans: A Study in the Sociology of Deviance*, Wiley, New York, 1966.

[4] Quoted in Inciardi, *Reflections on Crime*, p. 31.

[5] A Marxist criminologist, Hobsbawm, sees the outlaw as a rural social bandit who appears during periods of abnormal hardship such as wars, famines, and industrialization and expresses a "prepolitical" social consciousness. Outlaws have emerged in many societies in which there has been rapid industrialization. See: Eric J. Hobsbawm, *Primitive Rebels*, Norton, New York, 1959.

[6] Gustavus Myers, *History of the Great American Fortunes*, Modern Library, New York, 1964, part II, chap. II–VII.

[7] Ibid., part III, chap. III–VIII. Quotation appears on p. 281.

[8] Matthew Josephson, *The Robber Barons: The Great American Capitalists*, 1861–1901, Harcourt, Brace and World, New York, 1962.

[9] Edwin H. Sutherland, *White Collar Crime*, Holt, Rinehart and Winston, New York, 1949, p. 28.

[10] Daniel Bell, "Crime as an American Way of Life," in *The End of Ideology: On the Exhaustion of Political Ideas in the Fifties*, Collier, New York, 1961, p. 133.

[11] Ibid.

[12] Richard Maxwell Brown, "Historical Patterns of American Violence," in Graham and Gurr, *Violence in America*, p. 41.

[13] Like the history of crime, that of violence was rediscovered. This rediscovery came in the late 1960s. See: Richard Hofstadter and Michael Wallace, eds., *American Violence: A Documentary History*, Vintage, New York, 1970. See also: Graham and Gurr, *Violence in America*.

[14] Brown, "Historical Patterns of American Violence."

[15] Ibid., p. 31.

[16] Hofstadter and Wallace, *American Violence*, p. 20.

[17] Ibid., pp. 21–22. See also: Richard Maxwell Brown, "The American Vigilante Tradition," in Graham and Gurr, *Violence in America*, chap. 6.

[18] On the types and themes of violence, see: Hofstadter and Wallace, *American Violence*.

[19] Ibid., p. 11.

[20] Brown, "Historical Patterns of American Violence," pp. 25–27.

[21] On southern violence, see: Raymond D. Gastil, "Homicide and a Regional Culture of Violence," *American Sociological Review*, vol. 36, June 1971, pp. 412–427.

[22] Inciardi, *Reflections on Crime*, pp. 50–53.

[23] Richard Hofstadter, "Reflections on Violence in the United States," in Hofstadter and Wallace, *American Violence*, pp. 3–43.

[24] H. H. Gerth and C. Wright Mills, *From Max Weber: Essays in Sociology*, Oxford University Press (Galaxy), New York, 1958, p. 78.

[25] On the prosecutor, see: Joan E. Jacoby, *The American Prosecutor: A Search for Identity*, Heath (Lexington Books) Lexington, Mass., 1980. See also: Chapter 17 of the present text.

[26] Richard Quinney, *Class, State, and Crime: On the Theory and Practice of Criminal Justice*, McKay, New York, 1977, p. 112.

[27] On the implications of localism for crime reporting, see: Mae Churchill, "Carter's Born-Again War on Crime," *Social Policy*, vol. 9, no. 3, November-December 1978, pp. 40–45.

[28] James Willard Hurst, *The Growth of Law: The Law Makers*, Little, Brown, Boston, Mass., 1950, pp. 85–87.

[29] Ibid., pp. 176–177.

[30] Peter H. Rossi, Emily Waite, Christine E. Bose, and Richard E. Berk, "The Seriousness of Crimes: Normative Structure and Individual Differences," *American Sociological Review*, vol. 39, no. 2, April 1974, pp. 224–237.

[31] Bell, "Crime as an American Way of Life," p. 132.

[32] See: Joseph R. Gusfield, *Symbolic Crusade: Status Politics and the American Temperance Movement*, University of Illinois Press, Urbana, 1963. See also: Chapter 13 of the present text.

[33] On the variation of these laws by state, see: Nicolette Parisi et al., *Sourcebook of Criminal Justice Statistics—1978*, U.S. Department of Justice, Criminal Justice Research Center, Washington, D.C., June 1979, pp. 271–279.

[34] Theodore Sarbin, "The Myth of the Criminal Type," in Theodore R. Sarbin and Daniel Adelson, eds., *Challenges to the Criminal Justice System: The Perspectives of Community Psychology*, Human Sciences Press, New York, 1979, pp. 1–27.

[35] Edwin M. Schur, *Crimes without Victims: Deviant Behavior and Public Policy*, Prentice-Hall, Englewood Cliffs, N.J., 1965.

[36] Alexander B. Smith and Harriet Pollack, *Some Sins Are Not Crimes: A Plea for Reform of the Criminal Law*, Franklin Watts (New Viewpoints), 1975; and Norval Morris and Gordon Hawkins, *The Honest Politician's Guide to Crime Control*, University of Chicago, 1970, especially chap. 1.

[37] David J. Rothman, *The Discovery of the Asylum: Social Order and Disorder in the New Republic*, Little, Brown, Boston, 1971, p. 58.

[38] Ibid., chap. 7.

[39] Sarbin, "The Myth of the Criminal Type."

[40] Charles Loring Brace, *The Dangerous Classes of New York and Twenty Years Work among Them*, Wynkoop and Hallenbeck, New York, 1872, p. 35.

[41] John S. Brown, "The Increase of Crime in the United States," *The Independent*, 1907, pp. 832–833.

[42] This point is discussed in Chapter 18 of the present text. See also: Marvin E. Wolfgang, Robert M. Figlio, and Thorsten Sellin, *Delinquency in a Birth Cohort*, University of Chicago Press, Chicago, Ill., 1972.

[43] See Ferdinand Lundberg, *The Rich and the Super-Rich: A Study in the Power of Money Today*, Bantam, New York, 1968, especially chap. III, "Crime and Wealth."

[44] Bell, "Crime as an American Way of Life."

[45] These studies have their limitations. One is that they produce artificially large percentages, since they typically ask whether the respondent has *ever* committed an offense. Another is that respondents may lie or forget. For a discussion of their methodology, see Chapter 3 of the present text.

[46] Jay R. Williams and Martin Gold, "From Delinquent Behavior to Official Delinquency," *Social Problems*, vol. 20, Fall 1972, pp. 209–299.

[47] For a review of the issues and results of self-report surveys, see: LaMar T. Empey, *American Delinquency: Its Meaning and Construction*, Dorsey, Homewood, Ill., 1978, chap. 7, pp. 141–166.

[48] Charles R. Tittle and Wayne J. Villemez, "Social Class and Criminality," *Social Forces*, vol. 56, no. 2, December 1977, pp. 474–502.

[49] Charles R. Tittle, Wayne J. Villemez, and Douglas A. Smith, "The Myth of Social Class and Criminality: An Empirical Assessment of the Empirical Evidence," *American Sociological Review*, vol. 43, October 1978, pp. 643–656.

[50] Steven Box and Julienne Ford, "The Facts Don't Fit: On the Relationship between Social Class and Criminal Behavior," *Sociological Review*, vol. 19, 1971, p. 48.

[51] Stephen Schafer, *The Victim and His Criminal: A Study in Functional Responsibility*, Random House, New York, 1968, chap. 1.

[52] President's Commission on Law Enforcement and Administration of Justice, *The Challenge of Crime in a Free Society*, Avon, New York, 1968, pp. 135–136. One notable exception to neglect of the victim is: Hans von Hentig, *The Criminal and His Victim*, Yale University Press, New Haven, Conn., 1948.

[53] See, for example: Morton Bard and Dawn Sangrey, *The Crime Victim's Book*, Basic Books, New York, 1979; and Janet Bode, *Fighting Back: How to Cope with the Medical, Emotional, and Legal Consequences of Rape*, Macmillan, New York, 1973.

[54] Philip H. Ennis, *Criminal Victimization in the United States*, University of Chicago, National Opinion Research Center, 1967.

[55] See: Stephen E. Feinberg, "Victimization and the National Crime Survey: Problems of Design and Analysis," in Stephen E. Feinberg and Albert J. Reiss, Jr., eds., *Indications of Crime and Criminal Justice: Quantitative Studies*, U.S. Department of Justice, Washington, D.C., 1980. For a further discussion of

victim surveys, especially their methodology, see: Chapter 3 of the present text.

[56] Wesley G. Skogan, "Crime in Contemporary America," in Graham and Gurr, *Violence in America.*

[57] Richard Hofstadter, "Reflections on Violence in the United States," pp. 6–7.

[58] Ibid.

[59] John Godwin, *Murder U.S.A.: The Ways We Kill Each Other*, Ballantine, New York, 1978, p. 281.

[60] President's Commission on Law Enforcement and Administration of Justice, *The Challenge of Crime in a Free Society*, p. 101.

[61] Ted Robert Gurr, "On the History of Violent Crime in Europe and America," in Graham and Gurr, *Violence in America*, pp. 353–374.

[62] Inciardi, *Reflections on Crime*, pp. 50–51.

[63] Skogan, "Crime in Contemporary America," especially pp. 380–382.

[64] Ibid.

[65] Kenneth E. Boulding, *The Organizational Revolution: A Study in the Ethics of Economic Organization*, Quandrangle, Chicago, Ill., 1968.

[66] C. Wright Mills, *The Power Elite*, Oxford University Press, New York, 1959.

[67] Ibid., p. 347.

3

Crime Statistics

Obtaining systematic information about crime has long been a matter of concern to criminologists. In the United States, court statistics date back to colonial times. Police statistics have been collected since the 1830s, and information about prisoners has been included in census counts since 1850. Attempts to generate statistics about crime rates began in the late 1920s; these attempts have included uniform crime reporting, victim surveys, and self-report studies.

Despite the extensive efforts devoted to their collection, crime statistics are the subject of much dispute and controversy. There is concern about what kind of statistics should be collected, who should collect them, how accurate they are, and, most generally, what they mean. In this chapter we will examine the major types of crime statistics and the debates about them. The chapter begins with an overview of the different types of statistics and then considers how statistics can be used to assess the amount of crime in American society. As we shall see, each major form of crime statistics has its strengths and limitations, its supporters and critics.

It should be noted that the focus of this chapter is the methods used to gather statistics. The substantive findings—i.e., what the particular statistics tell us about crime—will be included in subsequent chapters. Generally, crime statistics entail so many "ifs, ands, and buts" that it is quite appropriate to discuss and analyze the methods by which they are collected before considering the statistics themselves.

OVERVIEW OF CRIME STATISTICS

To obtain an overview of crime statistics in the United States, we should first take a historical perspective, to see how the statistics evolved. Then we can consider the present-day agencies that collect and report the various crime statistics.

Historical Perspective

The original impetus for crime statistics came from European thinkers who were concerned with crime.[1] In England, as early as 1778, Jeremy Bentham urged publication of data about prisoners, as a political barometer to gauge the effectiveness of the legislative function. In France, in the 1830s, A. M. Guerry and Adolphe Quetelet first attempted to conceptualize phenomena such as crime rates and use crime statistics to understand fluctuations and variations in the rates.

Although inspired by the European interest, the United States, an emerging nation at the time, was slow to become involved in the collection of crime statistics. The earliest efforts were at the state level. New York State began publishing court statistics in 1829; Massachusetts and Maine, in 1830. Massachusetts and New York published police statistics as early as 1834 and 1839, but these statistics covered only those who were incarcerated by the police. The federal government became involved in 1850, but its interest was mainly in generating data about people in prison. For several decades, the Census Bureau generated its information about prisoners by including a question in the general population census about family members who were in prison.

The early efforts at collection of crime statistics can only be described as scattered and fragmentary. Control at the state level allowed for enormous variation both in kinds of data and in methods of data collection. Control by police, courts, or correctional agencies meant that they collected specialized data of interest to themselves but not necessarily useful in understanding patterns of crime.

Federal concern with crime statistics did not begin until 1870, when the Department of Justice was created. One section of the law establishing the department stated that it was

> the duty of the Attorney General to make an annual report to Congress . . . [on] the statistics of crime under the laws of the United States, and, as far as practicable, under the laws of the several states.[2]

However, this section fell into disuse almost immediately. Not until 1929, after much lobbying by the International Association of Chiefs of Police and other interested groups, was there an effort to establish uniform crime reporting that attempted to standardize record-keeping practices and provide an overall perspective on the amount of crime in the United States.[3]

Present-Day Statistics

Since 1930, the Federal Bureau of Investigation has published annual Uniform Crime Reports (UCR) that employ the standardized record-keeping practices advocated in the late 1920s. The Uniform Crime Reports quickly became a key source of crime statistics. They provide official statements about the amount of crime in the United States by reporting figures on the number of crimes reported to state and local police agencies. They also report the proportion of crimes known that are cleared by arrest, the number of arrests, and the social characteristics of persons who are arrested.[4]

However, limitations of the UCR, many of which will be discussed below, have resulted in the development of many other crime statistics programs. Problems in methodology have led to attempts to assess overall crime rates by using approaches other than uniform crime reporting—in particular, by using victimization and self-report surveys. At the same time, criminal justice agencies, many of which emerged in the decades following the 1930s, have found the need for data that are more specific and more appropriate to their concerns. The result is a proliferation of crime statistics programs. An overview of those operating at the federal level is given in Table 3.

Despite the number of crime statistics programs, many of the historical problems remain. For one, standardization of reporting is elusive, since most of the programs rely upon voluntary use by state and local agencies of recommended uniform crime reporting procedures. For another, there is still fragmentation in the overall statistics on crime. Victimization studies show only indirectly the amount of crime that has come to police attention. Agency statistics reflect only one component of the criminal justice system. Criminal justice statistics and statistics from specialized and limited programs relate to efforts of federal agencies, whereas the majority of those convicted of felonies have violated state

TABLE 3. Major National and Federal Criminal Statistics Programs by Type of Program, 1979

Victimization statistics	Agency statistics	Criminal justice record statistics	Specialized and limited programs	Federal criminal statistics
National Crime Survey (NCS)	Uniform Crime Reports (UCR)	Computerized Criminal History (CCH)	Homicide (Mortality) Statistics	DEA Defendant Statistics
Victimizations reported by national samples of the US population. NCJISS-Census	Police reports of offenses known to them and arrests made by them. FBI	An automated file of records of persons charged with criminal conduct. FBI	Reports from medical examiners on deaths caused by homicide. NCHS	A file on persons arrested for federal drug law violations. DEA
	Juvenile Court Statistics	Offender Based Transaction Statistics (OBTS)	Addict Reporting Program	Federal Defendant Statistics
	Juvenile and other court reports on the number of children referred. NIJJDP-NCJJ	State level automated disposition reporting programs linked to FBI-CCH. NCJISS	Information about persons identified as addicts/abusers by police agencies. DEA	Data supplied by federal clerks of court for persons and cases tried. U.S. Courts
	National Prisoner Statistics (NSP)	State Judicial/ Corrections Information System	Drugs Awareness Warning Network	Automated Inmate Information System
	Annual counts of state and federal prisoners, admissions and releases. NCJISS-Census	State level automated court and correctional data systems. NCJISS	Coroner, emergency room, and crisis center reports of drug user contacts. DEA NIDA	An automated file on all persons in the federal prison system. EPS
	Uniform Parole Reports (UPR)	Prosecutor's Management Information System	Client-Oriented Data Acquisition Program	Federal Supervision Statistics
	Data on state and federal parole systems and their parole populations. NCJISS-NCCD	Automated judicial data system designed for use by prosecutors. NCJISS-INSLAW	Admissions and releases from federally funded drug treatment programs. NIDA	Data from federal probation offices on persons under supervision. U.S. Courts

SOURCE: Roland Chilton, "Criminology: Criminal Statistics in the United States," *Journal of Criminal Law and Criminology*, vol. 71, no. 1, 1980, p. 55.

laws. Finally, there is no central agency designed to coordinate data-gathering efforts and to provide a complete overview of crime in the United States.[5]

Bearing these problems in mind, let us turn to the key question facing criminologists: how to determine the amount of crime in our society.

STATISTICS ON CRIME IN THE UNITED STATES

Although we shall have occasion to use the data obtained from several of the programs shown in Table 3, our primary concern lies with estimating the amount and rate of crime in the United States. To that end, our focus will be on the

Uniform Crime Reports, the National Crime Surveys of victims, self-reported crime surveys, and other types of estimates. Let's take a closer look at the methodology and rationale of these several methods that are used to estimate the amount of crime and crime rates for the United States.

Uniform Crime Reports

The most frequently used publication concerning the amount of crime in the United States is the Uniform Crime Reports (UCR), published annually by the Federal Bureau of Investigation. Since the 1930s these reports have been the basis for nearly all official statements about the crime problem (such as Figure 4). The reasoning behind publishing UCR can be seen in the foreword to a recent volume, by the director of the FBI:

> UCR statistics have become a valuable research source for a myriad of constituents—sociologists, legislators, municipal planners, scholars, the press, and criminal justice practitioners. The general public, too, has become increasingly interested in the periodic assessments of crime in the nation.[6]

FIGURE 4.
The "crime clock" should be viewed with care. It is the most aggregate representation of UCR data; and it is designed to convey annual reported crime in terms of relative frequency of index offenses. But this mode of display should not be taken to imply that Part I offenses are committed with regularity; rather, it represents the annual ratio of crime to fixed time intervals. (SOURCE: Federal Bureau of Investigation, *Uniform Crime Reports—1981*, Government Printing Office, Washington, D.C., 1982, p 5.)

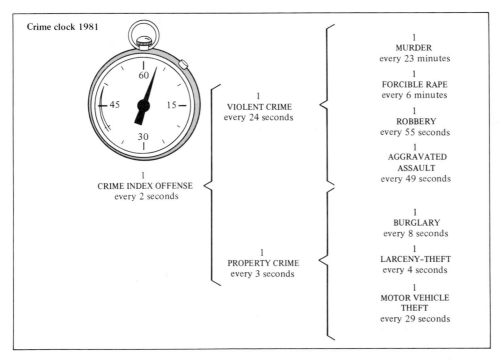

The nature of UCR statistics

In that they purport to be authoritative concerning the amount of crime in the United States, the Uniform Crime Reports make a number of assumptions of which we need to be aware. To begin with, they include selected criminal acts. Second, they single out some criminal acts that are regarded as more significant than others. Third, they report different types of information about the more significant criminal acts.

The 29 selected criminal acts included in the Uniform Crime Reports are listed in Box 1. They are broken down into Part I and Part II offenses. The eight Part I offenses (criminal homicide, forcible rape, robbery, aggravated assault, burglary, larceny-theft, motor vehicle theft, and arson) are designed to serve as an index of crime because of their ''seriousness as well as their frequency of occurrence and likelihood of being reported to law enforcement.''[7] Whereas data on arrests are reported for all offenses, two additional forms of statistics are maintained for the Part I offenses: (1) the number of crimes reported to the police and (2) the number of crimes cleared by arrest. A crime becomes ''reported'' when the police are informed about it, usually by the victim. The police investigate to make certain that the alleged crime actually did occur; if they find that it did, about 97 percent of the time it becomes listed as a ''reported crime'' or a ''crime known.'' The reported crime becomes ''cleared by arrest'' when an arrest is made. The step-by-step procedure is skipped for the offender arrested at the scene of the crime. In that case, the counts for crimes known, crimes cleared by arrest, and arrests all simultaneously increase by one. It is also possible that

Box 1: Offenses in Uniform Crime Reporting

Part I:

1. Criminal homicide
2. Forcible rape
3. Robbery
4. Aggravated assault
5. Burglary-breaking or entering
6. Larceny-theft (except motor vehicle theft)
7. Motor vehicle theft
8. Arson

Part II:

9. Other assaults (simple)
10. Forgery and counterfeiting
11. Fraud
12. Embezzlement
13. Stolen property: buying, receiving, possessing
14. Vandalism
15. Weapons; carrying, possessing, etc.
16. Prostitution and commercialized vice
17. Sex offenses (except forcible rape, prostitution, and commercialized vice)
18. Drug abuse violations
19. Gambling
20. Offenses against the family and children
21. Driving under the influence
22. Liquor laws
23. Drunkenness
24. Disorderly conduct
25. Vagrancy
26. All other offenses
27. Suspicion
28. Curfew and loitering laws
29. Runaway

SOURCE

Federal Bureau of Investigation (FBI), *Uniform Crime Reports*, Government Printing Office, Washington, D.C., app. II.

Although this mugging victim is reporting the crime to the police, it may not be cleared by an arrest.   (JILL FREEDMAN/ARCHIVE)

one arrest may clear many crimes; for example, an arrested burglar may confess to other burglaries.

It is important to note that the purpose of UCR is to provide an informed statement concerning how much crime occurs and how many arrests are made by police. The Uniform Crime Reports are used for crime statistics and are not directly related to police operations. That police have investigated complaints to see that they are genuine still does not mean that the incidents would be defined as crimes in a court of law. That police arrest persons does not mean that these people will subsequently be proven guilty in court. That some offenders confess to crimes other than the ones for which they were arrested may clear reported crimes, but it does not mean that the offenders are or will be found guilty of them.

Data on crimes reported and arrests are subject to a number of calculations. Crimes reported are broken down by place so that certain differences can be seen: regional, state, city, and urban-suburban-rural. Arrests are broken down by age; sex; race; and urban, suburban, or rural location. Rates are calculated both for crimes reported and for arrests. They are obtained by dividing the number of crimes reported or the number of arrests made by the number of people in the population divided by 100,000. The rates are annual. For example, in 1981 there were 22,520 reported murders. When this figure is divided by the total population of somewhat under 230 million to the nearest 100,000 (i.e., by 2300 people), the rate is 9.8 for the year. (See Table 4.) Rates can be calculated for any particular age, race, sex, or place and can be made specific to a group by using its smaller population base.

**TABLE 4.   Part I Crime Index Statistics: Number, Rate per 100,000,
and Percent Cleared by Arrest, by Particular Crime—1981**

Part I offense	Number of crimes reported	Rate per 100,000	Percent cleared by arrest
Criminal homicide	22,520	9.8	72
Forcible rape	81,540	35.6	48
Robbery	574,130	250.6	24
Aggravated assault	643,720	280.9	58
Burglary	3,739,800	1632.1	14
Larceny-theft	7,154,500	3122.3	19
Motor vehicle theft	1,074,000	468.7	14
Total Part I offenses	13,290,210	5,800.0	19

SOURCE: Federal Bureau of Investigation (FBI), *Uniform Crime Reports—1981*, Government Printing Office, Washington, D.C., 1982, pp. 36 and 152.

Limitations of Uniform Crime Reports

Although the Uniform Crime Reports are our most extensive source of data about crime in the United States, they have been the subject of much criticism and debate. Controversy has centered on three major areas: (1) the particular offenses which should be included; (2) the gaps between crimes which occur and crimes which are reported, and the gaps between reported crimes and arrests; and (3) statistical errors related to the techniques and scope of the data-gathering efforts. Since UCR data are so widely used and since some of them will be quoted in later chapters, it is important to examine these criticisms in some detail.

1. Uniform crime offenses   The most important criticism of UCR concerns the offenses that are or should be included in the reports. For the most part, the Uniform Crime Reports measure "person-to-person" offenses. Although the category "all other offenses" makes it appear that the figures are complete, the crimes which fall into the scope of UCR are typically those committed by the poor, the young, and the relatively powerless. Certain serious crimes such as kidnapping and skyjacking are not listed separately by type. Some significant corporate crimes—such as violation of antitrust laws, environmental pollution, and marketing of unsafe products—are not listed, because they are enforced by other federal agencies. Neither do most crimes against organizations find their way into the reports, because they are usually handled by private rather than public police agencies. Still other crimes, such as income tax evasion, are left out altogether. Nor is there a separate category for organized crime, although arrests of organized crime figures may appear under gambling, drug abuse, or prostitution and commercialized vice.

The definitional problems are exacerbated if one examines only the Part I offenses that are often used as an index of crime in the United States. A careful reading of the list in Box 1 shows that while serious crimes such as fraud, embezzlement, and buying, receiving, and possessing stolen property are Part II offenses, the category "larceny-theft" is included in Part I, with the result that many comparatively minor theft crimes can be classified as Part I offenses. For instance, one may question whether thefts of bicycles and motor vehicle accessories, which together account for 30 percent of all larcenies, should be considered as a problem comparable to murder, assault, rape, or robbery.

instance, one may question whether thefts of bicycles and motor vehicle accessories, which together account for 30 percent of all larcenies, should be considered as a problem comparable to murder, assault, rape, or robbery.

2. Gaps The second criticism of the Uniform Crime Reports concerns the gap between crimes that really occur and those that are reported and the gap between crimes that are reported and arrests.

There is, to begin with, an immense amount of unreported and uncounted crime. It occurs but it is not reported or, if reported to the police, it is not recorded for UCR purposes. Unreported crime can range from trivial thefts to murders which may be discovered only by chance (for example, when a river bed is dredged).[8] In order to obtain estimates of the amount of crime that really occurs, criminologists have developed victim surveys, which will be discussed below. Generally, victim surveys have found that reported crime is only one-half or one-third of the amount mentioned to survey interviewers.

In addition to the gap between real and reported crime, there is another between reported crime and arrests. In a given year police make well over 10 million arrests, a rate of 4705 per 100,000 people. However, the large number of arrests can be misleading. Since arrest statistics measure the number of *arrests*, the number of *individuals* involved may be considerably less than the 10 million noted, because some persons may be arrested more than once during a given year. Moreover, nearly one out of every four arrests is for alcohol-related offenses, especially "driving under the influence" and "drunkenness." Only about one in five arrests (22 percent, to be exact) is for a Part I index offense.

The gap between reported crime and arrests is evident in the low percentage of crimes cleared by arrest. For the serious Part I offenses, the overall arrest clearance rate is about one in five. The clearance rate varies for the specific offenses that make up the crime index, from a high of 72 percent for murder to a low of 14 percent for motor vehicle theft (in 1981; see Table 4). The proportion of all reported Part I crimes cleared by arrest has, interestingly enough, remained near 20 percent for each of the past 20 years despite enormous increases in the number of reported crimes.

The fact that only a small proportion of crimes are cleared by arrest means that the characteristics of arrested persons may not be indicative of all persons who are actually committing crimes. Those who are arrested tend to be male, young, black, and poor; but who commits the four out of five Part I offenses which are not cleared by arrest? To answer this question, criminologists have developed "self-report" crime surveys, which will be discussed later.

3. Statistical problems The third criticism concerning UCR data has to do with methods of data gathering, which can play an important part in the compilation of crime statistics. Perhaps the most basic problem is that statistics are gathered by the more than 15,000 local law enforcement agencies which voluntarily cooperate in the uniform crime reporting system administrated by the Federal Bureau of Investigation. This approach is made necessary because police departments are organized locally rather than federally or by states. In the early years of uniform crime reporting, fewer local agencies chose to cooperate in the system, so that UCR statistics covered only half of the United States population (rural areas, especially, were unlikely to report). However, over the years the number of participating agencies has increased, so that the reports now cover about 98 percent of the total population.

Gathering the UCR statistics locally means that they are subject to errors, differences in interpretation of incidents or arrests, and manipulation on the part of officials. In past years, officially reported crimes in various localities have shown some sharp changes from one year to another. For example, following reporting reforms in 1959 in Kansas City, the volume of crimes increased 202 percent in two years. In Chicago the change was 72 percent in one year. Other changes have been downward. In Washington, D.C., during a "war on crime," police began designating some larcenies as "under $50" so that they would not classify as Part I offenses.[9] While these instances may not have affected national rates dramatically, the FBI now exerts greater diligence in the effort to standardize crime reporting. In particular, it checks for error when it receives reports indicating any significant increase or decrease over the previous reporting period. It also compares agency reports against the experience of similar agencies and conducts seminars and workshops in crime reporting.[10]

Increased technical sophistication in counting has influenced the number of crimes reported. Centralized reporting, often with the use of special telephone numbers, has taken reporting out of the hands of local precinct commanders and given police chiefs centralized control over it. Many departments have computerized their reporting processes. The necessity of reporting some crimes to insurance companies and the widespread publicity about crime also encourage

Sophisticated equipment enables police to learn about and respond quickly to citizens' requests for help.   (RENE BURRI/MAGNUM)

people to report victimizations. All these changes promise a more efficient official crime reporting system. At the same time, they may also mean that the apparently higher reported crime rates of recent years may in part be the result of reporting factors rather than an increase in crime itself.[11]

Finally, the way the Part I index is computed can be immensely misleading. Simply adding the number of incidents or rates of different types of crimes together in effect makes the major offenses equal. However, can we really give homicide and larceny-theft equal ranking? Note also that 90 percent of reported Part I offenses are property crimes: burglary, larceny, and motor vehicle theft. Only 10 percent are violent crimes: homicide, rape, assault, and robbery. In other words, although we often think of violent crime when we hear the term "crime rate," the crime rate is basically composed of property crimes. Changes in violent crime—for example, a doubling of the homicide rate—would have virtually no impact on the overall Part I rate. On the other hand, since larceny-theft constitutes over half of the total crime index, relatively small changes in its rate may have considerable impact on the total rate.

Even with their limitations, the UCR data are still the most extensive source of information on crime and on police activities, especially arrest; and the trend is toward more reporting and more uniformity in methods of reporting. At the same time, it must be said that whether the Uniform Crime Reports are useful sources of data for criminology and criminological research is an open question. While some have claimed that UCR data cannot be used for research purposes,[12] others have argued that they may be quite useful if "modest demands" are made of them; for instance, they can provide clear indications of which cities have more crime than others.[13]

The limitations of UCR statistics, and debates about them, have stimulated a great deal of research designed to develop other ways to estimate the amount of crime in the United States. One such method is the victim survey; another is the study of self-reported criminal behavior; a third is the attempt to generate dollar estimates of crime. Since these other approaches have produced estimates of crime rates that differ markedly from those of the Uniform Crime Reports, it is important to take a look at them. In the following examination, additional arguments related to the debate over crime statistics will also be presented.

Victim Surveys

How victim surveys are made

As we saw in Chapter 2, victim surveys were first sponsored in 1965 by the Presidential Commission on Crime. The National Opinion Research Center survey of 10,000 households was followed up by National Crime Surveys (NCS), in which a nationwide panel sample of occupants of 65,000 randomly selected households are questioned every six months to produce quarterly estimates of the crime rate for the United States as a whole. These interviews cover rape, robbery, assault, burglary, and theft. Respondents are asked to remember past events, recall exact data and details, describe assailants, tell of financial loss or physical injury, report whether or not insurance claims were filed, and indicate whether the events were reported to the police.[14]

Victim surveys have found crime rates that are substantially higher—in some cases, more than triple—those of the Uniform Crime Reports. Such findings have led many to conclude that there is a vast reservoir of unreported crime which does not appear in the official figures. Known as the "dark figure" of crime, the tremendous amount of unreported crime suggests that crime in America is far more extensive than is publicly acknowledged.[15]

Limitations of victim surveys

Although victim surveys do show that much crime remains unreported, their findings need to be qualified by a closer look at how their methodology differs from that of the Uniform Crime Reports. There are several ways in which UCR statistics and victim surveys are not comparable. Moreover, victim surveys are (like the UCR figures) subject to errors of overreporting and underreporting. Let's briefly review the issues.

The lack of comparability between the Uniform Crime Reports and victim surveys is attributable to the following factors: (1) Rates of crime developed through victim surveys are based on numbers of persons victimized; for UCR, rates are calculated by numbers of incidents. (2) Victimization may be a condition rather than an incident; e.g., a businessperson may be repeatedly subject to robbery or a spouse may be subjected to repeated beating. One estimate is that 20 percent of all personal victimizations may be of this nature; counting them as separate incidents tends to inflate victimization counts. (3) Victimization rates are based on numbers of people age 12 and over, while UCR rates cover the entire population of the United States. (4) Finally, the categories of crimes do not correspond exactly. Victim surveys count attempts separately, whereas UCR figures include attempts with incidents. One crime, personal larceny, is considered a crime against the person by the victim surveys but a property crime by UCR.[16]

Victim surveys are subject to overreporting of crimes by respondents, who may purposely fabricate incidents or, not being familiar with legal technicalities, may make errors in interpreting or classifying incidents. Moreover, they may forget exactly when or where crimes occurred. Interviewers are also a source of error. They may consciously or subsconsciously report more crime than is warranted in order to produce outcomes consistent with hypotheses.[17]

It has also been noted that victim surveys, like the Uniform Crime Reports, can understate the amount and rate of crime. Respondents may forget or fail to report their victimizations. Personal crimes such as rape and assault may be underreported because of reluctance to speak about them. Property crimes may be seen as too small to report. Finally, the answers are voluntary, and there is no penalty for not reporting victimization. Factors such as these lead observers such as Wesley Skogan to speak of a "doubly dark" figure of crime, reported neither to police nor to survey interviewers.[18]

The people who conduct victimization surveys have not been unaware of the problems stemming from overreporting and underreporting. There have been studies that attempt to control for "recall decay," where events are forgotten because of time lapse, and for "telescoping," where events are reported for incorrect time periods.[19] In one study, it was found that of 400 persons known to have called police to report victimizations, 20 percent failed to volunteer the events in a follow-up interview. It has also been found that minor variations in the wording and timing of questions have substantial effects upon response patterns.[20]

Self-Reported Crime Surveys

How self-report surveys are made

Like victim surveys, surveys of self-reported crime represent attempts to develop estimates of crime that go beyond the official Uniform Crime Reports. They too have attempted to bring to light the "dark figure" of crime that remains unreported to police. However, rather than ask the victim, self-report surveys ask their respondents to voluntarily report—one might say "confess"—criminal or delinquent behavior in which they have been involved.

Dating back to the 1940s, self-reported crime surveys have typically queried samples of juveniles concerning a variety of delinquent and criminal offenses.[21] Different studies have often dealt with different offenses, although the generalized instrument shown in Box 2 has been used in several investigations. Most self-report studies have been limited to particular states; but there have been two national surveys, one taken in 1967 and the other in 1972.[22] Among the very few self-report surveys that have used samples of adults are those which studied self-admitted criminal behavior in New York State in the 1940s[23] and a more recent one which employed random samples in New Jersey, Iowa, and Oregon.[24] There are no national surveys of self-reported crimes based on samples of adults.

Specific findings of self-report surveys will be examined later (see Chapter 10), but it should be noted here that these surveys have detected an enormous amount of unreported crime. In fact, nearly every juvenile has admitted to breaking some law at one time or another. Adult lawbreaking is also much more widespread than official figures would suggest. For juvenile offenses in particular—even for serious ones—it has been estimated that eight out of ten offenses go undetected and nine out of ten do not result in court action.[25]

Box 2: Instrument for a Self-Reported Crime Survey

Each of the following questions is answered yes or no:

1. Have you ever taken little things (worth less than $2) that did not belong to you?
2. Have you ever taken things of some value (between $2 and $50) that did not belong to you?
3. Have you ever taken things of large value (worth over $50) that did not belong to you?
4. Have you ever taken a car for a ride without the owner's permission?
5. Have you ever banged up something that did not belong to you on purpose?
6. Not counting fights you may have had with a brother or sister, have you ever beaten up on anyone or hurt anyone on purpose?

SOURCE

Travis Hirschi, *Causes of Delinquency*, University of California Press, Berkeley, 1969, p. 54.

Limitations of self-report surveys

While pointing to an immense reservoir of unreported crime, self-reported crime surveys can also be misleading. To begin with, they are even less comparable to Uniform Crime Report figures than victim surveys are. For one thing, only two self-report surveys have been based on nationwide samples, and neither of these included adults broken down by age groups. For another, surveys which have asked repondents if they *ever* committed a particular act may drastically inflate estimates of crime as compared with the Uniform Crime Reports. Finally, the self-report surveys have tended to concentrate on relatively minor crimes such as status offenses (e.g., truancy from school, defiance of parental authority, running away), which are crimes only when committed by juveniles, and on smaller property offenses.

Self-report surveys are also subject to problems inherent in interviews and questionnaire methods. Since so little delinquent behavior comes to official attention, the accuracy of self-report data is difficult to assess. Respondents may forget, may lie, or may fail to interpret their past behavior as criminal or delinquent. On the other hand, they may fabricate crimes for fun or to impress interviewers. As with victim surveys, the answers are voluntary and may reflect pressures on interviewers to produce positive findings.[26]

Other Estimates of Crime

In addition to uniform crime reporting, victim surveys, and self-report surveys, there have also been attempts to estimate the extent of crime in the United States by generating "dollar figures" for crime. This technique of estimating the cost of crime is especially prevalent in the areas of corporate crime, crimes against organizations, and organized crime—forms of crime for which incident statistics are difficult, if not impossible, to compute. Although such dollar figures are quoted in later chapters, it should be borne in mind that they are at best estimates, often collected by nongovernmental sources. Most have not been subjected to the kind of scrutiny that other measurement techniques have received. For the most part, their accuracy should remain suspect, although the figures are useful for appreciating the relative size of the various forms of crime in the United States.

SUMMARY

Attempting to measure rates and trends of crime in the United States has proved to be a difficult and elusive task. The earliest efforts began at the state level for courts and police; the federal government first collected statistics on prisoners in the 1850s. The use of standardized, nationwide procedures to calculate rates of crime and gather systematic information about arrests did not begin until 1930, when a system of uniform crime reporting was developed and administered by the FBI. Since 1930, the Uniform Crime Reports have been a comprehensive source of data about crime even though they have been much criticized for (1) the particular offenses which should be included, (2) gaps between crimes which occur, crimes which are reported, and arrests, and (3) a number of statistical problems.

Lack of satisfaction with the Uniform Crime Reports as accurate measures of crime has led criminologists to seek other ways of assessing the amount of crime in American society. The two main alternative approaches are victim surveys and surveys of self-reported crime. Investigators using victim surveys have attempted to survey a cross section of the public concerning the nature and extent of its victimization. Investigators using self-report surveys have asked samples of respondents, often youths, to confess the nature and extent of crimes they have committed. Both approaches have uncovered a "dark figure" of unreported crime that appears far more extensive than the amount in the Uniform Crime Reports. However, these other approaches also have been the object of much criticism. Victim surveys may be influenced by overreporting and underreporting. Self-report surveys have been criticized for concentrating too much on limited samples (especially juveniles) and on minor offenses, and in some instances for asking respondents whether they have *ever* committed a given offense.

Nevertheless, it is safe to say that victim and self-report surveys have added a new dimension to crime statistics and the measurement of crime. They have shown conclusively that much crime is neither officially reported nor officially acted upon, even though it may be impossible to specify exactly how much. Victimization studies have also shown that young people, minorities, and the poor are disproportionately the victims of crime and that age is the key social variable influencing the reporting of crime (see Chapter 9). Self-report studies have shown that considerable numbers of people have committed criminal acts, especially minor ones, even though relatively few are ever punished or put in prison (see Chapter 10).

Discrepancies between estimates of crime based on official reports and those based on victimization or self-report surveys raise fundamental questions concerning the amount of crime in the United States. Historically, the trend from judicial statistics to police statistics, covering both arrests and crimes reported, and then to estimates from victim and self-report surveys, has meant that the data base has become larger and larger.[27] While it is often believed that crime has increased in recent years, it may well be that part or all of this increase may simply reflect our increased knowledge about the crime that actually exists. By the same token, increased official attention to any particular type of crime can lead to increases in its rate simply because law enforcement agencies dip "ever deeper into the vast reservoir of unreported crime."[28]

While acknowledging that victim surveys produce crime rates substantially higher than those reflected in the Uniform Crime Reports, a few recent investigators have found that the different methods can produce comparatively similar results when they are used to analyze particular crime patterns. Wesley Skogan, for example, found that UCR data and data from victim surveys lead to similar conclusions about variations between cities in robbery and motor vehicle theft.[29] Similarly, a study by Robert O'Brien and his associates found some convergence between UCR data and data from victim surveys for person-to-person (as opposed to business) larceny, rape, and aggravated assault, while data from victim surveys were more likely than UCR data to be correlated with urban structural characteristics such as density and crowding for person-to-person larceny and rape.[30] In other words, when specific variations in crime rates are compared, UCR and victim data may produce parallel findings. To the extent that they do, it can be said that both are satisfactory measures of crime.

The similarities and variations in findings among the three major methods of measurement have led different investigators to different conclusions. On the one hand, one might cite Alan Booth and his associates, who note, "Both the UCR and victim indices need to be refined to make them more useful indicators."[31] On the other hand, some criminologists have spoken out in defense of UCR statistics; as Skogan notes, "Official crime statistics may be quite useful as such, if we make modest demands of the data."[32] Finally, one might also cite the conclusion of Michael J. Hindelang and his associates:

> Both official data and self-reports provide valid indicators of the demographic characteristics of offenders, *within the domain of behavior effectively tapped by each method.*[33]

Hindelang's conclusion seems a most sensible one that deserves to be given further consideration. In fact, it will be the recommendation of this text that each piece of crime data be evaluated in terms of how it supports or challenges a particular argument at hand. No one type of data is definitive. Rather, it is necessary to recognize that different forms of data can be used to gain different insights into the various types of crime in American society.

NOTES

[1] Two key articles on the history of crime statistics are: Michael D. Maltz, "Crime Statistics: A Historical Perspective," *Crime and Delinquency*, vol. 23, 1977, pp. 32–40; and Scott H. Decker, "The Evolution of Crime Statistics as a Police Problem," *Journal of Police Science and Administration*, vol. 6, no. 1, 1978, pp. 67–73.

[2] U.S. Congress, *Acts and Resolutions of the United States of America Passed at the Second Session of the Forty-First Congress*, 1870.

[3] International Association of Chiefs of Police (IACP), *Uniform Crime Reporting*, IACP, New York, 1929.

[4] E.g., see: Federal Bureau of Investigation (FBI), *Uniform Crime Reports—1981*, Government Printing Office, Washington, D.C., 1981.

[5] Roland Chilton, "Criminal Statistics in the United States," *Journal of Criminal Law and Criminology*, vol. 71, no. 1, 1980, pp. 56–67.

[6] FBI, *Uniform Crime Reports—1981*, p. 1.

[7] Ibid., p. 1.

[8] Wesley G. Skogan, "Dimensions of the Dark Figure of Unreported Crime," *Crime and Delinquency*, vol. 23, June 1977, 41–50.

[9] President's Commission on Law Enforcement and the Administration of Justice, *The Challenge of Crime in a Free Society*, Government Printing Office, Washington, D.C., 1967, p. 25.

[10] FBI, *Uniform Crime Reports—1978*, pp. 1–5.

[11] For a discussion of the issues, see: Albert J. Reiss, Jr., "Assessing the Current Crime Wave," in Barbara N. McLennan, ed., *Crime in Urban Society*, Dunellen, New York, 1970, pp. 23–42.

[12] See: Ronald H. Beattie, "Criminal Statistics in the United States," *Journal of Criminal Law, Criminology, and Police Science*, vol. 51, May-June 1960, pp. 49–65; and Donald J. Black, "Production of Crime Rates," *American Sociological Review*, vol. 35, August 1970, pp. 723–748.

[13] Wesley G. Skogan, "The Validity of Official Crime Statistics: An Empirical Investigation," *Social Science Quarterly*, vol. 55, June 1974, pp. 25–38. See also: Charles R. Tittle, "Crime Rates and Legal Sanctions," *Social Problems*, vol. 16, Spring 1969, pp. 409–423.

[14] Stephen E. Fienberg, "Victimization and the National Crime Survey: Problems of Design and Analysis," in Stephen E. Fienberg and Albert J. Reiss, Jr., *Indicators of Crime and Criminal Justice: Contributions of American Sociology*, 2d ed., Rand McNally, Chicago, Ill., 1976, pp. 131–148.

[15] Skogan, "Dimensions of the Dark Figure of Unreported Crime."

[16] See: John B. Cordrey, "Crime Rates, Victims, Offenders: A Victimization Study," *Journal of Police Science and Administration*, vol. 3, no. 1, March 1975, pp. 100–110; Scott H. Decker, "Official Crime Rates and Victim Surveys: An Empirical Comparison," *Journal of Criminal Justice*, vol. 5, no. 1, 1977, pp. 47–54; and Albert D. Biderman, "Notes on Measurement by Crime Victimization Surveys," in Fienberg and Reiss, *Indicators of Crime and Criminal Justice*, pp. 29–32.

[17] James P. Levine, "The Potential for Crime Overreporting in Criminal Victimization Surveys," *Criminology*, vol. 14, November 1976, pp. 307–327.

[18] Skogan, "Dimensions of the Dark Figure of Unreported Crime." See also: Cordrey, "Crime Rates, Victims, Offenders."

[19] For a review, see: Fienberg, "Victimization and the National Crime Survey," p. 36.

[20] Albert J. Reiss, Jr., "Measurement of the Nature and Amount of Crime," in President's Commission on Law Enforcement and Administration of Justice, *Studies in Crime and Law Enforcement in Major Metropolitan Areas: Field Surveys III,* vol. 1, Government Printing Office, Washington, D.C., 1967. See also: Simon I. Singer, "A Comment on Alleged Overreporting," *Criminology,* vol. 16, May 1978, pp. 99–107.

[21] Fred J. Murphy et al., "The Incidence of Hidden Delinquency," *American Journal of Orthopsychiatry,* October 1946, pp. 686–696.

[22] Martin Gold and Donald J. Reimer, "Changing Patterns of Delinquent Behavior among Americans 13 to 16 Years Old: 1967–1972," *National Survey of Youth,* report 1, University of Michigan Institute for Social Research, mimeographed, 1974.

[23] James A. Wallerstein and J. C. Wyle, "Our Law-Abiding Law-Breakers," *Federal Probation,* vol. 25, April 1947, pp. 107–112.

[24] Charles R. Tittle and Wayne J. Villemez, "Social Class and Criminality," *Social Forces,* vol. 56, December 1977, pp. 474–502.

[25] Maynard I. Erickson and LaMar T. Empey, "Court Records, Undetected Delinquency, and Decisionmaking," *Journal of Criminal Law, Criminology, and Police Science,* vol. 54, December 1963, pp. 456–469. See also: Jay R. Williams and Martin Gold, "From Delinquent Behavior to Official Delinquency," *Social Problems,* vol. 20, Fall 1972, pp. 209–229.

[26] On the methodological problems of self-reported crime surveys, see: Michael Hindelang, "Race and Involvement in Common Law Personal Crimes," *American Sociological Review,* vol. 43, February 1978, pp. 93–109, especially pp. 103–104; Michael J. Hindelang, Travis Hirschi, and Joseph G. Weis, "Correlates of Delinquency: The Illustration of Discrepancy between Self-Report and Official Measures," *American Sociological Review,* vol. 44, December 1979, pp. 995–1014; and Michael J. Hindelang, Travis Hirschi, and Joseph G. Weis, *Measuring Delinquency,* Sage, Beverly Hills, Calif., 1981, especially chap. 11.

[27] Harold E. Pepinsky, "The Growth of Crime in the United States," *Annals,* vol. 423, January 1976, pp. 23–30.

[28] Eugene Doleschal, "Crime—Some Popular Beliefs," *Crime and Delinquency,* vol. 25, January 1979, pp. 1–8, quotation from p. 3.

[29] Skogan, "The Validity of Official Crime Statistics."

[30] Robert M. O'Brien, David Shichor, and David Decker, "An Empirical Comparison of the Validity of UCR and NCS Crime Rates." *Sociological Quarterly,* vol. 21, Summer 1980, pp. 391–401.

[31] Alan Booth, David R. Johnson, and Harvey M. Choldin, "Correlates of City Crime Rates: Victimization Surveys versus Official Statistics," *Social Problems,* vol. 25, December 1977, pp. 187–197.

[32] Skogan, "The Validity of Official Crime Statistics," p. 25.

[33] Hindelang et al., "Correlates of Delinquency," p. 995.

Part One introduced some of the basic issues in criminology. We saw that crime has both a legal definition and a social nature. We looked at criminology as a discipline relying on scientific methodology and drawing upon a number of scholarly perspectives to study criminal acts, criminal offenders, victims of crime, social contexts of crime, and the criminal justice system. In addition, we explored the notion of a societal perspective on crime and identified seven major types of crime: person-to-person, violent; person-to-person, property; corporate crime; crimes against organizations; social-order crimes; organized crime; and political crime.

We also began to explore the field of criminology. In looking at the problem of crime in the United States, we found that crime and violence have long been part of an American society characterized by continuous change. While many offenders who are arrested come from outsider groups and from groups of low social and economic status, crime has been a "highroad to wealth" for others. Victims of crime have often been ignored and neglected. Attempts to develop ways of assessing rates and trends of crime have

proven difficult and elusive. The official Uniform Crime Reports are the most comprehensive source of information about crime. However, disagreements over how well they measure crime have led some criminologists to develop surveys of victims and others to develop self-report surveys of crime. These measures suggest that actual crime rates may be considerably in excess of officially reported ones. As a result, crime statistics is a field that remains in dispute.

Having considered some of the basic criminological issues, we now need to deal in depth with the theories that have been advanced to explain or offer insights into crime. Substantial contributions have been made by social scientists as well as by natural scientists. The result is a great wealth of theories.

To say that there is a wealth of theories is not to say that there is consensus among criminologists. To the contrary, criminology is characterized by sharp divergences and debates on every front. Absence of consensus is also evident in the noncumulative nature of much criminological work. One study of 3690 criminological works published between 1945 and 1972 found that over half received no subsequent citation while 82—only 2.2 percent of the total—received 50 percent of the subsequent citations.[1]

In the discussions of criminological theory, we shall begin a systematic examination of four important topics: criminal acts, criminal offenders, victims of crime, and social contexts within which crime occurs. Discussing criminal acts separately from offenders and victims implies that *how* certain types of acts came to be defined as crimes must be kept analytically distinct from *why* certain offenders commit crimes.[2] Considering victims separately from offenders calls attention to the development of victimology, an emerging area of study and research. Finally, reserving social context for separate discussion implies that the amount of crime, typically expressed in terms of rates, is distinctly related to various characteristics of groups and societies.

Approaching criminology in terms of these four topics does pose a risk of duplication in the discussions of various schools of criminological thought. Economic thinking about crime, for example, appears in both Chapter 6, on criminal offenders, and Chapter 8, on social contexts. Critical criminologists' challenge to classical thought about criminal acts is discussed in Chapter 4; their challenge to positivist thought about criminal offenders is discussed in Chapter 6; and their attempt to redefine the social context of crime is discussed in Chapter 8. However, even though there is some overlap, explaining criminology in terms of these four key topics seems justified because it helps us to deal with the complexity of crime. As we shall see, each topic poses a different set of questions; each generates a different set of answers.

Whether we examine criminal acts, criminal offenders, victims, or social contexts, we find evidence of fundamental changes in criminological interpretations in recent years. Variously termed "new criminology," "Marxist criminology," "materialist criminology," "dialectical criminology," "radical criminology," "socialist criminology," and—the term used in this text—"critical criminology," the new interpretations have challenged the more traditional classical and positivist modes of thought that preoccupied criminologists in earlier decades.[3] Indeed, some criminologists have described the field of criminology as one in the midst of a fundamental paradigmatic change.[4] Although the veracity of this description remains to be seen, we shall find that criminal acts, criminal offenders, victims of crime, and social contexts are viewed very differently by the recently emerged critical criminologies.

In Part Two, one chapter is devoted to the criminal act, two to criminal offenders, one to the victims of crime, and one to the social contexts of crime. In each chapter, we shall (1) identify the appropriate theories in their early form, (2) examine modern arguments, (3) review related research, and (4) make an assessment. Having done that, we shall be able to understand how the theories shed light on the major types of crimes to be discussed in Part Three.

NOTES

[1] Marvin E. Wolfgang, Robert M. Figlio, and Terence P. Thornberry, *Evaluating Criminology*, Elsevier-Oxford, New York, 1978. See also: Gary S. Green, "A Test of the Ortega Hypothesis in Criminology," *Criminology*, vol. 19, no. 1, May 1981, pp. 45–52.

[2] Clayton A. Hartjen, "Crime as Commonsense Theory," *Criminology*, vol. 18, no.4, February 1981, pp. 435–452.

[3] For a review, see: Robert M. Bohm, "Radical Criminology: An Explication," *Criminology*, 19, 4 (February, 1982), 565–589.

[4] Charles E. Reasons, "Social Thought and Social Structure: Competing Paradigms in Criminology," *Criminology*, vol. 13, no. 3, November 1975, pp. 332–365. See also: William V. Pelfrey, "Mainstream Criminology: More New than Old," *Criminology*, vol. 17, no. 3, November 1979, pp. 323–329. Others do not agree that the new interpretations are fundamentally different. See: Robert F. Meier, "The New Criminology: Continuity in Criminological Theory," *Journal of Criminal Law and Criminology*, vol. 67, no. 4, 1977, pp. 461–469. See also: David Schichor, "The New Criminology: Some Critical Issues," *British Journal of Criminology*, vol. 20, January 1980, pp. 1–19.

PART TWO

Theories
of Crime

Perspectives on Criminal Acts

4

The criminal act is the oldest of four criminological concerns—act, offender, social context, and victim. As such, the criminal act is a logical starting point for criminology. It is only after certain acts are defined as crimes that some people are officially made criminals, others are made victims, and it becomes possible to talk about the social context of crime. As we shall see in this chapter, using the criminal act as the starting point for criminology has led one group of thinkers to argue for a legalistic, control-oriented criminology based on deterrence and another group to conceptualize criminalization as a process by which the powerful groups in a society control those who are less powerful.

To appreciate the importance of the criminal act for criminology, one need only recognize that as new criminal law is created, new groups of criminal offenders and new groups of victims also emerge. The narcotics addict, for example, became a criminal with the passage and subsequent court interpretations of the Harrison Act of 1914 and the Marijuana Tax Act of 1937.[1] In their classic criminology text, Harry Elmer Barnes and Negley K. Teeters characterized the United States as an "overcriminalized society," noting that 500,000 new state laws were enacted between 1900 and 1930, and that 76 percent of all prison inmates in 1931 were incarcerated for acts that had not been crimes 15 years earlier.[2] Today, too, thousands of laws continue to be enacted each year by our 50 states and our federal legislature.[3]

In this chapter we will examine the diverse ways in which criminology has dealt with the criminal act. As we shall see, consideration of criminal acts was foremost for the classical school of criminology which emerged in the late 1700s. Criminal acts have also been a major concern in the period since 1960; in fact, a fascinating variety of insights and perspectives have been explored.

This chapter will review the early arguments of the classical thinkers, their subsequent elaboration, and then their apparent decline in popularity among professional criminologists. Following that, we turn to the period after 1960, in which there are two sharply contrasting approaches to the criminal act. One can be called the "deterrence approach." It has put the classical argument into modern form. The other, "critical criminology," has argued that crime is best seen as a political phenomenon. We will need to examine the research which supports or fails to support each of these approaches. Finally, we will consider how each can be applied to the types of crime discussed in Part Three.

EARLY CRIMINOLOGY

Spurred by the works of Cesare Beccaria (1738–1794) and Jeremy Bentham (1748–1832), the first school of modern criminology emerged in the late 1700s; it is known as the "classical school." The classical school made the criminal act the focal point of criminology. Classicists argued (1) that crimes needed to be defined legally, (2) that punishment needed to be apportioned to crimes, (3) that people acted out of free will, and, hence, (4) that criminal law would operate to deter—i.e., prevent—crime. The classical school was enormously influential in its day. Yet, even after undergoing neoclassical modifications, it fell into disfavor until it was resurrected in the post-1960 period.

The Classical School

Beccaria

The most important thinker of the classical school, Cesare Beccaria, was an Italian nobleman who received his university training in mathematics. Working with the Veri brothers, who were concerned with penal reform in Milan, Italy, Beccaria became interested and involved in the question of crime and punishment. In 1764, at the age of 26, he wrote *An Essay on Crime and Punishments*, a book that was to have enormous influence throughout the entire world.[4]

In his *Essay*, Beccaria was influenced by the social-contract theory of society expressed in the works of the French authors, especially Jean Jacques Rousseau (1712–1778). Furthermore, he was driven by the dream of a peaceful society in which justice would prevail. Thus, he came to argue that laws are the conditions under which we sacrifice part of our liberty in order to enjoy the rest in peace and security. For Beccaria, the authority of making penal laws could reside only with legislators who represented the whole society and were united with the people they represented by a social compact.

According to Beccaria, laws had to be written. Crimes were to be defined in terms of their injury to society rather than the intention of the person committing them or the dignity of the person offended. Punishments were to be proportioned to the crime ("let the punishment fit the crime" became the maxim) and to be administered with certainty, fairness, and humanity. From this point of view, the central interest of criminology becomes law and the violation of specific legal codes.

At the core of classical school thought is the assumption of free will, in which people are seen to act in a responsible manner, to be aware of their actions, and to understand the consequences of their actions. Indeed, at one point, Beccaria proposed to prevent crime by perfecting the system of education.[5] Yet the overall thrust of his argument is *deterrence*. *If* individuals act out of free will, *if* crimes are defined legally in terms of the injury to society, and *if* punishments are proportional to the crimes and administered with certainty, fairness, and humanity, *then* criminal law will operate to deter or prevent crime. Although punishments were to be spelled out in the law, deterrence—prevention—was the desired outcome. As Beccaria wrote, "It is better to prevent crimes than to punish them."[6]

Bentham

Beccaria's work was further developed by Jeremy Bentham, an English utilitarian philosopher, who wrote during the same period. As a utilitarian, Bentham argued that persons engaged in a "felicity calculus" in which they rationally assessed the relative pains and pleasures of an act and its consequences.[7] Applied to criminal behavior, utilitarianism meant that it was necessary to have a legal code which prescribed the specific punishments for specific crimes. Orienting their conduct to such a code, potential offenders would be deterred or prevented from committing acts in which the pain of the consequences exceeded the pleasure gained from them.

DARTMOOR PRISON.

Classical school theorists argued that prisons allowed punishments to be proportional to crimes; Dartmoor Prison is modeled after Jeremy Bentham's panopticon. (NEW YORK PUBLIC LIBRARY)

Bentham also went beyond Beccaria in arguing that the aim of punishment was not only to deter others but also to prevent what today is called "recidivism." However, he also felt that punishment should be avoided in cases in which (1) there is no criminal offense, because consent has been given (Bentham was against using the criminal law to regulate personal morality); (2) punishment has no power to affect the will (e.g., when dealing with the very young or the insane); (3) the evil of the punishment exceeds that of the offense; and (4) the same purpose may be obtained at a cheaper price. In particular, he considered capital punishment unsatisfactory because the pain it imposes is greater than the purpose it accomplishes.[8]

Finally, Bentham articulated a reformative and utilitarian justification of punishment. Like Beccaria, he argued that it should be apportioned to the crime and administered humanely. However, he went on to propose the "panopticon," a model prison in the form of a circular building which kept prisoners enclosed but gave the prison director complete surveillance of prisoners as well as staff. Inside the model prison there was provision for prisoners to work and to be taught profitable trades. Bentham also anticipated today's prerelease programs, classification of offenders, and religious training in prisons. In short, he made punishment a science, one that was to be rational, impersonal, and humane.[9]

In its day, the classical school had enormous influence. It emerged as Europe and the United States were undergoing dramatic social changes. The medieval order—with its fixed hierarchies that offered immense privilege for some elite groups, its powerful hereditary monarchs, and its labor system that kept peasants as serfs—was in its final stages. A new, industrial society was rapidly emerging. Democracy and social reforms were called for. Subjects were to become citizens. Serfs were to become laborers. In the process, old regimes fell; new governments emerged.

In Europe, reforms of the criminal law were a most important part of the widespread social changes. After the French Revolution of 1789, the Constituent Assembly's first order of business was to revise the criminal code. In the new code of 1791, judicial discretion was eliminated and penalties were to be applied equally to all violators of the law. England accomplished a similar revision with gradual reforms that lasted well into the 1800s. Moreover, reflecting Bentham's influence, there was considerable movement toward codification of the common law.[10]

Europe also witnessed a major shift away from torture to the use of imprisonment under codes in which time spent in prison was proportioned to severity of the criminal offense. In 1786, for example, a number of Italian cities instituted a code in which punishments were proportioned to crimes; the number of treasonable acts was reduced; and hard labor and the lash replaced fire, the wheel, and other forms of torture. The 1800s also saw prisons reshaped by many of the reforms suggested by Bentham.

In the United States during the 1790s, Beccaria's essay enjoyed great popularity. Optimistic in the aftermath of independence and nationhood, Americans argued that the origin and persistence of deviant behavior lay in the defective colonial criminal codes, which reflected British insistence on severe and cruel punishment. Reform became the order of the day. Laws were to be clear and simple. Punishments were to be moderate but certain. Imprisonment was seen as more humane than hanging and less brutal than whipping. In general, the enthusiasm was enormous. As David J. Rothman writes of the period:

> They located the roots of deviancy not in the criminal, but in the legal system. Just as colonial codes had encouraged deviant behavior, republican ones would now curtail, or even eliminate it. To pass the proper laws would end the problem.[11]

In short, good law became an end in itself, a cure for crime.

Neoclassicism

Logical and rational though they appeared, the reforms advocated by the classical school were found to be problematic when put into practice. To begin with, many of the punishments were still severe and harsh; long prison sentences, for example, were common. Moreover, questions such as the following arose: How could the law take into account the differences between individual offenders—differences such as age, previous criminal record, and soundness of mind? Should there be a range of penal measures available to the court? Should experts other than lawyers be called to testify in cases? To resolve these kinds of questions, legal scholars writing in the early and middle 1800s developed what came to be known as the "neoclassical school" or, as it has been called more recently, "neoclassical revisionism."[12]

The neoclassicists' major modification of classical thought was their questioning of the way free will was exercised and the circumstances under which it was exercised. The neoclassicists argued that (1) children under age 7 and the aged were incapable or less capable of making their own decisions; (2) the insane and the feebleminded were incapable of freedom of action; and (3) the courts should take into account factors such as mitigating circumstances, incompetence, pathology, and past record of offenders. In so doing, the neoclassicists saw the criminal actor as "no longer the isolated, atomistic rational man of pure reason." Their thinking also paved the way for the use of nonlegal experts, such as psychiatrists and social workers, by the courts.[13]

The modifications made by the neoclassicists found ready acceptance. The very severe French penal code of 1791 was revised in 1810 to allow for less severe penalties and more judicial discretion. Questioning the rationality of the criminal actor, the McNaughton rule of 1843 in England permitted a defense on the grounds of insanity if it were proved that

> at the time of the committing of the act, the party was labouring under such a defect of reason, from disease of the mind, as not to know the nature and quality of the act he was doing; or if he did know it, that he did not know he was doing what was wrong.[14]

In the United States the New Hampshire rule went even further in that it absolved an accused person from criminal responsibility if the unlawful act was the product of mental disease or defect.[15] The middle 1800s also saw the beginnings of probation and parole, which involved serving sentences in the community rather than in the prison (see Chapter 18).

The broader significance of the neoclassical modifications was that they began to take criminal offenders into account. In allowing for the law to take individual differences into account, the neoclassicists implied that there were multiple causes of crime and that the doctrine of free will was no longer a satisfactory explanation for criminal behavior. This viewpoint helped to create the academic climate for the positivist school of criminology, which came to dominate thinking about crime throughout the late nineteenth and early twentieth centuries. (See Chapters 5 and 6.) At the same time, the greater flexibility of neoclassicism allowed classical principles to have a continuing influence on the practice of criminal justice.

Indeed, it is safe to say that the principles of classicism, along with their neoclassical adaptations, have exerted an enormous influence on criminal justice. Speaking generally of the classicists' reforms, Coleman Phillipson wrote in 1923:

> The triumph of Beccaria's teaching has been complete. His principles are now embodied in every criminal code in Christendom; and they have penetrated into the distant Orient. Indeed, no civilized code of criminal law, wherever promulgated, can now disregard them.[16]

Or, as it has been put in the more recent writing of Ian Taylor, Paul Walton, and Jock Young:

> It is this (neoclassical) model—with minor corrections—which remains the major model of human behavior held to by agencies of social control in all advanced industrial societies (whether in the West or the East).[17]

Indeed, in any assessment of criminality in today's society one can hardly ignore the legacy of the classical school: the "compendious body of written criminal law which prescribes negative sanctions for people found individually responsible for causing social injury."[18]

Decline of Classicism

Although classicism and neoclassicism exerted an enormous influence upon criminal justice, professional criminologists of the latter 1800s became disenchanted with classical thought. For one thing, there was great disillusionment with the prison system, especially with its harmful effects upon those subjected to its discipline. In particular, rates of recidivism were high (see Chapter 18). For another, classical theory advanced no proposition concerning the causes of criminal behavior.

Finally, professional criminologists of the latter 1800s, confronted by what they saw as rising crime rates, lost faith in the classical argument that the criminal law would deter crime if administered with certainty, fairness, and humanity. Loss of faith in deterrence grew to the point where deterrence was no longer taken as an issue for serious scholarly study. In fact, as two later writers have noted, by 1950 "the bulk of the research seemed to indicate to most scholars that the idea of deterrence was not empirically valid."[19]

CRIMINOLOGY AFTER 1960

During the 1960s, there was a dramatic turnaround in criminology. The criminal act once again became a focal point. This turnaround happened in two sharply different ways: (1) through the reemergence of classical ideas and (2) through the debate over which acts should be crimes, a debate engendered by critical criminology. Let's look at each of these modern developments in thinking about criminal acts.

Modern Classicism

Since the 1960s, serious scholarly attention has once again been devoted to classical concerns. There are several diverse factors behind this change. For one, public demands for "law and order" have led to increased calls for definite sentences, for certainty rather than discretion in the administration of law (e.g., see Chapter 17), and for greater use of imprisonment rather than suspended sentences, probation, and parole. For another, economists whose theoretical orientation includes a view of people as "rational" and acting out of free will have begun to examine crime. Finally, the advanced statistical techniques now available permit a more sophisticated calculation of the relationships between crime rates and other factors. The new classical emphasis can be seen in deterrence research and in renewed calls for determinate sentencing.

Deterrence research

Following the widely accepted definition given by Franklin E. Zimring and Gordon J. Hawkins, "deterrence" refers to situations "where a threat causes individuals who would have committed the threatened behavior to refrain from doing so."[20] It follows that "net deterrence" is "the total number of threatened behaviors it (the threat) prevents less those it creates."[21] The problem for research is that deterrence and net deterrence cannot be observed or measured. As Jack P. Gibbs put it, "Common sense to the contrary, we never *observe* someone omitting an act because of the perceived risk and fear of punishment."[22] How can we study behavior that we cannot observe?

One way to get around this problem is to focus on crime rates. Problematic though these may be, we can reason that deterrence would be operating if one jurisdiction with strict law enforcement showed a crime rate which was dramatically lower than that of another where the enforcement was lenient. From this line of approach, the classical deterrence argument would be restated as follows: "The rate for a particular type of crime varies inversely with the celerity, certainty, and severity of punishments of that type of crime."[23] In other words, crime rates go down when celerity (swiftness with which offenders are prosecuted), certainty, and severity increase. People act rationally and see that the costs or possible consequences of crimes exceed the benefits obtainable by those crimes.

The research on deterrence has reflected the classicists' concern with certainty and severity. In this research, certainty is measured by statistics such as crime clearance rates, proportion of cases prosecuted, proportion of prosecuted cases found guilty, and, more generally, the proportion of reported crimes for which offenders are imprisoned. As each of these increases, the certainty that the offender will be punished increases. Severity is typically measured by length of prison sentences served for the crimes under consideration.

Some findings of deterrence research One aspect of deterrence research has been a preoccupation with the relationship between homicide rates and capital punishment. In the late 1950s, Thorsten Sellin compared homicide rates for the years 1920–1955 in matched groups of states which had and had not retained the death penalty. According to his calculations, the homicide rates of states that retained the death penalty differed little from those of states which did not retain it. Sellin was led to the conclusion that "the presence of the death penalty—in law or practice—does not influence the homicide death rates."[24]

However, research on capital punishment as a deterrent took a different turn in the 1970s with the work of the economist Isaac Ehrlich. Criticizing Sellin for failing to consider the extent of actual enforcement of the death penalty, alternative punishments, and incapacitation of offenders who were punished, and for various methodological shortcomings, Ehrlich related capital punishment to the murder rate utilizing an elaborate model with a regression analytic technique. Of six measures of actual risk of execution, he found that all were negatively

Preparing the electric chair.
Despite much debate, there
is little clear evidence that
death sentences deter crime.
(DOUG MAGEE/EDITORIAL
PHOTOCOLOR ARCHIVES)

related to the murder rate (four of these were statistically significant beyond chance), a finding which implies that the greater the risk—i.e., certainty—of execution, the lower the murder rate.[25]

Ehrlich's work has stimulated a great deal of controversy and further research. Critics questioned the regression analysis he used when attempts to replicate his findings were frustrated by rounding error,[26] choice of years selected, and use of FBI rather than Vital Statistics data.[27] In other analyses, unemployment rates and duration of unemployment have been found to be more related to rates of homicide and rape than executions are.[28] Capital punishment has also been found to be "brutalizing" in that there is a "spillover effect" of two additional homicides in the month after an execution.[29] Finally, an analysis focused on police found no consistent relationship between provision for capital punishments and killings of police.[30] Yet it must also be noted that in a subsequent cross-sectional analysis comparing states, Ehrlich claimed to find additional support for the hypothesis that capital punishment deters murder.[31]

Some deterrence research has moved beyond preoccupation with capital punishment and homicide rates. A landmark study by Charles R. Tittle used indices of certainty (the number of admissions to state prisons divided by the number of crimes known to police), and severity (especially the average length of time served by felony offenders) and correlated them to crime rates (as indicated in the Uniform Crime Reports for various states). Tittle's major finding was that there was a negative correlation of .45 between certainty and the overall crime rate. In other words, as the rate of certainty increases, the level of crime decreases by about half as much. If one examines particular offenses, certainty is more strongly related to the crime rates for sex offenses and assault than to those for homicide and motor vehicle theft. Severity, on the other hand, is positively related to the general crime rate and rates for specific crimes (with the exception of murder) in that as severity increases, so do crime rates. However, relationships are smaller and almost disappear if highly urbanized states are compared with less urbanized states.[32]

Subsequent work on deterrence has gone in several directions. In two studies of skyjacking, for example, it was found that increasing the probabilities of apprehension and incarceration—in other words, increasing certainty—led to significant reductions in hijackings.[33] One study of shoplifting found that a low risk of apprehension was associated with higher amounts of shoplifting.[34] The threat of punishment was found to generate higher reported income among income tax violators (although about a third of those responding to threat also attempted to make up through greater deductions what had been lost through more honest reporting of income).[35]

Deterrence has also been subjected to critical scrutiny. Increasingly, it is recognized that individual actors need to be taken into account. If this is done, the fear of sanctions is readily seen to be only one determinant of behavior. The study of shoplifting cited above also found that informal sanctions (i.e., approval or disapproval from friends) appeared to be stronger deterrents than formal sanctions. A study of marijuana use found that extralegal factors exercise a stronger effect than legal ones.[36] An exploratory study of actual versus perceived certainty of punishment found that people's estimates of arrest rates are significantly influenced if they have experienced an arrest.[37] Finally, in a survey using data on nearly 2000 individuals from randomly sampled households in three states, which examined nine offenses (assault, $50 theft, $5 theft, income tax cheating, lying to an intimate, occupational-specific deviance, sitting during a rendition of the national anthem, smoking marijuana, and illegal gambling), Tittle found the perceived certainty of punishment to be

> apparently of relatively less import in accounting for abstinence from marijuana use, tax cheating, and sitting during the national anthem, but . . . of relatively large significance in explaining unwillingness to gamble illegally or to commit the serious crimes assault and theft.[38]

However, he also goes on to stress the importance of informal social controls, to note that there are considerable differences among persons (such as age, sex, size of place of residence, and religious participation) that lead to variations in deviant behavior, and to assert the need for a theory to identify the process by which threat of sanctions might affect behavior.[39]

Another unresolved problem in deterrence research is causation. To say that uncertainty and crime rates are correlated does not necessarily mean that increased certainty causes a lower crime rate. In fact, it could well be the other way around: that high crime rates cause decreased certainty. This is because there are limits to the capacity of the criminal justice system; in particular, there are only a fixed number of prison cells. Indeed, it must be noted that since 1960 the considerable increase in number of recorded crimes has meant that the average certainty of punishment, if defined by imprisonment, has declined dramatically. The increase in crime rate has preceded—one might say "caused"—the decrease in certainty.[40]

To sum up, there has been an abundance of research supporting deterrence in the period since 1960. Ehrlich's work advanced the provocative finding that certainty of execution lowers the murder rate. Working with index crimes generally, Tittle also found certainty to be related to lower crime rates. Other researchers found that increased certainty could serve to deter skyjacking, shoplifting, and income tax violations. At the same time, it must also be said that the deterrence argument is open to question. Some criminologists would question the research methodology used in deterrence research. Some would argue that informal social controls are more powerful influences over behavior than legal controls. Finally, some would question whether a criminal justice system operating at capacity can increase certainty to the point of deterrence. These "ifs, ands, and buts" in deterrence research lead us to the following critique.

Critique of deterrence research Although deterrence research has proliferated in recent years, Tittle's assessment appears to be a most reasonable one:

> Although this collection of evidence has renewed confidence that sanctions play an important part in human conduct, it also revealed how little we actually know and it has raised many more question than it has answered.[41]

While some of the gaps in our knowledge are the result of poor statistical data, there is also need for a theory that will deal with the complex questions of the type discussed above. In particular, what is the relationship between formal and informal social controls? Why are there differences between persons? How does the threat of sanctions affect behavior? Is it possible that high crime rates "cause" decreased certainty?

In short, much remains to be done before the deterrence argument can be accepted. In thinking about the implications of deterrence, it will be useful to bear in mind Daniel Nagin's words of caution:

> Policy makers in the criminal justice system are done a disservice if they are left with the impression that the empirical evidence, which they themselves are frequently unable to evaluate, strongly supports the deterrence hypothesis.[42]

Nevertheless, the recent interest in deterrence research has breathed new life into the classical school of criminology.

Determinate sentencing: An application of policy

Classical rationales are also clearly evident in the many calls for determinate or fixed sentencing that have emerged in recent years. People who take this position would seek to base sentencing of the offender on the criminal act rather than on the offender's characteristics as indicative of his or her potential for rehabilitation. They would also seek to place the authority for sentencing in the hands of legislatures rather than judges and parole boards.

There are several dimensions to the modern arguments for fixed or determinate sentencing. One is that punishment is "moral insofar as it affirms the social order."[43] Indeed, if administered with fairness, consistency, and humanity, the law is a tool of moral learning.[44] Another is that society needs to defend itself against dangerous offenders;[45] Ernest van den Haag, for one, argues that the death penalty should be used even though we lack proof of its deterrent effect.[46] Others would argue that without punishment there is no viable legal system.[47]

Finally, determinate sentencing based on categories of "demonstrated risk" has been seen as bringing "more certainty and fairness *to the prisoner*."[48]

It is in the modern arguments for fixed or determinate sentencing that one sees the long-run staying power of classical thinking about crime. The criminal law is a point of focus; the criminal act and the sanctions attached to it are placed at the center of criminological thought. Punishment is legitimate, especially if administered with certainty and fairness. Its actual use and theoretical use are necessary for a viable social order. Assuming that offenders are rational and able to calculate their actions, determinate sentences are fair to offenders and, at the same time, provide predictable social responses to criminal behavior, thereby deterring it.

Critical Criminology

While some present-day criminologists are studying criminal acts by returning to classical arguments, others—the "critical" criminologists—have begun to deal with criminal acts in an entirely different manner. Questioning the rightfulness of criminal law, they have asked how it is that some acts come to be defined as crimes while others, perhaps equally harmful, remain noncriminal. They have also discerned a clear relationship between crime and social power and advanced the notion that crime is a political phenomenon.[49]

Modern critical criminology offers two main perspectives on the criminal act: the labeling perspective and the conflict perspective. The labeling perspective calls attention to the manner in which societies define criminal and deviant behaviors. The conflict perspective emphasizes the manner in which the definition of criminal acts is the product of struggle among competing social groups. Let's examine these perspectives in greater detail, noting the research related to them, and then consider the critiques to which they have been subjected.

Labeling perspective

Stemming from symbolic interactionism, a theory developed by the social philosopher George Herbert Mead, the labeling perspective (or, as it is sometimes called, the "interactionist" perspective) emphasizes the social construction of crime and deviance.[50] It sees no act as inherently criminal. It sees criminalization as proceeding from social needs and cultural patterns of a society.

A number of theorists have taken the labeling perspective. Among the earliest and most prominent was Edwin Lemert, who argued that it was more useful to see social control as leading to deviance than to see deviance as leading to social control.[51] Later, in an often-quoted statement, Howard. S. Becker wrote:

> *Social groups create deviance by making the rules whose infraction constitutes deviance*, and by applying those rules to particular people and labeling them as outsiders.[52]

His statement was further elaborated in the work of Kai T. Erikson:

> People who gather together into communities need to be able to describe and anticipate those areas of experience which lie outside the immediate compass of the group.[53]

Erikson then went on to assert that the deviant is the person who personifies the forces of evil which lie outside the boundaries of the group and "that in doing so, he shows us the difference between the inside of the group and the outside."[54]

The idea that deviance is a group product has a number of interesting ramifications. In modern society the mass media become "mystifiers of social deviance" in that they "reinforce, legitimate, and partly create the images and myths of a basically consensual and just society."[55] Furthermore, the actions of agencies which attempt to define and control crime often become more critical in shaping the problem of crime than the motives and intentions of those who are labeled criminal.[56] Finally, deviance is often amplified when less social tolerance of deviant behavior leads to:

> More acts being defined as crimes
> > *leads to*
> More action against criminals
> > *leads to*
> More alienation of deviants
> > *leads to*
> More crime by deviant groups
> > *leads to*
> Less tolerance of deviants by conforming groups
> > *and round again*[57]

The labeling perspective is especially useful in examining what often appear to be arbitrary and capricious definitions of crimes. It helps explain why certain acts are designated as crimes in some places and at some times while in others they are not (see Chapter 13). Moreover, the labeling perspective is most suggestive in its argument that the definition of criminal acts is a fundamental process flowing out of group needs to set boundaries for behavior. Mass media and control agencies themselves may be elements of that process. The irony is that deviant behavior itself may be amplified where there is less tolerance of it.

Conflict perspective

While the labeling perspective emphasizes the social construction of crime and deviance, the conflict perspective sees the definition of crime as the product of struggle among competing groups. There are two viewpoints within the conflict perspective—one focusing on group interaction and struggle, the other taking a radical or Marxist position.

Group interaction and struggle   As advanced by George B. Vold in the late 1950s, the "group interaction" perspective sees people as both part and product of their group associations. Society, in turn, consists of groups which are in constant interaction and struggle with each other. Each group aims constantly to improve its own position vis-à-vis other groups. Groups come into conflict when the interests and purposes of one group overlap, encroach upon, or compete with those of others.[58] According to Vold, criminality flows out of the conflicts between groups:

> As one political group lines up against another, both seek the assistance of the organized state to help them defend their rights and protect their interests. Thus the familiar cry, 'there ought to be a law' (to suppress the undesirable) is understandable as the natural recourse of one side or the other in a conflict situation.[59]

From this point of view, crime can be seen as behavior of a minority group, and much criminal behavior can be seen as political. Vold's perspective is illustrated by conscientious objectors who serve prison sentences for the crime of having convictions that lead them to refuse to participate in war. It is also seen in the criminalizing of political protest, management-labor conflicts, and attempts to upset systems of racial segregation.[60] In advancing conflict criminology, Vold is careful to note that he is dealing with "those kinds of situations in which the individual criminal acts flow from the collision of groups whose members are loyally upholding the in-group position."[61]

Although it is advocated by a number of criminologists,[62] conflict criminology today is most often identified with the work of Austin T. Turk.[63] Like Vold, Turk proposes that the study of criminalization begin by considering the relative position of various groups in society. His interest, however, lies in considering how those in power achieve and maintain their authority and legitimacy. According to Turk, social order is complex in that it requires a balance between consensus or agreement and coercion or force. The task of authorities is to prevent the balance from shifting excessively to either side. As he puts it, the stability of authority is secure as long as people have "been conditioned to accept as a fact of life that authorities must be reckoned with as such."[64]

Taking this view of society, Turk argues that a theory of crime must deal with the question of the types of conflict which are and are not criminalized. One factor affecting criminalization is the cultural or social difference between authorities and subjects: where such differences are minimal, less behavior will be criminalized; where the differences are maximal, the subjects will have both language and philosophy to justify their behavior. Another factor combines the degree of organization and level of sophistication of authorities and "norm resisters"; conflict is more likely when subjects are organized into groups and associations and also more likely when there is less sophistication, i.e., less "knowledge of patterns in the behavior of others which is used in the attempts to manipulate them."[65] This is because sophisticated authorities and subjects can achieve their goals without overt conflict. A third factor is the relative power of the two groups; generally, criminalization will be greater when enforcers have more power and resisters have less. A final factor is the "realism of conflict moves," i.e., maintaining or resisting authority with relatively little investment of

resources; here criminalization will tend to increase when "conflict moves" lack
realism.

85

*Perspectives on
Criminal Acts*

Radical or Marxist viewpoint Attempting to go beyond consideration of group
interaction and struggle, criminologists of the radical or Marxist persuasion have
asked two key questions: (1) Which acts should be crimes? (2) Which acts should
criminologists take as appropriate for study? They have claimed that it is
necessary to see the origin of deviant acts in the economic system of capitalism.
From their viewpoint, crime is the pathological product of a pathological social
system. Indeed, the existing criminal law is arbitrary and suspect, since it is a tool
of the ruling classes.

Radical and Marxist criminologists base their work on the thought of Karl
Marx and William Bonger (see Chapter 6) and take the position that the political
initiatives that give rise to or abolish legislation are "intimately bound up with the
structure of the political economy of the state."[66] As Richard Quinney puts it,
"law became the ultimate means by which the State secures the interests of the
ruling class."[67] In a more detailed formulation, Steven Spitzer has argued that
populations in capitalistic societies become

> eligible for management as deviant when they disturb, hinder or call into question
> any of the following: (1) capitalist modes of appropriating the product of human labor
> (e.g., when the poor "steal" from the rich), (2) the social conditions under which
> capitalist production takes place (e.g., those who refuse or are unable to perform
> wage labor), (3) patterns of distribution and consumption in capitalist society (e.g.,
> those who use drugs for escape and transcendence rather than sociability and
> adjustment), (4) the process of socialization for productive and non-productive roles
> (e.g., youth who refuse to be schooled or those who deny the validity of "family
> life") and (5) the ideology which supports the functioning of capitalist society (e.g.,
> proponents of alternative forms of social organization).[68]

In other words, it is the acts which pose a threat to the state that come to be
defined as criminal; the question of individual or social harm is secondary.

From a radical or Marxist perspective it is necessary to recognize that there
are many harmful acts which are either not part of or not enforced under the
present criminal law. The following statement of the American Friends Service
Committee states the case:

> Actions that clearly ought to be labeled "criminal," because they bring the greatest
> harm to the greatest number, are in fact accomplished officially by agencies of the
> government. The overwhelming number of murders in this century has been
> committed by governments in wartime. Hundreds of unlawful killings by police go
> unprosecuted each year. The largest forceful acquisitions of property in the United
> States have been the theft of lands guaranteed by treaty to Indian tribes, thefts
> sponsored by the government. The largest number of dislocations, tantamount to
> kidnapping—the evacuation and internment of Japanese-Americans during World
> War II—was carried out by the government with the approval of the courts. Civil-
> rights demonstrators, struggling to exercise their constitutional rights, have been
> repeatedly beaten and harassed by police and sheriffs. And in the Vietnam war,
> America has violated its Constitution and international law.[69]

Acts which pose a threat to the state often become defined as criminal; this
1982 demonstration for nuclear disarmament resulted in the largest mass arrest
in the history of New York City.   (WIDE WORLD PHOTOS)

In developing the case further, one might also consider Schwendinger and
Schwendinger, who would cite human rights violations, imperialism, war, racism,
sexism, and poverty as forms of crime;[70] or Quinney, who sees three major types
of crimes of domination: (1) crimes of control (e.g., felonies or misdemeanors
committed by law enforcement agents as they enforce the law), (2) crimes of
government (e.g., the Watergate crimes and other crimes committed by elected
and appointed officers), and (3) crimes of economic domination (e.g., price fixing,
pollution, and other crimes committed by corporations).[71] These forms of crimes
are seen by radicals as tolerated under capitalism because they are necessary to its
survival.

The radical or Marxist perspective on the criminal act has expanded a long-
standing criminological debate over the proper dimensions of criminological
inquiry. One approach, very much along the lines of the classical school
(discussed earlier in this chapter), would have criminology deal specifically with
crimes that are violations of criminal law. As Paul Tappan put it:

> Crime is an intentional act or omission in violation of criminal law (statutory and case
> law), committed without defense or justification, and sanctioned by the state as a
> felony or misdemeanor.[72]

An alternative approach was put forth by Edwin Sutherland and others who sought during the 1940s to extend the scope of criminology to include unethical business practices, even though such practices were in many cases considered violations of civil or administrative rather than criminal law.[73] Today, the radical or Marxist approach of a criminology that would examine crimes against human rights proposes to do what might be called an "end run" around both Tappan and Sutherland.[74] In advocating the study of imperialism, war, racism, sexism, and poverty, it would open an enormous number of areas to criminological inquiry.

It should be noted that definition of crime is an issue which continues to divide the critical criminologies we have been discussing. In seeing crime as a social construct, labeling theorists are accepting the legitimacy of what the authoritative agencies of the society have defined as crime. In seeing crime as the outcome of struggle among social groups, conflict theorists taking a view based on group interaction and struggle also see the criminal law as a normal, legitimate part of society. However, for radical or Marxist criminologists criminal law is not the appropriate definition of crime. Indeed, as was mentioned earlier, they consider the existing criminal law arbitrary and suspect, since it is a tool of the ruling classes.[75]

Having outlined the perspectives comprising modern-day critical criminology, we now need to turn to the research that has been stimulated by the questions it has raised. Although this research is not voluminous, we shall see that there is an interesting set of findings contributing to our understanding of how criminal acts are socially defined.

Research in critical criminology

Critical criminology has stimulated two important lines of research related to criminal acts. One has dealt with the creation of law, attempting to show how lawmaking is the product of struggle between antagonistic interests and social classes. The other has provided an empirical assessment of the extent of social agreement on the seriousness of given criminal acts.

Both lines of research have been advanced to demonstrate the superiority of critical criminology over competing arguments. In particular, critical criminology has been pitted against consensus explanations. Whereas critical criminology emphasizes control of the state (and hence the criminal law) as the "prize for which antagonistic interests struggle," consensus explanations argue that lawmaking reflects a fundamental consensus about values among members of society.[76] The classical school of criminology (discussed earlier in this chapter) and the positivist school (to be discussed in Chapters 5 and 6) are consensus explanations in that both assume that there is little social struggle and little social debate over which acts *should be* included in the criminal law.

Studies of creation of law   The studies of creation of law have looked to historical analyses to support the perspective of critical criminology. England of the Middle Ages provides a number of instances in which law was specifically used to support commercial interests. Beginning in the 1400s and expanding greatly in the 1700s, laws against theft, especially larceny, were developed and promoted by merchants and industrialists who needed new ways of protecting their property.[77] Vagrancy laws, first developed in the interest of landlords, were later modified to protect merchants from wandering bands of displaced peasants. In 1530, the vagrancy statutes were modified further to give authorities even more control over "rogues," "vagabonds," and "ruffians"; in fact, the authorities were permitted to arrest persons suspected to be capable of committing crimes.[78] Finally, there were the enclosure laws, which had the effect of removing peasants from the land, and laws prohibiting workers from organizing.[79] Together, the laws against theft, the vagrancy laws, and the enclosure laws guaranteed a continuous supply of laborers at low wages and served to create conditions under which the newly emergent capitalist interests could obtain high profits.

Other critical analyses of creation of law have gone along several lines of inquiry. Child welfare laws promulgated as humanitarian reforms at the turn of the century have been found to be "more concerned with restriction than with liberation, eliminating 'foreign' and radical ideologies, and preparing youth as a disciplined and devoted work force."[80] In the mid-1960s, negotiations over modifications of New York State's prostitution law saw the interests of welfare, civil liberties, and the bar association coming to dominate over those of police and businesspeople; the general public was not even considered.[81] One study of the meat-packing industry found, paradoxically, that laws appearing to conflict with the interests of the ruling class may in fact maintain them; the net result of more sanitary meat packaging was that added costs forced small firms out of the industry.[82]

Interactionists have been particularly concerned with the manner in which deviance comes to be socially perceived. In his work developing the interactionist perspective, Becker called attention to the role of moral entrepreneurs, i.e., individuals, groups, or organizations who define new categories of deviance as crime. The efforts of moral entrepreneurs are dramatically clear in the development of the Prohibition movement, in which the Women's Christian Temperance Union played the leading role;[83] and in the development of narcotics legislation, in which the Federal Narcotics Bureau itself waged an intensive campaign of propaganda and lobbying.[84] In other research into the perception of deviance, it has been shown how the changed vocabulary of deviance has influenced social reaction to corporate behavior[85] and how irrational public fears about sexual crime led to enactment of unworkable laws concerning sexual psychopaths.[86]

Other studies of creation of law have reached conclusions that would call one or more of the critical criminologies into question. Contrary to Anthony M. Platt's findings on child welfare laws, noted above, John Hagan and Jeffrey Leon found that the debate over delinquency legislation in Canada flowed from organizational interests rather than from attempts of capitalists to control juvenile labor markets and that the emphasis was on probation work, not imprisonment.[87] In other work, Hagan and two associates argue that elites may take the lead in endorsing more tolerant viewpoints toward certain crimes (e.g., homosexual acts) and that dominant groups form the cutting edge of social consensus.[88] Similarly, in an assessment of changes in the California penal code from 1955 to 1971, Richard Berk and his associates argue that while the consensus model cannot explain the specific changes that were made, it is true that, "at one time or another virtually everyone gained through the making of laws."[89]

Perhaps the most general perspective on the creation of law has been taken by William Chambliss and Robert Seidman. In their review of studies of law creation, they are critical of both consensus and conflict explanations. Specifically concerning conflict theories, they argue that conflict theories based on group interaction and struggle cannot explain why a given group succeeds and that conflict theories based on radical or Marxist ideas cannot explain why the ruling class is often divided in its interests. They therefore conclude that both types of conflict theories tend to be tautological in their pure forms, that a combination of the two is in order, and that each society, nation, economic system, and historical period contains "certain contradictory elements which are the moving force behind social changes—including the creation of law."[90] They go on to stress that people—not the "system," "society," or the "legal order"—make laws.

Empirical assessment of societal consensus   The other important line of research developed by critical criminology stems from attempts to show that there is disagreement, especially between social classes, on the seriousness of criminal acts. As it turns out, the research findings suggest otherwise. In one study, Peter H. Rossi and his associates conducted a questionnaire survey of 200 randomly selected households in Baltimore and found that (1) the general ordering of crimes by seriousness corresponds with commonsense expectations (crimes against persons are regarded as highly serious, crimes against property as significantly less serious, and white-collar crimes and crimes without victims as not particularly serious); and (2) agreement among various subgroups was quite high, with the possible exception of black males having less than a high school education.[91] Similarly, Charles W. Thomas and his associates, using a sample of over 3300 randomly selected people in the southeastern area of the United States, found high correlations among respondents' rank orderings of types of crime as well as high agreement on the appropriate length of sentences for the given types of crime. Again, there were some differences among blacks, who preferred more lenient sentences for homicide, rape, and sale of drugs to minors but more severe sentences for gambling, prostitution, and use of marijuana.[92]

Tittle's study of deterrence, mentioned earlier, included a question concerning "how deviant" nine offenses were regarded. All but one of them were considered morally wrong by more than 50 percent of the people in each of the three states. Generally, despite some revealing differences by age (e.g., twice as many older people as younger people found smoking marijuana to be morally wrong), offenses were ranked similarly by respondents in all three states and respondents of differing sex, race, socioeconomic status, and size of place of residence. A subsequent question concerning "how serious" the deviant acts were regarded found only slightly less similarity among residents, with the exception of respondents of differing ages.[93] Finally, V. Lee Hamilton and Steve Rytina found substantial agreement that "the punishment should fit the crime," although some respondents dissented out of principle and there was some dissent on the part of lower-income and black respondents.[94]

In short, the studies attempting to show disagreement on the seriousness of criminal acts have been less than supportive of the critical criminological viewpoint. In fact, although there are some exceptions, the studies suggest that consensus theory may be closer to the mark. There are several possible explanations for the failure of research studies to support the position of critical criminology. For one, the data may be inadequate; these are limited samples drawn from different places at different times. Second, people may have been misled about the really serious crime in American society; the apparent consensus may have been molded or manipulated by elite interests. Third, if the real elite in American society is the 1 percent of Americans who own 50 percent of all the property, these people will not be picked up as a significant part of the small samples which have been surveyed. Finally, as was noted earlier, it may well be that modern societies have a fair amount of consensus and some pockets of dissent, and rest on a balance between the two.

Critique of critical criminology

In analyzing the definition of criminal acts in terms of the wider social structure, there is no doubt that the critical criminologists have advanced a socially informed critique of traditional criminology, both of the classical school discussed earlier in this chapter and of the positivist school to be discussed in Chapters 5 and 6. They have pointed out that criminologists need to look beyond official definitions of crime. They have made it clear that powerful social groups manipulate definitions of crime to increase their own power. They have moved criminology away from preoccupation with pathology of individual offenders and toward consideration of political pathology of social systems, especially capitalism. In short, they have demonstrated that crime can be meaningfully interpreted as a political phenomenon.

Whether the critical criminologists have adequately addressed the questions they have raised is the subject of much debate. One line of criticism has questioned the methodological adequacy of one or another of the critical criminologies. Indeed, they have been criticized by some as being "moralistic," "unempirical," and "rhetorical"[95] and by others as being imprecise about "conflict" and "power."[96] Labeling theory, in particular, has been subject to attack for weak conceptualization and sloppy research, and for being "ossified."[97] Moreover, as was noted with regard to the debate over conflict and consensus, the research findings do not provide clear support for critical criminological arguments; it does appear that there is a fair amount of consensus concerning the seriousness of criminal acts.

A second line of criticism would cast doubt on the wisdom of seeing crime as a political phenomenon. If politicalization is overemphasized, the distinction between political and criminal behavior becomes blurred.[98] At the same time, it may well be that certain acts *are* intrinsically criminal and *would* nearly always be criminalized regardless of the power structure of a society—murder, assault, incest, spreading infectious diseases intentionally, etc.[99]

Finally, there is uncertainty about the direction of action advocated by the critical criminologies, especially radical or Marxist criminology. One part of their argument would appear to call for repeal of laws where there is an absence of clear consensus, especially laws regarding use of narcotics, illegal gambling, and various sexual practices (decriminalization of these social-order crimes is discussed further in Chapters 13 and 19). Yet the inclusion of imperialism, racism, and sexism as crimes would considerably expand the purview of criminology, not to mention the criminal law and the power of the state, into areas in which there is not necessarily greater social consensus.

Generally, there is a need for sharper theorizing and further empirical research before the critical criminologists' insights about the political nature of crime can be fully accepted. The creation of law is a complex process; we have seen earlier the attempts of Turk to combine consensus and coercion theories and of Chambliss and Seidman to blend group interaction and struggle with radical or Marxist formulations. Moreover, there is also need for greater understanding of how law is related to other mechanisms of social control.

In short, as was noted of deterrence research, much remains to be done. The critical criminologists have brought needed attention to the political nature of crime. To be sure, their arguments may be overstated at points, and there may be weaknesses in the methodologies and conceptualization of their studies. Nevertheless, there are, as we shall see, many types of crime which can be more fully appreciated if there is an understanding of the sociopolitical context in which particular acts come to be criminalized.

APPLICABILITY OF CLASSICAL AND CRITICAL PERSPECTIVES ON ACTS TO MAJOR FORMS OF CRIME

In Part Three, seven major types of crime will be discussed; the presentation of each type of crime will begin with consideration of the criminal act. This form of presentation reflects a classical emphasis in that the statutes defining the behavior as criminal will be quoted. But it also reflects a critical criminological emphasis in that the historical situation will be examined and competing definitions of the criminal act will be taken into account.

It is noteworthy that classical school criminologists, as well as those involved in deterrence research, have been most interested in person-to-person violent crimes (especially homicide, rape, assault, and robbery) and person-to-person property crimes (burglary, larceny, and motor vehicle theft). Stating appropriate legal definitions, setting appropriate penalties, and deterring these crimes have been continuing concerns of the classical school. However, the preoccupation with these two types of crime does not mean that classical approaches could not also be applied to other types.

In contrast to the classical school, critical criminology has been more concerned with corporate crime, social-order crime, organized crime, and political crime. As we shall see, it is for these types that political factors are important in the very definition of the criminal act. For corporate and social-order crime, in particular, there is so much disagreement about the acts involved that the law and appropriate punishments have been vague, full of loopholes, and unenforceable or arbitrarily enforced. Organized crime and political crime are so closely related to power that it becomes essential to understand the political dynamics concerning how and why certain acts are or are not criminalized. Critical criminological arguments could also be applied to the definition of person-to-person criminal acts (although in fact this has been done less often). For example, it might be argued that the expanded definition of rape reflects the increased power of women in American society. (On rape, see Chapter 9.)

SUMMARY

The criminal act was the focus of the earliest school of modern criminological thought, the classical school. This school had its roots in the works of Beccaria and Bentham, two eighteenth-century thinkers who sought major reforms in the criminal law. In particular, they held that crimes needed to be defined legally, that punishments should be apportioned to crimes, that people act out of free will, and thus that criminal law with appropriately defined punishments would in and of itself deter crime. Bentham also envisioned a model prison and advanced reforms concerning the internal operation of prisons. Classicism was enormously influential in Europe and in the newly emerging American states, where passage of proper laws was seen as the solution for the problem of crime.

In neoclassicism, classical principles were modified somewhat to accommodate different standards of criminal responsibility for the very young or very old and for the insane and feebleminded, and where there were other mitigating factors such as the previous record of offenders. Neoclassicism also provided for the courts to use nonlegal experts such as psychiatrists and social workers. With these neoclassical adaptations, classicism came to be "the major model of human behavior held to by agencies of social control in all advanced industrial societies."[100] Nevertheless, among criminologists interested in the study of crime, classical thought declined in the latter 1800s and during the first half of the 1900s. During those many years, criminology became almost completely preoccupied with criminal offenders (see Chapters 5 and 6).

The period since 1960 has seen criminologists again orienting their thinking to the criminal act. There are two sharply contrasting schools of thought. One is modern classicism. Built upon its eighteenth-century predecessor, it has emphasized deterrence research and called for determinate sentencing. Deterrence research has been extensive although not conclusive. Ehrlich's finding that capital punishment deterred murder has been challenged on various methodological grounds. It is also challenged by other research findings that (1) unemployment is more related to rates of homicide and rape than executions are and (2) capital punishment produces increases in homicides in the month after executions. Studies of offenses other than murder have found that increases in certainty are associated with decreases in crime rates within certain limits. Other deterrence research has called attention to the very critical role of informal social controls in deterrence and to the unresolved issue of whether certainty "causes" decrease in crime or high crime rates "cause" decreased certainty.

Deterrence research has breathed new life into the classical school. However, it is fair to say that it has raised more questions than it has answered and that there is need for more theory and related research to deal with the complex question of the conditions under which threat of sanctions will influence people to refrain from committing criminal acts.

The second school of thought since 1960 that has dealt with the criminal act is critical criminology. It has questioned how and why certain acts become crimes, and it has emphasized the relationship between crime and social power. Critical criminology has advanced two major perspectives on the criminal act:

labeling and conflict. The labeling theorists have emphasized the social construction of crime and deviance and taken a relativistic view that would stress the arbitrariness in defining certain acts as criminal. Conflict criminologists have seen the definition of crime as the product of struggle among competing groups. Conflict theorists who focus on group interaction and struggle have stressed the manner in which social groups seek laws to protect their own interests. Criminalization can thus be seen as the outcome of a power struggle between authorities and "norm resisters." Conflict theorists who take a radical or Marxist perspective have seen deviant acts as originating in the economic system of capitalism, crime as pathological, and criminal law as the tool of the ruling class. Some radical or Marxist criminologists would greatly expand the scope of criminology by having it consider violations of human rights as well as various crimes of domination typically committed by ruling-class interests.

Critical criminology has opened two important lines of research concerning the criminal act: studies of creation of law and studies of the extent of social agreement on the seriousness of certain criminal acts. Studies of creation of law have thrown criminology into a host of historical analyses dealing with older laws such as those concerning vagrancy, larceny, and the enclosure acts and newer ones such as those concerning child welfare, prostitution, meat packaging, alcohol, narcotics, corporate deviance, and sexual psychopathy. Most of these studies confirm or illustrate the conflict hypothesis: that laws grow out of group power and serve the interests of social elites. Research on social agreement about the seriousness of crimes has found, on the contrary, that there is much public consensus on the seriousness of criminal acts.

Critical criminology is important because it has advanced a socially informed critique of traditional criminology. It has made it clear that criminology cannot accept the criminal law as a given and that power is part of the criminalization process. At the same time, weaknesses in methodology and conceptualization have pushed critical criminology into clarifying its position. Some critical criminologists have developed a formulation that would combine coercion and consensus theories; others have sought to blend conflict and Marxist ideas.

Both of the major perspectives taken since 1960 have implications for the particular forms of crime we shall take up in Part Three. The classical school demands that we take into account the legal definition of crime and the possibility of deterrence. Critical criminology demands that we take into account the political context of crime. While classical perspectives have most often been applied to person-to-person crimes, critical criminological arguments are especially appropriate for corporate, social-order, organized, and political crime.

Having dealt with the criminal act, we now need to turn our attention to the criminal offender. As we shall see in Chapters 5 and 6, study of the criminal offender has for many years commanded the lion's share of criminological time and energy.

NOTES

[1] Charles E. Reasons, "The Addict as a Criminal: Perpetuation of a Legend," *Crime and Delinquency*, vol. 21, January 1975, pp. 19–27.
[2] Harry Elmer Barnes and Negley K. Teeters, *New*

Horizons in Criminology, Prentice-Hall, Englewood Cliffs, N.J., 1959, p. 74.
[3] See: Harold E. Pepinsky, *Crime and Conflict: A Study of Law and Society*, Academic Press, New York, 1976,

chap. 7; and Charles E. Reasons, "Law and the Making of Criminals," in C. E. Reasons, ed., *The Criminologist: Crime and the Criminal*, Goodyear, Pacific Palisades, Calif., pp. 99–105.

[4] Cesare Beccaria-Bonesana, *An Essay on Crimes and Punishments*, Academic Reprints, Stanford, Calif., 1953; first published 1776.

[5] Ibid., p. 156.

[6] Ibid., p. 148.

[7] Jeremy Bentham, *An Introduction to the Principles of Morals and Legislation*, Pickering, London, 1923; first published 1789.

[8] Gilbert Geis, "Pioneers in Criminology: VII. Jeremy Bentham (1748–1832)," *Journal of Criminal Law, Criminology, and Police Science*, vol. 46, July-August 1955, pp. 164–67.

[9] Michael Ignatieff, *A Just Measure of Pain: The Penitentiary in the Industrial Revolution*, Pantheon, New York, 1978.

[10] Coleman Phillipson, *Three Criminal Law Reformers: Beccaria, Bentham, Romilly*, Dent, London, and Dutton, New York, 1923, chap. IV.

[11] David J. Rothman, *The Discovery of the Asylum: Social Order and Disorder in the New Republic*, Little, Brown, Boston, Mass., 1971, pp. 59–62; quotation on p. 61.

[12] For an overview, see: Ian Taylor, Paul Walton, and Jock Young, *The New Criminology: For a Social Theory of Deviance*, Routledge and Kegal Paul, London, 1973, pp. 7–11.

[13] Ibid., p. 8.

[14] Abraham S. Goldstein, *The Insanity Defense*, Yale University Press, New Haven, Conn., 1967, p. 45.

[15] For a discussion, see: Winfred Overholser, "Isaac Ray, 1807–1881," in Hermann Mannheim, ed., *Pioneers in Criminology*, 2d ed., Patterson Smith, Montclair, N.J., 1972, pp. 177–198.

[16] Phillipson, *Three Criminal Law Reformers*, p. 101.

[17] Taylor, Walton, and Young, *The New Criminology*, p. 10.

[18] Pepinsky, *Crime and Conflict*, p. 113.

[19] Charles R. Tittle and Charles H. Logan, "Sanctions and Deviance: Evidence and Remaining Questions," *Law and Society Review*, vol. 7, Spring 1973, p. 372.

[20] Franklin E. Zimring and Gordon J. Hawkins, *Deterrence: The Legal Threat in Crime Control*, University of Chicago Press, Chicago, Ill., 1973, p. 71.

[21] Ibid., p. 71.

[22] Jack P. Gibbs, *Crime, Punishment, and Deterrence*, Elsevier, New York, 1975, p. 3.

[23] Ibid., p. 5.

[24] Thorsten Sellin, *The Death Penalty*, American Law Institute, Philadelphia, Pa., 1959.

[25] Isaac Ehrlich, "The Deterrent Effect of Capital Punishment: A Question of Life and Death," *American Economic Review*, vol. 65, June 1975, pp. 397–417.

[26] P. Passell and J. B. Taylor, "The Deterrent Effect of Capital Punishment: Another View," discussion paper 74-7509, Columbia University, Department of Economics.

[27] William J. Bowers and Glenn L. Pierce, "The Illusion of Deterrence in Isaac Ehrlich's Research on Capital Punishment," *Yale Law Journal*, vol. 85, December 1975, pp. 187–208.

[28] Burley V. Bechdolt, Jr., "Capital Punishment and Homicide and Rape Rates in the United States: Time Series and Cross Sectional Regression Analyses," *Journal of Behavioral Economics*, Summer-Winter, 1977, pp. 33–66.

[29] William J. Bowers and Glenn L. Pierce, "Deterrence or Brutalization: What Is the Effect of Executions?" *Crime and Delinquency*, vol. 26, October 1980, pp. 453–484.

[30] William C. Bailey, "Capital Punishments and Lethal Assaults against Police," *Criminology*, vol 19, no. 4, February 1982, pp. 608–625.

[31] Isaac Ehrlich, "Capital Punishment and Deterrence: Some Further Thoughts and Additional Evidence," *Journal of Political Economy*, vol. 25, August 1977, pp. 741–788.

[32] Charles R. Tittle, "Crime Rates and Legal Sanctions," *Social Problems*, vol. 16, Spring 1969, pp. 409–423.

[33] Robert Chauncey, "Deterrence: Certainty, Severity, and Skyjacking," *Criminology*, vol. 12, February 1975, pp. 447–473; and William M. Landes, "An Economic Study of U.S. Aircraft Hijacking, 1961–1976," *Journal of Law and Economics*, vol. 21, no. 1, April 1978, pp. 1–31.

[34] Robert E. Kraut, "Deterrent and Definitional Influences on Shoplifting," *Social Problems*, vol. 23, February 1976, pp. 358–368.

[35] Richard D. Schwartz and Sonya Orleans, "On Legal Sanctions," *University of Chicago Law Review*, vol. 34, 1967, pp. 274–300.

[36] Robert F. Meier and Weldon T. Johnson, "Deterrence as Social Control: The Legal and Extralegal Production of Conformity," *American Sociological Review*, vol. 42, 1977, pp. 292–304.

[37] Jerry Parker and Harold G. Grasmick, "Linking Actual and Perceived Certainty of Punishment," *Criminology*, vol. 17, no. 3, November 1979, pp. 366–379.

[38] Charles R. Tittle, *Sanctions and Social Deviance: The Question of Deterrence*, Praeger, New York, 1980; quotation from p. 191.

[39] Ibid., chap. 11.

[40] Henry H. Pontell, "Deterrence: Theory versus Practice," *Criminology*, vol. 16, May 1978, pp. 3–22. However, see also: methodological criticisms of Pontell's research offered by Gibbs, Tittle, and Richard L. Henshel, *Criminology*, vol. 16, May 1978, pp. 22–44. Finally, see: Daniel Nagin, "Crime Rates, Sanction Levels, and Constraints on Prison Population," *Law and Society Review*, vol. 12, Fall 1977, pp. 341–366.

[41] Tittle, *Sanctions and Social Deviance*, p. 24.

[42] Daniel Nagin, "General Deterrence: A Review of the Empirical Evidence," in Alfred Blumstein, Jacqueline Cohen, and Daniel Nagin, eds., *Deterrence and Incapacitation: Estimating the Effects of Criminal Sanctions on Crime Rates*, National Academy of Sciences, Washington, D.C., 1978, p. 136.

[43] Graeme Newman, *The Punishment Response*, Lippincott, Philadelphia, Pa., 1978, especially p. 279.

[44] Jan Gorecki, *A Theory of Criminal Justice*, Columbia University Press, New York, 1979.

[45] James Q. Wilson, *Thinking about Crime*, Basic Books, New York, 1975.

[46] Ernest van den Haag, "On Deterrence and the Death Penalty," *Journal of Criminal Law, Criminology, and Police Science*, vol. 60, June 1969, pp. 141–147.

[47] Hyman Gross, *A Theory of Criminal Justice*, Oxford

University Press, New York, 1979, especially pp. 400–412; and Hyman Gross and Andrew von Hirsh, eds., *Sentencing*, Oxford University Press, New York, 1981.

[48] David Fogel, " . . . *We Are the Living Proof* . . . ": *The Justice Model for Corrections*, Anderson, Cincinnati, Ohio, 1975, especially p. 247.

[49] Gresham M. Sykes, "The Rise of Critical Criminology," *Journal of Criminal Law and Criminology*, vol. 65, no. 2, June 1974, pp. 206–213. On critical criminology, see also: George B. Vold, *Theoretical Criminology*, 2d ed., prepared by Thomas J. Bernard, Oxford University Press, New York, 1979, pp. 11–14 and part 4.

[50] George Herbert Mead, *On Social Psychology: Selected Papers*, Anselm Strauss, ed. and intro., Phoenix, Chicago, Ill., 1956.

[51] Edwin Lemert, *Human Deviance: Social Problems and Social Control*, 2d ed., Prentice-Hall, Englewood Cliffs, N.J., 1967, p. v; 1st ed. appeared in 1951. See also: *Social Pathology: A Systematic Approach to the Theory of Sociopathic Behavior*, McGraw-Hill, New York, 1951, especially chap. 9.

[52] Howard S. Becker, *Outsiders: Studies in the Sociology of Deviance*, Free Press, New York, 1963, p. 9.

[53] Kai T. Erikson, "Notes on the Sociology of Deviance," in Howard S. Becker, ed., *The Other Side*, Free Press, New York, 1964, p. 15.

[54] Ibid., p. 15.

[55] Stuart L. Hills, *Demystifying Social Deviance*, McGraw-Hill, New York, 1980, p. 21.

[56] Jason Ditton, *Controlology: Beyond the New Criminology*, Macmillan, London, 1979.

[57] Leslie T. Wilkins, *Social Deviance*, Tavistock, London, 1965, p. 90–91.

[58] George B. Vold, *Theoretical Criminology*, chap. 13.

[59] Ibid., p. 287.

[60] Ibid., p. 292–296.

[61] Ibid., p. 296.

[62] E.g., see: Thorsten Sellin, *Culture, Conflict, and Crime*, Social Science Research Council, New York, 1938; and Richard Quinney, *The Social Reality of Crime*, Little, Brown, Boston, 1970.

[63] The following discussion is based on: Austin Turk, *Criminality and Legal Order*, Rand McNally, Chicago, Ill., 1969; and Austin T. Turk, "Conflict and Criminality," *American Sociological Review,* vol. 31, no. 3, June 1966, pp. 338–352.

[64] Turk, *Criminality and Legal Order*, p. 44.

[65] Ibid., p. 59.

[66] Taylor, Walton, and Young, *The New Criminology*, p. 273.

[67] Richard Quinney, "Crime Control in Capitalist Society: A Critical Philosophy of Legal Order," in Ian Taylor, Paul Walton, and Jack Young, eds., *Critical Criminology*, Routledge and Kegal Paul, London, 1975, p. 198.

[68] Steven Spitzer, "Toward a Marxian Theory of Deviance," *Social Problems*, vol. 22, no. 5, June 1975, pp. 638–651.

[69] American Friends Service Committee, *Struggle for Justice*, Hill and Wang, New York, 1971, pp. 10–11.

[70] Herman Schwendinger and Julia Schwendinger, "Defenders of Order or Guardians of Human Rights?" *Issues in Criminology*, vol. 5, no. 2, Summer 1970, pp. 123–157.

[71] Richard Quinney, *Class, State, and Crime: On the Theory and Practice of Criminal Justice*, McKay, New York; 1977, pp. 50–52.

[72] Paul W. Tappan, *Crime, Justice, and Correction*, McGraw-Hill, New York, 1960, p. 10.

[73] Edwin H. Sutherland, "Is 'White Collar Crime' Crime?" *American Sociological Review*, vol. 10, April 1945, pp. 132–139.

[74] Schwendinger and Schwendinger, "Defenders of Order or Guardians of Human Rights?"

[75] Thomas J. Bernard, "The Distinction between Conflict and Radical Criminology," *Journal of Criminal Law and Criminology*, vol. 72, no. 1, 1981, pp. 362–379.

[76] William Chambliss and Robert Seidman, *Law, Order, and Power*, 2d ed., Addison-Wesley, Reading, Mass. 1982, pp. 33–38.

[77] Jerome Hall, *Theft, Law, and Society*, Bobbs-Merrill, Indianpolis, Ind., 1952; originally published in 1935.

[78] William J. Chambliss, "A Sociological Analysis of the Law of Vagrancy," *Social Problems*, vol. 12, Summer 1964, pp. 67–77.

[79] Georg Rusche and Otto Kirchheimer, *Punishment and Social Structure*, Columbia University Press, New York, 1939, chap. 3.

[80] Anthony M. Platt, *The Child-Savers: The Invention of Delinquency*, University of Chicago Press, Chicago, Ill., 1969, p. 36.

[81] Pamela A. Roby, "Politics and Criminal Law: Revision of the New York State Penal Law on Prostitution," *Social Problems*, vol. 17, Summer 1969, pp. 83–109.

[82] Gabriel Kolko, *The Triumph of Conservatism*, Free Press, New York, 1963.

[83] Joseph Gusfield, *Symbolic Crusade: Status Politics and the American Temperance Movement*, University of Illinois Press, Urbana, 1963.

[84] Reasons, "The Addict as a Criminal: Perpetuation of a Legend." See also: Troy Duster, *The Legislation of Morality: Law, Drugs, and Moral Judgment*, Free Press, New York, 1970; and C. Reinarman, "Moral Entrepreneurs and Political Economy: Historical and Ethnographic Notes on the Construction of the Cocaine Menace," *Contemporary Crises*, vol. 3, 1979, pp. 225–254.

[85] Victoria Lynn Swigert and Ronald A. Farrell, "Corporate Homicide: Definitional Processes in the Creation of Deviance," *Law and Society Review*, vol. 15, no. 1, 1980–1981, pp. 161–182.

[86] Edwin H. Sutherland, "The Sexual Psychopath Laws," *Journal of Criminal Law and Criminology*, vol. 40, January-February 1950, pp. 543–554.

[87] John Hagan and Jeffrey Leon, "Rediscovering Delinquency: Social History, Political Ideology, and the Sociology of Law," *American Sociological Review*, vol. 42, August 1977, pp. 587–598.

[88] John Hagan, Edward T. Silva, and John H. Simpson, "Conflict and Consensus in the Designation of Deviance," *Social Forces*, vol. 56, December 1977, pp. 320–340.

[89] Richard A. Berk, Harold Brackman, and Selma Lesser, *A Measure of Justice*, Academic Press, New York, 1977, p. 300.

[90] Chambliss and Seidman, *Law, Order, and Power*, p. 144.

91 Peter H. Rossi, Emily Waite, Christine E. Bose, and Richard E. Berk, "The Seriousness of Crimes: Normative Structure and Individual Differences," *American Sociological Review*, vol. 39, April 1974, pp. 224–237.

92 Charles W. Thomas, Robin J. Cage, and Samuel C. Foster, "Public Opinion on Criminal Law and Legal Sanctions: An Examination of Two Conceptual Models," *Journal of Criminal Law and Criminology*, vol. 67, no. 1, 1976, pp. 110–116.

93 Tittle, *Sanctions and Social Deviance*, chap. 3.

94 V. Leo Hamilton and Steve Rytina, "Social Consensus on Norms of Justice: Should the Punishment Fit the Crime?" *American Journal of Sociology*, vol. 85, no. 5, March 1980, pp. 1117–1144.

95 Jeff Coultner, "What's Wrong with the New Criminology?" *Sociological Review*, new series, vol. 22, no. 1, February 1974, pp. 119–135; Carl B. Klockars, "The Contemporary Crises of Marxist Criminology," in James A. Inciardi, ed., *Radical Criminology: The Coming Crises*, Sage, Beverly Hills, Calif., 1980, pp. 92–123; and David Schichor, "The New Criminology: Some Critical Issues," *British Journal of Criminology*, vol. 20, January 1980, pp. 1–19.

96 Piers Beirne, "Empiricism and the Critique of Marxism on Law and Crime," *Social Problems*, vol. 26, no. 4, April 1979, pp. 373–385.

97 Charles R. Tittle, "Labelling and Crime: An Empirical Evaluation," in Walter R. Gove, ed., *The Labelling of Deviance: Evaluating a Perspective*, Wiley, New York, 1975, chap. 6; and Peter K. Manning, "Deviance and Dogma: Some Comments on the Labelling Perspective," *British Journal of Criminology*, vol. 15, no. 1, January 1975, pp. 1–20.

98 Schichor, "The New Criminology: Some Critical Issues."

99 Charles Wellford, "Labeling Theory," *Social Problems*, vol. 23, no. 3, Feburary 1975, pp. 332–345.

100 Taylor, Walton, and Young, *The New Criminology*, p. 10.

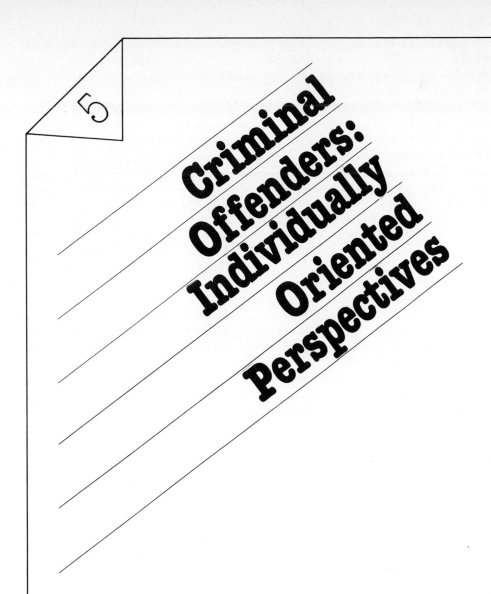

Criminal Offenders: Individually Oriented Perspectives

5

Much of our thinking about crime has centered on criminal actors, especially offenders. Over and over again, Americans have attempted to discover personal defects that supposedly lead people to crime. They have asked: Do offenders have defective bodies? Are they mentally unbalanced? Are they products of poverty or of slums? Is there something wrong with their socialization? Did they grow up in "bad" families, receive improper schooling, associate with the "wrong" people? Did they learn social values predisposing them toward crime?

Studying individual offenders began in the 1830s, when officials started to examine biographies of prisoners in the attempt to understand why they had turned to crime. It flourished in the latter 1800s, when criminologists turned to scientific positivism, which sought to use the methodology of the emerging natural sciences to understand, to predict, and to attempt to control criminals. Over the years, many theories have been advanced. As we shall see, some have been disproved, others have been discarded, and still others have given rise to more complex formulations.

Criminological positivists argue that the causes of crime are to be found in the personal characteristics of offenders. In this argument, there are two interrelated assumptions: (1) that offenders are different from nonoffenders, and (2) that offenders are led into crime by forces over which they have less than complete control. The search for unique personal characteristics and these two assumptions are themes which run through the four major types of criminological positivism which we shall consider: (1) biological and (2) psychological (in this chapter); and (3) economic and (4) sociological (in Chapter 6).

In recent years positivistic theories seeking to understand crime by studying individual offenders have been sharply challenged. As with the criminal act, this challenge has come from the diverse group of writers whom we are calling "critical criminologists." They have made three major points: (1) Criminologists must examine the process by which people come to be called "criminal." (2) There are no unique characteristics that distinguish criminals from noncriminals. (3) People are fully human actors who make commonsense interpretations of reality rather than suffer predisposition to crime as a result of outside forces.

The study of offenders has received a great deal of criminological attention. To understand it, we shall need to consider individually oriented perspectives in this chapter and group-, culture-, and system-oriented perspectives in Chapter 6. This chapter begins examining nineteenth-century perspectives on criminal offenders and goes on to consider the voluminous twentieth-century work in biological and psychological positivism. Chapter 6 continues the discussion of twentieth-century positivism by considering its economic and sociological forms. Chapter 6 will also present the details of the critical attack on positivism. Finally, Chapter 6 considers how the positivist and critical perspectives on the criminal offender can be applied to the major forms of crime discussed in Part Three.

NINETEENTH CENTURY

To understand the nineteenth-century perspectives on crime and criminals, it will be useful first to examine American thinking and then to turn to a consideration of European positivism.

The first several decades of American society were characterized by immense social change. The total population increased dramatically; from about 4 million in 1790, it tripled to well over 12 million in 1830. This dramatic increase was accompanied by geographical movement into cities and in and out of territories as well as movement up and down the social ladder. This period also saw the beginnings of the industrial revolution and the challenge of Enlightenment ideas to the older Calvinist doctrines. In short, the period saw enormous demographic, economic, and intellectual changes in the newly emerged society.[1]

With these enormous social changes came a dramatic shift in thought about crime. By the 1820s, Americans came to be very concerned about crimes as well as other social problems. As David J. Rothman has put it, they asked:

> What . . . was to prevent society from bursting apart? From where would the elements of cohesion come? More specifically, would the poor now corrupt the society? Would criminals roam out of control? Would chaos be so acute as to drive Americans mad?[2]

Shifting away from their earlier emphasis on the legal system, they now sought the answers to these questions in the deviant and in the criminal rather than in good law and moderate but certain punishment. In their quest, they went to the prison, attempting to find the origins of crime in the life stories and personal characteristics of convicts.

Several models of behavior were advanced. Some investigators looking into the life stories of convicts found the answer in early childhood, arguing that incorrectly disciplined children became especially prone to a life of crime. In fact, many people claimed that breakdown of the household was one of the leading causes of crime.[3] In professional circles, medical doctors such as Charles Caldwell (1772–1854) applied phrenology to the study of criminals. Claiming that certain parts of the head controlled the tendencies to combativeness, destructiveness, acquisitiveness, and other characteristics often regarded as criminal, one phrenologist

> examined fifteen prisoners in the St. Louis jail, described each head and what it betokened, predicted the character of the crime, and was thereupon informed of the charge against the prisoner. The description and the prediction corresponded remarkably![4]

Others, such as Isaac Ray (1807–1881), attempted to distinguish criminals from insane people.[5] A few of these early thinkers, many of whom were physicians, attempted to consider both characteristics of the individual and social or environmental factors as elements in the predisposition toward crime.[6]

In considering the shifting perspectives on crime during the 1830s, two points ought to be kept in mind. One is the disillusionment with certain aspects of classicism. The more rational legal codes neither led to a decrease in crime nor solved the problem of what to do with criminals. To many, there was need for a new approach that would go beyond the rationality of certain punishment.[7] The other point is that despite the disillusionment with classicism, no distinctly

American school of criminology emerged during this period. Indeed, it can be said that the American contribution to the problem of the criminal lay in penology, not in theoretic understanding of criminal behavior.[8] For this type of understanding, it is necessary to turn to positivism, which has its roots in European, especially Italian, thought of the latter decades of the nineteenth century.

European Positivism

Study of the individual criminal has long been part of European thought. In the sixteenth century, J. Baptiste della Porte (1535–1615) claimed that there was a relationship between types of crimes and body characteristics of criminals. In the eighteenth century Johan Lavater (1741–1801) attempted to apply physiognomy, the study of facial features, to the understanding of criminal behavior.[9] Later in the eighteenth century, Franz Joseph Gall (1758–1824), a famous surgeon, pioneered in the application of phrenology to the study of criminals. Gall conducted extensive studies of bumps and other irregularities in the skulls of inmates of prisons and mental asylums and also of comparable noninstitutionalized groups. In retrospect, it is interesting to note that Gall's work was quite exhaustive, highly recognized in its day, and never really disproven. Indeed, there are some who would claim that Gall should be regarded as the first criminologist.[10]

Lombroso

However, the distinction of being the first criminologist is usually accorded to Cesare Lombroso (1836–1909). It was Lombroso who, along with his followers Enrico Ferri (1856–1929) and Rafaele Garofalo (1852–1934), developed a study of

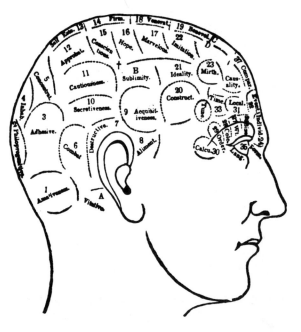

Phrenologists believed that specific parts of the brain controlled various emotional and intellectual capacities, and they confidently interpreted these capacities by measuring the shape of a person's skull. (PHRENOLOGICAL JOURNAL, 1842; NEW YORK PUBLIC LIBRARY)

crime which was based on Charles Darwin's theory of evolution and was diametrically opposed to the classicism of Beccaria. The differences were sharp: (1) Instead of free will, it advocated a deterministic model of behavior. (2) Instead of legalistic definitions of crime, it argued for natural ones. (3) Instead of equating the punishment to the crime, it sought to tailor punishment to the offender. (4) Moreover, it sought to redefine punishment as treatment. (5) It argued for the application of scientific methods to the study of criminal behavior.[11] So encompassing was the work of Lombroso, Ferri, and Garofalo that it gave birth to a school of criminology, the "positivist" school, which enormously influenced both European and American criminological thought for decades and which remains influential today. Given the importance of the school they created, it will be most useful to examine these three positivist pioneers in greater depth.

Lombroso was a medical doctor with interests in history and philosophy. He was a university professor for many years and had experience as an army doctor and in administering medical services to the insane at various mental hospitals in Italy. Intellectually Lombroso was deeply influenced by Charles Darwin (1809–1882), whose books *Origin of Species* (1859), *Descent of Man* (1871), and *Expression of Emotion in Man and Animals* (1872) tied human beings to the animal kingdom and saw a continuous link between humans and the simpler forms of animal life. Lombroso also was intellectually oriented to the work of Auguste Comte (1798–1853), a French thinker known as the "father of sociology." Comte advocated the application of scientific methods to the study of society and advanced the notion of social progress. Moreover, many of Comte's ideas were solidly grounded in biology.[12]

Dissatisfied with the abstract legalism of the classical school, and with its emphasis on the offense, Lombroso set out to discover physiological differences among lunatics, criminals, and normal people. His most striking insight came upon examining the skull of a famous brigand, Vilella. In a postmortem examination, Lombroso found Vilella to have a "median occipital fossa" on the interior of the lower back part of the skull, a characteristic found in inferior animals. In addition, he found a depression correlated with an overdevelopment of the vermis, known in birds as the middle cerebellum. To Lombroso, this case opened up immense possibilities:

> This was not merely an idea, but a revelation. At the sight of that skull, I seemed to see all of a sudden, lighted up as a vast plain under a flaming sky, the problem of the nature of the criminal—an atavistic being who reproduces in his person the ferocious instincts of primitive humanity and the inferior animals.[13]

A few years later, Lombroso was speaking of the commonality between the criminal, the insane, and the epileptic, claiming that all were suffering from atavism, or biological reversion to a primitive or earlier type of human being. In so doing, he gave birth to a field of study subsequently called "criminal anthropology."

Later, at Ferri's suggestion, Lombroso began using the term "born criminal." After all, if an atavism is a biological reversion, it would follow that criminal tendencies are inherited. As Lombroso put it:

> Many of the characteristics presented by savage races are very often found among born criminals. Such, for example, are: the slight development of the pilar system;

low cranial capacity; retreating forehead; high developed frontal sinuses; great frequency of Wormian bones; early closing of the cranial sutures; the simplicity of the sutures; the thickness of the bones of the skull; enormous development of the maxillaries and the zygomata; prognathism; obliquity of the orbits; greater pigmentation of the skin; tufted and crispy hair; and large ears. To these we may add the lemurine appendix; anomalies of the ear; dental disastemata; great agility; relative insensibility to pain; dullness of the sense of touch; great visual acuteness; ability to recover quickly from wounds; blunted affections; precocity as to sensual pleasures. . . .[14]

Concerning the proportion of criminal offenders possessing these biological characteristics, Lombroso had in his early work claimed that born criminals constituted between 65 and 70 percent of the criminal population. However, this proportion dropped to 33 percent by the time of his last major work; and several other types of criminals were also delineated: criminaloids (those drawn into crime by opportunity), latent criminals (those who are venerated as chiefs of society but whose depraved nature emerges while in power), and criminals by passion (those committing crime out of love or politics).[15] In this last work, Lombroso also took into account a multiplicity of causes of crime that included factors such as climate, race, alcoholism, education, and wealth, to mention only a few.[16]

Ferri

The second major figure of the positive school was the colorful Enrico Ferri. Ferri was the son of a poor shopkeeper, and his early education was quite erratic. However, he became interested in legal medicine, took a degree in criminal law, and came to be influenced by Lombroso, who was 20 years older. Aside from his academic pursuits, Ferri was an active public speaker as well as a lawyer. A few years before his death, he estimated that he had delivered 2300 university lectures, 600 public lectures of a scientific nature on about 40 topics, countless addresses in court, and thousands of political speeches.[17]

Essentially a legal reformer, Ferri believed that crime was inevitable in society. However, in his opinion the law was equally inevitable; and society, in its expression of the will of the majority, was justified in reserving the right to defend itself against aggressors and, hence, to punish. Ferri fought the individualism of the classical school, arguing that it "failed to distinguish between dangerous and not dangerous, atavistic and evolutive delinquents."[18] Given his stance, it followed that the sentencing task of a judge was "to fix the form of social preservation best suited to the defendant according to the anthropological category in which he belongs."[19] Ferri's position provided a justification for indeterminate sentencing (to be discussed further in Chapter 17). He also delineated five or six classes into which offenders could be put and suggested a system in which expert judges, prosecutors, defenders, psychiatrists, and anthropologists would periodically revise prisoners' sentences. In other words, Ferri anticipated parole boards.[20]

Although he vigorously questioned the basic classical assumptions—free will and letting the punishment fit the crime—Ferri was not a simple biological determinist. In fact, he was a committed socialist—politically and intellectually a follower of Karl Marx (1818–1883). For Ferri's criminological work, this orientation meant that the human being was seen as a "puppet of the forces of environment and of physical heredity" and that social accountability should replace moral responsibility.[21] In understanding evolution, he shifted from the physical and biological factors stressed by Darwin to the social and environmental factors stressed by Marx. In the final analysis, his theory of crime causation is "synthetic" in that it relates crime to physical or geographical factors (race, climate, fertility of the soil, etc.), to the constitution of the individual (age, sex, civil status, anatomical features, etc.), and to social factors (increase or decrease of population, migration, customs, etc.).

Finally, it should also be mentioned that Ferri's work reflects the considerable optimism of many of the early positivists. Believing that social defense could be achieved scientifically, Ferri argued that criminal science would dig its own grave because "it will reduce the number of delinquents to an irreducible minimum."[22] Moreover, he envisioned a civilized society with less penal justice and more social justice, although he saw that every society, even a socialist utopia, would have its own form of criminality.

Garofalo

The third major figure of Italian positivist criminology was Raffaele Garofalo. A member of the Italian nobility and a lawyer, prosecutor, and magistrate, Garofalo, like Ferri, was very much concerned with the practical reforms of the criminal law and legal institutions associated with the administration of criminal justice.[23] He was influenced by Darwin and argued for direct study of the criminal; and his most significant contribution was his attempt to reorient positivist thinking to crime rather than the criminal. His key concept was "natural crime," by which he meant that crime is an act which offends the sentiments of the average moral sense of the community. He placed "natural crime" into two categories: (1) offenses to the sentiment of pity (attacks upon human life tending to produce physical harm, suffering, or moral suffering); and (2) offenses to the sentiment of probity (attacks upon property involving violence, extortion, negligence, and fraud). Interestingly, acts menacing the state or attacking social power would be excluded from "natural crime."[24]

Although Garofalo did not argue that governments legislate only against natural crime, he did assert that natural crime should be the area of major or even exclusive concern to the scientific criminologist. In making this assertion, he anticipated later schools of criminological thought that have seen crime in terms of unethical business practices or violations of human rights (see Chapter 4). Garofalo's view also allowed for a criminology that would be independent of the study of law.

It is in the work of Lombroso, Ferri, and Garofalo that we see the emergence of the positivist mode of thinking that came to influence much subsequent criminological thought. Turning the classical school on its head, positivism made the offender rather than the criminal act the focal point for criminology. The positivist criminologists argued that offenders have personal characteristics which distinguish them from nonoffenders and that offenders are led into crime—some would say "predisposed" toward crime—by forces or factors beyond their control.

Positivist criminologists also pioneered the application of scientific methods to the study of offenders. Claiming to be unbiased, they pursued an analytical quest for the characteristics that separated offenders from nonoffenders. With positivism, experts other than lawyers—in particular, psychiatrists, social workers, and natural and social scientists—became involved in criminology and in criminal justice. The emphasis on crime as legally defined shifted to an emphasis on crime as an act offending the moral sense of the community. Hope that deterrence would solve the problem of crime was replaced by faith that treatment based on a scientific approach would reduce the number of criminals and social delinquents.

TWENTIETH CENTURY

The twentieth century saw an enormous expansion of the positivist criminology pioneered by Lombroso, Ferri, and Garofalo. This expansion occurred both in Europe and in America. It was especially great in the earlier years of this century, but it has continued until the present. Moreover, the expansion has been marked by great diversity; literally every branch of the emerging natural and social sciences has, sooner or later, advanced a new theory or perspective from which to study the individual criminal. In focusing on biological, psychological, economic, and sociological approaches, we will be able to consider a representative although by no means exhaustive account of twentieth-century perspectives on criminal offenders.[25]

It should be mentioned that there is little consensus among criminologists on any one theory. Despite the fact that each theory has been sharply criticized, both by other positivists and by critical criminologists, each continues to have its supporters. The field of criminology seems to be characterized by fads and foibles. Theories are advanced, become popular, flourish, and then decline. Sometimes theories decline as a result of research which clearly disproves them; but sometimes a theory will decline simply because professional attention has turned to other theories. Bearing this in mind, let us first examine the various approaches which have characterized criminological thought in this century, then examine critical criminologists' challenge to positivism, and finally assess the various perspectives. In the remainder of this chapter we shall consider biological and psychological approaches, most of which are in the traditions of European positivist criminology. In Chapter 6 we will consider economic and sociological approaches, and the critical attack on positivism.

Biological Approaches

Twentieth-century biological approaches to the study of offenders have moved in several directions. An early direction stems from Goring's critique of Lombroso, and from Hooton's reassessment of Goring. Although diverse, present-day biological work is united in the strong emphasis it gives to the role of neurochemical factors in the genesis of criminal behavior.

Goring

Lombroso's work stimulated much heated debate in its day. One significant challenge came from Charles Goring (1870–1919). Although he also sought the answer to criminal behavior in the body characteristics of criminals, Goring was disturbed both with criminal anthropology and with the scientific methods used by Lombroso. In a study sponsored by the British government, he set out to gather and analyze data on 96 traits of more than 3000 English convicts and smaller numbers of noncriminals. Goring's book *The English Convict* has been called "the classic example of the application of biometrics to the study of the criminal."[26]

Goring's critique of Lombroso was directed mainly at his research methodology. To begin with, he insisted on precise measurement. Second, he argued that Lombroso had treated deviations from the mean as abnormal rather than unusual phenomena. Finally, he felt that Lombroso had used measuring techniques which provided a low rate of reproducibility. Goring's approach was to examine statistically the kinds and degrees of criminality evidenced in the 3000 convicts. He took 37 physical traits and 6 mental traits and compared them with types of crimes that had been committed and degrees or extent of criminality.[27]

Of the traits examined by Goring, few were significantly related to criminal behavior. Of the 37 physical traits, only 6 were related to the type or degree of criminality with correlation coefficients above .15 (on a scale of 0 to 1.00). On the other hand, Goring did find a high degree of association, .6553, between criminality and what he called "defective intelligence." Moreover, in extensive comparisons with noncriminal groups categorized into four social and seven occupational classes, Goring found criminals to be inferior to the general population in terms of stature and weight. After making extensive calculations, he was led to conclude that the "anthropological monster (of Lombroso) has no basis in fact" but that there is a physical, mental, and moral type of normal person who tends to be convicted of crime and who shows "defective physique" and "defective mental capacity."[28]

Goring also found the following to be true:

1. Environmental conditions are unrelated to crime.
2. Only to a trifling extent is crime the product of social inequalities.
3. Imprisonment has no effect upon physique, but mortality from suicide is greater for those imprisoned than for the general population.
4. Criminals are products of the most prolific stocks of the community. Their decline in fertility is due to a psychological reaction to imprisonment.
5. Criminal predispositions are influenced by heredity but in the same way as physical and mental qualities and conditions.[29]

Finally, in sharp contrast to Ferri's dream that scientific treatment would reduce the number of delinquents to an irreducible minimum, Goring wrote:

> Assuming that by the segregation of all criminals, crime might be reduced to nothing: yet parents with the least social proclivities would still go on begetting offspring who, on the average would commit the greatest number of anti-social offenses. . . .[30]

This statement would stand today as a positivist criminological rebuke to those who would seek to solve the problem of crime instantaneously by "locking criminals up and throwing the key away."

Hooton

Goring's detailed statistical work did not resolve scientific concerns about Lombrosian positivism. Decades later, in the 1930s, an American anthropologist, Earnest Hooton (1887–1954), reexamined Goring's work and concluded that his extensive statistical manipulations only served to confuse the issues and neither substantiated nor refuted Lombroso's theories. Setting out to prove Lombroso correct, Hooton studied (for over three years) the anthropological characteristics of offenders in Massachusetts jails and prisons and compared them with samples of noncriminals—a somewhat disparate group consisting of militia officers, bathing house patrons at a public resort, outpatients from the Massachusetts General Hospital, and Nashville firemen.[31]

Comparing the offenders and noncriminals on more than 100 characteristics, Hooton found the following kinds of differences:

Sociological

1. Apart from age considerations, these criminals are less often married, more often widowed, and more frequently divorced than comparable civilians.
2. After due allowance is made for the partially rural character of our criminal series and for the almost exclusively urban provenience of our check sample, there remain in the criminals probable excesses of extractive, laborer, and personal service occupations, and deficiencies of trade, professional, and clerical occupations.
3. Criminals are greatly inferior to civilians of the same ethnic origin in educational attainments.

Morphological

1. Tattooing is commoner among criminals than among civilians.
2. Criminals probably have thinner beard and body hair and thicker head hair.
3. Criminals have more straight hair and less curved hair.
4. Criminals have more red-brown hair and less gray and white hair.
5. Dark eyes and blue eyes are deficient in criminals, and blue-gray and mixed eyes are in excess. Homogeneous irides are rare in criminals, and zoned and speckled irides are excessively present. Eyefolds are commoner in criminals and thin eyebrows occur more frequently.
6. Low and sloping foreheads are excessively present among criminals.
7. High narrow nasal roots, high nasal bridges, undulating nasal profiles, nasal septa inclined upward and deflected laterally, extreme variations in thickness of the nasal tip, are more frequent in criminals than in civilians.
8. Thin lips and compressed jaw angles are commoner in criminals.
9. Marked overbites are rarer in criminals than in civilians.
10. The ear of the criminal is more likely to have a slightly rolled helix and a perceptible Darwin's point than is that of the civilian. More extreme variations of ear protrusion are found in criminals than in civilians. The criminal ear tend to be small.
11. Long, thin necks and sloping shoulders are in excess among criminals.[32]

It should also be noted that Hooton was concerned about crime because he saw it as evidence of "degenerative trends in human evolution" that needed to be checked.[33] Unlike the evolutionists of his day, he felt it misleading to believe that culture "evolves by itself ever onward and upward."[34]

Sheldon

Another biologically positivist approach is represented in the work of William H. Sheldon (1899–1977). He attempted to establish "biological humanities," which he defined as "a science of man resting on biological descriptions and procedures."[35] To do this, he developed a descriptive device—"somatotype," i.e., "body type"—which served to quantify physiques and related temperaments. He found three basic types: endomorphs, mesomorphs, and ectomorphs. Endomorphs tended to have physiques featuring great development of the digestive viscera, i.e., to be fat, soft, and rotund; their temperaments featured relaxation, love of comfort, and extraversion. Mesomorphs showed predominance of bones, muscles, and connective tissue; their temperaments featured activity, dynamism, and bodily aggressive behavior. Ectomorphs showed predominance of skin, nerves, sense organs, and brain; their temperaments featured restraint, inhibition, a tendency toward fatigue, and introversion. In all, Sheldon and his associates studied the physiques of about 46,000 men to arrive at this typology.[36]

Applying this "science of biological humanities" to delinquent youths,

William Sheldon developed the descriptive device of the somatotype; the photograph illustrates the three basic somatotypes: a skinny ectomorph, an athletic mesomorph, and a heavy endomorph. (WASYL SZKODZINSKY/PHOTO RESEARCHERS, INC.)

Sheldon and his associates followed a sample of 200 young men through the eight-year period 1939–1946. The young men were chosen from a group of 400 who had contact with the Mayden Goodwill Inn, a rehabilitation agency in the South End of Boston. After rigorously presenting case histories, Sheldon found the 200 to be "decidedly mesomorphic," having no tendencies toward endomorphy and few toward ectomorphy. By comparison, 200 college students he had studied earlier shared a significant tendency toward ectomorphy.[37] It might be added that William Sheldon's approach was taken up by Sheldon Glueck and Eleanor Glueck, who systematically compared 500 persistent delinquents with 500 proven nondelinquents. After matching the two groups in variables such as age, intelligence, ethnic-racial derivation, and residence in underprivileged areas, they found that 60 percent of the delinquents as opposed to 31 percent of the nondelinquents were mesomorphic.[38] Subsequent work by Juan B. Cortes also claimed to find an association between delinquency and mesomorphy.[39]

Present-day biological approaches

Today's biologically oriented criminology has attempted to move well beyond the work of the earlier criminologists. Its general perspective is that there is continuous interaction between the human organism and its environment. Thus, biologically oriented criminologists consider it necessary to take both biological and sociological factors into account:

> The very social groups which account for high rates of officially recorded delinquency and crime are also markedly overrepresented in the "continuum of reproductive casualties." Certain prenatal, perinatal, and postnatal factors (complications of pregnancy, prematurity, and malnutrition) are associated with a variety of neurological and related disorders in the child. These problems are exacerbated by postnatal social experiences which add further stress to the affected youngsters from the aforementioned population groups, and make them more vulnerable to a variety of difficulties in adapting to existing societal situations.[40]

One prominent work in the field suggests that genetic and psychological factors may provide weak explanations for lower-class criminality but strong explanations for middle-class criminality.[41]

The research to support today's biologically oriented criminology has proceeded along a number of lines. The theme of some work has been the notion that the proclivity to crime is inherited. Other work has looked to the autonomic nervous system, to alpha brain waves, and to a variety of other biochemical or pharmacological traits. Let's take a closer look at some of this research.

Crime as inherited behavior The idea that criminal tendencies are inherited is by no means new. In fact, one earlier piece of research, very popular among American criminologists, was Richard L. Dugdale's book *The Jukes*, written in 1877. Dugdale traced more than 700 of the 1200 members of the Jukes family over a period of 125 years.[42] (The Jukes family is the largest family of criminals and paupers ever studied.) Further support for the notion that criminal tendencies are inherited and run in families was reflected in studies conducted by Henry H.

Goddard and A. H. Estabrook, as well as in Goring's finding of a substantial relationship between crimes of parents and their offspring if the parents had been imprisoned.[43]

Modern research has also detected a link between criminality of parents and criminality of their offspring.[44] One recent review of these studies found that between 30 and 45 percent of offspring with criminal records had one or both parents with criminal records. However, there is a problem with these findings in that the possibility that any person will be arrested is very high. For example, one study in Philadelphia found that over 30 percent of the males sampled had at least one police contact before age 18; another investigation found that about 40 percent of all males in the United States would probably be arrested once during their lifetime. Since the general probability of arrest is this high, the percentage of parent-child criminality would have to be much higher to be significant. It should also be noted that there is need to consider whether criminal parents and offspring are linked maternally or paternally and whether female and male offspring are similarly affected.[45]

Another direction of research attempting to establish the idea that criminal tendencies are inherited may be seen in studies of adoptive as opposed to natural or biological children. Barry Hutchings and Sarnoff A. Mednick followed up all the males born in Copenhagen between 1927 and 1941 and adopted by someone outside the family in order to compare the conviction records of adopted sons with those of their biological and adoptive fathers. They found that

1. 49 percent of the biological fathers of adoptees who later became criminal had criminal records.
2. 28 percent of the biological fathers of adoptees who remained noncriminal had criminal records.
3. 23 percent of the adoptive fathers of adoptees who later became criminal had criminal records.
4. 14 percent of the adoptive fathers of adoptees who remained noncriminal had criminal records.[46]

Comparison of groups 1 and 2 suggests that criminal tendencies might to some extent be inherited. At the same time, where the adoptive father is criminal, criminality of the adoptee is also considerably more likely, as is shown by comparison of groups 3 and 4.[47]

A third direction of research on inherited criminality is the attempt to identify genetic factors in criminality. Two lines of approach have been taken: one has sought to show the genetic transmission of criminal tendencies by studying pairs of twins; the other has examined chromosome patterns. Twin studies were first carried out by Johannes Lange, a German psychiatrist. In 1930, he found that prisoners who were identical male twins were much more likely than prisoners who were fraternal twins to have twins outside the prison who had also been in prison.[48] A leading example of contemporary research in this area is the work of Karl O. Christiansen. Studying over 7000 male twins during the 1960s, he found that 35 percent of the identical twins, as opposed to 13 percent of the fraternal twins, were concordant in their behavior (i.e., both were criminal or both were noncriminal).[49] However, another study of male twins in Norway, which took account of both biological factors and environmental relationships, found that while identical twins showed more concordance than fraternal twins, the similarities depended upon their subjective feeling of closeness and identity.[50]

The chromosome theory has attracted a great deal of scientific attention. It holds that an extra Y chromosome is associated with aggressive or violent behavior, which in turn is linked with crime. One of several possible unusual genetic patterns, the extra Y chromosome produces a "supermale" who has an XYY pattern rather than the XY pattern normal for males. The extra Y chromosome in males was first observed by Patricia A. Jacobs and her colleagues; they studied 197 inmates at a Scottish maximum security hospital and described the XYY males as having "dangerous violent or criminal tendencies."[51] The "XYY theory" has stimulated literally hundreds of studies and has become the subject of much debate.[52] Perhaps the most definitive study was conducted by Herman A. Witkin and his associates, who examined all male Danish citizens born to women who lived in Copenhagen between 1944 and 1947, a total of 28,884 men. From this group they took the tallest 4591 men—i.e., all those over 184 centimeters—as their sample. They were then able to obtain blood samples and buccal smears on 4124 of the tall men. Of the 4124, the researchers found only 12 XYY males (4096 were XY males; 16 showed an XXY pattern). Checks of the penal registers showed that 41.7 percent of the XYY males—i.e., 5 of the 12—had been convicted of one or more criminal offenses. The comparable figures are 9.3 percent of the 4096 XY males and 18.8 percent of the XXY males. However, although the percentage of convictions was significantly higher for the XYY males, all but one of the convictions were for property offenses. The notion that XYY males are inclined toward aggressive criminal acts was not supported by the data.[53]

Crime and the autonomic nervous system   Another line of biologically oriented research has seen the autonomic nervous system of the body as the key factor in criminality. The autonomic nervous system controls many of the body's involuntary functions and is largely responsible for the "fear response" which inhibits behavior. Behavior is inhibited if there is a rapid autonomic nervous system response to an anxiety-provoking situation. Such a response can be assessed by examining the electrodermal recovery rate seen in a skin conductance response, a method used in lie detector tests. The theory is that "the combination of hyporesponsiveness and slow electrodermal recovery rate should give the maximum Autonomic Nervous System predisposition to delinquency."[54] In a study which tracked 311 males between 1962 and 1976, Sarnoff A. Mednick found that the 36 falling into disagreements with the law had considerably slower electrodermal recovery rates than those who did not.[55] Hans J. Eysenck, a British psychologist, has also found that psychopaths (to be discussed later in this chapter) show slower arousal rates than persons who are more likely to feel guilt.[56] One review of studies taking this approach concluded:

> The results concerning SCR (electrodermal) recovery and antisocial behavior appear to be quite consistent. Subjects who display antisocial behavior (psychopaths, adult criminals, and adolescent delinquents) also display significantly slower SCR (electrodermal) recovery than do matched controls.[57]

In interpreting these findings, it is useful to bear in mind that the autonomic nervous system may predispose certain people to criminal behavior, but such a predisposition does not mean that a person will necessarily commit a crime. In fact, one observer has found circumstances in which the autonomic nervous system is clearly under voluntary control.[58]

Other biological approaches   Other biologically oriented criminological research has looked to neurophysiological, biochemical, and pharmacological factors. Neurophysiological researchers have been concerned with electroencephalogram measures of brain activity which attempt to show that slower alpha patterns are characteristic of persons who later become delinquent.[59] Biochemical and pharmacological researchers have claimed that the behavior associated with crime and delinquency is "caused by chemical deficiencies in the body or by brain toxicity." Such chemical deficiencies can originate from genetic factors, improper nutrition of mother or fetus, vitamin deficiency, vitamin dependence, or food allergies.[60] Although the systematic research relating chemical deficiencies or brain toxicity to crime is weak, the approach might be described as "suggestive." Its proponents have argued that it is applicable to diverse groups such as alcoholics, delinquents, penitentiary inmates, and "social misfits."[61]

Psychological Approaches

Having considered some of the ways in which criminality has been related to bodily characteristics, we now need to examine how theorists and researchers have related criminality to mental traits. Such an examination leads us into psychological positivism.

In psychological positivist approaches we see the attempt to apply scientific perspectives in order to establish a link between mental disorder and criminal behavior. To appreciate psychological positivism, it will be useful to take a brief look at the history of thinking about the criminal mind and mental disorder—in particular, the work of Sigmund Freud. Then we can consider the work of William Healy and Augusta Bronner, two psychiatrists who applied Freud's approach to the study of delinquents. Finally, we shall review some of the present-day criminological research which takes the vantage point of psychological positivism.

The question addressed by psychologically oriented criminologists is an age-old one: Is there a criminal mind? Throughout the ages, there have been many different answers. Some people have seen the criminal mind as one possessed by evil spirits. Others have talked of its relationship to feeblemindedness or emotional disturbance. Magic, exorcism, flogging, and lobotomy have all been used in the attempt to rid people of evil spirits or cure them of feeblemindedness.

In the 1800s the older views about the mind began to change. Studies of anatomy, physiology, and other branches of medicine led to the discovery that much physical illness was organically based. At the same time, mental disorders also came to be seen as organically based or as the product of psychological problems. The changed views of the mind are also reflected in thinking about criminal behavior.[62] As was noted earlier, the American thinker Isaac Ray attempted to make a distinction between criminals and insane people. The shift in thinking is also reflected in the famous McNaughton case, in which the court argued that a criminal had to know the difference between right and wrong in order to be held blameworthy for committing a crime. (See Chapter 4.)

Freud

The changed perspectives on the human mind became systematized in the work of Sigmund Freud (1856–1939) and his pupils, especially Alfred Adler (1870–1937) and Carl Jung (1875–1961). They saw the mind generally, and the personality in particular, as subject to unconscious, irrational forces. Childhood experiences, especially the relationship with the mother, were held to play a considerable role in personality development. From this viewpoint, the genesis of criminal or deviant behavior lay in the mind, and such behavior was the product of sickness or maladjustment.

Although better known as a psychologist than as a criminologist, Freud did give some consideration to criminals. He saw the criminal as one who has a defective self. According to Freud, the self is composed of three parts: the id, the ego, and the supergo. The id is the reservoir of unconscious drives and feelings. The superego is the conscience or demands of society which are inculcated as the result of training and education. In the middle stands the ego, the rational or conscious part of the self which balances the demands of the id with those of the superego and mediates between the personality as a whole and the outside environment.[63]

If we take Freud's approach, we can see crime as the result of weak ego control over the id and corresponding repressed guilt. The criminal gets psychic relief from being punished and in fact commits a criminal act in order to be caught and punished. In other words, the normal pattern in which guilt or discomfort keeps people away from crimes is reversed. The basis for all this is to be found in childhood, when inner needs and impulses, especially those of a sexual or aggressive nature, were not adequately met. In short, criminal behavior is a substitute response for a part of the personality that has been repressed.[64]

Healy and Bronner

Although Freud's approach formed a starting point for the many psychiatrists who treated people manifesting some form of crime or deviance, it was William Healy and Augusta Bronner who first attempted to combine the psychiatric case approach with an emphasis on statistics in order to understand causes of crime. Disagreeing with the biological positivists who saw delinquency as the result of defective organisms, Healy and Bronner stressed personality and environmental factors as well as biological ones. First in *The Individual Delinquent* and later in *Delinquents and Criminals*, Healy and Bronner studied samples of delinquents which ran into the thousands. Among other things, they found that delinquents had a higher frequency than nondelinquents of what they called "personality defect" (as seen in emotional disturbances) and "personality disorder." They also stressed the home environment as a key factor in delinquent behavior.[65]

The lead of Healy and Bronner was followed by considerable numbers of psychiatrists who became concerned with the diagnosis and treatment of offenders. Using projective tests and interviews, they conducted diagnoses by delving

Kenneth Bianchi sobs in a
courtroom in Washington
State after pleading guilty
to the 1979 slaying of two
students. Bianchi's case is
an example of crimes that
seem to be explicable only
in psychological terms.
(WIDE WORLD PHOTOS)

into family history, early childhood, relationships with parents and siblings, attitudes and personality characteristics, and subsequent experiences of offenders with an eye to prescribing treatment plans for them. Treatment was to involve psychoanalysis. The psychiatric approach also became part of the medical model in which criminality or deviance was seen as an illness to be diagnosed and then treated.[66]

The psychiatric approach based on the work of Freud, Healy and Bronner, and others has been quite popular. There are 24,000 psychiatrists in the United States, not to mention clinical psychologists and other professional groups who generally support the viewpoint. Moreover, there has been a popular culture which is supportive of psychiatry and of the view that the criminal or deviant is one who is sick and in need of treatment. Indeed, there are many crimes, especially certain bizarre ones, which appear to be explicable only in terms of factors rooted deep in the personality. (For an example, see Box 3.)

Present-day psychological approaches

In recent years psychologically oriented criminologists have continued to emphasize various characteristics of the offender's mind. One line of research has sought to establish traits of the criminal personality. A second has attempted to deal with the psychopathic personality. A third has sought to find relationships between crime and delinquency and other psychological traits such as intelligence and learning disabilities.

Personality studies   Psychologists have put a great deal of effort into exploring the relationship between deviant personality and deviant behavior. Among the

Was the Hillside Strangler a Jekyll and Hyde? He hated and despised Kenneth Bianchi, 27, a security guard in Bellingham, Wash. "Ken doesn't know how to handle women," he snarled. "You gotta treat 'em rough." He spoke crudely of his sexual exploits with women and then said of Bianchi: "Boy, did I fix that turkey. I got him in so much trouble, he'll never get out."

The voice, according to Psychologist John Watkins of the University of Montana, came from a sort of *Doppelganger*, a second and hidden personality of the same Kenneth Bianchi, "a very pure psychopath." It expressed the personality's "general underlying hatred of women" and from time to time seized complete control of the normally mild-mannered Bianchi. It did indeed get him into serious trouble. In January, Bianchi was arrested and charged with strangling two young women, whose bodies were found that month stuffed into the rear of a car in Bellingham. Last week Los Angeles Police Chief Daryl Gates announced that he had enough "hard physical evidence" to seek murder charges against Bianchi for ten of the 13 murders ascribed to the notorious "Hillside Strangler."

The brutal murders took place between September 1977 and February 1978 and brought a reign of terror to Los Angeles. Women were afraid to walk alone at night, even in residential areas. The strangler's victims included a prostitute and a runaway, whose nude bodies were found tossed into wooded areas. His eighth and ninth victims, however, were twelve-year-old girls, school chums at a Catholic elementary school who disappeared while out shopping. The killer dumped their bodies near Dodger Stadium.

When Bianchi stands trial in Los Angeles and Washington he is expected to plead not guilty by reason of insanity because of a dual personality. At first even Bianchi's defense attorney, Dean Brett, rejected the plea. "That's the stuff of novels," he told an associate. But when Brett had trouble communicating with Bianchi, he called in a team of psychologists and psychiatrists. One of them, Watkins, hypnotized Bianchi and discovered the second personality. Watkins told TIME Correspondent Edward J. Boyer that while hypnotized, Bianchi identified ten of the 13 Hillside victims and admitted killing them. In subsequent sessions with Watkins, Bianchi's second personality emerged without hypnosis. Says Watkins: "The underlying personality would threaten me a good deal. He would get up and stride around. I was never quite sure but that he would attack me."

Bianchi's case, reminiscent of the bestselling book and hit movie *The Three Faces of Eve*, is similar to that of William Milligan, who was accused of raping four women students at Ohio State University two years ago. Defense psychiatrists reported that Milligan had ten personalities and that only one of them was responsible for the crimes. A judge found Milligan not guilty by reason of insanity, and he was committed to a mental hospital.

Watkins claims that Bianchi was not aware of his second personality until told about it by the experts. The psychologist insists that the *Doppelganger* is no alibi; it probably first emerged, he says, when

instruments utilized, probably the most popular are the Minnesota Multiphasic Personality Inventory (MMPI), a test consisting of 550 items originally designed to help diagnose people in need of psychiatric help. Other tests are the California Psychological Inventory (CPI), the Murray Thematic Apperception Test, and the Rorschach test. Whereas the MMPI and CPI are self-administered attitudinal tests, the Murray and Rorschach tests are performance and free-association tests that call upon subjects to react as the tests are administered.

Some of the results of the research into the relationship between delinquency and crime have been quite suggestive. In his review of the literature, Juan B. Cortes concludes that personality traits such as aggression, hostility, overactivity, and individualistic thinking are predictive of delinquent activity, while those such as withdrawal, depression, and a tendency toward identification with the opposite

Bianchi was nine years old. Other medical experts are now examining Bianchi to determine whether his disorder is organic, caused by a brain tumor. But Watkins and an associate believe that the dual personality stems from Bianchi's unhappy childhood.

He was adopted in infancy by Nicholas and Frances Bianchi of Rochester, N.Y. Nicholas, who was a welder, died when Kenneth was 14. Throughout his childhood, Kenneth often suffered from amnesia, which Watkins says is a symptom of dissociative reaction, the medical term for dual personality. Bianchi had frequent nightmares of being in a dark room with a strange presence, perhaps an awareness of the second personality, and severe migraine headaches. Says Watkins: "Headaches often occur when the personality underneath is trying to get out and the one on top is trying to maintain control. The battle is experienced as a severe headache." Friends from high school remember him as a loner. As an adult Bianchi was considered a ladies' man. With dark hair and a thick, slick mustache, he had no trouble attracting women.

Throughout high school Bianchi had one obsession: to become a policeman. He studied police science at Monroe Community College in New York but dropped out before finishing. He tried to find a job as a policeman in upstate New York and failed. When he moved to Los Angeles in 1975, he sought, again in vain, for police jobs while living with his cousin, Angelo Buono, 44. Finally, Bianchi got a position at a land title company, but he pretended to colleagues that he was an undercover cop on the side. He carried an attache case in which he kept a phony highway patrolman's badge and identification, handcuffs, and photos of nude women. A neighbor recalls him as "sometimes too friendly, always trying to impress." At times, however, he had violent outbreaks of temper and threw heavy objects against the walls of his apartment.

One day he remarked to a coworker, "What would you think if I told you I'm the Hillside Strangler?" Someone passed the comment along to the police, but it was one of thousands of tips, and was ignored. After Bianchi's arrest in Bellingham, Los Angeles police took another look and discovered some remarkable coincidences. For six months he had lived in the same Glendale apartment building as Kristina Weckler, the Hillside Strangler's seventh victim. He lived across the street from Cindy Hudspeth, victim No. 13, and once lived in the Hollywood apartment building where Kimberly Martin, victim No. 12, was killed.

So far only the psychiatrists charged with defending Bianchi have spoken. Los Angeles police have not commented on the defense claim of a dual personality. In the meantime, the judge in Bellingham has appointed six experts to examine Bianchi and make their own diagnosis. When they are done, Bianchi will be tried in Washington, in late summer at the earliest. If he is convicted, the prosecutor will ask for the death penalty.

SOURCE

Time, May 21, 1979.

sex have an inhibitory effect upon delinquency. However, he goes on to note that these relationships do not allow us to conclude that personality traits cause delinquency:

> In many instances, one is never sure whether particular traits were present before the deviant behavior developed or whether experiences encountered as a result of the deviation produced or increased the traits. Those traits or dimensions are also socially determined. . . .[67]

As specific studies, one might also cite Michael J. Hindelang's study of self-reported criminal behavior, in which he found that the Psychopathic Deviate (PD) Scale of the Minnesota Multiphasic Personality Inventory was significantly associated with fighting, use of "soft" drugs, malicious destruction, theft, and use of drugs in a high school population.[68] However, a recent attempt to replicate Hindelang's findings reported correlations between personality variables and theft, and between use of "soft" drugs and destruction of property; but these correlations were significantly reduced when the F scale (sensitive to the exaggeration of deviant behaviors and psychotic symptoms) was introduced as a control.[69]

Sociologists have generally been skeptical of attempts to relate personality traits to criminal or delinquent behavior. An early review found that 47 out of 113 studies (42 percent) conducted before 1950 reported differences between criminal and noncriminal populations.[70] A later review following the same methodology used in the earlier study found that 76 out of 94 studies (81 percent) conducted between 1950 and 1965 reported differences.[71] Finally, the most recent update, dealing with the period 1966–1975, found that 35 out of 44 (80 percent) studies reported differences.[72] High though these percentages may appear, one cannot conclude that a criminal personality exists. Aside from the remark by Cortes quoted above, the biggest problem is in the various scales. Investigations before 1950 used many scales; middle-period investigations used mainly the Minnesota Multiphasic Personality Inventory–Psychopathic Deviate Scale and the California Personality Inventory–Socialization Scale; and later investigations have again turned to a variety of scales. The MMPI is particularly problematic, since it includes an item—"I have never been in trouble with the law"—to which the response would in and of itself discriminate statistically between delinquents and nondelinquents.[73] There are also other problems in that differences within delinquent groups are greater than those between delinquents and nondelinquents (or criminals and noncriminals). As the most recent review study concluded, "Cursory personality testing has not differentiated criminals from noncriminals."[74]

Psychopathic personality A second way to handle the question of the relationship between crime and personality is to assert that there is a criminal personality type—a view held by many psychiatrists. The type has been described by terms such as "sociopathic personality," "antisocial personality," "criminal psychopath," "psychopathic personality," and "habitual antisocial deviant." The American Psychiatric Association has defined "antisocial personalities" as

> individuals who are basically unsocialized and whose behavior pattern brings them repeatedly into conflicts with society. They are incapable of significant loyalty to individuals, groups, or social values. They are grossly selfish, callous, irresponsible, impulsive, and unable to feel guilt or to learn from experience and punishment. Frustration tolerance is low. They tend to blame others or offer plausible rationalizations for their behavior.[75]

Neat though it may appear, this definition of the antisocial personality raises a number of questions. It does not specify whether sociopathic personalities must have all, some, or only one of the traits listed in the definition. Moreover, it does not specify whether such a personality type is necessarily violent. Some would claim that sociopaths are unable to modify behavior in light of experience, unable to formulate long-term goals, unable to form meaningful relationships with others, unable to experience shame or remorse, and unable to experience sex with emotional involvement. However, at the same time it can also be said that sociopaths are often nonviolent, may be quite intelligent, do not suffer from delusion, and do not appear nervous. In fact, many are sane under the traditional tests for insanity. Hervey Cleckley goes so far as to argue that the typical psychopath does not usually commit major crimes and may be found in any profession, including business, science, medicine, and psychiatry.[76]

The definitional problems are especially evident in the various estimates concerning the proportion of the population that would fall into the category "sociopath." As Simon Dinitz has suggested, somewhere between 2 and 5 percent of the general population—from 4.5 million to 11.2 million people—could possibly be considered sociopaths.[77] Among the correctional population in particular, a commonly accepted estimate is 20 percent of adult prison inmates. However, the problems of defining sociopathic personality become apparent when two writers with backgrounds in law enforcement quote estimates that sociopaths make up 40 percent of the criminal population.[78] Although sociopathic behavior is not necessarily dangerous, its unpredictable nature has led psychiatrists to link it to dangerousness. The problem is that the link has been a factor in overprediction of dangerousness.[79]

Nevertheless, definitional problems have not prevented psychologically oriented positivists from theorizing about and conducting research on the sociopath. Eysenck's argument that sociopathy has a physiological manifestation and presumably a physiological basis has already been noted; according to this theory, sociopaths' lower level of cortical arousal does not allow them to inhibit deviant or criminal behavior.[80] The notion that sociopathy has a physiological basis has led some researchers to argue that sociopaths can be "resocialized" only after "biomedical intervention," one method being the drug imipramine hydrochloride.[81]

Intelligence   The third area of interest for present-day psychological criminology is intelligence. The belief that intelligence is related to crime and delinquency was very popular in the early decades of the twentieth century, subsequently declined in popularity, and is presently on the rise. The most important early adherent was Henry H. Goddard, who wrote in 1920:

> Every investigation of the mentality of criminals, misdemeants, delinquents, and other antisocial groups has proved beyond the possibility of contradiction that nearly all persons in these classes, and in some cases all, are of low mentality. . . . It is no longer to be denied that the greatest single cause of delinquency and crime is lowgrade mentality, much of it within the limits of feeble-mindedness.[82]

In recent years, criminologists such as Travis Hirschi and Michael J. Hindelang are once again speaking of a link between intelligence and delinquency. In an important article, they argue that sociologically oriented criminologists have ignored or minimized the relationship between intelligence quotient (IQ) and delinquency, even though studies have clearly shown that delinquents have lower IQs than nondelinquents, regardless of their race or social class. Hirschi and

Hindelang assert that IQ should be considered as important as race and class in a sociological theory of delinquency. However, in contrast to psychologically oriented criminologists, they see IQ from a social viewpoint in that low IQ is associated with poor school performance, which in turn is associated with delinquency.[83] Another example of this type of research can be seen in a somewhat varied group of studies showing some links between learning disabilities and juvenile delinquency.[84]

SUMMARY

In this chapter, the first of two chapters on the criminal offender, we have seen how criminological thinking in the 1800s turned from the crime to the criminal, from classicism to positivism. In the United States during the 1830s, life stories of convicts, phrenology, and new conceptions of insanity were all part of the changed criminological thinking. In Europe during the latter 1800s, positivism emerged. Positivists advocated examining the characteristics that would distinguish offenders from nonoffenders, using natural definitions of crime, tailoring punishment to the offender, redefining punishment as treatment, and applying unbiased scientific methods to the study of criminal behavior.

In the twentieth century, positivist criminology has undergone enormous expansion; literally every branch of the emerging natural and social sciences opened up a new positive perspective.

Biological approaches, seen in the work of Lombroso, Goring, Hooton, and Sheldon, find the roots of criminal behavior in bodily characteristics. Today's biologically oriented criminology has moved in the direction of taking both biological and sociological factors into account. The research designed to support biological criminology has proceded along several lines. One is that criminal tendencies are inherited, a notion which finds limited support in studies of adoptive and natural children, studies of twins, and studies of the XYY chromosome pattern in males. Another is studies of the autonomic nervous system which find that subjects displaying antisocial behavior have slower arousal or response rates. A third line, still in its infancy, has looked to neurophysiological, biochemical, and pharmacological factors.

Psychologically oriented criminologists have attempted to link mental traits to criminal behavior. Their perspective emerged in the late 1800s as science began to undermine older ways of thinking about the human mind. The work of Freud is pivotal, although he was not primarily a criminologist. Freud saw the criminal as a person suffering from weak ego control over the id and obtaining psychic relief from being caught and punished. His insight was applied by Healy and Bronner, who emphasized personality and environmental factors as causes of juvenile delinquency. The viewpoint was also adopted by psychiatrists who became concerned with the diagnosis and treatment of offenders.

Today, psychological approaches to crime have taken several paths. One is the attempt to utilize personality tests to explore the relationship between personality and deviant behavior; while many studies have reported correlations, critics have questioned their methodology and the logic of their findings. Another is exploration of the psychopathic personality; here too we have a line of thought that has been attacked generally for vagueness in definition. Finally, there are some thinkers who have sought to refocus scholarly attention on the relationship between intelligence and delinquency—in particular, on IQ and learning disabilities.

It should be noted that the biological and psychological perspectives discussed in this chapter have been sharply criticized. Some of the grounds for these criticisms will become evident as we examine group-oriented and culture-oriented perspectives, which focus on environmental factors rather than bodily characteristics or mental traits. Others will become evident as we examine the system-oriented critique of all positive perspectives. It is to these matters that we turn our attention in Chapter 6.

NOTES

[1] For the historical observations in this section, see: David J. Rothman, *The Discovery of the Asylum: Social Order and Disorder in the New Republic*, Little, Brown, Boston, Mass., 1971, chap. 3.

[2] Ibid., p. 58.

[3] Ibid., pp. 65–78.

[4] Arthur E. Fink, *Causes of Crime: Biological Theories in the United States, 1800–1915*, Barnes, New York, 1962. See: chap. 1 for a discussion of phrenology. Quotation appears on p. 14.

[5] Winfred Overholser, "Isaac Ray," in Hermann Mannheim, ed., *Pioneers in Criminology*, 2d ed., Patterson Smith, Montclair, N.J., 1972, pp. 177–198. See also: Fink, *Causes of Crime*, chap. II.

[6] E.g., see: Joseph Mouledoux, "Edward Livingston, 1764–1836," in Mannheim, *Pioneers in Criminology*, pp. 69–83.

[7] Rothman, *The Discovery of the Asylum*, p. 62.

[8] Fink, *Causes of Crime*, chap. XI.

[9] On the early criminologists, see: Stephen Schafer, *Theories in Criminology*, Random House, New York, 1969, chap. V.

[10] Leonard Savitz et al., "The Origins of Scientific Criminology: Franz Joseph Gall as the First Criminologist," in Robert F. Meier, ed., *Theory in Criminology: Contemporary Views*, Sage, Beverly Hills, Calif., 1977, pp. 41–56.

[11] Clarence Ray Jeffery, "The Historical Development of Criminology," in Mannheim, *Pioneers in Criminology*, pp. 458–498.

[12] On Lombroso, see: Marvin Wolfgang, "Cesare Lombroso," in Mannheim, *Pioneers in Criminology*, pp. 232–291.

[13] Quoted by Wolfgang, ibid., p. 248.

[14] Cesare Lombroso, *Crime: Its Causes and Remedies*, Little, Brown, Boston, Mass., 1918, pp. 365–366.

[15] Ibid., part III.

[16] Ibid., part I.

[17] Thorsten Sellin, "Enrico Ferri," in Mannheim, *Pioneers in Criminology*, pp. 361–384.

[18] Enrico Ferri, *Criminal Sociology*, Little, Brown, Boston, Mass., 1917, p. 443.

[19] Ibid.

[20] On the reforms proposed by Ferri, see: Sellin: "Enrico Ferri," pp. 375f.

[21] Ferri, *Criminal Sociology*, p. xxix.

[22] Ibid., p. 569.

[23] Francis A. Allen, "Raffaele Garofalo" in Mannheim, *Pioneers in Criminology*, pp. 318–340.

[24] Raffaele Garofalo, *Criminology*, Patterson Smith (Reprint Series), Montclair, N.J., 1968, pp. 33f.

[25] For a more complete account of the theories discussed here, see: Schafer, *Theories in Criminology*, chaps. VIII–XIII; or George B. Vold, *Theoretical Criminology*, 2d ed. prepared by Thomas J. Bernard, Oxford University Press, New York, 1979, chaps. 4–7.

[26] Edwin D. Driver, "Charles Buckman Goring," in Mannheim, *Pioneers in Criminology*, pp. 429–442; quotation appears on p. 429.

[27] Charles Goring, *The English Convict: A Statistical Study*, Patterson Smith (Reprint Series), Montclair, N.J., 1972; first published 1913.

[28] Ibid., p. 370.

[29] Ibid., pp. 370–373.

[30] Ibid., p. 373.

[31] Earnest Albert Hooton, *The American Criminal: An Anthropological Study—The Native White Criminal of Native Parentage*, Greenwood, New York, 1939.

[32] Ibid., p. 301.

[33] Earnest Albert Hooton, *Crime and the Man*, Greenwood, Westport, Conn., 1939, p. 395.

[34] Ibid., p. 370.

[35] William H. Sheldon, *Atlas of Man: A Guide for Somatyping the Adult Male at all Ages* (with the collaboration of C. Wesley Dupertuis and Eugene McDermott), Gramercy, New York, 1954, preface.

[36] Ibid.; and William Sheldon with S. S. Stevens, *The Varieties of Temperament: A Psychology of Constitutional Differences*, Hafner, New York, 1970; originally published 1942, 2 vols.

[37] William Sheldon with Emil Hartl and Eugene McDermott, *Varieties of Delinquent Youth*, Hafner, Darien, Conn., 1970; originally published 1949.

[38] Sheldon Glueck and Eleanor Glueck, *Physique and Delinquency*, Harper, New York, 1956, and *Unraveling Juvenile Delinquency*, Harvard University Press, Cambridge, Mass., 1950.

[39] Juan B. Cortes with Florence M. Gatte, *Delinquency and Crime: A Biopsychosocial Approach*, Seminar Press, New York, 1972.

40 Saleem A. Shah and Loren H. Roth, "Biological and Psychophysiological Factors in Criminality," in Daniel Glaser, ed., *Handbook of Criminology*, Rand McNally, Chicago, Ill., 1974, p. 153.

41 See: preface to Sarnoff A. Mednick and Karl O. Christiansen, eds., *Biosocial Bases of Criminal Behavior*, Gardner, New York, 1977, pp. ix–x.

42 Richard L. Dugdale, *The Jukes: A Study in Crime, Pauperism, Disease, and Heredity*, 4th ed., Putnam, New York, 1942; originally published 1877.

43 Henry H. Goddard, *The Kallikak Family*, Macmillan, New York, 1912; and A. H. Estabrook, *The Jukes in 1915*, Carnegie Institution of Washington, Washington, D.C., 1916.

44 E.g.: Sheldon Glueck and Eleanor Glueck, *Of Delinquency and Crime*, Thomas, Springfield, Ill., 1974; and Lee Robins et al., "Arrests and Delinquency in Two Generations: A Study of Black Urban Families and Their Children," *Journal of Child Psychology and Psychiatry*, vol. 16, 1975, pp. 125–140.

45 For a discussion, see: Lee Ellis, "Genetics and Criminal Behavior: Evidence through the End of the 1970s," *Criminology*, vol. 20, no. 1, May 1982, pp. 45–46.

46 Barry Hutchings and Sarnoff A. Mednick, "Criminality in Adoptees and Their Adoptive and Biological Parents: A Pilot Study," in Mednick and Christiansen, *Biosocial Bases of Criminal Behavior*, pp. 127–141.

47 For a review of adoptive studies, see: Ellis, "Genetics and Criminal Behavior," pp. 52–56.

48 Johannes Lange, *Crime as Destiny*, Boni, New York, 1930.

49 Karl O. Christiansen, "A Preliminary Study of Criminality among Twins," in Mednick and Christiansen, *Biosocial Bases of Criminal Behavior*, pp. 89–108. See also: Christiansen, "A Review of Studies of Criminality among Twins," pp. 89–108.

50 Odd S. Dalgard and B. Einar Kringlen, "A Norwegian Twin Study of Criminality," *British Journal of Criminology*, vol. 16, 1976, pp. 213–232.

51 Patricia A. Jacobs, Muriel Brunton, and Marie M. Melville, "Aggressive Behavior, Mental Subnormality, and the XYY Male," *Nature*, vol. 208, December 1965, pp. 1351–1352.

52 See: Ellis, "Genetics and Criminal Behavior," pp. 49–51.

53 Herman A. Witkin et al., "Criminality in XYY and XXY Men," *Science*, vol. 193, August 13, 1976, pp. 547–555.

54 Sarnoff A. Mednick, "A Bio-Social Theory of Learning of Law-Abiding Behavior," in Mednick and Christiansen, *Biosocial Bases of Criminal Behavior*, p. 4.

55 Ibid., pp. 4f.

56 Hans J, Eysenck, *Crime and Personality*, Houghton Mifflin, Boston, Mass., 1964, especially chap. 4.

57 David A. T. Siddle, "Electrodermal Activity and Psychopathy," in Mednick and Christiansen, *Biosocial Bases of Criminal Behavior*, pp. 206–207.

58 Robert Edelber, "Electrodermal Recovery Rate, Goal-Orientation, and Aversion," *Psychophysiology*, vol. 6, 1970, pp. 527–539.

59 Sarnoff A. Mednick et al., "EEG as a Predictor of Antisocial Behavior," *Criminology*, vol. 19, no. 2, August 1981, pp. 219–229.

60 Leonard J. Hippchen, "The Need for a New Approach to the Delinquent-Criminal Problem," in Leonard J. Hippchen, ed., *Ecologic-Biochemical Approaches to Treatment of Delinquents and Criminals*, Van Nostrand and Reinhold, New York, 1978, chap. 1; quotation from p. 13.

61 See: the other selections in Hippchen, *Ecologic-Biochemical Approaches to Treatment of Delinquents and Criminals*. See also: B. E. Ginsburg, "The Violent Brain: Is It Everyone's Brain?" in C. R. Jeffery, ed., *Biology and Crime*, Sage, Beverly Hills, Calif., 1979, pp. 47–64.

62 On the changed approaches to mental behavior, see: Nolan Don Carpenter Lewis, *A Short History of Psychiatric Achievement*, Norton, New York, 1941.

63 Sigmund Freud, *The Ego and the Id*, trans. Joan Riviere, Norton, New York, 1960.

64 Sigmund Freud, "Criminals from a Sense of Guilt," in *The Standard Edition of the Complete Psychological Works of Sigmund Freud*, vol. 14, Hogarth, London, p. 332.

65 William Healy, *The Individual Delinquent*, Little, Brown, Boston, Mass., 1915; and William Healy and Augusta F. Bronner, *Delinquents and Criminals: Their Making and Unmaking*, Macmillan, New York, 1928.

66 E.g., see: Robert M. Lindner, *Rebel without a Cause*, Grune and Stratton, New York, 1944; and Seymour L. Halleck, *Psychiatry and the Dilemmas of Crime*, Harper and Row, New York, 1967.

67 Cortes, *Delinquency and Crime*, p. 186.

68 Michael Hindelang, "The Relationship of Self-Reported Delinquency to Scales of the CPI and MMPI," *Journal of Criminal Law, Criminology, and Police Science*, vol. 63, 1972, pp. 75–81.

69 Spencer A. Rathus and Larry J. Siegel, "Crime and Personality Revisited: Effects of MMPI Response Sets in Self-Report Studies," *Criminology*, vol. 18, no. 2, August 1980, pp. 245–251.

70 Karl F. Schuessler and Donald B. Cressey, "Personality Characteristics of Criminals," *American Journal of Sociology*, vol. 56, March 1950, pp. 476–484.

71 Gordon P. Waldo and Simon Dinitz, "Personality Attributes of the Criminal: An Analysis of Research Studies, 1950–1965," *Journal of Research in Crime and Delinquency*, vol. 4, 1967, pp. 185–202.

72 David J. Tennenbaum, "Research Studies of Personality and Criminality: A Summary and Implications of the Literature," *Journal of Criminal Justice*, vol. 5, no. 3, 1977, pp. 1–19.

73 Waldo and Dinitz, "Personality Attributes of the Criminal," p. 482.

74 Tennenbaum, "Research Studies of Personality and Criminality," p. 17.

75 *Diagnostic and Statistical Manual of Mental Disorders*, American Psychiatric Association, Washington, D.C., 1968, p. 41.

76 Hervey Cleckley, *The Mark of Sanity*, 5th ed., Mosby, St. Louis, Mo., 1976.

77 On the sociopath, see: Simon Dinitz, "Chronically Antisocial Offenders," in John P. Conrad and Simon Dinitz, *In Fear of Each Other: Studies of Dangerousness in America*, Heath (Lexington Books), Lexington, Mass., 1977, pp. 21–42.

78 Thomas Strentz and Conrad V. Hassel, "The Sociopath—A Criminal Enigma," *Journal of Police Science and Administration*, vol. 6, no. 2, 1978, pp. 135–140.

[79] Stephen J. Pfohl, *Predicting Dangerousness: The Social Construction of Psychiatric Reality*, Heath (Lexington Books), Lexington, Mass., 1978.

[80] See: "Crime as Inherited Behavior" in the present chapter. See also: Sybil B. G. Eysenck and H. J. Eysenck, "Crime and Personality: An Empirical Study of the Three-Factor Theory," *British Journal of Criminology*, vol. 10, July 1970, pp. 225–239; and Robert D. Hare and Daisy Schalling, *Psychopathic Behavior: Approaches and Research*, Wiley, New York, 1978.

[81] Harry E. Allen, Simon Dinitz, et al., "Sociopathy: An Experiment in Internal Environmental Control,"

American Behavioral Scientist, vol. 20, no. 2, December 1976, pp. 215–226.

[82] Harry H. Goddard, *Human Efficiency and Levels of Intelligence*, Princeton University Press, Princeton, N.J., 1920, p. 73–74.

[83] Travis Hirschi and Michael J. Hindelang, "Intelligence and Delinquency: A Revisionist Review," *American Sociological Review*, vol. 42, 1977, pp. 572–587.

[84] Charles A. Murray, *The Link between Learning Disabilities and Juvenile Delinquency*, National Institute of Juvenile Justice and Delinquency Prevention, Law Enforcement Assistance Administration, U.S. Department of Justice, April 1976.

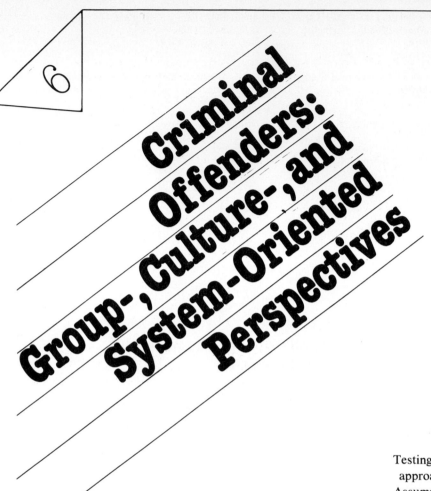

Criminal Offenders: Group-, Culture-, and System-Oriented Perspectives

While some criminologists in the positivist tradition have emphasized bodily characteristics and mental traits of offenders, others have stressed the environmental factors which are associated with individual proclivity to crime. Among the environmental factors, most attention has been given to the social and economic ones. In calling attention to social and economic factors, criminologists taking these perspectives have placed group or cultural influences on offenders at the core of criminological thought. As we shall see, a considerable part of twentieth-century criminology reflects group and culture-oriented perspectives on criminal offenders. In opposition to these and other positivist views are the system-oriented perspectives of critical criminologists.

As with the individually oriented perspectives, much of the thinking relating group and cultural factors to criminal behavior falls into the tradition of criminological positivism. That is, it puts the offender rather than the act at the core of criminology. It seeks to find the characteristics, in this case social and economic, which distinguish offenders from nonoffenders. It too assumes that offenders are influenced by forces over which they have little or no control, and it purports to study these forces by the unbiased application of scientific methodology.

In recent years both individual and group or cultural positivist perspectives have been attacked by criminologists called "critical." They have argued that criminology can understand the offender only by examining the criminal justice system in which offenders are caught and processed; that a sharp distinction between offenders and nonoffenders is unwarranted; and that people are common-sense theorizers, not puppets of larger forces. We shall examine the critique of system-oriented critical criminologists after we look at the economic and sociological approaches of group- and culture-oriented criminologists.

GROUP-ORIENTED AND CULTURE-ORIENTED PERSPECTIVES

Economic Approaches

Inspired by Karl Marx, economically oriented criminologists have emphasized capitalism and social class as the key to understanding why individuals commit crimes. To understand their approach, we need to examine the work of Karl Marx and early Marxist criminologists and some present-day work on the relationship between social class and crime.

Marx

Karl Marx (1818–1883), who wrote during the mid-1800s, lived during a period in which society was immensely changed by the industrial revolution. In this revolution, machines came to replace human work; and capitalism, based on the pursuit of private profit, came to replace the highly structured feudal system, which had been based on long-standing personal ties between nobility and serfs. Marx's main concern was with the struggle between the social groups he called "classes" and with the revolution necessary for still further change which would see capitalism replaced by communism. However, as we shall see, Marx did touch upon crime; and a Marxist approach has provided a useful framework for understanding crime, not only for economic positivists but also for critical criminologists.

123

The analytic keys to Marx's approach are his concepts of social class and class struggle. Social classes are determined by the relationships that people have within the mode of production. In capitalist society, there are basically two classes: the bourgeoisie, or employers, who possess capital and own the means of production; and the proletariat, or workers, who sell their labor to capitalists. Because capitalism allows for profit—the right of capitalists to retain the difference between the cost of products and their selling price in the market—it is a system which exploits the worker. Not only does the capitalist take the surplus value produced by workers, but workers as consumers are forced to buy the products of their own (or other workers') labor at a price which includes the capitalist's profit.[1]

Marx's main interest was in revolution. He reasoned that capitalist societies would experience continual class struggle because of the opposed interests of bourgeoisie and proletariat. As the struggle evolved, workers would become aware of the conditions of their exploitation and unite in collective action against the capitalist class.[2] Eventually, the capitalist class would be overthrown. Such a development would pave the way for a society in which workers would collectively own and control the means of production. In the new communist society the institutions—especially the states upon which the capitalists relied to maintain their dominance over workers—would no longer be needed and would thus "wither away." Marx called on all to work for the social revolution that would make this possible.[3] Marx touched upon crime at a number of points in his analysis of society. Perhaps most basic is his view that capitalists and landlords

In the fifteenth and sixteenth centuries, people whose lands were expropriated were forced to survive as beggars, vagabonds, and thieves, because there were no jobs to be had.
(BETTMAN ARCHIVE)

used criminal methods in the large-scale expropriation of land from the people. In fact, he notes that, ironically,

> the law itself becomes now the instrument of the theft of the people's land, although the large farmers make use of their little independent methods as well. The parliamentary form of the robbery is that of Acts for enclosures of Commons, in other words, decrees by which the landlords grant themselves the people's land as private property, decrees of expropriation of the people. . . .[4]

Moreover, Marx notes how the people whose lands were expropriated were

> turned *en masse* into beggars, robbers, vagabonds, partly from inclination, in most cases from stress of circumstances. Hence, there was at the end of the 15th and during the whole of the 16th century, throughout Western Europe a bloody legislation against vagabondage. . . . Legislation treated them as "voluntary" criminals, and assumed that it depended on their own good will to go on working under the old conditions that no longer existed.[5]

Carrying the argument one step further, Marx's collaborator, Frederick Engels (1820–1895), saw crime as an early, although unsuccessful, form of social protest carried out by workers in the early days of the industrial revolution.[6]

Early Marxist criminologists

Marx's insights on crime were most systematically developed by Willem Bonger (1876–1940), a Dutch criminologist. As Bonger saw it, crime was a direct result of the economic system of competitive capitalism which fostered "egoism" and weakened the moral feelings of people in society. The capitalist system engendered different forms of criminal behavior in different social groups. It led *capitalists* of the merchant, industrial, and professional classes to think only of their own advantage, to the detriment of those with whom they did business. It led to bad domestic conditions among the *proletariat*, which in turn led to high rates of juvenile delinquency. Finally, through exploitation, it demoralized the *lower proletariat*, who then became void of feelings for other people.[7]

Bonger's cure for crime—stemming from his stress on the relationship between crime and economic conditions—was to change the social and economic environment of society. The key, in his estimate, was a change to a society "based upon the community of the means of production": i.e., one in which property was distributed according to the maxim "to each according to his needs." In such a society each person would be more interested in helping others than in harming them. The causes of social demoralization would disappear. Crimes might still be committed; but they would be committed by "pathological individuals" and would fall "rather within the sphere of the physician than that of the judge."[8]

In other work, Bonger was an early critic of theories attempting to relate crime and race. Noting that some crime occurs in all races, he argued that people may have criminal inclinations that go against the general interest of the community but that these inclinations are brought out only "under certain circumstances." Hence, differences in crime rates are at best relative. Bonger finds criminal statistics to be too poor to allow conclusions about race and crime.[9] Furthermore, noting that there is much variation within any one race with respect to predisposition to crime, he concludes that "no definite results have been obtained in the study of 'race and crime,' and that much still remains unsettled."[10] In taking this position, Bonger anticipated much of the uncertainty that has characterized the contradictory conclusions about crime and race which emerged from later research. (See, for example, Chapter 17.)

Besides Bonger, there were a number of Marxist scholars in the late nineteenth century and early twentieth century who also sought to tie crime to economic causes. In many respects they were like the European positivists (discussed in Chapter 5), except that they paid far more attention to the economic causes of crime:

> To them, crime was an exclusively lower-class phenomenon, invariably harmful to society. They described criminals as being driven to crime by poverty or pernicious social conditions, but not as seeking it out for personal gain.[11]

Although latter-day Marxist criminology has gone far beyond these early formulations, the idea that a person's position in the economic and social order is an important predictor of proclivity to crime has received an enormous amount of attention.[12]

Present-day economic research

Plausible though it may sound, the idea that criminals are people driven to crime by poverty or pernicious social conditions is one which receives, at best, only mixed support in present-day research. To be sure, there are many ecological studies which have correlated poverty and crime rates, especially official rates (to be discussed in Chapter 8). However, this does not mean that poor people are necessarily more likely to commit crimes.

There are several reasons why one cannot make the blanket statement that poor people are more likely to commit crimes. For one, findings of self-report studies have often conflicted with those based on official crime statistics.[13] Second, it may well be that lower-class adults are more likely to commit crime but that delinquency is spread equally throughout all social groups.[14] Third, even the statement that lower-class adults are more likely to commit crimes is misleading, because middle- and upper-class people may well commit different forms of crime. (See Chapter 2.) Finally—as we shall see later—social class or status sometimes plays a role in the way courts dispose of criminal cases (see Chapter 17).

In short, to say that poverty produces crime is simplistic. At a minimum, we need to specify what types of crime we are talking about and what we mean by the ideas of social class and social status.

Aside from problems concerning the relationship between crime and social class, it may also be that criminal behavior is better explained in terms of the intervening cultural and social factors than simply in terms of the economic environment of the offender. Seeing offenders as part of their cultural and social environment leads us to our fourth approach to the study of offenders.

Sociological Approaches

127

Criminal Offenders:
Group-, Culture-, and
System-Oriented
Perspectives

Keeping a positivist concentration on the offender as the core of a theoretical explanation of crime and delinquency, sociological approaches dominated criminological thinking during the middle decades of the twentieth century. In contrast to the biologically and psychologically oriented theorists, criminologists of this persuasion have argued that criminal behavior is learned rather than innate. In contrast to economic theorists, they see cultural values and intermediate-level institutions (such as the family and schools) rather than social class as critical to the genesis of criminal behavior.

There is much diversity in the sociological approaches. While some branches reflect a strong ecological and ethnographic orientation, others are interested in the implications of social norms and patterns of socialization. Much sociological work has struggled with ways to incorporate theoretical insights into empirical research. This discussion imposes some order on that diversity by classifying sociological theories of crime into three types: cultural-deviance theories, strain (or motivational) theories, and control (or bond) theories. For each type of theory, research which supports or does not support it will be noted. Finally, we shall look at further research designed to test one type of theory as opposed to another.

Cultural-deviance theories

Theories of cultural deviance see the offender as one who conforms to a set of values or standards not accepted by the society at large. Such theories claim that criminal behavior is learned from others involved in it and the critical questions for criminological investigation relate to the conditions under which and the ways in which criminal behavior is learned. These theories arose from a strong background of empirical research carried out by sociologically oriented researchers at the University of Chicago. They have subsequently been elaborated by a number of criminologists.

Chicago school   The ecological and ethnographic research pursued at the University of Chicago dates back to the 1900s. Concerned with rapid urban development brought about by immigration and expansion, members of what came to be known as the "Chicago school" sought answers to problems such as housing, employment, health, poverty, and crime. Their investigatory focus was practical. They sought concrete answers to what they saw as real problems. Much of their research was funded by state and city governments, especially by welfare organizations and criminal justice agencies, which were interested in developing workable policies.

The general perspective of the Chicago school was "social disorganization." This perspective was supported by research in cities in which it was found that there were "zones of transition" surrounding central business districts. While such zones might contain some wholesale or light manufacturing businesses, they tended to be characterized by physical deterioration as well as real estate speculation based on the hope that the central business district would expand. Socially, zones of transition had high rates of school truancy, families on relief, and tuberculosis, in addition to high rates of delinquency and crime. (See Chapter 8.) Moreover, communities in zones of transition lacked viable institutional resources and often contained conflicting norms:

> Thus, within the same community, theft may be defined as right and proper in some groups and as immoral, improper and undesirable in others.[15]

Growing up in a community with conflicting norms, the individual child or young person would encounter competing systems of values. In such a situation, a career in delinquency and crime becomes a viable alternative, one that offers the promise of economic gain, prestige, and companionship. It is interesting to note that within his or her own social world, the child "may be a highly organized and well adjusted person."[16]

In an ethnographic work using a life-history approach to show the problems of a young person encountering competing value systems, Clifford R. Shaw tells the story of Sidney, who began stealing at age 7—without even realizing that this was the legal offense "theft"—and then went on to learn delinquency from older boys in the neighborhood. According to Shaw, Sidney lacked appreciation of the "moral significance of his crime" because most of his contacts outside the home "were limited largely to delinquent and criminal groups." Shaw goes on to contrast Sidney with a brother seven years older who, though living in the same family and neighborhood, was able to form ties with groups in his synagogue and did not develop into a juvenile delinquent.[17]

Sutherland and differential association   The cultural-deviance perspective of the Chicago school was subsequently elaborated by Edwin H. Sutherland (1883–1950) into his well-known theory of differential association. Sutherland, who became the foremost of American criminologists, began his professional career at the University of Chicago. He followed the reform orientation and the practical focus of the Chicago school; his doctoral thesis was on the problem of unemployment. However, Sutherland subsequently became involved in a large number of criminological studies that went far beyond those of the ecologists. In 1924, he published his first criminology text, one that was to remain a major force in American criminology for many years. In the 1939 edition, he introduced the theory of differential association, through which he sought to interpret both the findings of the ecologists and other work in areas such as white-collar crime, professional theft, embezzlement, and laws concerning sexual psychopathy.

In the theory of differential association the conflict of cultures becomes "the fundamental principle in the explanation of crime."[18] People are exposed to different cultural values and are as it were drawn to or from crime, depending on the values to which they are exposed. In Sutherland's words, the theory is based on nine propositions:

1. Criminal behavior is learned; or stated another way, criminal behavior is not inherited. The person who is not trained in criminal behavior does not invent it any more than a person who had not been trained in mechanics makes mechanical objects.

2. Criminal behavior is learned in interaction with others in a process of communication, both verbal and nonverbal (gestures).
3. The principal learning of criminal behavior occurs within intimate personal groups. Impersonal agencies of communication, such as movies, newspapers, etc., play a relatively minor part in the genesis of criminal behavior.
4. The learning of criminal behavior includes:
   a. The techniques of committing the crime—sometimes complicated, sometimes simple
   b. The specific direction of motives, drives, rationalizations, and attitudes
5. The specific direction of motives and drives is learned from favorable or unfavorable definitions of the legal codes. An individual may be surrounded by persons whose definitions are favorable to the violation of legal codes. In American society these definitions are almost always mixed with consequences that produce culture conflict with respect to the legal codes.
6. A person becomes delinquent because of an excess of definitions favorable to law violation over definitions unfavorable to violation of law.
7. Differential association may vary in frequency, duration, priority, and intensity. Priority means it developed early; intensity has to do with the prestige of the source.
8. The process of learning criminal behavior by association with criminal and anticriminal patterns involves all of the mechanisms required in any other learning; this learning is not restricted to imitation.
9. Although criminal behavior is an expression of general needs and values, it is not explained by those general needs and values since noncriminal behavior is an expression of the same needs and values.[19]

It should be noted that the theory of differential association assumes a society consisting of a multiplicity of groups and subcultures, some of which are at variance with the legal system. In such a society, rules of conduct may be derived from the smaller, intimate groups with their unique subcultures. The critical factors in becoming criminal are the nature and extent to which an individual is intimately involved with groups and the posture of the group versus the law, as expressed in Sutherland's proposition 6.

As a leading theory of criminal behavior, differential association has stimulated a great deal of sociological interest and research. It finds indirect support in the many studies describing the process of socialization into criminal and deviant groups; becoming a prostitute or a skilled burglar, for example, is seen as the result of an interaction process in which ties are created with others already involved in the activity and broken with conventional associates.[20] It found direct support in early research in which James F. Short addressed the hypothesis that boys and girls who are most seriously involved in delinquent behavior will indicate that their best friends are "delinquency producing" while those least seriously involved will see their best friends as "delinquency inhibiting."[21] In later research, Gary F. Jensen also found a strong positive relationship between the number of delinquent friends and delinquency, a relationship which remained even when respondents' definitions of delinquency were controlled.[22]

In later work, differential association has been elaborated into "social-learning theory" and found to be considerably supported by research dealing with adolescents' drug-related and alcohol-related behavior. One study using self-report data on 3065 male and female adolescents attending grades 7 through 12 in seven communities in three midwestern states found:

> As predicted by the theory (social learning), the adolescents in our sample use drugs or alcohol to the extent that the behavior has been differentially reinforced through association in primary groups and defined as more desirable than, or at least as justified as, refraining from use.[23]

A further analysis using the same data discerned differences between marijuana and alcohol. In the case of marijuana, adolescents learned definitions of the behavior from peers while those of parents remained a constant. In the case of alcohol, definition of the deviant behavior was learned from both peers and parents; thus, parents' definitions were more important for alcohol. As the researcher goes on to note, conformity to the norms of peer group, while important during adolescence, may well decrease as people get older.[24]

However, other research has failed to support a theory of differential association. When Albert J. Reiss and A. Lewis Rhodes investigated the behavior of 299 delinquent boys and each boy's two best friends, they found:

> Close friendship choices are more closely correlated with delinquency *per se* than with participation in specific patterns of delinquency presumably learned from others.[25]

This finding calls attention to some of the difficulties with differential-association theory. One problem is that demonstrations that delinquents associate primarily

Teenagers of the south Bronx, abandoned by their parents, formed the Nobody's Children Club.   (ED LETTAU/PHOTO RESEARCHERS, INC.)

with other delinquents may simply mean that juveniles who are already delinquent seek out associations with other delinquents.[26] Another is that the variables suggested as important by the theory have proven to be difficult to quantify. For example, one might well ask how an excess of definitions favorable or unfavorable to violating the law could be counted.

The problems with differential-association theory have led several criminologists to attempt restatements of differential association. C. R. Jeffery developed what he called a "theory of differential reinforcement" in which he maintains that criminal behavior is "operant behavior, that is, it is maintained by the changes it produces on the environment."[27] It then follows that crime can be prevented by changes in the physical environment.[28] Daniel Glaser suggests a "differential anticipation" theory which he sees as both combining differential association with control theory (to be discussed later in this chapter) and taking biological and social factors into account. As he put it:

> Differential-anticipation theory assumes that a person will try to commit a crime wherever and whenever the expectations of gratifications from it—as a result of social bonds, differential learning, and perceptions of opportunity—exceed the unfavorable anticipations from these sources.[29]

Other work based on cultural deviance The argument that a criminal offender is someone who conforms to norms not accepted by the society at large has also been advanced by other criminologists. Surveying world literature on crime and deviance, Marvin E. Wolfgang and Franco Ferracuti were led to conclude that there are subcultures of violence in which significant lessons are transmitted from generation to generation within ethnic groups.[30] Another application of this argument is to see the subculture of violence as a regional phenomenon, one that is especially evident in the southern part of the United States (for a discussion, see Chapter 9).

Finally, Walter B. Miller has advanced the notion that lower-class values are in and of themselves conducive to high crime rates. Grouped around the "focal concerns" of trouble, toughness, smartness, excitement, fate, and autonomy, such values contrast markedly with middle-class values, which emphasize ambition, cultivation of skills and talents, ability to postpone gratification, and preparation for the future. Being brought up in the lower class means learning a culture different from that on which the criminal law is based. Miller estimated that 40 to 60 percent of Americans may be influenced by lower-class values, with perhaps 15 percent being "hard-core" lower-class—i.e., people for whom lower-class values constitute a lifestyle.[31]

Strain (or motivational) theories

Strain theories, the second of our three sociological approaches, see offenders as pushed into deviance by legitimate desires that conformity cannot satisfy. They relate the offender's inclination to crime both to culture and to social structure. Moreover, rather than seeing an American society composed of diverse subcultures, they picture an overriding American culture, one which places a high value upon monetary success. Theorizing in this vein began with the publication of

Robert K. Merton's essay "Social Structure and Anomie" in 1938[32] and was advanced in the work of Albert K. Cohen as well as that of Richard A. Cloward and Lloyd R. Ohlin. It too has led to research, which will be discussed later in this chapter.

Merton Merton's understanding of crime was based on a reformulation of the work of the French thinker Émile Durkheim. Durkheim had advanced the concept of "anomie" or "normlessness" to describe modern societies, which he felt had so much occupational specialization that spontaneous consensus of their various parts is lost. (For a more complete discussion, see Chapter 8.) For Merton, anomie in American society is seen in the disparity between its ideal of monetary success as a "goal worth striving for" and its limitations on the possibilities of attaining success legitimately.

For Merton, the offender is a person who is pressured to engage in nonconforming rather than conforming conduct, and this pressure is a result of anomie in American society. To encourage people to obtain success and at the same time limit the possibility of success is to create a dilemma that can be resolved only by nonconforming, often criminal, conduct. The pressure is greater on the lower classes, since their opportunities are more limited; and this explains what Merton assumes to be the higher crime rates of the lower classes.

Actually, five kinds of behavioral adaptations are possible for individuals under the pressures exerted by social structure (see Table 5). Of the five, four are in some way deviant. Type 3 is simply giving up; this describes the person who "plays it safe" and just puts in his or her own time. Type 4 is the response of the vagrant, vagabond, alcoholic, or drug addict who has dropped out of society (see Chapter 13). Type 5 is the political criminal, the dissenter involved in criminal acts in which he or she attempts to substitute new goals or means for existing ones (hence the plus and minus in Table 5; see Chapter 15).

Of Merton's behavioral types, it is type 2 which is the key to explaining the criminality of the lower classes. In order to achieve monetary success, they need to be innovators, i.e., to circumvent the culturally approved means of attaining success. An example is Al Capone, who was seen by many not only as a successful criminal but also as a folk hero representing "the triumph of amoral intelligence over morally prescribed 'failure,' when the channels of vertical mobility are closed or narrowed."[33] One might also cite the nineteenth-century

TABLE 5. A Typology of Modes of Individual Adaptation

Modes of adaptation	Cultural goals	Institutional means
1. Conformity	+	+
2. Innovation	+	−
3. Ritualism	−	+
4. Retreatism	−	−
5. Rebellion	±	±

KEY: + acceptance; − rejection.
SOURCE: Robert K. Merton, *Social Theory and Social Structure*, enlarged ed., Free Press, New York, and Collier Macmillan, London, 1968, p. 194.

"robber barons" and today's corporate criminals, who are often regarded as shrewd, smart, and successful because they get away with sharp business deals. The irony is that there are many instances in which deviant or criminal activity is seen by many Americans as paying off, especially when it appears to be done in excess by other people.[34]

Cohen Strain theory took another direction in the work of Albert K. Cohen, who attempted to apply it to understand gang delinquency.[35] To Cohen, the United States was a class society marked by a conflict between the middle class and the working class. This viewpoint contrasts with Merton's, which emphasizes goals held by all members of society, and with the cultural-deviance theories, which emphasize a pluralistic society with sometimes conflicting subcultures.

In Cohen's terms, the United States is a society which subjects its children to continual evaluations. In these evaluations it is middle-class, not working-class, values which are the "measuring rod." Citing as middle-class values ambition, individual responsibility, cultivation of personal skills and performance, asceticism, rationality, manners and personality, control of aggression and violence, and respect for property, Cohen notes that middle-class socialization is, "conscious, rational, deliberate and demanding. Relatively little is left to chance."[36] Useful though these values may be for getting ahead in a society that encourages impersonal competition, they contrast sharply with those of an easygoing, spontaneous working-class subculture that places much less emphasis on achievement.

One result of the conflict between middle-class and working-class values is a delinquent subculture which becomes for the working-class child "a way of dealing with the problem of adjustment" to middle-class culture. The delinquent subculture is reactive and oriented toward peer groups. Its values are directly contrary to those of the middle class. Gang boys are truant because good boys aren't. Some of their activity is purposeless and nonutilitarian rather than goal-directed. Other activity has a purpose but not one that is economically or socially useful; for example, delinquents will vandalize a school in the evening because the teacher gave them a low grade earlier in the day.

From Cohen's viewpoint, the working-class gang is an illustration of Merton's behavioral type of rebellion. Turning inward, with a sense of solidarity in which its members find protection, the working-class gang is usually hostile to outsiders. It has rejected middle-class values and has established a new set of values more acceptable to its members. The rebellious attitude is especially apparent in the considerable amount of purposeless and nonutilitarian crime and delinquency.

Cohen's theory of working-class delinquency is directly antithetical to Miller's theory (described earlier). Whereas Miller saw delinquent behavior as a direct expression of lower-class subcultural values, Cohen saw it as *reactive*. Thus Cohen is implicitly asserting that middle-class values are the only viable ones in American society. Moreover, his views of delinquents as malicious disregards some of the positive aspects of delinquent activities. It may well be that much delinquent behavior is not reactive or defiant in a negative sense but rather is done for "kicks," e.g., rolling drunks, snatching purses, staying out all night, and doing what one wants without adult supervision.[37]

Vandals smashed this statue of a drummer boy that had stood for 100 years in the Chickamauga-Chattanooga National Military Park, Tennessee, as a monument to soldiers of the Civil War. (WIDE WORLD PHOTOS)

Cloward and Ohlin   The next major statement of strain theory emerged from the work of Richard A. Cloward and Lloyd E. Ohlin. In that Cloward had studied under Merton at Columbia and Ohlin at Chicago and at Indiana while Sutherland was there, their collaboration represented a merger of the two dominant sociological perspectives of their time. Moreover, their ultimate aim was practical and applied. They were researchers for a project on the lower east side of New York City. Funded by the National Institute of Mental Health, this "action project" was designed to address delinquency by expanding educational and economic opportunities and by developing community organization. In expounding a theory, Cloward and Ohlin hoped to formulate a stronger rationale for programmatic efforts.

Like Cohen, Cloward and Ohlin felt that delinquent subcultures needed to be more fully understood if the rationale for delinquency was to become clear. In this spirit, they open their book *Delinquency and Opportunity* by discussing three types of delinquent subcultures: (1) criminal subcultures oriented toward theft, extortion, and illegal income; (2) conflict subcultures characterized by a manipulation of violence; and (3) retreatist subcultures in which the consumption of drugs is featured. Many so-called slum areas are in effect organized by criminal subcultures which are often linked to adult criminal groups (e.g., organized crime). Such areas provide opportunities to neighborhood children even though these opportunities may well be illegitimate. In comparison, conflict and retreatist subcultures are seen in disorganized slums which offer neither legitimate nor illegitimate opportunity.[38]

Turning to the issue of what motivates delinquents, Cloward and Ohlin extend Merton's formulation by portraying the lower-class delinquent as an innovator, one who accepts the goal of success but, because of limited means, cannot possibly achieve it. Their position is:

> The disparity between what lower-class youth are led to want and what is actually available to them is the source of a major problem of adjustment. . . . Faced with limitations on legitimate avenues of access to these goals, and unable to revise their aspirations downwards, they experience intense frustrations; the exploration of nonconformist alternatives may be the result.[39]

Although all American young people may experience frustration, "the poor desire a proportionately larger increase in income than do persons in higher strata."[40] The problem is, on the one hand, that they are limited in their access to legitimate means; and, on the other hand, that illegitimate means may well be available to them.

Cloward and Ohlin's approach received extensive attention when it became the basis for "Mobilization for Youth," a major federally funded project designed to put "expanding opportunity" into practice.[41] From a theoretical viewpoint, their work is important because it effectively combined two branches of sociological criminology: cultural-deviance theory and strain theory. Although criticized for its vagueness (note the phrase "may be the result" and the several meanings for the terms "frustration" and "nonconformist alternatives"), it did show that cultural values alone could not explain delinquency; that the social structure of the neighborhood community should be an object of focus; and that it is necessary to look beyond cultural values to examine opportunities available in the larger social systems in which people are located.

Control theories

Control theory, the third line of sociological work, has sought to apply knowledge about processes of socialization to the study of crime and delinquency. Its basic argument is that delinquent acts occur when ties to the conventional social order are broken. As one early writer put it, delinquency can best be seen as a "failure of personal and social control."[42]

Control theorists, like Merton, draw their inspiration from Durkheim's work; but their formulation of the problem contrasts markedly with Merton's. Control theorists take the concept of anomie developed in Durkheim's later work, *Suicide*:

> . . . Society cannot disintegrate without the individual simultaneously detaching himself from social life. . . . The more weakened the groups to which he belongs, the less he depends on them, the more he consequently depends only on himself and recognizes no other rules of conduct than what are founded on his private interests.[43]

Travis Hirschi, a contemporary sociologist, rewords Durkheim somewhat when he states: "Control theories assume that delinquent acts result when an individual's bond to society is weak or broken."[44] There are four elements of the bond:

attachment (caring about others, their opinions, and their expectations), commit-ment (time, energy, and self invested in conventional behaviors), involvement (engrossment in conventional activities), and belief (attribution of moral validity to conventional norms). As one or more elements of the bond become weakened, delinquency becomes possible, although not inevitable.[45]

Control theory differs from differential association and strain theory on several key points. For one, it asks why most people refrain from criminal behavior rather than why some people engage in crime. For another, it empha-sizes social factors of the bond rather than the exposure to favorable or unfavorable definitions of the legal code. For a third, it omits consideration of delinquent subcultures, preferring to examine variations in the extent to which people are bound to their society.

Hirschi's research, designed to test his theory, was conducted at high schools in the San Francisco Bay area from which he drew a sample of approximately 4000 students. Measuring delinquency by self-reported as well as officially reported behavior, Hirschi found that attachment to parents and school is associated with lawful conduct and resistance to delinquency. Attachment to peers is predictive of delinquency, except that boys with other significant attachments are rarely inclined toward juvenile gangs. Involvement in conven-tional activities leads to less involvement in self-reported delinquency. Finally, more delinquent young people, as compared with those who are less delinquent, are likely to agree with the following statements:

> "Most criminals shouldn't really be blamed for the things they have done."
> "I can't seem to stay out of trouble no matter how hard I try."
> "Most things that people call 'delinquency' don't really hurt anyone."
> "Policemen do not try to give all kids an even break. . . . It is alright [*sic*] to get around the law if you can get away with it."[46]

Hirschi concludes his study by claiming that his data support a control theory rather than cultural deviance or strain theory:

> In every case, the conclusion is the same: the absence of control increases the likelihood of delinquency regardless of the presence of group traditions of delinquen-cy. Although social support increases the likelihood that delinquent acts will be committed, the view that the child must somehow be taught in intimate, personal groups greatly overstates the case.[47]

Other attempts to support control theory through empirical research, however, have not come to definitive conclusions. Hindelang's study in rural New York State failed to replicate a positive relationship between attachment to parents and attachment to friends, failed to show that attachment to friends increases the likelihood of delinquent behavior, and found a slight positive relationship between identification with peers and delinquency, one which control theory would not be able to account for.[48] Designing a study to incorporate these problems, Rand D. Conger found not so much that control theory is incorrect but that it is incomplete because the critical issue was not identification with peers as such but what type of peers individuals identified with.[49] Finally, Michael D.

Wiatrowski and his associates used Hirschi's theories to analyze data from a longitudinal "Youth in Transition" study of over 2000 tenth-grade boys in the United States. Their analysis led to a reformulation of Hirschi's theories which argues that bonds to society are formed both in the family and in educational contexts and that "acceptance of conventional social values may be the consequence of a youth's belief in the efficacy of education in pursuing future goals."[50]

Testing the sociological approaches: Research

Two major research efforts have attempted to compare the adequacy of the explanations advanced by the three main lines of sociological thinking. One is that of Eric Linden and James C. Hackler, who were concerned with linking differential association and control theory. In their research on 200 boys, ages 13 to 15, from a low-cost housing project in Seattle, Washington, they found that it was most useful to examine the "affective ties"—i.e., the ties these boys had to other persons—rather than the generalized normative commitment stressed by Sutherland. When they examined these ties, they found that boys with weak or nonexistent ties to conventional associates (either peers or parents) but moderate ties to deviant peers were most involved in delinquency. They conclude, "one of the factors conducive to delinquency involvement is attachment to deviant peers."[51] Such a finding provides more specificity than Sutherland's notion of an excess of definitions and, at the same time, questions control theory by arguing that delinquents maintain ties to a value system, although not one of the conventional social order.

The other important research effort testing the adequacy of explanations offered by the sociological approaches was made by Delbert S. Elliott and Harwin L. Voss. They begin by seeing delinquency in terms of four variables taken from the major theories: disjunction between aspiration and opportunity, external attribution of blame, alienation and normlessness, and access to delinquent groups.[52] Combining these four variables, their hypothesis is:

. . . Failure to achieve valued goals, when attributed to injustice or inequities in the social system, leads to normlessness.[53]

They also note that young people do not engage in normlessness unless exposed to it and that to be consistent the hypothesis should apply to all social classes. Finally, according to Elliott and Voss, delinquency is similar to dropping out in that both are "adaptations to failure."[54]

As the setting for research into delinquency, Elliott and Voss chose the school because "delinquency and dropout are primarily adaptations to school-related problems."[55] Tracking a sample of 2309 students in a California school district from ninth to twelfth grade and analyzing the data in considerable detail, Elliott and Voss reported a number of findings, many of which challenged existing theories or what was believed to be known about delinquency. Among them were:

1. There was no support for Cloward and Ohlin's hypothesis, because few young people anticipated failure to achieve long-range results.
2. There was no consistent blame of self or system.

3. Normlessness in school and at home, but not in the community, was related to delinquency. Normlessness and social isolation were predictive of dropping out.
4. Association with dropouts was conducive to dropping out. Similarly, association with delinquent friends, combined with weak commitment to parents, was predictive of delinquency.
5. Although rates of police contact were higher for dropouts than for graduates, both groups had lower rates of police contact than young people in school. Presumably, these lower rates reflected the transition to marriage and employment.
6. There was limited support for the relationship between failure and delinquency, although there was a stronger relationship for males than for females. However, academic failure and parental rejection were "mutually reinforcing."
7. Delinquent behavior did not appear to be related to social class or ethnic origin. On the other hand, dropping out was related to social class: lower-class young people were more likely to drop out.
8. The level of participation in the school's extracurricular activities was not related to delinquency, perhaps because so few participated in them. At the same time, delinquent behavior was not restricted to a few "hoods" or "outsiders" but appeared to be "a more general feature of adolescent culture."
9. Failure, normlessness, and association with delinquent friends were both causes and consequences of involvement in delinquent behavior.[56]

From this suggestive body of findings, Elliot and Voss draw the conclusion that campaigns to keep young people in school should be reconsidered, since staying in school "often aggravates a youth's problems rather than alleviating them."[57]

Assumptions of the sociological approaches

Sociological approaches to the study of offenders reflect some fundamental changes in assumptions made about human nature. For the biological, psychological, and economic approaches, the explanation of criminality lies in the unique qualities possessed by the offender—genes, intelligence, socioeconomic status, etc. In comparison, for the sociological theories—especially cultural-deviance and control theories—the explanation lies in the kinds of social associations a person experiences. As David Matza puts it, the shift is from an explanation of criminality based on affinity to one based on affiliation. In explanations based on affiliation, the subject becomes "*converted* to conduct novel for him but already established for others."[58]

The sociological theories also raise questions about the extent to which behavior is determined by forces external to the individual. As we noted earlier, classical theorists (see Chapter 4) generally assumed that people act out of free will when committing crimes, while positivist theorists attempted to study various factors believed to predict or determine individual behavior. On the surface, the two positions appear incompatible.[59] However, Matza, in an earlier work than the one cited above, argued that the sociological model was one of "soft determinism'' which saw persons neither as wholly free nor as completely constrained or determined. To Matza, the appropriate image for the delinquent was one of drift:

> . . . an actor neither compelled nor committed to needs nor freely choosing them . . . conforming to certain traditions in American life while partially unreceptive to other more conventional traditions . . . [60]

Moreover, Daniel Glaser has suggested that the legal responsibility implied by free will and the lack of responsibility implied by determinism are, in fact, compatible with each other. In his opinion, both are

> socially derived linguistic representations of reality, free will to justify holding people morally responsible for their conduct, and determinism to explain or predict and hence to rationalize attempting to influence or control behavior.[61]

In short, many sociologists would argue that offenders can be legally responsible even if they have drifted or come to be involved in criminal activity because of factors of which they were not completely aware.

SYSTEM-ORIENTED PERSPECTIVES: CRITICAL CRIMINOLOGISTS' CRITIQUE OF POSITIVISM

In recent years, all four positivist approaches—sociological, biological, psychological, and economic—have come under sharp attack. Several of the fundamental assumptions of positivism have been thrown open to debate. Hence, it is important to complete our discussion of perspectives on individual offenders by examining the critique of positivism represented by system-oriented approaches.

The past two decades have seen a number of attempts to change the focus of criminology by posing fundamentally different types of questions for research and scholarly analysis. This shift in thinking about the offender parallels the shift in thinking about the act which was discussed in Chapter 4. It too is "critical" in that it advocates fundamentally new directions for criminological inquiry and proposes to take inequalities of social power—of the social system—into account. Moreover, it seriously questions the efficacy of even studying the characteristics of individual offenders.[62]

Critical criminologists' critique of positivist approaches revolves around three questions: (1) What is the process by which people come to be called "criminal"? (2) Who is the criminal? (3) What is the rationale by which people act? Although there is some overlap, let's examine these questions one at a time.

The first question the critical criminologists ask is: *By what process do people come to be called "criminal"?* Rather than adopting the positive approach of studying characteristics of individual offenders, critical criminologists prefer to consider the ways in which people react to the allegedly deviant or criminal behavior of others. As Howard S. Becker put it in a now classic work, social rules are not enforced until

> those who want the rule enforced publically bring the infraction to the attention of others. . . . People blow the whistle, making enforcement necessary, when they see some advantage in doing so. . . . [63]

Similarly, Edwin M. Lemert argued that society's response to deviants was a far more important object of study than the deviants themselves, or their behavior. As he put it, the idea that deviant behavior leads to social control was one that needed to be turned around:

> I have come to believe that the reverse idea (i.e., social control leads to deviance) is equally tenable and the potentially richer premise for studying deviance in modern society.[64]

Taking this perspective, we would need to ask why it is that some people consistently violate legal norms but escape public recognition while others are caught and punished for actions which cause relatively little social harm. To put it in other words, does an arrest tell us more about the policies and practices of those making the arrest than it does about the person arrested? In asking these kinds of questions, Becker and Lemert gave birth to what is often called the "labeling" perspective on criminal behavior.[65]

From the viewpoint of labeling theorists, organizations are especially suspect in designating and conferring indentities on those they process. Following what they consider to be an impersonal, detached, or "professional" approach, organizations in the police, court, and correction system often serve to confirm deviant or criminal social identities by recasting the self-images of those whom they process in case histories and allowing for negotiation in which power plays are possible.[66]

The labeling perspective finds evidence in many different areas. Police arrest policies are enormously influenced by factors such as respect shown by suspected offenders and race of suspected offenders, especially in minor criminal matters (this point is discussed in Chapter 16). How the courts prosecute depends on a number of factors other than the offense; race, class, and conformity to criminal stereotypes such as the "normal primitive" may markedly affect the course of prosecutions. What is more, a number of studies indicate that laws provide so much flexibility that justice becomes the result of a bargain among prosecutors, defense attorneys, and judges (see Chapter 17). In the view of labeling theorists, variables such as these so complicate the question whether a person is or is not processed as an offender that his or her underlying nature or behavior becomes far less relevant. The social reaction is more problematic, and more in need of study, than the underlying behavior which supposedly prompted it.

In studying social reaction, one very soon becomes aware of the political dimensions involved in the processing and labeling of offenders. As Eugene Doleschal and Nora Klapmuts write:

> Those caught up in the system are overwhelmingly the poor, the lower class, members of minority groups, immigrants, foreigners, persons of low intelligence, and others who are in some way at a disadvantage.[67]

Similarly, William J. Chambliss puts it as follows:

> We have come to realize that crime is not so much a matter of individuals differing in their social experiences. Crime is rather a political phenomenon whereby some

behaviors and some people are labeled "criminal," "delinquent," or "sick," while other behaviors and people are not.[68]

Finally, in an explicitly Marxist formulation, Steven Spitzer argues that the capitalist mode of production depends upon the regulation and management of problem populations whose "behavior, personal qualities, and/or position threaten the *social relations of production* in capitalist societies." In that the behaviors defined as problematic are widespread, there is a large problem population, an almost inexhaustible pool from which agencies of social control can draw candidates for processing as deviants.[69]

In examining the process by which people come to be called "criminal," we also find the answer to our second question: *Who is the criminal?* To put it in a nutshell, for the critical, or system-oriented, criminologist the criminal is the person who gets caught and comes to be processed through the machinery of criminal justice. The point is that the people who are typically caught and processed are not necessarily representative of the people who commit criminal or deviant acts. Corporate criminals (see Chapter 11), computer thieves (see Chapter 12), and political criminals—especially politicians who commit crimes by abuse of office (see Chapter 15)—provide striking examples of people who have committed serious crimes but are rarely processed as criminals.[70]

A related point is that there is no clear dividing line between criminals and noncriminals. This position finds much support in self-report studies, which show criminal behavior to be widespread among all social groups and classes (see Chapter 3). The absence of a clear dividing line between criminals and noncriminals has presented considerable problems for positivist criminology. For one thing, as Alex Thio notes, it has led positivist criminologists to assume erroneously that lower-class criminality is greater than middle- or upper-class criminality and hence that theories of crime need to explain lower-class criminality, especially lower-class delinquency.[71]

Another problem is that the lack of a clear dividing line between criminals and noncriminals has continually frustrated attempts at prediction. Despite its claims to be able to understand and predict (in order to control) behavior, positivism has yet to develop an adequate set of variables that would predict criminal behavior. In many instances, individual criminal behavior is overpredicted; i.e., persons are incorrectly identified as potential offenders.[72] In one survey of variables predicting recidivism, it was found that type of offense and number of previous convictions are better predictors than variables describing individual attributes.[73] One observer has argued that the powers of prediction offered by positivist theories are so gross that they are comparable to using a tool like a napalm bomb to discriminate guerilla targets.[74]

Critical criminologists have been much interested in the social construction of deviance. In fact, rather than focus on the distinction between criminals and noncriminals, critical criminologists, especially labeling theorists, are more concerned with the distinction between "primary" and "secondary" deviance. Primary deviance is represented by the person who commits one or more violations of rules but explains or rationalizes them while clinging to a nondeviant identity and role. Secondary deviance occurs when the social response is such that a person is provided with a new, negative social identity (e.g., "prostitute," "drug addict," "convict"). Feeling themselves to be negatively labeled, such people may well increase their deviant behavior. Moreover, once people have been negatively labeled, their identity becomes difficult to change: e.g., the "clean" person who once used drugs remains an "ex-addict," and the person who no longer sells sexual services for money is an "ex-prostitute." Through this further, "secondary" deviance—the result of negatively defining and rejecting the offender—societies inadvertently encourage the very activities they seek to eradicate.[75]

The third question posed by critical criminologists is: *What is the rationale by which people act?* This question challenges the assumptions that positivists make about the rationales of human action. As was noted earlier, the determinism implied in the positivist perspective stands in rather sharp contrast to the free will of the classicists. Critical criminologists are closer to free-will theorists than they are to deterministic theorists; they have stressed the view that human beings are "commonsense theorizers" or "constructors of commonsense reality." Moreover, critical criminologists would understand behavior by analyzing these constructs. From their viewpoint, the task for criminology is not to ask why people commit crimes but rather to discover

> how some behaviors come to be recognizable and therefore describable as crimes, either by the actors involved or by some observer.[76]

In an interesting application of this perspective, Lonnie H. Athens shows how violent criminal offenders typically "*self consciously construct* violent plans of action before they commit violent criminal acts. . . ."[77] To the extent that such a process occurs, it considerably undermines positivist explanations of crime, which picture offenders driven by biological, psychological, economic, or sociological forces.[78]

ASSESSING THE POSITIVIST APPROACHES

Sharp though the challenges of critical criminology have been, it is by no means clear that their arguments have prevailed. As was indicated at a number of points in this chapter and Chapter 5, positivism of all types continues to receive much scholarly attention. Since a number of diverse viewpoints have been presented, it may be useful to offer an assessment of the present state of criminological perspectives on individual offenders, and a few further issues for consideration.

Present-day criminological thinking finds itself caught between and among various specialized academic disciplines, each of which attempts to understand the criminal offender in terms of its own perspective on behavior. As we have seen, the four major positivist approaches are biological, psychological, economic, and sociological. These perspectives have competed against each other in the attempt to provide the most adequate explanation of crime. While sociological thinking has dominated the criminological scene for the past several decades, there are some signs of a swing back to the once-discredited biological criminology.[79]

Perhaps a more realistic position is to see each of the four positivist approaches as providing a partial perspective on crime. Thus, it might well be argued that biological, psychological, economic, and social variables are interactive and that all of them need to be considered for a complete explanation of crime. In this regard, it is interesting to note that some sociologists have called for theories which would take biological factors into account,[80] and that some biologically oriented criminologists have seen the need to consider sociological factors.[81]

Even if the four disciplinary perspectives were to be integrated, criminology would still have to deal with the critique of the critical criminologists. *If* the process by which people come to be criminalized is the best explanation of their proclivity to crime, *if* there is no clear dividing line between criminals and noncriminals, and *if* people are commonsense theorizers in full control of their actions, then the positivists' search for a complete explanation of crime might well be abandoned. The "causes" of crime would lie more in the arbitrary action of the criminal justice system than in the individual offender.

However, criminology has by no means seen the full acceptance of the arguments of critical criminologists. The labeling viewpoint has come under sharp attack,[82] and there are fundamental disagreements among the various schools of critical criminology.[83] Moreover, research findings do not always support the perspectives advanced by critical criminology (e.g., see Chapter 17). If positivism is to be discarded in favor of critical criminology, the latter will need to demonstrate clearly that the processing of criminals is so arbitrary that it is virtually meaningless to study offenders. Here too it may well be that there is some room for a middle ground between positivist and labeling approaches.[84]

There are also three further considerations concerning perspectives on criminal offenders. The first of these is that virtually all the theories conceptualize crime as if it were one type of behavior. This may well be an oversimplification; crime is heterogeneous and multifaceted. It may be that the offender who commits a multimillion-dollar computer theft acts out of a rationale far different from that of a rapist, who in turn acts for different reasons from a juvenile shoplifter out for some fun. First offenders who are juveniles have different characteristics from first offenders at later ages. In other words, criminology is a field in which there is much need for middle-range theories that deal with the dynamics of particular types of crime.[85]

The second consideration is that a theory of *criminal behavior* is not a theory of *crime*, because it does not explain why the act committed by the offender is criminal or noncriminal;[86] that is why theories focusing on criminal acts have been examined (in Chapter 4) separately from those focusing on offenders (in Chapters 5 and 6).

The third consideration is that there is no theory of criminal behavior which explains *all* criminal behavior.[87] As we have seen, the presently available theories appear at best to be partial perspectives on the behavior of offenders. It is also debatable whether or not criminal behavior is explained by the same theories which explain law-abiding behavior. In short, despite the tremendous effort that has gone into the study of offenders and into the critique offered by critical criminology, there is surprisingly little consensus on theories that attempt to explain the actions and rationales of individual criminal offenders.

It might also be mentioned at this point that criminology is not limited to the study of crime and the study of offenders. There are two other alternatives: the victim and the social context. These other possibilities are the subjects of Chapters 7 and 8.

APPLICABILITY OF POSITIVIST AND CRITICAL PERSPECTIVES ON OFFENDERS TO MAJOR FORMS OF CRIME

The enormous emphasis placed by criminology on the individual criminal offender means that offenders cannot be ignored when the major forms of crime are considered—as they are in Part Three of this text. Each of the chapters in Part Three devotes some attention to typical offenders. Nevertheless, as was indicated earlier, present criminological knowledge does not allow us to posit a direct relationship between type of crime and type of offender. Moreover, studies of offenders' rationales for committing particular types of crimes are generally lacking.

In that they are stated generally, any of the theories attempting to explain individual criminal behavior could be applied to any of the major forms of crime. However, the actual theorizing and research intended to support the theories have not worked that way. As we saw earlier, many positivist theories have a distinct class bias, suggesting that lower-class criminality is what is most problematic and most in need of explanation. They also have a bias toward certain types of crime: person-to-person violent crimes (especially homicide, rape, assault, and robbery); and, to a lesser extent, person-to-person property crimes (especially burglary, larceny, and motor vehicle theft). Rarely have positivist theories, especially biological and psychological positivism, been applied to corporate crime, crimes against corporations, crimes against the social order, organized crime, or political crime.

Critical criminological perspectives can be useful in explaining types of crime other than direct person-to-person crimes. As we shall see, it is with these other types that the criminal justice system can be most arbitrary and selective in terms of who does or does not get caught and processed. These crimes are committed by a wide range of people. However, many of those who commit them—especially the more powerful members of society—are never apprehended or convicted. Indeed, many do not think of themselves and are not regarded by others as criminals, even though they commit criminal acts (e.g., corporate executives who knowingly market defective products or workers who steal from their employers). Critical criminological perspectives may be more useful than positivism in studying these types of crimes.

SUMMARY

In contrast to biological and psychological approaches, economic and sociological approaches have stressed environmental factors which lead people to crime. Economic approaches can be traced to Karl Marx, a major nineteenth-century thinker who was concerned with class struggle and the antagonisms between bourgeoisie and proletariat. Marx saw as criminal the manner in which capitalistic and landlord interests expropriated peoples' land and believed that the criminalization of landless people was a direct consequence. Following in his footsteps, Bonger, an early Marxist criminologist, saw crime as the direct result of a capitalistic system that fostered "egoism" and weakened the moral feelings of people in society. Other early Marxist criminologists attributed crime to poverty or pernicious social conditions. Later research has been ambivalent about the relationship betwen crime and poverty, and sociologists have stressed the role of intervening cultural and social factors in the causation of crime and delinquency.

Sociological criminology is very diverse. This chapter presented three major schools of thought: cultural-deviance theories, strain (or motivational) theories, and control (or bond) theories. Cultural-deviance theories see the offender as one who conforms to a set of values or standards not accepted by the society at large. This viewpoint is reflected in the work of the Chicago school, which emphasized the point that children in a socially disorganized neighborhood may be socialized into delinquent norms at a very early age. It is also the basis for Sutherland's theory of differential association, the theory that delinquent or criminal behavior is learned in intimate social groups and that a person becomes delinquent because of an excess of definitions favorable to violating the law over definitions unfavorable to violating the law. The object of much attention, Sutherland's differential association has been supported by some but not all research. In later years it was reformulated into a "theory of differential reinforcement" by Jeffery and a "differential anticipation theory" by Glaser. Cultural-deviance theory of criminal behavior as learned through exposure to divergent sets of values is also reflected in Wolfgang and Feracutti's notion of "subcultures of violence," in descriptions of regional subcultures of violence, and in Miller's specifications of a lower-class value system.

Strain theories see the offender as pressured into nonconformity—the pressure coming from disparity between the American goal of monetary success and the lack of means available to attain it. In Merton's terms, strain theory sees lower-class people as deviating from culturally approved norms because they need to be "innovators" in order to succeed. Cohen emphasizes the clash between middle-class and working-class values, a clash which encourages young people at school to rebel. Cloward and Ohlin stress the limited access to legitimate means of getting ahead and the relative openness of illegitimate means. To them, frustration, and therefore delinquency, results from the disparity between what young people are led to want and what is actually available to them.

Control theories take a contrasting approach in that they see delinquent acts as the result of broken ties to the conventional social order. Focusing on attachment, commitment, involvement, and belief, control theories ask why most persons refrain from criminal behavior. These theories emphasize social factors in the ties to conventional values and omit consideration of delinquent subcultures. Control theory has found support in the work of Hirschi but has been questioned or refined in other investigations.

In research testing the relative adequacy of the three sociological approaches, Linden and Hackler found that delinquency can best be explained by "affective ties" between delinquents and their deviant peers. In a similar vein, Elliott and Voss found associations with delinquent friends, combined with weak commitment to parents, to be conducive to delinquency. In addition, they also found delinquency and dropping out to be adaptations to school-related problems.

The sociological approaches, which dominated criminological thought for decades, have been criticized on several grounds. One possibility is to keep the emphasis of positivism but see biological, psychological, economic, and sociological variables as interactive and to form a theory of criminal behavior that would integrate these diverse perspectives. A more radical attack has been made by the critical, or system-oriented, criminologists, who have sought (1) to focus on the process by which offenders are caught and punished, (2) to break down the sharp distinction between offenders and nonoffenders, and (3) to challenge the deterministic emphasis of the positivists.

It is necessary to recognize that crime is heterogeneous and multifaceted, that a theory of criminal behavior is not a theory of crime, and that there is no theory of criminal behavior which explains all such behavior.

Although each of the approaches discussed in Chapters 5 and 6 could in theory be applied to any form of crime (the various types are discussed in Part Three), positivist approaches have most often been applied, sometimes directly but more often indirectly, to offenders who commit person-to-person crimes. Critical, or system-oriented, approaches tend to have more applicability to the other types of crime, in which processing is crucial because it so seldom occurs.

Having looked at the various approaches to offenders, it is now necessary to examine how criminologists have formulated a criminology of victims. This is the subject of Chapter 7.

NOTES

[1] Karl Marx, *Capital: A Critique of Political Economy*, ed. by Frederick Engels, trans. by Samuel Moore and Edward Aveling, International, New York, 1967; originally published 1867.

[2] Reinhard Bendix and Seymour Martin Lipset, "Karl Marx's Theory of Social Classes," in Reinhard Bendix and Seymour Martin Lipset, eds., *Class, Status, and Power: A Reader in Social Stratification*, Free Press, Glencoe, Ill., 1953, pp. 6–11.

[3] Karl Marx, *The Communist Manifesto*, Regnery, Chicago, Ill., 1954, originally published 1848.

[4] Marx, *Capital*, vol. I, p. 724.

[5] Ibid., p. 734.

[6] Frederick Engels, *The Condition of the Working Class in England*, trans. and ed. by W. O. Henderson and W. H. Chaloner, Basil Blackwell, Oxford, 1958.

[7] Willem Bonger, *Criminality and Economic Conditions*, trans. by Henry P. Morton, Little, Brown, Boston, Mass., 1916, pp. 401–449; reprinted by Agathon, New York, 1967.

[8] Ibid., p. 672.

[9] William A. Bonger (Willem Bonger), *Race and Crime*, Patterson Smith, Montclair, N.J., 1969, chap. 3.

[10] Ibid., p. 103

[11] David F. Greenberg, ed., *Crime and Capitalism: Readings in Marxist Criminology*, Mayfield, Palo Alto, Calif., 1981, p. 11.

[12] E.g., see: John Braithwaite, *Inequality, Crime, and Public Policy*, Routledge and Kegan Paul, London, 1979, especially part III.

[13] Charles R. Tittle et al., "The Myth of Social Class and Criminality: An Empirical Assessment of the Empirical Evidence," *American Sociological Review*, vol. 43, 1978, pp. 643–656.

[14] Terence P. Thornberry and Margaret Farnworth, "Social Correlates of Criminal Involvement: Further Evidence on the Relationship between Social Status and Criminal Behavior," *American Sociological Review*, vol. 47, August 1982, pp. 505–518. For another approach, see: Richard A. Berk, Kenneth J. Lenihan, and Peter H. Rossi, "Crime and Poverty: Some Experimental Evidence from Ex-Offenders," *American Sociological Review*, vol. 45, October 1980, pp. 766–786.

[15] Clifford R. Shaw and Henry D. McKay, *Juvenile Delinquency and Urban Areas: A Study of Rates of Delinquency in Relation to Differential Characteristics of Local Communities in American Cities*, University of Chicago Press, Chicago, Ill., 1942, rev. ed. 1969, p. 171.

[16] Ibid., p. 316.

[17] Clifford R. Shaw in collaboration with Maurice E. Moore, *The Natural History of a Delinquent Career*, Greenwood, New York, 1968; originally published 1931; quotation from p. 233. The Chicago school gave rise to an extensive body of ecological work dealing with the social context of crime. This work will be discussed in Chapter 8 of the present text.

[18] Karl Schuessler, "Introduction," in Karl Schuessler, ed., *Edwin H. Sutherland on Analyzing Crime*, University of Chicago Press, Chicago, Ill., 1973, p. xiv.

[19] Edwin H. Sutherland, *Principles of Criminology*, 4th ed., Lippincott, Philadelphia, Pa., 1947, pp. 5–9.

[20] On prostitutes, see: Tanice G. Foltz, "The Process of Becoming a Prostitute: A Comparison Between Lower-Class and Middle-Class Girls," in Tanice G. Foltz, "Escort Services: An Emerging Middle Class Sex-for-Money Scene," *California Sociologist*, vol. 2, no. 2, Summer 1979, pp. 121–128. On skilled burglars, see: Neal

Shover, "The Social Organization of Burglary," *Social Problems*, vol. 20, no. 4, Spring 1973, pp. 499–514.

[21] James F. Short, Jr., "Differential Association as a Hypothesis: Problems of Empirical Testing," *Social Problems*, vol. 8, Summer 1960, pp. 14–25.

[22] Gary F. Jensen, "Parents, Peers, and Delinquent Action: A test of the Differential Association Perspective," *American Journal of Sociology*, vol. 78, 1972, pp. 562–575.

[23] Ronald L. Akers et al., "Social Learning and Deviant Behavior," *American Sociological Review*, vol. 44, August 1979, pp. 635–655; quotation from p. 647.

[24] Susan M. Jaquith, "Adolescent Marijuana and Alcohol Use: An Empirical Test of Differential Association Theory," *Criminology*, vol. 19, August 1981, pp. 271–280.

[25] Albert J. Reiss, Jr., and A. Lewis Rhodes, "An Empirical Test of Differential Association Theory," *Journal of Research in Crime and Delinquency*, vol. 1, January 1964, pp. 5–18.

[26] Sheldon Glueck, "Theory and Fact in Criminology: A Criticism of Differential Association," *British Journal of Delinquency*, vol. 7, October 1956, pp. 92–109.

[27] C. R. Jeffery, "Criminal Behavior and Learning Theory," *Journal of Criminal Law, Criminology, and Police Science*, vol. 56, September 1965, pp. 294–300.

[28] C. R. Jeffery, "Criminal Behavior and the Physical Environment," *American Behavioral Scientist*, vol. 20, no. 2, November-December 1976, pp. 149–174.

[29] Daniel Glaser, *Crime in Our Changing Society*, Holt, Rinehart and Winston, New York, 1978, p. 127; italics omitted.

[30] Marvin E. Wolfgang and Franco Ferracuti, *The Subculture of Violence: Towards an Integrated Theory in Criminology*, Tavistock, London, 1967.

[31] Walter B. Miller, "Lower Class Culture as a Generative Milieu of Gang Delinquency," *Journal of Social Issues*, vol. 14, 1958, pp. 5–19.

[32] For an updated version of the seminal article, see: Robert K. Merton, "Social Structure and Anomie," in Robert K. Merton, *Social Theory and Social Structure*, enlarged ed., Free Press, New York, and Collier Macmillan, London, 1968, pp. 185–215. See also: "Continuities in the Theory of Social Structure and Anomie," ibid., pp. 215–248.

[33] Merton, "Social Structure and Anomie," p. 200.

[34] Steven Box, *Deviance, Reality, and Society*, Holt, Rinehart and Winston, London, 1971, chap. 2.

[35] Albert K. Cohen, *Delinquent Boys: The Culture of the Gang*, Free Press, Glencoe, Ill., 1955.

[36] Ibid., chap. IV; quotation from p. 98.

[37] Gwynn Nettler, *Explaining Crime*, McGraw-Hill, New York, 1974, p. 165. See also: Gwynn Nettler, *Explaining Crime*, 3d ed., McGraw-Hill, New York, 1984.

[38] Richard A. Cloward and Lloyd E. Ohlin, *Delinquency and Opportunity: A Theory of Delinquent Gangs*, Free Press, Glencoe, Ill., 1960, chap. 1.

[39] Ibid., p. 86.

[40] Ibid., p. 89.

[41] Harold H. Weissman, *Community Development in the Mobilization for Youth Experience*, Association Press, New York, 1969, and *Employment and Educational Services in the Mobilization for Youth Experience*, Association Press, New York, 1969.

[42] Albert J. Reiss, "Delinquency as the Failure of Personal and Social Control," *American Sociological Review*, vol. 16, April 1951, pp. 196–207.

[43] Émile Durkheim, *Suicide: A Study in Sociology*, trans. by John A. Spaulding and George Simpson, Free Press, Glencoe, Ill., 1951, p. 209; originally published 1897.

[44] Travis Hirschi, *Causes of Delinquency*, University of California Press, Berkeley, 1969, p. 16.

[45] Ibid., pp. 16–34.

[46] Ibid., pp. 203–211.

[47] Ibid., p. 229.

[48] Michael J. Hindelang, "Causes of Delinquency: A Partial Replication and Extension," *Social Problems*, vol. 20, Spring, 1973, pp. 471–487.

[49] Rand D. Conger, "Social Control and Social Learning Models of Delinquent Behavior: A Synthesis," *Criminology*, vol. 14, May 1976, pp. 17–40.

[50] Michael D. Wiatrowski et al., "Social Control Theory and Delinquency," *American Sociological Review*, vol. 46, October 1981, pp. 525–541; quotation from p. 534.

[51] Eric Linden and James C. Hackler, "Affective Ties and Delinquency," *Pacific Sociological Review*, vol. 16, no. 1, January 1973, pp. 27–46; quotation from p. 43.

[52] Delbert S. Elliott and Harwin L. Voss, *Delinquency and Dropout*, Heath (Lexington Books), Lexington, Mass., 1974. It will be recognized that the first variable is the one advanced by Cloward and Ohlin, the third is the one stressed by Merton, and the fourth is Sutherland's contribution. Concerning the second variable, see: Gresham M. Sykes and David Matza, "Techniques of Neutralization," *American Sociological Review*, vol. 22, December 1957, pp. 664–670.

[53] Elliott and Voss, *Delinquency and Dropout*, p. 10.

[54] Ibid., p. 10.

[55] Ibid., p. 36.

[56] Selected findings are listed here. For the complete set of findings, see: Elliott and Voss, *Delinquency and Dropout*.

[57] Ibid., p. 207. For a related discussion, see: Delbert S. Elliott et al., "An Integrated Theoretical Perspective on Delinquent Behavior," *Journal of Research in Crime and Delinquency*, vol. 16, no. 1, January 1979, pp. 3–27.

[58] David Matza, *Becoming Deviant*, Prentice-Hall, Englewood Cliffs, N.J., 1969; quotation from p. 101.

[59] Stephen Schafer, "The Problem of Free Will in Criminology," *Journal of Criminal Law and Criminology*, vol. 67, no. 4, 1977, pp. 481–485.

[60] David Matza, *Delinquency and Drift*, Wiley, New York, 1964, p. 29.

[61] Daniel Glaser, "The Compatability of Free Will and Determinism in Criminology: Comments on an Alleged Problem," *Journal of Criminal Law and Criminology*, vol. 67, no. 4, 1977, pp. 485–490.

[62] Gresham M. Sykes, "The Rise of Critical Criminology," *Journal of Criminal Law and Criminology*, vol. 65, no. 2, 1974, pp. 206–213.

[63] Howard S. Becker, *Outsiders: Studies in the Sociology of Deviance*, Free Press, New York, 1963, p. 122.

[64] Edwin M. Lemert, *Human Deviance, Social Problems, and Social Control*, Prentice-Hall, Englewood Cliffs, N.J., 1976, p. ix.

[65] The perspective has its roots in sociology; see: Richard V. Ericson, *Criminal Reactions: The Labelling Perspective*, Saxon House, Westmead, England, and

Heath (Lexington Books), Lexington, Mass., 1975, chap. 1.

66 Edwin M. Schur, *Radical Nonintervention: Rethinking the Delinquency Problem*, Prentice-Hall, Englewood Cliffs, N.J., 1973, pp. 120–126.

67 Eugene Doleschal and Nora Klapmuts,"Toward a New Criminology," *Crime and Delinquency Literature*, vol. 5, no. 4, 1973, pp. 607–626.

68 William J. Chambliss, *Criminal Law in Action*, Hamilton, Santa Barbara, Calif., 1975, preface.

69 Steven Spitzer, "Toward a Marxian Theory of Deviance," *Social Problems*, vol. 22, no. 5, June 1975, pp. 638–651; quotation from p. 642. See also: Chapter 4 of the present text, "Radical or Marxist Viewpoint."

70 E.g., see: Frank Pearce, *Crimes of the Powerful: Marxism, Crime, and Deviance*, Pluto, London, 1976.

71 Alex Thio, "Class Bias in the Sociology of Deviance," *American Sociologist*, vol. 8, February 1973, pp. 1–12.

72 Beverly Koerin, "Violent Crime: Prediction and Control," *Crime and Delinquency*, vol. 15, July 1978, pp. 148–171. See also: Stephen J. Pfohl, *Predicting Dangerousness: The Social Construction of Psychiatric Reality*, Heath (Lexington Books), Lexington, Mass., 1978.

73 David A. Pritchard, "Stable Predictors of Recidivism: A Summary," *Criminology*, vol. 17, no. 1, May 1979, pp. 15–21.

74 Harold E. Pepinsky, "The Irresponsibility of Explaining Criminality," paper presented at the Academy of Criminal Justice Sciences Meeting, Cincinnati, Ohio, March 14–16, 1979.

75 See: Edwin Lemert, *Social Pathology*, McGraw-Hill, New York, 1951, chaps. 3 and 4; and Frank Tannenbaum, *Crime and the Community*, Ginn, Boston, Mass., 1938, chap. I, especially pp. 19–22.

76 Clayton A. Hartjen, "Crime as Commonsense Theory," *Criminology*, vol. 18, no. 4, February 1981, pp. 435–452; quotation on p. 443.

77 Lonnie H. Athens, *Violent Criminal Acts and Actors: A Symbolic Interactionist Study*, Routledge and Kegan Paul, Boston, Mass., 1980.

78 See: Ericson, *Criminal Reactions;* and Ian Taylor, Paul Walton, and Jock Young, *The New Criminology: For a Social Theory of Deviance*, Routledge and Kegan Paul, London, 1973, especially p. 271.

79 Alberta J. Nussi and Stephen L. Abramowitz, "From Phrenology to Psychosurgery and Back Again: Biological Studies of Criminality," *American Journal of Orthopsychiatry*, vol. 46, no. 4, October 1976, pp. 591–607.

80 C. R. Jeffery, "Criminology as an Interdisciplinary Behavioral Science," *Criminology*, vol. 16, no. 2, August 1978, pp. 149–169; Glaser, *Crime in Our Changing Society*, pp. 126–127; and Lee Ellis, "The Decline and Fall of Sociology, 1975–2000," *American Sociologist*, vol. 12, April 1977, pp. 56–66.

81 Sarnoff A. Mednick and Karl O. Christiansen, *Biosocial Bases of Criminal Behavior*, Gardner, New York, 1977, especially Sarnoff A. Mednick, "A Biosocial Theory of the Learning of Law-Abiding Behavior," pp. 1–8. See also: Saleem A. Shah and Loren H. Roth, "Biological and Psychophysiological Factors in Criminality," in Daniel Glaser, ed., *Handbook of Criminology*, Rand McNally, Chicago, Ill., 1974, pp. 101–173.

82 See: Charles Wellford, "Labelling Theory and Criminology: An Assessment," *Social Problems*, vol. 22, no. 3, February 1975, pp. 332–345; Peter K. Manning, "Deviance and Dogma: Some Comments on the Labelling Perspective," *British Journal of Criminology*, vol. 15, no. 1, January 1975, pp. 1–20; and Charles R. Tittle, "Labelling and Crime: An Empirical Evaluation," in Walter R. Cove, ed., *The Labelling of Deviance: Evaluating a Perspective*, 2d ed., Sage, Beverly Hills, Calif., 1980, chap. 6.

83 See: James A. Inciardi, ed., *Radical Criminology: The Coming Crises*, Sage, Beverly Hills, Calif., 1980.

84 E.g., see: Edwin M. Lemert, "Beyond Mead: The Societal Reaction to Deviance," *Social Problems*, vol. 21, no. 4, April 1974, pp. 457–468.

85 Wouter Buikhuisen, "An Alternative Approach to the Etiology of Crime," in Sarnoff A. Mednick and S. Giora Shoham, eds., *New Paths in Criminology: Interdisciplinary and Intercultural Explorations*, Heath (Lexington Books), Lexington, Mass., 1979, pp. 27–43.

86 Clarence Ray Jeffery, "The Historical Development of Criminology," in Hermann Mannheim, ed., *Pioneers in Criminology*, 2d ed. enlarged, Patterson Smith, Montclair, N.J., 1972, pp. 471–472.

87 Ibid., p. 472.

Perspectives on Victims of Crime

7

Of our four criminological concerns—acts, offenders, victims, and social context—focus on victims is the newest. It was not until the mid-1960s that victimology emerged as a distinct area of study. Before that time, studies and systematic data about crime victims were virtually nonexistent. Nor was much attention paid to the plight of victims in the criminal justice system. The overriding concern with individual offenders was complemented by an almost complete lack of concern with understanding the victims of crime.

The field of victimology was first delineated in 1963 by Benjamin Mendelsohn, who proposed to study "victimity," or the

> whole of the socio-bio-psychological characteristics, common to all victims in general, which society wishes to prevent and fight, no matter what their determinants are (criminals or others).[1]

A later proponent saw victimology as a general area of study that would involve

> the study of the social processes through which individuals and groups are maltreated in such a way that social problems are created.[2]

Defining victimology in the broad terms that have been proposed by Mendelsohn and others would allow it to encompass studies of war, genocide, slavery, natural disasters, and certain aspects of social inequality. Although there have been many studies in these areas, the field of victimology has concentrated almost exclusively on the victims of crime. In this sense, victimology is a subdiscipline of criminology.

After this Chesapeake Bay resident objected to commercial fishing near his home, his car was struck by shotgun blasts that wounded him in the head. (WIDE WORLD PHOTOS)

Interest in victimology was spurred by the work of the President's Commission on Crime and a series of National Crime Panel surveys (see Chapter 3). As we shall see, these studies have provided a strong empirical base for victimology. The work in victimology can be categorized into five major topics: (1) the victim's contribution to the criminal offense, (2) the characteristics of victims of crime, (3) the situations in which victimization occurs, (4) the treatment of the victim in the criminal justice system, and (5) some basic questions about victims. It might also be added that the findings of victimization studies have been used to qualify and correct official crime statistics.

In this chapter we shall consider the five major topics that lie at the core of victimology. In considering them, we shall focus on the general points of the victimological perspective, since many of the particular research findings will be covered in later chapters, especially Chapters 9 and 10.

THE VICTIM'S CONTRIBUTION TO THE CRIMINAL OFFENSE

Thinking of the victim as a possible contributor to the crime was first suggested by Hans von Hentig: ". . . The victim shapes and moulds the criminal [and] . . . may assume the role of determinant" in the criminal act.[3] In a subsequent elaboration of this position, Marvin E. Wolfgang argues that certain homicides are "victim-precipitated" in that

> . . . the victim is a direct, positive precipitator in the crime. The role of the victim is characterized by his having been the first in the homicide drama to use physical force directed against his subsequent slayer. The *victim-precipitated* cases are those in which the victim was the first to show and use a deadly weapon, to strike a blow in an altercation—in short, the first to commence the interplay or resort to physical violence.[4]

Applying the concept to property crime—that is, crime involving property— Michael Fooner speaks of "victim-induced criminality" in which people create a temporary opportunity for crime by not acting reasonably to protect their money, jewelry, or other valuables.[5]

Victim-precipitation is an approach which has informed several significant pieces of sociological research. Its most significant application has been to the study of person-to-person violent crime (to be discussed in Chapter 9). At the same time, the victim-precipitation approach has some serious problems: one being that the concept is too vague and, hence, too difficult to operationalize;[6] another being that it tends to blame the victim for the crime.[7] Nevertheless, taking victim-precipitation into account is important to criminology. For one thing, some victims are not simply the passive objects of acts perpetrated by offenders. For another, cases involving victim-precipitation or complicity in the criminal act raise questions of guilt and innocence under the criminal law. (For a discussion of the role of previous relationships in plea bargaining, see Chapter 17.[8])

CHARACTERISTICS OF CRIME VICTIMS

Like the positivist studies of criminal offenders, victimological studies have attempted to delineate characteristics that would identify persons who are likely to be crime victims. In an early study on this subject, von Hentig mentioned being young, female, old, mentally defective or deranged, intoxicated, an immigrant, a member of a minority group, and of dull to normal intelligence as traits that would be likely to predispose one toward victimization. He also saw the depressed or apathetic, the acquisitive or greedy, the wanton or sensual, the lonesome or heartbroken, the tormentor, and the "blocked" person in a "losing situation" as people prone or vulnerable to victimization.[9] While some of von Hentig's predisposing characteristics are difficult to define and test in empirical research, the victimization studies based on data from the National Crime Panel surveys have found generally higher rates of victimization among males and young people, and for certain crimes among blacks and lower-income groups. (See Chapters 9 and 10.)

In other empirically oriented work, there have been attempts to delineate types of victims. Ezzat A. Fattah, for one, has suggested that there are five types of victims: nonparticipating victims, latent or predisposed victims, provocative victims, participating victims, and false victims (who either are not victims or victimize themselves).[10] Burt Galaway and Joe Hudson have argued for a typology based on the victim's responsibility for the crime: unrelated victims, provocative victims, precipitative victims, biologically weak victims, socially weak victims, self-victimizing victims, and political victims.[11] Albert J. Reiss has advanced the concept of repetitive victimization, noting that within a population of victims there are considerable numbers of individuals and households prone to repeated victimization, often by the same type of crime.[12]

Both the offenders and the victims of person-to-person violent crimes are likely to be male, young, and poor.   (LEONARD FREED/MAGNUM)

A further insight on the characteristics of victims has been advanced by
Michael J. Hindelang and his associates in the form of the following proposition:

> An individual's chances of personal victimization are dependent upon the extent to
> which the individual shares demographic characteristics with offenders.[13]

As they go on to note, for person-to-person crimes such as rape, robbery, assault,
and larceny, there are a number of studies supporting the view that both offenders
and victims are disproportionately male, young, urban, black, of lower socioeconomic status, unemployed, and unmarried. What is more, they argue, groups of
individuals who possess two of these social characteristics are especially likely to
experience high rates both of victimization and of offending.[14]

SITUATIONS IN WHICH VICTIMIZATIONS OCCUR

While some work in victimology has stressed the characteristics of victims, other
efforts have attempted to develop knowledge about typical situations in which
person-to-person victimizations occur. Again, the work of Hindelang and his
associates illustrates the direction this work has taken. Two of the propositions
they advanced are most indicative:

> The probability of suffering a personal victimization is directly related to the amount
> of time that a person spends in public places (e.g., on the street, in parks, etc.), and
> particularly in public places at night.[15]

And:

> The probability of personal victimization, particularly personal theft, increases as a
> function of the proportion of time that an individual spends among nonfamily
> members.[16]

Both of these propositions are supported by findings from a number of studies.[17]
More generally, taking a situational approach to victimization is analogous to
taking a situational approach to crime, a line of reasoning that will be developed
further as we examine perspectives on social contexts in Chapter 8.

TREATMENT OF VICTIMS IN THE CRIMINAL JUSTICE SYSTEM

The fourth major topic developed by victimologists concerns the way victims are
handled in the criminal justice system. In recent years the long-standing neglect of
the victim has been increasingly recognized. Researchers have found that
characteristics of victims may well influence whether or not offenders are
convicted,[18] decisions about case processing,[19] and decisions about sentencing.[20]
A number of writers have advocated changes in the legal system that would
improve the status of the victim—changes such as expanded use of civil liability,[21]
use of self-defense for battered wives accused of killing their husbands,[22] and
victim-compensation programs.[23] While far from being fully implemented, such
proposals would mean some dramatic changes in our system of criminal justice.[24]

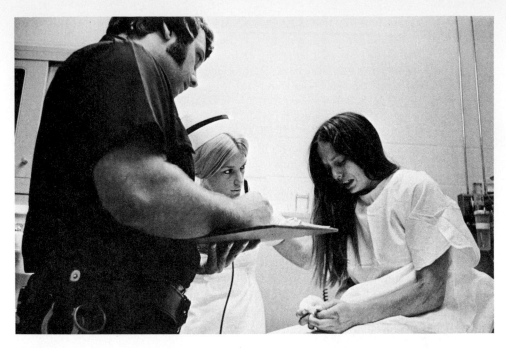

The criminal justice system is paying increasing attention to crime victims; here, an officer is interviewing a victim of rape. (ROBERT GOLDSTEIN/PHOTO RESEARCHERS, INC.)

BASIC QUESTIONS ABOUT VICTIMIZATION

Aside from the four major topics discussed above, the study of crime victims has opened up some fundamental questions for consideration by criminologists. Perhaps the most basic question is: Who is the victim? Jeffrey H. Reiman notes that to answer this question a victimologist must determine if a crime has been committed, who has been harmed in or by the crime, and who has set the crime in motion. In taking these factors into account, there is the underlying question whether victimologists should consider "crime" and "harm" as they are legally defined or according to some other criterion. There is another consideration: if the legal system itself is unjust, then those subject to its injustice are victims of the system.[25]

Critical criminologists concerned with social injustice have also advanced expanded conceptualizations of the victim. Richard Quinney would place the burden of conceptualizing the victim on the criminologist:

> . . . Whenever the criminologist confronts the victim, he is presenting his world view of reality. . . . To regard one class of persons as victims and another not as victims is thus an appeal to one's own morality.[26]

In Quinney's opinion, it is necessary to consider victims of police forces, correctional systems, violence by the state, and oppression of any sort.

In a similar vein, William Ryan has advanced the notion that inequality breeds victims:

> The victims in American society are not simply the 10 percent of us who are Black, the 15 percent or so who are officially below the "poverty line." The majority of us who are non-Black and, officially, at least, non-poor, are also victims. At least two-thirds, perhaps three-fourths of us are relatively poor compared to the standards of the top 10 or 5 percent, and relatively vulnerable.[27]

Conceptualizations such as these provide the rationale for a greatly expanded criminological enterprise.

Other writers have also argued for expanded or altered conceptions of the victims of different types of crime. Thorsten Sellin and Marvin E. Wolfgang, for example, have advanced a fivefold typology of victimization: (1) "primary victimization," referring to individual victims; (2) "secondary victimization," referring to impersonal victims such as organizations; (3) "tertiary victimization," referring to the public or society as victim; (4) "mutual victimization," referring to victims who themselves are offenders in consensual criminal acts; and (5) "no victimization," referring to situations in which there is no recognizable victim.[28]

Finally, Edwin M. Schur has advanced the notion of victimless crime, in which the so-called crime is a consensual transaction involving a willing exchange of illicit goods and services and the persons engaging in the exchange do not see themselves as victims.[29] However, the idea of victimless crime has been challenged by Hugo A. Bedau, who argues that people such as alcoholics, addicts, and others may well be harmed or caused to suffer from the exchange and that the supposed consent is often uninformed. He goes on to recommend that people be allowed privacy but that "sober public discussion and private reflection" be used to consider "the difficult question of what is to be done with and for those who have engaged in immoral conduct that harms themselves after all."[30]

ASSESSMENT

Although a comparatively new field of study, victimology has opened many new avenues of criminological inquiry. In calling attention to the victim, it has furnished a useful balance to criminology's extensive concern with the offender. It has led criminologists to appreciate patterns of interaction in which the victim may be a possible contributor to the crime. It has led criminologists to question why victimization rates for person-to-person crimes are higher for people such as males, youths, blacks, and lower-income groups. It has led criminologists to develop typologies of situations in which victimizations and, hence, crimes occur. It has led to a reexamination of the way victims are treated in the criminal justice system. Finally, it has provocatively advanced some basic questions concerning the nature of victimization: whether it needs to be legally defined, whether it is a function of social inequality, whether impersonal victimization needs to be examined, and whether victimless crime is a useful concept. In short, although comparatively new, victimology has provided a number of significant perspectives from which to view crime-related issues.

APPLICABILITY OF PERSPECTIVES ON VICTIMS TO MAJOR FORMS OF CRIME

As with perspectives on criminal acts and offenders, victimological perspectives have often been applied to the study of person-to-person violent crimes and person-to-person property crimes. In fact, as we examine these types of crime in greater detail in Chapters 9 and 10, we shall find that victim surveys offer a wealth of information on which social groups experience high crime rates, who reports crime, and how victims sometimes precipitate crime. In offering this kind of information, victim surveys also provide a useful correction to official crime statistics.

The victimological approaches discussed in this chapter can also enhance our understanding of crimes other than those of a person-to-person nature, although they have been less systematically employed in these areas. The impersonal or nonpersonal victimization implicit in these other forms of crime demands that we understand the typology of "secondary," "tertiary," and "no" victimization advanced by Sellin and Wolfgang. In fact, type of victimization provides part of the rationale for the breakdown of types of crime in Part Three of this book. In particular, it demands that we consider several types of crime which are unique by virtue of the victim's situation: crimes against organizations, in which organizations are the victims of crime; social-order crimes, in which some victims are willing participants; and political crimes, in which the political or social system is the victim.

SUMMARY

Spurred by the work of the President's Commission on Crime and by a series of National Crime Panel surveys, the study of crime victims—victimology—came of age during the 1960s. Empirically oriented, it has addressed five major topics. Specifically, it has (1) pictured the victim as a possible contributor to crime, (2) identified social characteristics and types of victims, (3) identified situations in which victimization and hence crimes occur, (4) analyzed the plight of the victim in the criminal justice system, and (5) raised fundamental questions concerning the victim, the relationship between inequality and victimization, and typologies of victimization that are linked to different types of crimes. Victimology is a comparatively new area that has opened up a number of important questions for criminological inquiry.

Now that we have examined criminological perspectives on criminal acts, offenders, and victims, we can turn to our fourth concern, the social context of crime. That is the subject of Chapter 8.

NOTES

[1] Benjamin Mendelsohn, "Victimology and the Technical and Social Sciences: A Call for the Establishment of Victimology Clinics," in Israel Drapkin and Emilio C. Viano, eds., *Theoretical Issues in Victimology*, vol. 1, *Victimology: A New Focus*, Heath (Lexington Books), Lexington, Mass., 1975, p. 27. Mendelsohn's original article was "The Origin of the Doctrine of Victimology," *Excerpta Criminologica*, vol. 3, 1963, pp. 239–244.

[2] Vahakn Dadrian, "An Attempt at Defining Victimology," in Emilio C. Viano, ed., *Victims and Society*, Visage, Washington, D.C., 1976, p. 40.

[3] Hans von Hentig, *The Criminal and His Victim: Studies in the Sociobiology of Crime*, Yale University Press, New Haven, Conn., 1948, p. 384.

[4] Marvin E. Wolfgang, *Patterns of Criminal Homicide*, University of Pennsylvania Press, Philadelphia, 1958, p. 252.

[5] Michael Fooner, "Victim-Induced Criminality," *Science*, vol. 153, September 2, 1966, pp. 1080–1083.

[6] Robert A. Silverman, "Victim Precipitation: An Examination of the Concept," in Drapkin and Viano, *Theoretical Issues in Victimology*, pp. 99–109.

[7] On the general perspective of blaming victims for their problems, see: William Ryan, *Blaming the Victim*, rev. updated ed., Vintage, New York, 1976.

[8] On the implications for compensation of victims, see: Fooner, "Victim-Induced Criminality."

[9] Von Hentig, *The Criminal and His Victim*, p. 433.

[10] Ezzat A. Fattah, "Towards a Criminological Classification of Victims," *International Journal of Criminal Police*, vol. 209, 1967.

[11] Burt Galaway and Joe Hudson, eds., *Perspectives on Crime Victims*, Mosby, St. Louis, Mo., 1981, pp. 22–23.

[12] Albert J. Reiss, Jr., "Victim Proneness in Repeat Victimization by Type of Crime," in Stephen Feinberg and Albert J. Reiss, Jr., *Indicators of Crime and Criminal Justice: Quantitative Studies*, U.S. Department of Justice, Washington, D.C., June 1980.

[13] Michael J. Hindelang, Michael R. Gottfredson, and James Garofalo, *Victims of Personal Crime: An Empirical Foundation for a Theory of Personal Victimization*, Ballinger, Cambridge, Mass., 1978, p. 257.

[14] Ibid., pp. 257–259. See also: Chapter 9 of the present text.

[15] Hindelang et al, *Victims of Personal Crime*, p. 251.

[16] Ibid., p. 260.

[17] Ibid., pp. 251–253 and pp. 260–262.

[18] Donald J. Newman, *Conviction: The Determination of Guilt or Innocence without Trial*, Little, Brown, Boston, Mass., 1966.

[19] Kristen M. Williams, "The Effects of Victim Characteristics on the Disposition of Violence Crimes," in William F. McDonald, ed., *Criminal Justice and the Victim*, Sage, Beverly Hills, Calif., 1976, pp. 177–207.

[20] Deborah Denno and James A. Cramer, "The Effects of Victim Characteristics on Judicial Decision Making," in McDonald, *Criminal Justice and the Victim*, pp. 215–226. See also: Chapter 16 of the present text.

[21] Ruben Castillo, Thomas W. Dressler, Richard Foglia, and Michael J. Faber, "The Use of Civil Liability to Aid Crime Victims," *Journal of Criminal Law and Criminology*, vol. 70, no. 1, 1979, pp.. 57–62.

[22] Nancy Wolfe, "Victim Provocation: The Battered Wife and Legal Definition of Self Defense," *Sociological Symposium*, vol. 25, Winter 1979, pp. 98–118.

[23] Roger E. Meiners, *Victim Compensation: Economic, Legal, and Political Aspects*, Heath, Lexington, Mass., 1978; and Herbert Edelhertz and Gilbert Geis, *Public Compensation to Victims of Crime*, Praeger, New York, 1974.

[24] For a further discussion, see: Chapter 17 of the present text.

[25] Jeffrey H. Reiman, "Victims, Harm, and Justice," in Drapkin and Viano, *Theoretical Issues in Victimology*, pp. 77–87.

[26] Richard Quinney, "Who Is the Victim?" in Israel Drapkin and Emilio Viano, eds., *Victimology*, Heath (Lexington Books), Lexington, Mass., 1974, p. 107.

[27] Ryan, *Blaming the Victim*, pp. xiii–xiv.

[28] Thorsten Sellin and Marvin E. Wolfgang, *The Measurment of Delinquency*, Wiley, New York, 1964, pp. 150–156.

[29] Edwin M. Schur, *Crimes without Victims: Deviant Behavior and Public Policy*, Prentice-Hall, Englewood Cliffs, N.J., 1965, p. 30; Edwin M. Schur and Hugo Adam Bedau, *Victimless Crimes: Two Sides of a Controversy*, Prentice-Hall, Englewood Cliffs, N.J., 1974. See also: the discussion in Chapter 13 of the present text.

[30] Schur and Bedan, *Victimless Crimes,* p. 102.

8

Perspectives on Social Contexts of Crime

Our fourth major criminological concern looks to the group, society, or social situation to explain crime rather than to the legal system, the individual offender, or the individual victim. It stresses the manner in which crime responds to social or situational factors. Focusing exclusively on crime rates, it seeks to understand the various social and environmental factors which influence these rates.

As we shall see, the perspectives that have been advanced to understand the social context of crime are quite varied. They include some of the oldest systematic research on crime carried out by cartologists, beginning in the mid-1820s. Also included are the seminal work of Émile Durkheim (1858–1917), a French sociologist; ecologically oriented research carried out at the University of Chicago; strain theories developed by American sociologists; economic approaches; historically oriented criminological work; and contributions from critical criminologists. To appreciate the full scope of criminological work dealing with the social context, we will need to consider these perspectives one at a time.

In examining the social-context perspectives on crime, it is useful to keep W. S. Robinson's "ecological fallacy" in mind. Briefly put, Robinson's point is that there is no simple one-to-one correspondence between the characteristics of an area or a social unit and the people who live in the area or who are members of the social unit. Aggregate data can be quite useful in understanding area- or group-related phenomena, but they are by no means meant to describe the behavior of particular individuals in the area or group. Thus, for example, crime and poverty may be related for a group of census tracts, but the relationship might not hold for the individuals living in those tracts.[1] The possibility of committing the ecological fallacy demands that care be taken in the interpretation of data on social contexts—particularly when data on crime are involved, since crime is a statistically rare occurrence among large areas or groups of people. It is in part to avoid the ecological fallacy that we are considering social-context perspectives independently of perspectives on individual offenders, even though we shall find some overlap between the two.

CARTOLOGICAL APPROACHES

The earliest group of writers interested in studying the social context of crime were the cartologists of the early nineteenth century. Their approach is exemplified in the work of Adolphe Quetelet (1796–1874), a Belgian statistician who was intrigued by the year-to-year continuity in the French national crime statistics which were maintained beginning in 1825. He argued that the continuity was attributable to factors such as age, sex, and climatic conditions. Another proponent of cartology was A. M. Guerry (1802–1866), a French criminologist who attempted to account for different crime rates in different localities, and changes in crime rates over time, by analyzing differences in social conditions and in legislation.[2]

In contrast to the biologically oriented Italian positivist school that was to appear in the latter nineteenth century (see Chapter 5), the early cartologists took a distinctly sociological approach to the study of crime. Instead of looking to defects within people, Quetelet looked to society as the key to an explanation of crime. In his words:

> Society carries within itself, in some sense, the seeds of all the crimes which are going to be committed, together with the facilities necessary for their development.[3]

Expanded and elaborated by Durkheim and many other sociologically oriented thinkers, this statement of Quetelet's forms the basis for what we are calling ''social-context'' perspectives on crime.

DURKHEIM'S APPROACH: SOCIAL COHESION

Living in nineteenth century France—a society profoundly influenced by the political revolution of 1789 and the more gradual economic effects of the industrial revolution—Durkheim was primarily concerned with the manner in which industrial societies would be able to maintain social cohesion. He visualized two ideal types of societies. One was ''mechanical'': in such a society each group was similar, independent, and relatively isolated from the remaining groups. The other was ''organic'': in an ''organic'' society each social group was specialized by virtue of occupation, interdependent, and relatively close to the other groups. While cohesion in mechanical societies was based on uniformity of individuals, it could well become problematic for organic societies. In thinking about Durkheim, it should be noted that mechanical and organic societies are ideal, polar-opposite types; actual societies contain features of each type.[4]

Durkheim saw industrial societies as tending toward the organic type and used the term ''anomie''—meaning ''normlessness''—to describe a society that has reached an advanced state of organic solidarity. In such a society the division of labor is characterized by so much specialization that the spontaneous consensus of its parts is lost. The society is formless and fragmented; restraints on people's passions weaken markedly; the individuals in it become isolated and lost. As one later commentator put it:

> This is the milieu which produces crime and anti-social disorders. There are no constraints and the cult of individualism cuts away all inhibitions. This breaks down the cohesive forces and each man becomes a ''law unto himself.'' This is ''Anomie''—the dead end of meaningless living.[5]

Durkheim applied his perspective both to law and to crime. He saw law as important in maintaining social cohesion in both mechanical and organic societies, but in quite different ways. In mechanical societies it functions in a repressive manner in that it is oriented toward punishing deviation from social norms. In organic societies it is restitutive in that it seeks to correct wrongs which occur between individuals. In the mechanical society, punishment is a passionate reaction in which society avenges and the criminal expiates his or her outrage to social morality. In the organic society, the use of punishment declines and the law provides for a ''return in state'' (restoration of the social relationship) or for ''correction'' of individuals.[6]

In applying his perspective to crime, Durkheim made a number of strikingly original statements. Taking a cue from the cartologists, he argued that crime is normal in mechanical societies, since there will always be differences between individuals which the law seeks to repress. To illustrate this point, he cites the following extreme example:

> Imagine a society of saints, a perfect cloister of exemplary individuals. Crimes, properly so called, will there be unknown; but faults which appear venial to the layman will create there the same scandal that the ordinary offense does in ordinary consciousnesses. If, then, this society has the power to judge and punish, it will define these acts as criminal and will treat them as such.[7]

Another indicator of the normality of crime is the development of new types of crime in response to changing social sentiment and morality. So normal is crime in mechanical societies that it is unrealistic to think of a society without it:

> A society without criminality would necessitate a standardization of the moral conceptions of all individuals which is neither possible nor desirable.[8]

Finally, the normality of crime is complemented by the normality of punishment. Punishment is important because it assumes social cohesion and implants the notion of good and evil in the minds of people. When criminals are punished, law-abiding citizens feel rewarded for their good behavior.[9]

To appreciate Durkheim, two further points ought to be noted. One is that while crime is normal for a society, it may well be abnormal for the person who commits it. For example, a certain rate of murder will be "normal" for a society at a given point in time even if some or all of those who commit murder are mentally abnormal people. The other is that the questions how much crime and what types of crime are normal and functional for society were never satisfactorily answered by Durkheim. He did seem appalled by, and called "abnormal," the unusually high crime rate in France, which had experienced a 300 percent increase between the beginning and end of the nineteenth century.[10] Generally, he saw anomic social conditions as productive of a variety of social maladies, including high rates of suicide and crime.[11]

Durkheim's ideas on law and crime have had enormous influence on the work of sociologically oriented criminologists. They led directly to the strain theories as well as the control theories discussed in Chapter 6. They have also influenced much of the research to be discussed in this chapter. More specifically in Durkheim's tradition, Kai T. Erikson, for one, has shown (1) how definitions of deviance helped shape the boundaries of the Puritan community in early America and (2) how deviance within the Puritan community remained fairly constant over time.[12] Stephen D. Webb, using urban data for the United States, found some support for the hypothesis "that deviance or crime increases concomitant with an increasing division of labor."[13] Edward Sagarin has assembled papers showing how crime and deviance contribute to social and political change.[14]

However, to say that Durkheim's ideas have been enormously influential is not to say that his thinking has been universally accepted. Empirically minded researchers have found the concept of anomie to be difficult to define.[15] Some later commentators have noted that Durkheim's statement that crime and deviance are useful for society has led sociologists to deemphasize the conditions under which they are detrimental.[16] Another critic has argued that Durkheim's arguments are flawed because they confuse inevitability with necessity, confuse the functions of crime with those of social control, and fail to answer the question why humans need crime to adapt to future forms of society.[17]

Moreover, some of the later research has not supported Durkheim's theories. In contrast to Webb, Marvin Krohn examined whole societies and found that total crime rates and rates of property crime were explained in part by population density (defined as percent of population in localities of over 100,000), industrialization (defined as use of energy per capita), and division of labor, but not by measures of anomie.[18] Richard A. Berk and his associates found no evidence that the number of people punished in California between 1851 and 1970 remained stable over a period of time.[19] Finally, John A. Conklin found in some cases that crime produces insecurity and distrust in communities rather than bringing people together or strengthening social bonds through response to it.[20]

That Durkheim's ideas continue to be debated and subjected to empirical tests is perhaps the best indicator of their potency. We will find them to be reflected directly in the "anomie perspective" developed by Robert K. Merton and indirectly in the other perspectives discussed in this chapter.

ECOLOGICAL APPROACHES

The ecological perspective on the social context of crime stems from the observation that certain zones or areas of cities are characterized by high rates of crime and delinquency as well as other social pathologies such as physical deterioration, school truancy, families on relief, infant mortality, and various diseases. The study of these zones or areas dates back to the latter nineteenth century, to the studies of London done by Henry Mayhew (1812–1887) and Charles Booth (1840–1916). In the United States it became formulated into an elaborate series of studies carried out by researchers at the University of Chicago beginning in the 1920s—in particular, Clifford R. Shaw (1895–1957) and Henry D. McKay. In recent decades ecologically oriented criminological research has strongly emphasized the importance of understanding the physical environment, the role of opportunity, and the temporal distribution of routine social activities.

Chicago School

We have already encountered the basic perspective of the Chicago school in Chaper 6. As we saw, the Chicago researchers were concerned with the fact that zones or areas of cities characterized by high rates of crime and delinquency (as well as other social pathologies) contained conflicting norms and competing systems of values. We saw how the existence of conflicting norms and competing value systems led criminologists such as Sutherland to argue that crime was learned through a process of social interaction. In the present chapter, our viewpoint is similar, but the emphasis is different. Rather than applying the arguments of the Chicago school to individuals, we need to ask how and why certain areas come to have and maintain high rates of crime and delinquency as well as an abundance of other social pathologies.

The Chicago school, as represented in the thought of Robert Park and Ernest

Burgess, took an ecological approach to explain the existence of urban areas with high crime, high delinquency, and general social pathology.[21] According to this approach, plants and animals are organisms which are interrelated and interdependent but which constantly struggle for individual survival. Two ecological concepts were especially important in understanding the city. The first concept was of communities in which plant and animal life tended to live together in a natural economy, a "symbiosis." In urban areas these natural symbiotic communities are seen in racial or ethnic areas (e.g., Chinatowns and "black belts"), income or occupational groupings, and industrial or business areas. The second concept was of invasion, dominance, and succession in which new plant, animal, or social groups might take over an existing area. In urban areas, such growth and change would find one organic community replacing another as cities expanded from their centers outward in a series of concentric circles.[22]

The urban ecological approach developed at the University of Chicago became the basis for an extensive study of delinquency by Shaw and McKay, utilizing data from the records of police and juvenile courts that spanned the years between 1900 and 1940. From these data, it was immediately apparent that there were enormous variations in the rates of delinquency in the various Chicago communities and suburbs regardless of whether delinquency was measured by police arrests or court commitments. Generally, the rates were high in areas adjacent to central business areas or to certain outlying industrial centers—in other words, in the "interstitial areas" and "zones of transition." Rates also showed a regular decrease as one went from the center of Chicago to its periphery. A number of other interesting findings also emerged from this research:

1. Delinquency is cumulative in that the higher the rate of delinquency in an area, the greater the probability that the offender will become a recidivist and eventually be committed to a training school.
2. High or low rates of delinquency are not permanent characteristics of any ethnic or racial group. Each population group experienced high rates of delinquency when it occupied the areas of first settlement, and the rates declined as groups moved out to better areas or toward stability in the same areas.
3. Areas showing high rates of delinquency were also characterized by high rates of school truancy, high rates of court offenders, large numbers of families on relief, high rates of tuberculosis, and low rates of home ownership.
4. Communities with high delinquency rates in 1900 also had high rates in 1940, despite complete changes in ethnic composition. Moreover, a subsequent follow-up study in 1966 produced remarkably similar results.
5. Comparative studies of Philadelphia, Boston, Cincinnati, Greater Cleveland, and Richmond, Virginia, also confirmed the pattern.[23]

In short, Shaw and McKay provided a well-documented description of slums—i.e., areas of low socioeconomic status and high delinquency which are still prevalent in many American cities today.

In interpreting their findings, Shaw and McKay used the concepts formulated by Park and Burgess. They saw the problems of delinquency, crime, and other social pathologies as related to "invasion, dominance, and succession." Rapid population growth meant that the equilibrium in natural communities would be destroyed; the natural symbiosis of a community would be lost. In such communities there would be a diversity of norms, standards of behaviors, and values. Careers in crime and delinquency would be viable options. As was noted in Chapter 6, the people living in such areas could more readily be socialized into delinquency and crime; indeed, such behavior might even appear normal to those involved in it.

Present-Day Ecological Research

Some recent work on the ecology of crime has continued in the tradition of Shaw and McKay and other researchers oriented toward the Chicago school.[24] Nevertheless, other recent work contains some important new elements. For one thing, the methodology has become more rigorous. Variables are more explicitly defined, samples are more carefully drawn, and calculations are more sophisticated now that computers make the simultaneous analysis of several variables possible. For another, the perspective has been broadened in at least three different ways: (1) some ecological studies have been based on victimization data; (2) some studies have stressed routine activities in everyday life; and (3) opportunity has become critical in the interpretation of crime rates.

The ecological studies based on victimization data have begun to identify situational factors in victimization. Indeed, we have already noted propositions concerning victimization situations that were advanced by Hindelang and his associates (see Chapter 7). To these propositions can be added the finding that people are most likely to be victims of violent crime in their own homes and least likely to be victims of violent crime in commercial buildings or on a public conveyance; for property crime the situation is reversed: people are more likely to be victims of property crime in less familiar surroundings.[25] In other research, John W. C. Johnstone found that all types of delinquent activity are linked to social location; in particular, the "situation of being a 'have not' in a community of 'haves' represents a context which can produce high levels of utilitarian delinquency."[26] Examining findings such as these, one writer was led to the following comment concerning the importance of ecological variables:

> If victims are chosen not because of the opportunities they present but because the opportunity is visible to potential offenders, then proximity to the behavioral world of offenders will be important.[27]

A second present-day approach has developed the concept of routine activity to understand crime. From this viewpoint, crime can be seen as a product of three elements: "motivated offenders, suitable targets, and absence of capable guardians against a violation." All three are necessary for crime to occur. Convergence in time and space of offenders and suitable targets, combined with the absence of capable guardians, may lead to increases in crime rates without changes in the motivation of offenders. In particular, the major shift of routine occupational and social activities away from the home cannot be ignored in explanations of increases in the crime rate in recent years.[28] Taking routine activities into account is an approach which we shall find to be of considerable

Crime tends to flourish when three elements come together: offenders, suitable targets, and an absence of capable guardians. In this instance, the capable guardians were just too late to keep this woman from being mugged.   (JILL FREEDMAN/ARCHIVE)

value in interpreting patterns of person-to-person violent crime and person-to-person property crime. (See Chapters 9 and 10.)

The third way in which the ecological perspective has been broadened is the development of the concept of opportunity. Although much ecological work is descriptive, the general concept of opportunity is central to the ecological approach. Opportunity is critical to the argument that abundance may explain much of the variation seen historically in rates of property crime.[29] It also contributes to the idea that there is a symbiotic relationship between "target areas" and nearby "offender areas."[30] In another form of this theory, opportunity is at the core of the notion of "defensible space"—the idea that in some situations the environment encourages inhabitants to assume control over space, thereby making it secure from crime.[31]

To sum up, the ecological perspective (or, as it was presented in Chapter 6, the cultural-deviance perspective) is one that has long been known and yet continues to be viable. Concerned with crime rates and social conditions, researchers at the University of Chicago used concepts such as symbiosis, invasion, dominance, and succession to understand urban growth and change. Shaw and McKay in particular were concerned with rapid population growth which destroyed natural community symbiosis. While owing much to the Chicago school, present-day ecological research has broadened its concepts by employing victimization data, stressing the role of routine activities in everyday life, and developing arguments about opportunity in the interpretation of crime rates.

STRAIN (OR MOTIVATIONAL) APPROACHES

While often applied to individuals, strain (or motivational) perspectives also have implications for the social context of crime. For one thing, they owe an intellectual debt to Durkheim's concept of anomie. For another, strain theorists argue that certain cultural and social structural conditions create problematically high crime rates for American society generally and for lower-class male youths in particular. In Chapter 6, we saw how strain theories were used to explain individual propensities toward crime. In this chapter we need to examine how they would account for differences in crime rates.

For strain theorists, crime and delinquency rates are best understood by looking at cultural values and social structures. According to Robert K. Merton, the key point is that there are

> processes through which infringement of social codes constitutes a "normal" (that is to say, an expectable) response.[32]

This response occurs because American society produces a strain toward anomie and deviant behavior by setting forth monetary success as a goal "worth striving for" and, at the same time, limiting the means of achieving this goal.

From Merton's perspective, it is the strain built into American society that produces the high rate of crime noted in Chapter 2:

> It is when a system of cultural values extols, virtually above all else, certain *common* success-goals *for the population at large* while the social structure rigorously restricts or completely closes access to approved modes of reaching these goals *for a considerable part of the same population*, that deviant behavior ensues on a large scale.[33]

The strain toward anomie and deviant behavior is particularly great for young people, males, and lower-class groups because the disparity between the goal of monetary success and the means of attaining it is greatest for these groups.[34]

In focusing on the higher crime rates of lower-class male youths, writers who followed Merton's lead were also led to focus on various aspects of the social context. For Albert K. Cohen, the problem was not how individuals became socialized into crime but rather how delinquent subcultures arose in the first place (see Chapter 6). In taking this approach, Cohen argued that (as he put it in a later work) deviant action is typically a collaborative social activity in which "a number of individuals with like problems and in effective communication with one another may join together to do what no one can do alone."[35] Richard A. Cloward and Lloyd E. Ohlin also argue from the social-context perspective in that they focus on criminal, conflict, and retreatist subcultures. "Criminal subcultures" are the product of organized slums; "conflict" and "retreatist" subcultures are the product of disorganized slums. Conflict and retreatist subcultures offer neither legitimate nor illegitimate opportunity.[36]

ECONOMIC APPROACHES

In contrast to the early cartologists, Durkheim, the ecologists, and the strain theorists, some criminologists have emphasized the importance of the economic aspect of social context in understanding crime rates. Their general perspective comes from the work of Karl Marx, who saw every aspect of social life as determined by the economic relationships between people. As he put it:

> The sum total of these relations of production constitutes the economic structure of society—the real foundation, on which rise legal and political superstructures and to which correspond definite forms of social consciousness.[37]

It follows that crime rates reflect the economic structure of society. Early Marxist criminologists argued that crime was a lower-class phenomenon, caused by poverty. (See Chapter 6.) Other criminologists, both Marxist and non-Marxist, have argued that the link between crime and poverty would mean higher rates during economic depressions and lower rates during periods of prosperity. Still others have held that economic inequality is accompanied by high rates of crime.

Plausible though the link between crime and poverty may appear, the results of research have been less than conclusive. Such research dates back to the 1800s. Some studies have found higher crime rates in times of economic hardship; others have reported exactly the opposite; still others have found no relationship.[38] For example, taking unemployment as a measure of hardship, Daniel Glaser and Kent Rice found that delinquency is high when unemployment is low and vice versa.[39] Larry D. Singell, on the other hand, found that delinquency increased when unemployment increased.[40] Moreover, a study of the Joint Economic Committee of the United States Congress calculated that a 1 percent increase in unemployment results in a 4 percent increase in admissions to state prisons and a 5.7 percent increase in murder. (The Joint Economic Committee examined the period 1940–1973.)[41]

Nor is crime directly related to poverty. As we saw in Chapter 2, the relationship between social class and crime is questionable, especially if self-report studies and upper-class types of crime are taken into account. However, some ecologically oriented research, using official measures of crime, has found higher crime rates in areas where a high percentage of the adult male population is in lower-class occupations, a high percentage of people are unemployed, a high percentage of people are on welfare, or a high percentage of people are below the poverty line.[42]

In recent years, several significant studies have found the amount of inequality to be related to crime rates. Thus, Paul Eberts and Kent P. Schwirian found that Standard Metropolitan Statistical Areas (SMSAs) having balanced class structures have lower crime rates than SMSAs with large upper-class or large lower-class concentrations.[43] In a study using data on SMSAs for 1967 and 1973, John Braithwaite found

> strong and consistent support for the hypothesis that cities in which there is a wide income gap between poor and average-income families have high rates for all types of crime.[44]

Finally, Judith R. Blau and Peter M. Blau found higher rates of criminal violence in SMSAs marked by socioeconomic inequalities. They argue that the amount of socioeconomic inequality, with its implied relative deprivation, is of more importance to understanding violent crime than the absolute number of people living in poverty or the existence of a subculture of violence.[45]

Examining the relationship between economic inequality and crime rates is a most promising line of research. As we shall see when we look at critical criminological perspectives later in this chapter, examination of the amount of social inequality provides important insights into the social context of crime.

HISTORICAL APPROACHES

A distinctly different appreciation of the social context of crime is provided by the historically oriented criminological research that has emerged in recent years. Employing a variety of theoretical viewpoints, historical criminology has explored patterns of crime in earlier periods in order to advance insights concerning the type and amount of crime and to understand the origins of present-day agencies of social control. Although several significant works have appeared, historical criminology has been described as a field of study which is still in its infancy and which lacks a distinct conceptual framework.[46]

One kind of insight offered by historical analysis concerns the amount of crime in earlier societies. Taking a historical as well as a comparative viewpoint, Ted Robert Gurr found that both England and the United States have experienced crime waves. In England the waves have occurred roughly a century apart: in the mid-1700s, in the 1830s and 1840s, and to a lesser extent in the 1970s. In the United States there was an upsurge in crime beginning in the 1850s which crested in the 1870s; then there was a long ebbing until the 1940s, when the upward trend of recent decades began. Gurr suggests three possible reasons for these crime waves: (1) Crime waves occur as a result of transformation from agricultural to industrial society. (2) Crime waves are the result of a spillover effect following wars. (3) Crime waves occur when there is a relatively large youthful population.[47] Although Gurr's work is far from definitive, it certainly calls attention to the need to take social context into account in understanding crime, and to the limitations of theories which account for crime at only one historical period.

Historically oriented criminology also offers a diversity of insights on the forms which crime has assumed. Marxist criminology is rich with historical insights on crime; indeed, in Chapter 6 we saw how capitalistic and landlord interests engaged in the organized theft of people's land, creating masses of beggars, robbers, and vagabonds. In an interesting extension of this perspective, the British Marxist historian Eric J. Hobsbaum sees social banditry as a "prepolitical" movement involving "little more than endemic peasant revolt against oppression and poverty."[48] In another interpretation, James A. Inciardi has traced criminal professions, finding that the highly skilled thieves of former ages are now very much on the wane.[49] We shall find these kinds of historical perspectives to be especially useful in understanding person-to-person property crimes (Chapter 10) and organized crime (Chapter 14).

In addition to insights concerning the type and amount of crime in earlier societies, historically oriented criminological research has generated fresh perspectives on modern crime-control agencies by examining their historical origins. Thus, police in New York can be seen as part of social changes such as rapid population growth; sharper class, ethnic, and religious distinctions; and a dizzying cycle of boom and bust. Police in the more conservative Boston can be seen as part of the response to social challenges posed by riots, increasing crime, and disorderly behavior related to drunkenness. (See Chapter 16.) American criminal courts can best be understood when their English legal origins are recognized and when the emergence of the key figure of the prosecutor in the 1830s is appreciated. (See Chapter 17.)

While they have been particularly important for studies of police and courts, historically oriented perspectives have also provided suggestive insights into correctional policies and practices. Several works have been especially significant. David J. Rothman has shown dramatically how the massive social changes of the early 1800s led Americans to adopt the institution of the prison. Georg Rusche and Otto Kirchheimer linked type of punishment to the economic system by showing how use of convict labor coincides with the decline of corporal punishment. Michel Foucault and Michael Ignatieff have developed powerful analyses demonstrating how prisons provided new means of imposing discipline over those marginal to industrial society.[50] (The historical analysis of corrections will be discussed in Chapter 18.) Finally, other historically oriented researchers have advanced diverse interpretations of crime control that would (1) see juvenile court reforms as the product of class warfare and xenophobia;[51] (2) associate criminality with political and religious dissent in Puritan America;[52] and (3) show how policies of crime control are linked to a view of offenders as members of the "dangerous classes."[53]

Insights such as these promise that the historically oriented criminological research will remain viable in the years ahead. At a minimum, the historical approach demonstrates the subtle, changing nature of the social context of crime. At a maximum, it provides a wealth of new data and advances new interpretations which can be used to develop and test social-context perspectives.

CRITICAL APPROACHES

As with criminal acts (Chapter 4) and individual criminal offenders (Chapter 5), critical criminologists have sharply challenged the various approaches to crime rates and the social context of crime. In criticizing ecological research, strain theories, economic theories linking crime to poverty, and some historical research, critical criminologists have seen a need to take larger political and economic structures into account. Two major, sometimes interrelated, themes are seen in their arguments: (1) Crime rates are explained by the actions of agencies of social control. (2) Economic and political factors determine the social context of crime. Let's examine each of these themes.

Control Agencies

For the critical criminologists, the key issue is how control agencies define and react to crime. They believe that crime rates are simply rates of deviance that are socially recognized by official agencies of social control.[54] Police decisions to arrest and to use force are so arbitrary that the quality of interaction between police and offenders is the critical determinant of the social context of crime (on police discretion, see Chapter 16). Moreover, conviction rates are suspect because court processing of offenders is (according to some studies) influenced by

"Contrology." Some criminologists believe that reported patterns of crime reflect the activities of crime-control agencies. (LEONARD FREED/MAGNUM)

social variables such as socioeconomic status, membership in minority groups, sex, and age. (See Chapter 17.)

The work of Aaron V. Cicourel on juvenile justice illustrates the conflict perspective on control agencies. Analyzing differences in rates of delinquency in two cities of similar size, he found that the city with the higher general rate of delinquency and the higher rate of recidivism also had a larger, better organized, more professional police department, one which maintained better records. The other city had higher rates of delinquency among Mexican Americans and blacks, a phenomenon Cicourel attributed to the police view that minorities were "troublesome" and to their more aggressive policing of these groups.[55] A different type of illustration is a review by David Seidman and Michael Couzens of the way the crime control program of the Nixon administration pressured police in Washington, D.C., to reduce crime. The police did respond to the pressure, but part of their response consisted in downgrading offenses; for example, larcenies of $50 or more were recorded as larcenies of under $50.[56]

Some critical criminologists would carry the argument a step further and see control agencies as active agents of crime and deviance. Gary T. Marx, for one, argues that control agencies can create what they set out to control. Generation of deviance by control agencies can take three forms: (1) "escalation," in which action taken by authorities unintentionally encourages violations of rules; (2) "nonenforcement," in which authorities unintentionally encourage violations by not taking action; and (3) "covert facilitation," in which authorities use hidden or deceptive actions to intentionally encourage violations.[57] In a more general statement of this perspective, Jason Ditton has coined the word "contrology" to capture the sense of his argument that the sources of crime lie in the action of control agencies: we should, he argues, be talking about "control waves" rather than "crime waves."[58]

Economic and Political Factors

The second theme that has characterized critical arguments is their emphasis on the relationship between crime and general economic and political factors. We have already seen that critical criminologists consider these factors as part of definitions of criminal acts (Chapter 4) and conceptualizations of the criminal offender (Chapter 6). Now, it is important to discuss their view of the role played by economic and political factors in the social context of crime.

One line of critical criminology, often indentified with the conflict school, has emphasized the relationship between economic inequality and imprisonment rates. In a test of a conflict proposition, David Jacobs compared states ordered in terms of economic inequality and found that greater inequality is associated with higher rates of imprisonment for larceny and burglary but not for motor vehicle theft, robbery, murder, and assault.[59] Matthew G. Yeager, in a study that used data on unemployment and prison populations for the period 1952–1978, found unemployment to be highly correlated with numbers of prisoners; in fact, a 1 percent increase in male unemployment resulted in 1395 additional prisoners in federal penal institutions.[60] In other research based on data for states, William G. Nagel found that higher crime rates were associated with higher per capita income and higher rates of unemployment, but with lower percentages of populations living in poverty.[61]

A second line of critical criminology would emphasize the need to "study crime in relation to the way societies organize their economic and political institutions."[62] This reflects economically oriented criminology which sees patterns of social inequality as criminogenic (see the discussion above). The modern Marxist view is explicitly stated by Steven Spitzer when he argues that capitalist societies create "problem populations" by excluding certain people from the labor market or by alienating them from institutions designed to secure class rule, such as the school.[63] In other work, Marxist-oriented critical criminologists have stressed the link between organized crime and political parties[64] and have argued that monopolistic holders of wealth increase that wealth through activities which are permitted even though they are illegal under antitrust laws.[65]

Although critical criminologists are united in their emphasis on the importance of political and economic factors, there is a fundamental divergence over whether crime is normal or pathological. Conflict theorists see crime as the normal actions of normal people who lack the power to control the criminalization process. However, Marxist theorists see crime as the pathological product of a pathological economic system—competitive capitalism.[66] The Marxist-oriented criminologist Richard Quinney asserts:

> The importance of criminal justice is that it moves us dialectically to reject the capitalist order and to struggle for a new society. We are engaged in socialist revolution.[67]

In other words, so important are economic and political factors that for critical Marxist criminologists there is no hope of finding a solution to crime short of radical economic and political changes.

ASSESSMENT OF SOCIAL-CONTEXT PERSPECTIVES

Having considered some of the major social-context perspectives, we will now find it useful to consider the criticisms to which they have been subjected and some of the possibilities for further theorizing along these lines.

Social-context approaches, like other criminological work, have been subjected to a variety of criticisms. Although focused on the ecology of the Chicago school, John Baldwin's four points of criticism could with a few exceptions also be applied to the other social-context approaches. The four points are: (1) Virtually all areal (ecological) studies have been based on officially recorded crime statistics drawn from police, court, or other institutional sources. (2) The possibility of the ecological fallacy means that the data are somewhat limited in their applicability. (3) The question whether slums produce deviants or deviants drift to slums is unresolved. (4) The deterioration and degradation of slum areas may be due less to social disorganization and lack of community control than to the indifference of landowners and industrialists who profit from slum conditions.[68] Point 4 is an exception in that it is a criticism which conflict criminologists have levelled specifically against the ecologists.[69]

In addition to these four problems, social-context approaches also suffer from some of the same limitations as the perspectives on criminal offenders discussed in Chapters 5 and 6. In that they are disciplinary perspectives, either sociological or economic, they tend to provide only partial explanations of crime. Moreover, if crime rates are manufactured by control agencies, as some critical criminologists have argued, the search for general economic and social conditions as causes may have little meaning. Finally, the three considerations mentioned in the assessment of approaches to offenders also apply to social-context approaches: (1) Crime is heterogeneous and multifaceted—not a unitary type of behavior. (2) Explanations of crime rates do not explain why behavior is criminal or not criminal in the first place. (3) No one theory explains all criminal behavior.

Nevertheless, despite the criticisms and limitations, there is much to be said for the social-context approaches to the study of crime. Crime rates do show enormous variations among different groups in a society, from one historical period to another, and from one society to another. At the same time, they also show stability and continuity over the short run. Analyzing variations in crime rates for differing social contexts enables us to appreciate the extent to which crime responds to situations or opportunities rather than to the motivations of offenders.

Taking a social-context approach provides an immensely promising way of understanding crime and dealing with the problem of crime. Although by no means simple, it is in principle easier to attempt to understand a relatively limited number of variables influencing crime rates in designated social contexts than to understand the much larger number of variables that may influence individuals. Moreover, once understood, manipulation of the social factors may be a far more realistic approach to dealing with crime than treatment of individuals. For example, using architectural design to prevent crime (as Oscar Newman suggests in his book *Defensible Space*[70]), or using knowledge of changes in routine activities to redeploy police (following the approach of Cohen and Felson[71]), may in the long run be more workable than attempts to "correct" individual offenders have been. (On correcting individuals, see Chapter 18; on changing social contexts, see Chapter 19.)

An increasingly sophisticated methodology also promises to make social-context approaches more useful. To begin with, there have been attempts to study particular crimes using ecological methods—car stripping, arson, and handling stolen goods, to name only a few.[72] Second, ecologists have also concerned themselves with distribution of justice and variations in law enforcement.[73] Third, as was discussed earlier, some studies have used victimization data to develop ecological perspectives. Fourth, the research potential of the ecological approach is enhanced by data from the National Crime Panel survey, collected from a victimization perspective, which support the correlations between sex, age, race, and crime rates that have long been observed for official data.[74]

Given the viability of a social-context perspective on crime, the question becomes which of the social-context approaches is most valid. All the approaches continue to have their advocates. The narrowly focused urban-area work of the Chicago school has, as we have seen, been expanded in present-day ecological research. Strain theorists, while focusing on lower-class male youths, have looked to broader social structural and cultural values to explain crime and delinquency. Marxist criminologists have sought an economic explanation. Critical criminologists, including some historians, have pointed to control agencies and larger economic and political factors as determinants of the social context of crime.

It is impossible to state definitively which of the social-context approaches is "correct." It is true that the ecological research of the Chicago school is the most narrowly focused and that the historical and critical approaches tend to be broadest in scope. However, as was true of theories about the individual offender, there is room for a plurality of viewpoints. Such a possibility is recognized by the critical criminologist David F. Greenberg:

> To criticize mainstream criminology for its tunnel vision is not to say that its findings are wrong. Specific claims can only be evaluated case-by-case. From a Marxist point of view, much of the trouble in mainstream criminology is of a different sort. In failing to consider the possibility that findings might be valid only within the context of given social arrangements one is apt to interpret them as if they had universal validity.[75]

In other words, so social a phenomenon is crime that universal, "monocausal" explanations may well be inappropriate. A thorough understanding of crime demands that we consider both its microecology and its macroecology—both the conflicts of cultural values and social structure and the larger economic and political factors that influence or determine crime rates.

APPLICABILITY OF SOCIAL-CONTEXT PERSPECTIVES TO MAJOR FORMS OF CRIME

As was true of perspectives on criminal acts, offenders, and victims, social-context perspectives have often been applied to the study of person-to-person violent crimes and person-to-person property crimes. As we examine these types of crime in greater detail in Chapters 9 and 10, we shall find that a number of social-context factors have been related to crime rates. In fact, we shall see that high crime rates are associated with urban environments, certain cultural values, availability of guns, amount and type of property, increases in youthful and urban populations, and the shift of routine social activities away from the home in the past several decades.

Social-context approaches are also of considerable value in understanding crimes other than person-to-person crimes. Corporate crimes, crimes against corporations, social-order crimes, organized crime, and political crime often assume forms that reflect their social context. As we shall see, there are certain cultural values, certain kinds of social organization, and certain types of opportunity structures that in effect support these forms of crime.

SUMMARY

Social-context perspectives focus primarily on crime rates and seek an explanation of crime in the group, society, or situation rather than in the legal system, the individual offender, or the individual victim. Encompassing some of the oldest systematic criminological research, social-context perspectives have been quite varied. They date back to the works of Quetelet and Guerry, early cartologists who looked to society as the key to an explanation of crime and were intrigued by the continuity of crime rates and their variability in time and place. Their perspective was greatly elaborated in the work of Durkheim, a French sociologist concerned with social cohesion. Arguing that crime and punishment are normal in mechanical societies seeking to repress differences between individuals, Durkheim saw crime as problematic in organic societies beset by anomie or normlessness. Supported by some and criticized by others, Durkheim's thinking has influenced much sociologically oriented criminological work.

Another major social-context perspective is ecological research that has sought to link crime rates to various social conditions. Researchers at the University of Chicago used concepts such as symbiosis, invasion, dominance, and succession to explain the diversity of norms, standards of behavior, and values which characterized urban areas with high crime, high delinquency, and social pathology. Present-day ecological research has considerably broadened the ecological approach to include studies based on victimization data, studies stressing routine activities in everyday life, and use of the concept of opportunity to interpret differences in crime rates. Present-day ecological approaches would include: (1) delineating situations in which victimization is likely to occur, (2) examining the shift in recent decades of routine occupational and social activities away from the home, and (3) understanding increases in property crime in light of abundance, explaining the symbiotic relationship between "target areas" and nearby "offender areas," and exploring the possibility of defensible space.

Other work on social contexts has been done by strain (or motivational) theorists, economic theorists, and historically oriented theorists. Strain theorists have been concerned with the relationship between crime rates, cultural values, and social structures. They hold that American society, especially that portion of it which is young, male, and lower-class, has had high crime rates because of the considerable disparity between the demands of the American goal of success and the means available to obtain it. Economically oriented criminologists have taken a contrasting approach, seeing economic factors as critical to understanding crime rates. However, studies relating crime to economic hardship and to poverty have shown mixed results. The most promising avenue of inquiry has pursued the proposition that the greater the inequality in an area, the greater its crime rate. Finally, historically oriented researchers, a group relatively new to the study of crime, have explored a diversity of approaches as they have analyzed the amount of crime in earlier societies and the origins of agencies of social control. Some have been explicitly Marxist while others have taken a broad range of social factors into account as they sought to understand crime rates.

The earlier schools of social-context thought have been sharply challenged by critical criminology. Critical criminologists have stressed the need to understand crime in terms of larger political and economic structures. Some critical theorists have seen control agencies as active agents in the creation of crime and crime rates. Others have examined crime in terms of economic and political factors. One approach—that taken by conflict criminologists—is to pursue the relationship between economic inequality and rates of crime or imprisonment. Another approach—that taken by modern Marxists—would see capitalist societies as criminogenic in that they create surplus populations, allow organized crime to be part of the political process, and allow monopolistic holders of wealth to increase their wealth through illegal practices. Although similar in their emphasis on economic and political factors, conflict criminologists and modern Marxist criminologists differ in that the former see crime as part of the normal action of normal people who lack power to control the criminalization process while the latter see crime as the pathological product of a pathological economic system, competitive capitalism.

The various social-context approaches have received a number of criticisms. For example, it is said that they rely too much on official crime rates; that they fail to appreciate the limitations imposed by the ecological fallacy; that they do not resolve the question whether contexts such as slums produce deviants or whether deviants drift to slums; and that they do not indicate whether slums are due to social disorganization or to the practices of landowners and industrialists who profit from them. In addition, there is the possibility that social-context perspectives provide partial rather than full explanations of crime and that crime rates are the artificial creation of control agencies. Moreover, as with approaches to offenders, there is the need to recognize that crime is a heterogeneous rather than a unitary type of behavior, that explanations of crime rates do not explain why behavior is criminal, and that no one theory explains all criminal behavior.

Despite the criticisms, social-context approaches are valuable to criminology. Crime rates do show short-run stability; but they also show considerable variation for different groups, historical periods, and societies. Studying these variations allows criminologists to understand how crime responds to opportunities as well as to the motivations of offenders. Moreover, it is in principle easier to understand a comparatively limited number of variables influencing crime rates for social contexts than a possibly unlimited number of variables that may influence individuals. Present-day methodologies also promise to enhance the viability of social-context approaches. Some present-day theories would also allow for a plurality of viewpoints to understand crime rates and the social contexts which influence them.

Like other criminological efforts, social-context perspectives have most often been applied to the study of person-to-person violent crimes and person-to-person property crimes. They offer a wealth of detail on the contextual factors that influence crime rates. Besides person-to-person crimes, social-context approaches are valuable in understanding corporate crime, crime against corporations, social-order crime, organized crime, and political crime. Indeed, as we shall see, dealing with these types of crimes has often involved changing the social context rather than apprehending and punishing offenders.

NOTES

[1] W. S. Robinson, "Ecological Correlations and the Behavior of Individuals," *American Sociological Review*, vol. 15, 1950, pp. 351–357.

[2] For a good discussion of the early cartologists, see: Leon Radzinowicz, *Ideology and Crime*, Columbia University Press, New York, 1966, pp. 29–42.

[3] As quoted in: Leon Radzinowicz and Joan King, *The Growth of Crime: The International Experience*, Basic Books, New York, 1977, p. 65.

[4] Émile Durkheim, *The Division of Labor in Society*, trans. by George Simpson, Free Press of Glencoe, Collier-Macmillan, London, 1933. The discussion of Durkheim is in part indebted to: George B. Vold, *Theoretical Criminology*, 2d ed. prepared by Thomas J. Bernard, Oxford University Press, New York, 1979, pp. 201–211.

[5] Walter A. Lunden, "Émile Durkheim" in Hermann Mannheim, ed., *Pioneers in Criminology*, 2d ed., Patterson Smith, Montclair, N.J., 1972, p. 395.

[6] Durkheim, *The Division of Labor in Society*, pp. 85–110 and 111–129.

[7] Émile Durkheim, *The Rules of Sociological Method*, 8th ed., trans. by Sarah A. Solovay and John H. Mueller, ed. by George E.G. Catlin, University of Chicago, 1938, pp. 68–69.

[8] Ibid., p. xxxviii.

[9] Durkheim, *The Division of Labor in Society*, pp. 85–110.

[10] Durkheim, *The Rules of Sociological Method*, p. 66.

[11] Émile Durkheim, *Suicide*, trans. by John A. Spaulding and George Simpson, Free Press, New York, 1951, pp. 246–253; originally published 1897.

[12] Kai T. Erickson, *Wayward Puritans: A Study in the Sociology of Deviance*, Wiley, New York, 1966.

[13] Stephen D. Webb, "Crime and the Division of Labor: Testing a Durkheimian Model," *American Journal of Sociology*, vol. 78, no. 3, November 1972, pp. 643–656.

[14] Edward Sagarin, ed., *Deviance and Social Change*, Sage, Beverly Hills, Calif., 1977.

[15] Herbert McClosky and John H. Schaar, "Psychological Dimensions of Anomy," *American Sociological Review*, vol. 30, February 1965, pp. 14–40.

[16] Steven Box, *Deviance, Reality, and Society*, Holt, Rinehart and Winston, London, 1971, chap. 2.

[17] Bob Roshier, "The Function of Crime Myth," *Sociological Review*, new series, vol. 25, 1977, pp. 309–323.

[18] Marvin Krohn, "A Durkheimian Analysis of International Crime Rates," *Social Forces*, vol. 27, no. 2, December 1978, pp. 654–670.

[19] Richard A. Berk, David Rauma, Sheldon L. Messinger, and Thomas F. Cooley, "A Test of the Stability of Punishment Hypothesis: The Case of California, 1851–1970," *American Sociological Review*, vol. 46, December 1981, pp. 805–829.

[20] John E. Conklin, *The Impact of Crime*, Macmillan, New York, and Collier Macmillan, London, 1975. chap. 4.

[21] The following discussion is indebted to: Vold, *Theoretical Criminology*, chap. 9.

[22] See: Robert E. Park, *Human Communities*, Free Press, Glencoe, Ill., 1952; and Robert E. Park, Ernest W. Burgess, and Roderick D. McKenzie, *The City*, University of Chicago Press, Chicago, Ill., 1928.

[23] Clifford R. Shaw and Henry D. McKay, *Juvenile Delinquency and Urban Areas: A Study of Rates of Delinquency in Relation to Differential Characteristics of Local Communities in American Cities*, University of Chicago Press, Chicago, Ill., 1942, rev. ed. 1969, especially pp. 383–388.

[24] For a review, see: John Baldwin, "Ecological and Areal Studies in Great Britain and United States," in Norval Morris and Michael Tonry, eds., *Crime and Justice: An Annual Review of Research*, vol. 1, University of Chicago Press, Chicago, Ill., 1979, pp. 29–66.

[25] Michael J. Hindelang, Michael R. Gottfredson, and James Garofalo, *Victim of Personal Crime: An Empirical Foundation for a Theory of Personal Victimization*, Ballinger, Cambridge, Mass., 1978, especially pp. 241–274.

[26] John W. C. Johnstone, "Social Class, Social Areas, and Delinquency," *Sociology and Social Research*, vol. 63, 1978, pp. 49–72.

[27] R. N. Davidson, *Crime and Environment*, St. Martin's Press, New York, 1981, p. 113.

[28] Lawrence E. Cohen and Marcus Felson, "Social Change and Crime Rate Trends," *American Sociological Review*, vol. 44, August 1979, pp. 588–608; quotation from p. 589. See also: Lawrence E. Cohen, Marcus Felson, and Kenneth C. Land, "Property Crime Rates in the United States: A Macrodynamic Analysis, 1947–1977; with Ex Ante Forecasts for the Mid-1980s," *American Journal of Sociology*, vol. 86, no. 1, July 1980, pp. 90–118; and Lawrence E. Cohen, James R. Kluegel, and Kenneth C. Land, "Social Inequality and Predatory Criminal Victimization: An Exposition and Test of a Formal Theory," *American Sociological Review*, vol. 46, October 1981, pp. 505–524.

[29] Leroy C. Gould, "The Changing Structure of Property Crime in an Affluent Society," *Social Forces*, vol. 48, September 1969, pp. 50–59.

[30] C. Ray Jeffery, *Crime Prevention—Through Environmental Design*, Sage, Beverly Hills, Calif., 1977, chaps. 10 and 11.

[31] Oscar Newman, *Defensible Space*, Macmillan, New York, 1972. For other work on the ecological perspective, see: Davidson, *Crime and Environment*; Keith D. Harries, *The Geography of Crime and Justice*,

McGraw-Hill, New York, 1974; and Daniel E. Georges Abeyie and Keith D. Harries, eds., *Crime: A Spatial Perspective*, Columbia University Press, New York, 1980.

[32] Robert K. Merton, *Social Theory and Social Structure*, enlarged ed., Free Press, New York, and Collier Macmillan, London, 1968, pp. 185–186.

[33] Merton, *Social Theory and Social Structure*, p. 200.

[34] For a discussion, see: Paul C. Friday and Jerald Hage, "Youth Crime in Post-Industrial Societies: An Integrated Perspective," *Criminology*, vol. 14, no. 3, November 1976, pp. 347–366.

[35] Albert K. Cohen, "The Sociology of the Deviant Act: Anomie Theory and Beyond," *American Sociological Review*, vol. 30, February 1965, pp. 5–14; quotation on p. 8.

[36] Richard A. Cloward and Lloyd E. Ohlin, *Delinquency and Opportunity: A Theory of Delinquent Gangs*, Free Press, Glencoe, Ill., 1960.

[37] Karl Marx, *Capital: A Critique of Political Economy*, ed. by Frederick Engels, trans. by Samuel Moore and Edward Aveling, Swan Sonnenschein, Lowry, London, 1887.

[38] For a review, see: Vold, *Theoretical Criminology*, pp. 165–171.

[39] Daniel Glaser and Kent Rice, "Crime, Age, and Employment," *American Sociological Review*, vol. 24, October 1959, pp. 679–686.

[40] Larry D. Singell, "An Examination of the Empirical Relationship between Unemployment and Juvenile Delinquency," *American Journal of Economics and Sociology*, vol. 26, no. 4, 1967, pp. 377–386.

[41] Harvey Brenner, *Estimating the Social Costs of National Economic Policy*, Government Printing Office, Washington, D.C., 1976.

[42] For an overview, see: Duncan Timms, *The Urban Mosaic: Towards a Theory of Residential Differentiation*, University of Cambridge Press, Cambridge, England, 1971.

[43] Paul Eberts and Kent P. Schwirian, "Metropolitan Crime Rates and Relative Deprivation," *Criminologica*, vol. 5, no. 4, February 1968, pp. 43–52.

[44] John Braithwaite, *Inequality, Crime, and Public Policy*, Routledge and Kegan Paul, London, 1979, p. 216.

[45] Judith R. Blau and Peter M. Blau, "The Cost of Inequality: Metropolitan Structure and Violent Crime," *American Sociological Review*, vol. 47, February 1982, pp. 114–129.

[46] Michael S. Hindus, "The History of Crime: Not Robbed of Its Potential, but Still on Probation," in Sheldon L. Messinger and Egon Bittner, eds., *Criminology Review Yearbook*, vol. I, Sage, Beverly Hills, Calif., 1979, pp. 217–241.

[47] Ted Robert Gurr, "On the History of Violent Crime in Europe and America," in Hugh David Graham and Ted Robert Gurr, eds., *Violence in America: Historical and Comparative Perspectives*, rev. ed., Sage, Beverly Hills, Calif., 1979, pp. 353–374.

[48] Eric J. Hobsbaum, *Primitive Rebels: Studies in Archaic Forms of Social Movement in the Nineteenth and Twentieth Centuries*, Norton, New York, 1959.

[49] James A. Inciardi, *Careers in Crime*, Rand McNally, Chicago, Ill., 1975.

[50] David J. Rothman, *The Discovery of the Asylum: Social Order and Disorder in the New Republic*, Little, Brown, Boston, Mass., 1971; Georg Rusche and Otto Kirchheimer, *Punishment and Social Structure*, rev. ed., Russell and Russell, New York, 1968, originally published 1939; Michel Foucault, *Discipline and Punish: The Birth of the Prison*, Vintage, New York, 1977; and Michael Ignatieff, *A Just Measure of Pain: The Penitentiary in the Industrial Revolution, 1750–1850*, Pantheon, New York, 1978.

[51] Anthony M. Platt, *The Child Savers: The Invention of Delinquency*, University of Chicago Press, Chicago, Ill., 1969.

[52] Erikson, *Wayward Puritans*. See also: Chapter 7 of the present text.

[53] Eric H. Monkkonen, *The Dangerous Class: Crime and Poverty in Columbus, Ohio, 1860–1885*, Harvard University Press, Cambridge, Mass., 1975.

[54] Donald J. Black, "Production of Crime Rates," *American Sociological Review*, vol. 35, August 1970, pp. 773–747.

[55] Aaron V. Cicourel, *The Social Organization of Juvenile Justice*, Wiley, New York, 1968, especially pp. 58–110.

[56] David Seidman and Michael Couzens, "Getting the Crime Rate Down: Political Pressure and Crime Reporting," *Law and Society Review*, vol. 8, no. 3, Spring 1974, pp. 457–494.

[57] Gary T. Marx, "Ironies of Social Control: Authorities as Contributors to Deviance through Escalation, Nonenforcement, and Covert Facilitation," *Social Problems*, vol. 28, no. 3, February 1981, pp. 221–246.

[58] Jason Ditton, *Contrology: Beyond the New Criminology*, Humanities Press, Atlantic Highlands, N.J., 1979.

[59] David Jacobs, "Inequality and the Legal Order: An Ecological Test of the Conflict Model," *Social Problems*, vol. 25, June 1978, pp. 515–525.

[60] Matthew G. Yeager, "Unemployment and Imprisonment," *Journal of Criminal Law and Criminology*, vol. 70, Winter 1979, pp. 586–588.

[61] William G. Nagel, "A Statement on Behalf of a Moratorium on Prison Construction," *Crime and Delinquency*, vol. 23, no. 2, April 1977, pp. 154–172.

[62] David F. Greenberg, ed., *Crime and Capitalism: Readings in Marxist Criminology*, Mayfield, Palo Alto, Calif., 1981, p. 18.

[63] Steven Spitzer, "Toward a Marxian Theory of Deviance," *Social Problems*, vol. 22, no. 5, June 1975, pp. 638–651. See also: David F. Greenberg, "Delinquency and the Age Structure of Society," *Contemporary Crises*, vol. 1, April 1977, pp. 189–223.

[64] Frank Pearce, *Crimes of the Powerful: Marxism, Crime, and Deviance*, Pluto, London, 1976, especially pp. 124–164.

[65] Harold Barnett, "Wealth, Crime, and Capital Accumulation," *Contemporary Crises*, vol. 3, April 1979, pp. 171–186.

[66] The distinction between conflict and radical (Marxist) criminology is based on: Vold, *Theoretical Criminology*, pp. 313–314.

[67] Richard Quinney, *Class, State, and Crime: On the Theory and Practice of Criminal Justice*, McKay, New York, 1977, p. 165.

[68] Baldwin, "Ecological and Areal Studies in Great Britain and the United States," pp. 34–37.

[69] Jon Snodgrass, "Clifford R. Shaw and Henry D. McKay:

Chicago Criminologists," *British Journal of Criminology*, vol. 16, 1976, pp. 1–19.

[70] Newman, *Defensible Space*.

[71] Cohen and Felson, "Social Change and Crime Rate Trends."

[72] For an overview, see: Davidson, *Crime and Environment*, chap. 1.

[73] Ibid., chap. 5; and Harries, *The Geography of Crime and Justice*, chap. 5.

[74] Michael J. Hindelang, "Variations in Sex-Race-Age-Specific Incidence Rates of Offending," *American Sociological Review*, vol. 46, August 1981, pp. 461–474.

[75] Greenberg, *Crime and Capitalism*, p. 17.

Review and Preview...

PART TWO AND PART THREE

Viewed in their entirety, present-day theories of crime are a curious mixture of the major currents of thought detailed in Part Two: classicism; positivism; individually oriented perspectives using biological, psychological, sociological, economic, and critical approaches to understand offenders; victimology; and ecological, strain, economic, historical, and critical approaches to relate crime to social contexts. These various currents of thought often espouse contrasting assumptions about human nature, emphasize different aspects of the study of crime, and propose different strategies for dealing with the problem of crime. It is perhaps amazing that all of them are in vogue today, attempting to be taken seriously as people seek solutions to the problem of crime.

Let us briefly review the major directions that criminological thought has taken. Using an eighteenth-century frame of reference, classical criminology focused the study of crime on the legal definition of criminal acts, assumed that all people were rational, and advocated deterrence as the way to deal with crime. In a distinct reorientation, late-nineteenth-century positivism turned criminology to the study of offenders, many of whom were assumed to be irrational and in need of treatment. In the early decades of the twentieth century, economists and sociologists—especially the latter—began to devote extensive efforts to the study of both offenders and the social contexts of crime. Since the 1960s, critical criminology has challenged classicism, positivism, and much of the work done by sociologists. It argues for a criminology that focuses on the act, that understands offenders in terms of how they are processed through the criminal justice system, that takes victims into account, and that sees a relationship between crime and power. Indeed, in its estimate, crime is a political phenomenon.

To recognize the diversity of perspectives is not to despair about the state of criminology today. Criminology is not a monolithic science. Indeed, it is worth noting that theoretical structures are never accepted or rejected on empirical grounds alone but are modified by new findings or discarded if other theories explain the facts better.[1] It may be that all the evidence is simply not available, so that we do not have a complete picture. It may also be that the problem of crime is itself so complex that it is amenable to several different approaches. In fact, in order to deal with this complexity, Part Two considered theories of crime in four major categories. In any event, the diversity of theories should serve as warning that instant solutions to the problem of crime are not to be found. However, this is not to say that progress is impossible. Rather, much research and thought have been cited which do increase our understanding of crime and criminal justice.

Nevertheless, that so many major theoretical perspectives are argued today is an indication that criminological knowledge remains very unsettled. As it turns out, none of the policies and programs espoused by any of the schools has enjoyed a striking success. In the search for answers, modern deterrence theory and biosocial positivism have emerged as revivals of approaches that had fallen into disuse and disrepute. Yet the more popular sociological and critical approaches are by no means fully supported by research. In fact, differential association, the dominant sociological theory for many years, was not even stated in a form that could be readily tested with known methodologies. Parts of critical criminology are equally "visionary."

It can be said that present-day criminology is richer than the purely sociological approaches which dominated the field during the early and middle decades of the twentieth century. At present, it appears that criminology may well move away from sociological approaches. It can go in the direction of the modern biological or "biosocial" approaches. It can become "rational" and look for models of deterrence. It can

become "radical" and interpret criminological phenomena in terms of their relationship to the larger structures of society. All these trends are now evident. The risk is that those who choose to concentrate on the offender may ignore the social context from which offenders typically come, while those who concentrate on social contexts may lose sight of the actual offenders.

Whatever direction criminology takes, there are several important considerations that ought to be kept in mind.

1. There is need for theories that explain particular forms of crime. Talking about crime in general often clouds a discussion, and in all probability there is no one theory or perspective that embraces all types of crime. Thus, we need to develop theories that apply to particular types of crime rather than continually attempt to seek out the one theory that will explain crime in general. For example, it may well be that *some* crimes are best seen as political while others are best understood in terms of social contexts and still others as the product of disturbed personalities. It may well be that labeling theory provides the most useful approach to what we shall call "social-order" crimes, while deterrence theory works for crimes such as hijacking airplanes.

2. Any approach may lead to excesses in application. Treatment methods developed in the light of new biological and psychological knowledge must be applied only in the context of constitutional rights. Vague definitions of crime developed from radical views about society must be applied with full attention to the rights of those perceived as "guilty." Deterrence must not be used to develop social repression.

3. Recently developed research methods now permit alternative theoretical models to be tested. For example, we can now design research that will demonstrate whether strain or control theory better explains criminal or delinquent behavior. We can also use multiple factor analysis to consider large numbers of variables simultaneously.

4. The social context in which crime occurs often gets lost when we begin criminology from the perspective of the criminal offender or the criminal act. However, if we start theorizing from the perspective of the social and physical environment, we might well find that the critical factor in crime is opportunity afforded by the environment. We do know that certain types of environments produce high crime rates: for example, easily accessible banks, close proximity of upper- and lower-class residential areas, and shifts of routine activities away from the home. Modern ecological research is currently exploring these areas. In the end, it may be that the environmental context is the most readily controlled aspect of crime.

The chapters dealing with theories of crime included sections on the applicability of those perspectives to the major forms of crime. These sections anticipate our next task: to take a systematic look at the major forms of crime in the United States today.

Part Three organizes the complexity of crime in two different ways. The first involves identifying seven major types of crime: person-to-person, violent; person-to-person, property; corporate crime; crimes against organizations; social-order crimes; organized crime; and political crime. As we shall see, it is only the first two types that involve individuals directly both as criminal offenders and as victims of crime. The remaining five types are in some sense creatures of social organization. In corporate crime, the organized entity is the criminal offender. In crimes against organizations, the organized entity is the victim. In social-order crime, society is the supposed victim while many of the individual participants are involved in "willing exchanges." In organized crime, there is a unique form of collusion between criminal offenders. In political crime, the political or social system itself is threatened. The highly organized nature of modern American society demands that we analyze crime by taking all seven major types into account. Thus, in Part Three one chapter will be devoted to each type of crime.

The second device for organizing the complexity of crime is to take our four criminological topics and utilize them as a basis for the structure of each chapter in Part Three. Thus, for each of the seven major types of crime, we shall analyze the criminal act, criminal offenders, victims, and the social contexts within which the crime occurs. This form of organization will allow for a ready integration of the theories of crime discussed in Part Two with the discussions about the types of crime in Part Three.

NOTES

[1] Piers Beirne, "Empiricism and the Critique of Marxism on Law and Crime," *Social Problems*, vol. 26, no. 4, April 1979, pp. 373–85.

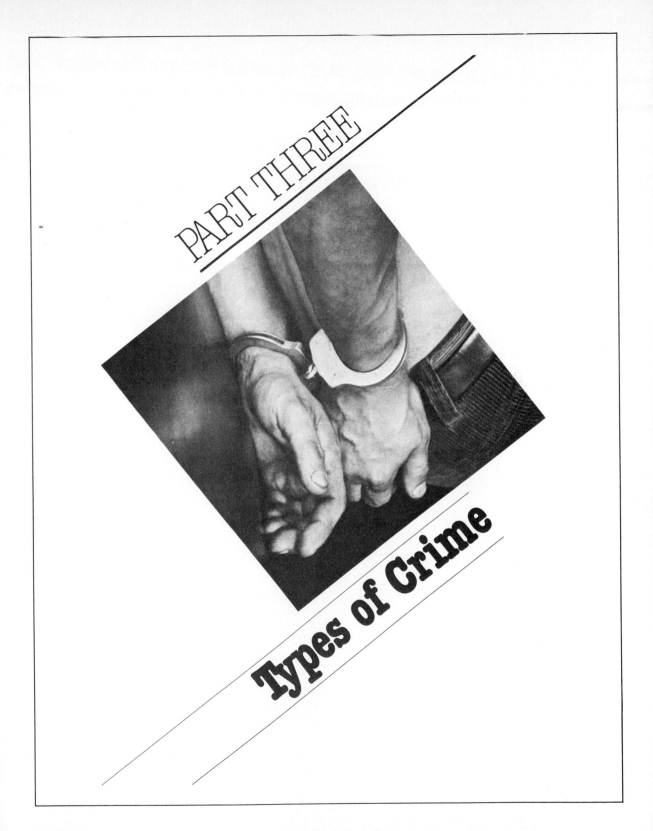

PART THREE

Types of Crime

Person-to-Person Violent Crimes

9

In today's society crime takes many forms. Let's begin our study by examining the form often identified as "the crime problem": crimes in which one person inflicts violence upon another. The main person-to-person violent crimes are murder, aggravated assault, rape, and robbery. However, other assaults, kidnapping, abuse of spouses and children, and (in that it potentially involves people as victims) arson could also be included.

Person-to-person violent crimes evoke much public concern and fear. Since the 1960s, "crime in the streets" has been a politically explosive issue. Crime in the streets is usually identified with robbery, a highly visible crime that involves direct confrontation between an offender and a victim who are typically strangers to each other. Yet, as we shall see, this concern with robbery obscures a critical issue. Most violent crime occurs in the home rather than on the streets. Furthermore, the numbers of relatives, neighbors, and acquaintances exceed the numbers of strangers involved in the most serious violent crimes.

Whether in the streets or in the home, violent crime is, indeed, a social problem. There are about 22,000 homicides each year in the United States; what this figure means is that one's chance of dying violently in a given year is more than 1 in 10,000. Those statistical odds may sound small; but there are other alarming aspects to the picture of violent crime. Although the United States has experienced "homicide waves" earlier in its history, increases in homicide since 1965 have brought the overall rate back to the all-time peak of 1933. Despite the fact that most homicides involve relatives, neighbors, and acquaintances, there has been a startling increase in killings of strangers—especially in felony murders, which are committed during the course of another crime (e.g., murders committed in the course of robberies). Moreover, multiple or "mass" murders have also become more commonplace.[1] For some groups the trends are especially alarming: among inner-city black males aged 15 to 44, homicide is the leading cause of death.[2]

In addition to its costs in terms of death and injury, violent person-to-person crime also contributes to neighborhood decline. Since the actual chances of being harmed by a violent crime are statistically small, concern for neighborhoods and communities may underlie the fear of crime.[3] In any case, it seems apparent that many traditional urban ethnic areas have broken up as their inhabitants have moved to higher-income, suburban, or predominantly white areas in order to "feel safer." This trend has an enormous social cost of mutual distrust and reinforced segregation.[4]

In analyzing violent person-to-person crime, recognizing that it is found both in our neighborhood streets and in our homes is an important first step. A more comprehensive overview of its importance and various dimensions can be obtained by examining acts of violence, violent offenders, victims of violence, and social contexts of violence.

ACTS OF VIOLENCE

Violence has long been part of the human condition. Our social myths, history, and literature imply that it is not unusual and may even be "inevitable." In the Bible, Cain murdered Abel because God did not respect Cain's offering. In the Roman myth, Romulus killed his twin brother Remus because Remus ridiculed his strength and authority. The Greek myth of Oedipus tells of parricide, filicide, fratricide, and multiple suicide.[5] Our bedtime "fairy tales" for children tell of felonious homicide ("Jack and the Beanstalk") and parental neglect and abuse ("Hansel and Gretel").

Literary violence continues to entertain us today. The murder mysteries written by authors such as Agatha Christie and Mickey Spillane provide "relaxing" reading. The mind of the murderer is the subject of much serious literature. Writers such as C. P. Snow, Norman Mailer, and Truman Capote have attempted to uncover how it works in books such as *A Coat of Varnish, The Executioner's Song,* and *In Cold Blood.* Television networks broadcast an enormous variety of stories that involve murders, rapes, robberies, and family violence. Many of the stories seen as fiction and entertainment correspond so closely to news broadcasts shown over the same networks that fact and fiction can easily become blurred.

In contrast to their myths, history, and literature, societies have attempted to control interpersonal violence by outlawing its various forms. Criminal law has astonishing durability. So extensive has been the borrowing from one society to another that it makes sense to speak of the "evolution" of law and order.[6] Despite variations in specific definitions of crimes, most systems of criminal law are clear in their attempt to outlaw violent acts such as killing and assaulting other persons, violent sexual assault, and robbery—i.e., theft accompanied by violence.

Our legal system in the United States is derived for the most part from common law. Common law emerged in the 1200s, when the English kings, in particular Henry II, managed to take control of the courts away from the nobility. Before that, acts seen as "crimes" were avenged by blood feuds between family clans or, beginning in the 700s, were responded to by local clan councils. With Henry II's control over the courts, a "common law" rapidly emerged. By 1225, in his book *De legibus Angliae,* Henry de Bracton—perhaps the first common-law scholar—was able to establish the important concepts of law related to the violent crimes of homicide, assault, and robbery. Today, although other new crimes of violence have emerged, these basic definitions remain virtually unchanged.[7]

Homicide

Let us begin with criminal homicide, which has been considered a serious offense in virtually all times and places. Criminal homicide is perhaps the most extreme form of crime in that it involves loss of life. Following the Uniform Crime Reports, criminal homicide may be defined as follows:

> *Murder and nonnegligent manslaughter:* the willful (nonnegligent) killing of one human being by another. Deaths caused by negligence, attempts to kill, assaults to kill, suicides, accidental deaths, and justifiable homicides are excluded. Justifiable homicides are limited to: (1) the killing of a felon by a law enforcement officer in the line of duty; and (2) the killing of a felon by a private citizen.
>
> *Manslaughter by negligence:* the killing of another person through gross negligence. Traffic fatalities are excluded. While manslaughter by negligence is a Part I crime, it is not included in the crime index.[8]

In reflecting on this definition, it should be noted that some homicides are "justifiable" in that they are committed by police officers or by private citizens who kill felons in self-defense. (Homicides by police officers will be discussed further in Chapter 16.) Furthermore, the charge of manslaughter by negligence is specifically for person-to-person crimes, thereby circumventing the enormous issue of violations of laws concerning occupational health and safety (to be discussed further in Chapter 11).

The distinction between murder and manslaughter rests on the question of intent. For an act to be *murder,* there must be *mens rea,* i.e., a guilty state of mind or "malice aforethought." Further distinctions not reflected in the definitions used for purposes of crime reporting are based on whether or not a killing was "premeditated," that is, considered beforehand; and on whether or not it was "deliberate," that is, conceived and decided upon through careful thought rather than impulse.

Without malice aforethought, premeditation, or deliberation, a killing is *manslaughter.* It may be "voluntary manslaughter" if the act was committed in the heat of passion or excited by a quarrel. Or it may be "involuntary manslaughter" if the act occurred unintentionally during the course of a minor criminal act.

Finally, there are *felony murders,* killings committed during certain felonies—including robbery, burglary, rape, sexual assault of a child, certain narcotics offenses, and kidnapping.[9]

Unfortunately, the statistics on criminal homicide that are maintained in the Uniform Crime Reports do not fully reflect these distinctions. However, the statistics do indicate substantial increases in the homicide rate; in recent years about 10 of every 100,000 Americans has been a homicide victim. Moreover, both the crime reports and other evidence suggest that the "run of the mill" homicide is a far cry from the premeditated murder that has been the subject of so much fiction and literature. Rather, the typical homicide would appear to be voluntary manslaughter committed in the heat of passion and during quarrels. (See Box 4.)

The notion of the typical homicide as voluntary manslaughter committed in the heat of passion and during quarrels is supported in the statistics of the Uniform Crime Reports. Take, for example, the homicides which occurred during 1981. Although the relationships were unknown in 30 percent of the cases, in the remaining 70 percent the breakdown is as follows: 17 percent involved family members; 38 percent involved friends, acquaintances, and neighbors; and only 15 percent were clearly identifiable as "stranger killings." When the cases are classified by circumstances and motive, a somewhat similar picture emerges: 42 percent concerned romantic triangles, the influence of alcohol or narcotics, or arguments over property or money; 17 percent involved other motives; and in 18 percent the motive was unknown. The remaining 23 percent—fewer than one in four—were classified as known or suspected felony murders.[10]

As if to emphasize the extent to which homicide is tied into American social life, its occurrence is directly related to the pace of social activity. Seasonally, the number of homicides rises somewhat in the summer months, when people tend to be involved in leisure activities; and in December, when families typically get together. The association with days of the week and hours of the day is even greater. The weekend in general (Saturday in particular) and the hours between 8 P.M. and 2 A.M. are the times when most homicides occur.[11] These are also the times when people are most likely to be involved in activities in their homes and neighborhoods.

Box 4: Three Typical Cases of Homicide (Nonnegligent Manslaughter) and One Typical Assault

Homicide (Nonnegligent Manslaughter)

Between Neighbors

. . . At 3:15 P.M., the reporting officer arrived on the scene and found a circular five-inch hole in the screen made by a shot gun blast. The victim was found lying on his back on the bedroom floor. The pattern made by the shot on the living room wall indicated that the subject was hit in the hallway approximately twelve and one-half feet from the screen. A witness said the victim had complained to the suspect about talking too loud in front of his apartment. The victim then drew a gun, pointed it at the suspect's head, and pulled the trigger three times, without the gun going off. The suspect ran toward the project across the street, and the victim fired one shot at him. The suspect then came back with a shot gun, fired through the victim's door, and fled the scene.[a]

Between Husband and Wife

. . . A husband threatened to kill his wife on several occasions. In this instance, he attacked her with a pair of scissors, dropped them, and grabbed a butcher knife from the kitchen. In the ensuing struggle that ended on their bed, he fell on the knife.[b]

Between Parties with a Previous Relationship

. . . Novella Gilmore, a 30 year old woman, had a court order directing her former boy friend, Eddie Martin, to stay away from her. But Eddie didn't obey. He was in her apartment, . . . and she says he started beating her. She allegedly grabbed a gun, shot him, and then called the police. It was 12:10 A.M. When the cops arrived, they found Eddie Martin, 26, lying face down on a bed, clad in his undershorts and a T-shirt. The bullet had gone through his right ear and exited through the front of his head. A few hours later, Novella Gilmore, who has a four year old child, was charged with homicide.[c]

Assault (a "Near Homicide") between Husband and Wife

. . . The victim was interviewed at the hospital. She related that she had been cut by her husband, who had picked a fight with her and then slashed her on the left side of the stomach without reason or provocation. She had just come home from work and found her husband in an intoxicated condition. Following the quarrel, the husband allegedly picked up a kitchen butcher-type knife and slashed her. The offender was also interviewed. After advising him of his constitutional rights, the reporting officer decided that the offender was under the influence of alcohol to the point where interviewing him would be useless. The offender did admit cutting his wife, however. His version was that both he and his wife had been drinking and that he had cut his wife with the aforementioned knife, following the argument that she had instigated.[d]

SOURCES

[a] Lynn A. Curtis, *Criminal Violence: National Patterns and Behavior,* Heath (Lexington Books), Lexington, Mass., 1974, p. 1.
[b] Marvin E. Wolfgang, "Victim-Precipitated Criminal Homicide," *Journal of Criminal Law, Criminology, and Police Science,* vol. 48, June 1957, pp. 1–11.
[c] "Murder in New York: A Case-by-Case Look at Week's Slaughter," *Daily News,* October 23, 1977, p. 109.
[d] Curtis, *Criminal Violence,* p. 1.

The solution of a typical homicide case is relatively simple. Except for people who commit felony murders, few of those who commit homicides try to escape or avoid detection. Often they remain at the scene of the killing; they may even call the police. Hence, criminal homicide shows a high clearance rate: nationally, 76 percent of homicides are cleared by arrest. In about two-thirds of all homicides, the suspect is taken into custody within 24 hours. However, if a homicide is not solved within 24 hours, the chances of its ever being solved drop markedly.[12]

Although most homicides involve family members, friends, or acquaintances, there is some evidence that the feared "stranger murders" are on the increase, especially in urban areas. For example, in 1977 the police department of New York City made an analysis of murders and found that relationships between parties could be determined in only half of the cases. For these cases, about 35 percent involved murder by strangers, committed most often during the course of robberies. If the percentage of "stranger murders" was higher in the cases where the relationship between the parties was listed as unknown, the overall proportion of "stranger murders" could easily have been more than 40 percent. It also appears that the percentage of homicides cleared by arrest is dropping, as would be expected if "stranger murders" are on the increase.[13]

Assault

Much of what has been said about criminal homicide could also be said for our second major form of person-to-person violent crime, aggravated assault. Again according to the Uniform Crime Reports, aggravated assault can be defined as follows:

> An unlawful attack by one person upon another for the purpose of inflicting severe or aggravated bodily injury. This type of assault usually is accompanied by the use of a weapon or by means likely to produce death or great bodily harm. Simple assaults are excluded.[14]

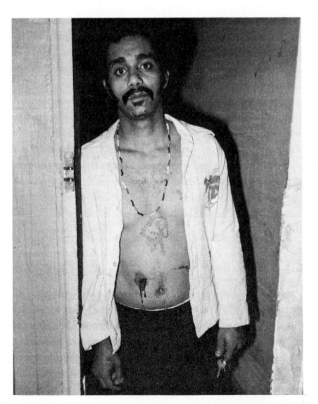

A victim of aggravated assault, this man has been stabbed twice in the stomach. (JILL FREEDMAN/ARCHIVE)

Aggravated assault is distinguished from "other" or "simple" assault, which is a Part II offense defined as "assault or attempted assault where no weapon was used or which did not result in serious or aggravated injury to the victim."[15]

There is a tremendous amount of assault in American society. First, the rate of reported aggravated assault is 280.9—more than 28 times the homicide rate, 9.8. Second, if we can judge from the number of arrests, simple assault occurs even more frequently than aggravated assault. In fact, according to victim surveys, there are in all more than 4.5 million assaults each year. Assuming that there were no repeat victimizations, this would mean that nearly 2 percent of the entire American population are assault victims each year. According to some observers, assault is often part of an ongoing relationship characterized by recurrent violence in which the intention is to do some harm but not necessarily to kill.[16]

The social aspects of assault are more difficult to piece together than the statistical aspects, since less information is available. The Uniform Crime Reports do not give detailed information comparable to that given for criminal homicide; as a result, the situations and social relationships of the parties are unknown. Nor are time of day and day of week reported. However, a handful of studies of assaults in specific cities have attempted to fill this gap.

Although not as consistent as the data for homicide, the patterns of aggravated assaults in the four selected studies shown in Table 6 (page 192) are somewhat similar. For the District of Columbia and the 17 American cities studied, relatives, friends, or acquaintances are involved in the majority of assaults where the relationship between offender and victim is known. As is stated in one of the footnotes to Table 6, the percentage of "stranger assaults" in St. Louis may be high because of the classification system used by the researchers. However, with nearly half of its aggravated assaults classified as "stranger assaults," Westchester County appears to be an exception.

Rape

Person-to-person violent crime takes a rather different form when it is a matter of forcible rape. Its definition is:

> The carnal knowledge of a female forcibly and against her will. Included are rapes by force and attempts or assaults to rape.[17]

Forcible rape is distinguished from statutory rape in which the "victim" is under the age of consent and no force is used.

The number of rapes reported to police has shown considerable increase in recent years. Currently, the rate of reported rape stands at 69 per 100,000 females, up from 36 per 100,000 females in 1970.

Of all the major crimes of interpersonal violence, rape shows the greatest ambiguity in its social definition. In some societies it has been regarded as a property crime in which one man committed an offense against another by abusing the other man's "property."[18] In the United States today, rape is undergoing considerable redefinition. Until recently, the definition has been quite narrow: "the penetration of a penis into the vagina against the will of a female who is not

TABLE 6. Offender-Victim Relationship in Aggravated Assaults, Selected Studies

Offender-victim relationship	St. Louis (N = 241)	District of Columbia (N = 131)	17 American cities (N = 1493)	Westchester County (N = 317)
Kinship	19.5	20.6	13.9	9.8
Husband-wife		(10.7)	(9.4)	
Other family		(9.9)	(4.5)	
Close friend, lover, common-law spouse, or acquaintance	NA	60.3	32.0[a]	16.4
Stranger or no relationship	80.5[b]	19.1	30.7[c]	44.8
Unknown, or not reported	NA	NA	24.3	29.0
Total[d]	100.0	100.0	100.0	100.0

[a] Includes close friend, paramour, homosexual partner, prostitute, acquaintance, neighbor, business relation, and sex rival or enemy.

[b] This percent of undoubtedly high. In their table 6 (p. 456), Pittman and Handy present kin relationship dichotomized as "kin"-"not kin." The percent shown above (80.5) is that for "not kin." However, in a subsequent table (their table 15, p. 468), Pittman and Handy describe (for a limited number of cases, N = 50) the relationship between "offender-victim acquaintance" and "sex of offender and victim." One category of "offender-victim relationship" is given as "former close relation." The marginal total of 25 cases for this class does not exhaust the possible number in that class, since the data in the table pertain only to assaults in which offenders and victims were of opposite sexes. Thus, at least 10.4 percent and quite possibly more of the total (N = 241) had "former close relationships."

[c] Includes 20.6 percent "stranger" and 10.1 percent "felon" or "police officer."

[d] Percentages may not sum to 100, because of rounding.

SOURCES:

1. Reprinted from: Christopher S. Dunn, "The Patterns and Distribution of Assault Incident Report Characteristics—Among Social Areas," pamphlet, U.S. Department of Justice, LEAA Report, Government Printing Office, Washington, D.C., 1976, p. 13.

2. David J. Pittman and William Handy, "Patterns in Criminal Aggravated Assault," *Journal of Criminal Law, Criminology, and Police Science*, vol. 55, 1964, p. 465.

3. Data for District of Columbia from: President's Commission on Crime in the District of Columbia, *Report of the Commission*, Government Printing Office, Washington, D.C., 1966, p. 78.

4. Data for 17 American cities from: Donald J. Mulvihill, Melvin M. Tumin, and Lynn A. Curtis, *Crimes of Violence: A Staff Report Submitted to the National Commission on the Causes and Prevention of Violence*, Government Printing Office, Washington, D.C., p. 287.

5. Data for Westchester County from: Christopher S. Dunn, "The Analysis of Environmental Attribute/Crime Incident Characteristic Interrelationships," Ph.D. dissertation, State University of New York at Albany, 1974, p. 252.

the assailant's wife."[19] However, recent legislation in some states is altering this definition in several ways:

1. The intercourse need not be vaginal, but can be oral or anal.
2. The penetration need not be by a penis, but can be accomplished by any object, including the tongue.
3. The victim need not be female.
4. The victim can be the assailant's wife.[20]

In studies of rape, investigators report that in practice there are very different definitions of what constitutes rape in different parts of the United States. For example, Los Angeles utilizes a far more comprehensive definition of what constitutes forcible rape than Boston does.[21]

In particular cases, the definition of forcible rape depends heavily on the situation. One survey of 343 females found less than complete unanimity on the perception that rape had occurred in selected hypothetical situations presented to respondents (see Table 7). We can note particularly that for the two acts involving dating—"dating in man's apartment" and "date with respected bachelor"—more than 40 percent of those surveyed felt that the act was not or probably was not rape. There were also substantial minorities who did not agree that rape had occurred in the situations "meeting in bar and taken to deserted road" and "woman's boss after working late." More than most other crimes, rape places the burden of definition of the situation on its victim; and in many instances the victim is blamed for the crime.[22]

In the situations described in the survey cited above, there was least unanimity about rape where a previous relationship existed between the male and female. Although the relevant data are not collected systematically in the Uniform Crime Reports, two different studies have found that a previous relationship exists in 40 to 50 percent of forcible rapes; the remainder take place between complete strangers.[23] In rapes where victim and offender had a previous relationship, about two-thirds involve acquaintances, and the rest involve close friends or relatives.[24] It should be noted that the two studies quoted here are based on rapes reported to the police. In the nationwide surveys of crime victims, the proportion of victim-reported rapes that are "stranger rapes" is 61 percent.[25]

In short, among violent crimes, rape is most ambiguous in its social

TABLE 7. Results of a Survey: Females' Perception that Rape Has Occurred in Seven Selected Situations (*N* = 343)[a]

	Yes		Possibly		Uncertain		Probably not		No	
	Percent[b]	*(N)*	*Percent*	*(N)*	*Percent*	*(N)*	*Percent*	*(N)*	*Percent*	*(N)*
Accosted in parking lot and beaten	91.8	(190)	3.4	(7)	3.8	(8)	0.0	(0)	1.0	(2)
Meeting in bar and taken to deserted road	40.5	(83)	27.8	(57)	9.3	(19)	12.2	(25)	10.2	(21)
Dating in man's apartment	18.8	(37)	20.8	(41)	15.7	(31)	23.4	(46)	21.3	(42)
Man entered through window with knife	80.3	(163)	9.4	(19)	3.9	(8)	3.0	(6)	3.4	(7)
Telephone repairman who slaps woman	78.2	(158)	13.9	(28)	4.0	(8)	1.5	(3)	2.5	(5)
Woman's boss after working late	48.8	(99)	19.7	(40)	12.8	(26)	11.3	(23)	7.4	(15)
Date with respected bachelor	20.3	(41)	17.8	(36)	17.3	(35)	19.3	(39)	25.2	(51)
Total	54.3	(771)	16.1	(228)	9.5	(135)	10.0	(142)	10.1	(143)

[a] The sum of *N* for each row is not always equal to 208, because some respondents failed to answer some questions. Of a possible total of 1456, 1419 valid responses were obtained.

[b] Percentages are always based on the row total.

SOURCE: Reprinted from Susan H. Klemmack and David L. Klemmack, "The Social Definition of Rape," in Marcia J. Walker and Stanley L. Brodsky, eds., *Sexual Assault: The Victim and the Rapist*, Heath (Lexington Books), Toronto, 1976, p. 141. The seven selected situations are described in detail in the source.

definition. The rape situation itself proves to have a very elusive definition, heavily dependent upon how the victim perceives the situation. However, rape is like murder and assault in that many rapes involve people between or among whom a previous social relationship exists.

Robbery

Unlike other violent crimes, robbery almost always occurs between strangers. It is defined as follows:

> The taking or attempting to take anything of value from the care, custody, or control of a person or persons by force or threat of force or violence and/or by putting the victim in fear.[26]

A crime of high visibility that combines force and theft, robbery involves direct, face-to-face confrontation between offender and victim. In this confrontation there is no guile, deceit, or trickery: the victims are well aware that they are being robbed.[27] The basic definition of robbery has remained unchanged for many centuries.

In recent years, the rate of robbery reported to the police has shown substantial increases. It now stands at 250.6 per 100,000 persons, its all-time high.

Although robbery has a picturesque history—famous robbers such as Robin Hood, Jesse James, Bonnie and Clyde Barrow, and Willie Sutton have delighted our imaginations—great robberies are in fact rare. Bank robbery, although sensational, accounts for only about 1 percent of the total reported robberies. Nearly half of the reported robberies take place on the streets (see Box 5) or highways. One-fourth occur in commercial establishments, gasoline or service stations, and convenience stores. The remaining robberies take place in residences or other locations. The average loss for reported robberies was placed at $665 in 1981.[28]

In the societal reaction to robbery it is the force involved, rather than the theft itself, that has become the focus of public concern. Much of the fear of "crime in the streets" is really fear of violence inflicted by strangers. In that robbery rates have shown enormous increases throughout the past two decades, these fears have some basis in fact. Yet there are some ironies in this fear of robbery. For one thing, the monetary loss is typically small. Far more is lost through other theft crimes such as burglary, motor vehicle theft, and various forms of "white-collar" theft. For another, in the aggregate the amount of violence and death inflicted by relatives, acquaintances, and friends exceeds that inflicted by robbers.

Other Violent Crimes

Person-to-person violence does not end with the four major crimes discussed above. In particular, in recent years a great deal of attention has been given to violence in families. When it falls short of murder, family violence does not usually find its way into the picture of crime. Although offenses against the family and children have long been included as Part II offenses, the number of crimes of this nature reported to police is thought by some to represent only a small part of

Box 5: A Perspective on Street Robbery (Mugging)

Ask virtually any American city-dweller today what crime he most fears, and feels he is most apt to be the victim of some day; in all likelihood he will answer: a mugging.

Yet vaster and far more dreadful crimes exist all around him: the savage acts and relentless extortions of Mafia "families" seeking and maintaining control over businesses, unions, and even political clubs; the white-collar crimes, so destructive of the moral premises on which our society is built, that are daily practiced by businessmen, politicians, and office employees; the widespread trafficking in heroin by dealers and pushers, actively aided by some of the very police assigned to narcotics control; and the bombing, arson, sniping, and other revolutionary acts by means of which urban guerrillas are turning parts of our major cities into battlefields.

But despite the magnitude and seriousness of these forms of crime, what most alarms us and most gravely damages our faith in our society is the ever-present threat of some sudden, unpredictable, savage assault upon our own body by a stranger—a faceless, nameless, fleet-footed figure who leaps from the shadows, strikes at us with his fists, an iron pipe, or a switchblade knife, and then vanishes into an alley with our wallet or purse, leaving us broken and bleeding on the sidewalk. Headlines are made by riots, rapes, dope-smuggling, embezzlement, and kidnapping, while the mugging—moronically simple in execution and trifling in yield—is relegated to inside pages or ignored altogether; yet it is this, rather than the more complex and newsworthy crimes, that is responsible for the flight of millions of Americans to the suburbs, the nightly self-imprisonment of other millions behind locked doors and barred windows, and the mounting attacks of law-and-order advocates upon constitutionally guaranteed rights that are fundamental to our concept of democracy.

SOURCE

Morton Hunt, *The Mugging,* Atheneum, New York, 1972, prologue, p. vii.

---

those that are committed. The "discovery" of child abuse awaited the realization by pediatric radiologists during the 1950s that children's injuries such as bone fractures were often the result of parental "misconduct and deliberate injury."[29] Even more recently, abuse of spouses has come to the forefront of public awareness; and two authors have gone so far as to label the family a "cradle of violence."[30] While their position may be overstated, we have already seen that much violence does occur within the family.

As with rape, the criminal nature and extent of family violence depend on how particular situations are defined. Again, situational definitions can be very subjective. In spouse and child abuse, whether a situation is considered "violent" by the participants may be even more influenced by understandings built up through close relationships over a period of years. In one national survey, 2143 husbands and wives were asked by Richard Gelles whether they had engaged in one or more of eight violent acts. Of the respondents, 16 percent had been involved in one of the acts in the previous year. In the entire length of marriage, 28 percent had been involved in one of the acts. It should be noted that although Gelles described the eight acts as "violent," it is questionable whether the parties themselves always did. Which of these acts should be regarded as "criminal" is also questionable. To claim that 28 percent of American families have been involved in the course of marital life in criminally violent acts seems extreme.

Our overview of person-to-person violent crimes would be incomplete without some mention of crimes which occur less frequently but can be very serious: kidnapping for ransom, skyjacking, and arson. Each of these crimes involves property theft or damage as well as personal injury. The first two are uniquely twentieth-century crimes: kidnapping was socially defined as a crime during the 1930s, and skyjacking during the 1960s.[31] Despite its implications for property, arson is considered a crime of personal violence, since the potential for injury is always present. Although arson is older in social definition than kidnapping or skyjacking, recent refinements in techniques used to determine whether arson is the cause of fire have led the FBI to classify it as a Part I rather than a Part II offense, beginning in 1980.

To sum up, although the major crimes of interpersonal violence—especially murder, assault, and robbery—have long been defined as criminal acts, the nature of interpersonal violence continues to undergo redefinition. In particular, rape has come to be seen as a personal rather than a property crime, and its definition is becoming much broader in scope. Crimes of family violence, especially spouse and child abuse, are emerging into public consciousness and being redefined legally. Although they occur less frequently, kidnapping and skyjacking have emerged as twentieth-century crimes. Most recently, the definition of arson as a Part I offense means that it will receive considerably more attention as a serious crime. In other words, even though the criminal laws designed to regulate person-to-person violence have long been established, old laws are being reformulated and new ones created in the attempt to respond to changing social conditions.

Having examined the person-to-person acts of violence that are defined as crimes, we can now take a look at the people who are involved in violent crimes. Our interest is in their social characteristics. Let's consider offenders first, and then victims.

VIOLENT OFFENDERS

Characteristics of Violent Offenders

Large though the number may appear, the police make approximately 1 million arrests each year for the person-to-person violent crimes outlined above. About half of these arrests are for the four major crimes: murder, aggravated assault, rape, and robbery. The other half are for the remaining violent offenses, especially other assaults, family offenses, and arson. In addition, there are over 175,000 arrests for carrying and possessing weapons. In order to obtain information about offenders, police classify arrests by sex, age, and race of the persons arrested. Recognizing the limitations and problems of such data, criminologists have undertaken further studies based on arrested offenders in order to provide a more accurate and complete profile of the typical violent offender. In this section we shall take a look at the demographic profile of the offender as seen in arrest patterns and then discuss the criminological studies of offenders' "careers."

Sex

Starting with breakdowns of arrested offenders in the Uniform Crime Reports, we readily see that the typical violent offender is male.[32] Although males make up only 49 percent of the population, they account for more than 85 percent of arrests

Offense	Sex	Age			Race	
	Male	Under 18	Under 21	Under 23	Black	All others[a]
Criminal homicide	87	9	24	43	49	1
Forcible rape	99	15	31	52	48	2
Robbery	93	29	51	71	60	1
Aggravated assault	87	14	28	47	37	1
Other assaults	86	17	31	50	33	2
Arson	89	42	55	67	21	1
Offenses against family and children	89	5	15	33	36	1
Weapons, carrying, possessing, etc.	93	15	31	50	37	1
Percent of group in total population		(13–17)[b]	(13–20)[b]	(13–24)[b]		
	49	9	15	23	12	2

[a] Excluding whites and blacks but including Indians, Chinese, Japanese, and "all other."

[b] Those age 12 and under have been omitted from this calculation because the percentage of arrests for this age group is extremely low.

SOURCE: Figures calculated from: Federal Bureau of Investigation (FBI), *Uniform Crime Reports—1981,* Government Printing Office, Washington, D.C., 1982, sec. IV.

for each of the violent crimes listed in Table 8. When arrests of males are compared with arrests of females for each of the major crimes, the results are as follows:

> Robbery: 12 males for every female
> Criminal homicide: 6 males for every female
> Aggravated assault: 6 males for every female

Since rape usually involves a male offender and a female victim, virtually all those arrested for forcible rape are male. The few females arrested for this crime are often accessories to rapes being committed by males upon other females.

These male-to-female arrest ratios for violent crimes have remained virtually the same for the past two decades, despite marked changes in the role of females in American society. That the arrest ratios have remained so distinctly weighted on the side of males suggests either that men are by nature more violent or that cultural or environmental factors tend to keep men in violent crime and women out of it. While both views have their adherents, it is also possible that both are correct.

Age

Aside from being usually male, the arrested violent offender is usually young. Although they make up only 9 percent of the American population, 13- to 17-year-olds account for 48 percent of those arrested for arson; 34 percent of those arrested for robbery; and over 15 percent of those arrested for forcible rape, aggravated assault, other assaults, and weapons offenses. When the under-25 age group is examined, it can be seen that well over half of those arrested for virtually every violent crime fall into this category. Yet people in the age group 13–24 are only 23 percent of the total population. (See Table 8.) In the arrest patterns for crimes and age groups, a phenomenon known as the "age of maximum criminality" stands out. Once the highest number of arrests is reached, the numbers of arrests decline for each subsequent age group. Arrests for violent crimes peak at relatively young ages. For robbery, the peak age is 18; for forcible rape, 20; for assault and murder, 21. Arrests for offenses against family and children peak in the middle years of the life cycle.[33]

Race

The third factor in arrests for violent crime is race. In comparison with their numbers in the American population, blacks are far overrepresented in arrests for violent crimes. Although blacks make up 12 percent of the population, 60 percent of those arrested for robbery, 49 percent of those arrested for criminal homicide, 48 percent of those arrested for rape, and (with the exception of arson) more than 30 percent of all those arrested for other violent crimes are black. By comparison, the percentage of arrests for offenders of "all other" races is roughly comparable to the percentage of these other groups in the total population. (See Table 8.)

Sex, age, and race

A few studies based on officially recorded police contacts have examined the cumulative impact of sex, age, and race. Probably the most extensive and best known of these was conducted by Marvin Wolfgang and his associates, who tracked a sample of 10,000 boys in Philadelphia from ages 10 through 18.[34] (Girls were excluded because of their low delinquency rates.) Of the 10,000 boys, no less than 3475 had come to police attention as delinquents, and in all they had committed 10,214 delinquent acts.[35]

Analyzing the comprehensive data, Wolfgang et al. found distinct racial differences in patterns of delinquency. To begin with, 50 percent of the nonwhites, as opposed to 29 percent of the whites, were delinquent. Moreover, 14 percent of the nonwhites, as opposed to 3 percent of the whites, were "chronically delinquent," i.e., had committed five or more offenses during this period of their lives. Nonwhites became delinquent at a much younger age and were more likely to have committed a violent crime at any age.[36] For specific violent offenses, rates for nonwhites were substantially higher than those for whites: for robbery, the difference was 21 times; for aggravated assault, it was 11 times.[37]

Sharp though the racial differences in arrest rates may be, it is unfair to conclude that blacks are inherently more criminal or violent than whites. To begin with, there is some overlap with the age factor. The nonwhite population is somewhat younger than the white population: 24 percent of nonwhites, as opposed to 20 percent of whites, are in the age group 14–24, which is prone to violent crime. Second, patterns of housing segregation have had the effect of keeping a large proportion of blacks in inner-city, high-crime urban areas. Third, throughout the 1970s arrest rates of blacks for murder showed declines while those of whites were on the increase.[38] Fourth, it may well be that blacks are more likely than whites to be arrested: a number of studies relying on self-reports of delinquent or criminal behavior show smaller racial differences in crime rates than studies utilizing arrest statistics.[39] Finally, blacks are more likely to fall into groups of lower socioeconomic status, which have higher rates of arrest.

Socioeconomic status

While the FBI classifies arrests by sex, age, and race, investigators using more focused data drawn from smaller samples have attempted to relate arrests and convictions to other social factors. Most important among these factors has been socioeconomic status (SES), which is reflected in measures such as type of occupation, median years of school completed, and median income. Some of these investigators have argued that violent offenders are far more likely to come from lower-SES groups than from middle- or upper-SES groups.

Data based on arrested offenders support the argument that those of lower SES are more likely to come from poor than from middle-class neighborhoods.[40] Wolfgang's study found that assault and robbery rates were consistently higher for lower-SES males, regardless of their race.[41] It might also be added that, since convictions are more likely for violent crimes, prisons and jails are filled with people who rank low on various measures of SES.[42]

Repeaters: The Problem of Prediction

Many people think that society would be safer if violent offenders were simply rounded up and put in prison or out on some remote island. This simple solution to the problem of crime assumes (1) that there are a limited number of violent offenders who can be easily identified, (2) that violent offenders will regularly repeat their behavior, and (3) that previously nonviolent people will not become violent. Each of these assumptions is debatable.

In support of the "lock them up and throw the key away" argument, it can be said that substantial percentages of alleged offenders arrested for homicide and assault have previous records of arrest. In fact, well over 50 percent of alleged offenders appear to have had previous contact with the law. However, many of these previous contacts or arrests are not for violent crimes but rather for property or social-order crimes. It might also be added that a large proportion of victims of homicide and assault also have arrest records, although the percentage of victims with previous arrest records is somewhat less than that of offenders with previous arrest records.[43]

It has also been found that relatively small numbers of "chronic offenders," those committing five or more offenses, can commit large numbers of criminal or delinquent acts. In a cohort study which examined all males born in Philadelphia in 1945 for their involvement with crime, it was found that "chronic offenders" included only 18 percent of the delinquents but accounted for 52 percent of the total delinquencies committed. Furthermore, the mean "seriousness" score, an indicator of the extent to which violence was involved, was 127.45 for the chronic offenders as opposed to 118.83 for other, less frequent repeat offenders and 80.65 for one-time offenders.[44] Similarly, in another cohort study of those born in Columbus, Ohio, in the years 1956–1960, "chronic offenders" included 34 percent of the delinquents but accounted for 44.8 percent of the serious or major crimes against the person committed by the total group.[45]

Social factors do predict to some extent which offenders will become chronic. The most clear are sex and age. Males are far more likely than females to become chronic delinquents; and the general rule for age is the lower the age of first police contact, the greater the number of offenses and the more serious the offenses. Lower-SES boys are more likely to become chronic delinquents, but the evidence on race is unclear. In the Philadelphia study, nonwhites were considerably more likely to be chronic offenders; but in the Columbus study, equal proportions of black and white offenders were found in the "chronic" category or among those committing violent offenses.

When we shift our focus from chronic offenders to offenders arrested for violence, it is important to note that violent offenders are relatively unlikely to repeat their violence. In the Columbus study, which focused on violent juvenile offenders, it was found that over four-fifths were arrested only once on a charge of violence; only 3.8 percent were arrested on charges of violence on three or more occasions. This small group accounted for a small percent (10.4) of the arrests for violent crimes. In a study of arrested adults that paralleled the study of juveniles in Columbus, it was found that over half of all those arrested for violent crimes during the year 1973 had no record of previous felony conviction and 82 percent had no record of previous violent felony conviction.[46]

One thing that has been learned from these studies is that predicting exactly which offenders will repeat violent criminal behavior is virtually impossible. As the Columbus study of violent juvenile offenders concluded: "If Columbus has a mutant breed of young monsters who are repetitively and wantonly violent, they do not make their appearance in our statistics."[47] Generally, although there is a fair likelihood of rearrest for property crime, the probability of rearrest for violent crime is about four in ten.[48] One in-depth study drew the following conclusion:

> The prediction of violent behavior is difficult under the best of circumstances. It becomes more so when powerful social contingencies pull and push the clinician now in one direction, then in another.[49]

The study of adult violent offenders in Columbus found that patterns of violent crime are not sufficiently predictable and recurrent to justify a policy of severe sentences: in fact, a five-year sentence for each of the convicted felons (which would increase prison commitments by 500 or 600 percent) would have prevented only 3.6 percent of the reported crimes for which convictions would have been obtained.[50]

Robbery is somewhat different from other violent crimes; there are some offenders who pursue robbery as if it were an occupation. Indeed, some are true "professionals" in that they have a long-term, deep-seated commitment to robbery, utilize much skill and planning, and work in groups in which different members assume particular roles.[51] Other recidivist robbers "graduate" into robbery from motor vehicle theft and burglary because robbery requires little preparation and offers much freedom and unlimited potential targets. Recidivist robbers can commit large numbers of offenses: in one study, 49 offenders reported a total of 10,500 crimes (including a variety of types)—an average of 20 per year

An opportunistic robbery. A 67-year-old drifter is beaten and robbed of $31
near downtown Dallas, Texas.   (WIDE WORLD PHOTOS)

during the times they were out on the streets. On the other hand, their rate of
serious crimes per month dropped from 3.2 when they were juveniles to 1.5 as
young adults and to 0.6 for the adult period of their lives.[52]

However, not all robbers are heavily or continually involved in robbery.
Some offenders engage in robbery intermittently and can be regarded as "opportunistic." The opportunist robber robs less frequently and uses little careful
planning, often pursuing unprotected vulnerable victims. The monetary gains are
often minimal, and weapons are typically not used. In addition to opportunists,
there may also be robbers who are drug addicts or alcoholics. Addict robbers have
a high commitment to theft as a means of getting money to support their addiction;
alcoholic robbers engage in robbery on an irregular, sporadic basis.[53]

With robbery, as with other types of violent crime, we have no way to
predict who the offenders will be or which ones will be recidivists. In the case of
robbery, the arrested offender is more likely to be male, young, black, and poor.
Yet the professional robber, who is more likely to be white, commits a substantially larger number of offenses involving larger amounts of money, if self-reported

"confessions" are to be believed.[54] Moreover, while it is true that some offenders graduate from petty crime into robbery, the much larger proportion of offenders do not.

To sum up briefly, the irrational nature of violent crime is again evident in our analysis of the offender. We can state that arrested violent offenders are generally more likely to be male, in their early twenties, black, and poor. However, of the total numbers of people in these social categories, only a small proportion ever commit a serious violent crime. Most of those who commit the less serious property crimes do not "graduate" into violent crime. With the exception of professional robbers, comparatively few of those who are arrested for violent crime repeat their criminally violent behavior.

That the majority of delinquents and criminals reduce the extent of their criminal behavior as they become older points to a significant "maturing" out of crime. Violent crime is a young person's activity. By definition, to undertake it one must have physical strength or ability, and the nerve to use a gun. Indeed, one of the most hopeful aspects of the picture of crime is that substantial numbers of those involved in crime seem to "get over it." After age 21, arrest rates for nearly all the violent crimes drop for the remainder of the life cycle. According to self-confessions, rates drop as age increases, even for recidivist robbers. This maturing out of criminal behavior is a most optimistic part of the picture, one that is often overlooked by professional criminologists.[55]

VICTIMS OF VIOLENCE

To extend our perspective on person-to-person violent crime, we also need to study the victim. Fortunately, data gathered in the nationwide victim surveys conducted in the late 1970s enable us to examine the social characteristics of the victim, just as we examined those of the offender.

Surveys of crime victims, as well as other studies, allow us to get a perspective on how the often-forgotten victim fits into the picture of crime. With regard to person-to-person violent crime, several interesting conclusions have emerged: (1) victims come from social groups remarkably similar to those of offenders; (2) the age and sex groups most likely *not* to report crimes to the police are the ones most likely to be victimized; and (3) some violent crimes may be "victim-precipitated." Let us examine each of these conclusions in greater detail. Our focus is on the four major violent crimes, since most of the victimization studies have dealt primarily with them.

Characteristics of Victims

Sex

That victims of violent person-to-person crimes come from social groups remarkably similar to those of offenders is a conclusion that readily emerges from an examination of victim surveys and Uniform Crime Reports data.[56] Let us begin with sex. Generally, two-thirds of those victimized by person-to-person crimes are male. For criminal homicide, the proportion rises to more than three-fourths.

Looking at the number of male victims compared with the number of female victims, we find the following ratios:

Murder: 3.4 males for every female
Robbery: 2.2 males for every female
Assault: 2.0 males for every female

Because of its traditionally narrow definition, forcible rape nearly always has a female victim.

Age

As with the age of maximum criminality for offenders, there is an age of maximum victimization. Once that age has been reached, victimization rates drop for subsequent age groups. Like the age for offending, the age of maximum victimization comes early in the life cycle. For the crimes we are considering, it is as follows:

Murder: 25–29
Assault: 20–24
Robbery: 20–24
Rape and attempted rape: 16–19[57]

It is interesting to note that murder, the most serious of the offenses, has the highest maximum victimization age. Nevertheless, violent crime victimization still peaks early in the life cycle. Recent concern for crimes against the elderly should not obscure the fact that it is young people who are disproportionately the victims of crime.[58]

Race and socioeconomic status

Race and socioeconomic status are important characteristics of crime victims. The extent to which black people are victimized by crime was dramatically illustrated in a special issue of *Ebony* magazine.[59] Perhaps the most telling figure is that more blacks were murdered in the United States in 1977 (5734) than died in the entire nine years of the Vietnamese war (5711, or 634 per year). As was mentioned earlier, homicide is "*the leading cause* of death of inner city Black males 15 to 44."[60] One extensive analysis of the medical problems of the victims of violent assault shows that blacks are more likely to be the victims of violent crimes, especially serious ones, and more likely to require overnight hospitalization because of injury suffered in crime.[61] In assessing the overall picture, the editors of *Ebony* put it as follows:

When we started work on this special issue, we knew that Black on Black crime was a critical problem. What we did not know—primarily because no one had presented an up-to-date picture—was the awesome and tragic dimension of the problem. And as we dug beneath the surface and processed statistics and reports from experts and victims, we found ourselves reeling with shock and consternation.[62]

Ebony's concern is also reflected in the statistics derived from crime victimization surveys and the Uniform Crime Reports. When victimization rates are computed separately by race, the ratios of black to white victims are as follows:[63]

Murder: 8.9 to 1
Robbery: 1.9 to 1
Rape and attempted rape: 1 to 1
Assault: 0.9 to 1

In other words, for the most serious crime, murder, the victimization rate for blacks is nearly nine times as high as that for whites. On the other hand, victimization rates for rape and assault are about the same. Robbery is in between, with rates of victimization for blacks being close to double those for whites.

Surveys have also found that the chances of victimization are related to socioeconomic status, especially when status is measured by family income. People who are members of families having incomes of less than $3000 per year are especially likely to be victimized by rape and attempted rape, robbery, and assault. The following figures give some idea of the differences. Members of white families with incomes under $3000 per year are victimized by rape nearly 5 times as frequently as those with incomes exceeding $25,000. For robbery, the difference is 1.7 times. For assault, the difference is about 2 times. At any income level, black families experience higher rates of victimization for robbery than white families do.[64]

The factors of race and income are independent of each other. In other words, for both blacks and whites, family income makes a considerable difference in victimization rates. In fact, family income is probably a more important factor than race in determining the probability of becoming a crime victim. However, a far larger proportion of black households than white households fall into the lower-income category. The net result is the differences in black and white victimization rates discussed above.

To sum up, although not as sharply drawn, the demographic profile of the victim is remarkably similar to that of the offender. For violent person-to-person crimes, both groups show overrepresentation of males, young people, blacks, and the poor. Age is somewhat of an exception in that the age of the typical victim, although still young, is slightly higher than that of the typical offender. Nevertheless, with the exception of males, it can be said that violent person-to-person crimes involve the groups with least power in American society.

Crime Reporting by Victims

The second major issue with which victimization surveys have dealt is the reporting of crime, specifically, *why* crimes are reported and *who* reports them. Concern about crime reporting dates back to the NORC survey conducted by the President's Crime Commission in the middle 1960s, when it was concluded that the major reason for the dramatic differences between crimes reported in victim surveys and the official statistics on crime was the failure of citizens to report offenses.[65]

Because of its seriousness and the existence of the victim's body, there is good reason to think that murder is the most frequently reported major crime. If we look at the percent of unreported crime for each of the other major offenses, the most recent panel survey by LEAA shows the following percentages of unreported crime:

Assault: 54 percent unreported
Rape and attempted rape: 48 percent unreported
Robbery: 42 percent unreported[66]

More to the point than *type* of offense, close analysis of the data shows that the key factor in reporting of crime by citizens is the *seriousness* of the offense. Seriousness is a complex factor to evaluate; but it has at least four dimensions: (1) the value of stolen or damaged property, (2) the extent of personal injury, (3) the use of a weapon which threatens bodily harm, and (4) the extent to which the crime violates the victim's feeling of personal security. The rule is, "The greater the loss, harm, threat or insecurity generated by an event, the more likely it is to be reported to the police."[67]

When asked why offenses were not reported to the police, victims gave two kinds of reasons. One, the perception that "nothing could be done," was an important reason for not reporting rape and robbery. The other, the victim's belief that the matter was "private" or "not important enough," was cited as one of the important reasons for not reporting rape, robbery, and assault (see Table 9). While the first reason may reflect low expectations for the police and the criminal justice system, the other raises the question whether some criminal acts deemed serious under the law are actually judged as serious by those involved in them.

When broken down by offense, sex, age, race, and SES, the data suggest that age is the most important factor in reporting or not reporting crime. Younger people are less likely to report crimes than older people are. There are also sex differences: males are somewhat less likely than females to report. Blacks and whites at various income levels are about equally likely to report crimes involving

TABLE 9. Two Reasons Most Frequently Given for Not Reporting Crimes to Police, and Percent of Respondents Giving Them, by Type of Victimization

Type of victimization[a]	Reasons for not reporting	Percent of respondents
Rape	"It was a private matter."	27
	"Nothing could be done."	13
Robbery	"Victimization was not important enough."	20
	"Nothing could be done."	18
Assault	"It was a private matter."	32
	"Victimization was not important enough."	29

[a] The category "other" is excluded.

SOURCE: Data from: Timothy J. Flanagan, David J. von Alstyne, and Michael R. Gottfredson, *Sourcebook of Criminal Justice Statistics—1981*, Government Printing Office, Washington, D.C., 1981, pp. 242–243.

personal victimizations.[68] It is interesting to note that for age as well as sex, there are sharp differences between crime victimization and reporting. The groups least likely to be victimized are the ones which are most likely to report their victimization.

Resemblance between Victims and Offenders and Victim-Precipitation

The final issue about crime victims concerns the victim's involvement in the crime. In discussing offenders and victims separately, the impression is that offenders are active doers while victims are passive recipients of criminal acts. However, for violent person-to-person crime the picture of the active offender and passive victim is often not accurate. First of all, offenders and victims in particular cases are often alike in terms of their social characteristics. Second, many are involved in some kind of previous relationship. Finally, in some violent crimes it is even appropriate to call the criminal act "victim-precipitated." Each of these points needs to be considered further.

The *social resemblance* between offenders and victims of violent crime is striking. According to the Uniform Crime Reports data for "single victim–single offender" criminal homicides in 1978, 88 percent of whites were killed by other whites and 95 percent of blacks by other blacks. Similarly, 82 percent of male victims were killed by other males; but, in an exception to the general pattern, only 9 percent of females were killed by other females.[69] Other, more detailed examinations of homicide have painted a similar picture: roughly nine out of ten homicides involve people of the same race; roughly two out of three involve people of the same sex. Although data on age are affected by the way age categories are broken down, the typical murder involves a person in the twenties killing another only slightly older.[70]

In extending analysis of offenders and victims to aggravated assault, it has been found that the proportions of offenders and victims of the same social category are similar to those in criminal homicide.[71] Ninety percent of rapes also involve two people of the same race.[72] However, there are some age differences among the people involved in rape: on the average, offenders are four to five years older than their victims.[73]

Robbery, the "stranger crime," stands out in that, of all the violent crimes, it is most likely to bring people of different social categories into contact with each other. It is very likely to be interracial: of the armed robberies in 17 American cities, 47 percent involved black offenders and white victims. Similarly, 44 percent of unarmed robberies were of this type.[74] Robbery is also considerably more likely to find male offenders and female victims and younger offenders and older victims.[75]

Not only do victims and offenders in serious person-to-person violent crimes (especially homicide, forcible rape, and assault) have similar social characteristics; as we have already seen, they are also often involved in a *previous interactive relationship*. A further point needs to be made here: the "victim" may have had direct involvement and complicity in the sequence of actions that led to the crime. As Stephen Schafer puts it:

> Doer and sufferer often appear in crime in a close interpersonal relationship where the victim may be one of the determinants of the criminal action.[76]

In their study of murderers, Victoria Swigert and Ronald Farrell found that in most murders classified as "stranger murders" there was some interaction before the killing. Typically, the interaction was an

> argumentative encounter in a public place. Discussions of politics, religion, and similar topics in bars and pool rooms occasionally resulted in the death of one of the parties.[77]

Finally, in some cases, the interaction between offender and victim is so involved that the crime can best be classified as *victim-precipitated*. For homicide, the victim may have been "the first in the homicide drama to use physical force directed against his subsequent slayer."[78] No less than one out of every four Philadelphia murders studied by Wolfgang was victim-precipitated. In other studies, the figure has been put at 38 percent in Chicago.[79] The national commission on violence surveying data in 17 American cities found victim-precipitation in 22 percent of the 668 cleared murders it analyzed.[80]

Victim-precipitation also characterizes other person-to-person violent crimes. In an extensive study of rape, Amir attempted to estimate the percentage of victim-precipitated rapes. To begin with, he noted that most rapes were planned and typically occurred at the residence of one of the participants. Forty-eight percent of the victims were known to the offender. In these cases, he reported, the women generally had a reputation for being "loose" or were vulnerable because of their age. Over half of the rape victims displayed only submissive behavior; by comparison, 27 percent of the victims resisted the offender, and 18 percent put up a strong fight. Curiously, "the closer the relationship was between the victim and offender, the greater was the use of physical force against the victim." Of the rapes studied, Amir classified nearly one in five as "victim-precipitated," in which "the victim enters vulnerable situations charged with sexuality."[81]

However, Amir's application of victim-precipitation to rape has been challenged. As was noted earlier, of all the crimes of interpersonal violence, rape is most heavily dependent on the subjective definition of the parties in the situation. It can be argued that Amir's definition of the situation is overinfluenced by traditional stereotypes that men have of women:

> Thus, hitchhiking and walking alone at night in a rough neighborhood may be considered behavior encouraging a sexual attack. This view of what a *man* can assume to be a sexual invitation is unreasonable. . . . In its failure to accord any considerations to the woman victim's intentions, victim precipitation becomes nothing more than a male view of the circumstances leading up to the incident.[82]

In that definitions of crime are dependent on situations, victim-precipitation may prove to be a concept which, although suggestive, is very difficult to quantify and apply to the study of violent crimes other than homicide.

Some writers have attempted to extend the idea of victim-precipitation to assault and robbery. Using national data, Curtis claims that 14 percent of cleared aggravated assaults and 21 percent of the noncleared aggravated assaults were victim-precipitated. He even goes so far as to regard a portion of armed robberies as victim-precipitated; for example, old people who are out alone at night, truck drivers who want a share of the goods that will be stolen, and bank managers who want to cover their embezzlements.[83] Similarly, Normandeau estimates that 11 percent of the robberies he studied were victim-precipitated in the broad sense that victims used careless or "casual money-handling habits." Another 12 percent of the victims were more or less inebriated when the offense occurred.[84]

Although difficult to apply to crimes other than murder, the concept of victim-precipitation does suggest that some of the most violent crime is tied into the web of everyday social life. Murderers do not have a "typical psychological profile."[85] Most often they know their victims, perhaps even live with them, and possibly in one of four cases could have been the victim. Similarly, rape, assault, and robbery may in part be influenced not only by the offender's motivation but also by the attitude of the victim toward the offender and by the nature of the situation in which offender and victim find themselves.

That common crimes are part of the web of everyday life leads us to conclude that they are conditions or incidents which "surface," or come to public attention. For this reason, an analysis which counts only numbers of crimes, offenders, and victims—whether by official reports or victim surveys—can lead to mistaken impressions which make it difficult to appreciate the extent and trend of crime in the United States today. Hence, this descriptive overview of person-to-person violent crime needs to go beyond violent offenders and victims of violence to examine the social context of violent crime.

SOCIAL CONTEXTS OF VIOLENCE

Social context is a very important part of our analysis of crime. In focusing on it, we are calling attention to the link between situations and crimes. The argument here is that there are certain kinds of situations which bring offenders and victims who are "suitable targets" together without guardians or "policing agents" to prevent criminal acts from occurring.[86] Some clues to the important differences in situations are provided by examining differences in crime rates. In violent crime, the city, cultural values, and guns can be seen as important aspects of the social context. In addition, there are also certain dynamic aspects to the social context.

The City

Urban areas report much higher rates of violent crime than suburban or rural areas do. (See Table 10.) For urban areas, rates show an almost consistent increase as one goes from cities with populations of less than 10,000 to cities with populations of more than 1 million. Overall rates of violent crime are nearly 6 times higher in the larger cities than in the small ones. For robbery—the most distinctly urban crime in that it typically involves strangers—the difference is *20 times*. Although smaller, there are similar substantial differences for each major violent crime. Suburban areas resemble medium-sized cities; and rural areas show lower rates than urban areas of any size. Sharp rural-urban differences are also apparent in the findings of the LEAA victimization surveys.[87]

Not only do larger cities show higher rates of violent crime; but within any city, certain neighborhoods have dramatically higher rates than others. Almost

TABLE 10. City Size and Crime Rates: Overall Violent Crime, Murder, Forcible Rape, Robbery, and Aggravated Assault

City size	Number of cities	Crime rates				
		Overall violent	Murder	Forcible rape	Robbery	Aggravated assault
1,000,000+	5	1726.6	27.8	62.2	1108.8	527.8
500,000–999,999	18	1211.1	20.2	76.2	687.4	427.2
250,000–499,999	32	1286.4	20.9	84.5	640.6	540.3
100,000–249,999	112	826.4	13.1	56.4	349.6	407.3
50,000–99,999	272	583.7	7.4	37.9	228.0	310.4
25,000–49,999	594	451.9	5.7	29.0	154.8	262.5
10,000–24,999	1500	342.3	4.5	20.1	92.5	225.3
−10,000	5670	291.0	4.0	16.4	54.5	216.0
Suburban areas	1104	392.2	7.3	31.7	112.0	241.1
Rural areas	2626	179.4	7.0	15.7	22.1	134.6

SOURCE: Federal Bureau of Investigation (FBI), *Uniform Crime Reports—1981*, Government Printing Office, Washington, D.C., 1982, pp. 144–145.

invariably, these neighborhoods are also characterized by poverty, poor education, high truancy, unemployment, low per capita income, bad health, overpopulation, and inadequate housing. Much addiction to alcohol and narcotics is also present. Transiency is common. In such "slums" or "ghettos" it can readily be seen that "poverty, illness, injustice, idleness, ignorance, human misery and crime go together."[88] The sheer frustration of living often produces large numbers of highly motivated offenders and the existence of relatively powerless people who become easy targets. Moreover, the high transiency means that there is a never-ending succession of motivated offenders and suitable targets.

Research on the "slum" as a social unit has been a concern of the ecological school of criminology. Perhaps the most famous of the ecological studies was conducted by Clifford Shaw and Henry McKay at the University of Chicago in 1942. They found indices measuring poverty in residential zones in 20 cities to be highly correlated with official crime rates. A greater number of families dependent upon state aid and higher rates of infant mortality, tuberculosis, and mental disorder were also associated with the higher crime rates.[89] Subsequent studies not only have confirmed this picture but have also found that these characteristics will persist in neighborhoods over long periods of time. Even though a neighborhood may sustain population changes, the grouping of the social indicators and the crime rate will remain quite constant.[90]

Cultural Values

A second important aspect of the social context of crime is the cultural values people hold. On one level, these values may influence people's interpretation of situations as criminal or noncriminal and their decisions as to whether matters should be kept private or reported to police. On another level, cultural values may permit, tolerate, approve, or even foster interactions that are defined by the law as criminal. In this latter sense the cultural values can be called "criminogenic."

Many criminologists have argued that there are subcultures of violence which are conducive to high crime rates in certain localities or among certain groups. One worldwide survey showed that there are a number of communities, regions, tribes, and subcultures in which violence is not only respected but also demanded as people respond to disputes in which honor is involved.[91] Closer to home, in Europe and America dueling was a means of resolving disputes between "gentlemen" well into the nineteenth century. Today, there is the cultural value of "machismo," or compulsive masculinity, in which males are encouraged to express themselves through athletics, fighting, drinking, being competitive, and controlling females. In his study of homicides in Philadelphia, Wolfgang commented upon the power of this value:

> Quick resort to physical combat as a measure of daring, courage, or defense of status appears to be a cultural expression, especially for lower socio-economic class males of both races. When such a culture norm response is elicited from an individual engaged in social interplay with others who harbor the same response mechanism, physical assaults, altercations, and violent domestic quarrels that result in homicide are likely to be common.[92]

The influence of cultural values on crime rates has also been utilized to explain the considerably higher rates of violent crime in the southern and western regions of the United States. While these regional differences are not as sharp today as in the past, recent Uniform Crime Reports rates show that they continue to persist. (See Table 11.) This pattern has led some criminologists to argue that there is a regional culture of violence which originated in southern cultural traditions and later spread to the western states. In support of this argument, it is noteworthy that the south was typically a frontier society, and one in which extreme class differences could be maintained only by violence. Hence, southern values and culture readily accepted a militaristic tradition, carrying of guns and knives, the street duel, mob lynching, and lax law enforcement.[93] An important exception to the southern influence on violent crime rates is robbery, the "stranger crime," which is much higher in the more urbanized northeastern states.

In addition to subcultures of violence and regional cultures, there are also a variety of other cultural values that may condone or even encourage crime.

TABLE 11. Region and Crime Rates for Murder, Forcible Rape, Robbery, and Aggravated Assault

Region	Crime rates per 100,000			
	Murder	Forcible rape	Robbery	Aggravated assault
Northeastern	8.0	27.2	390.9	261.8
North central	7.3	28.8	176.5	205.0
Southern	12.7	37.8	200.3	313.3
Western	10.2	50.2	280.2	350.4

SOURCE: Federal Bureau of Investigation (FBI), *Uniform Crime Reports—1981*, Government Printing Office, Washington, D.C., 1982, pp. 40–45.

Looking at homicide rates for 110 nations since 1900, Dane Archer and Rosemary Gartner found that nations involved in wars experienced increases in homicide rates more often than nations not involved in wars. After considerable review of the different ways of explaining this increase, they were led to conclude:

> The one model which appears to be fully consistent with the evidence is the legitimation model, which suggests that the presence of authorized or sanctioned killing during war has a residual effect on the level of homicide in peacetime society.[94]

Persuasive as the "subculture of violence" theory may sound, it has also been sharply questioned. Critics have argued that instead of seeing violence as caused by values, it is more accurate to say that frustrating poverty, unemployment, and congested housing underlie the violent subculture. In other words, the situation gives rise to the values rather than the other way around. In the case of the regional subculture of violence, it is also worth noting that the murder rate in a state is as closely related to its rate of extreme poverty as to its "southernness."[95]

As an alternative to the subcultural approach, it might be noted that small communities and simpler societies appear able to control crime and deviance by informal social means. In complex societies and urban neighborhoods, these informal controls no longer operate to deter potential offenders from crime. The cycle is cumulative:

> High crime rates will be found where formal control agents lack public support and where informal controls are not strong enough to effectively restrain deviants in the community. Whether formal controls alone can reduce crime rates without the aid of informal controls is doubtful.[96]

Moreover, crime itself generates suspicion and mistrust, thereby weakening the social fabric of the community.[97] From this point of view, the cultural values of personal responsibility and care for others that are expressed through informal social controls may be more important determinants of crime than cultural values that may appear to support crime.

Guns

Although there is no necessary connection between possession of a firearm and its utilization for a violent crime, the gun, especially the handgun, is a most effective weapon for criminal homicide and robbery. It is easily concealable and allows the offender to harm the victim without engaging in direct personal contact. As it turns out, the handgun is the most popular weapon for criminal homicide; half of reported homicides are committed with handguns. Three out of five homicides are committed with some type of firearm. And four out of ten robberies are committed with firearms, many of which are handguns.[98]

Given the link between guns and serious violent crime, the number of handguns and firearms owned by Americans may appear alarming. Beginning in the 1950s and coinciding with trends in urban violence, the production and import of handguns alone has been estimated at 2 million per year by the mid-1970s.

The handgun is often used for robbery; in this photo, a masked gunman, surprised by police while robbing a jewelry store, takes a passerby hostage. (UPI)

Currently, the total number of weapons of all types owned by Americans is estimated to be between 90 million and 200 million.[99]

While Americans own weapons for a number of reasons, one of the ironies in the picture of crime is that the "house gun" kept for self-defense is six times more likely to be used to kill someone by accident or in a quarrel than to defend against an intruder. It is also estimated that 100,000 firearms are stolen each year, primarily during household burglaries. Despite these problems, the United States is very permissive about gun ownership and even regards it as a constitutional right. Although the exact distribution of weapons is unknown, it would be hard to disagree with the comment of Daniel Glaser that "the distribution of such lethal devices must be considered in explaining the dimensions and location of violent crime."[100]

Dynamic Aspects of Social Context

In addition to considering the city, cultural values, and guns as part of the social context of violent crime, it is necessary to examine some of the social changes that characterize the postindustrial United States. This requires an ecological approach which considers not only a *spatial* analysis of crime rates (e.g., urban and regional differences) but also a *temporal* analysis that takes into account the rhythm, tempo, and timing of everyday routine activities. Such an approach will make it clear that in recent years the number of motivated offenders, suitable targets, and situations without guardians has increased dramatically.[101]

The key social changes are increased youthful population, increased urban population, and a shift of routine activities away from the home.

Increased youthful population

Until recently, the United States has been faced with continued increases in the size of its 14- to 17-year-old population. In fact, between 1960 and 1970, the number of people in this age group, which is highly prone to crime, grew over 42 percent—to more than 15 million. Although the number appears to have leveled off during the 1970s, the sheer size of the youthful population has been a factor in the increases in recorded crime after 1960.

Increased urban population

Like the youthful population, the urban population is prone to crime and has shown increases both in numbers and in percent of the American population. In 1950, 64 percent of Americans were classified as living in urban areas. By 1960, the figure was 70 percent; and by 1970, it had risen further, to 73 percent. Although the 1980 figure of 74 percent appears to represent a leveling off of the urban increase, it is important to note that the United States is one of the most urbanized societies in the world today.[102]

Major shift of routine activities away from the home

Perhaps the real key to explaining the increases in rates of violent crime since 1960 is the shift of routine activities away from the home. For one thing, there have been increases in travel and vacations. For another, college enrollments have increased; between 1970 and 1975 alone, the increase was 16 percent. The shift of routine activities for females has been even greater. Since 1960, there has been a 31 percent increase in rate of participation in the labor force by married women. The number of women college students increased by 118 percent. Generally, trends such as these mean that more people spend more of their life outside the home.[103]

Spending more time outside the home places more people in more situations where they can become targets of crime. In that persons who keep house have noticeably lower rates of victimization, the outside involvement of women, traditionally the housekeepers, automatically exposes them to greater risk. Similarly, in that married people have considerably lower rates of victimization, the increase in single-family households puts more people in categories with higher victimization rates for violent crimes such as rape, robbery, and assault.[104]

In short, there is a strong possibility that the social changes of the past two decades have drastically undermined traditional mechanisms of social control. Increased youthful populations, increased urban populations, and a shift of routine activities away from the home have meant that there are more offenders as well as more opportunities for offenders and victims to come together. Even though the number of suitable guardians—i.e., police—has increased and the police are better equipped and trained, the problems created by these social changes have not proved amenable to police work as it is currently practiced. As the FBI says of murder, the most serious of the violent crimes, "Criminal homicide is primarily a social problem over which law enforcement has little or no control."[105]

SUMMARY

Person-to-person violent crimes, defined hundreds of years ago in the common law, still arouse much public concern and fear. Most violent crimes—especially homicide, assault, and rape—involve family members, friends, acquaintances, and neighbors. Robbery is somewhat different in that it typically involves strangers and also combines force with theft. In recent years, new person-to-person crimes such as child abuse, spouse abuse, kidnapping for ransom, skyjacking, and arson have been defined or redefined as law responds to changing social conditions.

In the United States, police make about 1 million arrests per year for person-to-person violent crimes. Those who are arrested are disproportionately male, under age 21, black, and of lower socioeconomic status. Although there are some chronic offenders, many violent offenders are arrested only once. Predicting which people will be violence-prone without erroneously identifying a much larger number of nonviolent persons is virtually impossible. Here too, robbery is an exception in that there is much recidivism among robbers, and indeed there are many who pursue robbery as an occupation or "profession." For the major violent crimes, offenders appear to "mature out" as they become older; arrest rates for violent crimes drop significantly for each successive group over the age of 21.

The victim surveys of the 1970s have provided new knowledge about victims and new perspectives on victims. For one thing, analysis in terms of social characteristics shows victims to be remarkably similar to offenders. For another, the groups most likely to be victimized are least likely to report their victimization to police. Finally, substantial proportions of violent crimes may in fact be precipitated by those who subsequently become victims.

Person-to-person violent crimes are also much influenced by the social situations or contexts that bring offenders and victims into contact with each other. The city, cultural values conducive to crime, and the ready availability of guns are social contexts that tend to produce higher rates of violent crime. In addition, increases in the youthful population, increases in the urban population, and shifts of routine activities away from the home appear to have undermined many of the traditional mechanisms of social control.

NOTES

[1] John Godwin, *Murder U.S.A.: The Ways We Kill Each Other,* Ballantine, New York, 1978, pp. 9–12.
[2] "Black on Black Crime—The Causes, the Consequences, the Cures," *Ebony,* vol. 34, no. 10, August 1979, p. 144.
[3] James Garofalo and John Laub, "The Fear of Crime:

Broadening Our Perspective," *Victimology: An International Journal,* vol. 3, 1978, pp. 242–253.

[4] Donald J. Mulvihill, Melvin M. Tumin, and Lynn A. Curtis, *Crimes of Violence: A Staff Report Submitted to the National Commission on the Causes and Prevention of Violence,* Government Printing Office, Washington, D.C., 1969, chap. 6, p. 405.

[5] M. D. A. Freeman, *Violence in the Home,* Saxon House (Teakfield), Westmead, England, 1979, p. 4.

[6] A. S. Diamond, *The Evolution of Law and Order,* Greenwood, Westport, Conn., 1951.

[7] See: Frank R. Prassel, *Criminal Law, Justice, and Society,* Goodyear, Santa Monica, Calif., 1979, chap. 2.

[8] So that the statistics presented in the present text will be consistent with the definitions of criminal acts, the definitions given follow: Federal Bureau of Investigation (FBI), *Uniform Crime Reports—1981,* Government Printing Office, Washington, D.C., 1982, app. II, p. 316.

[9] Donald T. Lunde, *Murder and Madness,* Stanford Alumni Association, Stanford, Calif., 1975, pp. 3–4.

[10] FBI, *Uniform Crime Reports—1981,* p. 12.

[11] Marvin E. Wolfgang, "A Sociological Analysis of Criminal Homicide," *Federal Probation,* vol. 25, no. 1, March 1961, pp. 48–55; and Alex Pokorny, "A Comparison of Homicides in Two Cities," *Journal of Criminal Law, Criminology, and Police Science,* vol. 56, no. 4, 1965, pp. 479–487.

[12] Lunde, *Murder and Madness.*

[13] Citizens Crime Commission of New York City, "Crossroads on Crime," January 1980, mimeographed.

[14] FBI, *Uniform Crime Reports—1981,* app. II, p. 316.

[15] Ibid.

[16] Christopher S. Dunn, "The Patterns and Distribution of Assault Incident Characteristics among Social Areas," U.S. Department of Justice, Law Enforcement Assistance Administration Report, Government Printing Office, Washington, D.C., 1976.

[17] FBI, *Uniform Crime Reports—1981,* app. II, p. 316.

[18] E.g., see: Kate Millett, *Sexual Politics,* Equinox ed., Avon, New York, 1971.

[19] National Institute of Law Enforcement and Criminal Justice, LEAA, U.S. Department of Justice, *Forcible Rape: Police Administrative and Policy Issues,* Government Printing Office, Washington, D.C., 1978, p. 5.

[20] Ibid.

[21] Duncan Chappell, "Forcible Rape and the Criminal Justice System: Surveying Present and Future Trends," *Crime and Delinquency,* April 1976, pp. 125–136.

[22] Marilyn E. Walsh and Donna D. Schram, "The Victim of White-Collar Crime: Accuser or Accused?" in Gilbert Geis and Ezra Stotland, eds., *White-Collar Crime: Theory and Research,* Sage, Beverly Hills, Calif., 1980, pp. 52–76.

[23] National Institute of Law Enforcement and Criminal Justice, *Forcible Rape;* and Menachem Amir, "Forcible Rape," *Federal Probation,* vol. 31, March 1967, pp. 51–58.

[24] Ibid.

[25] Timothy J. Flanagan, David J. von Alstyne, and Michael R. Gottfredson, eds., *Sourcebook of Criminal Justice Statistics—1981,* Government Printing Office, Washington, D.C., 1981, p. 267.

[26] FBI, *Uniform Crime Reports—1981,* app. II, p. 316.

[27] Werner Julius Einstadter, *Armed Robbery: A Career Study in Perspective,* Ph.D. dissertation, University of California, Berkeley, University Microfilms, Ann Arbor, Mich., 1966.

[28] FBI, *Uniform Crime Reports—1981,* pp. 15–18.

[29] Stephen J. Pfohl, "The 'Discovery' of Child Abuse," *Social Problems,* vol. 24, February 1977, pp. 310–323.

[30] Suzanne K. Steinmetz and Murray A. Straus, "The Family as Cradle of Violence," *Society,* vol. 10, September-October 1973, pp. 50–56.

[31] Ernest Kahlar Alix, *Ransom Kidnapping in America, 1874–1974: The Creation of a Capital Crime,* Southern Illinois University Press, Carbondale, 1978; and Robert Chauncey, "Deterrence: Certainty, Severity, and Skyjacking," *Criminology,* vol. 12, February 1975, pp. 447–473.

[32] FBI, *Uniform Crime Reports—1981.* The basis for this discussion of data on arrests is contained in: sec. IV.

[33] Calculated from: arrest data in FBI, *Uniform Crime Reports—1981,* sec. IV.

[34] Marvin E. Wolfgang, Robert M. Figlio, and Thorsten Sellin, *Delinquency in a Birth Cohort,* University of Chicago Press, Chicago, Ill., 1972.

[35] Ibid., p. 68.

[36] Ibid., p. 123.

[37] Ibid., pp. 68–69.

[38] Joseph G. Weis and James Henney, "Crime and Criminals in the United States in the 1970s: Statistical Appendix," in Sheldon L. Messinger and Egon Bittner, eds., *Criminology Review Yearbook,* vol. 1, Sage, Beverly Hills, Calif., 1979, p. 764.

[39] For a discussion, see: Chapter 10 of the present text.

[40] E.g., see: Lynn A. Curtis, *Criminal Violence,* Heath (Lexington Books), Lexington, Mass., 1974, chap 7. For a recent work, see: Donna Martin Hamparian, Richard Schuster, Simon Dinitz, and John P. Conrad, *The Violent Few: A Study of Dangerous Juvenile Offenders,* Heath (Lexington Books) Lexington, Mass., 1978, especially chap. 3.

[41] Wolfgang et al., *Delinquency in a Birth Cohort,* pp. 72–73.

[42] President's Commission on Law Enforcement and Administration of Justice, *The Challenge of Crime in a Free Society,* Avon, New York, 1968, p. 151. See also: Nicolette Parisi et al., *Sourcebook of Criminal Justice Statistics—1978,* Government Printing Office, Washington, D.C., 1979; and U.S. Department of Justice, Bureau of Justice Statistics, *Profile of Jail Inmates: Sociodemographic Findings from the 1978 Survey of Inmates of Local Jails,* Government Printing Office, Washington, D.C., 1980.

[43] Wolfgang, "A Sociological Analysis of Criminal Homicide"; and David J. Pittman and William Handy, "Patterns in Criminal Aggravated Assault," *Journal of Criminal Law, Criminology, and Police Science,* vol. 55, December 1964, pp. 462–470. See also: Victoria Lynn Swigert and Ronald A. Farrell, *Murder, Inequality, and the Law: Differential Treatment in the Legal Process,* Heath (Lexington Books), Lexington, Mass., 1976, chap. 4.

[44] Wolfgang et al., *Delinquency in a Birth Cohort,* p. 95.

[45] Hamparian et al., *The Violent Few,* p. 128.

[46] Stephen Van Dine, John P. Conrad, and Simon Dinitz, *Restraining the Wicked: The Incapacitation of the*

Dangerous Criminal, Heath, Lexington, Mass., 1979.

[47] Hamparian et al., *The Violent Few*, p. 54.

[48] Roger Hood and Richard Sparks, *Key Issues in Criminology*, McGraw-Hill, New York, 1970, pp. 134–38.

[49] John Monahan, *Predicting Violent Behavior: An Assessment of Clinical Techniques*, Sage, Beverly Hills, Calif., 1981, p. 169.

[50] Van Dine et al., *Restraining the Wicked*, p. 125.

[51] Einstadter, *Armed Robbery*. See also: John E. Conklin, *Robbery and the Criminal Justice System*, Lippincott, Philadelphia, Pa., 1972.

[52] Joan Petersilia, Peter W. Greenwood, and Marvin Lavin, *Criminal Careers of Habitual Felons*, National Institute of Law Enforcement and Criminal Justice, LEAA, Government Printing Office, Washington, D.C., 1978.

[53] Conklin, *Robbery;* and Petersilia et al., *Criminal Careers of Habitual Felons*.

[54] Petersilia et al., *Criminal Careers of Habitual Felons*.

[55] Harold E. Pepinsky, "The Irresponsibility of Explaining Criminality," paper presented at a meeting of the Academy of Criminal Justice, Cincinnati, Ohio, March 14–16, 1979.

[56] Flanagan et al., *Sourcebook of Criminal Justice Statistics—1981*, p. 250. Data for murder from: FBI, *Uniform Crime Reports—1981*, p. 9.

[57] Flanagan et al., *Sourcebook of Criminal Justice Statistics—1981*; Parisi et al., *Sourcebook of Criminal Justice Statistics—1978*, p. 255; and FBI, *Uniform Crime Reports—1981*, p. 10.

[58] Jack Goldsmith and Sharon S. Goldsmith, eds., *Crime and the Elderly: Challenge and Response*, Heath, Lexington, Mass., 1976.

[59] "Black on Black Crime—The Causes, the Consequences, the Cures."

[60] Ibid., p. 144.

[61] Wesley G. Skogan, "The Victims of Crime: Some National Survey Findings," in Anthony L. Guenther, ed., *Criminal Behavior and Social Systems: Contributions of American Sociology*, 2d ed., Rand McNally, Chicago, Ill., 1976, pp. 131–148.

[62] "Black on Black Crime—The Causes, the Consequences, the Cures," p. 144.

[63] Calculated from: Flanagan et al., *Sourcebook of Criminal Justice Statistics—1981*, pp. 256–257. Murder victimization rate calculated from: FBI, *Uniform Crime Reports—1981*, p. 10.

[64] Flanagan et al., *Sourcebook of Criminal Justice Statistics—1981*, p. 258. Criminal homicide statistics by SES are not available.

[65] Philip H. Ennis, *Criminal Victimization in the United States*, University of Chicago, National Opinion Research Center, 1967, chap. 5.

[66] Flanagan et al., *Sourcebook of Criminal Justice Statistics—1981*, p. 233. Because of the preserved infrequency of nonreporting, murder was not included among the offenses studied in the LEAA survey.

[67] Skogan, "The Victims of Crime," p. 145.

[68] Flanagan et al., *Sourcebook of Criminal Justice Statistics—1981*, pp. 236–239.

[69] FBI, *Uniform Crime Reports—1981*, p. 8.

[70] Wolfgang, "A Sociological Analysis of Criminal Homicide"; Swigert and Farrell, *Murder, Inequality, and the Law: Differential Treatment in the Legal Process*, chap. 2.

[71] Curtis, *Criminal Violence;* and Pittman and Handy, "Patterns in Criminal Aggravated Assault."

[72] Curtis, *Criminal Violence*.

[73] National Institute of Law Enforcement and Criminal Justice, *Forcible Rape*, p. 2.

[74] Curtis, *Criminal Violence*, p. 21.

[75] Ibid., pp. 32 and 35.

[76] Stephen Schafer, *The Victim and His Criminal: A Study in Functional Responsibility*, Random House, New York, 1968, p. 3.

[77] Swigert and Farrell, *Murder, Inequality, and the Law*, p. 47.

[78] Marvin E. Wolfgang, "Victim-Precipitated Criminal Homicide," *Journal of Criminal Law, Criminology, and Police Science*, vol. 48, June 1957, pp 1–11.

[79] Harwin L. Voss and John R. Hepburn, "Patterns in Criminal Homicide in Chicago," *Journal of Criminal Law, Criminology, and Police Science*, vol. 59, December 1968, pp. 499–508.

[80] Curtis, *Criminal Violence*, p. 82.

[81] Amir, "Forcible Rape."

[82] Camille E. LeGrand, "Rape and Rape Laws: Sexism in Society and Law," *California Law Review*, vol. 61, May 1973, pp. 929–930.

[83] Curtis, *Criminal Violence*, pp. 92–93.

[84] André Normandeau, "Trends and Patterns in Crimes of Robbery (With Special Reference to Philadelphia, Pennsylvania, 1960 to 1966)," Ph.D. thesis, University Microfilms, Ann Arbor, Mich., 1968, especially pp. 29lf.

[85] Lunde, *Murder and Madness*, p. 105.

[86] Lawrence E. Cohen and Marcus Felson, "Social Change and Crime Rate Trends: A Routine Activity Approach," *American Sociological Review*, vol. 44, August 1979, p. 589.

[87] See: Flanagan et al., *Sourcebook of Criminal Justice Statistics—1981*, p. 244. Some investigators using other analytical approaches have been led to question certain aspects of the relationship between city size and crime rates. See: David Shichor, David L. Decker, and Robert M. O'Brien, "Population Density and Criminal Victimization: Some Unexpected Findings in Central Cities," *Criminology*, vol. 17, no. 2, August 1979, pp. 184–193.

[88] Ramsey Clark, *Crime in America: Observations on Its Nature, Causes, Prevention, and Control*, Pocket Books, New York, 1970, p. 50.

[89] Clifford R. Shaw and Henry D. McKay, *Juvenile Delinquency and Urban Areas*, University of Chicago Press, Chicago, Ill., 1942.

[90] R. C. Tryon, "Predicting Group Differences in Cluster Analysis: The Social Area Problem," *Multivariate Behavioral Research*, vol. 2, 1967, pp. 453–476. See also: Curtis, *Criminal Violence*, chap. 7.

[91] Marvin Wolfgang and Franco Ferracuti, *The Subculture of Violence*, Tavistock, London, 1967, pp. 271–284.

[92] Marvin Wolfgang, *Patterns in Criminal Homicide*, University of Pennsylvania Press, Philadelphia, 1958, pp. 188–189.

216

[93] See: Raymond D. Gastil, "Homicide and a Regional Culture of Violence," *American Sociological Review,* vol. 36, no. 3, June 1971, pp. 412–426.

[94] Dane Archer and Rosemary Gartner, "Violent Acts and Violent Times: A Comparative Approach to Postwar Homicide Rates," *American Sociological Review,* vol. 41, December 1976, pp. 937–963; quotation from p. 961.

[95] Colin Loftin and Robert H. Hill, "Regional Subculture and Homicide: An Examination of the Gastil-Hackney Thesis," *American Sociological Review,* vol. 39, October 1974, pp. 714–724. For further debate on the merits of the concept of a regional culture of violence, see: William G. Doerner, "The Index of Southernness Revisited: The Influence of Wherefrom upon Whodunit"; Colin Loftin and Robert H. Hill, "Comments"; and R. D. Gastil, "Comments," *Criminology,* vol. 16, no. 1, May 1978, pp. 47–66.

[96] John E. Conklin, *The Impact of Crime,* Macmillan, New York; and Collier Macmillan, London, 1975, p. 137.

[97] Ibid., p. 248.

[98] FBI, *Uniform Crime Reports—1981,* pp. 10 and 18.

[99] See: James D. Wright and Linda L. Marston, "The Ownership of the Means of Destruction: Weapons in the U.S.," *Social Problems,* vol. 23, October 1975, pp. 93–107.

[100] Daniel Glaser, *Crime in Our Changing Society,* Holt, Rinehart and Winston, New York, 1978, p. 214.

[101] The approach to social change and crime given in the present text follows: Cohen and Felson, "Social Change and Crime Rate Trends."

[102] *Current Population Reports: Population Characteristics,* series P-20, no. 336, April 1979. See also: *Historical Statistics of the United States,* series A73-81, U.S. Department of Commerce, Bureau of the Census, Washington, D.C., 1975.

[103] Cohen and Felson, "Social Change and Crime Rate Trends."

[104] Ibid., p. 596.

[105] FBI, *Uniform Crime Reports—1981,* p. 10.

Person-to-Person Property Crimes

The term "person-to-person property crimes" refers to crimes involving people and their property. Robbery, a person-to-person property crime which involves theft as well as violence, was discussed in Chapter 9. In this chapter we shall consider burglary, which is a crime of trespass; and larceny, which is the most general type of theft. One type of larceny, theft of motor vehicles, will demand special attention. Other special types of larceny are confidence games, forgery, and the passing of worthless checks.

Although less feared than violent crimes, person-to-person property crimes occur far more frequently. In fact, in the United States 90 percent of the index crimes reported to police involve loss of property. Police make well over 2 million arrests for property crimes each year, and victims report losses of more than $9 billion for the major property offenses. Yet these official data far underestimate the extent of property crimes. Well over half of the person-to-person property crimes which occur are never officially reported to police. Of those which are reported, only about one in five is cleared by arrest. Many of those arrested are never prosecuted. Some of those prosecuted are never convicted. Of those convicted, relatively few receive jail or prison sentences.[1]

In contrast to violent crimes, interpersonal property crimes more often than not involve offenders and victims who are strangers to each other. In burglary, there is no direct interaction between offender and victim. Larceny can involve personal contact, but it often does not. Crimes such as confidence games (con games), forgery, and passing worthless checks are characterized by a false or exploitative social relationship between offender and victim. The prevalence of property crime is in part a subtle statement that we live in a society in which we often confront one another as strangers.

Two aspects of person-to-person property crime are of special importance: (1) the fact that ours is a materialistic society with an abundance of money and goods, which provides immense opportunities for theft; and (2) the fact that much theft is organized. Regarding the latter point, it may be noted that thefts are often committed by teams or groups. For some, theft is an "occupation" or even a "profession." From a social point of view, theft is a recycling of property. Stolen goods are purchased from the offenders by fences, who in turn market them back to the public at "discounted" prices. A new form of social organization has developed in response to theft: insurance systems which help cushion victims of certain types of theft.

With these themes in mind, we can turn to a more detailed analysis of person-to-person property crimes. Like violent crime, person-to-person property crime can be discussed in terms of our four perspectives: acts, offenders (burglars and thieves), victims (of trespass and theft), and social contexts.

ACTS AGAINST PROPERTY

As with crimes of violence, the basic laws attempting to control theft of property have their origins in the common law which emerged in England during the 1100s. The concepts of burglary and theft were defined by Henry de Bracton in 1225, when he systematized the English Common Law in his work *De legibus Angliae*.[2] However, concepts and types of property have changed tremendously since that time; and with these changes, laws concerning theft have undergone considerable development.

Burglary

Burglary was the first defined area in laws dealing with theft. The definition reflects its medieval origins: burglary is a crime of trespass upon another person's property, a trespass which often involves theft. Indeed, the present-day official definition used in crime reporting continues to suggest both trespass and theft:

> The unlawful entry of a structure to commit a felony or a theft. Attempted forcible entry is included.[3]

The term "burglary" originally meant "entry at night," but the present-day definition includes unlawful entry at any time, day or night. Statistics are kept on how the unlawful entry is accomplished; and distinctions are made among forcible entry, unlawful entry where no force is used, and attempted forcible entry. Forcible entry accounts for 73 percent of all reported burglaries; unlawful entry without force for 19 percent; and attempted forcible entry for 8 percent. Present-day burglary laws include structures as diverse as telephone booths and motor vehicles, reflecting a concern not only with trespass but also with protection of private property in general.[4]

Now numbering more than 3.5 million reported incidents per year for the United States, burglary makes up 28 percent of the index crimes. At present, the number of reported burglaries is six times that of reported robberies. Like other index crimes, burglary has shown tremendous increases during the past 20 years. In fact, the rate of reported burglaries has tripled in that time period. The dollar loss for burglary now totals $3.5 billion per year. Although it is not so directly threatening to the person as robbery, burglary is the cause of much concern because it is primarily a stranger-to-stranger crime which in two-thirds of the reported cases violates the sanctity of people's homes. It may well be that this violation of the home overrides concern about lost property. As it turns out, many burglaries are committed by juveniles and net small amounts of money. The average dollar loss per reported burglary was $924 in 1981.[5]

Larceny

Laws concerning larceny—unlike those concerning burglary and robbery—have changed considerably over the centuries. The modern law of larceny can be traced to the Carrier's case of 1473, which extended the definition of larceny from the direct, overt taking of goods to the illegal removal and conversion of another person's property, an offense that previously would have been treated as a civil matter. In England, the eighteenth century saw a very rapid development of the law of larceny, designed to clarify ownership of property in the emerging commercial, industrial society. Making larceny a criminal matter made it possible to use criminal penalties against shoplifters, confidence artists, swindlers, dishonest employees, and others who would undermine the integrity of commercial and trading exchanges. Hence, in this period, larceny and, more generally, theft without violence came to be seen as a major type of crime. Specific forms of larceny received special legal definition and attention: e.g., receiving stolen property, larceny by trick, obtaining goods by false premises, and embezzlement.[6]

Although laws dealing with larceny are now well established, the definition of larceny used for purposes of reporting index crimes was changed as recently as 1973. Until that time, larceny was classified as an index offense only if the value of the property taken was $50 or more. In 1973, larceny was renamed "larceny-theft" and expanded to include offenses of any dollar value:

> The unlawful taking, carrying, leading, or riding away of property from the possession or constructive possession of another. Examples are thefts of bicycles, automobile accessories, shoplifting, pocket-picking, or any stealing of property or article which is not taken by force and violence or by fraud. Attempted larcenies are included. Embezzlement, "con" games, forgery, worthless checks, etc., are excluded.[7]

This expanded definition allows the reporting system for index crimes to include large numbers of minor thefts, distinguishable from robbery and burglary in that there is no use of force or violence and from other thefts in that they are not accomplished by deception. (In this text the terms "larceny" and "larceny-theft" are used interchangeably.)

The expanded definition of larceny has served to make it the most frequent index offense: not only is it the most frequently reported crime, but half of the arrests for index crimes are for larceny. Each year more than 7 million larcenies are reported to police. The rate for larceny is nearly twice that for burglary and 12 times that for robbery. However, this greater frequency is accompanied by

Larceny is the most frequently reported index crime. (ARTHUR TRESS/PHOTO RESEARCHERS, INC.)

TABLE 12. Types of Larceny, Percent of All Larcenies, Average Value of Stolen Property

Type	Percent of all larcenies	Average value of stolen property
Motor vehicle accessories	19	$192
From buildings	17	$518
From motor vehicles	18	$366
Bicycles	9	a
Shoplifting	11	$ 72
Coin machines	1	a
Pocket picking	1	$235
Purse snatching	2	$196
All other	22	a
	100	Overall average: $340

ᵃ Figures not available.

SOURCE: Federal Bureau of Investigation (FBI), *Uniform Crime Reports—1981*, Government Printing Office, Washington, D.C., 1982, pp. 26 and 28.

comparatively less seriousness of particular incidents. For each reported theft, the average value of property stolen in 1981 was $340, and the total loss to victims nationally was $2.4 billion; both figures are considerably lower than the comparable figures for burglary. The somewhat less serious nature of larcenies is seen in Table 12, which shows the major types, how often each occurs, and the average value of property stolen. Of all larcenies, 37 percent—more than one in three—are motor vehicle–related in that they involve thefts of motor vehicle accessories or thefts from motor vehicles. (Theft of the motor vehicle itself is a separate type of larceny, which we shall consider shortly.) Comparatively few involve personal contact such as pocket picking and purse snatching.

As with other index crimes, the long-run trend of larceny is upward and shows continuing increases in recent years. There is about three times more reported larceny today than there was in 1960, even after the changed definition is taken into account. What does this mean? Like burglary and robbery, larceny is a stranger-to-stranger crime. In a society in which "rip-off" has become part of everyday language, it might even be said that larceny is legitimate in the eyes of some people. Yet, although larceny does not arouse the same fears as robbery and does not involve violation of the home as burglary does, it nevertheless violates laws. To some, it may be little more than a nuisance; but to others, it can mean substantial losses.

Motor Vehicle Theft

One type of larceny deserves special attention: theft of motor vehicles. Motor vehicle theft has several unique features. First, automobiles and other motor vehicles are, with the exception of housing, the most expensive items purchased by most people. Second, a motor vehicle is very movable. Often it is left on the streets, physically removed from its owner, for long periods of time. Third, theft of a motor vehicle is the property offense most likely to be reported and the one in which the property is most likely to be returned to the owner, although its condition may be poorer. Fourth, when a stolen vehicle is recovered, it is usually found that the owner has either left the key in it or left the ignition switch open.[8] Finally, losses from motor vehicle theft are most likely to be cushioned by insurance.

One journalist has called motor vehicle theft the "happy crime."[9] Although such thefts are often reported to the police, few offenders are arrested. In fact, only 14 percent of motor vehicle thefts are cleared by arrest—the lowest percentage for any of the index crimes. Offenders who are arrested often are not prosecuted or, if prosecuted, are given lenient sentences by judges who are faced with what they regard as more serious crimes. Nor is the victim hurt much. Virtually all motor vehicles are covered by insurance, and the proceeds from insurance can be used for a new vehicle. Only the insurance company appears to lose, but it can recover its losses in higher premiums to policyholders.

However, from another viewpoint, motor vehicle theft is far from "happy." More than 1 million vehicles are stolen each year, with an average value of $3173; the total losses, more than $3.4 billion, are considerably in excess of losses from robbery, burglary, or larceny. This money, as noted above, is recaptured through increased insurance premiums paid by the public. In addition, stolen vehicles are involved in a large number of accidents. If left abandoned, they incur cleanup costs borne by taxpayers. Finally, many stolen vehicles are used as is or for parts by vehicle theft rings, some of which are controlled by organized crime.

Historically, motor vehicle theft is a new arrival, a twentieth-century form of

Motor vehicle theft is the most costly form of reported larceny. (TONY O'BRIEN/TRICORN)

crime. The total number of registered motor vehicles rose from fewer than 8000 in 1900 to more than 150 million by 1980. With this increase, motor vehicle theft— like its historical antecedent, horse theft—became defined as a special type of larceny, usually carrying a more severe penalty than grand larceny. There were also special statutes regulating the criminal receiving of motor vehicles as well as the ownership of garages and repair shops.[10] Today, the basic definition in the Uniform Crime Reports is simply:

> The theft or attempted theft of a motor vehicle. A motor vehicle is self propelled and runs on the surface and not on rails.[11]

The statistics on motor vehicle theft indicate that it is the one major crime which does not show continual increases. The number of vehicles reported stolen has fluctuated between 900,000 and slightly over 1.1 million each year since 1970. When measured by population, the rate has remained around 450 per 100,000. However, a different perspective emerges if rates are calculated by number of registered automobiles rather than number of persons. From this viewpoint, motor vehicle theft reached a high of 1100 per 100,000 registered automobiles in 1933, dropped to 800 in 1945 and to 550 in 1965, and currently stands at 697.[12] In other words, the number of registered vehicles has increased so much that the rate of theft is lower in recent years if it is measured in terms of number of vehicles.

Special Types of Larceny

The last type of person-to-person property crime which we shall consider here involves the use of deceit to commit theft. The particular form varies: forgery, con game, swindling, dealing in stolen property. Again, these are acts that came to be defined as crime in eighteenth-century England as modern forms of property emerged. Today, for statistical purposes they are considered Part II offenses. Since statistics on the number of crimes reported are not given for these offenses, it is virtually impossible to give any indication of the trends for these property crimes. However, it can be said that the number of arrests for these offenses has shown an increase, but nowhere near the increase for Part I offenses. It should also be said that con games and swindles of one form or another have long been pursued as criminal occupations.

The acts of receiving and fencing stolen goods are often overlooked in discussions of person-to-person property crimes. The thief who is involved in the "separation" of property other than cash from a victim needs to dispose of the stolen goods. It is the receiver or the fence who provides markets for the stolen property to members of the general public who are willing to do business. The fence, a parasitic intermediary, has an immense amount of power over thieves and their activities. Yet the fence has been curiously ignored by the law. For many centuries, receiving stolen goods knowingly did not make a person an accessory to a crime. Even today, law enforcement tends to be directed against the thief rather than the semirespectable "businessperson" who remarkets the stolen goods.[13]

In conclusion, a final but important point about property crimes is that many are never reported and officially recorded. As we shall see in the discussion of its victims, property crime often goes unreported, especially if the value of the property involved is small. It should also be said that little property crime is cleared by arrest: for burglary, the clearance rate is 14 percent; for larceny-theft, 19 percent; and for motor vehicle theft, 14 percent. If clearance rates took unreported property crimes into account, they would be as low as 5 or 10 percent. These low clearance rates, combined with general acceptance of the activities of the fence, imply that property crime can be seen as a massive system for recycling of property in our society, one that is tolerated if not condoned. This is a theme which we must explore further later in this chapter.

However, before turning to the recycling of property in our society, it will be useful to take a closer look at the offenders and victims of property crime. As with violent crime, we shall focus on their social characteristics; in particular, their sex, age, race, and socioeconomic status. Let's look first at the offender and then at the victim.

PROPERTY OFFENDERS: BURGLARS AND THIEVES

Characteristics of Offenders

Even though few person-to-person property crimes are cleared by arrest, police make more than 2 million arrests each year for property crimes. As with the violent crimes, those arrested for property crimes are more likely to be male, young, black, and of lower socioeconomic status than their numbers in the population would suggest. (See Table 13.) However, persons arrested for property crimes differ in several respects from those arrested for violent crimes. For one thing, an increasing proportion are female. For another, there is a larger proportion showing a clear pattern of repeated arrests. This pattern points up a broader issue,

TABLE 13. Percentages of Those Arrested Falling into Various Social Categories

Offense	Sex	Age			Race	
	Male	Under 18	Under 21	Under 25	Negro	All others[a]
Burglary	94	43	64	79	30	1
Larceny	71	35	52	66	32	2
Motor vehicle theft	91	41	61	76	30	2
Forgery and counterfeiting	68	11	27	49	36	1
Stolen property: buying, receiving, possessing	89	27	48	66	34	1
Percent of group in total population		(13–17)[b]	(13–20)[b]	(13–24)[b]		
	49	9	15	23	12	2

[a] Excluding whites and Negroes but including Indians, Chinese, Japanese, and "all others."

[b] Those age 12 and under have been omitted from this calculation because the number of arrests for this age group is extremely low.

SOURCE: Federal Bureau of Investigation (FBI), *Uniform Crime Reports—1981*, Government Printing Office, Washington, D.C., 1982, sec. IV.

the fact that certain types of property theft reflect centuries-old techniques, arts which are pursued as occupations or "professions."

Sex

The offender arrested for a property crime is most likely to be male. Arrest ratios for the major crimes are as follows:

> Burglary: 15 males for every female
> Motor vehicle theft: 10 males for every female
> Larceny-theft: 2 males for every female

Of these three crimes, larceny-theft stands out in that its sex ratio is distinctly lower than that of burglary and motor vehicle theft. This lower sex ratio represents a trend that dates back to the 1950s: larceny arrest rates for females have increased between three and four times as rapidly as those of males.[14] The considerable increase in arrests of females for larceny can be attributed to the increased opportunities for crime that have come about as a result of the greater involvement of women in social activities outside the home. In fact, there has been some movement toward equalization of larceny rates for males and females, as well as rates for other types of crime, as women are offered more opportunities in American society.[15] However, this point needs to be qualified: it is possible that increases in arrests and prosecutions of females may reflect greater willingness on the part of police, prosecutors, judges, and juries to recognize criminality in women.

Age

Youth is an even more important factor in arrests for property crimes than in arrests for violent crimes. Of those arrested for the major crimes of burglary and motor vehicle theft, 41 percent are under age 18; of those arrested for larceny, 35 percent are under age 18. Even larger percentages are under 21. The under-25 group accounts for over 75 percent of those arrested for burglary and motor vehicle theft and 66 percent of those arrested for larceny. (See Table 13.) The age group with the largest numbers of arrests—i.e., the "age of maximum criminality"—is 17 for burglary and 16 for motor vehicle theft. This is even younger than it is for any of the violent crimes.

Again, the Part II offenses show somewhat contrasting patterns with respect to sex and age of those arrested. Like larceny, forgery and counterfeiting are somewhat more "feminized" than they were in earlier years, although offenders are typically older. Buying and receiving stolen property is more "masculine," although here the offenders are somewhat older that those who are typically arrested for burglary and motor vehicle theft.

Race

As with violent crime, the official arrest rates for property crimes show blacks to be overrepresented in comparison with their numbers in the population. This overrepresentation is much less for property crime than it is for violent crime; but blacks still account for 31 percent of arrests for property crimes. Arrests of people of other races occur in numbers that are proportionate to their percentage of the population. (See Table 13.)

Socioeconomic status

Although socioeconomic status of arrested offenders is not specifically noted in the Uniform Crime Reports, it is generally agreed that the typical offender arrested and convicted for property crime comes from the lower classes. As we saw in Chapter 9, prison populations have a large proportion of people of lower socioeconomic status who are young, male, and black or members of other minorities. A study by Marvin Wolfgang and his associates, which followed a cohort of males born in 1945 and residing in Philadelphia between their tenth and eighteenth birthdays, found that (1) nearly two-thirds of the delinquencies committed involved some form of theft, and (2) although secondary to race, low socioeconomic status was characteristic among both those who were to become one-time delinquents and those who were to become recidivists.[16] More recent work has also called attention to the relationships between unemployment, low income, and arrest (as well as rearrest) for property crime.[17]

Problems with Sex, Age, Race, and Socioeconomic Status

There are several problems with arrest statistics which convey the impression that the typical property offender is male, young, black, and of lower socioeconomic status. One is that, according to self-report surveys, theft is widespread and occurs throughout all groups in the population. Another is that there are some offenders who show very high rates of repeated theft. Finally, some offenders pursue theft as an occupation or even a profession. Let's take a look at each of these problems.

Findings of self-report surveys

That theft is widespread and occurs throughout all groups in the population is a conclusion which has emerged from self-report surveys conducted by sociologists.[18] In examining self-reported theft among 1993 randomly sampled adults in New Jersey, Iowa, and Oregon, Charles Tittle and Wayne Villemez found that 21 percent said they had taken something that did not belong to them valued at about $5, and that 7 percent had taken something valued at about $50.[19] An earlier study conducted in New York State in the 1940s had found even higher percentages admitting to criminal behavior for larceny (theft under $50), grand larceny (theft over $50), motor vehicle theft, and burglary. The percentages of men admitting these offenses were 89, 13, 26, and 17 respectively; for women, they were 83, 11, 8 and 4 respectively.[20]

Studies of juveniles have also shown substantial numbers, among both working- and middle-class subjects, who will admit to some type of theft.[21] From another perspective, Walter Miller observed an enormous amount of theft in gangs in a city he called "Midcity." He reports 3½ "theft-oriented" acts for every "hard"—or actual, arrestable—act of theft and 10 incidents of theft for every court appearance on theft charges. About 50 percent of the boys and 20 percent of the girls in the group were involved in such acts. Theft was, as Miller puts it, the "dominant" form of behavior in the gangs he observed.[22]

Characteristics of recidivists

Although self-report surveys have been persuasive in suggesting that theft offenders come from every sector of society, there is reason to believe that persistent or chronic offenders have distinctive social characteristics. Generally, it should be borne in mind that while substantial proportions of young people report *some* theft, very few report frequent or serious involvement. However, when we consider recidivist offenders, it is this smaller group that needs to be examined.

The question whether the frequent or serious offender has distinctive social characteristics is more easily answered for delinquency in general than for theft in particular (although theft, as has been noted, is an important part of delinquency). Wolfgang's study of arrested delinquents found that recidivists (those arrested more than once) and chronic offenders (those arrested more than five times) were more likely to be nonwhite and of lower socioeconomic status. Chronic offenders made up 18 percent of the birth cohort but accounted for 52 percent of the delinquent acts committed by the entire cohort. Chronic offenders were likely to begin their delinquent "careers" at an earlier age; to move more frequently; and to show a poorer level of ability, performance, and achievement in school.[23]

In contrast to Wolfgang's study of arrested offenders, the self-report studies cited above have, as we saw, generally concluded that class and race play a lesser role or no role at all in delinquent behavior. However, Delbert Elliott and Suzanne Ageton have recently attempted to resolve some of the methodological issues that have plagued self-reported studies of delinquency. Their research findings, based on a nationwide probability sample of over 1700 young people age 11–17, represented a distinct break with those of previous self-report surveys in that self-reported delinquencies were somewhat higher for blacks than for whites (the ratio was 3:2). Property crimes accounted for much of the difference: black respondents reported twice as many property crimes as white respondents. There were also class differences: lower-class respondents had a higher rate of self-reported delinquency than working-class respondents, who in turn had a higher rate than middle-class respondents. Age and sex differences were consistent with other large-scale self-report surveys.[24]

Elliott and Ageton go on to note that the race and class differences are "the result of relative differences at the high end of the frequency continuum." As they put it:

> Not only are the relative *proportions* of blacks and lower-class youth higher at the high end of the frequency continuum but also, within the high category, blacks and lower-class youth report substantially higher *frequencies* than do whites and middle-class youth.[25]

In other words, while nonoffenders and one-time offenders may have similar race and class characteristics, multiple or chronic offenders show a distinct race and class bias. If these findings are accurate, they would confirm the race and class bias of the official arrest statistics. However, since they are out of line with much previous research, further studies are necessary before definite conclusions can be drawn about multiple or chronic offenders.

Theft as an occupation

People who commit property crimes are a diverse group. Some are juveniles who try such crimes on one or more occasions; others pursue them as an occupation or career. Moreover, some offenders are part of "organized crime," in which case the theft is pursued in collaboration with a network of others who are also involved in criminal activity. To understand the diversity of offenders, it is useful to look at the criminal occupations that emerged as societies experienced industrialization and to examine the typologies of offenders that have been advanced in recent studies of burglary and motor vehicle theft. Having done this, we will be in a position to make some conclusions about recidivism.

Professionals   Specialized criminal occupations developed in Europe when industrialization left a social class of landless, masterless, and penniless people. Thus, fifteenth-century England saw stealing develop into a business with areas of specialization by distinct types of offenders: burglary (safe burglary and house burglary); sneak theft, i.e., theft without violence or breaking in (bank sneak theft, house sneak theft, shoplifting, pennyweighting, pocket picking, and lush working); confidence swindling (the short con, the big con, circus grifting); forgery and counterfeiting; and extortion.[26]

With the emergence of specialized criminal occupations, professional criminals also emerged. The professional criminal is unique in that he or she pursues crime with such a degree of commitment that it replaces work as the central life orientation. Theft can be seen as "professional" to the extent that there is (1) a complex of techniques necessary to pursue theft, (2) a status among professional peers, (3) groups with shared feelings and sentiments, (4) a feeling of segregation from the rest of society, and (5) an organization which provides help and support.[27]

The well-developed criminal specializations in England (described above) were transported across the ocean to the United States as it too experienced the social changes associated with industrialization. In the United States theft also became professionalized. In fact, James Inciardi estimates that by 1900 professional criminals in the United States numbered about 100,000. However, he sees professional crime as on the decline today and estimates that the entire professional underworld numbered only about 2000 by the close of the 1970s.[28]

To say that the professional underworld is on the decline is not to say that specialization in and organization of property crime have disappeared. Burglary, larceny, and motor vehicle theft continue to be practiced as occupations by many in our society. Neal Shover divides the social organization of burglary into its internal and external aspects. "Internal organization" refers to burglary crews of perhaps three or four—one a lookout, one a driver who also monitors police calls, one or more who are actually involved in the theft, and a tipster who receives a 10 percent fee. The "external organization," set up to deal with the outside world, provides an outlet for stolen goods as well as "protection" in the event of arrest. Burglary crews are formed at bars and lounges where thieves hang out or through tipsters and fences.[29]

More recently, Marilyn Walsh has argued that the fence plays a dominant, if not the most powerful, role in the organization of burglary and property theft in today's society. With more than three-fourths of all thefts involving merchandise rather than cash, there is a continual need for thieves to dispose of stolen goods. The fence meets this need, but in so doing assumes enormous control over the activities involved in theft. Fences keep contacts in both the legal and the illegal world and can cope with the police or courts when necessary. In marked contrast to the arrested burglar, who is male, young, black, and poor, the typical fence (although also male) is middle-aged (median age, 46.5), white, and quite well-to-do. Fences are often considered legitimate, productive members of society. About 29 percent of the 115 fences identified by Walsh could be classified as "most respected"; 37 percent could be classified as "marginal" businesspeople. Of these fences, 64 percent owned and 10 percent worked for a legitimate business entity.[30]

Other types of offenders While property crime is an occupation or profession for some offenders, it by no means works that way for all offenders. We have already seen that the age of maximum criminality for arrested offenders is 16, hardly one at which a person would have a developed occupation, much less a career. That some people can pursue property crime as an occupation while most of those arrested are juveniles implies that there are different types of offenders. Describing these types has been a concern of criminologists. Let's take a look first at a general typology of property offenders developed by Don C. Gibbons and then at particular typologies of burglars and motor vehicle thieves.

In his general typology of property offenders, Gibbons distinguishes four categories: (1) professional thief, (2) professional "heavy," (3) semiprofessional property offender, and (4) one-time loser. We have already looked at the professional thief, who has well-developed skills, is involved in theft full-time, and has a long-term commitment to a particular type of theft. Professional "heavies" are also involved in full-time careers in criminality and employ complex skills, but they are more likely to threaten the use of force to accomplish their crimes. Furthermore, their background is more likely to be urban and lower-class, with some gang involvement; by contrast, professional thieves come from a variety of social-class backgrounds. The semiprofessional uses much simpler skills and is more likely to engage in direct assaults upon personal or private property. The crimes committed by semiprofessionals do not involve the complex interactional processes of professional property crimes; and semiprofessionals' criminal careers are episodic, often alternating with periods of employment at "straight" jobs. Generally, their background is working- or lower-class. Finally, there are "one-time losers"—relatively naive and unsophisticated offenders who steal some property and get caught; naive check forgers who write bad checks when the need arises; and automobile joyriders.[31]

While Gibbons's typology is suggestive, it does not deal in depth with particular types of property theft and does not furnish information concerning the numbers of offenders who would fall into the particular categories. Studies of burglary and theft have led to the development of more detailed typologies. Marilyn C. Walsh, for example, identifies a "pecking order" or social ranking of thieves which is based not only on skill but also on age and use of narcotics: "good burglar"—a specialist who selects high-value targets, plans well, and rarely uses a weapon; "known burglar"—one who burglarizes consistently but with minimal planning, frequently uses a weapon, and is arrested often; "young burglar"—one who is like the known burglar but young; "juvenile burglar"—one who is rarely encountered by detectives; "booster"—one who is heavily into larceny and is often addicted to narcotics; and "junkie"—one who has the longest arrest record and concentrates on theft of small items. It is worth noting that the "junkie," or drug user, tends to commit more crime but derives smaller profit from each crime and is more likely to be arrested.[32]

Motor vehicle theft has also been the subject of attempts to develop specific typologies of offenders. In a study conducted both in Toledo, Ohio, and in Virginia, Charles McCaghy and his associates found that a sizable proportion of cars stolen (although not the largest proportion) are stolen by juveniles who are white, of higher socioeconomic status, and from better neighborhoods. Their typology of motor vehicle thieves reflects perhaps even more complex motivations for vehicle theft than those reported for burglary. In all, they found five types of offenses, which would involve different kinds of offenders: "joyriding"—in which the theft is primarily recreational and nonutilitarian; "short-term transportation"—in which the vehicle is taken for personal use in the city in which it is stolen; "long-term transportation"—in which the vehicle is retained for personal use in another city; "profit"—in which professionals or amateur "strippers" are involved; "theft"—in which the vehicle is used for commission of another crime.[33] Again, the percentages falling into the categories are not given.

Although typologies of offenders can be criticized for failing to include information about what percentage of offenders would fall into each category, it should be noted that this information is virtually impossible to obtain. At best, general estimates of the numbers are available. However, certain trends in types of offenders can be identified. The decrease in number of professional criminals has already been noted. One analyst would carry this line of thought a step further, to argue that the sheer abundance of property in American society has brought increasing numbers of amateurs into crime. Presenting data on the specific crime of bank robbery, Leroy Gould notes that before 1940 most bank robbers were professional and full-time. Since then, a new, nonprofessional criminal element has entered, so that today close to half of the arrested bank robbers were not pursuing a criminal career beforehand. Bank robbery has also been made easier because banks employ fewer armed guards (relative to the number of branch outlets) and fewer banks have adequate alarm systems. Concerning motor vehicle theft, Gould finds a growing involvement of young people in the 1950–1965 period.[34]

According to one recent analysis, motor vehicle theft is once again showing a trend toward professionalization, or at least toward increased involvement of organized theft rings. There has been a decrease in the percentage of juveniles arrested for motor vehicle theft (from 62 percent in 1967 to 53 percent in 1977); in the proportion of vehicle thefts "solved" (in 1967, 24 percent were cleared by arrest; in 1977, only 16 percent were); and in the average value of a recovered vehicle as a percentage of its value at the time of arrest (from 86 percent in 1967 to 60 percent in 1977). At the same time, there has been an increase in the proportion of stolen vehicles that are trucks and buses (from 6 percent in 1974 to 9 percent in 1977). In light of these trends, the National Association of Attorneys General, in a report on motor vehicle theft, sees "clear evidence" that the involvement of juveniles and amateurs is declining while that of adults, professionals, and organized crime is increasing.[35] Since this analysis is based on officially reported data, there may be some problem with the exact percentages quoted. However, the general idea of this and other analyses that different types of offenders may be attracted to different types of crime, depending on social factors, is an important one that criminologists need to develop further.

Problems with typologies   There are two important qualifications which must be made concerning typologies of offenders. One is that relatively few offenders have clear-cut, "one-crime" careers. When a person is arrested for robbery, burglary, or larceny and subsequently rearrested, there is an 80 percent chance that the rearrest will be for a property crime; but the probability of rearrest for the *same* property crime is considerably less. Of the property crimes, burglary is the most likely to be repeated; but even for burglary the probability is less than one in two. For larceny and motor vehicle theft, the probability is barely one in four. If conviction and reconviction (rather than arrest and rearrest) are taken as criteria, the probability declines even further. In short, despite the tendency of property offenders to continue to engage in property crime, there is a great deal of "crime switching."[36]

The second qualification concerning typologies is that a tremendous proportion of those arrested for crimes are first-time arrestees. Thus, Wolfgang's study of a cohort of nearly 10,000 delinquents between the ages of 10 and 18 found that no less than 46 percent of those arrested were being arrested not only for the first time but also for the only time.[37] Another cohort study, conducted by the British Home Office Statistical Research Unit in 1964, found that 46 percent of its sample of all those convicted of an offense in March or April 1957 had been arrested only once.[38] Focusing specifically on burglary, one study found that 60 percent of arrested burglars had no previous criminal record as adults (juvenile records were unavailable) at the time of their arrest; and 71 percent had no previous arrest record for burglary.[39] It hardly seems justifiable, then, to develop typologies of offenders who have committed their offense, or at any rate have been arrested for it, only once.

The problems with typologies raise a larger issue. For most property offenders, crime declines with age, a phenomenon which was already noted in connection with violent crime.[40] Even though property crime is more likely than violent crime to be repetitive, arrest rates for property offenses are markedly lower for adults than for juveniles. As it turns out, the older the age group, the lower the arrest rate for person-to-person property crime. As with violent crime, for many of these property crime offenders there is a maturation out of criminal behavior.

There is no good way to predict repeat offenders—that is, those who will *not* "mature out of crime." In a long-range study, Farrington found that the strongest predictor was self-reported delinquency. However, if self-reported delinquency is uscd for this purpose, an enormous number will be incorrectly predicted to remain delinquents while many others who would have remained delinquents will not be identified.[41] Perhaps the problem is that criminal behavior occurs infrequently in large populations—in other words, it is a rare event. Attempting to find characteristics of individuals that will predict rare events

> amounts to using a gross tool like a napalm bomb to discriminate unusual targets like several guerillas staying in a village of several hundred non-combatants.[42]

The phenomenon of maturation is one of the "unexplained mysteries" of criminality. Significantly, it is often those who are undetected or left alone by the criminal justice system who mature out of criminal behavior to become law-abiding citizens.[43] Bearing this in mind, Wolfgang has argued that social intervention would be most effective if it could stop delinquents before they go beyond their fourth arrest for delinquency.[44] However, waiting for maturation to occur does not save the victim—to whom attention must now be given.

VICTIMS OF PROPERTY CRIMES

Through victim surveys, criminologists have acquired data about the victims of property crime much more refined than the data contained in the Uniform Crime Reports.[45] To begin with, far more property victimizations are reported to survey

These residents of Prospect Heights, Illinois, returned from a vacation to find the interior of their home almost completely destroyed by vandals. (WIDE WORLD PHOTOS)

interviewers than to the police. Second, the surveys make a distinction between personal, household, and business victimization—a distinction which is not made by the Uniform Crime Reports. Finally, the surveys offer a wealth of detailed data concerning the sex, age, race and socioeconomic status of those who are victimized by property crime.

In thinking about victims of property crime, it must be noted that in most burglaries, larcenies, and motor vehicle thefts the offender and the victim are strangers to each other. Generally, the thief and property owner do not even see each other. Some property crimes do involve personal interaction—e.g., personal larceny with contact (purse snatching or pocket picking) and the confidence game, or con game, in which the victim is taken in as an accomplice to the crime.[46] However, such personal interaction is seen in only a small proportion of all property crimes.

Number of Victimizations

Examining property crime from the viewpoint of its victims, one is immediately struck by the tremendous amount of such crime that is reported to survey interviewers but not to the police. In 1979, for example, surveys by the Law Enforcement Assistance Administration (LEAA) showed more than 34 million victimizations for burglary, larceny, and motor vehicle theft—more than 2½ times the number reported to police in that year. When victimization rates are recalculated from the survey data, they are dramatically higher than those in the Uniform Crime Reports. The LEAA surveys found a personal larceny rate of 8899 per 100,000 persons 12 years of age or older. Rates per 100,000 households were 8409 for burglary, 13,375 for larceny, and 1752 for motor vehicle theft. Including the data from victim surveys in conjunction with calculating rates from the bases indicated here leads to dramatically higher crime rates for all categories.[47] The Uniform Crime Reports for 1976 showed rates of 1632, 3122, and 469 per 100,000 people for burglary, larceny, and motor vehicle theft respectively.

Victimized Households: Age, Race, and Socioeconomic Status

The general rates tell us that property crime is far more extensive than police reports would indicate; more specific breakdowns on the basis of age and race of head of household (sex is not given) and family income provide detailed information on who is victimized. Several interesting findings emerge.

The most clear-cut differences have to do with the age factor: whether for burglary, larceny, or vehicle theft, the rate of victimization declines as the age of the head of the household increases. Households headed by people 65 and over have victimization rates between one-fourth and two-fifths of those headed by 20- to 34-year-olds.[48]

For burglary and motor vehicle theft, households headed by blacks or other nonwhites have higher victimization rates than households headed by whites: 50 percent higher for burglary, and 30 percent higher for vehicle theft. However, larceny rates are somewhat higher for households headed by whites.[49]

The most complex relationships emerge when race and income are combined for households. Households can be broken down into six income levels: (1)

under \$3000, (2) \$3000 to \$7499, (3) \$7500 to \$9999, (4) \$10,000 to \$14,999, (5) \$15,000 to \$24,999, and (6) \$25,000 or more. Several differences in rates are apparent. For burglaries, rates for households headed by whites are highest for the low-income group, drop for the middle-income groups, and then rise again for the upper-income groups. Households headed by blacks show a different pattern for burglaries: rates drop as income rises. For larceny, it is the other way around: with only one exception (black families with incomes of \$15,000 to \$24,999), rates increase as family income rises, for both white and black families. Motor vehicle theft resembles larceny, but the differences between groups are greater. Rates are lowest for white families in the under-\$3000 group and generally increase as family income rises, so that those with incomes of \$25,000 or more report nearly 2½ times the number of victimizations.[50] For black families, the victimization rates for vehicle theft rise with family income, peak in the category \$7500 to \$9999, and then decline.[51] Finally, victimization rates for personal larceny without contact are similar to those of household larceny. They decrease as age increases; they are higher for whites than for blacks; and generally, they increase as family income increases.[52]

It is interesting to speculate about the reasons for some of the differences in rates that are reported in the LEAA victim surveys. In general, it can be said that the least powerful groups in society are the most likely to be victimized. Indeed, these are the same groups from which arrested offenders come. Such a statement would explain the higher victimization rates for younger age groups as well as the higher rates for black as compared with white households. However, it is not true that those of lower family income are more likely to be victimized. In fact, for larceny and motor vehicle theft it is higher-income groups, and for burglary both lower- and higher-income groups, that show high rates.

To interpret family income as it relates to rates of victimization for property crimes demands that a "contextual" approach be taken. It must be recognized that crime requires likely offenders, suitable targets, and an absence of capable guardians.[53] To steal, the likely offender must go where the money is—in other words, identify a suitable target. It is also easier if the target is unprotected, that is, if there is an absence of capable guardians. Victimization rates for businesses may be much higher than those for households simply because a business is a highly visible, "suitable" target. Rates for personal larcenies, household larcenies, and motor vehicle theft may increase with family income simply because the more affluent have more to steal and are therefore better targets. Somewhat of an exception, burglary seems to respond to several of the factors. It may be that the burglary rate is high for low-income families because likely offenders have easy access to their homes, and for upper-income families because they are suitable targets. Middle-income families may have lower victimization rates because they are physically removed from likely offenders. The contextual approach is one which will be developed further later in this chapter.

Nonreporting of Property Crimes

In considering the findings of victim surveys, we must question the seriousness of the property crimes reported to survey interviewers. Aside from the tremendous numbers of victimizations, it is striking that such large proportions are never reported to the police. Consider larceny, the most common of the property crimes. Nearly three-fourths of the more than 15 million personal larcenies without contact, and nearly three-fourths of the more than 10 million household larcenies, were never reported to the police. Similarly, slightly over half of household burglaries went unreported. Rates of unreported crime are considerably lower for motor vehicle theft, presumably because these losses are more likely to be covered by insurance. Yet survey interviewers found that three out of ten vehicle thefts were never reported to police. (See Table 14.)

Not reporting property crimes is related in part to social factors and in part to how the victim perceived the situation. In reporting, the key social factor is age: younger victims are less likely to report their victimizations than older ones. For most age groups, males are somewhat less likely than females and blacks are somewhat less likely than whites to report victimizations. However, these sex and race differences in reporting are secondary to the much sharper age differences.[54]

How the victims perceived the situation can be seen in their responses to the question why the crime was not reported. Two reasons dominate: "Nothing could be done" and "The victimization was not important enough." For burglary and larceny, these reasons account for more than half of the nonreporting. For motor vehicle theft, they account for one-third. Other, less common, reasons were "The police would not want to be bothered," "It was a private matter," "I did not want to get involved," and "Fear of reprisal."[55]

That so many victims felt that nothing could be done or that their victimization was of insufficient importance to report points either to low expectations about the criminal justice system or to casual feelings about property crime. As far as a casual attitude is concerned, it might be said that there is some factual basis for it. Close to half of the personal larcenies and more than half of the household larcenies—the most common offense—involved property worth less than $50; fewer than one in ten involved property worth more than $250. Even household burglaries, where there is the element of violation of the home, involved comparatively small amounts of money; fewer than one-fourth of the reported victimizations involved property worth $250 or more. The main exception is motor vehicle theft, for which 58 percent of the victimizations involved property worth at least $250.[56]

TABLE 14.   LEAA Victim Survey: Estimated Number of Victimizations and Percent Not Reported to Police for Personal and Household Victimizations, by Type of Crime

Type of victimization and type of crime	*Estimated victimizations*	*Percent not reported to police*
Personal victimizations		
Personal larceny with contact	510,790	64
Personal larceny without contact	15,861,378	74
Household victimizations		
Burglary	6,684,018	51
Larceny	10,631,289	74
Vehicle theft	1,392,837	30

SOURCE: Timothy J. Flanagan et al., *Sourcebook of Criminal Justice Statistics—1981*, Government Printing Office, Washington, D.C., 1982, p. 232.

Taking the perspective of the victim leads us to question the seriousness of the property crimes uncovered by survey interviewers. The large percentage of unreported personal and household victimizations, combined with the feelings on the part of nonreporters that nothing could be done or that the victimization was not important enough to report, means that property crime, especially in small amounts, is a common, possibly even an accepted, part of American life. To understand why property crime can be acceptable, we need to examine the social context in which it occurs.

Before we turn to the social context, it should be noted that this examination of the victims of person-to-person property crime has relied heavily on the LEAA victim surveys conducted in the mid-1970s. These surveys were selected because they represent the most extensive and most up-to-date work on victims. Moreover, with few exceptions, they have produced findings similar to those of the innovative victim surveys undertaken by the President's Crime Commission.[57] Unlike the victims of violent crime, victims of property crime have seldom been the focus of studies other than the LEAA surveys.

SOCIAL CONTEXTS OF PROPERTY CRIMES

Although consideration of the act, the offender, and the victim is basic to understanding property crime, its dynamics can be fully appreciated only when the social context is examined. Four background factors are of immense importance: (1) the amount and type of property available to be stolen; (2) attitudes toward property; (3) the city; and (4) unemployment. There are also dynamic aspects of the social context. Examining these social factors will shed light on why there is so much property crime in American society (both reported and unreported), why rates of property crime differ with time and place, and what possibilities exist for changing rates of property crime.

Background Factors

Amount and type of property

Property crimes are crimes of opportunity. In bemoaning the tremendous increases in rates of property crimes, we often lose sight of the equally tremendous increases in the amount of property—movable property in particular—that is available to be stolen or at risk of being stolen. The situation was much different in earlier times. One commentator—writing of Brooklyn, New York, in the 1880s—expressed it as follows:

> There was almost nothing to steal and neither place nor person to receive the booty after it had been secured. Wealth was quite evenly distributed, and consisted almost exclusively of real estate, live stock and slaves. Marriage settlements were drawn as late as 1810, in which the jointure consists largely of farming land. There were no banks nor other means of investing money securely. Money itself was scarce. Nearly all the account books of both farmers and merchants of that time show that money transactions were infrequent and that barter was the basis of a large proportion of all the business done. It is not to be inferred that people were more honest then than now. They simply had no opportunities. The change from twenty-eight arrests in

1790 to thirty thousand in 1886 means not so much the increase of wrong-doers as it does the increase of portable wealth and of its concomitant temptations.[58]

Nor is it any secret that movable wealth has increased many times since the 1800s. The number of automobiles alone has risen to over 150 million. Cash and currency in banks have also shown tremendous increases. To put it in a word, we have a society of "abundance"; and this abundance in and of itself may explain much of the dramatic increase in rates of property crime, especially when rates are calculated in terms of number of persons rather than in terms of total amount of property.[59]

Some forms of property are particularly easy to steal. For example, consider motor vehicles and electronic appliances. About 30 percent of all thefts in the Uniform Crime Reports involve motor vehicles or their parts or accessories, or thefts from motor vehicles. Radio and television sets, plus electronic components and accessories, make up a small part of total truckload tonnage, but they account for a larger proportion of goods stolen. Increases in expenditures for motor vehicle parts and lighter weights of durable consumer goods suggest that the consumer goods market "may be producing many more targets suitable for theft."[60]

Attitudes toward property

Aside from the sheer abundance of property, there is the importance we attach to property. Our laws protect the right of individual ownership even though we own so many items that few people keep a written inventory of the things they own. At the same time, we often become casual concerning property; and some of us fail to take elementary precautions to secure our possessions. The strictness of the law as it contrasts with our casual attitude toward our property is the only way to account for one of the greatest disparities in the picture of crime: there is an immense amount of larceny, much of it involving small amounts of money; but little is reported to the police. This disparity can be expressed by figures cited earlier. In 1980 more than 16 million personal larcenies (estimated) were reported to LEAA interviewers, more than half involving property worth less than $50; of these, close to three-fourths were never reported to the police. Similarly, more than 10,000 household larcenies were reported to interviewers, over half of them involving property worth less than $50; 74 percent went unreported. Looking at these figures, we might ask whether petty theft is exceptional or routine behavior.

Other important aspects of our attitudes and values concerning property can be seen in the desire for a bargain and the willingness to be relatively impersonal in property transactions. It is a combination of these two factors which permits us to tolerate the fence, who appears to be a key figure in what can best be described as a well-organized, extensive system of recycling property. On one hand, the fence controls thieves in that he or she sets prices and may even place orders for particular kinds of stolen property. On the other hand, the fence deals with willing businesspersons or with the consuming public, who are not accustomed to asking questions about the origins of merchandise and are at times lured by the prospect of lower prices. It is to these people that the fence sells illegally acquired property. This process of property recycling can work only if those in the system benefit from it and tolerate and condone the activities of the fence. In fact, fences have had few problems in gaining social acceptance or carrying on their work. Many are regarded as "legitimate." Others who are regarded "semilegitimate" or "shady" have little difficulty remaining in business. Even law enforcement tends to be directed much more strongly against the thief than against the fence or the receiver of stolen property.[61]

The city

As was true of violent crime, the city emerges as an important background factor explaining differences in rates of property crime. Generally, the larger the city, the higher the overall rate of property crime. However, property crime is more diffused throughout American society, so that differences among cities of various sizes are not so pronounced as they are for violent crime. In cities with populations over 150,000, rates even decline somewhat. The rate for a city of 250,000 to 499,999 people is only about double the rate for a city of less than 10,000. Despite increases in recent years, suburban and rural areas continue to show lower overall rates than cities of any size. Larceny is a significant factor in property crime. Its rates show the least variation among localities of different sizes. By comparison, rates for motor vehicle theft increase sharply as city size increases. Burglary rates also increase with city size (although less sharply); but, as with the general rate of property crime, the increase occurs only up to populations of 250,000 to 499,999—for larger populations the rate declines. (See Table 15.)

Seizing upon the general relationship between size of city and crime rate, some researchers have argued that crime rates are directly associated with population density. Although this may be true for violent crime, for property crime the association is by no means simple or direct. As the Uniform Crime Reports data (cited in the foregoing paragraph) indicate, with the exception of

TABLE 15. City Size and Crime Rates: Overall Property Crime, Burglary, Larceny, and Motor Vehicle Theft

		Crime rates			
City size	Number of cities	Overall property	Burglary	Larceny	Motor vehicle theft
1 million +	5	7337.9	2473.4	3466.6	1397.9
500,000–999,999	18	8252.8	2621.9	4715.4	915.6
250,000–499,999	32	8757.7	2923.4	5064.5	769.8
100,000–249,999	112	7944.7	2476.0	4874.0	594.7
50,000–99,999	272	6370.6	1927.2	3881.0	562.3
25,000–49,999	594	5857.8	1625.1	3810.0	422.7
10,000–24,999	1500	4935.9	1309.2	3307.9	318.8
−10,000	5670	4466.2	1093.1	3135.9	237.2
Surburban areas	1104 agencies	3954.0	1411.9	2238.3	303.8
Rural areas	2626 agencies	2119.1	836.7	1157.7	124.7

SOURCE: Federal Bureau of Investigation (FBI), *Uniform Crime Reports—1981*, Government Printing Office, Washington, D.C., 1982, pp. 144–145.

motor vehicle theft, rates do not continue to increase for cities of 500,000 or more population. More specifically, detailed analysis shows the highest crime rates to be in the central business districts of urban areas; the highest rates of offenders are found in lower-class, slum neighborhoods. Particularly vulnerable to burglary are businesses in areas adjacent to areas where many offenders live.[62] Finally, recent research has shown that (1) decreases in population density in physical locations produce increases in property crimes;[63] and (2) according to a reanalysis of data from victimization surveys, household burglary and household larceny in central cities are negatively correlated with population density—i.e., the less dense the population, the higher the rate of property crime.[64]

That the relationship between crime rates and population density is not clear-cut for property crime is attributable to the interplay of the three factors noted earlier: motivated offenders, suitable targets, and absence of capable guardians. If motivated offenders come from urban slum neighborhoods with high concentrations of offenders, they will not have ready access to the more lucrative residential targets in suburban areas. As a result, they will go either to adjacent businesses and well-to-do urban areas or to nearby slum urban areas. Such a rationale would underlie the finding that burglary rates are highest for families who are on the upper and lower rungs of the income ladder. Those in the middle-income range are more likely to be physically removed from the potential offender.

Also clouding the relationship between crime rates and population density is a change in guardianship. It may be that with the increase in property there has also been more extensive use of security guards, locking devices, alarm systems, and public information campaigns encouraging the average citizen to take precautions against crime. Those with more valuable property are more likely to take measures to protect it, thereby reducing the opportunity for property theft.

Unemployment

A fourth background factor is unemployment. It is often assumed that unemployment leads to crime. Again, however, the evidence is not clear-cut. On the one hand, there is general, if not uniform, support for a correlation between prison admissions and unemployment. Rearrest has also been shown to be related to unemployment.[65] On the other hand, a higher unemployment rate would in and of itself produce a greater number of convicted criminals who are unemployed.[66] Moreover, one interview study of inmates of Riker's Island (New York City) found that the cumulative number of cases which departed from the simple model of "unemployment leads to crime" probably exceeded half of the entire sample. Over 30 percent of the cases showed a pattern of alternating or concurrent work and criminal activity.[67] In unemployment we once again have a background factor that is somewhat, but by no means directly, related to the rate of property crime.

Dynamic Aspects of Social Context

Like rates of violent crime, rates of property crime are very much affected by social changes. In today's society, the increased youthful poulation has probably influenced rates of property crime even more than rates of violent crime, since (as we have seen) property offenders engage in criminal behavior at an earlier age than violent offenders. There is also an increased urban population; and insofar as rates are higher in medium-size and larger-size cities, the overall rate of property crime is higher. Another factor is the somewhat higher rates of unemployment in the 1970s, although (as noted above) these are only indirectly related to crime. Finally, the major shift of routine activities away from the home (see Chapter 9) should mean that more suitable targets are at risk. Homes are more likely to be left unattended as more people engage in out-of-town travel, more married women work outside the home, and vacation periods are longer. At the same time, being out of the home makes people themselves potential targets for theft more often.

One dynamic aspect of the social context was noted earlier but needs to be restated here: the increased involvement of females in property crime. The shift of routine activities away from the home has meant both that more property targets are at risk and that more females are in situations that offer opportunities for crime. Hence there have been increases not only in the number of females arrested each year for property crimes but also in the proportion of arrestees who are female. As noted earlier, female involvement is greatest in larceny, the most common of the property crimes.

SUMMARY

Several forms of property crime were basic to the common law which emerged in England over 700 years ago. Robbery and burglary were the earliest to be defined. Larceny in its modern form appeared with the Carrier's case of 1473 and underwent extensive development as England became a commercial, industrial society.

Today, person-to-person property crime, while less of a focus of public concern than person-to-person violent crime, accounts for 90 percent of all reported index crimes. Larceny alone accounts for half of the arrests made by police for index crimes. Yet much property crime remains unreported, and clearance rates are low. The most costly of the three major property crimes, motor vehicle theft, can be characterized as a "happy crime" in that few offenders are prosecuted and victims' considerable losses are cushioned by insurance. Motor vehicle theft is also unique in that it is somewhat on the decline. Although often neglected, the fence plays a key role in property crime in marketing or "recycling" stolen goods.

Property offenders who are arrested are more likely to be male than female, although males and females are moving toward equality in arrest rates for larceny. Arrested offenders tend to be young, black, and of lower socioeconomic status. Self-report studies show theft to be widespread throughout all social groups; but some recent research based on self-reported behavior has found that blacks and young people of lower socioeconomic status are still overrepresented among multiple or chronic offenders. For some people, property crime is an occupation or even a "profession."

Victims of property crime are numerous. Households headed by younger people are more likely to be victimized by property crime than those headed by middle-aged or older people. Households headed by blacks and other nonwhites have higher victimization rates for burglary and motor vehicle theft; those headed by whites have higher rates for larceny. Despite the extensive victimization, much property crime remains unreported to police.

The presently high rates of person-to-person property crime, both reported and unreported, can be attributed to several background factors and to various dynamic aspects of the social context. To begin with, American society has an enormous amount of property that is available to be stolen. Although ownership of personal property is protected by law, Americans can be relatively casual about items they own, especially items of little value. There is a secondary property distribution market, controlled by fences who resell stolen property, often on a large scale. With some exceptions, large cities have higher rates of property crime than smaller ones, probably because they provide more opportunity for theft. When suitable targets are located near motivated offenders, rates are particularly high.

Certain dynamic aspects of the social context have also served to draw ever-increasing numbers of motivated offenders and suitable targets together in the absence of guardians or policing agents to prevent thefts from occurring. Youthful and urban populations are on the increase. Unemployment rates, although indirectly related to crime, have been higher in recent years. As activities are more often oriented away from the home, more property is at risk. At the same time, it appears that more females have been drawn into property crime.

NOTES

[1] On the attrition of arrests for robbery, burglary, and larceny, see: Vera Institute of Justice, *Felony Arrests: Their Prosecution and Disposition in New York City's Courts,* Vera Institute of Justice, Longman, New York, 1977, 1981, chaps. 3–5.

[2] See: Frank R. Prassel, *Criminal Law, Justice, and Society,* Goodyear, Santa Monica, Calif., 1979, chap. 2.

[3] Federal Bureau of Investigation (FBI), *Uniform Crime Reports—1981,* Government Printing Office, Washington, D.C., 1982, p. 316.

[4] Carl E. Pope, "Crime-Specific Analysis: An Empirical Examination of Burglary Offender Characteristics," monograph, U.S. Department of Justice, Law Enforcement Assistance Administration, analytic report no. 10, p. 12.

[5] See: FBI, *Uniform Crime Reports—1981,* pp. 21–23.

[6] Jerome Hall, *Theft, Law, and Society,* Little, Brown, Boston, Mass., 1935. On the evolution of the law of theft, see also: Lloyd L. Weinreb, *Criminal Law: Cases, Comment, and Questions,* 3d ed., Foundation Press, Mineola, N.Y., 1969, part 2.

[7] FBI, *Uniform Crime Reports—1981,* p. 316. Note that embezzlement, "con" games, forgery, worthless checks, etc., are excluded from the counts of index crime. These forms of larceny are regarded as Part II offenses; see: Box 1 in the present text.

[8] Charles H. McCaghy, Peggy C. Giordano, and Trudy Knicely Henson, "Auto Theft: Offender and Offense Characteristics," *Criminology,* vol. 15, no. 3, November 1977, pp. 367–385.

[9] Thomas Plate, *Crime Pays!* Ballantine, New York, 1975, pp. 37–38.

[10] Jerome Hall, *Theft, Law, and Society,* chap. 6.

[11] FBI, *Uniform Crime Reports—1981,* p. 316.

[12] See: Leroy C. Gould, "The Changing Structure of Property Crime in an Affluent Society," *Social Forces,* vol. 48, September 1969, pp. 50–59.

[13] Marilyn E. Walsh, *The Fence: A New Look at the World of Property Theft,* Greenwood, Westport, Conn., 1977; and Duncan Chappell and Marilyn Walsh, " 'No Questions Asked': A Consideration of the Crime of Criminal Receiving," *Crime and Delinquency,* vol. 20, April 1974, pp. 157–168.

[14] Rita James Simon, *Women and Crime,* Heath (Lexington Books), Lexington, Mass., 1975. See also: Darrell J. Steffensmeier and Charles Jordan, "Changing Patterns of Female Crime in Rural America, 1962–1975," *Rural Sociology,* vol. 43, 1978, pp. 87–102.

[15] Simon, *Women and Crime,* p. 47. See also: Freda Adler, *Sisters in Crime: The Rise of the New Female Criminal,* McGraw-Hill, New York, 1975.

[16] Marvin E. Wolfgang, Robert M. Figlio, and Thorsten Sellin, *Delinquency in a Birth Cohort,* University of Chicago Press, Chicago, Ill., 1972, chap. 5.

[17] Richard A. Berk, Kenneth J. Lenihan, and Peter H. Rossi, "Crime and Poverty: Some Experimental Evidence from Ex Offenders," *American Sociological Review,* vol. 45, October 1980, pp. 766–786.

[18] See: Chapters 2 and 3 of the present text.

[19] Charles R. Tittle and Wayne J. Villemez, "Social Class and Criminality," *Social Forces,* vol. 56, December 1977, pp. 474–502.

[20] James A. Wallerstein and J. C. Wyle, "Our Law-Abiding Law-Breakers," *Federal Probation,* vol. 25, April 1947, pp. 107–112.

[21] For a review, see: LaMar T. Empey, *American Delinquency: Its Meaning and Construction,* Dorsey, Homewood, Ill., 1978, chap. 7.

[22] Walter B. Miller, "Theft Behavior in City Gangs," in Malcolm W. Klein, ed., *Juvenile Gangs in Context: Theory, Research, and Action,* Prentice-Hall, Englewood Cliffs, N.J., 1967, pp. 25–37.

[23] Wolfgang et al., *Delinquency in a Birth Cohort,* chaps. 5 and 6.

[24] Delbert S. Elliott and Suzanne S. Ageton, "Reconciling Race and Class Differences in Self-Reported and Official Estimates of Delinquency," *American Sociological Review,* vol. 45, February 1980, pp. 95–110.

[25] Ibid., p. 104.

[26] James A. Inciardi, *Careers in Crime,* Rand McNally, Chicago, Ill., 1975, pp. 12–13.

[27] Edwin H. Sutherland, *The Professional Thief: By a Professional Thief,* University of Chicago Press, Chicago, Ill., 1937, chap. 9.

[28] Inciardi, *Careers in Crime,* chap. 7.

[29] Neal Shover, "The Social Organization of Burglary," *Social Problems,* vol. 20, no. 4, Spring 1973, pp. 499–514.

[30] Marilyn E. Walsh, *The Fence.* See also: Carl B. Klockars, *The Professional Fence,* Free Press, New York, 1974; and Illinois Legislative Investigating Commission, "Fencing: Criminal Redistribution of Stolen Property," report to the Illinois General Assembly, May 1978.

[31] Don C. Gibbons, *Society, Crime, and Criminal Careers: An Introduction to Criminology,* 3d ed., Prentice-Hall, Englewood Cliffs, N.J., 1977, chaps. 12–13.

[32] Walsh, *The Fence,* pp. 61–62.

[33] McCaghy et al., "Auto Theft; Offender and Offense Characteristics."

[34] Gould, "The Changing Structure of Property Crime in an Affluent Society."

[35] National Association of Attorneys General, Committee on the Office of Attorney General, "Organized Auto Theft," monograph, 1979.

[36] Roger Hood and Richard Sparks, *Key Issues in Criminology,* McGraw-Hill, New York, 1970, pp. 135–138.

[37] Wolfgang et al., *Delinquency in a Birth Cohort,* p. 65.

[38] British Home Office Statistical Research Unit, *The Sentence of the Court,* Her Majesty's Stationery Office, London, 1964.

[39] Pope, "Crime-Specific Analysis," analytic report no. 11.

[40] See: Chapter 9 of the present text.

[41] David P. Farrington, "Self-Reports of Deviant Behavior: Predictive or Stable?" *Journal of Criminal Law and Criminology,* vol. 64, March 1973, pp. 99–110.

[42] Harold E. Pepinsky, "The Irresponsibility of Explaining Criminality," paper presented at a meeting of the Academy of Criminal Justice, Cincinnati, Ohio, March 14–16, 1979, p. 3.

[43] Ibid., p. 12.

[44] Wolfgang et al., *Delinquency in a Birth Cohort,* p. 105.

[45] For an overview of victim surveys, see: Chapter 2 of the present text. On their methodology, see: Chapter 3 of the present text.

[46] Robert Louis Gasser, "The Confidence Game," *Federal Probation,* vol. 27, no. 4, December 1963, pp. 47–54.

[47] Timothy J. Flanagan et al., eds., *Sourcebook of Criminal Justice Statistics—1981,* U.S. Department of Justice, LEAA, 1981, Government Printing Office, Washington, D.C., pp. 232, 248–249.

[48] Nicolete Parisi et al., eds., *Sourcebook of Criminal Justice Statistics—1978,* U.S. Department of Justice, LEAA, Government Printing Office, Washington, D.C., 1979, p. 398. Comparable figures are not given in the 1981 *Sourcebook.*

[49] Ibid., p. 397. Comparable figures are not given in the 1981 *Sourcebook.*

[50] The relationship between family income and motor vehicle theft is probably exaggerated somewhat because higher-income families tend to have more automobiles per family.

[51] Parisi et al., *Sourcebook of Criminal Justice Statistics—1978,* p. 398.

[52] Ibid., pp. 380, 378, and 384.

[53] Lawrence E. Cohen and Marcus Felson, "Social Change and Crime Rate Trends: A Routine Activity Approach," *American Sociological Review,* vol. 44, August 1979, pp. 588–608.

[54] Flanagan et al., *Sourcebook of Criminal Justice Statistics—1981,* pp. 236–239.

[55] Ibid., p. 372.

[56] Ibid., pp. 242–243.

[57] Phillip H. Ennis, *Criminal Victimization in the United States: A Report of a National Survey,* President's Commission on Law Enforcement and Administration of Justice, Washington, D.C., 1967.

[58] William E. S. Fales, *Brooklyn's Guardians,* Brooklyn, New York, 1887. No publisher identified.

[59] Gould, "The Changing Structure of Property Crime in an Affluent Society."

[60] Cohen and Felson, "Social Change and Crime Rate Trends," pp. 596 and 599.

[61] Walsh, *The Fence.* See also: Klockars, *The Professional Fence.*

[62] Sarah L. Boggs, "Urban Crime Patterns," *American Sociological Review,* vol. 30, no. 6, December 1966, pp. 899–908.

[63] Lawrence E. Cohen, Marcus Felson, and Kenneth C. Land, "Property Crime Rates in the United States: A Macrodynamic Analysis, 1947–1977, with Ex Ante Forecasts for the Mid-1980s," *American Journal of Sociology,* vol. 86, no. 1, July 1980, pp. 90–118.

[64] David L. Schichor, David L. Decker, and Robert M. O'Brien, "Population Density and Criminal Victimization: Some Unexpected Findings in Central Cities," *Criminology,* vol. 17, no. 1, August 1979, pp. 184–193.

[65] Peter H. Rossi, Richard A. Berk, and Kenneth J. Lenihan, *Money, Work, and Crime: Experimental Evidence,* Academic Press, New York, 1980.

[66] For a general discussion, see: Robert W. Gillespie, "Economic Factors in Crime and Delinquency: A Critical Review of the Empirical Evidence," final report submitted to the National Institute of Law Enforcement and Criminal Justice, September 15, 1975.

[67] Michelle Sviridoff and James W. Thompson, "Linkages between Employment and Crime: A Qualitative Study of Rikers Releases," Employment and Crime Project, Vera Institute of Justice, New York, September 10, 1979.

11

Corporate Crime

To discuss corporate crime, we need to change our emphasis from "crime in the streets" to "crime in the suites." Though the patterns may differ, corporations—and, for that matter, other types of organizations—are hardly strangers to crime. In this chapter on corporate crime, we shall see that corporations may be offenders. In Chapter 12, we shall take a look at the other side of the coin and observe that they can also be victims of crime.

AN OVERVIEW

When asked about crime, few Americans think of large corporations. After all, are not corporations in the business of making a profit? Do they not need to deal fairly and honestly with customers, employees, and competitors so that they can maintain goodwill? Are not corporate executives already affluent? Why should they need to commit crime? What can they gain from it?

Not thinking about corporations in connection with crime is in part due to the absence of systematic statistics on the overall extent of corporate crime. The FBI does not publish a "corporate crime index," and no reports of corporate crime are published annually so that trends can be observed. Nor are there victimization surveys or self-report studies. One of the ironies of corporate crime is that victims often remain unaware of their victimization. Another is that corporate criminals in many instances neither see themselves nor are seen by the public as criminals (Figure 5).

FIGURE 5.
Corporate crime is not always considered "criminal." (SOURCE: *Village Voice*, April 6, 1972.)

Some Examples of Corporate Crime

However, a great deal of piecemeal evidence suggests that we must concern ourselves with corporate crime. Nearly every week, some large national corporation is mentioned in newspapers or magazines in connection with some type of criminal activity. Consider the following instances that have appeared in the press:

Illegal dumping of pesticides by *Hooker Chemical Company* in California poisoned local drinking wells. In Florida, Hooker was convicted of polluting the air with fluoride. In New York, Hooker was cited for dumping toxic wastes into the Love Canal. In each of these cases, top managers were reportedly aware of the illegal activity. (*New York Times,* August 5, 1979; August 6, 1979; and June 8, 1980.)

The corporate records of *Firestone* showed that its top management was aware from the outset of flaws in the "500" steel-belted radial tire. The House Committee on Oversight and Investigations determined that the tire had been "the major cause or chief contributing factor in accidents involving 41 deaths, about 60 injuries, and hundreds of incidents of property damage." (*Time,* June 25, 1979.)

Although *Ford* executives have not been convicted of reckless homicide, internal corporate memos indicate that they knew before marketing the Pinto that its design made it more vulnerable to fire in low-speed, rear-end crashes than other cars. An $8 part would have reduced the risk of fire but was not added until 1976 so that the corporation could save $20.6 million. An estimated 500 people were killed over an eight-year period. (*Village Voice,* October 25, 1979.)[1]

American Airlines paid a $500,000 fine for improper maintenance of DC-10

Representatives John Moss and James Collins of the House Committee on Oversight and Investigations examine a Firestone steel-belted radial 500 tire.   (UPI)

jumbo jets, including one plane which crashed in Chicago with a loss of 273 lives. (*New York Times,* November 17, 1979.)

Illegal payments to secure business in foreign countries, illegal political campaign contributions, and secret slush funds appear to be a way of life for many major corporations. Among those cited for these offenses and subsequently pleading guilty are *Westinghouse, Lockheed, Gulf Oil, Phillips Petroleum,* and *Diamond International,* to name only a few. (*Village Voice,* October 25, 1979.)

The *International Systems and Controls Corporation,* designed to help third world countries develop their energy and agriculture, was accused by the Securities and Exchange Commission of making more than $23 million of illegal payments and having outstanding commitments for another $10 million of such payments in order to get $750 million in orders over the past decade. Such payments are criminally liable under the Foreign Corrupt Practices Act and United States securities laws. (*Time,* July 23, 1979.)

In its rush to market an intrauterine contraceptive device (IUD), to women, the *A.H. Robbins Company* used faulty statistics and improper tests. As a result, 17 women died and hundreds needed painful operations because of ''side effects'' produced when the device was inserted. The company earned $16 million from the IUDs, although it subsequently incurred substantial litigation costs.[2]

The list of examples of corporate crime could go on and on. Moreover, there is another chilling aspect of corporate crime: the routine violation of occupational safety regulations. Some years ago, the Occupational Safety and Health Administration (OSHA) reported that 100,000 Americans die annually from occupationally related diseases.[3] Many, if not most, of these deaths could be avoided with adequate precautions. In some instances, the neglect is legendary. Legislation providing for safety in coal mining was not passed until more than 120,000 workers had been lost in 100 years of mining accidents.[4] Although asbestos and vinyl chloride have long been known as carcinogens, workers have continued to be employed in their manufacture without adequate precautions. Such precautions could readily be taken but would severely cut into corporate profits.[5]

Extent of Corporate Crime

Although the economic cost of corporate crime is almost impossible to estimate, it is enormous. In addition to environmental and health hazards, each of the cases mentioned above involved millions or even billions of dollars. There are other rough estimates. In the mid-1970s, for example, it was estimated that businesses were paying a total of $5 billion per year in illegal kickbacks. These kickbacks were made partly as direct cash payments; but many other methods were also used: paying for automobile rentals, providing paid vacations, providing credit cards and charge accounts, paying rents on vacation dwellings and at resorts, providing unsecured loans, providing free goods as samples, buying from a business owned or run by relatives, putting relatives on the payroll as ''consultants,'' giving scholarships to children, paying country club dues, furnishing company aircraft, and rigging company contests.[6]

One investigation of illegal practices dealt specifically with the oil industry. It found illegal price collusion among intermediaries ("daisy chaining"), other illegal price manipulations, and falsification of reports to the government. Citing these findings, Representative John Conyers, Jr., a Michigan Democrat and chairman of the Judiciary Subcommittee of the House of Representatives, was led to say that the government is "sitting on top of the largest criminal conspiracy in America, . . . costing the American people millions of dollars."[7]

Finally, in a general estimate of the cost of corporate crime, Senator Philip Hart of the Senate Judiciary Subcommittee on Antitrust and Monopoly was quoted as saying: "Faulty goods, monopolistic practices, and similar law violations annually cost consumers between $174 billion and $231 billion."[8] To put these figures into perspective: in the year in which the estimate was made, the estimated total annual cost to consumers of corporate violations exceeded the total budget for national defense and amounted to between 7 percent and 10 percent of the gross national product. In any event, no matter how one calculates the economic cost of corporate crime, its total is far in excess of the approximately $5 billion involved in the "street crimes"—robbery, burglary, larceny, and motor vehicle theft.

Few scholarly studies have attempted to estimate the incidence of corporate involvement in criminal behavior. Of those that have, the most striking is a classic study by Edwin Sutherland, who, in a book published in 1949, examined the "criminal history" of 70 of the largest manufacturing, mining, and mercantile corporations in the United States.[9] In all, he found a total of 980 decisions against these corporations, with a maximum of 50 and an average of 14 per corporation. A breakdown by type of adverse decision is as follows:

307	Restraint of trade (monopoly)
222	Patent infringement
158	Unfair labor practice
130	Other
97	Misrepresentation in advertising
66	Illegal rebate
980	Total[10]

Of the 980 decisions, 158 were executed in criminal court, 296 in civil court, 129 in equity court, 361 by commission order, 25 by commission confiscation, and 11 by commission settlement. However, even if the analysis were limited to decisions by criminal courts, "it would show that 60 percent of the 70 larger corporations have been convicted in criminal courts and have an average of four convictions each."[11] In fact, Sutherland adds, 30 of the 70 corporations either were illegal in origin or began illegal activities immediately after their origin; and 8 were probably illegal in origin or in initial policies.

Although Sutherland's work received much acclaim, it was not until 1979 that another large-scale, comprehensive investigation of corporate violations of the law was conducted. Under the direction of Marshal B. Clinard, this investigation examined the criminal behavior of 582 of America's publicly owned corporations, with annual sales between $300 million and $45 billion. Taking the years

1975–1976, the researchers examined all enforcement actions obtainable, initiated, and enforced by 24 federal agencies.[12] Like Sutherland, Clinard and his associates found an immense amount of corporate activity that was illegal, criminal, or both. More than 60 percent of the corporations had at least one legal action initiated against them during the relatively brief period of the study (two years). For firms with one or more violations, the average was 4.4 per corporation. More than 40 percent of the manufacturing corporations engaged in *repeated* violations. As Clinard and Yaeger report:

> Fully one-quarter of the 477 manufacturing corporations, or 120, had multiple cases of non-minor violations charged against them during 1975–1976; five or more such cases were brought against 32 firms.[13]

In certain industries, illegal corporate behavior appears to be quite common. The motor vehicle, pharmaceutical, and oil refining industries accounted for almost half of all violations, and four out of every ten violations the researchers characterized as "serious" or "moderate." In these industries about 90 percent of the firms violated the law at least once; 80 percent had one or more serious or moderate violations.

Corporate Crime versus Other Organizational Crime

In focusing on corporate crime in this chapter, we should note that two phenomena are *not* included. First, corporate crime is not the same as "white-collar crime." Although the term "white-collar crime" can include corporate crime, it is a more general term that covers crimes such as embezzlement, computer crime, frauds against corporations, and (according to some authors) political corruption and misconduct. These topics are most important; but it seems best to discuss them as other types of crime (see Chapters 12 and 15).

Second, corporate crime as discussed here does not include instances where business is organized specifically for criminal activity. Rackets, land swindles, "front organizations," and bogus insurance schemes are, of course, also part of criminology. However, in dealing with corporate crime, the point is that we find a great deal—indeed, an enormous amount—of criminal activity in organizations that are legitimate, often highly respected institutions of our society.

Having considered the importance of corporate crime, we can turn now to its analysis in terms of corporate criminal acts, corporate criminal offenders, victims of corporate crime, and social contexts of corporate crime.

CORPORATE CRIMINAL ACTS

Generally, corporate crime can be defined as follows:

> Illegal acquisitive behavior engaged in for the immediate purpose of increasing corporate (as distinguished from personal) wealth.[14]

As we have already seen, the range of acts that can fit into the category of corporate crime is considerable. However, it is also useful to note that there has

Some corporate actions against the environment have become major concerns in the United States. This 66-year-old man, a long-time resident of the Love Canal area, had to abandon his home because poisonous chemicals from a nearby landfill seeped into his basement. (UPI)

been a historical line of development. Beginning in the late 1800s, there was an emphasis on monopoly or antitrust law. Subsequently, unfair labor practices were added. At present, actions against the environment and the consumer have become major concerns.[15]

Controlling corporate crime has been neither easy nor successful. Unlike street crime, corporate crime has always occasioned much public debate over what particular acts should be defined as "criminal." Nor does the debate stop with definition; it usually extends to enforcement of the law—in particular, to what penalties should be administered.

Let us look first at monopoly, probably the most important corporate crime; and then at the range of other acts that subsequently became defined as corporate crimes.

Monopoly and Antitrust Violations

The apparent need to develop legislation applicable to corporations resulted from the enormous expansion of corporate business interests and activities in the post-Civil War period. This "dark age" of American history was a period in which there was a dramatic transformation not only in American technology but also in the creation of large, nationwide, "capitalistic" corporations. Two particular developments, the invention of the trust device and New Jersey's legalization of the holding company, paved the way for the rise of monopolies—that is, organizations which dominate whole markets for various types of products. After the establishment of the Rockefeller-dominated Standard Oil Trust, which monopolized the oil refining industry, a host of other monopolistic trusts also emerged: cottonseed oil in 1884; linseed oil in 1885; whiskey, lead, and sugar in 1887; matches in 1889; tobacco in 1890; and rubber in 1892.[16]

The enormous concentration of power in the monopolistic trusts came into direct conflict with the traditional American values of individualism and competition. These values, well established in American society, had in fact been brought to America by the colonists. Antimonopoly sentiment can be traced back to businesspeople in Europe, who struggled against crown monopolies in the late Middle Ages. The "business revolutions" of 1688 in England and 1789 in France were important statements on behalf of "free" and "open" trade—statements that became important values in the emerging American society.[17] In part, the Revolutionary War was fought because colonists objected to an absentee government which protected British traders from colonial expansion. Later, after the republic was fully established, Andrew Jackson broke up the Second Bank of the United States because it threatened to become too powerful.[18]

In light of these values, it is no wonder that there was widespread public opposition to the newly formed trusts. As if to add insult to injury, many of the trusts were put together with business methods that can best be described as ruthless if not outright criminal. The Rockefeller Standard Oil Trust, for example, was predicated on illegal, secret rebates with the leading railroads of the country. Indeed, in the development of the great American fortunes, laws were routinely flouted and corruption was common.[19]

The Sherman Act

Opposition to the trusts came from a number of groups—especially farmers, who felt squeezed by the "new monopolists." The political battle lines became drawn. In 1888, both the Republican and the Democratic parties had antimonopoly planks in their platforms. In addition, the Populist party expressed the sentiment very clearly:

> The fruits of the toil of millions are boldly stolen to build up the colossal fortunes for a few. . . . From the same prolific womb of governmental injustice we breed the two great classes—tramps and millionaires.[20]

The result of all this feeling was the Sherman Antitrust Act, passed by Congress in 1890. It prohibited "every contract, combination . . . or conspiracy in restraint of trade" and made it criminal to "monopolize or attempt to monopolize" any line of commerce in the United States.[21]

Despite the popular sentiment for its passage, the Sherman Antitrust Act became one of the most unenforced pieces of legislation in the history of the United States. Few cases were filed under the act. Of the first seven that were filed, the government lost six. The Justice Department did not even appropriate funds for antitrust activities until 1903. At that time, five lawyers and four stenographers began the Antitrust Division of the Justice Department.

In retrospect, it can be seen that the Sherman Act was full of loopholes. For one thing, interlocking directorates and stock acquisitions among competitors were still permitted. For another, the vagueness and generality of the Sherman Act permitted the courts to make interpretations that dramatically reduced its impact. Perhaps the most damaging court interpretation was the Supreme Court's "rule of reason" test, by which intent had to be proved. Under this interpretation, the only illegal trusts that could be prosecuted were "bad" trusts formed by people "intending to monopolize" and engaging in predatory practices.

Subsequent legislation

Each attempt to close some loopholes left others open. The Clayton Act, which also established the Federal Trade Commission, prohibited stock acquisitions but not asset acquisitions. The latter soon proliferated. It was not until the Celler-Kefauver Act of 1950, which prohibited asset acquisitions, that "horizontal" mergers (between competitors) and "vertical" mergers (between suppliers, producers, and dealers) were effectively controlled. However, the loophole then became "conglomerate" mergers, in which corporations joined forces with other corporations in nonrelated areas of business activity and argued that this involved no conspiracy or restraint of trade.[22]

The result of loopholes in antitrust laws and unenforcement of antitrust policy is a relentless increase both in the number of mergers and in the size of large corporations. Most observers distinguish three waves of mergers: 1898–1902, 1925–1929, and 1955–1969. These waves generally coincide with bull markets in stocks; and each wave has seen increased numbers of firms involved in mergers. In fact, in the period 1967–1969 there were more mergers per year than in the entire wave of 1898–1902.

The largest 500 manufacturing corporations, the "Fortune 500," reported over $1.4 trillion in sales in 1979 and $78.2 billion in profits. They employ more than 15 million people. The largest 200 account for two-thirds of industrial sales and three-fourths of all manufacturing assets. Moreover, it would appear that the large corporations are continuing to grow. In 1950, the largest 200 controlled "only" half of all manufacturing assets. By another count, between 1960 and 1974 the sales of all corporations grew by 135 percent; those of the 25 largest grew by 772 percent.

It is in the failure of the Sherman Act and the Clayton Act, and in the long history of relative unenforcement of antitrust laws, that one can see some of the key issues in corporate crime. Corporate crime is less visible than street crime; and there is less social consensus about how to deal with it. Moreover, its very definition conflicts with the activities of substantial business interests. Thus, there has been a continuing debate over whether monopoly should be defined as a crime, and if so how.[23]

Some problems of antitrust enforcement

Compounding the general absence of consensus about antitrust laws is the difficulty of defining issues and injuries involved in particular cases. The size of the task is dramatically apparent in large cases such as the recent government actions to break up American Telegraph and Telephone (AT&T) and International Business Machines (IBM). The latter, called the "case of the century" has already involved the accumulation of over 30 million pages of material and incurred a vast amount of professional work. (See Box 6.) It is reported that IBM's legal expenses for its defense exceed the entire annual budget of the Antitrust Division of the Justice Department.[24]

The difficulties in defining monopoly, both generally and in specific cases, underlie the pattern of weak enforcement. For one thing, there are few resources devoted to the enforcement of antitrust laws. Even though the staff of the Antitrust Division is much larger today than it was in 1903, it is still relatively small compared with the size of the problem. Indeed, it is almost ludicrous to imagine a staff of 427 professionals with a budget of $40 million attempting to oversee the activities of 203 industrial firms each worth over $1 billion in assets, 85,000 worth over $1 million in assets, and 1.8 million firms in all.[25]

It is also true that in the cases which have been prosecuted, actual penalties for violating the law are both weak and rarely applied. Between 1955 and 1974, the maximum penalties were a $50,000 fine for a corporation and one year in prison for an individual. Although these were raised in 1975 to $1 million and three years in prison, the penalties are still light; the fine especially is minimal compared with the billions of dollars in assets held by many firms. Moreover, as it turns out, few executives ever go to prison. In fact, in the first 82 years of the Sherman Act, in only four instances did an executive actually spend time in jail or prison.[26]

The weakness of the Sherman Antitrust Act and its subsequent underenforcement point up a more general problem: the attempt to define criminal acts in the absence of widespread social consensus. Richard Hofstader argues that

Box 6: The Case of the Century

On the last working day of the Johnson Administration in January 1969, the Justice Department filed suit against International Business Machines, accusing it of monopolizing the "general purpose" computer business. Specifically, IBM was charged with trying to force customers to buy entire IBM systems for commercial use, and with keeping competitors out of the market. A decade later *U.S. v. IBM* is still droning on, a costly monument to the law's delay. The frustrating case, Yale Professor Robert Bork told TIME's conference, is the antitrust division's "Viet Nam." Thomas Barr, the Cravath, Swaine & Moore attorney who is leading the IBM defense, explained at the meeting why he sees no light at the end of the tunnel.

For three years after its complaint was filed, Barr recounted, the Government did almost nothing. Pretrial "discovery," which allows lawyers to search for facts and find out what evidence the other side plans to use, did not begin until 1972. For the next two

years, each side deluged the other with paper, 30 million pages worth. After several delays, the trial began in 1975 in U.S. District Court in Manhattan. It took the Government almost three years to present its case; one witness alone testified for 78 days.

Yet, Barr said, the case is now "almost dead in the water." Reason: the Government insisted on yet another round of discovery starting last year. Federal attorneys began deposing IBM witnesses again and requesting even more documents. Queried by TIME, the Government's chief lawyer in the case, Robert Staal, insisted that in order to cross-examine IBM's witnesses, the Government needs to know what IBM has been doing in the computer industry since 1974, when the first round of discovery ended. But Barr contended that since the case started, the Government has brought in a whole new team of lawyers, who had

Continued on next page.

to educate themselves. Scoffed Barr: "This is a continuous reinvention of the wheel."

The case has also been a man-eater for IBM and its law firm. In order to recruit top law school graduates, Cravath has constantly had to boost starting salaries (this year, at least $30,000); the grads fear becoming stuck on the IBM case, which is widely seen as a black hole for fledgling legal careers. Those who are assigned to the case get up to $5,000 extra combat pay annually.

Assistant Attorney General John Shenefield has repeatedly told Congress that his antitrust division is trying to speed the case. But it is difficult to see how. This winter, Barr recounted, the Government subpoenaed IBM Chairman Frank Cary to produce virtually every document relating to computers accumulated by the company since 1973. That amounts to 5 billion pieces of paper, said Barr, who claims that to comply would take 100 lawyers 620 years working full time. Staal, however, called Barr's figures "grossly exaggerated" and contended that the parties could easily work out a compromise, but that IBM refuses to negotiate.

John Diebold, the noted computer consultant, who was asked by IBM to be a witness, gave the TIME conference "a peasant's view of what it is like to have the Justice Department's B-52s drop napalm on me." First, at Government request, he turned over 300,000 pages of documents from his company, the Diebold Group, relating to the computer industry. Said Diebold: "That is a minor ripple in the ocean of paper that has been delivered by IBM, but I wasn't even a party to the case!" Then he was tied up full time for two months giving depositions to the Government. Diebold was asked not only about the fees IBM paid his firm but about his personal net worth. Finally, Diebold reported, the Justice Department lawyers told him to produce more than 1,000 lengthy and confidential reports that Diebold's consulting company had made for its clients, including some plans for IBM's competitors to compete with IBM.

At that point, Diebold withdrew as a witness rather than disclose reports to clients "on things genuinely unconnected with the case for the sake of a fishing expedition on the part of the Justice Department." As he told the TIME conference, "Gradually, I realized that the Government lawyers don't understand what they're doing." For example, according to

the Government's definition of the "general purpose" computer market, there were only eight competitors in 1969, said Diebold. "Since that date, we have clocked something on the order of 300 new players in the game—Japanese, French, American. During that time, has the Government changed its definition of the industry? Indeed they have. Today they no longer maintain there are eight competitors; today they say there are four. Yet the reality is that there is very wide-scale competition in that industry, ease of entry and rapidly declining costs to customers."

Staal, who says Diebold dropped out rather than produce more evidence damaging to IBM's case, responds that the other companies do not make general purpose computers; they manufacture smaller or specialized computers or parts.

But change in technology and the computer market is a major obstacle to the Government's case. None of the IBM computer systems that were on the market when the Government filed suit are still being made by the company. The trustbusters claim that the same pattern of IBM monopoly persists, but they must constantly seek new facts to prove it. The Government has never spelled out just how it wants to break up IBM to foster competition. Any "relief" that the court eventually may grant must be based on up-to-date information. So last January—ironically on the tenth anniversary of the case—the Government made yet another discovery request for current information and IBM's plans for the future. IBM is resisting; it argues that this third round of discovery would bare its trade secrets and further delay the trial.

IBM has also been sued 20 times on antitrust charges by private companies since 1969. So far, none of the plaintiffs have won, though many cases are on appeal or still pending. None of the private cases got bogged down during trial like *U.S. v. IBM*. If that case is ever definitely resolved, it could be a legal landmark. Not only might it dismantle the seventh biggest U.S. industrial corporation, but it might also set new limits on the way that big companies grow internally. The IBM case is already "the case of the century," says Barr. The problem, he adds, is that it may also become the case of the 21st century.

SOURCE

Time, May 21, 1979.

many politicians of the day saw the Sherman Act as "a gesture, a ceremonial concession to an overwhelming public demand for some kind of reassuring action against the trusts."[27] Another historian, Gabriel Kolko, argues that the antitrust movement was basically conservative. Rather than representing a victory of the public over the trusts, it provided an opportunity for the trusts to hold onto what they had already acquired through cutthroat competition.[28] In this sense, the economy became "rationalized" and "regulated," even if it was somewhat less competitive.

Perhaps the fact that so few cases are prosecuted suggests that our society is engaging in what Ferdinand Lundberg calls a "ceremonial use of sacrifice." Although concentration continues to increase and competition continues to decline, there is still much lip service to the value of competition. By singling out a few as "criminals," we can maintain that value even though reality has dramatically changed.[29]

Other Corporate Crimes

Much of what has been said about monopoly is also true of other corporate crimes, in areas which have come to attention more recently: labor relations, the environment, and the consumer. In each of these areas, a large number of corporate acts have come to be defined as criminal.

The definition of particular corporate acts as crimes has been piecemeal. Over the past 50 years, criminal acts have come to include the following: foreign payoffs, illegal financial manipulations, misrepresentation in advertising, issuance

Foreign payoffs are another aspect of corporate crime. Here, Japanese demonstrators carry a mock airplane and a cartoon of a politician implicated in the Lockheed payoff scandal. (UPI)

of fraudulent securities, falsification of income tax returns, unsafe work conditions, manufacture of unsafe foods and drugs, illegal rebates, unfair labor practices, illegal political contributions, discriminatory employment practices, and environmental pollution.[30]

There is no single agency or bureau to deal with these violations; nor is there any coordinated enforcement effort. Instead, a host of governmental agencies have attempted to control these activities, including the Federal Trade Commission, the Food and Drug Administration, the Securities and Exchange Commission, the Environmental Protection Agency, and the Consumer Product Safety Commission, as well as the Antitrust Division of the Department of Justice. With such a variety of agencies, often working at cross-purposes, it is an understatement to call enforcement efforts "fragmented."

As with antitrust legislation, enforcement has been weak. The most recent (and very thorough) study, by Clinard, covered the 582 largest publicly held corporations for the two years, 1975–1976. It found that

> of 56 convicted executives of large corporations, 62.5 percent received probation, 21.4 percent had their sentence suspended, and 28.6 percent were incarcerated.[31]

Such lenient penalties can hardly be considered a "crackdown" on corporate crime.

Like antitrust violations, corporate crimes are crimes of the powerful. Whether or not a given corporate act is defined as criminal often represents the outcome of a political struggle. The compromises made in the definition of corporate crimes dramatically influence enforcement efforts in specific cases. Considering this situation, it is perhaps hardly surprising that corporate crime is as extensive as it reportedly is. Moreover, the situation is reflected in similar ways when we look at corporate criminal offenders and victims of corporate crime.

CORPORATE CRIMINAL OFFENDERS

It is in thinking about corporate criminal offenders that we begin to become aware of the intricate way in which crime is embedded in the larger network of social relationships. Who is the offender—the corporation or its agents? If corporations are not deliberately criminal, why do they get involved in crime? What do corporate agents think about their criminal behavior?

With so much of our life in modern society revolving around corporations and other organizations, the question who is the offender in corporate crime is most critical. The law recognizes two kinds of persons: "natural" and "juristic." "Natural person" refers to a living, biological individual; "juristic person" refers to a corporation or other organization such as a church, a club, or even a football franchise.[32]

The Juristic Person

The development of the juristic person proved to have enormous implications for the development of western European and American society. Although the legal concept dates back to Roman law, it was not until the twelfth century that the law allowed organizations to act in their own right. Giving this freedom of action to organizations paved the way for the emergence of the modern corporation in the fifteenth century. It also served as the basis for the "organizational revolution" that has so profoundly changed American society since the nineteenth century.

The juristic person turned out to be a very powerful organizational device. In the case of the corporation, it allowed the possibility of a continuous or autonomous life, regardless of the particular investors or managers who happened to be involved in it at any given time. This meant that it could survive the death of its founder or founders. It also meant that the corporation could enter into contracts and be responsible for its own debts. As a public entity, it could bring together a large number of individual investors, each of whom contributed a small amount of money and risked only the money invested in the enterprise. With this device, huge capitalistic enterprises, some with considerable risk, could readily be assembled and operated.[33]

Although it provided a powerful organizational device, the concept of the juristic person has posed problems concerning criminal responsibility. Corporations may commit crimes, but it is the individuals who run them who form criminal intent and should be liable for the crimes. Yet the courts have often relied on fines as penalties for corporate criminal behavior, even though fines may hurt the corporation rather than the individuals responsible for its actions.

Some writers would argue that there are "criminogenic organizations," i.e., organizations which are "of such a nature as to allow for possible criminal activities."[34] Much depends on the situation in which an organization or corporation finds itself. Where there is difficulty in meeting profit goals, organizations may resort to crime in order to do so. They may also attempt to reduce uncertainty by creating orderly markets and overriding price competition, even if that entails paying fines. In fact, fines may simply be regarded as a "business cost." Pressures may also come from department or subsidiary goals in which a large company will assign each of its units a responsibility for attaining profits, virtually ignoring questionable behavior that may be necessary to attain these goals.

It should be noted that there is no inherent need for organizations to be criminogenic. In fact, the comprehensive study by Clinard and his associates found that: (1) Many firms compete successfully without resorting to illegal behavior; 40 percent of those studied had no legal action initiated against them during the two-year period of the study. (2) There are few clear relationships between characteristics of firms or industries and corporate violations. The researchers concluded, "Economic pressures and other factors operate in a corporate environment that is conducive to unethical and illegal practices."[35]

The Natural Person

Even though it has its own legal personality, a corporation is operated by real people who develop and implement policies. However, over the years corporations have become so complex that it is often difficult to determine which individuals are responsible for corporate policies and what form their responsibility takes. Moreover, most corporate executives, even those convicted of rather serious violations, do not see themselves as "criminals"—perhaps as a consequence of their social characteristics. Let's take a look at each of these points.

Responsibility for corporate acts

Around the turn of the century, things were much simpler. When the owner of the corporation was also its chief executive and general manager, that one person played a tremendous role in all phases of corporate activity. From the accounts of Gustavus Myers and Matthew Josephson, two historians of early capitalism, we have little doubt that the major firms were effectively run by single individuals who often acted autocratically.[36] Most of the early capitalists singlehandedly controlled vast resources and personnel, unilaterally making decisions on every phase of corporate activity that came to their attention.

In today's world, corporations have become exceedingly complex. To begin with, there may be many stockholders: for example, AT&T has close to 3 million stockholders and over 500 million shares; Exxon has 800,000 stockholders and 250 million shares. Some observers have long argued that there is a clear separation between ownership, in which owners remain passive investors merely interested in getting a good return on their money, and control, where managers make the decisions and form the policies that govern corporate behavior.[37]

However, this argument has not convinced everyone. Some people have maintained that even though it may appear otherwise, a small number of families actually do control corporations through a number of corporate devices.[38] In addition, at least one researcher has found that managers do not behave differently from owners, because they too consider "profit" to be the major criterion of organizational success and one consistent with their efforts to advance their own careers.[39] Ralph Nader argues that corporations can be dominated by a chief executive or an executive clique; this executive or clique "chooses the board of directors and, with the acquiescence of the board, controls the corporation."[40] In his view, the corporate executive's decision to expand, to merge, or even to violate the law "can be made without accountability to outside scrutiny."

The issue of responsibility extends much further than the separation of ownership and management. Decisions concerning a company product may involve very diverse groups. For example, in one case in which test data were faked to produce a profitable but defective safety brake, there was collusion on the part of several B.F. Goodrich engineers, the project manager, the data analyst and technical writer, the manager of the design engineering section, the manager of the technical services division, and possibly the typist who saw the changes from negative to positive in the conclusion of the report. Yet when the case came to light, each of these people denied responsibility for falsifying the test results. Top executives claimed that it just could not have happened. No one was "punished." However, "the following day the Department of Defense made sweeping changes in its inspection, testing and reporting procedures."[41]

Responsibility is an issue that needs further legal and social debate. As it stands now, corporations often cover their directors and officers with legal liability insurance or indemnify them against fines and judgments by reimbursing them with stockholders' money. However, there is need for a review or "autopsy" of actual situations in which corporate behavior gets out of control. As one writer concludes:

> The law is going to have to become much more sophisticated about the special institutional features of corporations that make the problems of controlling them (and of controlling the men in them) a problem distinct from controlling human beings in ordinary situations.[42]

Social characteristics of corporate offenders

So few are the indictments or prosecutions of corporate criminals that there are no comprehensive statistics concerning offenders. However, from the few cases that have emerged, the social characteristics of corporate criminals reflect those of corporate executives generally; they are, virtually without exception,

Male
Middle-aged
White
Middle- or upper-class

In other words, corporate crime is committed by people who are normally accorded high status in American society.

In part because of their high status, corporate criminals who are caught do not think of themselves as criminals. The reactions of the General Electric executives trapped in the most serious antitrust case ever prosecuted are most indicative. One of them responded as follows to a question about knowing that price-fixing meetings with competitors were illegal:

> Illegal? Yes, but not criminal. I didn't find that out until I read the indictment. . . . I assumed that criminal action meant damaging someone, and we did not do that. . . . I thought that we were more or less working on a survival basis in order to try to make enough to keep our plant and our employees.[43]

Using what Gilbert Geis calls "vocabularies of adjustment," most of those involved described what they were doing as "stabilizing prices" or as falling into gray areas where there was reasonable doubt. One was quoted as saying, "It is the only way a business can be run. It is free enterprise." Others protested that they were the fall guys of American business, since "conspiracy is just as much a 'way of life' in other fields as it was in electrical equipment."[44]

There are at least three reasons why corporate criminals do not think of themselves as criminals. One is that they are insulated from those who are victimized. Corporate executives do not regularly come into contact with lower-echelon employees, customers, or even the "environment." Instead, they work through intermediaries who bear the brunt of dealing with outside groups.[45] Second, executives are typically well-mannered, highly trained people who are also respected members of the community. (See Box 7.) Third, they do not lose status among business associates for their violations; in fact, they are more likely to receive sympathy and support.[46]

As a group, they looked like just what they were: well-groomed corporation executives in Ivy League suits, employed by companies ranging in size from Joslyn Manufacturing and Supply Co., whose shop space is scarcely larger than the courtroom itself, to billion-dollar giants like General Electric and Westinghouse. There was J. E. Cordell, ex-submariner, sales vice president of Southern States Equipment Corp., pillar of the community in a small Georgia town, though his net worth never exceeded $25,000; and urbane William S. Ginn, G.E. vice president at $135,000 a year, a man once thought to be on his way to the presidency of the corporation. There was old, portly Fred F. Loock, president of Allen-Bradley Co., who found conspiring with competitors quite to his taste ("It is the only way

a business can be run. It is free enterprise."), and G.E.'s Marc A. deFarranti, who pocketed his repugnance on orders from his boss. There was M. H. Howard, a production manager of Foster Wheeler, who found it hard to stay in the conspiracy (his company's condenser business ran in the red during two years of it), and C. H. Wheeler Manufacturing's President Thomas, who found it hard to quit—he'd been told his firm couldn't survive if he left the cartel.

SOURCE

Richard Austin Smith, "The Incredible Electrical Conspiracy," *Fortune,* April 1961, pp. 132–180, and May 1961, pp. 161–224.

Criminologists have experienced much difficulty in thinking about the corporate criminal. Although corporate criminals commit by far the largest dollar volume of crime—and although their acts may undermine public health and safety—they are *not* like the stereotypic "biosocial criminal" or "undereducated male, sloppy and dirty in appearance and a loner or gang member." Nor are they "maladjusted" or "transgressors."[47] In fact, it is ridiculous to picture the corporate criminal as coming from poverty, having a poor family background, or experiencing any of the other numerous social factors often held to be related to crime.

The existence of corporate offenders has demanded that criminologists change their definitions of criminals. Early in the century, the sociologist Edward A. Ross coined the term "criminaloid" for law-defying monopolists, fraud promoters, product adulterers, rebaters, and other capitalists involved in marginally legal or actually illegal business dealings.[48] Sutherland, whose work has already been quoted, argued that the conventional theories of crime simply didn't apply to "white-collar criminals." More recently, Erwin Smigel and H. Laurance Ross put it as follows:

> The [corporate] criminal is not an alien creature, governed in his behavior by strange or special forces. Rather, he is the ordinary or even the respected man, perhaps a pillar of the business community, who is doing the job he thinks expected of him.[49]

If Smigel and Ross are correct in saying that corporate criminals are only doing what they think is expected of them, we must conclude that societal norms governing business behavior are very ambiguous.

Finally, Geis would argue that corporate crime is "avocational"—that is, committed by people (1) who do not think of themselves as criminals, (2) whose income or status is derived primarily from activities other than crime, and (3) who can be deterred if they are publicly labeled as criminals.[50] Geis makes the point about criminal self-image by noting a sharp disparity: stockbrokers who made illegal "insider transactions" would see themselves as *businesspeople* whereas factory workers who committed robbery would see themselves as *armed robbers*. It is perhaps the ultimate insult to society that criminal businesspeople are allowed the luxury of regarding themselves as entrepreneurs, as executives rather than as criminals.

VICTIMS OF CORPORATE CRIME

If corporate crime is as serious as the foregoing pages have implied, it is curious that there is virtually no systematic information about victims of corporate crime. There are no official crime reports, no crime surveys that would allow us to compute anything resembling a rate of victimization.

Yet overall victimization is great. If we accept Senator Hart's estimate (quoted earlier) that faulty goods, monopolistic practices, and similar violations annually cost American consumers between $174 billion and $231 billion, the cost per person would be between $805 and $1069 per year. For a family, the cost would range between $3107 and $4125, or more than 20 percent of an average family's income. As mentioned earlier, there are also victims who die or suffer injury or other health impairment from occupationally related diseases, unsafe products, and environmental pollution.

The reason why we have extensive overall victimization but virtually no information about victims is that of all forms of crime, corporate crime is the most impersonal. In most cases, there is virtually no involvement or interaction between offenders and victims. In many cases, victims do not even realize that they are being victimized. One wonders, for example, whether the millions of owners of the Pinto automobile marketed by Ford see themselves as victims of a corporate crime.

Nor is there much sharing or mutual awareness on the part of victims. Victims of corporate crime are typically weak, disorganized, and not in a position to fight back. Consider this quotation from Daniel Drew, one of the most ruthless of the early capitalists, who wrote in the 1880s:

> When I am fighting a money-king, even my victories are dangerous. Take the present situation. I had scooped a fine profit out of the Erie deal and it was for the most part in solid cash. But—and here was the trouble—it had all come out of one man—Vanderbilt. Naturally it had left him very sore. And being so powerful, he was able to fight back. As has been seen, he did fight back. . . . On the other hand, if I had taken these profits from outsiders, it would in the aggregate have amounted to the same sum, but the losers would have been scattered all over the country and so wouldn't have been able to get together and hit back. By making my money from people on the outside, an insider like myself could make just as much in the long run, and not raise up any one enemy powerful enough to cause him discomfort.[51]

As Sutherland notes, since consumers tend to be scattered, unorganized, lacking objective information, and sustaining small losses in particular transactions, they often have little need or desire for action against corporations. Similarly, even if stockholders suspect illegal behavior by management, they too are "scattered

[and] unorganized, and frequently cannot even secure access to the names of other stockholders.''[52] The result is that we are left with victims who are voiceless.[53]

In addition to being unorganized, some victims of corporate crime may even be blamed for their victimization.[54] If the dominant rule is *caveat emptor*—''let the buyer beware''—it is the buyer who is to blame for purchasing defective goods. But it seems absurd to blame the buyer for purchasing the Pinto, with its defective design that made it susceptible to fire in rear-end collisions; or to blame the women who used IUDs marketed on the basis of faulty test data.[55]

It is clear that if corporate crime is to be taken seriously, a much more sophisticated concept of the victim is required.[56] In antitrust violations, we are victimized collectively by administered prices, which increase inflation and unemployment; and by increased concentration of wealth, which widens the gap between rich and poor. We are also victimized by an economic system with organizational units so large that economies of scale and efficiency, as well as the capacity to innovate, are lost.[57] With regard to labor relations and crimes against the environment and consumers, there is need for a typology of victims that would enable investigators to get a handle on the importance and extent of these corporate crimes. In their study of corporate crimes, criminologists need a breakthrough similar to that represented by the class action suit, a recently developed legal tool that has the potential of allowing victims to pursue cases not simply on their own behalf but on behalf of a group who experienced the same type of victimization.

As is also true of the person-to-person crimes considered in Chapters 9 and 10, corporate criminal offenders and victims of corporate crime act within certain social contexts. To further our understanding of corporate crime, we must examine the social contexts in greater detail.

SOCIAL CONTEXTS OF CORPORATE CRIME

Of all forms of crime, corporate crime is the most problematic and paradoxical. The penalties for corporate crime evolved from an antibusiness sentiment that has at times been very strong in American society, and they are potentially severe, but they have remained underenforced. Despite the enormous costs of corporate crime, there is little public outcry against it; rarely is corporate crime connected with the ''crime problem.'' Even when they are caught, corporate offenders do not see themselves as ''criminals.'' Nor is there much concern for the victim; ''caveat emptor'' puts the onus of responsibility on the buyer rather than the seller.

Although the costs in terms of dollars and damages may be large, so few are the actual cases of corporate crime that it is impossible to make any definitive statements about the impact of particular social contexts on the rates or amount of corporate crime in different industries or different areas. The study by Clinard (quoted earlier) produced data which suggest that financial strain may lead to increased violations. This study also found that the motor vehicle, pharmaceutical, and oil refining industries accounted for almost half of all violations and 40 percent of the serious or moderate violations. As was noted, the study concluded that economic factors operate in a "corporate environment" conducive to unethical and illegal practices. Let's take a look at this environment.

American Values

The issue of corporate crime can be seen as corporate ethics versus violations of the law. Corporate ethics must in turn be seen in the broader social context of American capitalism. As a capitalist society, the United States has allowed an immense amount of economic resources and power to be left in the control of private rather than public interests. This policy reflects traditional values of "individualism" and "competition," as well as "free and open" trade. It also reflects the thinking of Adam Smith, who argued that the capitalistic system would be "self-regulating" if each person were allowed to pursue his or her own private interests. According to this philosophy, there should be a minimum of public control of business enterprise so that an "invisible hand" in the form of a free and open market would work to produce the best possible outcome.[58] Smith's philosophy fully legitimated profit seeking, not only as proper but also as a socially desirable activity.

The American values expressed in Adam Smith's philosophy paved the way for a literally unprecedented development of American society in the late 1800s. Even though their actions violated some of the older common-law restraints, and even though some of their corporations were actually formed illegally, capitalists were left remarkably free to exploit natural resources, to build railroads, and to set up the other basic industries that were to become an important part of our economic system. The freedom allowed to the capitalistic entrepreneurs and their corporations undoubtedly played a large role in the rapid emergence of the United States as an industrial nation and world power.

But the question became: How much freedom should be given to the capitalists? Should they be left free to merge and combine their corporations into ever-larger concentrations of wealth and power? Freedom could lead to monopoly, or at best oligopoly, where one or a handful of firms effectively dominate a given industry—an outcome precisely the opposite of the one intended by Adam Smith. Should capitalists be left free to arbitrarily set wages at whatever levels they desire and not be limited in terms of what they should expect of their workers? Should they be held accountable for faulty products, for misleading advertising, for pollution of the environment, or for illegal payments to obtain business or political favors?

Each of these issues became significant for the development of antibusiness sentiment. That sentiment was expressed first in the Sherman Antitrust Act of 1890, and later in the Fair Labor Standards Act of 1938 and much other New Deal legislation. Since the late 1960s, issues related to the environment, illegal contributions, and faulty products have served to coalesce antibusiness sentiment. The number of regulations and agencies gives the appearance that corporations are being held increasingly accountable for their actions and are being controlled by increasingly stricter rules. Indeed, the threat is that if these rules are overstepped, the violations will in many cases be treated as "criminal."

The extent of antibusiness sentiment is evident in the findings of surveys of attitudes toward business and business crimes.[59] Earlier sociologists asserted that the public does not regard corporate crime as "real crime"; but several more recent polls show that the public is quite aware of some of the critical issues. A nationwide Louis Harris poll conducted in 1969 asked respondents to identify the worse action in various pairs, and received the following answers:

> A manufacturer of unsafe cars (68 percent)
>   *or*
> A robber (22 percent)
>
> A white grocer who sells bad meat to a black customer (63 percent)
>   *or*
> A black rioter (22 percent)
>
> A businessperson who illegally fixes prices (54 percent)
>   *or*
> A burglar (28 percent)[60]

Although this survey was conducted during a time of public concern with "crime in the streets," significantly more people saw the crimes of establishment figures as worse than street crime. In a somewhat different vein, a 1976 poll conducted by George Gallup asked people to rate the honesty of various occupational groups. It found that only 19 percent of those surveyed felt that business executives had "high or very high" ethical standards.[61] Finally, a recent nationwide survey of 60,000 Americans showed that they considered illegal price fixing to be more serious than robbery and industrial pollution of a city's water supply to be more serious than burglary.[62]

Other studies with more limited samples have found that when people are asked about hypothetical business crimes and appropriate responses to them, many would impose harsher penalties than are actually imposed by the courts. For example, when Donald Newman asked 178 people to recommend penalties in specific cases violating the Food, Drug, and Cosmetic Act, he found that nearly 80 percent believed that the penalty actually imposed should have been greater than it was.[63] A more recent extensive reanalysis of a public opinion survey about crime conducted by Peter Rossi and others found that in the public's evaluation of crime, both "organizational" crime and "street" crime are generally seen as serious *if* they have a "physical" impact. In other words, "People appear to evaluate both common and organizational offenses in terms of impact."[64] Finally, another recent study of public opinion about "white-collar crime" in general concluded that its perceived seriousness had increased during the 1970s, although it was still not considered as serious as other forms of illegality.[65]

In short, the broader context of values is one in which there is public sentiment for placing more and more areas of corporate behavior under public scrutiny and accountability. In many instances, corporate practices formerly considered only unethical, or even ethical, have been made illegal. One result is that many managers feel themselves caught between the "profit ethic" and their own personal morality. Another result is the belief that the "profit ethic" can no longer remain the sole basis of American business.[66]

If it is true that the public now takes corporate crime seriously, then we must ask why enforcement efforts have not increased accordingly. We have already seen that the lack of full social consensus undercut enforcement of the antitrust legislation. To the factors mentioned in that discussion must be added the conclusion drawn by John Conklin:

> Public attitudes have failed to coalesce in part because of the complex and diffuse nature of business crime, the absence of obvious victims, the small monetary losses for each victim, and the lack of continuing media attention to business crime. Because of the absence of a strong countervailing force, business offenders are subject to neither informal control by public opinion nor formal legal controls which would result from citizen action to have new laws passed and old ones enforced. Such circumstances set the stage for the perpetration of crime in the business world.[67]

Finally, there is also an organizational factor which would suggest that despite some antipathy between government and business, there is a remarkable marriage between the two.

The organizational factor is that the logic of industry regulation assumes that government makes the rules independently of business or, in other words, that business will allow government alone to set down "rules of the game." This logic has turned out to be markedly flawed. Instead of government regulation of business, it has very often been the case that "rules-making agencies of government are almost invariably captured by the industries which they are established to control."[68] Conklin cites a significant example: when President Gerald Ford called for less federal regulation of the airlines in 1975, a spokesperson for the Air Transportation Association argued that such a change would

> adversely affect millions of passengers and shippers, thousands of businesses in hundreds of communities, the reliable transportation of the mail, the welfare of 300,000 airline employees, millions of shareholders, investors holding billions of dollars of airline debt, aircraft manufacturers and suppliers and will endanger the financial integrity of the nation's vital airport system.[69]

It seems incredible that a return to Adam Smith's utopia could lead to such disastrous consequences. Government and business have become so intertwined that one can easily lose sight of who is regulating whom.

Current Issues

The problems and paradoxes posed by corporate crime do not lend themselves to easy solutions. In retrospect, it can be seen that the underenforcement—indeed, unenforcement—of antitrust legislation exacerbated the problems of corporate crime in that it allowed corporations to grow far larger and more powerful than they needed to be. As it stands now, corporations are so large and complex that it may be literally impossible for them to act in a manner that is completely fair, not only to their stockholders but also to their managers, customers, and employees and to the environment. Because of the size and power of corporations, corporate actions inevitably have public implications which, whether good or bad, simply cannot be ignored. The days of maximum freedom—of virtual absence of restraint for corporation owners and managers—are now in the past.

The problem today is how to regulate corporate behavior and at the same time permit capitalists to earn fair profits and assume innovative risks. If it went too far, the current trend toward more regulation could have the affect of retarding capitalistic development. Yet if regulation of corporations continued to be ineffective, there would be a risk of further concentration of power and continued violations against employees, consumers, and the environment. Clearly, some middle ground must be sought.

There have been a variety of proposals for this "middle ground" that would alter the social context of corporate crime. Conklin, for one, suggests the creation of a "countervailing force" by consolidation of existing agencies—for example, those in consumer protection. This would give the agencies more of an impact. Conklin also suggests that publication of an annual report comparable to the FBI's Uniform Crime Reports would give more visibility to corporate crimes.[70] Various changes could also be made in the penalties for corporate crime and in democracy for shareholders. There could also be increased use of class action suits and federal chartering of corporations.[71]

More radical solutions to corporate crime would involve fundamental changes in the economic system. In a socialist society, corporations would presumably be more responsive to public demand, since they would be run by the state.[72] Another type of change would be a drastic reorientation toward small-scale economies which would cut through the problem of size and social complexity.[73] In considering these more radical solutions, one must decide whether the current system has "criminal" tendencies serious enough to require the proposed change. One might also ask whether the proposed change would eliminate or substantially reduce "crime."

SUMMARY

Corporate crime arouses less public concern than person-to-person crime. Nevertheless, it is quite extensive and incurs enormous economic and human costs. Violations of occupational safety regulations, which involve much injury and even death, appear routine in many industries. The total dollar cost of corporate crime, according to one official estimate, is between $174 billion and $231 billion a year.

Defined as "illegal acquisitive behavior engaged in for the immediate purpose of increasing corporate wealth," corporate criminal acts have undergone extensive definition and redefinition since the 1880s. Monopoly-antitrust law was an early emphasis and has remained so. Over the past 50 years many other criminal corporate acts have also been defined, such as illegal financial manipulations, misrepresentation in advertising, issuance of fradulent securities, falsified income tax returns, unsafe work conditions, manufacture of unsafe foods and drugs, illegal rebates, foreign payoffs, unfair labor practices, illegal political contributions, discriminatory employment practices, and environmental pollution. However, enforcement has proved to be problematic, and comparatively little in personnel or resources has been committed to it. Cases tend to be complex and costly to prosecute. Monopoly and other crimes have eluded precise legal definition. Finally, the courts have failed to apply strong penalties either in fines or in prison terms.

On one level, the corporation itself is the offender. The law sees the corporation as a juristic person, one subject to fines. Some corporations appear to be criminogenic or of such a nature as to allow for criminal activities. On another level, the people who are responsible for running corporations, either as owners or as managers, are the offenders. Yet the complexity of ownership and management of modern corporations has made responsibility difficult to pin down. Those cases which have emerged show the typical corporate offender to be male, middle-aged, white, and middle- or upper-class. Rarely do such people think of themselves as criminals, even if they commit serious corporate crimes.

Other than overall estimates of injury, death, and dollar costs, there is virtually no systematic knowledge of the victims of corporate crime. Corporate crime is impersonal, so that victims are far removed from offenders. Victims are also weak and disorganized as a group. Furthermore, rules such as "let the buyer beware" implicitly place the blame for corporate crime on its victims. Recognizing problems such as these, several observers have argued that there is need for a more sophisticated concept of the victim.

Finally, corporate crime is influenced by its social contexts. The traditional values of "individualism," "competition," "free" trade, and "open" trade have been called into question as public concern with problems such as monopoly, unfair competition, misleading advertising, unfair labor practices, and damage to the environment has increased. At the same time, government and business have become so intertwined that it is incorrect to think that government can simply set down "rules of the game" according to which business can then operate.

At present, the problem is how to regulate corporate behavior and, at the same time, allow capitalists to earn fair profits and assume innovative risks. Moderate solutions lie along the lines of consolidation of existing regulatory agencies, publication of annual reports on corporate crime, stiffer sanctions, increased democracy for shareholders, increased use of class action suits, and more federal chartering of corporations. More radical proposals include a socialist society, which presumably would make corporations responsive to public concerns, since they would be run by the state; and a society based on a small-scale economy, which would solve some of the problems created by corporate size and complexity.

NOTES

[1] For a sociological approach to the Pinto case, see: Victoria Lynn Swigert and Ronald A. Farrell, "Corporate Homicide: Definitional Processes in the Creation of Deviance," *Law and Society Review,* vol. 15, no. 1, 1980–1981, pp. 161–182.

[2] Mark Dowie and Tracy Johnston, "A Case of Corporate Malpractice," in Peter Wickman and Phillip Whitten, eds., *Readings in Criminology,* Heath, Lexington, Mass., 1978, pp. 256–262. This article originally appeared in: *Mother Jones,* November 1976.

[3] *Report to the President on Occupational Health,*

Government Printing Office, Washington, D.C., May 1972. See also: Daniel M. Berman, "Death on the Job: Occupational Health and Safety Struggles in the United States," *Monthly Review Press,* vol. 4, 1980, pp. 239–266.

[4] Ben A. Franklin, "The Scandal of Death and Injury in the Mines: More Than 120,000 Miners Have Died Violently," *New York Times Magazine,* March 30, 1969, pp. 25–27 and 122–130.

[5] Joel Swartz, "Silent Killers at Work," *Crime and Social Justice,* vol. 3, Spring-Summer 1975, pp. 15–20. See

also: Paul Brodeur, *Expendable Americans,* Viking, New York, 1974.

[6] Abraham S. Blumberg, *Criminal Justice: Issues and Ironies,* 2d ed., New Viewpoints (Franklin Watts), New York, 1979, p. 28. On bribes and kickbacks in business, see also: Lester A. Sobel, ed., *Corruption in Business,* Facts on File, New York, 1977.

[7] *New York Times,* June 5, 1979.

[8] Quoted by: Marshall B. Clinard and Peter C. Yeager, *Corporate Crime,* Free Press, New York, and Collier MacMillan, London, 1980, p. 8.

[9] Edwin H. Sutherland, *White Collar Crime,* Holt, Rinehart, and Winston, New York, 1949.

[10] Ibid., p. 22.

[11] Ibid., p. 25.

[12] Clinard and Yeager, *Corporate Crime,* chap. V.

[13] Ibid., p. 118. N.B.: Violations were classified by the investigators as minor, moderate, or serious. In contrast to moderate or serious violations, minor violations involved paperwork only.

[14] James T. Carey, *An Introduction to Criminology,* Prentice-Hall, Englewood Cliffs, N.J., p. 355.

[15] Robert L. Heilbroner, Morton Mintz, Colman McCarthy, Sanford U. Ungar, Kermit Vandivier, Saul Friedman, and James Boyd, *In The Name of Profit,* Warner Paperback Library ed., Doubleday, New York, 1972, pp. 196f.

[16] This discussion of the history of antitrust follows: Ralph Nader, Mark Green, and Joel Seligman, *Taming the Giant Corporation,* Norton, New York, 1976, chap. VII.

[17] Ferdinand Lundberg, *The Rich and the Super-Rich: A Study in the Power of Money Today,* Bantam (Grosset and Dunlap), New York, 1968, pp. 144–145.

[18] Nader et. al., *Taming the Giant Corporation,* p. 198.

[19] See: Gustavus Myers, *History of the Great American Fortunes,* Modern Library, New York, 1964; and Matthew Josephson, *The Robber Barons: The Great American Capitalists, 1861–1901,* Harcourt, Brace and World, New York, 1962.

[20] Nader et. al., *Taming the Giant Corporation,* p. 199.

[21] Ibid.

[22] Ibid., pp. 199–202.

[23] David Dale Martin, *Mergers and the Clayton Act,* University of California Press, Berkeley, 1959.

[24] Nader et. al., *Taming the Giant Corporation,* p. 203.

[25] Ibid.

[26] Ibid., p. 208.

[27] Richard Hofstadter, *The Age of Reform: From Bryan to FDR,* Knopf, New York, 1955.

[28] Gabriel Kolko, *The Triumph of Conservatism: A Reinterpretation of American History 1900–1965,* Free Press, New York, 1963.

[29] Lundberg, *The Rich and the Super-Rich,* p. 148.

[30] Clinard and Yeager, *Corporate Crime,* pp. 113–116.

[31] Ibid., p. 287. The figures total more than 100 percent because some violators received both partially suspended sentences and probation.

[32] James G. Coleman, *Power and the Structure of Society,* Norton, New York, 1974, pp. 13–37.

[33] Edward Gross, "Organization Structure and Organizational Crime," in Gilbert Geis and Ezra Stotland, eds., *White-Collar Crime: Theory and Research,* Sage, Beverly Hills, Calif., 1980, pp. 52–76.

[34] Ibid., p. 63.

[35] Clinard and Yaeger, *Corporate Crime,* p. 132.

[36] Myers, *History of the Great American Fortunes;* and Josephson, *The Robber Barons.*

[37] Adolph A. Berle and Gardiner C. Means, *The Modern Corporation and Private Property,* Macmillan, New York, 1933.

[38] For a recent statement, see: Maurice Zeitlin, "Who Owns America: The Same Old Gang," in Annual Editions, Robert L. David, ed., *Social Problems 80/81,* Dushkin Publishing Group, Guilford, Conn., 1980, pp. 153–157. This article originally appeared in: *The Progressive,* June, 1978.

[39] R. J. Larner, *Management Control and the Large Corporation,* Junellen, New York, 1970.

[40] Nader et al., *Taming the Giant Corporation,* p. 76.

[41] Kermit Vandivier, "Why Should My Conscience Bother Me?" in Heilbroner et al., *In the Name of Profit,* pp. 11–33; quotation from p. 33.

[42] Christopher D. Stone, "Corporations and Law: Ending the Impasse," in John M. Johnson and Jack D. Douglas, eds., *Crime at the Top: Deviance in Business and the Professions,* Lippincott, Philadelphia, Pa., 1978, p. 331.

[43] Gilbert Geis, "White Collar Crime: The Heavy Electrical Equipment Antitrust Cases of 1961," in Marshall B. Clinard and Richard Quinney, eds., *Criminal Behavior Systems: A Typology,* Holt, Rinehart and Winston, New York, 1967, p. 144.

[44] See also: Richard Austin Smith, "The Incredible Electrical Conspiracy," *Fortune,* April 1961, pp. 132–180, and May 1961, pp. 161–224.

[45] On the isolation of business executives, see: Sutherland, *White Collar Crime,* pp. 247–253.

[46] Ibid., pp. 235–241 and 219–220.

[47] On the images of criminals, see: John P. Reed and Robin S. Reed, "Status, Images, and Consequences: Once a Criminal, Always a Criminal," in Terence Thornberry and Edward Sagarin, eds., *Images of Crime: Offenders and Victims,* Praeger, New York, 1974, pp. 123–134.

[48] Edward A. Ross, "The Criminaloid," in Gilbert Geis and Robert F. Meier, eds., *White Collar Crime,* Free Press, New York, 1977, pp. 29–37.

[49] Erwin O. Smigel and H. Laurance Ross, *Crimes against Bureaucracy,* Van Nostrand, New York, 1970, p. 2.

[50] Gilbert Geis, "Avocational Crime," in Daniel Glaser, eds., *Handbook of Criminology,* Rand McNally, Chicago, Ill. 1974, pp. 273–298.

[51] Sutherland, *White Collar Crime,* p. 230.

[52] Ibid., pp. 230–231.

[53] Joseph A. Page and Mary-Win O'Brien, *Bitter Wages,* Grossman, New York, 1973.

[54] Marilyn E. Walsh and Donna D. Schram, "The Victim of White-Collar Crime: Accuser or Accused?" in Geis and Stotland, *White-Collar Crime,* pp. 32–51.

[55] See: examples at beginning of the present chapter.

[56] Diane Vaughan, "Crime between Organizations: Implications for Victimology," in Geis and Stotland, *White Collar Crime,* pp. 77–97.

[57] Nader et. al., *Taming the Giant Corporation,* pp. 212–227.

[58] Adam Smith, *An Inquiry into the Nature and Causes of the Wealth of Nations,* Dent, London, 1910.

[59] These are discussed by: John E. Conklin, *Illegal but Not Criminal: Business Crime in America,* Prentice-Hall, Englewood Cliffs, N.J., 1977, chap. 2.

60 "Changing Morality: The Two Americas: A *Time*–Louis Harris Poll," *Time*, June 6, 1969, p. 26.

61 "High Rating Given to Doctors in Poll," *New York Times*, August 22, 1976.

62 See: Marvin E. Wolfgang, *New York Times*, March 2, 1980.

63 Donald J. Newman, "Public Attitudes toward a Form of White-Collar Crime," *Social Problems*, vol. 4, January 1953, pp. 228–232.

64 Laura Shill Schrager and James R. Short, Jr., "How Serious a Crime? Perceptions of Organizational and Common Crimes," in Geis and Stotland, *White-Collar Crime*, pp. 14–31; quotation from p. 26.

65 Francis T. Cullen, Bruce G. Fink, and Craig W. Palanzi, "The Seriousness of Crime Revisited: Have Attitudes toward White-Collar Crime Changed?" *Criminology*, vol. 20, no. 1, May 1982, pp. 83–102.

66 Marshall B. Clinard and Peter C. Yeager, "Corporate Crime: Issues in Research," *Criminology*, vol. 16, no. 2, August 1978, pp. 255–272.

67 Conklin, *Illegal but Not Criminal*, p. 33.

68 Heilbroner et. al., *In the Name of Profit*, p. 204.

69 Conklin, *Illegal but Not Criminal*, p. 95. See also: Mark J. Green, Beverly C. Moore, Jr., and Bruce Wasserstein, *The Closed Enterprise System*, Grossman, New York, 1972.

70 Conklin, *Illegal but Not Criminal*, chap. 6.

71 Again, the work of the Nader group gives an excellent overview of the possible solutions. See: Nader et al., *Taming the Giant Corporation*; and Green et al., *The Closed Enterprise System*.

72 For a Marxist view, see: Richard Quinney, *Class, State, and Crime: On the Theory and Practice of Criminal Justice*, McKay, New York, 1977, chap. 5.

73 See: E. F. Schumacher, *Small Is Beautiful: Economics As If People Mattered*, Harper and Row, New York, 1973.

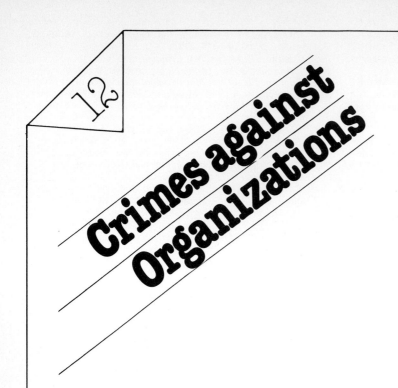

Crimes against Organizations

The other side of organizational involvement in crime finds the organization as victim. Organizations, especially business corporations, are victimized by criminal acts ranging from sabotage and vandalism to theft by employees, shoplifting, and—most recently—computer crime. As with corporate crime, the dollar amounts involved in crimes against organizations far exceed those involved in street crime. Moreover, crimes against organizations play an important role in business losses and bankruptcy.

AN OVERVIEW

As organizations become larger, more impersonal, and "faceless," crimes against them seem to be on the upswing. Committed by Americans of both sexes and all ages, classes, and racial and ethnic groups, crimes against organizations are, for the most part, easy to do, seldom detected, seldom prosecuted, and lightly penalized. Proceeds from these crimes feed into an "informal," "hidden," or "underground" economy outside of government control and virtually tax-free.

The total picture is awesome. However, even though acts such as embezzlement, theft by employees, shoplifting, and fraud have long been defined as crimes, their enforcement has been left largely in the hands of private, nongovernmental agencies. For this reason, solid data are hard to get. Although suggestive, official crime reports grossly underestimate the scope and extent of crimes against organizations. Data in private hands are scattered and uncoordinated. Hence, in assessing the total picture of crimes against organizations, it is necessary to rely upon estimates or "educated guesses."

Extent of Crime against Organizations

Surprising though it may appear, business organizations themselves do not know the exact amount of money they lose to crime. Most industries attempt to calculate an "inventory shrinkage" figure, which is estimated to be somewhere between 2 and 6 percent—for some stores, up to 9 or 10 percent—of the total inventory, depending upon the nature and location of the business.[1] Although "inventory shrinkage" can also include clerical and billing errors, much of it may be attributable to crime. If 2 percent sounds like a small figure, it must be realized that annual sales of the Fortune 500 corporations alone exceed $1 trillion. Hence, "shrinkages" can easily run into tens of billions of dollars.

The most general cost estimates of crimes against organizations have been offered by the United States Department of Commerce. Basing its estimate on consultations with industry, this agency reported that crimes cost an estimated $26 billion in 1976. It noted that American business lost more to crime than the combined sales of Sears, Wards, and Penny's, the nation's three largest retailers.[2] A comprehensive survey conducted in 1978 by the American Management Association on industry estimates of crimes against business put the total estimated cost between $30 billion and $40 billion per year.[3] Had these crimes not been absorbed as business costs, pretax profits of American business would have been about 17 percent greater in 1977.

One Piece at a Time

(As recorded by Johnny Cash and the Tennessee 3)
WAYNE KEMP

Well, I left Kentucky back in forty-nine
Went to Detroit workin' on assembly lines
The first year they had me puttin' wheels on Cadillacs
Ev'ryday I'd watch them beauties roll by
And sometimes I'd hang my head and cry
'Cause I always wanted me one that was long and
    black.

One day I devised myself a plan
That should be the envy of most any man
I'd sneak it outta there in a lunch box in my hand
Now gettin' caught meant gettin' fired
But I figured I'd have it all by the time I retired
I'd have me a car worth at least a hundred grand.

I'd get it one piece at a time and
It wouldn't cost me a dime
You'll know it's me when I come through your town
I'm gonna ride around in style
I'm gonna drive ev'rybody wild
'Cause I'll have the only one there is around.

So the very next day when I punched in
With my lunch box and the help from a friend
I left that day with a lunch box full of gears
I've never considered myself a thief
But G.M. wouldn't miss just one little piece

Especially if I strung it out over several years.
Now the first day I get me a fuel pump
The next day I got me an engine and a trunk
The little things I could get out in my lunch box
Like nuts and bolts and all four shocks
But the big stuff we snuck out in my buddy's
    mobilehome.

Up to now the plan went all right
Till we tried to put it together one night
And that's when we noticed that something was
    definitely wrong

The transmission was a fifty-three and

The motor turned out to be a seventy-three
And when we tried to put the bolts in, all the holes
    were gone
So we drilled them out so they would fit
And with a little help from an adapter kit
We had that engine runnin' like a song.

Now the head lights was another sight
We had two on the left and one on the right
But when we pulled the switch out
All three of 'em came on
The back-end looked kinda' funny too
But we put it together and when we got through
That's when we noticed we only had one tail fin
About that time, my wife walked out
I could see in her eyes she had her doubts
But she opened the door and said, "Honey, take me
    for a spin."

So we drove it up town to get the tags
And I headed her right on down the main drag
But up there at the court house, they didn't laugh
'Cause to type it up, it took the whole staff
And when they got through, the title weighed sixty
    pounds

I got it one piece at a time and it didn't cost me a dime
You'll know it's me when I come through your town
I'm gonna ride around in style:
I'm gonna drive everybody wild
'Cause I'll have the only one there is around.

(Ad lib)
"Yeah, Red Rider, this is the Cottonmouth in the
Psychobilly Cadillac, com'on? This is the Cottonmouth, a negatory on the cost of this mo-chine there,
Red Rider, you might say I went right up to the factory
and picked it up, it's cheaper that way. What model is
it? . . , Well, it's a '49, '50, '51, '52, '53, '54, '56, '57,
'58, '59 automobile . . . '60, '61, '63, '64, '65, '66, '67,
'68, '69 automobile . . . '70, '71, '72, '73 . . .

SOURCE:

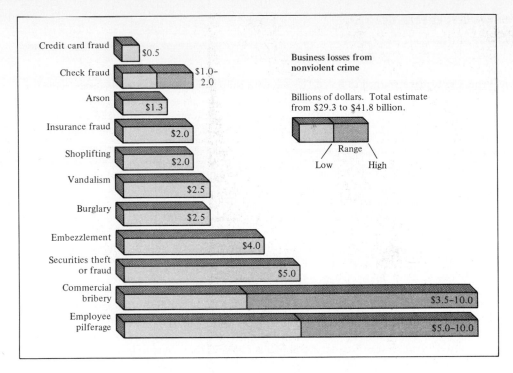

Business losses from nonviolent crime

Billions of dollars. Total estimate from $29.3 to $41.8 billion.

FIGURE 6.
Estimated dollar value of crimes against business, 1975; from a study by the American Management Association. (SOURCE: *New York Times*, January 27, 1978.)

Figure 6 illustrates the range of crimes that businesses may experience. It is useful to make a distinction between "internal losses," which result through breaches of faith by dishonest employees and management (e.g., embezzlement, commercial bribery, and pilferage); and "external losses," involving those outside the organization (the remaining crimes listed in Figure 6).[4] The higher-range cost estimates for internal losses suggest that these are the more costly of the two.

Internal losses: Theft by employees

According to a number of observers, theft by employees appears to be common, widespread, and even acceptable. The thefts may range from objects of minimal value such as stationery supplies to embezzlements that run into millions of dollars. One rough overall estimate is that 50 percent of the nation's work force engages in some form of theft.[5] Another observer sees a "better than a 50 percent chance of sizable dishonesty and a 75 percent chance of costly malpractice in the average business."[6] The employee thief may wear a "white collar" or a "blue collar."[7] He or she may be a manager or high executive. In fact, some of the most spectacular cases of theft by employees have involved executives. The nation's largest railroad line was looted of more than $21 million by executives. (See Box 9, pages 274–275.)

$21-Million Fraud at Penn Central Is Charged to 3

Bevan, Ex-Finance Officer, and Business Associates Accused of Conspiracy

PHILADELPHIA, Jan. 4—The former finance chairman of the bankrupt Penn Central Transportation Company and two of his business associates were charged today in criminal warrants with illegally diverting more than $21-million from America's largest railroad.

District Attorney Arlen Specter alleged that David C. Bevan conspired with Charles J. Hodge, a Wall Street broker, and Albert F. Lassiter, a retired Air Force brigadier general, and "substantially drained the resources of the Penn Central, contributing to its bankruptcy in June, 1970."

The railroad now is undergoing reorganization under the supervision of the United States District Court here. It reported today a net loss for the first 11 months of 1971 of $248.9-million. The deficit for the 1970 period was more than $290-million. . . .

Bevan Denies Charges

Mr. Bevan denied any wrongdoing, calling the accusations "incredible" and "a grave mistake." He demanded an immediate trial "so that I can at least be vindicated."

"I have been the scapegoat long enough," he stated, referring to the Penn Central's collapse, and added:

"Except for the fact that I am experiencing it myself, I would say that this sort of thing just cannot happen in America . . . Surely there is something wrong with the system which permits an individual to be publicly accused on such baseless charges."

General Lassiter and Mr. Hodge were not immediately available for comment. A spokesman said Mr. Hodge would issue a statement tomorrow.

The 57-page complaint specifically accused the three men of joining together to cheat and defraud the railroad. It alleged two major schemes:

A plan to invest more than $21-million in Executive Jet Aviation, Inc., a charter airline based in Columbus, Ohio, and then headed by General Lassiter. Such an investment violated a Civil Aeronautics Board ruling that forbade a railroad from controlling an air carrier.

"The manipulating of over $85-million in Penn Central investments" to benefit Penphil, a private investment club formed by Mr. Bevan and Mr. Hodge, who was the railroad's chief investment adviser. The complaint charged that, by the investment in Executive Jet, the three men hoped to profit through a travel agency owned and controlled by them, their relatives and friends.

The fraud warrant, signed by Common Pleas Judge Ethan Allen Doty, alleged that Penphil made $1.7-million in profits by buying and selling stocks in which the railroad had interests.

Penn Central trustees now are considering a proposal that would wipe out its $21-million investment in Executive Jet for less than $1-million. The C.A.B. in 1969 fined Penn Central $65,000, one of the largest in the C.A.B.'s history for the company's illegal control of Executive Jet.

Mr. Specter said that arrangements were being made for the three men to surrender here Thursday, with arraignment set for Thursday morning. Each man

The articles stolen vary from industry to industry. In a recent study in which 4985 people were asked to provide anonymous answers to a questionnaire on theft by employees, the researchers found that in retail stores the most common form of theft was unauthorized use of employees' discount privileges. Although this is often not defined as criminal, it is interesting to note that no less than 57 percent had done it at some time, and 28 percent had done it on a monthly or more faces a maximum prison term of four years—two years on the charge of conspiracy to cheat and defraud and two years on the charge of fraudulent conversion.

The complaint alleges that stock manipulation occurred in the dual investment in the Great Southwest Corporation by Penphil and the railroad. Penphil first bought into Great Southwest, a Texas-based real-estate developer, pouring in $165,000. Then Penn Central began buying huge blocks that forced up the price of the shares, and Penphil got out with a profit of $212,500, according to the complaint. Penn Central's investment totaled $80-million, and Great Southwest now is valued at less than $50-million.

"Various Junkets"

The complaint also alleges that General Lassiter arranged "dates" for Mr. Bevan and Mr. Hodge to continue the flow of railroad funds to Executive Jet.

"The steady flow of Penn Central money to Executive Jet was maintained by Lassiter's procuring of young women to accompany Bevan and Hodge on various junkets in the United States and Europe," the complaint said, adding:

The Penn Central itself has accused Mr. Bevan, Mr. Hodge, and the railroad's former treasurer, William R. Gerstnecker, of an unlawful conspiracy that drove the giant transportation company—less than two years after the merger of the Pennsylvania and New York Central Railroads—into bankruptcy court.

The railroad's lawsuit was filed last April. It accused the defendants of conspiring for "personal profit, gain and unjust enrichment" and said monetary damage was at least $66-million.

"It was one of the purposes of the conspiracy, by the exploitation of Penn Central's resources, to build Penphil into a large worldwide conglomerate by making Penphil the recipient of all of the advantages, gains, benefits, profits, and unjust enrichment which were intended to result from the conspiracy," the railroad's suit alleged.

"As a result of the conspiracy, Penphil stockholders, including Bevan, Hodge and Gerstnecker, realized a 600 percent profit on their investment in less than eight years," the suit added.

Mr. Bevan was dismissed from his $132,000-a-year position two weeks before the railroad filed for reorganization on June 8, 1970.

Mr. Hodge, who lives in Short Hills, N. J., formerly was a partner of duPont, Glore Forgan, Inc., New York City.

Ruling on Lien Made

Federal Judge John P. Fullam, in the United States District Court in Philadelphia, has ruled that Richard Joyce Smith, the trustee of the New York, New Haven & Hartford Railroad, has a tentative lien, indeterminate in amount, against Penn Central.

The lien is upon all real property, all readily identifiable personal property, except rolling stock, formerly owned by the New Haven and conveyed to the Penn Central as of Dec. 31, 1968, and still in possession of the Penn Central on June 11, 1971.

The New Haven is a corporate shell, having turned over its railroad assets to the Penn Central on Dec. 31, 1968. Mr. Smith holds 950,000 shares of Penn Central common stock, $34-million of the road's bonds and about $14-million in cash. Judge Fullam's court is in charge of the Penn Central's reorganization.

SOURCE

New York Times, January 5, 1972.

frequent basis. In manufacturing firms, 21 percent of the respondents reportedly took raw materials or components, 4 percent on a monthly or more frequent basis. In hospitals, the activity most often reported was taking medical supplies such as bandages and linens. Of the respondents, 37 percent had done this, and 11 percent did it monthly or more frequently. There were also a variety of other thefts in addition to these "most common activities."[8]

So common is theft by employees that some people believe it has changed the concept of honesty:

> Times have changed. No longer is theft a deviant activity. It has become so normal that honesty, not dishonesty, may well become the new deviance.[9]

Another management consultant argues: "Crime does pay for dishonest employees. It is the fastest-growing, tax-free segment of the economy."[10] In a more general way, theft by employees may be part of a general "rip-off" in which stealing, especially from large corporations and government, has become "legitimate"—or at any rate rationalized—because "they" are doing it to "us" through inferior products and dishonest prices.[11]

Whether or not morality has changed, there are enormous costs to theft by employees. To recover the losses, businesses increase prices somewhere in the area of 12 percent.[12] For those firms unable to pass the costs along, the result may well be bankruptcy. Dishonest employees can play a substantial role in bankruptcy. Between 1950 and 1971, as many as 100 bank failures were directly attributable to fraud or embezzlement.[13] Dun and Bradstreet reported that in one year "internal dishonesty was responsible for approximately 7 percent of commercial bankruptcies reported."[14] The spectacular Penn Central case reported in Box 9 shows that even the corporate giants are not immune to the impact of dishonesty by employees or, in this case, management.[15] Nor is this phenomenon new. Edwin Sutherland reported the estimate of the Controller of the Currency that 50.4 percent of the bank failures between 1869 and 1899 and 61.4 percent of those between 1900 and 1919 were attributable to dishonesty on the part of their officers or employees.[16]

With the advent of the computer, theft by employees has assumed dramatically new forms. The computer has made it possible to store records of physical assets in electronic and magnetic form. More than 60 percent of American banks, with over 90 percent of the nation's negotiable assets, are automated. Computers are even more impersonal than organizations. In fact, they are replacing people at a remarkable rate. For example, one of the nation's largest banks transmits records of transactions totaling $30 billion to $60 billion every day from one computer to another over a telephone line.[17]

Although there were only 630 known cases of computer "abuse" as of 1978, computer crimes have a number of remarkable features. First of all, the offender and victim are far removed from each other—even more so than in corporate crime. In addition, computer criminals utilize entirely new methods, some of which can be neither detected nor prevented with the present technology. (See Box 10.) Computer crimes can be set up to occur after the offender leaves an organization, so that the offender need not be present at the scene of the crime. Also, a computer crime can be repeated automatically at periodic intervals. If set up properly, a computer crime is neither preventable nor detectable even if it is suspected. Finally, as if to make things all the more easy for criminals, legal complexities make computer crime extremely difficult to prosecute.[18]

Somewhat less evident than theft, but also involving acts of employees directed against organizations, is "production deviance." Although not always criminal, this form of antiorganizational behavior can take distinctly criminal

Box 10: The New Terminology of Computer Crime

- Data diddling: The unauthorized modification, replacement, insertion, or deletion of data before or during its input to a computer system.
- Superzapping: The unauthorized use of utility computer programs to modify, destroy, disclose, or use data or computer programs in a computer system.
- Impersonation: Taking and using the identity of an authorized computer user to use the computer in his stead.
- Piggybacking: The unauthorized interdiction of a communication curcuit to covertly replace an authorized user.
- Wire tapping: Covertly tapping into a communication circuit but the circuit carries digitized data instead of voice data.
- Trojan horse: Covertly inserting computer instructions into a computer program that is authorized for use in a computer.
- Asyncronous attack: Compromising a computer system by taking advantage of weaknesses in its asyncronous functions.
- Trap door: A weakness or error introduced into or left in a computer program that can be exploited at a later time to compromise a computer system.
- Salami methods: Transferring small amounts of assets (slices of salami) from a large number of accounts into a favored account which then can be converted to a fraudulent gain.
- Logic bomb: A computer program or part of a program that is automatically repeatedly executed to test the state and contents of a computer system.
- Data leakage: A method for covertly obtaining data from a computer system by leaking it out in small amounts.
- Simulation: A common computer application that can be used to simulate a fraud for planning purposes or as an aid in regulating, monitoring, or accounting in the perpetration of an ongoing complex fraud.

SOURCE

Donn B. Parker, "Computer-Related White-Collar Crime," in Gilbert Geis and Ezra Stotland, eds., *White-Collar Crime: Theory and Research*, Sage, Beverly Hills, Calif., 1980, pp. 203–205.

---

forms. One criminal form of production deviance is industrial sabotage.[19] Ironically, in some instances crime may be a way of fulfilling organizational work requirements. According to one report, workers in an aircraft factory used illegal "taps" to get their jobs done, and cooperative relationships between line supervisors and inspectors supported this illegal practice.[20] Production deviance can also take the form of internal subversion in nuclear installations.[21]

In a recent study which examined both theft by employees and production deviance, 500 self-administered questionnaires were mailed to retail clerks. Each questionnaire asked the clerks about their involvement in such deviance. The questionnaires were returned by 269 of the 500. Of those responding to the survey, 15 percent were involved in various kinds of thefts, and 27 percent had engaged in unauthorized sale of merchandise to a friend at a reduced rate.[22]

External losses: Shoplifting

In addition to internal losses, organizations, especially businesses, are also the victims of crime from sources outside the organization. For the most part, these crimes involve fraud (involving credit cards, checks, insurance, or securities) or are "street crimes" (arson, vandalism, and burglary). (See Figure 6.) Although these crimes are important and costly, it is shoplifting, which is also costly, that has received most attention from criminologists.

From the available evidence, it appears that shoplifting is widespread. Again, the exact amount is unknown because, as with theft by employees, shoplifting losses are part of "inventory shrinkage." Shoplifting appears to be quite common or "ordinary."[23] In a thorough study of shoplifting conducted in the 1960s, Mary Owen Cameron estimated annual shoplifting losses to run between 2 and 5 percent of inventory.[24] More recently, one expert in the security field estimated that there are over 100 million shoplifting incidents per year and that the total lost each year to shoplifters is $3 billion—even greater than the $2 billion reported in Figure 6.[25]

As an "ordinary" crime, shoplifting is committed by a cross section of the American public. By definition, its victims are retail stores. In recent years there have been a number of studies in which people entering stores have been "followed" and observed. The findings of these studies appear to substantiate the assertion that shoplifting is an ordinary activity:

> Of 1700 customers selected at random in downtown metropolitan stores in New York, Philadelphia, Chicago, and Boston, one out of 15 customers (about 6 percent) stole about $5.50. Ninety percent who stole did so on the main floor.[26]
>
> In one New York store, out of 500 shoppers, 42 (or 1 in 12) stole something.[27]
>
> In one year an estimated 3.8 million shoplifters were apprehended across the country, one every 19 seconds. Yet no more than 1 in 35 shoplifters is apprehended.[28]

Like theft by employees, shoplifting incurs costs which are added to the price of products. Again, although these costs can only be estimated, they are substantial. Perhaps as much as 15 percent of the cost of supermarket goods includes an allowance for shoplifting. A retailer operating on a low profit margin often must receive $30 in sales to break even after a $1 theft. One 474-outlet chain, John's Bargain Stores, was driven into bankruptcy when shoplifting reached a reported 10 percent of sales.[29]

Private Security

Crimes against organizations have spawned a large private security force which grew tremendously throughout the 1970s. Of the 800,000 full-time security personnel in the United States, half are in the field of private security. However, the figure 800,000 does not include the part-time personnel who make up 25 to 50 percent of the private security work force. To put it succinctly, "In all probability, the private police industry greatly exceeds the public police sector."[30]

To sum up, considering crimes against organizations opens up some new perspectives. First, criminal acts—ranging from sabotage and vandalism to theft by employees, computer crime, and shoplifting—are widespread, indeed "ordinary." Second, the cost of crimes against organizations—$30 billion to $40 billion per year—is substantial, and many times greater than that of street crime. There are also hidden costs, which are reflected in inflated prices of products and

The upsurge of crimes against
organizations has inspired an
equally rapid growth in
security forces. (LEONARD
FREED/MAGNUM)

business bankruptcies. Third, a cross section of the American public is involved.
Fourth, despite their prevalence, criminal acts against organizations are kept out
of the central focus of criminal justice because they are handled almost exclusively by private rather than public police. Moreover, because they are impersonal,
crimes against organizations have relatively low visibility.

Having looked at some of the key issues in this overview, let us now turn to
consideration of criminal acts against organizations, antiorganizational criminal
offenders, organizations as victims, and social contexts of crimes against organizations.

CRIMINAL ACTS AGAINST ORGANIZATIONS

Background

From a social point of view, crimes against organizations are a significant part of
"white-collar crime," which can be defined as follows:

> An illegal act or series of illegal acts committed by nonphysical means and by
> concealment or guile, to obtain money or property, to avoid the payment or loss of
> money or property, or to obtain business or personal advantage.[31]

For crimes against organizations, it is personal advantage that is clearly involved.
The individual benefits, and the organization loses.

Although the definition offered above is useful in conceptualizing the general
category of crimes against business, we also need to examine the legal definitions
of specific offenses. These legal definitions also have an interesting and informa-
tive history. For one thing, most of the legally defined crimes against property
were set down in the eighteenth century. For another, although the offenses are
defined publicly, they are usually enforced privately in specific cases. This leads
to a considerable interplay between public and private legal systems.

One might be tempted to think that theft is theft and has always been treated
as such. However, a closer reading of the history of the law of theft shows that
this is simply not the case. Until 1473, larceny was rather narrowly defined as the

overt taking of goods. The Carrier's case, in which goods in transit were removed and converted to the personal use of the transporter, served to extend the definition of larceny to include the illegal removal and conversion of another person's property. This changed definition of larceny meant that

> the door was thus opened for the inclusion of many types of behavior which had previously been treated as relatively innocuous.[32]

In other words, a fair number of acts that would previously have been civil offenses (in which one party could sue for damages against another) now became criminal acts (which could be prosecuted by the state).

During the 1700s, the development of property law went far beyond this enlarged definition of larceny. In particular, receiving stolen property, larceny by trick, obtaining goods by false premises, and embezzlement came to be defined as crimes. Acts passed by the British Parliament progressively extended criminal definitions in these areas. The first embezzlement statute, for example, applied only to the Bank of England. Later statutes applied to the South Sea Company and the Post Office. In 1799, a general embezzlement statute applied to all servants and clerks.[33] It should also be borne in mind that as the United States developed, it adopted the British common-law system and the legal precedents that had been established.

It was no coincidence that the 1700s showed such a marked development of law relating to property and commerce. These years saw the beginning of the industrial revolution as well as an enormous expansion of commerce, trade, and banking. With this expansion came the growth of the corporate form of organization, which put individuals into an employer-employee relationship rather than a master-servant relationship. Corporate interests also needed contracts which were free of guile and deceit so that they could carry on an ever-increasing number of exchanges.

When criminal laws were set down against broadly defined larceny, various types of fraud, and embezzlement, a whole new series of acts became crimes. Larceny, fraud, and embezzlement had no doubt taken place previously; but now they were no longer civil offenses. Instead, they were redefined as criminal and then subject to punishment by the state. In one sense, the government of England was using its power to foster commerce and trade. At the same time, existence of these laws served to foster the interests of trading and commercial groups. These laws guaranteed that violations of property rights would be treated as criminal matters. To realize the impact of these laws on crime today, one has only to bear in mind that 90 percent of all reported index crimes are crimes against property. In fact, about 50 percent of all index crimes are larcenies.

Internal Crimes

Today, theft by employees falls into several legal categories. (See Table 16.) Despite its importance to business, however, it is very difficult to locate in the official crime reporting system.

Year	Arson	Forgery and counterfeiting	Fraud	Embezzlement	Stolen property: buying and selling	Vandalism
1970	6.2	28.9	50.7	5.4	40.6	73.7
1971	7.2	29.2	61.5	4.6	48.6	78.4
1972	6.6	27.6	60.3	4.2	44.7	80.9
1973	7.2	27.1	55.1	3.6	45.3	78.1
1974	8.0	29.6	68.0	4.4	57.4	100.1
1975	8.1	32.3	81.6	5.2	56.3	98.1
1976	8.3	31.8	92.0	4.7	52.5	90.8
1977	8.7	35.6	113.6	3.5	54.7	103.1
1978	8.7	35.4	120.4	3.7	54.2	107.9
1979	9.0	34.7	119.0	3.9	52.6	116.9
1980	8.9	34.9	125.7	3.8	55.5	112.3
1981	9.0	38.0	127.3	3.8	57.1	106.8

SOURCE: Federal Bureau of Investigation (FBI), *Uniform Crime Reports—1981*, Government Printing Office, Washington, D.C., 1982, sec. IV, "Persons Arrested," for the selected years.

Probably the most straightforward form of internal crime is embezzlement, which is defined as follows:

> Misappropriation or misapplication of money or property entrusted to one's custody or control.

The most important point here is that one must be employed in a position of trust in order to commit embezzlement.[34] Unfortunately, systematic information about the frequency of embezzlement is difficult to obtain. Employers may not realize that they are losing funds to embezzlers. If they do, they may not report losses to the police or may report losses only in cases when an arrest is sought. Because of unsystematic reporting, police consider embezzlement as a Part II offense, for which only arrests are recorded. As it turns out, there are relatively few arrests for embezzlement. The number of arrests for embezzlement in 1981 was 8700—far below the number of arrests for larceny-theft (1.2 million).

Pilferage, which would include theft of company supplies, theft of merchandise from stockrooms, etc., is even more difficult to locate in the uniform crime reporting system. Not only is it unsystematically reported (as is also true of embezzlement), but there is no listing of pilferage separately from other types of larceny. However, some employees might be included among the arrests for buying and receiving stolen property, which appeared to be on a slight upswing throughout the 1970s. Although some writers would also include "chiseling" (minor cheating or swindling) and production deviance among crimes against organizations, there is no way of tracking their frequency through the uniform crime reporting system.

The newly emerging area of computer crime presents some complex definitional issues. If the situation is one in which an employee takes funds from a company, a computer theft may be defined as larceny or embezzlement. However, in some instances the distinction between petty larceny and grand larceny is lost because the stolen property is information whose monetary value may be difficult for the court to determine. And suppose that a computer tape is stolen. What is its value?[35] Finally, consider the following two cases:

> In Pennsylvania, two computer programmers stole $144,000 of computer services from their employer to engage in a business of automatically rescoring sheet music and were convicted of mail fraud.
>
> Over a telephone circuit from a terminal at his home in Virginia, a programmer stole a copy of a computer program out of the storage of his former employer's computer in Maryland. He was convicted of wire fraud.[36]

No wonder that the federal government has developed legislation on computer fraud and abuse to attempt to deal with this new area of crime.[37]

External Crimes

Shoplifting

Crimes committed by people external to the organization pose similar ambiguities in the way they are defined and counted in the public legal system. Perhaps most straightforward in its definition is "shoplifting," which can be defined as "theft from a retail store by people who pose as legitimate customers of the store."[38] For crime reporting purposes, shoplifting is treated as a type of larceny-theft. As it turns out, about 11 percent of reported larcenies are for shoplifting.

Other external crimes

In addition to shoplifting, business is also the victim of several other kinds of crime from external sources. According to the Uniform Crime Reports, about 25 percent of reported robberies are directed against commercial establishments, gasoline or service stations, convenience stores, and banks. And 33 percent of reported burglaries are nonresidential. In addition to these crimes, business also incurs losses through the following:

> Arson: any willful or malicious burning or attempts to burn, with or without intent to defraud, a dwelling house, public building, motor vehicle or aircraft, personal property of another, etc.
>
> Forgery and counterfeiting: making, altering, uttering, or possessing, with intent to defraud, anything false which is made to appear true. Attempts are included.
>
> Fraud: fradulent conversion and obtaining money or property by false pretenses. Included are larceny by bailee and bad checks except forgeries and counterfeiting.
>
> Vandalism: willful or malicious destruction, injury, disfigurement, or defacement of any public or private property, real or personal, without consent of the owner or person having custody or control.[39]

Although the exact proportion of arrests for these offenses that stem from crimes against organizations is unclear, it is important to note that (with the exception of embezzlement and vandalism) the arrest trends for each of these crimes are on the upswing (see Table 16). However, the increases have been much less dramatic than those for person-to-person violent crime and person-to-person property crime (see Chapters 9 and 10).

Private Law Enforcement: Some Issues

If we compare the legal definitions and official reports of crimes against organizations with estimates of its extent, we find extreme differences. For example, 11 percent of reported larcenies are for shoplifting. Numbering less than 1 million, these reported shoplifting larcenies are far less than the estimated 100 million "shoplifting incidents," involving $3 billion, each year. Nor would embezzlement seem to be a "problem," with only 8700 reported arrests per year. Moreover, the more general category of theft by employees is nearly untraceable in the officially reported crime figures, whereas unofficial estimates indicate that possibly 50 percent of employees steal.

Part of the reason for the differences between officially reported figures and observers' estimates of crimes against organizations lies in the dual criminal justice system that operates in the United States. Statistics on the size of the private police have already been noted. The point to be made here is that while criminal acts are defined in the public law, their application to specific crimes against organizations is handled by the "private" police. The result is a large area of criminality that remains literally untouched by public authority. Even basic information about the exact numbers and types of crime remains in private rather than public records.[40]

In that they must uncover crimes which may be difficult to detect, many private police are thrown into an "aggressive, proactive law enforcement role" which contrasts with the more "reactive . . . or 'order maintenance' function" of the public police.[41] Although theft by employees appears to be far more extensive than shoplifting, most private law enforcement efforts appear to be directed toward "external security," perhaps because it is easier to handle. Either way, there is a problem of which cases to focus on and which to refer to the police for prosecution.

At the outset, there is reluctance to refer any cases, especially those about which there is uncertainty and those in which small amounts of money are involved. Private security personnel appear especially anxious to avoid false or improperly handled arrests, since they are subject to costly and embarrassing lawsuits on charges of "mental anguish," "false imprisonment," "defamation of character," etc. Proof of forgery demands that "intent" be shown.[42] In light of these legal complications, the prime factor in the decision to refer shoplifting cases for prosecution is the retail value of the item stolen. Although race, age, and sex also seem to make a difference (nonwhite, older, and male shoplifters are more likely to be referred), several studies have found these differences to be secondary when the retail value of the item is taken into account.[43]

Little is known about the number or type of thefts by employees or other crimes by employees that are referred to the police. However, one study found that of 1681 known trust violators in three companies, only 278 (17 percent) were prosecuted; 8 were retained and "given another chance." Significantly less likely to be prosecuted were employees rated as excellent or good workers and those who had been with the company five years or more. In determining likelihood of prosecution, the total dollar value of merchandise ever embezzled by the employee emerged as the single most important "determinant of disposition."[44]

Probably the most notorious nonprosecution of cases has been in the costly area of computer crime. Faced by complex legal issues in prosecution and worried about unfavorable publicity that might result in public loss of confidence, many managements have let known computer criminals go virtually unpenalized. As one writer recently assessed the situation:

> Some offenders have been merely reprimanded. Some have been fired, but without being forced to make restitution. Others have even been given good references for future employment. An extreme example came in the case of a young executive in England who, when confronted with evidence, admitted he had been stealing from his company's computer. For fear of bad publicity, the company gave the man a letter of recommendation to help him find a new job. He soon went to work for another company as executive director and proceeded to raid the new company's computer, embezzling some $2,000 a week for three-and-a-half years. For a second time, the embezzler was uncovered but not prosecuted. Again the victimized company did not ask for restitution and provided the thief with a good employment reference.[45]

To sum up, somewhat in contrast to corporate crime, offenses against organizations revolve around well-defined criminal acts—such as embezzlement, fraud, and larceny—which emerged as crimes during the eighteenth century. From the estimates available, it would appear that only a small fraction of the offenses which occur are ever reported to the police or prosecuted in the public legal system. Thus, crimes against business, even though they are violations of substantive criminal law, are usually handled outside the criminal justice system. They constitute what we might call a "covert," "sub rosa," or "subliminal" type of criminal behavior in our society which, although not directly violent, is immensely costly.

ANTIORGANIZATIONAL CRIMINAL OFFENDERS

We can now turn our attention to offenders who commit crimes against organizations. As we shall see, just as criminal acts against organizations involve unique conceptual and legal issues, so too do antiorganizational offenders differ from the offenders we have considered in previous chapters.

As is suggested by their frequency and "ordinariness," crimes against organizations are committed by a cross section of Americans. Included among the offenders are children out for some fun and nonagenerians (see Box 11). Both males and females, whites and blacks are involved. As with corporate crime, most offenders are "avocational criminals," who—as "respectable," "solid," or "good middle-class" citizens—have a noncriminal self-image. But unlike corporate crimes, crimes against organizations are typically committed by both sexes and all age, racial, and class groups.

Box 11: Portrait of a Shoplifter

Shoplifter, 91, Receives Food, Gifts, and Sympathy

SAN ANTONIO, July 29 (UPI)—An outpouring of sympathy for Mattie Schultz, who said she wanted God to "close her eyes" because her plight had forced her to shoplift $15 worth of food to keep from starving, has improved the 91-year-old woman's outlook on life, a minister said today.

Stan Ferrar, pastor of the First Church of God, said he spoke with Mrs. Schultz yesterday and she appeared to be in a better frame of mind.

"She's beginning to get over being so depressed," Mr. Ferrar said today, "I think it is because of all the help."

Mrs. Schultz had said she wanted to die—to have God "close my eyes"—after she was arrested and jailed overnight last week on charges of stealing $15 worth of ham, sausage and butter from a grocery. Reports in the news media of her arrest resulted in contributions of food, money, and sympathy from across the nation.

"She's received calls from all over the United States, even up to Canada," said Mr. Ferrar, who helped the widow answer phone calls at her home.

She was hospitalized late Friday after she complained of severe stomach pain, but officials refused to disclose her whereabouts, saying she was exhausted and needed a rest from the publicity. She was believed to be in fair condition today at Baptist Memorial Hospital, but hospital spokesmen declined to release any information.

"She has some stomach problems and some heart problems," Mr. Ferrar said. "But I haven't talked to the doctor personally so I don't know if there is anything else."

Mrs. Schultz lost all but $10 of her $4,900 life savings to a swindler in October 1978. After that, her income was limited to Social Security and her late husband's veteran's benefits, but she often rejected welfare. State officials said she refused an offer last fall to be boarded at a nursing home and had rejected offers of aid.

SOURCE

New York Times, July 30, 1979.

Employees as Thieves

There have been three recent attempts to discover whether certain types of people are more likely than others to be involved in thefts from their employers. A study of retail store clerks by Richard Hollinger (cited earlier in this chapter) found that while all categories of clerks were involved, younger clerks (those between ages 16 and 21) were more likely than older clerks (ages 22 to 64) to have committed an act of "employee deviance." Aside from age, sex also made a difference: 58 percent of males compared with 43 percent of females were above the middle point on an "employee deviance" scale constructed by Hollinger. Employees with less seniority, those working fewer hours, and those dissatisfied with work and promotional opportunities were also more likely to be involved in "deviance." On the other hand, level of education, type of firm, rate of pay, whether or not the employee was a supervisor, and how management dealt with "deviance" appeared to make little difference in employees' involvement.[46]

The second study focused on sex as a variable. In examining a file of 447 "dishonest employees" who were involved in the theft of cash, merchandise, or both, Alice Franklin found that males committed more thefts than females: 40 percent of the employees but 56 percent of the violators were male. Males were also more likely to commit thefts involving more money. Like Hollinger, Franklin found that younger employees (ages 18 to 22) were most likely to steal. On the other hand, older women (41 and over) were more likely to steal than older men. Interestingly, the rate of theft was higher in jobs characterized by sex stereotyping. In particular, women who stole were usually in clerical and sales positions.[47]

The third study was a very comprehensive one of thefts by employees in retail stores, manufacturing firms, and hospitals (also cited earlier in this chapter). Regarding offenders' characteristics, these researchers found higher levels of theft by:

> Younger and never-married employees
> Employees who had both an opportunity to steal and knowledge about things to be taken
> Employees who were concerned with improving themselves and with meeting career goals
> Dissatisfied employees, especially younger ones

The most consistent predictor of theft was the employee's "perceived chance of being caught." However, informal sanctions by coworkers appeared to be about twice as influential in shaping behavior as the more formal responses of management.[48]

These three studies provide some suggestive although puzzling leads. All three point to age as a significant variable. Young people have less seniority and, it would seem to follow, less commitment to their work organizations, especially if they are dissatisfied with their work. Yet—apparently inconsistently—employees who have the opportunity to steal and knowledge about things to be taken, as well as those concerned with self-improvement, are also more likely to steal. The explanation may be (in part) that although more inclined to steal, younger employees may not have significant opportunities for theft and knowledge of what to steal. On the other hand, fewer older employees may steal, but those who do are involved in thefts of much greater magnitude.

Sex as a variable also needs some qualification. While it is true that male employees are more likely than females to be involved in theft, it should be noted that the difference found in these studies is minor compared with that found for person-to-person crimes generally and for violent crimes in particular, where the ratios of male to female arrests are more than 3 to 1 and 8 to 1 respectively. Theft by employees is a form of crime in which involvement of males and females can be expected to become more and more equal, especially as females participate more actively in the work force and achieve positions of greater responsibility.[49]

Shoplifters

Shoplifting has been studied more often than theft by employees. However, most studies have attempted to characterize shoplifters reported to the police rather than shoplifters in general. Such an approach may be misleading. For one reason, frequency of arrests, as well as age and sex of offenders, may show great variation from store to store.[50] For another, shoplifting may be common to all groups, but store personnel may be instructed to watch for a particular group, such as juveniles. If so, arrested offenders may be markedly different from actual offenders.

In a classic study based on observed behavior of customers, Mary Cameron argued that 10 percent of shoplifters are professional thieves, or "boosters," and 90 percent are "snitchers," who steal items for their own consumption. She found no particular population concentrations in her observations, although she concluded that most shoplifters are "respectable" people.[51] One study that did attempt to deal with types of offenders is the Management Safeguards study, which followed 1700 customers selected at random in downtown metropolitan department stores in New York, Philadelphia, Chicago, and Boston. This study found that shoplifting was equally likely to be committed by any of three age groups: under 21, 21–35, and over 35. It went on to conclude that by their concentration on teenage shoplifters, store detectives missed two-thirds of the actual shoplifting and the group which stole more dollar value per incident.[52]

The involvement of women in shoplifting has long been known; and some sociologists have argued that shoplifting is basically an extension of the woman's role as family shopper. However, this appears to be changing as American women approach equality with American men. During the 1960s and 1970s, arrest rates of females for larceny increased more rapidly than arrest rates for males, although only 11 percent of larceny arrests are for shoplifting. Similar increases in arrests of females are also evident for embezzlement, fraud and forgery, and counterfeiting.[53] As Freda Adler put it, when opportunities open up, the "new woman moves in—and she makes her entrance at all economic levels."[54] Darrell Steffensmeier and Charles Jordan also found a considerable increase in the proportion of arrests of females for larceny between 1962 and 1975 in urban as well as rural areas; but they argue that the increase "is very likely due to greater female participation in the traditional female offense of shoplifting."[55]

To say that shoplifting by females has increased is not to say that shoplifting is a uniquely female crime. It is worth noting that about 70 percent of larceny arrests are arrests of males. In the thorough study by Cameron cited earlier, no particular population concentrations (including sex differences) were found. And recently, after a thorough study of shoplifters in six matched pairs of department stores, Dean Rojek concluded, "The only meaningful finding was that the shoplifting rate was not greater for females than for males."[56] As with theft by employees, what distinguishes female involvement in shoplifting is that it is comparable to, not substantially less than, that of males.

Self-Images of Offenders

When we turn to the self-image of offenders, we find ourselves led to conclude that many people believe that crimes against organizations are not "real crimes" and those who commit them are not "real criminals." Consider the following comments of blue-collar workers:

> Occasionally I'll bring something home accidentally. I'll stick it in my pocket and forget it and bring it home. I don't return those 'cause it's only a small part and I didn't take it intentionally.

> Not as a rule they don't feel guilty. I know I don't—some may have guilt feelings—some may get neurotic over it but I don't. A good theoretical question is—"Is this theft?" I don't know what the answer would be though. I think that if it's for personal use it isn't but if it's for sale then it is theft.[57]

Donald Cressey argues that embezzlers who steal large sums of money rationalize their behavior by calling it "borrowing" rather than "stealing."[58] Some shoplifters also rationalize, like the woman who sobbed as she said, "Yes, I took the dress, . . . but that doesn't mean I'm a thief." In fact, one study of shoplifters found few differences in self-image between the shoplifters who were apprehended and those who were not.[59] Such "techniques of neutralization" and "vocabularies of adjustment" provide a most useful way for offenders to continue to see themselves as honest, "respectable" people. This perception is reinforced by the relative infrequency with which their acts are punished.

Actually, any offender may use techniques of neutralization to rationalize his or her behavior and thus avoid a criminal self-image. However, with crimes against organizations the argument can be pushed one step further: the corporation is so big anyway that it really doesn't matter. Again, this can be seen in the comments of workers:

> People have a different attitude toward the Company than they do toward each other or you. . . . They wouldn't come into your home and take thirty cents, but they will take from the Company. They figure it's got plenty of money and a few cents don't mean nothing to them, . . . but for you they figure there's not so much of it.[60]

> Never heard of anybody stealing anything from others. That's one thing. You can leave something laying around down there and no one will risk their job for taking things from others. They would be more severe on you if they caught you taking things from the workers than if you were taking from the Company. The people seem to realize most workers are rather poor and couldn't afford to lose something. A Company won't miss it like a person would. This don't make it right but it justifies it in their mind.[61]

> Well, Safeway, or a chain store, you just didn't care because you know that you are not stealing from somebody personal; you know they are going to make it up, but when you're stealing from an individual grocery, you have some compunction about it. . . . The unfortunate part about it is that the people you'd rather steal from first are some of the chain stores, and they're successful because they're son-of-a-bitches. . . . They are the most careful, they watch you.[62]

In some instances people's attitudes neatly link corporate crime to crimes against organizations:

> It's a corporation. . . . It's not like taking from one person. . . . The people justify it that the corporation wouldn't be hurt by it; . . . they just jack the price up and screw the customer. They're not losing anything. The Company told us that last year they lost $30,000, . . . but that was for losses of all types. It gives them a nice big tax write-off. I'll bet you a goddamn day's pay that they jack that son-of-a-bitchin' write-off way up too.[63]

The case portrayed in Box 12 shows clearly how offenders' behavior and self-image can be tied to management's behavior. This final link produces the attitude that since organizations—"they"—are so big and criminal anyway, anything I might do to them doesn't really matter. Therefore, I am not a criminal; "real" criminals are out in the streets.[64]

Two cousins in Dallas, Texas, owned and operated a company doing approximately $4 million business a year. Each partner drew $17,500 a year in salary. Both drove luxury automobiles and lived in expensive houses. Each of them spent four weeks hunting in Mexico each year, as well as two weeks in Arizona during the winter. That kind of living could not be done, of course, on $17,500 a year.

Considerable quantities of scrap copper, brass, and aluminum were accumulated in the company's production area. This scrapped metal was sold to a salvage company, and checks were issued to the business. The two partners endorsed the checks in the names of their firm and added their own names. These checks were then taken to the bank and converted into cash, with no record of the transaction ever appearing in the company books or the partners' tax returns. This side income totaled about $35,000 a year for each of the partners.

One of the sidelights to this study is that office employees usually reported to work about 9:30 or 10:00 o'clock. The hour that was allowed for lunch was seldom respected. Quite often stenographic and clerical employees had left for home by 4:00 or 4:30. There were eight employees on the office staff and in an indirect manner, all of them were taking advantage of their knowledge of the partners' schemes for lining their own pockets.

The truth is that in abusing the business, management destroys the respect that individual employees have for company assets. . . . If the individual workers observe that management has no respect for the company, its time, and its assets, they ask, "Why should I be concerned holding down losses or reducing costs if the boss doesn't care?"

SOURCE

Charles F. Hemphill, Jr., *Management's Role in Loss Prevention*, American Management Association, New York, 1976, pp. 56–57.

ORGANIZATIONS AS VICTIMS

If we take seriously the claim of offenders that they are not really criminals, it might at first sight appear that crimes against organizations have no real victims. After all, as Gerald Robin puts it, "the loss for these crimes is sustained by that nebulous entity the *company* rather than any *individual* in it."[65] Such a loss is "written off" as a cost of doing business or charged back to customers in the form of higher prices.

While it is true that companies rather than individuals are the immediate victims of crimes against organizations, there is a definite subsequent or "secondary" level of victimization. One aspect of "secondary" victimization is that losses which are written off come out of pretax profits and hence reduce the taxes paid by corporations. Another aspect is that losses are passed along to the consumer. Indeed, it must be recognized that crime is an integral part of the inflation currently plaguing American society. In either aspect, we see victims who are scattered, unorganized, lacking in objective information, and sustaining small losses in particular transactions—in a word, "voiceless." (See Chapter 11.)

Moreover, as it turns out, immediate and secondary victimization may not be entirely separate and distinct. Some corporate organizations may fail because they are unable to write off their losses or pass the extra costs along quickly enough. Also, if insurance claims are involved, insurance premiums are also a cost of doing business. Finally, losses which are readily written off during a period of rising profits may become glaringly obvious and too expensive to write off when profits decline. Bankruptcy ensues, and the corporation is the victim.

Box 13: Advertisement for a "Crimes against Business" Service

It is interesting to note that we are now seeing the beginnings of organization by corporate victims to fight crime. "Crimes against Business" seminars held in a number of cities have been organized by the Department of Commerce. Pamphlets and handbooks have been published.[66] Finally, there are "loss prevention" consultants and other consultants who offer services to business to combat "white-collar crimes." (See Box 13.) Whether or not these measures will substantially reduce crimes against business remains to be seen.

In regard to organizations as victims of crime, several other points of note have emerged from national surveys of crime victims (see Chapter 7). First, if the "street crimes" of robbery and burglary are broken down into those affecting businesses and those affecting persons, the rates of business victimization (number of victimizations per 100,000 businesses) are substantially higher than the rates of personal victimization (number of victimizations per 100,000 persons). For 1976, the figures were 25,579 for business victimizations and 12,866 for personal victimization.

Second, business victimizations by robbery and burglary are far more likely to be reported to police than personal victimizations. In 1976, only 12 percent of robberies and 25 percent of commercial burglaries went unreported.[67]

Finally, business victimizations for robbery and burglary are related to both type and size of business. As Tables 17 and 18 show, wholesale businesses have the highest rate of burglary victimizations and service businesses the lowest rate. For robbery, it is clearly retail businesses that are most likely to be affected. Business victimization rates for burglary and robbery increase as organizations get larger, but only up to a certain point. For burglary, the rate starts to decline with businesses that have $1 million or more in receipts. For robbery, the rate declines when the $500,000 level is reached. This pattern supports the general belief that small firms suffer more from crime of all types than larger businesses do.[68] It may well be that large organizations can better insulate themselves from crime. On the other hand, as we shall see in the following section, people are more willing to steal from large organizations or the government than from small ones.

TABLE 17. Estimated Rate (per 100,000 businesses) of Business Victimization, by Type of Business and Victimization, United States, 1976.

Type of business	Base	Business victimization rate	Type of victimization	
			Burglary rate	Robbery rate
Total businesses	7,245,657	25,579	21,733	3846
Retail, total	2,381,412	35,893	28,303	7590
Wholesale, total	505,085	33,351	31,312	2040
Real estate, total	225,786	a	a	a
Service	2,848,329	19,747	17,752	1995
Manufacturing	367,539	23,696	21,806	1890
Banks	69,961	a	a	a
Transportation	117,612	a	a	a
All other	729,933	14,251	12,838	1414

^a Data insufficient to compute rate.

SOURCE: Nicolette Parisi, Michael R. Gottfredson, Michael J. Hindelang, and Timothy Flanagan, eds., *Sourcebook of Criminal Justice Statistics—1978*, U.S. Department of Justice, Law Enforcement Assistance Administration, Washington, D.C., 1979, p. 399.

TABLE 18. Estimated Rate (per 100,000 businesses) of Business Victimization, by Receipt Size of Business and Type of Victimization, United States, 1976

Receipt size of business	Base	Business victimization rate	Type of victimization	
			Burglary rate	Robbery rate
Total businesses	7,245,662	25,279	21,733	3846
$1 million or more	515,049	28,922	23,958	4964
$500,000–$999,999	320,739	35,018	30,377	4640
$100,000–$499,999	1,219,397	31,235	25,621	5614
$ 50,000–$99,999	856,155	30,693	25,187	5506
$ 25,000–$49,999	645,232	27,306	23,376	3930
$ 10,000–$24,999	654,534	24,505	21,427	3078
Under $10,000	886,992	21,240	18,918	2323
No sales	654,278	14,083	13,797	287
Not available	1,493,286	22,186	18,259	3657

SOURCE: Nicolette Parisi, Michael R. Gottfredson, Michael J. Hindelang, and Timothy Flanagan, eds., *Sourcebook of Criminal Justice Statistics—1978*, U.S. Department of Justice, Law Enforcement Assistance Administration, Washington, D.C., 1979, p. 400.

SOCIAL CONTEXTS OF CRIMES AGAINST ORGANIZATIONS

Having considered criminal acts against organizations, antiorganizational criminal offenders, and organizations as victims, we can round out our study of crimes against organizations by examining their social contexts. Like other crimes, those against organizations are much influenced by the social contexts in which they occur.

In thinking about crimes against organizations, there are three kinds of social contexts that need to be taken into consideration: (1) values, norms, and attitudes; (2) expectations of management; and (3) marketing methods. The first context is characteristic of American society in general. The second has to do with theft by employees. The third has to do mainly with shoplifting. Let's look at each of these in turn.

Values, Norms, and Attitudes

The discussion so far has already touched upon many of the cultural values related to crimes against business. Earlier in this chapter the view was cited that theft is so normal that honesty may have become the new deviance. The attitude was also cited that "rip-offs" are common and people feel that stealing from corporations is legitimate because corporations victimize consumers through poor products and dishonest prices. Later, the same themes emerged in the discussion of offenders' vocabularies of adjustment and noncriminal self-images.

In looking at the "rip-off" in its social context, individual honesty becomes problematic. If corporations are ripping off people, and becoming larger and more impersonal in the process, people who rip off corporations either as employees or as outsiders can be seen as fighting back. One of the enduring themes in Anglo-American culture is that of Robin Hood, who ripped off the establishment of his time in order to fight the injustices it perpetrated. Less romantically, theft by employees can also be seen as a means of coping or catching up with inflation. Interpreted politically, it has overtones of a modern-day populism, in which the little people revolt against the enormous power of the large organizations. Indeed, there is a distinct ring of populism in the argument that if the "big guys" are getting "theirs," then I ought to get "mine."[69]

One older but very interesting study of a random sample of 212 people in a midwestern community suggests a link between public attitudes toward stealing and size of the victim organization.[70] Although there was general disapproval of stealing among those surveyed, an analysis of attitudinal scores showed greatest disapproval of stealing from small business and less disapproval of stealing from large businesses and government. Of the respondents, 50 percent disapproved or strongly disapproved of stealing from small businesses. The comparable figures for large businesses and government were 34 percent and 31 percent respectively. The most common reason for tolerance of stealing from large businesses was that a large business "can afford it best, or has tremendous capital." The most common reason for tolerance of stealing from government was that government "can afford it best, or collects a great amount of tax money." This study does not record a "fighting back" attitude; but it was made during the 1950s. With the growth in concentration and size of organizations since that time, it can be expected that the differences in attitude toward stealing from large and small organizations would be even sharper than those reported and that the "fighting back" theme might be present.

Another part of the general social context (also noted above) is the infrequent prosecution of employee thieves and shoplifters. Although factors such as social status of the offender, lack of previous record, and absence of violence or injury may be involved, it must be also remembered that crimes against organizations, despite their cost and importance, are rarely handled by the criminal justice system. For the most part, police do not come into contact with these crimes, and most are kept out of the prosecutorial system. Hence, it may appear to many that these crimes are innocuous or simply not "real crimes." On the other hand, Conklin argues that recently conducted surveys "indicate a fairly high degree of public condemnation of employee theft and embezzlement."[71] There are also indications of more emphasis by law enforcement agencies on "white-collar crimes." Yet since such small numbers are prosecuted, there is a long way to go before these offenses are taken as seriously as street crime.

Expectations of Management: Theft by Employees

The meaning of "honesty" as it relates to theft by employees becomes problematic if management expects its employees to steal. Yet it would appear that this is often the case. Workers have long been accustomed to "wages in kind" or "extras to supplement their objective dollar or material earnings."[72] In this sense, occupational theft can be tolerated as an informal type of fringe benefit. One study of managers suggested that such "unofficial rewards" are quicker and more convenient to dispense than more formal rewards, such as promotions.[73] Then there is the case of the "street-corner man" who was paid $35 per week and was assumed to be stealing another $35:

> The employer is not in wage-theft collusion with the employee. . . . Were he to have caught Tonk in the act of stealing, he would, of course, have fired him from the job and perhaps called the police as well. . . . The employer knowingly provides the conditions which entice (force) the employee to steal the unpaid value of his labor, but at the same time, he punishes him for theft if he catches him doing it.[74]

Another story is told of an executive hearing about a theft of $2000 per year by one of his employees. He responded by asking how much the employee was paid. When told it was $10,000, he replied, "Then keep quiet about it. He's worth at least $15,000."[75]

In this context, theft by employees is functional—i.e., useful—to management. In effect it serves as a "safety valve" for employees' frustration. Workers are given a means of getting back at management while management evades its responsibility for job enrichment or dealing with job dissatisfaction in a meaningful way. This interpretation fits in with the finding that many employees steal things they do not really need because they are stealing for personal "revenge" and "dignity." Managers, for their part, may calculate an "allowable amount of theft."[76]

Aside from management's involvement or complicity, theft by employees may be promoted by informal norms of work groups. Blue-collar workers make a clear distinction between company property, personal property, and property of uncertain ownership—for example, scrap and waste material, broken or defective components, and broken tools. In one study, it was found that items of uncertain ownership were especially likely to be "stolen."[77] As the case of "Joan," shown

Box 14: The Impact of Informal Work Group Norms

Case Example—The Retailing Executive Trainee

A young lady, we'll call [her] Joan, was graduated from a leading university with an MBA. She applied and obtained a job with one of the prestige department stores in New York as an executive trainee. She was assigned to a department head who was told by a superior, "I want you to break her in," and that's exactly what they did.

The supervisor took the young lady from school on her first day on the job and showed her around. While in the Sportswear Department, the supervisor selected a garment and said, "Isn't this beautiful?" Joan replied, "Yes, it's lovely." The supervisor asked Joan, "Do you really like it?" and Joan exclaimed, "Oh, it's out of this world." With this the supervisor plucked at a button on the $189 import and said, "This button is falling off," as she ripped it off the garment, and then let it fall onto the floor. The supervisor looked at Joan and said, "Oh my, now it's damaged and 'as is,' which means I can now mark it down for you. But, I can't give you an employee's discount because you are not here 30 days. I'll tell you what I'll do, I'll mark it down and write up the sale to myself." So, Joan obtained the garment at a 50% markdown less a 30% employee discount, the first day on the job.

Two weeks later she received an invitation to the wedding of a friend and was thinking about what she was going to send as a gift. As she passed through the Appliance Department, she saw an attractive electric percolator for $49.50—she thinks for a moment and then takes out a bobby pin and scratches the percolator, thinking to herself, "Good. This is what I understand is 'as is.'" Joan takes it to the appliance buyer and tells him, "A customer wants to buy it, but it's damaged. Can we mark it down?" And he replied, "Yes, mark it down ⅓." But Joan wasn't satisfied with that. She took the percolator to the Repair Department as if it were a customer complaint; she wasn't satisfied with the repair, so she made a substitution of a new one at ⅓ off.

You could talk to this young girl and say, "You're dishonest. You should be fired." And her mother could exclaim, "My daughter?" The girl would say, "Why pick on me? Everybody's doing it."

SOURCE

U.S. Department of Commerce, *Crimes against Business: A Management Perspective* (pamphlet), Government Printing Office, Washington, D.C.; 1976, quotation from Jaspen, p. 10.

---

in Box 14, indicates, informal norms of work groups can be a powerful factor in socialization of employees into theft; most people do not take a job with the explicit intention of ripping off their employer. On the other hand, a closer look shows that work groups' norms also limit the amount of theft and keep it from getting "too far out of hand."[78]

In short, to understand and deal with theft by employees, it is necessary to examine its social context. To say that it is simply a question of honesty oversimplifies the issue. Thus, one management consultant would put the onus on the department head:

> If the supervisor or department head is honest; reliable; has no double standards; has time and patience for people, a hundred employees, including your child, will rise to the occasion and do an honest day's work for an honest day's pay.[79]

The problem here is why the department head should be "honest," especially if dissatisfied with his or her job. Moreover, suppose that the department head's superiors are involved in corporate crimes to gain favor for the company. A contrasting proposal would urge acceptance at least of "controlled theft" by employees. Thus, one industrial psychologist argues that management should adopt a less hypocritical attitude toward business "honesty" and "publicly recognize that there is benefit to be obtained by utilizing employee theft as a motivational tool."[80]

Marketing Methods: Shoplifting

Social context also has a decided impact on the amount of shoplifting currently seen in American society. To begin with, the United States is a consumer society. Materialistic values are held by large numbers of people. Advertising plays on these values to encourage ever-greater consumption. After all, consumption is good for business.

One of the significant marketing innovations of the past few decades has been self-service department stores and discount stores. Goods of all types are attractively displayed on shelves; and members of the general public are encouraged to enter the store, buy whatever they need, and pay for it at a checkout counter. Merchandise turnover is greatly accelerated by such a system. Personal interaction between customers and salesclerks is reduced to a minimum. Indeed, there are considerable savings to the stores in that fewer salesclerks are needed.

Self-service stores are particularly vulnerable to shoplifting. (ROHN ENGH/PHOTO RESEARCHERS, INC.)

The self-service department store would be immensely profitable if everyone were totally honest and there were no shoplifting. Instead, people do shoplift, and stores have been left with the question how to "control" shoplifting. The methods of control have taken some time to develop. Initially, the focus was on prosecution; but apprehension and prosecution are extremely difficult and expensive. One store detective can watch continuously only six to ten customers per day, approximately one per hour. For a store with hundreds or thousands of customers per day, of whom one out of ten might be a shoplifter, such detective work would be extremely costly. Moreover, there often appears to be no correlation between apprehension statistics and the size of losses experienced by stores.[81]

Since prosecution is unworkable, private security has shifted its focus to prevention. One set of recommended guidelines for retailers included antishoplifting devices such as the following: sealing customers' packages; identifying "sold" merchandise in cartons; safeguards to prevent ticket switching and price changing (e.g., use of distinctive colored staples for applying price tickets); closed-circuit television; reflector mirrors; alarm activators (e.g., electronic tags attached to merchandise, security display cases, and concealed observation posts). The same guidelines also included suggestions for store layouts, employee training, company policies, practices of security personnel, and shoplifting indicators.[82] Although each of these ideas seems to be common sense, it is important to note that these guidelines are attempting to change the situation in which shoplifters find themselves rather than to do something to people who shoplift. In this area of criminal behavior, widespread as it is, such an approach is very practical.

SUMMARY

In crimes against organizations, the organization finds itself in the role of crime victim. The estimated total cost of crimes against organizations is between $30 billion and $40 billion per year—a sizable percentage of the pretax profits of American business. Such crime takes two major forms: internal losses, especially theft by employees; and external losses, especially shoplifting. Legally, crimes against organizations include several types of property crime: larceny, arson, forgery and counterfeiting, fraud, embezzlement, buying and selling stolen property, and vandalism. Although defined in public law, most crimes against organizations are handled by private police. Relatively few cases are ever reported to public police. Relatively few are prosecuted.

Antiorganizational criminal offenders come from a cross section of American society: both sexes and all ages, classes, and racial and ethnic groups are included. Most offenders use techniques of neutralization to rationalize their behavior; few have a criminal self-image. Many see organizations as so big or so remote and impersonal that theft makes little difference.

Victimization is twofold. On one level, profits are lost. On another level, losses that are written off either reduce taxes paid or are passed on to the consumer in the form of higher prices. There are some indications that victimized organizations are beginning to coordinate efforts to curb crimes directed against them.

To fully appreciate crimes against organizations, the social context needs to be taken into account. Certain American values appear to support or normalize antiorganizational crime, especially if the organization is large. Theft by employees is also fostered by expectations of management, especially the acceptance of controlled theft as a type of fringe benefit. Modern marketing methods have also made shoplifting easier.

Crimes against organizations can be expected to increase in the 1980s. The reasons are neatly summarized in the following quotation:

> Increasingly people work for, buy from, and administer the affairs of impersonal corporations. People who would never consider stealing articles from a friend's home or even from the "corner" grocer may have very different feelings about stealing merchandise displayed for sale in a branch of a large retail chain store. Someone who would be scrupulous about returning borrowed money to a friend can rationalize till-tapping from an employing organization, especially if he believes that the executives above him are taking bribes, padding their expense accounts, or otherwise "getting their cuts."[83]

The trends are sharper today than in 1964, when this passage was written. Widespread mergers of American corporations during the past decade have resulted in even greater concentration of corporate assets and power. Computers have dramatically increased "impersonalization." Employees are more aware of being "ripped off." And depersonalized self-service department and discount stores are even more widespread.

NOTES

[1] Saul D. Astor, *Loss Prevention: Controls and Concepts*, Security World, Los Angeles, Calif., 1978, pp. 12f; and Mary Owen Cameron, *The Booster and the Snitch: Department Store Shoplifting*, Collier Macmillan and Free Press of Glencoe, London, 1964, chap. 1.

[2] U.S. Department of Commerce, *Crimes against Business: A Management Perspective* (pamphlet), Government Printing Office, Washington, D. C., 1976.

[3] These estimates have not been replicated in more recent years.

[4] Bob Curtis, *Security Control: External Theft*, Chain Store Publishing, New York, 1971, p. 1.

[5] Mark Lipman, *Stealing*, Harper's Magazine Press, New York, 1973.

[6] Remarks by Norman Jaspan quoted in: U.S. Department of Commerce, *Crimes against Business*, p. 8.

[7] Donald N. M. Horning, "Blue-Collar Theft: Conceptions of Property, Attitudes toward Pilfering, and Work Group Norms in a Modern Industrial Plant," in Erwin O. Smigel and H. Laurence Ross, eds., *Crimes against Bureaucracy*, Van Nostrand, New York, 1970, pp. 46–64.

[8] John P. Clark, Richard C. Hollinger, et al., "Theft by Employees in Work Organizations: A Preliminary Final Report—Executive Summary," mimeographed.

[9] Astor, *Loss Prevention*, p. 59.

[10] Jaspan, in U.S. Department of Commerce, *Crimes against Business*, p. 8.

[11] Abraham S. Blumberg, *Criminal Justice: Issues and Ironies*, 2d ed., New Viewpoints, New York, 1979, pp. 37f.

[12] Richard Clifton Hollinger, "Employee Deviance Acts against the Formal Work Organization," Ph.D. thesis, University of Minnesota, 1979, p. 3.

[13] John E. Conklin, *Illegal but Not Criminal: Business Crime in America*, Prentice-Hall, Englewood Cliffs, N. J., 1977, p. 7.

[14] Astor, *Loss Prevention*, p. 13.

[15] James E. Sorensen, Hugh D. Grove, and Thomas L. Sorenson, "Detecting Management Fraud: The Role of the Independent Auditor," in Gilbert Geis and Ezra Stotland, eds., *White-Collar Crime: Theory and Research*, Sage, Beverly Hills, Calif., 1980, pp. 221–251.

[16] Edwin H. Sutherland, *Principles of Criminology*, Lippincott, Philadelphia, Pa., 1947, pp. 36f.

[17] Donn B. Parker, "Computer-Related White-Collar Crime," in Geis and Stotland, *White-Collar Crime*, pp. 199–220.

[18] On computer crime, see: ibid.; and Donn B. Parker, *Crime by Computer*, Scribner's, New York, 1976. See also: Thomas Whiteside, *Computer Capers: Tales of Electronic Thievery, Embezzlement, and Fraud*, New American Library, New York, 1978.

[19] Laurie Taylor and Paul Walton, "Industrial Sabotage: Motives and Meanings," in Stanley Cohen, ed., *Images of Deviance*, Penguin, London, 1971, pp. 219–245.

[20] Joseph Bensman and Israel Gerver, "Crime and Punishment in the Factory: The Function of Deviance in Maintaining the Social System," *American Sociological Review*, vol. 28, August 1963, pp. 588–598.

[21] Herbert Edelhertz and Marilyn Walsh, *The White-Collar*

Challenge to Nuclear Safeguards, Heath (Lexington Books), Lexington, Mass., 1978.

[22] Hollinger, "Employee Deviance Acts against the Formal Work Organization."

[23] The term used by: J. Arbaleda-Florez, Helen Durie, and John Costello, "Shoplifting—An Ordinary Crime," *International Journal of Offender Therapy and Comparative Criminology*, vol. 21, 1977, pp. 201–207.

[24] Cameron, *The Booster and the Snitch*, p. 10.

[25] Astor, *Loss Prevention*.

[26] Study by Management Safeguards, Inc., quoted in: Astor, *Loss Prevention*, p. 162.

[27] U.S. Department of Commerce, *Crimes against Business*.

[28] Curtis, *Security Control*, p. 12.

[29] Sherman E. Fein and Arthur M. Maskell, *Selected Cases on the Law of Shoplifting*, Thomas, Springfield, Ill., 1975, p. vii.

[30] Dean G. Rojek, "Private Justice Systems and Crime Reporting," *Criminology*, vol. 17, no. 1, May 1979, pp. 100–111.

[31] H. E. Edelhertz, E. Stotland, M. Walsh, and M. Weinberg, *The Investigation of White-Collar Crime: A Manual for Law Enforcement Agencies*, U.S. Department of Justice, Office of Regional Operations, Law Enforcement Assistance Administration, Government Printing Office, Washington, D. C., 1977.

[32] Jerome Hall, *Theft, Law, and Society*, Little, Brown, Boston, Mass., 1935; quotation on p. 4.

[33] Ibid., pp. 6–9.

[34] Federal Bureau of Investigation (FBI), *Uniform Crime Reports—1981*, Government Printing Office, Washington, D.C., 1982, p. 316.

[35] Whiteside, *Computer Capers*; legal issues discussed on pp. 82–87.

[36] Parker, "Computer-Related White-Collar Crime," p. 208.

[37] Whiteside, *Computer Capers*, app. A.

[38] Cameron, *The Booster and the Snitch*, p. 61.

[39] FBI, *Uniform Crime Reports—1981*, pp. 316–317.

[40] Cameron, *The Booster and the Snitch*, chap. 3.

[41] Rojek, " Private Justice Systems and Crime Reporting," p. 101.

[42] Curtis, *Security Control;* see: app.

[43] Richard J. Lundman, "Shoplifting and Police Referral: A Reexamination," *Journal of Criminal Law and Criminology*, vol. 69, no. 3, 1978, pp. 395–401, especially pp. 399–400.

[44] Gerald D. Robin, "The Corporate and Judicial Disposition of Employee Thieves," *Wisconsin Law Review*, 1967, pp. 685 f.

[45] Marc Leepson, "Computer Crime," in *Editorial Research Reports on Crime and Justice*, Government Printing Office, Washington, D.C., 1978, p. 61.

[46] Hollinger, "Employee Deviance Acts against the Formal Work Organization."

[47] Alice Franklin, "Criminality in the Workplace: A Comparison of Male and Female Offenders," in Freda Adler and Rita James Simon, eds., *The Criminology of Deviant Women*, Houghton Mifflin, Boston, Mass., 1979, pp. 167–170.

[48] Clark, Hollinger, et al., "Theft by Employees in Work Organizations."

[49] See: Freda Adler, *Sisters in Crime: The Rise of the New Female Criminal*, McGraw-Hill, New York, 1975.

[50] Rojek, "Private Justice Systems and Crime Reporting."

[51] Cameron, *The Booster and the Snitch*, pp. 159f.

[52] Study quoted in: Astor, *Loss Prevention*, p. 163. See also: Curtis, *Security Control*, p. 31.

[53] Rita James Simon, *Women and Crime*, Heath (Lexington Books), Lexington, Mass., 1975.

[54] Adler, *Sisters in Crime*, p. 166.

[55] Darrell J. Steffensmeier and Charles Jordan, "Changing Patterns of Female Crime in Rural America, 1962–1975," *Rural Sociology*, vol. 43, 1978, pp. 87–102.

[56] Rojek, "Private Justice Systems and Crime Reporting," p. 109.

[57] Horning, "Blue-Collar Theft," pp. 55 and 56.

[58] Donald R. Cressey, *Other People's Money*, Free Press of Glencoe, New York, 1953.

[59] Robert E. Kraut, "Deterrent and Definitional Influences on Shoplifting," *Social Problems*, vol. 23, February 1976, pp. 358–368.

[60] Horning, "Blue-Collar Theft," p. 55.

[61] Ibid., p. 55.

[62] David L. Altheide, Patricia A. Adler, Peter Adler, and Duane A. Altheide, "The Social Meanings of Employee Theft," in John M. Johnson and Jack D. Douglas, eds., *Crime at the Top: Deviance in Business, and the Professions*, Lippincott, Philadelphia, Pa., 1978, p. 119.

[63] Horning, "Blue Collar Theft," p. 55.

[64] On the way employee thieves perceive street criminals, see: Altheide et al., "The Social Meanings of Employee Theft," pp. 119f.

[65] Robin, "The Corporate and Judicial Disposition of Employee Thieves," p. 690.

[66] Whitney North Seymour, Jr., *Fighting White Collar Crime: A Handbook on How to Combat Crime in the Business World"* (pamphlet), United States Attorney, Southern District of New York, 1972.

[67] Nicolette Parisi, Michael R. Gottfredson, Michael J. Hindelang, and Timothy Flanagan, eds., *Sourcebook of Criminal Justice Statistics—1978*, U.S. Department of Justice, Law Enforcement Assistance Administration, Washington, D. C., 1979, tables 3.7 and 3.34. See also: FBI, *Uniform Crime Reports*. N.B.: The business portion of the LEAA Victim Survey was not conducted in 1977 or 1978. Hence, no further data are available at this time.

[68] U.S. Department of Commerce, *Crimes against Business*.

[69] Altheide et al., "The Social Meanings of Employee Theft," pp. 102–108.

[70] Erwin O. Smigel, "Public Attitudes toward Stealing as Related to the Size of the Victim Organization," *American Sociological Review*, vol. 21, no. 3, June 1956, pp. 320–327.

[71] Conklin, *Illegal but Not Criminal*, p. 32.

[72] Altheide et al., "The Social Meanings of Employee Theft," pp. 95–96.

[73] Melville Dalton, *Men Who Manage*, Wiley, New York, 1959.

[74] Elliot Liebow, *Tally's Corner*, Little, Brown, Boston, Mass., 1967. See also: Altheide et al., "The Social Meanings of Employee Theft."

[75] Laurence R. Zeitlin, "A Little Larceny Can Do a Lot for Employee Morale," *Psychology Today*, vol. 5, no. 1, June 1971, pp. 22–26.

[76] Ibid. On the usefulness of "employee deviance," see also: Bensman and Gerver, "Crime and Punishment in the Factory."

[77] Horning, "Blue Collar Theft."

[78] Altheide et al., "The Social Meanings of Employee Theft," pp. 108–119.

[79] U.S. Department of Commerce, *Crimes against Business*; quotation from Jaspan, p. 9.

[80] Zeitlin, "A Little Larceny Can Do a Lot for Employee Morale," p. 64.

[81] Astor, *Loss Prevention*.

[82] Ibid., pp. 165–179.

[83] Cameron, *The Booster and the Snitch*, p. 172.

Social-Order Crime

13

Up to this point in our overview of crime in American society, we have examined types of crime that involve violence or theft. In this chapter, our attention shifts to acts which are defined as crimes because they are considered deviant and offensive to the social order. To put it in the language of the criminologist, social-order crimes are socially deviant acts which have come into the scope of the criminal law.

As we shall see, the key issue with regard to the social-order crimes is whether many of them should continue to be defined as crimes at all. Because our ideas about deviance are changing rapidly, social-order crimes have become the subject of much debate. Some people have questioned the harmfulness of these acts. Others have questioned the assumption that consent is involved. Still others have argued that offenders' and victims' roles are blurred, since the supposed victim is often a willing participant. Ambiguity about social-order crime has made possible a social context in which well-developed criminal organizations thrive while law enforcement is weak and subject to corruption.

In thinking about social-order crimes, it is worth noting that they account for more police activity than crimes of violence or theft. In fact, if arrest is taken as an indicator of police activity, 31 percent of the more than 10 million arrests made by police in 1981 were of offenders who had committed neither person-to-person violent crimes nor property crimes. In order of frequency, arrests for social-order crimes were for drunkenness, disorderly conduct, drug violations, liquor violations, prostitution and commercialized vice, violations of curfews and loitering laws, sexual offenses (other than forcible rape and prostitution), gambling, and vagrancy. It is also possible that the category "all other offenses" involved acts which were considered threats to the social order.[1]

Social-order crime is probably the most difficult form of crime to discuss rationally. To begin with, the written literature is enormous, although much of it is preoccupied more with describing types of deviance than with understanding their social function or criminal nature. Second, the law itself appears inconsistent at many points. As we shall see, it permits acts which are known to be quite dangerous but prohibits others which seem comparatively harmless. Third, the law varies enormously from state to state; and its enforcement may differ from locality to locality. Fourth, there is no other type of crime for which actual behavior and socially expected behavior are so far out of line with the criminal law. Despite the large number of arrests for social-order crimes, the laws governing them are "more honored in the breach than the observance."

Since the act itself and its legal definition are so important in social-order crime, it is necessary to discuss them at some length; this is done in the following section. After that, we can turn to offenders and victims, who will be considered together, since their roles are so often blurred. Finally, we can examine the well-organized, immensely supportive social context which allows deviance to function smoothly even when it is berated and condemned.

SOCIAL-ORDER OFFENSES

The first problem in understanding social-order crimes is to specify the criminal acts about which we are speaking. Few writers would include all the categories of police arrests mentioned earlier, probably because they involve too many diverse types of behavior. Discussions of "crimes without victims," a term often used interchangeably with "social-order crime," have foundered on the issue of which acts to include. The following acts have been included in discussions of these crimes: abortion, bribery, drug addiction, fornication, gambling, homosexuality, loitering, use of marijuana, use of narcotics, private fighting (dueling), prostitution, public drunkenness, and vagrancy. However, a review of five studies of "crimes without victims" found that no two studies examined the same crimes and no one crime appeared on all five lists.[2]

Disagreement about which crimes to include in the category of social-order crime reflects the difficulty of defining deviance in modern society. While there is a fair amount of agreement that acts of person-to-person violence and theft of property are crimes, the definition of social-order crimes is much more relative; that is, these acts are crimes only if the deviation from norms is

> in a disapproved direction and of sufficient degree to exceed the tolerance limits of a social group which the deviation elicits, or is likely to elicit if detected, a negative sanction.[3]

In order to avoid the problem of listing all social-order crimes, let us consider three major areas: sexual acts, drug use, and gambling. Our interest lies in the disparity between how often the behaviors occur, their social settings, and the laws designed to regulate them.

Sexual Acts

In the United States sexuality is caught in a paradox: standards and laws are restrictive, but they are routinely flouted.[4] Compared with many other societies, the United States is quite narrow in its attitudes toward sexual behavior. Reproduction rather than pleasure has traditionally been emphasized; and sex is generally seen as legitimate only if it takes place within marriage, in private, and for the primary purpose of reproduction.

Laws about sex

Through its criminal law, the United States has attempted to control various aspects of sexual behavior: the degree of consent, the nature of the object or person, the nature of the sexual act, and the setting in which the act occurs.[5]

For the most part, laws concerning *consent* have to do with forcible rape (a violent crime which was discussed in Chapter 9). However, there are also laws against consensual relations between minors, against intercourse between adult males and minor females (statutory rape), and against sexual coercion of minors by adults.

Concerning *persons*, about half of our states have laws against extramarital intercourse. All forbid incest. Sexual relationships with animals and excessive attraction to physical objects are also punishable under the criminal law.

The nature of sexual *acts* prohibited under the criminal law is also very inclusive. The majority of states have laws against sodomy. Oral-genital and anal-genital contacts, even between husband and wife, are illegal in most states. Until the late 1960s, homosexual acts were illegal in all states; and today they still carry severe penalties in many states. Some state laws regard any position for intercourse other than the conventional one of the man lying on the woman as a crime against nature. Moreover, as recently as 1976, the Supreme Court upheld the right of states to make laws that regulate the private sexual behavior of consenting adults.[6]

Finally, the law has attempted to regulate the *setting* in which the sexual act occurs. Prostitution, "the granting of sexual access on a relatively indiscriminate basis for payment,"[7] is illegal in every state except Nevada, where counties can decide to allow brothels if they so choose. Other criminal laws are more specifically focused on those who would maintain a house of prostitution, on pimps who would exploit prostitutes for their own personal gain, and on procurers who seek to lure others into prostitution.

Sexual attitudes and behaviors

In striking contrast to the highly restrictive standards expressed in the law, sexual attitudes and behaviors are becoming increasingly looser. Since Sigmund Freud's work in the 1890s, there has been increased public discussion and recognition of the importance of sex in shaping personality and culture. Alfred Kinsey's books on sexual behavior in the human male and female suggested to Americans of the late 1940s that behavior had moved considerably out of line with the law. As Kinsey put it:

> A call for a cleanup of sex offenders in the community is (in effect) a proposal that 5 percent of the population should support the other 95 percent in penal institutions.[8]

Since Kinsey's time, any number of books have discussed changes in sexual attitudes and behaviors. Among them are Ira L. Reiss, *The Social Context of Premarital Permissiveness* (1967); Hendrick M. Ruitenbeck, *The New Sexuality* (1974); Morton Hunt, *Sexual Behavior in the 1970s* (1974); John Gagnon, *Human Sexualties*; and Gay Talese, *Thy Neighbor's Wife* (1979). Compared with the attitudinal and behavioral shifts discussed in these books, changes in the law have been modest. On the other hand, it can also be argued that traditional values continue to be supported by many Americans.

Law versus practice

The full extent of criminal sexual behavior is difficult to measure.[9] However, a few findings will convey an idea of the size of the problem. As long ago as 1948, Kinsey found that nearly 85 percent of all men had experienced premarital intercourse, nearly 70 percent had visited a prostitute, nearly 60 percent had engaged in heterosexual oral-genital contacts, 50 percent had committed adultery, 37 percent had experienced at least one homosexual contact, and 8 percent had had sexual activity with an animal.[10] His subsequent study of women (in 1954) found that their sexual experience, while less than that of men, was also quite extensive: nearly half had experienced premarital intercourse (although most often with the prospective husband), 60 percent had engaged in heterosexual oral-

Although prostitution is illegal in every state except Nevada, it is estimated that
between 100,000 and 500,000 prostitutes are at work in the United States
today.   (BURT GLINN/MAGNUM)

genital contacts, 25 percent had committed adultery, 28 percent had had homosexual experiences or desires, and 4 percent had experienced sexual activity with animals.[11]

More recent studies have confirmed the picture given by Kinsey. Morton Hunt found that no less than 95 percent of males and 85 percent of females under age 24 had experienced premarital intercourse. Robert Sorenson found that by age 19, 59 percent of boys and 45 percent of girls had experienced intercourse, 13 percent by the age of 12 or under.[12] Concerning prostitution, Charles Winick and Paul Kinsie estimate there are between 100,000 and 500,000 prostitutes in the United States.[13] If each prostitute saw an average of 18 clients per week, in the course of a year between 93.6 million and 450 million criminal acts of this nature would be committed.

The reasons why the law is so far out of line with actual sexual practices are complex. On the one hand, there are underlying biological, physical, and social factors. Although there is some debate about the cause, the age of menarch for girls and puberty for boys is dropping. At the same time, formal education and preparation for careers serve to postpone marriage for many people. The development of birth-control pills has made it possible to engage in sexual relationships with little fear of unwanted children. Finally, in a society that sees itself as overpopulated, there is no functional reason why sexual desires cannot be expressed in ways other than those leading to procreation.

These underlying biological, physical, and social factors are reflected in population statistics. One of the most dramatic changes has been the increase in the numbers of single, widowed, and divorced people. In 1955, these people were only 26 percent of the population over age 14; in 1980, they were 34 percent of the population over 14 and numbered about 54 million. The biological needs of this group have been almost totally ignored by the law. Many of the sexual acts they commit are criminal under the law.

On the other hand, there is the law itself. The oldest and most primitive societies almost always had two kinds of legal prohibitions: one against treason and one against sexual taboos:

> These two prohibitions had to exist in order to preserve the very life of the society. To tamper with the nation's safety, or with its future—and a future there cannot be without normal sexual relations—has always been criminal, even when theft and mayhem were mere private wrongs. Next to the law of treason, then, the law of sexual offenses is of paramount importance to any society.[14]

In other words, abnormal sexual relations were traditionally seen as a threat to the family. To be sure, the rationale was cloaked in mystery and often subject to punishment by ecclesiastical courts, especially in medieval Europe. Moreover, that the deviant sexual practices were forbidden by law hardly meant that they were eradicated. To the contrary, most have continued throughout the centuries.

The particular offenses which emerged as sexual crimes in England and the United States have been strongly influenced by social and historical factors. In England, sexual offenses were traditionally handled by an ecclesiastical court system which operated independently of the common law. With the subsequent decline of the ecclesiastical courts, many of the sexual offenses faded out of English law, so that today adultery, fornication, and prostitution (with the exception of street solicitation) are not criminal offenses in England. The offense of buggery, which included homosexuality between two men as well as bestiality by men or women, was made a capital offense by Henry VIII in 1533; the reason may have had more to do with the king's attack on the church than any threat presented by the crime itself.[15] Today, however, homosexuality between consenting males has also been decriminalized in England.

American society never had a system of separate ecclesiastical courts; therefore, sex offenses became part of the business of the state. Indeed, most legislation was at the level of the states, which passed locally developed statutes that showed marked variation from one locality to another.[16] Over the years, many types of legislation were passed, all designed to deal with various sexual practices in one way or another. One of the twentieth-century waves of legislation involved dealing with sexual psychopaths; such laws were passed by about a dozen states between 1937 and 1950 and have since been passed by others.

The laws against sexual psychopathy illustrate some of the more irrational aspects of legislation about sexual offenses. To begin with, there is a clear sequence of development of these laws, characterized by (1) arousal in a community of a state of fear as a result of a few serious sex crimes, (2) agitated community response, leading to (3) the appointment of a committee which gathers information and makes recommendations that are generally accepted uncritically by the state legislature. Proceeding largely in the absence of facts, the committees drafting the laws have assumed that sexual offenders are all dangerous, that they are likely to repeat their offenses, and that they can be treated effectively by psychiatrists. Subsequent research has shown these assumptions to be largely unfounded; and subsequent administration of the law has shown the label "sexual psychopath" to be so vague that the practical application of the law is quite unreliable.[17]

Decriminalization

Today, some of the inconsistencies in laws related to sex are being dealt with by decriminalization. In the late 1950s, the American Law Institute drafted a Model Penal Code to guide legislative revision. With its recommendations in hand, Illinois decriminalized private acts between consenting adults in 1960, a move that has since been followed by 21 other states.[18] On the other hand, as of 1975, 25 states continue to have "sexual psychopath" statutes on their books, and these statutes cover a broad range of sexual behavior.[19]

Movement toward the decriminalization of sex offenses and more rational sex codes has not meant that debate over the criminality of sex has ceased. In the 1960s Lord Patrick Devlin argued that there is such a thing as public morality and that society has a right to legislate against immorality; but H. L. A. Hart, arguing from John Stuart Mill's position that the only purpose for which power may be exercised is to prevent harm to others, questioned whether it is morally permissible to enforce morality.[20] In the 1970s Hugo Adam Bedau argued that allegedly "victimless crimes" can incur social harm and damage individual victims even though the activity may be consensual; and that at times the state should be paternalistic—for example, where the criminal law protects children and juveniles against exploitation, manipulation, and injury at the hands of adults. Edwin Schur, on the other hand, argued for decriminalization because of difficulties in law enforcement, extensive demand for the prohibited services, creation of criminals by the existence of the law, and the corruption of law enforcement.[21] Perhaps the present situation is best summarized by the following passage from Donal MacNamara and Edward Sagarin's book *Sex, Crime, and the Law*:

> There are many illegal sexual acts that, by what has come to be common consent, are not treated as crimes but that, for various reasons, have not been removed from the penal codes. At the other end of the spectrum, there are acts that are widely, if not universally, condemned but that many contend are not the rightful business of the law and should be considered matters of private morality and dealt with by education or propaganda from public health, social, educational, or religious sources. Between these extremes there are a few acts that it is agreed ought to be condemned, discouraged, and punished (as forcible rape); others that can be seen as essentially harmless (although they may or may not be such) except to the person or persons involved, as teenage consensual sex, homosexual relations, and masturbation; and some that overwhelming evidence suggests are manifestations of psychological disturbance whether or not they are in and of themselves antisocial (as transvestism and exhibitionism).[22]

The use of drugs, whether to achieve relaxation and pleasure or to treat illness, has long been part of the human condition. Yet it is only within the past century or so that drug addiction and abuse have been regarded as major social problems. Although governments have attempted to criminalize various aspects of the use, possession, or sale of drugs, there are substantial numbers in the population who continue their drug-consuming habits in violation of the criminal law.

The specifics of drug use and abuse are complex, in part because of the tremendous scientific advances over the past several decades:

> The increased complexity of the drug problem is related to the tremendous scientific advances in the field of pharmacology over the last thirty years. Society today has at its disposal drugs that cover the whole spectrum of human behavior. Besides the "contraceptive pill" we have others to sedate us when we are nervous, excite us when we are dull, slim us when we are fat, fatten us when we are thin, awaken us when we are sleepy, put us to sleep when we are awake, cure us when we are sick, and make us sick when we are well. Thus, on the one hand, drugs can enhance our ability to function more effectively but, on the other side, they can carry our minds out of the realm of reality into loneliness, despair, and hopelessness.[23]

Despite the advances in technology, our knowledge of drug addiction, habituation, dependence, and abuse remains very limited. A classification of the basic types of drugs available today would include the following: amphetamines; barbiturates (nembutal, amytal and seconal); cannabis (marijuana and hashish); cocaine; ethyl alcohol; hallucinogens (mescaline, psilocybin, and lysergic acid); and opiates (morphine and heroin). Of these, amphetamines and cocaine tend to act as stimulants on the central nervous system; the others act as depressants.

Laws about drug use

The laws governing drug use have been inconsistent and often arbitrary. Indeed, it is sobering to note that in the 1700s and 1800s coffee and tobacco were considered drugs; the use of tobacco was punishable by death in certain parts of Europe, and by splitting or cutting off the nose of the offender in England. Today, some would argue that our approach to drugs is no more realistic and that the effort to deal with drug use through criminal law has produced "a far greater problem than have drugs themselves."[24]

Harrison Act: Opiates The sometimes arbitrary and inconsistent approach to drug abuse can be seen in the legislation directed at opiates, which have, except for alcohol, received most attention. Opiate use had become quite common in the United States in the late 1800s and early 1900s. Morphine was used to deaden physical pain and was part of many medications sold directly to consumers. Informed guesses by scholars estimate that "medical" addicts numbered about 200,000 and included perhaps 3 percent of the population. These addicts were a cross section of the population; many were female, middle-aged, and middle- or upper-class.[25]

It was, then, in a context of relatively free use of opiates that the Harrison

Act of 1914 was passed. The Harrison Act was originally designed as a piece of federal legislation responding to international pressures to establish systems for internal control of narcotics, and to concern over "too many" addicts. It required only that addicts obtain drugs from physicians registered under the act and that records be maintained. However, subsequent court interpretations drastically restricted the discretion of doctors to prescribe opiates. In the process, the act also became interpreted as a tax measure, and the Treasury Department became entrusted with its enforcement.[26]

Implementation of the Harrison Act and its subsequent interpretations made an enormous difference in the pattern of drug use in the United States. For one thing, the addict became characterized as a "dope fiend"; by 1920, the social characteristics of the users had begun to change from female, middle-aged, and middle-class to male, young, and poor or minority. For another, the continuing drug traffic became tainted with criminality. Some doctors who continued to prescribe drugs for their addicted patients were put into prison. Professional criminals and organized crime, operating on an international scale, took control over the drug traffic. Law enforcement showed signs of corruption.[27]

Laws about alcohol Another type of drug abuse involves ethyl alcohol. Use of alcohol is an old American tradition, brought over by the early colonists. In the early days, most alcohol was consumed in the form of beer and wine; but by the late 1700s about 90 percent of the alcohol consumed was in the form of distilled spirits. However, this percentage dropped as later European immigrants brought their national drinking customs with them, and by the 1900s there was consumption of all three forms of alcohol. Drinking has been widespread in American society—one estimate of the average consumption is 2.65 gallons per year for each American 15 years or older—and today is commonly practiced on numerous social occasions.[28] Moreover, this per capita figure does not reflect the fact that since many Americans do not drink at all, those who do drink consume significantly greater amounts of alcohol.

In light of the widespread consumption and public acceptance of alcohol, it is remarkable that the United States is the only industrial country that has ever attempted to go "cold turkey" and totally prohibit its use. Nevertheless, Prohibition was enacted in 1920, in the Eighteenth Amendment to the Constitution, plus some related laws, which made it illegal to manufacture, consume, or sell alcoholic beverages. Prohibition posed many problems and was relatively short-lived. Rigorous abstinence conflicted directly with well-established drinking patterns, so that evasion of the law was widespread. Thousands of speakeasies—illegal drinking establishments—accommodated the drinking public. Police corruption was encouraged. Organized crime received a great impetus, since it moved in to provide much-desired but illegal liquor. Repeal came in 1933, in the form of another constitutional amendment, the Twenty-First Amendment. Since then, liquor has been sold legally—subject to licensing, taxation, and sale to adults—although the details of the laws differ from state to state.[29]

Although the repeal of Prohibition gave recognition to the unworkability of a law which ran counter to widespread practice, certain behaviors related to drinking have continued to be criminalized. For the most part, criminalization has concentrated on public behavior related to drinking: driving under the influence of

In many localities, drunkenness in public still leads to arrest. (CHARLES GATEWOOD/EDITORIAL PHOTOCOLOR ARCHIVES)

alcohol (which can have very serious consequences), violation of liquor laws, and drunkenness in public continue to be crimes. In fact, although there has been some decline in recent years, these three offenses still account for more than one out of every four police arrests. In addition, many of the arrests for disorderly conduct, vagrancy, and violations of curfews and loitering laws may also involve alcohol-related behavior.

Other drug legislation The repeal of Prohibition meant that drugs other than alcohol became the center of national policy. In a sense, enforcement of narcotics prohibition filled the moral void left when alcohol prohibition ended.[30] Indeed, it is worth noting that the Federal Narcotics Bureau was created in 1930, just as prohibition was coming to an end, so that there could be more cooperative law enforcement between federal and local officers. At the same time, the bureau also defined and shaped the outlines of the "drug problem."

One drug heavily emphasized by the newly created Federal Narcotics Bureau was marijuana. Originally, its use had been largely confined to the Mexican community and some Native American groups; but since 1960 there has been an immense increase in the number of users. Now estimated at anywhere from 5 million to 20 million, users of marijuana include many middle-class adolescents and young adults. They are typically found on high school and college campuses; estimates are that 20 to 50 percent of high school and college students have tried marijuana a few times, and perhaps one-third of those who have tried it continue to use it occasionally or regularly. Marijuana use in the 1960s had a distinct age factor: those under 25 were far more likely than those over 25 to have tried it. Often its use in and of itself was symbolic of protest against the "establishment."[31]

Inconsistencies and problems   Today, after more than 60 years of attempts to regulate the use of drugs, policy problems abound. These problems fall into three major areas: (1) the sheer prevalence of illegal drugs, (2) the harm to the user, and (3) the relationship between drug use and person-to-person violent and property crime. Let's take a brief look at each of these areas.

First, despite the regulations against drugs, it appears that substantial numbers of people are able to gain access to them. As Table 19 shows, as of 1980 every one of the drugs had been used by high school seniors. Marijuana had been used by nearly one out of every two; cocaine had been used by one out of every ten. Stimulants, sedatives, and tranquilizers—most of which are prescription drugs—were also widely used. Finally, although subject to age limitations in many states, alcohol had been used by nearly nine out of every ten.[32]

It is especially interesting to note that rates of drug use have remained high and continued to increase despite law enforcement efforts. The number of arrests for drug violations has increased dramatically. Between 1965 and 1969 the increase was sixfold. There was a subsequent doubling between 1970 and 1980, with the result that in 1980 there were more than 550,000 arrests for drug violations. Most of these arrests appear to involve cannabis. Nevertheless, it is possible that patterns of drug use may change. In fact, the study reported in Table 19, conducted annually since 1975, noted that although drug use has remained widespread, there were some modest declines in recent years. The declines were attributed to factors such as growing concern about health risks among the young, mounting disapproval of peers, and the changing mood of the times, rather than to control of the supply through rigorous law enforcement.[33]

TABLE 19. Reported Drug Use within Last 12 Months among High School Seniors: Class of 1980

Type of drug	Percent using
Alcohol	87.9
Marijuana	48.8
Stimulants	20.8
Cocaine	12.3
Sedatives	10.3
Hallucinogens	9.3
Tranquilizers	8.7
Other opiates	6.3
Inhalents	4.6
Heroin	0.5

SOURCE: Lloyd D. Johnston, Jerald G. Bachman, and Patrick M. O'Malley, *Highlights from Student Drug Use in America, 1975–1980*, U.S. Department of Health and Human Services, National Institute on Drug Abuse, Government Printing Office, Washington, D.C., 1981, p. 29.

The second major problem is that policy concerning criminalization is not directly related to the harm experienced by the user, or for that matter to the prevalence of the drug. If criminalization were related to the harm suffered by the user, the most "criminal" of the substances would probably be ethyl alcohol. Certainly it is the most widely abused. There are an estimated 10 million alcoholics in the United States, people who are physically dependent upon alcohol and who experience a deterioration of body cells or serious impairment of social functioning with continued use.[34] By comparison, there are an estimated 500,000 heroin addicts, who suffer no damage to their central nervous system but do experience increased physical dependence in addition to psychological dependence.[35] Marijuana involves no physical dependence and is therefore nonaddicting, although there is still concern about harmful side effects.[36] Finally, there are various forms of addiction to drugs which can legally be prescribed by doctors.[37]

The third problem concerns the relationship between drug use and crime. Much has been made of the fact that many heroin addicts engage in robbery, burglary, and larceny to secure the funds necessary to support their habit. This is no doubt true; but the question is: How many addicts are involved and how much of property crime is involved? Estimates of the proportion of property crime vary from one-fourth to half. However, many addicts were involved in street crime before becoming addicted; and some others use a legal job or the earnings of a spouse or parent for support. It should also be said that there is some evidence that arrest rates of heroin addicts drop as they enter methadone treatment. Finally, some addicts are able to sustain normal work patterns even though addicted.[38]

There is a much closer relationship between alcohol and crime than between heroin and crime. To begin with, use of alcohol is far more widespread than use of other drugs. Second, with alcohol the crime is due not to the need to get money to purchase alcohol but rather to the behavior induced by consuming alcohol. We have already mentioned the public aspects of drinking behavior which have long been criminalized and which consume a substantial amount of police effort. It is also worth noting that alcohol is involved in many violent crimes: Marvin Wolfgang found that the victim, the offender, or both had been drinking immediately beforehand in two-thirds of the homicide cases he analyzed.[39] David Pittman and William Handy found drinking in one-fourth of their criminal assault cases, a figure they regard as a minimum estimate.[40] Finally, more than half of all automobile fatalities involve one or more people committing the crime of "driving while intoxicated." Despite these acknowledged links with crime, alcohol use has been quite legal in the United States since 1933.

Decriminalization

As with sexual offenses, there are efforts to decriminalize drug use. Following a recommendation of the President's Crime Commission in 1966, law enforcement agencies seem to be making fewer arrests for alcohol-related crimes. Although still substantial, these arrests have declined somewhat in recent years as a percentage of all arrests. Many observers would accelerate the decriminalization process. Norval Morris and Gordon Hawkins have argued for the following legal reforms:

> Public drunkenness shall cease to be a criminal offense.
>
> Neither the acquisition, purchase, possession, nor the use of any drug will be a criminal offense. The sale of some drugs other than by a licensed chemist (druggist) and on prescription will be criminally proscribed; proof of possession of excessive quantities may be evidence of a sale or of intent to sell.
>
> Disorderly conduct and vagrancy laws will be replaced by laws precisely stipulating the conduct proscribed and defining the circumstances in which the police should intervene.[41]

Alexander B. Smith and Harriet Pollack have argued that prosecutions for crimes related to alcohol have placed an inordinate burden on the criminal justice system and that the public needs to be made more sensitive to the problems caused by drunkenness and assaultive behavior due to drunkenness.[42] Sensible though the suggested reforms may appear, they are far from current practice. As it stands, many forms of drug use remain widespread even though criminal under the law.

Gambling

Prevalence

Our third area of social-order crime is gambling. Again, we are dealing with an area in which criminal law appears out of joint with socially acceptable behavior. As the Commission on the Review of the National Policy toward Gambling put it:

> Most Americans gamble because they like to, and they see nothing "wrong" with it. This being so, they see no real distinction between going to the track to place a bet and backing their favorite horse with the local bookmaker. And this truly free-wheeling logic—so consistent with the free enterprise philosophy of most Americans—permeates the country's judicial system—police, prosecutors, and courts.[43]

The number of people who gamble is enormous. According to a major survey sponsored by the commission, no less than 61 percent of the adult American population—about 88 million people—participated in some form of gambling in 1974. Forty-eight percent—about 69 million—patronized some form of legal or illegal gambling. Eleven percent—16 million—were illegal gamblers. Three percent—or 4 million—were heavy illegal gamblers. Although dollar amounts are difficult to estimate, it is agreed that billions of dollars are involved in gambling and specifically in illegal gambling. The commission felt that its survey estimate of $5 billion was "too low," especially if compared with estimates of the Department of Justice, which range between $29 billion and $39 billion per year.[44]

Gambling is an ancient activity that may date back to prehistory and was seen as a legal and social problem even in ancient Rome and Egypt. In America, with its "get-rich-quick dream," gambling has played a prominent role. Its social history is most picturesque: gamblers worked New Orleans and the Mississippi River. When the west opened up, the gamblers went west. So intense were the games that many deaths occurred across gambling tables. In the early twentieth century, the gambling establishment served as one setting for the good life; plush casinos were places where gambling, liquor, and sex were nicely blended for middle- and upper-class amusement and enjoyment.[45]

Social-Order Crime

Popular as gambling is, what to do about it has never been clear:

> Gambling has been ignored, outlawed, legalized, outlawed in some form and legalized in others; it has been taxed, licensed and made a government monopoly. No other problem has inspired so many solutions, none of which has had more than a temporary success.[46]

Despite its frequency, Americans have chosen not to ignore gambling, probably because it violates the moral norm that money and possessions need to be earned, not gotten by chance. There is also some feeling that gambling should be controlled because some people must be restrained from gambling too much, because gambling leads to corruption of public officials, because the poor lose more than they can afford, and because organized crime is involved.[47]

Laws about gambling

Although the English common law was quite permissive about gambling, from the time of Henry VIII various statutes were designed to control it in one way or another. In the United States there was much variation from state to state. Despite the Puritan tradition, lotteries were quite commonplace during colonial times. However, lotteries fell into disuse; and a variety of antigambling statutes passed by states were used to attempt to control (1) the running of a gambling house; (2) gambling in places such as taverns, bowling alleys, and restaurants; (3) the activities of the professional gambler, gamekeeper, or bookmaker; (4) the possession, maintenance, rental, or sale of gambling equipment such as slot machines; and (5) the activities of touts and shills (the tout sells tips on racehorses; the shill is a gambler's accomplice who pretends to buy, bet, or bid in order to lure onlookers into participating).[48]

Today, there is a trend back toward legalization. Table 20 lists types of gambling activities and the number of states in which each type has been legalized. It is worth noting that (1) even bingo and horse racing, the two most popular forms, have not been legalized in every state; and (2) no one state permits all forms of legalized gambling. Even Nevada, usually regarded as most permissive, has no legalized lottery, numbers, or card-game gambling. By comparison, Connecticut permits as many forms of gambling as Nevada but has not legalized sports betting, casinos, card games, or various other forms.

Federal legislation of gambling began only in 1961. It was strengthened in 1970 with the Organized Crime Control Act. Federal enforcement operates through interstate commerce; its intent has been to control illegal gambling operations in which there are five or more persons financing, directing, managing, or owning a gambling business with gross receipts of $2000 per day over a 30-day period.

Neither federal nor state statutes appear to be used extensively to stop gambling. The use of the Organized Crime Control Act at its peak in 1972 led to 1532 indictments, a figure which had declined to 673 by 1975. Of those convicted after these indictments, only 20 percent received prison sentences.[49] While

**TABLE 20. Legalized Gambling by
Type of Activity and Number of States**

Type of activity	Number of states in which legalized
Bingo	42
Horse racing	32
Lottery	16
Dog racing	14
Numbers	13
Card games	6
Jai alai	4
Sports betting	4
Off-track betting	3
Casinos	2

SOURCES: Data from Public Gaming Research Institute, Rockville, Md.; and Council of State Governments, *The Book of the States, 1982–1983*, table 6. See also earlier data in: Linda Bailey and Elaine Knapp, "Gambling," *State Government News*, vol. 20, September 1977, p. 5.

detailed state data are not available, the 40,700 arrests for gambling reported in the Uniform Crime Reports for 1981 are a drop in the bucket compared with the total amount of gambling activity. The number is also substantially less than the number of sex-related or drug-related arrests.

Decriminalization

Although the small number of arrests for gambling suggests that it is in effect decriminalized, there are again many who would assert that gambling statutes should be taken out of the criminal law. Again, Morris and Hawkins argue that sensible legal reform should adopt this rule:

> No form of gambling shall be prohibited by the criminal law; certain fraudulent and cheating gambling practices will remain criminal.[50]

Smith and Pollack would take a somewhat contrasting approach:

> Gambling can be made available, under public or private sponsorship, to those who wish it with *no* advertising permitted, in much the same way some states run liquor stores. The location of gambling outlets can be confined to appropriate areas sufficiently accessible to meet demand, but not intrusive enough to promote gambling that might not otherwise take place.[51]

Legalization has looked attractive to legislators who seek the revenues that could be obtained either by taxing winnings or by taking a percentage of the pot before the winners' shares are distributed. However, as Jerome Skolnick argues, legalized casino gambling is still subject to corruption of three kinds: direct corruption of officials by buying them off; indirect corruption resulting from industry pressures on legislative, judicial, and administrative authorities; and the

Where gambling is legal, it is popular; crowded slot machines at a casino in Atlantic City, New Jersey. (UPI)

susceptibility of the gambling industry to fraud and infiltration by criminal elements.[52]

Although the particulars may differ, each of the three major areas of social-order crimes—sex, drug abuse, and gambling—raises a similar set of questions which have never been satisfactorily answered.[53] What exactly is the harm involved in these acts? Does it make sense to speak of harm if only consenting adults are involved? Just how morally offensive are these acts? Does society have a right to punish those who transgress its moral boundaries? Does it make a difference whether the immoral act is done in private or public? Finally, since the behaviors are so widespread, it is inevitable that law enforcers have considerable discretion. Does not this discretion make corruption possible?

It may be that these questions have no satisfactory answers. However, it is useful to note that all criminal law raises "moral" issues. The immorality of violence and theft are more certain, although even here we have seen that there is public debate about the types or settings of interactions that should be criminal. Nevertheless, with sex, drug abuse, and gambling, the issue is whether the basic forms of these behaviors should be criminal in the first place. Without a resolution of this basic question, the laws governing these acts will remain inconsistent and arbitrary. Although technically on the books, they may remain underenforced or not enforced at all.

OFFENDERS AND VICTIMS: PARTICIPANTS IN SEXUAL ACTS, DRUG USERS, GAMBLERS

The unclear public morality of sex, drug use, and gambling has dramatic consequences for offenders' and victims' roles. In fact, since "offender" and "victim" are often bound together in a mutually desired interaction, separation of these roles becomes most difficult. For this reason, we will consider them jointly in this section.

Many social-order crimes challenge commonsense thinking about offenders and victims. This is especially true where the criminal act is agreed upon by adults who participate in it. Does it make sense to speak of offenders and victims in an act of prostitution or homosexuality? If so, who is the offender: prostitute or client, aggressor or receiver? Are drug users offenders or victims? Who is the gambler: the one who takes the chance or the one who runs the game? Is the gambler an offender or a victim?

Given this confusion, rather than discuss offenders and victims separately, let us follow the lead of sociologists who have examined sex, drug abuse, and gambling as forms of deviance and consider deviant roles, identities, occupations, and even professions. The reality of the situation is that many people engage in illegal, deviant acts without regarding themselves as criminal or even deviant. They are the "amateurs" upon whom "professionals" depend if they are to make a living. They are the "respectable members" of the community who frequent the prostitute, the drug pusher, or the bookie. In other words, deviance can be a highly developed form of social activity. It brings together the professional for whom deviance has become a way of life and the general public for whom deviance satisfies a desire that is illegal according to the criminal law. In most instances, the interaction between the two is mutually desired.

Deviant Roles

Although numbers are difficult to estimate, there are many in our society for whom deviance is a social role. Thus we can distinguish between a "primary deviant," who may occasionally engage in some form of illegal sexual act, drug use, or gambling; and a "secondary deviant," for whom such deviant activity is actually a social role. The secondary deviant is likely to pursue the deviant activity as an occupation or profession, to participate in a deviant subculture, to have little difficulty seeing himself or herself as a deviant, and to be involved in a network of role relationships with others in the deviant activity.[54] Let's look first at sex, drugs, and gambling specifically, and then consider secondary and primary deviants in general.

Sexual deviants

Take, for example, female prostitution, often called the "world's oldest profession." Being a prostitute involves a woman in a world of clients, steerers, procurers, pimps, bellhops, cab drivers, madams, other prostitutes, and the police. It also means that she needs to develop a new self-image; in this regard, accepting money for sexual services seems to be more of a problem than sexual promiscuity itself. In many instances there is also a need to learn a wider set of skills in social management, including how and where to approach men, which men to approach, and how to handle situations in which men get "out of hand."[55]

For homosexuality, primary and secondary deviance take on a somewhat different meaning. Except for homosexual prostitutes, most homosexuals do not use sexual deviance as an occupation or profession: that is, they are not secondary deviants. Rather, they will most often attempt to lead an otherwise normal life: that is, to play the role of a primary deviant. The problem is that once the homosexual pattern is known, the homosexual may be thrown into the role of secondary deviant, often involuntarily. He or she is then seen as a homosexual regardless of the legitimate statuses that may also be held.[56]

Drug addicts

Addiction is another aspect of the distinction between the primary and secondary deviant. Many alcoholics are primary deviants who attempt to maintain normality in the other aspects of their life. Yet secondary deviance related to alcohol can be seen in those who frequent the skid rows of American cities—or, for that matter, in those who regularly attend meetings of Alcoholics Anonymous.[57]

On the other hand, because of the intense feelings of Americans about addiction to drugs other than alcohol, the category "drug addict" almost always subsumes one's total identity, even with persons capable of leading a stable, middle-class family life. In other words, it is far more difficult in our society for a drug addict, especially a heroin user, to maintain a primary deviant role than it is for an alcoholic.[58]

As for prostitutes and homosexuals, identity plays an important part in the self-definition of addicts. In the case of heroin, physical dependence is by no means the equivalent of psychological craving. Addicts freed of physical dependence on heroin are quite likely to return to it, whereas medical use of heroin seldom leads to addiction. It is also possible that many people experiment once, twice, or occasionally but never become addicted.[59] In part, addiction is a social process which, in the words of Marshall B. Clinard and Robert F. Meier, operates as follows:

> The more the addict associates with other drug addicts and the drug subculture, and the more he finds he cannot free himself from drug dependency, the more he adopts the self-conception of being an addict and plays the social role of an addict. The final step in the process, of course is the self-identification as "addict" or "junkie."[60]

In short, the heroin addict comes to play a social role. Addiction, then, is both physical dependence on heroin and social role playing.

Marijuana differs from heroin in that it induces no physical dependence and is most often consumed in intimate groups. For many users, it represents primary deviance in that they typically carry on an otherwise normal life. Yet at the same time, it involves participation in groups that are often antagonistic to established society.[61] Secondary deviance for the marijuana user appears to be a function of having contact with many users, which increases the likelihood of becoming a seller. This in turn increases the isolation from the conventional world. The result is assuming the role of secondary deviant.[62]

Gamblers

Since gambling is so widely accepted, few would see the gambler as a secondary deviant. However, the illegality of gambling makes professional gamblers—those who operate the games—a marginal, if not deviant, occupational group. Except for their colorful past, relatively little is known about gamblers as an occupational group in today's society. However, it can be said that they are involved in a network of role relationships with other gamblers as well as with loan sharks. Many are also part of larger organizational networks.[63]

Secondary deviants

The absence of hard statistics on the numbers of secondary deviants makes it very difficult to offer any statements about their social characteristics. However, of the sociological factors, age is probably the most outstanding. As with person-to-person crime, involvement in social-order crimes appears to decline with age. The most common ages for prostitution are 17 to 24, with 22 being the peak earning age.[64] Drug addiction seems to decline with age: addicts reduce heroin usage substantially by the time they are in their forties.[65] Smoking marijuana is a young person's pastime. Only the gambler seems more likely to be middle-aged and career-involved.

Deviant roles do appear to be sex-typed. Although there are male prostitutes, most are female. However, the majority of drug users and gamblers are male.

Some types of deviance are rooted in ethnic subcultures. The male numbers runner is an accepted part of the black community; the call girl is typically middle-class and white. A subculture of heroin addiction characterizes the ghettos of many large cities.[66] Historical and demographic factors can lead to very different patterns of vice for different ethnic communities.[67]

Primary deviants

Focusing on secondary deviance should not make us overlook those in the general public who engage in illicit sex, drug use, and gambling. Most who do so might be considered primary deviants, i.e., people who live otherwise normal or "straight" lives. It is the demand created by the primary deviant that makes secondary deviant roles viable. It takes several million johns to support hundreds of thousands of female prostitutes. The millions who gamble are the ones who provide the money necessary to support those who make their living from gambling. The millions of marijuana smokers support the thousands of people who deal in the marijuana trade.

As we have seen, hard statistics on primary deviants are not available. However, in contrast to secondary deviants, primary deviants appear to span the entire spectrum of ages. Predominately younger female prostitutes are visited by adult men of all ages. Homosexual preferences develop in the teens and for those who remain single generally increase through middle age.[68] Drug use may begin in high school or college and decline with age. However, many adults may continue it on a regular or occasional basis; in one recent self-report survey of adult deviance, 15 percent acknowledged current use of marijuana.[69] As was noted earlier, 11 percent of all Americans engage in illegal gambling; all groups are involved, although rates are higher for males than for females and higher for nonwhites than for whites.[70] In short, despite some variation, participation in illegal sex, illegal drug use, and illegal gambling occurs throughout all major groups in American society.

Although all major groups are participants, style or type of deviance differs sharply with social class as well as with race and ethnicity. Prostitution, for example, may reach all groups; but there are at least four types of prostitutes: streetwalkers, house prostitutes, massage parlour prostitutes, and call girls. From streetwalker to call girl, the social status of prostitutes, as well as the status of their clientele, increases.[71] Some types of gambling show sharp ethnic differences: e.g., numbers among blacks, lotteries among hispanics, church bingo among Irish and Italian immigrants. By contrast, the gambling casino appears suited to middle- or upper-class tastes. Horse racing and sports betting draw gamblers from many walks of life. Finally, heroin addiction (since the full effects of the Harrison Act have been felt) has been located in the black and hispanic ghettos, although some observers see a trend toward more involvement of females, whites, and younger people in the drug scene.[72]

Socialization into Deviant Roles

Sociologists have long been interested in the process by which people become involved in deviance. For the most part, their interest has been in secondary deviants–those for whom the illegal activity has become a full-time role and social identity. Since much of their study has concentrated on prostitutes and drug users, it is possible to identify socialization patterns for these two groups.

Conventional wisdom about female prostitutes is that entry into prostitution is preceded by a severe traumatic experience, often dating back to childhood. However, a reading of some of the many available materials suggests otherwise. Thus, John H. Gagnon and William Simon argue that vacillation, drift, or even accidental events (such as a man leaving money upon completion of the sex act) are predecessors of a career in prostitution. As was noted above, accepting money may be more problematic than promiscuous sexual involvements. For some girls and women, however, prostitution may signify an entry into what appears to be a more leisurely and unpressured life.[73]

One important aspect of socialization into the role of prostitute is a period of apprenticeship. Apprenticeship once occurred in brothels or houses of prostitution; but today it is more likely to take place with a more experienced prostitute or a male who operates as a pimp. The apprenticeship involves both learning the techniques of presenting oneself as sexually available for money and, in the broader sense,

> a process of managing a new conception of the self, a new relationship to males, a new way of talking about the self, and learning to meet a new world populated by special kinds of others.[74]

At the same time, there is a decrease in the frequency of interaction with conventional people and a reduced capacity to return to the conventional world. The apprenticeship typically ends with a "turning out" point at which the prostitute begins working on her own.

Socialization through peer groups is the crucial factor in drug use. Peer groups are necessary both to neutralize fears about addiction and to counter feelings of moral degradation normally associated with drug use. As Howard Becker noted in his studies of marijuana users over 25 years ago, it is the support of peers and friends that enables marijuana users to (1) learn the proper smoking techniques, (2) recognize when the high is achieved, and (3) enjoy the pleasurable effects while negating less pleasant side effects.[75] Bruce Johnson's more recent study found that marijuana users encompassed people of many backgrounds; the variable that separated users from nonusers was whether or not most of their friends used marijuana.[76] Similarly, heroin addicts are introduced to use of the drug by friends, most of whom have used the drug before although they are not themselves addicted.[77] As with prostitution, addiction to drugs is by no means the product of a single experience or even occasional experiences. Rather, it depends upon increasing contact with other drug addicts and developing a self-identification as an addict or junkie. At the same time, there is a decreased attachment to conventional society.

The notion of being socialized into deviance raises some fundamental questions concerning the extent to which involvement in deviance is voluntary or consensual. Becoming a secondary deviant is a gradual process, although there are certain turning points. How the deviant sees himself or herself and how others react are of greatest importance. However, what may at one point have been a voluntary decision, or a series of decisions, becomes at a later point an identity, a lifestyle, an occupation, or an addiction. Once a person has gone through this process, subsequent acts are highly influenced by the earlier choices.

In the final analysis, deviant roles are not assumed without socialization. No one is born a deviant. Like normal behavior, abnormal sex, drug abuse, and gambling are learned behaviors. In some cases, the peer group provides a setting in which deviance is learned. In others, deviance is learned from those already involved in it. Either way, there is a clear distinction between performing a deviant activity and playing a deviant role. The primary deviant does only the former and thinks of himself or herself as a normal person. The secondary deviant not only performs the deviant activity but also is socialized into playing the deviant role.

To summarize this discussion of offenders and victims, not only is there much ambivalence about the basic definitions of deviance in sex, drug abuse, and gambling, but it is also impossible to speak of offenders and victims. If the act is voluntary and the participants are consenting adults, many would question whether the term "victim" should even be employed.[78] For this reason, this discussion has maintained that the key distinction is between primary and secondary deviants. This distinction is basically social. Very definite processes of socialization are involved in assuming a secondary deviant role.

THE SOCIAL CONTEXT OF DEVIANCE

Our discussion of social-order crime now needs to explore the social organization of secondary deviant roles. As we shall see, there is a subculture, an organizational network, and indeed an economy of deviance in our society. Let us examine this larger social context, which provides immense support to behaviors which our society also declares illegal.

To talk about illegal sex, drug use, and gambling is to discuss the "under-life" of American society. Often confined to a specific section of town, the underlife may also surface in the semirespectable setting of an after-hours rendezvous club or a "fun city" like Las Vegas. It would also appear that the underground economy, one generated by dealings in illegal goods and services, plays an important role in many localities and regions of the United States. To better understand the underlife of our society, let us look first at its subcultures, second at its organizational networks, and finally at the politics that are related to it.

Subcultures

Social scientists use the term "culture" to mean "the way of life of a people." Culture involves values (things that are felt to be desirable), norms (rules that prescribe behavior in certain situations), and artifacts (objects that take on special meaning). Every society–indeed, every social group–has a culture. The term "subculture" refers to the culture of a group that is part of the larger society. Generally subcultures share many of the values, norms, and artifacts of the general culture but differ in some.

Although the subcultures of the underlife of American society have been the subject of intensive study on the part of criminologists, their complexities are such that their full dimensions are only beginning to emerge. Nevertheless, it can be said that every organized form of deviance has a unique subculture. For some, it may be the "street life" of drug use and hustling which has been called "a complex amalgam of interactional networks."[79] For others, it is a homosexual underground that allows sexual exchanges between men in relatively public areas (called "tearooms") if certain norms are observed:

> Avoid exchange of biographical data.
> Watch out for chickens.
> Never enforce your intentions on anyone.
> Don't knock a trick. He may be somebody's mother (homosexual mentor).
> Never back down on trade agreements.[80]

For still others, middle- and upper-class vice is practiced in more comfortable settings such as the "after-hours" club (which sees itself as "a regular place for irregular people") or the plush gambling casinos of Las Vegas or Atlantic City.[81] Here too there are norms which prohibit certain overt criminal activities but at the same time allow for deals, contacts, and other discreet arrangements.

Although the subcultures may vary from group to group, they can be most powerful in bringing together people who are relative strangers to each other and who may have little in common other than their shared interest in the deviant activity. In this sense, the common values, norms, and artifacts of the subculture make it possible to carry on continuous, organized forms of deviance. The result is that different social worlds are linked:

> The customers of most deviant workers are drawn directly from the upper world of conventional roles, . . . so-called normal citizens who demand forbidden services that are provided by the deviant workers.[82]

Nor is it always a question of monetary exchange. The homosexual and "street life" cultures are bound together by commonly accepted norms, values, and artifacts.[83]

The subcultures of the underlife of American society are also reflected in the definite times and places of deviant activity. The "after-hours" club functions in the early morning hours. The homosexual "tearoom" setting for sex operates during the April–October "hunting season." Place may be even more sharply delineated. Particular restrooms or beach areas are often frequented by homosexuals. More generally, virtually every city in the United States has a slum area in which illegal sex, drugs, and gambling are available to those who desire them.[84] On a national level, there is Las Vegas, where legalized gambling operates together with an officially illegal but actually tolerated sex industry.

Organizational Networks

Complementing the subcultures of the underlife of American society is an organizational network designed to deliver illicit goods and services to people who want them. These networks may range widely: from local ones, such as those in which prostitutes find themselves giving kickbacks to cooperating taxi drivers, bellhops, or hotel managers; to international ones designed to deliver manufactured heroin and marijuana, harvested from crops grown in third world countries, to street addicts. In some but by no means all cases, syndicated or organized crime is involved. We shall look at organizational networks here and at organized crime in Chapter 14.

Perhaps the greatest diversity of organizational networks is seen in female prostitution. The four major types were noted earlier: streetwalkers, house prostitutes, massage parlour prostitutes, and call girls. In recent years there appears to be a shift from houses of prostitution to massage parlours and call girls. It is interesting to note that the call-girl form of prostitution, which makes use of the telephone and depends on ease of mobility in urban areas, allows for much greater individualization of operation and more part-time prostitution. However, massage parlours and commercial escort services provide prostitutes with a more direct link to men who desire their services.[85]

In contrast to the individual, freewheeling nature of prostitution is the much more tightly organized network of narcotics distribution. The reason for this high degree of organization is that a relatively small amount of poppies, perhaps less than would grow in 10 acres, can supply the entire addict population each year. There is enormous dilution as the narcotics go from the poppy field to the addict. Opium is harvested with the poppies; morphine is extracted from the opium and then converted to heroin. Then the heroin is "cut" by adding powders of similar color and consistency, "packaged" into capsules, and sold to the consumer. The dilution is such that an estimated 5 tons of pure heroin is sufficient to supply the entire addict population of the United States for one year.[86]

At one time, the heroin market was supplied almost totally by poppies grown in Turkey. In fact, while one part of Turkey's poppy crop went for illegal heroin, the other was sold to pharmaceutical companies for conversion to medicinal morphine. The illegal opium was shipped to France and Corsica, where it was converted to heroin, cut, and shipped to the United States.[87] However, according to some recent accounts, the traffic has changed. Opium is now grown in Mexico and southeast Asia, and the "French connection" no longer enjoys its monopoly over the hard drug traffic.[88]

Whatever the source, the reported profit in illegal heroin is enormous. When opium was sold at $25 per kilogram, the cost of the raw materials in a New York City bag of heroin was about one-fourth of a cent.[89] Obviously, this implies immense profits; but there are also intermediaries along the way. Aside from the foreign exporters, there are importers (rarely addicts themselves); professional wholesalers (also rarely addicts); peddlers or retailers (who may be addicted); and pushers (addicts who sell to get funds for their own drug supplies).[90] According to one study, the average importer supplies only eight wholesalers, each wholesaler only six retailers, each retailer only six pushers, and each pusher only fifteen addicts. Hence, the supplies from the original importer reach 4320 addicts.[91] One most interesting feature of this organization is that it functions extremely well on a continuous basis despite police interference and despite absence of extensive contact or communication among people on different levels of the distribution system.

The market for marijuana and other drugs is much larger than that for heroin. From all accounts, it too is decentralized but very active and most effective in delivering drugs to users. As one writer describes it:

> "Mother ships" stand off the coast of Florida with tons of marijuana more potent by far than that once cultivated by the Rebozo boys on Fisher Island in Biscayne Bay. Fast boats race out to bring it in, and trucks and motor homes carry it north. As the flood continues, veterans recall the rum-running days of Prohibition when the old syndicate was born.[92]

Newspaper reports tell of Coast Guard ships seizing 20- to 40-ton shipments of marijuana, cocaine, and Quaalude on fishing boats; of marijuana emerging as a billion-dollar cash crop; of agribusiness in California and El Paso as a "major hub for drug trafficking."[93] From this perspective, the production and distribution of drugs is but another form of big business in the United States.

The social organization of gambling varies considerably according to social class and ethnic group. Casinos serving a middle- and upper-class clientele are run as business organizations with croupiers, pit bosses, and blackjack players serving as well-paid employees. Two contrasting forms of social organization are seen in bookmaking and numbers. Serving a predominantly middle-class clientele, bookmaking lends itself to small, autonomous organizations that are somewhat unstable. Bookmakers also have to deal with sheetwriters, who take bets from the public (often by telephone) and can change bookmakers at will. Numbers finds its locus in the black community. Numbers, which evolved from policy during the 1940s, may have more racketeers involved but nevertheless is decentralized. Controllers who run the game coordinate the activity of "runners," who as agents of the controllers take the bets and provide a direct contact between seller and customer.[94]

Although its size is difficult to estimate, American society has a considerable underground economy of illegal sex, drugs, and gambling. According to the estimates quoted earlier, the total could run into billions or possibly tens of billions of dollars. Most of the money is tax-free, although income tax laws require payment of taxes even on money that is earned illegally. It is also interesting to note that the federal government has, perhaps unwittingly, recognized the legitimacy of gambling by collecting a gambling tax, even in states in which gambling is illegal. Another aspect of the underground economy is seen in the money used in otherwise legal activities or transactions. Under current income tax laws, sometimes it pays to lose money gambling in Las Vegas:

> The musician-drug dealer visits Las Vegas three times a year, loses $15,000, and claims winnings of $60,000, on which he pays taxes. Gambling provides a credible source for income otherwise derived. The "dirty" money is by such a process transformed into "clean" money. In the vernacular of Watergate, it is laundered.[95]

The *Miami Herald* has reported drug-money transactions in which Key West homes are sold at artificially low prices with the seller receiving a cash payment "under the table." Here too the buyer has effectively laundered money.[96]

Politics

The third aspect of social context is the politics of illegal sex, drugs, and gambling. Although in a broad sense all crime is political (see Chapter 15), there is much disagreement whether various types of illegal sex, drugs, and gambling should be criminal. As we have seen, many areas of these laws appear inconsistent: comparatively harmless acts are illegal (e.g., smoking marijuana) while some harmful ones are legal even though they cause considerable problems to law enforcement (e.g., drinking alcohol).

In part, the inconsistencies in laws about deviance can be seen in the politics of ethnicity and social class that have marked American life. Invariably it is the less powerful groups' deviance which is defined as illegal. Consider the following account of drug use:

> Thus, opium, condoned throughout the colonial period and the first century of independence, began to fall into disrepute when its use was connected with the masses of Chinese laborers imported to construct the railroads that spanned the American West. Antagonism toward "cheap Chinese labor" was translated into condemnation of their opium-smoking habit, which was undermining the "traditional" American way of life. In similar fashion, opposition to cocaine–once a favorite ingredient of medicines and soft drinks–arose when exaggerated reports appeared of the use of the drug by blacks in the South. . . . In the 1930s, concern about the dangers of marijuana was stirred by its reported widespread use among Spanish-speaking groups.[97]

Indeed, the seemingly incredible attempt to legislate a "dry" country makes sense only if one sees Prohibition as a symbolic attempt on the part of small-town Protestants to control immigrant, urban newcomers, the majority of whom were Catholics.[98] In some instances, politics may shift if a form of deviance spreads to other groups in the population; witness the recent calls for decriminalization of marijuana, which followed increases in the use of marijuana by middle-class young people.

Seeking the decriminalization of marijuana, students conduct a "smoke-in" on a university campus. (WIDE WORLD PHOTOS)

One result of the confused politics is that law enforcement efforts have often been selective or ineffective. In one typical midwestern city, the political structure allowed for neither complete elimination nor complete acceptance of the vice which had become part of the community's life. Finding themselves caught between highly organized deviance and unclear public morality, the police were predictably quite inconsistent:

> It was literally the case that drunks were arrested on the street for public intoxication while gamblers made thousands of dollars and policemen accepted bribes five feet away.[99]

Absence of clearly defined victims has also meant that police have had to be aggressive—that is, to take the initiative—in their enforcement of deviance-related crimes. Reliance on informers, use of sweep arrests, and assumption of deviant roles have marked police law enforcement policies, which are often "antagonistic to the principles of due process of law."[100]

Today, as was noted above, there are numerous calls for decriminalization of one or more of the social-order crimes. Such an approach appears sensible in that it would take away from the government the responsibility of enforcing one group's morality at the expense of another group. It would also permit the government to tax the money derived from various forms of deviancy, through income taxes, sales taxes, or some other special tax. Furthermore, the government could license or even participate in some activities, as it now does in the case of state-run lotteries.

However, decriminalization is by no means a simple matter. Prostitution, for example, is commercial as well as sexual; if it were legalized, could the government guarantee that consumers would be provided with the services for which they contracted? If drugs were legalized, should the government make their possible effects known, as it now does for cigarettes? If so, whose research and which advertising or public information methods should be used? Other issues involve age limits and whether or how the public aspects of deviant behavior should be policed. The entire issue of decriminalization is a complex one; greater attention will be devoted to it in Chapter 19.

SUMMARY

Social-order crimes are acts which are defined as crimes because they are considered deviant and offensive to the social order. Although there is much disagreement over what specific crimes to include in this category, three major areas can be distinguished: sexual acts, drug abuse, and gambling.

In each area of social-order crimes, there is a substantial disparity between the written law and public attitudes or behavior. Each has seen a call for decriminalization in one form or another. Sexual laws, while differing from state to state, continue to define as criminal acts committed by substantial segments of the population. Policy about drug use has varied immensely. After the attempt at Prohibition during the 1920s, alcohol became legalized. Possession, sale, and use of heroin and marijuana have been criminalized in recent decades. However, illegal drugs are quite prevalent. Policies concerning drugs are not directly related to harm to users; and legal drugs (such as alcohol) appear to be related to other forms of crime at least as much as illegal drugs are. Despite a variety of laws against gambling, it is estimated that 11 percent of Americans engage in illegal gambling.

Since social-order crimes often involve consenting adults, the roles of offenders and victims become blurred. However, sociologists do distinguish primary deviants from secondary deviants. Primary deviants are otherwise "respectable" members of society who do not see themselves as deviants. Secondary deviants are likely to pursue the deviant activity as an occupation, to participate in a deviant subculture, to have little difficulty seeing themselves as deviants, and to be involved in a network of relationships with others who participate in the deviant activity. The forms of primary and secondary deviance differ for sex acts, drug use, and gambling. Secondary deviance appears to decrease with age, except for gamblers. Prostitutes are predominantly female; drug users and gamblers are predominantly male. Primary deviants are of both sexes and all ages.

People are socialized into deviance. For prostitutes, there is often a period of apprenticeship during which a new self, based on sexual availability, is acquired. Socialization through peers and friends appears to be a necessary condition for drug abuse.

Illegal sex, drug abuse, and gambling are generally run as part of a well-organized "underlife" of American society. Every organized form of deviance has a unique subculture; intricate rules regulate activities such as "tearoom" sex and casino gambling. Times and places for the deviant activity are also understood by those who participate in the subculture. Related to the subculture is an organizational network which may be basically local (as with prostitution) or international (as with distribution of heroin and marijuana). The organizational network is reflected in an underground economy involving billions of dollars per year.

The very definition of social-order crimes is caught up in the patterns of ethnicity and social class that have marked American life. Most often it is the less powerful groups' deviance that has been defined as illegal.

In recognition of the problems in enforcement caused by the inconsistent, ineffective, or arbitrary definition of social-order crimes, there are at present numerous calls for decriminalization of one or more of these offenses. However, decriminalization is not as simple as it may at first sight appear. It can be argued that consumers of sexual services, drugs, and gambling establishments should be protected by government. One can also argue that governments should legalize certain deviant activities so that they can be taxed. Age limits and issues related to policy also need to be resolved before decriminalization can be implemented. (This is a complex matter; and decriminalization will receive further attention in Chapter 19.)

To complete our consideration of social-order crime, we now need to discuss another aspect of deviance: the organization or monopoly of its markets by criminal groups in the society. In other words, we must now consider "organized crime." Although new issues will emerge, many of the issues discussed in this chapter will come back to haunt us, issues such as: What is the social definition of organized crime? Who is the typical offender? Is there a victim other than the willing participant? How is organized crime tied into the political system of our society? It is to these questions that we will turn in Chapter 14.

NOTES

[1] Federal Bureau of Investigation (FBI), *Uniform Crime Reports—1981*, Government Printing Office, Washington D.C., 1982, p. 186.

[2] Edwin M. Schur and Hugo Adam Bedau, *Victimless Crimes: Two Sides of a Controversy*, Prentice-Hall, Englewood Cliffs, N.J., 1974, p. 61.

[3] Marshall B. Clinard and Robert F. Meier, *Sociology of Deviant Behavior*, 5th ed., Holt, Rinehart and Winston, New York, 1979, p. 14.

[4] Gerhard O. W. Mueller, *Sexual Conduct and the Law*, 2d ed., Oceana, Dobbs Ferry, N.Y., 1980, p. 23.

[5] Stanton Wheeler, "Sex Offenses: A Sociological Critique," *Law and Contemporary Problems*, vol. 25, no. 2, Spring 1960, pp. 258–278.

[6] For a general discussion of sex and the law, see: Donal E. J. MacNamara and Edward Sagarin, *Sex, Crime, and the Law*, Free Press, New York, and Collier Macmillan, London, 1977.

[7] John H. Gagnon and William Simon, *Sexual Conduct: The Social Sources of Human Sexuality*, Aldine, Chicago, Ill., 1973, p. 217.

[8] Alfred Kinsey et al., *Sexual Behavior in the Human Male*, Saunders, Philadelphia, Pa., 1948, p. 392.

[9] The big problem is sample bias. Most surveys have not included a true cross section of the population or have experienced very high rates of refusal to respond.

[10] Kinsey et al., *Sexual Behavior in the Human Male*.

[11] Alfred C. Kinsey et al., *Sexual Behavior in the Human Female*, Saunders, Philadelphia, Pa., 1953.

[12] Robert Sorensen, *Adolescent Sexuality in Contemporary America*, World, Cleveland, Ohio, 1973.

[13] Charles Winick and Paul M. Kinsie, *The Lively Commerce: Prostitution in the United States*, Aldine, Chicago, Ill., 1971.

[14] Mueller, *Sexual Conduct and the Law*, p. 7.

[15] Ibid., p. 40.

[16] Ibid., chap. 5.

[17] Wheeler, "Sex Offenses: A Sociological Critique." Wheeler's discussion of this question draws on: Edwin Sutherland, "The Diffusion of Sexual Psychopath Laws," *American Journal of Sociology*, vol. 56, 1950, pp. 142–148.

[18] Mueller, *Sexual Conduct and the Law*, chap. 8.

[19] Nicolette Parisi et al., eds., *Sourcebook of Criminal Justice Statistics—1978*, U.S. Department of Justice, Criminal Justice Research Center, 1979.

[20] Patrick Devlin, *The Enforcement of Morals*, Oxford University Press, London, 1965; and H.L.A. Hart, *Law, Liberty, and Morality*, Stanford University Press, Stanford, Calif., 1963.

[21] Schur and Bedau, *Victimless Crimes*.

[22] Macnamara and Sagarin, *Sex, Crime, and the Law*, p. 5.

[23] David J. Pittman, "Drugs, Addiction, and Crime," in

Daniel Glasser, ed., *Handbook of Criminology*, Rand McNally, Chicago, Ill., 1974, p. 209.

24 John A. Clausen, "Drug Use," in Robert K. Merton and Robert Nisbet, eds., *Contemporary Social Problems*, Harcourt Brace Jovanovich, New York, 1971, p. 188.

25 Troy Duster, *The Legislation of Morality: Law, Drugs, and Moral Judgment*, Free Press, New York, 1970, chap. 1.

26 Alfred R. Lindesmith, *The Addict and the Law*, Indiana University Press, Bloomington, 1965, chap. 1.

27 Ibid.; and Duster, *The Legislation of Morality*, chap. 1.

28 Robert Straus, "Alcohol and Alcoholism," in Merton and Nisbet, *Contemporary Social Problems*, pp. 227–269. The 2.65-gallon estimate is given in: Strategy Council on Drug Abuse, *Federal Strategy for Drug Abuse and Drug Traffic Prevention*, Government Printing Office, Washington, D.C., 1979.

29 On Prohibition, see also: Joseph R. Gusfield, *Symbolic Crusade*, University of Illinois Press, Urbana, 1963.

30 Charles E. Reasons, "The Addict as a Criminal: Perpetuation of a Legend," *Crime and Delinquency*, vol. 21, no. 1, January 1975, pp. 19–27.

31 Clausen, "Drug Use," p. 202.

32 Strategy Council, *Federal Strategy for Drug Abuse and Drug Traffic Prevention*, p. 6.

33 Lloyd D. Johnston, Jerold G. Bachman, and Patrick M. O'Malley, *Highlights from Student Drug Use in America, 1975–1980* (pamphlet), U.S. Department of Health and Human Services, Rockeville, Md., 1980.

34 National Institute on Alcoholism Abuse and Alcoholism, as reported in: *New York Times*, December 8, 1982.

35 Jeremiah Lowney, Robert W. Winslow, and Virginia Winslow, *Deviant Reality: Alternative World Views*, 2d ed., Allyn and Bacon, Boston, Mass., 1981, pp. 103–106.

36 Lester Grinspoon, M.D., *Marijuana Reconsidered*, 2d ed., Harvard University Press, Cambridge, Mass., 1977.

37 Duster, *The Legislation of Morality*, chap. 2.

38 James A. Inciardi, "Heroin Use and Street Crime," *Crime and Delinquency*, vol. 25, July 1979, pp. 335–346. See also: James Vorenberg and Irving F. Lukoff, "Addiction, Crime, and the Criminal Justice System," *Federal Probation*, vol. 37, no. 4, December 1973, pp. 3–7; David Caplovitz, *The Working Addict*, Sharpe, White Plains, N. Y., 1976; and Paul Cushman, Jr., "Relationship between Narcotics Addiction and Crime," *Federal Probation*, vol. 38, no. 3, September 1974, pp. 38–42.

39 Marvin E. Wolfgang, "A Sociological Analysis of Criminal Homicide," *Federal Probation*, vol. 25, no. 1, March 1961, pp. 48–55.

40 David J. Pittman and William Handy, "Patterns in Criminal Aggravated Assault," *Journal of Criminal Law, Criminology, and Police Science*, vol. 55, no. 4, 1964, pp. 462–470.

41 Norval Morris and Gordon Hawkins, *The Honest Politician's Guide to Crime Control*, University of Chicago Press, Chicago, Ill., 1970, p. 3.

42 Alexander B. Smith and Harriet Pollack. *Some Sins Are Not Crimes: A Plea for Reform of the Criminal Law*, Franklin Watts, New York, 1975, p. 3.

43 Commission on the Review of the National Policy toward Gambling, *Gambling in America*, Final Report, Government Printing Office, Washington, D.C., 1976, p. ix.

44 Ibid.

45 Stephen Longstreet, *Win or Lose: A Social History of Gambling in America*, Bobbs-Merrill, Indianapolis, Ind., 1977; and Henry Chafetz, *Play the Devil*, Patten, New York, 1960.

46 Ernest Havemann, "A Panorama of Gambling," in Herbert L. Marx, Jr., ed., *Gambling in America*, Wilson, New York, 1952, p. 11.

47 For a discussion, see: Smith and Pollack, *Some Sins Are Not Crimes*, pp. 136–142.

48 Morris Ploscowe, "The Law of Gambling," *Annals of the American Academy of Political and Social Science*, vol. 269, May 1950, pp. 1–8.

49 Commission on the Review of the National Policy toward Gambling, *Gambling in America*.

50 Morris and Hawkins, *The Honest Politician's Guide to Crime Control*, p. 3.

51 Smith and Pollack, *Some Sins Are Not Crimes*, p. 141.

52 See: Jerome H. Skolnick, *House of Cards: The Legalization and Control of Casino Gambling*, Little, Brown, Boston, Mass., 1978, chap. 21.

53 The crimes discussed here are not the only social-order crimes. Not included in the above discussion are abortion, bribery, and several others noted earlier in the present chapter.

54 Clinard and Meier, *Sociology of Deviant Behavior*, pp. 42–44. See also: Edwin M. Lemment, *Social Pathology*, McGraw Hill, New York, 1951, p. 75–76.

55 Gagnon and Simon, *Sexual Conduct*, pp. 225–233.

56 Ibid., chap. 5.

57 Howard M. Bahr, *Skid Row: An Introduction to Disaffiliation*, Oxford University Press, New York, 1973.

58 However, some heroin addicts are primary deviants. The largest number of professionals who are addicts are doctors. See: Michael J. Pescor, "Physician Drug Addicts," in John A. O'Donnell and John C. Ball, eds., *Narcotic Addiction*, Harper and Row, New York, 1966, pp. 164–167.

59 Duster, *The Legislation of Morality*, p. 72.

60 Clinard and Meier, *Sociology of Deviant Behavior*, p. 315.

61 Erich Goode, "Multiple Drug Use among Marijuana Smokers," *Social Problems*, vol. 17, 1969, pp. 48–64.

62 Bruce D. Johnson, *Marihuana Users and Drug Subcultures*, Wiley, New York, 1973, p. 164.

63 For a historical perspective on the occupation, see: David R. Johnson, "A Sinful Business: The Origins of Gambling Syndicates in the United States, 1840–1887," in David H. Bayley, ed., *Police and Society*, Sage, Beverly Hills, Calif., 1977, pp. 17–47.

64 Clinard and Meier, *Sociology of Deviant Behavior*, p. 400.

65 Charles Winick, "Maturing Out of Narcotics Addiction," *Bulletin on Narcotics*, vol. 14, no. 1, 1962, pp. 1–8.

66 Joan W. Moore et al., *Homeboys: Gangs, Drugs, and Prison in the Barrios of Los Angeles*, Temple University Press, Philadelphia, Pa., 1978.

67 Ivan Light, "The Ethnic Vice Industry, 1880–1944," *American Sociological Review*, vol. 42, 1977, pp. 464–479.

68 Kinsey, *Sexual Behavior in the Human Male*, pp. 258–261.

69 Charles R. Tittle and Wayne J. Villemez, "Social Class

and Criminality," *Social Forces*, vol. 56, no. 2, December 1977, pp. 474–502.

[70] Commission on the Review of the National Policy toward Gambling, *Gambling in America*.

[71] Lowney, Winslow, and Winslow, *Deviant Reality*, pp. 137–138.

[72] Ibid., p. 106.

[73] Gagnon and Simon, *Sexual Conduct*, pp. 225–229.

[74] Ibid., p. 228.

[75] Howard S. Becker, "Becoming a Marijuana User," in *Studies in the Sociology of Deviance*, Free Press, New York, 1963, chap. 3.

[76] Johnson, *Marihuana Users and Drug Subcultures*.

[77] Dan Waldorf, *Careers in Dope*, Prentice-Hall, Englewood Cliffs, N.J., 1973.

[78] Edwin M. Schur, *Crimes without Victims*, Prentice-Hall, Englewood Cliffs, N.J., 1965.

[79] R. B. Smith and Richard C. Stephens, "Drug Use and 'Hustling': A Study of Their Interrelationships," *Criminology*, vol. 14, no. 2, August 1976, pp. 155–176.

[80] Laud Humphreys, *Tearoom Trade: Impersonal Sex in Public Places*, Aldine, Chicago, Ill., 1970, chap. 1. For a description of the homosexual underground, see also: John Rechy, *The Sexual Outlaw: A Documentary—A Non-Fiction Account, with Commentaries, of Three Days and Nights in the Sexual Underground*, Grove, New York, 1977; and Edward William Delph, *The Silent Community: Public Homosexual Encounters*, Sage, Beverly Hills, Calif., 1978.

[81] See: Julian B. Roebuck and Wolfgang Frese, *The Rendezvous: A Case Study of an After-Hours Club*, Free Press, New York, and Collier Macmillan, London, 1976; and Skolnick, *House of Cards*.

[82] Gale Miller, *Odd Jobs: The World of Deviant Work*, Prentice-Hall, Englewood Cliffs, N.J., 1978, pp. 5–6.

[83] On street life, see: Leroy C. Gould, Andrew L. Walker, Lansing E. Crane, and Charles W. Lidz, *Connections: Notes from the Heroin World*, Yale University Press, New Haven, Conn., 1974.

[84] William J. Chambliss, "Vice, Corruption, Bureaucracy, and Power," *Wisconsin Law Review*, vol. 4, December 1971, pp. 1150–1173.

[85] Clinard and Meier, *Sociology of Deviant Behavior*, pp. 398–400.

[86] On the organization of the heroin trade, see: Edward M. Brecher and the Editors of Consumer Reports, *Licit and Illicit Drugs: The Consumers Union Report on Narcotics, Stimulants, Depressants, Inhalents, Hallucinogens, and Marijuana—Including Caffeine, Nicotine, and Alcohol*, Consumers Union of the United States and Little, Brown, Boston, Mass., 1972; and Lawrence John Redlinger, "Marketing and Distributing Heroin: Some Sociological Observations," *Journal of Psychedelic Drugs*, vol. 7, no. 4, October-December 1975, pp. 331–353.

[87] For a personal account, see: Michael Auger, *The Heroin Triangle: Marseilles—Montreal—New York (The Confessions of Michael Mastantuone as Told to Michael Auger)*, trans. by Gayner Fitzpatrick, Methuen, Toronto, 1976.

[88] E.g.: Moore et al., *Homeboys*. See also: Hank Messick, *Of Grass and Snow: The Secret Criminal Elite*, Prentice-Hall, Englewood Cliffs, N.J., 1979.

[89] Brecher and Consumer Reports, *Licit and Illicit Drugs*.

[90] Redlinger, "Marketing and Distributing Heroin."

[91] Arthur D. Little, Inc., *Drug Abuse and Law Enforcement: A Report to the President's Commission on Law Enforcement and Administration of Justice*, January 18, 1967.

[92] Messick, *Of Grass and Snow*, p. 2.

[93] *New York Times*, July 8, 1979; July 20, 1980; and June 17, 1979, respectively.

[94] Peter Reuter and Jonathan B. Rubinstein, "Fact, Fancy, and Organized Crime," *Public Interest*, vol. 53, Fall 1978, pp. 45–67; and Ivan Light, "The Ethnic Vice Industry, 1880–1944," *American Sociological Review*, vol. 42, 1977, pp. 464–479.

[95] Skolnick, *House of Cards*, p. 46.

[96] *Miami Herald*, March 16, 1980.

[97] Richard C. Schroeder, *The Politics of Drugs: Marijuana to Mainlining*, Congressional Quarterly, Washington, D.C., 1975, p. 5.

[98] Gusfield, *Symbolic Crusade*.

[99] Chambliss, "Vice, Corruption, Bureaucracy and Power," p. 1168.

[100] Jerome H. Skolnick, *Justice without Trial: Law Enforcement in Democratic Society*, Wiley, New York, 1966, especially chap. 10.

14

Organized Crime

As previous chapters have suggested, most criminal activity in American society is organized rather than individualistic or spontaneous. Although the form may differ, criminal organization is seen in phenomena such as the recycling of stolen goods, the collaboration among individuals involved in corporate crime, the understandings between employers and employees that underlie theft by employees, and the subculture and organizational networks of social-order crimes. In fact, crime cannot be understood without an awareness of how it is organized. The organizational focus of this text places much emphasis on the social contexts of the major types of crime in American society.

However, to speak of "organized crime" is to discuss a unique kind of criminal organization. Organized crime involves the gangster or racketeer, a crime professional who as part of a larger organization uses extortion or other methods based on force to monopolize the profits from certain types of crime. Organized crime has been called the "Syndicate," the "Mafia," "Cosa Nostra," and a variety of other names. Although it is a colorful part of American social life, there are serious questions about the nature, structure, size, and role of organized crime in American society. As with other forms of crime, we must examine organized criminal acts, organized criminal offenders, victims of organized crime, and social context—the relationship between organized crime and American society. First, let's consider organized criminal acts.

ORGANIZED CRIMINAL ACTS

Organized crime in American society has been studied extensively. Books and films such as *The Godfather*, *The Valachi Papers*, *The Don is Dead*, and *Honor Thy Father* have popularized and romanticized it. Government hearings have attempted to expose facts about its operations. A few former members of organized crime have "confessed" how it works as they dropped out of its ranks.[1] Academic criminologists have used tapes and documents of the federal government, and personal informants, to study it.[2]

To appreciate the study of organized criminal acts, it will be useful to take a look at problems in the definition of organized crime, its history, estimates of its present-day size, and laws designed to control it. Let's begin with definitional problems.

Problems of Definition

Despite all the attention received by organized crime, it is immensely difficult to separate fact from fiction and even to establish what is meant by the term "organized crime." The difficulties are evident in ways organized crime can be defined. Donald R. Cressey, for one, sees organized crime as

> any crime committed by a person occupying, in an established division of labor, a position designed for the commission of crime, providing that such division of labor also includes at least one position for a corrupter, one position for a corruptee, and one position for an enforcer.[3]

Francis A. J. Ianni, by contrast, sees organized crime in a much more informal or functional sense as

> an integral part of the American system that brings together a public that demands certain goods and services that are defined as illegal, an organization of individuals who produce or supply those goods and services, and corrupt public officials who protect such individuals for their own profit or gain.[4]

As we shall see, the two definitions underlie differing conceptions of organized crime. Cressey compares it to a national corporation like General Motors. Ianni compares it to a network of extended family, ethnic, and political relationships.

One reason for the difficulty in defining organized crime is that there is no limited number of specific acts committed by organized criminals. Organized crime has been considered as encompassing (1) predatory crimes such as hijacking, burglary, and labor and business racketeering, not to mention murder; and also (2) demand-oriented illegal enterprises which deal in criminal but highly desired activities related to gambling, loansharking, narcotics, and sex, especially prostitution.[5] There is also a possible third area: the penetration of legitimate business by organized crime. Yet if organized crime is to be considered a separate category of crime, the nature of the organization or collusion is of more importance than the specific criminal acts committed.

The problem here is that the nature of the organization or collusion is most elusive and difficult to pin down. Even the terminology lacks standardization and clarity. Common speech refers to the "Mafia." Since the federal government recognized the existence of organized crime in the late 1950s, it has referred to organized crime as "Cosa Nostra." Some writers prefer the term "syndicated crime" or "illegal enterprise."[6] Still others have used "combo," "outfit," or "association." Each of these terms carries different connotations. "Mafia" and "Cosa Nostra" in particular convey an ethnic overtone to which many Italian Americans have objected.

To analyze organized crime, it is necessary to go beyond terminology and discuss what type of organization ought to be considered criminal. Thomas C. Schelling has noted that organized crime is not simply a monoploy (indeed some legitimate businesses are monopolies), but one which uses criminal means, including extortion by threat or use of violence, to establish and maintain itself. In that organized crime skims off the profits of criminal operations, it is an especially parasitic form of crime. At the same time, it provides the underworld with a governmental structure, one which maintains peace, sets rules, arbitrates disputes, and enforces discipline. It may even provide services to those who cooperate with it, such as tax advice, credit, enforcement of contracts, and protection from the law.[7] To put it another way, organized crime can be seen as both illegal enterprise and illegal government.[8]

The issues concerning definition, name, and nature of organization are by no means settled. Their importance will be appreciated as we proceed now to examine the history of organized crime, estimates of its present-day size, and the laws attempting to control it.

Early forms of organized crime

There is general agreement that organized criminal activity in the United States has its historical roots in the gangs that have appeared at various times and places in American history. As was noted in Chapter 2, criminal gangs and even syndicates existed as early as the 1760s. Later, on the western frontier of the middle 1800s, the predatory James, Younger, and Dalton gangs—among others— were an important part of the social scene. In the cities, gangs were organized along ethnic lines. Irish gangs were among the first to emerge; in New York City Tammany Hall was a unique political organization that blended machine politics,

During the Prohibition era, "Duckboard" Butler, public safety director of Philadelphia, happily smashed confiscated kegs of beer. Prohibition was an important factor in the history of organized crime.   (BETTMAN ARCHIVE)

Irish settlements, street gangs, and organized vice. In the early 1900s, German, Jewish, and Italian gangs took their place alongside those of the Irish. For the most part, these early gangs confined their racketeering, predatory, and criminal activities to their own ethnic groups and local territories.[9]

The big change came during the 1920s, when Prohibition provided the opportunity for gangsters to expand their activities outside their own ethnic groups and local communities. Millions of people in the general public wanted liquor and—given the prohibition on manufacture, distribution, sale, and use of alcoholic beverages—the largest part of the liquor traffic simply fell into the hands of the criminals. The semiorganized criminal gangs began to combine their efforts for mutual advantage, forming supply lines and staking out avenues for retail trade. At the same time, rivalries and competition for the lucrative trade led to strife and open warfare between gangs.[10]

The Mafia

There is general agreement on the ethnic organization of gangs and the importance of Prohibition for the consolidation of criminal activity. But there is disagreement over whether or not the early 1930s saw the emergence of "a secret nationwide society of Italian Americans—a Mafia which controls organized crime in the United States."[11] On one side are those who follow Cressey's approach and see organized crime as an alien conspiracy that took hold in the early 1930s and has continued in the direction of centralization and bureaucratization. On the other side, as we shall see, are those who decry the "Mafia myth" and see organized crime as essentially localized networks of individuals involved in racketeering activities. Those taking the latter approach—which follows from Ianni's definition—argue that organized crime is a product of American social life and that Italian supremacy in crime is a phase that will pass as Italians are increasingly absorbed into the mainstream of American society.

Unfortunately, the facts of history do not serve to resolve the argument among criminologists, because even the facts are in dispute. Two events in the late 1800s illustrate some of the historical confusion about the Mafia. One was the murder of Lieutenant Hennessey of the New Orleans police department, whose investigation of several murders had reportedly uncovered much mafioso activity. The second was the murder of Petrosino, a New York police official who was killed in Sicily while investigating possible ties between American and Sicilian crime figures.[12] While some have seen the murders as the work of the Mafia, others have claimed that Hennessey's and Petrosimo's allegations of mafioso activity were never really established and that the immense public reaction to these events was part of the hatred and distrust of foreigners that has often marked American life.[13]

It is amazing how much disagreement there is about the nature of the Mafia even as it existed in Sicily. Frederick Sondern saw it as an underground political resistance movement dating back to the eighteenth century, when Sicily was dominated by the Bourbons.[14] Others hold that it originated in the fifteenth century and was a product of the internal disorder and decay which characterized Europe of that time. Following this viewpoint, Chandler traces its development from the Garduna to the Mafia, which he claims emerged in 1860, partly as a result of the efforts of Guiseppi Mazzini, an Italian revolutionist.[15] Burton B. Turkus and Sid Feder have argued that the Mafia became extinct in Italy by 1930 and was replaced by the Unione Sicilano, a group that was much more sophisticated than the Sicilian Mafia.[16]

It can be argued that a secret criminal society (whatever its exact origins or name) was able to exist in southern Italy because a weak centralized government left people in need of protection. Protection could be secured only by seeking out authoritative role relationships which were highly family-oriented and emphasized the owing and payment of favors. At the same time, there was a male role model stressing individual honor and a norm of silence about oneself and one's activities.[17]

It is remarkable that this secret criminal group, which may have functioned well in southern Italy, could come to dominate and, some would say, control crime in the United States. After all, the societies were vastly different. One was small, agrricultural, and rural; the other large, industrial, and urban. One had experienced oppressive foreign domination; the other was a free, independent, democratic state. Yet it would appear that this secret criminal group, transplanted from southern Italy, was to play a key role in organized crime in the United States.

The timing of Italian immigration was a factor in determining the role of the secret criminal society in organized crime. Although Italian immigration had started as early as 1820, it was not until the 1920s that Italians were to succeed the Irish and Jews in important political and social positions in the United States. Coincidentally, it was also during the 1920s that Mussolini purged the Mafia from Italy, a move which forced many mafiosi to emigrate to the United States. One writer estimates that at least 500 mafiosi went to the United States between 1922 and 1929 and that many of these immigrants later became quite powerful in organized crime.[18]

It should also be recognized that immigration of Italians and mafiosi to the United States during the 1920s occurred in a period marked by intense rivalry among Irish, Jewish, and Italian groups. To those who understood the situation, these gang rivalries, which often resulted in warfare (for example, the "beer wars") were unproductive and costly. There was a need to consolidate power and to provide social order. Such a syndication, or rationalization, of criminal rackets was probably inevitable; and it could be claimed that the underworld was simply following the lead of an earlier generation of American capitalists, who had also organized large business empires by methods that were often illegal.[19] In any event, the Italians with their crime families moved in. Their indirect ties to the Mafia in the home country were probably of less importance than (1) their being in a position to meet the needs brought about as the result of unique social conditions in the United States and (2) their desire to gain money, power, and social status in the society to which they had immigrated.

Capone

Al Capone—an interesting historical figure, called by some the "greatest organizer of crime"—was the first person to develop an extremely efficient network of rackets. He employed over 700 people, and his operations went far beyond

Indicted for income tax evasion in 1931, Al Capone is seen with his lawyers at a hearing of the federal grand jury in Chicago. (BETTMAN ARCHIVE)

Chicago, his base city. One of the most colorful figures in the history of crime, Capone was also a businessman who knew how to skim the profits from the rackets, keep the operators in line, and pay off political officials. In fact, he pictured himself as a modern-day Robin Hood and enjoyed immense popular support. Curiously, he was caught not for committing any violent offense but for income tax evasion. Even then, he probably would have been acquitted had it not been for the efforts of a judge who at the last minute switched a jury that Capone had rigged. Capone's rise to power came in the mid-1920s; his trial and conviction occurred in 1931.

To argue against the "Mafia myth," it must be noted that Capone's rise to a preeminent position of power in the American underworld was not related to the Mafia, or for that matter to any other secret criminal society. To begin with, Capone was born in Brooklyn, New York. Moreover, he was of Neopolitan rather than Sicilian descent. Finally, his rise to power came through his ability to organize and control his gang. Once he was in power, his business acumen enabled him to syndicate the rackets in which he was involved. In other words, he was able to combine the use of violence with up-to-date business and organizational techniques and turn the rather irregular profits of the rackets into sources of regular income.[20]

Cosa Nostra

Historically, the early 1930s were a most significant period for the consolidation of organized crime operations. Again, however, there is disagreement about the nature and extent of the consolidation. Cressey claims that in 1931 organized crime leaders met together to form the nationwide cartel or confederation "which today operates the principal illicit businesses in America."[21] Called "Cosa Nostra," the nationwide cartel was a result of (1) a rational decision to form monopolistic corporations and (2) peace treaties and agreements hammered out at the end of the 1930–1931 war between the Masseria and Maranzano factions, known as the "Castellammarese war." According to Valachi's account of this war, between 30 and 90 people were killed in a period of 24 hours.[22]

In Cressey's view, the modern Cosa Nostra that emerged in 1931 comprises 24 crime families, each of which has between 20 and 700 members in various positions: boss, consigliere (counselor), underboss, caporegima (lieutenant), and solider (member). In addition, there are also "corrupters" (who handle police or public officials), "buffers," "money movers," "enforcers," and "executioners." (See Figure 7.) There are in all about 5000 known participants. The families are

FIGURE 7.
Cressey's view of an organized crime family. (SOURCE: President's Commission on Law Enforcement and Administration of Justice, *The Challenge of Crime in a Free Society*, Government Printing Office, Washington, D. C., 1967, p. 452.)

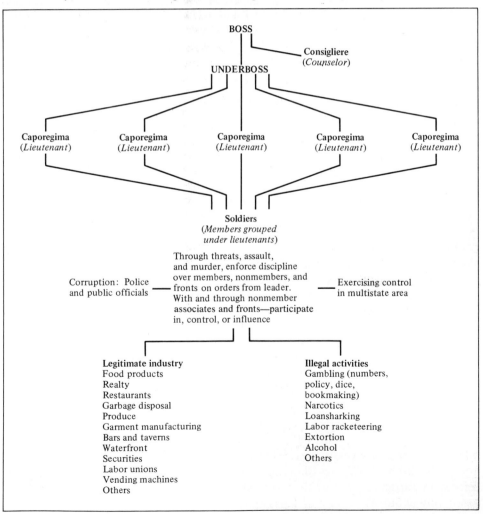

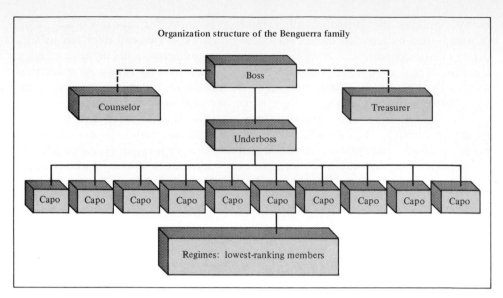

FIGURE 8.
Another view of an organized crime family. (SOURCE: Annelise Graebner
Anderson, *The Business of Organized Crime—A Cosa Nostra Family*, Hoover
Institute Press, Stanford, Calif., 1979, p. 35.)

linked to each other and to syndicates other than Cosa Nostra by understandings, agreements, and treaties. The highest ruling body is a national "commission" which is the ultimate authority, one that can set policy and arbitrate organizational and jurisdictional disputes.[23] (Figure 8 shows another view of a crime family.)

The aftermath of the 1930 war was a period of great change for Cosa Nostra. As Prohibition ended, it moved out of bootlegging liquor and into gambling, usury, and control of legitimate business, a move which increased its power and respectability.[24] At the same time, it set up an enforcement arm, popularly known as "Murder, Inc.," which was designed solely "for the preservation and improvement of the vast business interests: the rackets." Murder, Inc., has been described as a "fantastic ring of killers and extortionists" that was responsible for approximately 1000 murders in the decade 1930–1940. Its ruthless methods reportedly enabled it to take control over many of the local rackets.[25]

Again, the facts concerning the nature and extent of this consolidation have been called into question. Francis J. Ianni and Elizabeth Reuss-Ianni's study of one organized crime family concluded that crime families exist but are "traditional social systems, organized by action and by cultural values which have nothing to do with modern bureaucratic virtues."[26] They also argue that there is no national commission and that bosses resemble uncles to whom younger members give respect. In the same vein, both Joseph L. Albini and Dwight C. Smith believe that there is no one criminal organization with a national ruling body but rather a variety of illegal enterprises or crime syndicates that have been created to supply the illicit desires of Americans.[27] Their views have received empirical support in recent research by Alan A. Block and Peter Reuter and Jonathan B. Rubinstein.[28] Block, in particular, has criticized Cressey for relying too heavily on Valachi's testimony about the nature of Cosa Nostra organization.[29]

Whatever the nature or extent of consolidation, it is generally agreed that organized crime came to play a greater role in American life during the decades following its consolidation in the 1930s. Control of gambling appears to be a key part of this consolidation, with organized crime groups using force to skim off the profits of local operators. Numbers gambling is a case in point: a bet is placed on a three-digit number (often the last three digits of the total dollars bet at a racetrack or the total volume of stocks traded on a given day on the New York Stock Exchange). Thus, the odds are 1000 to 1. The corresponding payoff is between 500 and 600, with the remainder going to numbers runners and the "bank," i.e., those who run the game. Although the bets may be small, perhaps as small as 25 cents, the overall profits are enormous and provide a substantial cash flow. By all accounts, the involvement of organized crime in numbers, as well as other forms of gambling, has been an important factor in its growth in recent decades.

Organized Crime Today: Estimates of Size

There is general agreement that profits from gambling provide the basic source of income for present-day organized crime and give it the cash flow necessary to penetrate other businesses. However, estimates of the profits made from gambling differ widely, and estimates of the extent of penetration into legitimate business are even more speculative. There are also some who would claim that powerful organized crime families are now on the decline.

Gambling

Estimates of the extent of gambling, and the profit derived from it, are anything but exact. In conducting his hearings on crime in the early 1950s, Senator Estes Kefauver argued that 50 million Americans gambled a total of $30 billion per year, a sum which provided $6 billion in profits to entrepreneurs. This $6 billion was greater than the annual profits of the largest industrial enterprises at the time. After acknowledging the problems of judging the accuracy of the figures, the President's Crime Commission observed in 1967 that estimates of the annual intake from gambling varied from $7 billion to $50 billion. They too believed that the profit could be $6 billion or $7 billion.[30] More recent estimates are no more certain. As was noted in Chapter 13, the Department of Justice estimates illegal gambling to involve between $29 billion and $39 billion per year. However, a survey using the best social science research techniques, sponsored by the Commission on the Review of the National Policy toward Gambling, concluded that a much smaller amount—$5 billion—was involved in illegal gambling. Even the very conservative figure of $5 billion could yield well over $1 billion a year in profits, a substantial amount of money if divided among a limited number of people and not subject to income tax.

Other operations

Although gambling may be the logical starting point for organized crime, its operations are far broader. On the one hand, there are the demand-oriented illegal enterprises over which organized crime has been able to gain control: (1) selling of narcotics; (2) loansharking, either to gamblers or to small businesspeople unable to secure bank loans; (3) fencing of stolen property (see also Chapter 10); (4) cargo theft; (5) illegal trade in aliens; and (6) prostitution, which is generally provided as a "service" to clients.[31] On the other hand, there is its penetration into legitimate business as profits from illegal enterprises have been "laundered" and reinvested. The areas of its alleged involvement are many: (1) marketing of meat, cheese, and other food products; (2) trucking; (3) banking and finance; (4) restaurants; (5) labor racketeering; and (6) disposal of toxic wastes.[32]

According to some writers, organized crime has gained enormous influence in the United States. August Bequai, for one, writes:

> Organized crime, once a pawn of local political machines, has become a power in its own right. It controls multibillion-dollar businesses and elects agents to Congress. It has become a de facto government. In many urban slums it commands greater respect and authority than government. In fifty years the Capones and Lucianos have created America's fifth estate, a criminal confederation bound by political and economic needs and extending into every ethnic and racial group: Jews, Italians, Latins, blacks—all work together in this criminal cartel.[33]

In a similar vein, Cressey states:

> The members of this organization control all but a tiny part of the illegal gambling in the United States. They are the principal loan sharks. They are the principal importers and wholesalers of narcotics. They have infiltrated certain labor unions, where they extort money from employers and, at the same time, cheat the members of the union. The members have a virtual monopoly on some legitimate enterprises, such as cigarette vending machines and juke boxes, and they own a wide variety of retail firms, restaurants and bars, hotels, trucking companies, food companies, linen-supply houses, garbage collection routes, and factories. Until recently, they owned a large proportion of Las Vegas. They own several state legislators and federal congressmen and other officials in the legislative, executive, and judicial branches of government at the local, state, and federal levels. Some government officials (including judges) are considered, and consider themselves, members.[34]

Michael Gartner goes so far as to argue that crime and business are now so intertwined that it is quite normal for racketeers to put their booty into legitimate businesses and for businesspeople to put their profits into illegitimate enterprises.[35]

The view that organized crime is everywhere is difficult to assess. As with gambling, the extent of its penetration into legitimate business is impossible to determine. However, one study has identified at least five patterns: (1) legal holdings, legally operated; (2) predatory or parasitic exploitation of legitimate business (e.g., extortion of protection money or excessively high fees for garbage disposal); (3) monopoly; (4) unfair advantage; and (5) business activity supportive of illicit enterprise and reciprocally supported by it. The same study went on to observe that organized crime may control 50,000 commercial or industrial enterprises and $30 billion dollars (1 percent of the $3 trillion in business assets in the United States). This figure was described as far from a takeover but "impressive nonetheless." However, the study also noted that the firms which were controlled tended to be relatively small and restricted to pursuits involving simple production and marketing techniques.[36]

The impact of organized crime is also considerable by several other criteria. One is the income of organized crime members. Impressionistic accounts have suggested that incomes of individuals involved in organized crime can be substantial, especially since they are tax-free.[37] If official governmental estimates were correct (actually, they are probably overstated), there would be 5000 individuals who as full members of organized crime families each earned $1 million per year. This would mean that "some two-thirds of the national elite, in terms of annual income, consists of associates of organized crime."[38] In assessing the impact of organized crime by another approach, Harold D. Lasswell and Jeremiah B. McKenna were led to conclude that organized crime was grossing more revenue from its illegal policy and narcotics operations in Bedford Stuyvesant (a section of Brooklyn, New York) than the federal government was collecting from income taxes in the same area.[39]

National scope

In dealing with the issue of the extent of organized crime, one must also take into account its national scope. To begin with, organized crime families have their center of operation in relatively few selected cities. (See Figure 9.) Second, the President's Crime Commission, in attempting to understand the extent of orga-

FIGURE 9.
Centers of operations of organized crime families. Asterisk indicates number 2 in command. (SOURCE: Denny F. Pace and Jimmy C. Styles, *Organized Crime—Concepts and Control*, Prentice-Hall, Englewood Cliffs, N.J., 1975, p. 13.)

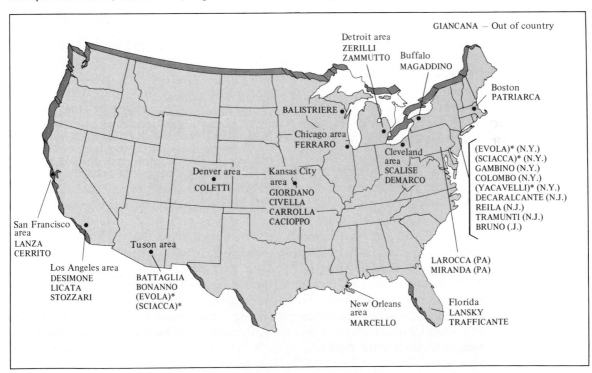

nized crime, surveyed officials in 71 cities. It found that the existence of organized crime was acknowledged in only 19 of the cities. There was a difference by size of city: organized crime was acknowledged to exist in 80 percent of cities of more than 1 million population but only 20 percent of those with 250,000 to 1 million population and 50 percent of those with 100,000 to 250,000 population. In other words, its operations were more prevalent in the largest and in the smallest cities, the medium-sized ones being comparatively immune.[40]

Judgments concerning the extent and profitability of organized crime are dependent on how one sees its structure. If one leans toward Cressey's position, which reflects the thinking of official governmental agencies, organized crime is immensely powerful because it controls the most profitable areas of criminal activity and concentrates its control in relatively few hands. On the other hand, it has already been noted that businesses in which organized crime has an interest tend to be relatively small and to involve simple production and marketing techniques. As far as is known, organized crime is not involved in IBM, GM, AT&T, or the other national or multinational corporations that dominate American business. Furthermore, organized crime seems to operate only in selected American cities. According to this contrasting view, while organized crime is immensely profitable and may control 1 percent of the total business assets in the United States, it does not appear to dominate American business. In this sense, it is the tail that occasionally wags the dog.

Another source of disagreement with Cressey's position is found among academic criminologists who see the tightly organized Italian crime families as a passing chapter in the social history of American crime. Two crime families have been studied in depth by academic criminologists. Ianni found that in the ''Lupollo'' family (a pseudonym) each succeeding generation was ''quietly but certainly'' moving out of crime; by the fourth generation, only four of 27 males remained involved. Some operations, for example, were passed on to black and Puerto Rican groups.[41] Similarly, Annelise Graebner Anderson studied the ''Benguena'' family and found much evidence of its decline since Prohibition, especially in the median age of its members (nearly half were over 60).[42] In another calculation, James A. Inciardi claims that of 5000 designated mafiosi, two-thirds are presently in jail, under indictment, or dead. He too argues that few are now recruited to the Mafia.[43]

In qualifying Cressey's position, these academic criminologists are not saying that organized crime is disappearing. Rather, they are saying that its form is changing. Because of increasing assimilation into American life, the Italians are either losing control or exercising less direct control of organized crime. To maintain control over ghetto-based rackets is more difficult as blacks, Puerto Ricans, Cubans, and other groups exercise power in the ghettos. Moreover, these newer groups are much less centrally controlled. Their ties are through neighborhood and prison friendships, not through extended family. This means that gambling may again be moving toward localization and decentralization.[44] As Denny F. Pace and Jimmy C. Styles put it, there are ''thousands of smaller independently organized groups operating.''[45] In these localized groups we can see some ethnic succession, but it tends to be away from the Italians, with their unique form of crime families.

Developing laws to control or regulate organized crime has been anything but easy. As was noted at the outset of the chapter, the very term "organized crime" has at least three meanings. If it refers to predatory crimes, why make these a separate category of law when they are already criminal? If it means demand-oriented illegal enterprises, how can organized crime be controlled when members of the public are willing to flout the law so that they can engage in their "vices"? If it means penetration of legitimate business, how can one design or enforce laws when legitimate and illegitimate businesses are so intertwined?

Ambiguities and problems

One problem is that many organized criminal activities operate in the "gray area" of law and morality. The demand-oriented but illegal enterprises that make possible the social organization of gambling, loansharking, selling of narcotics, prostitution, etc., are the prime cases in point. Moreover, there are constitutional limits on the use of methods that would aid the investigation and prosecution of members of organized crime; for example, wiretapping, eavesdropping, self-incrimination, and invasions of personal privacy. In other words, the same laws that protect ordinary businesspeople and citizens also provide a useful cover under which members of organized crime can carry on their activities.

In addition, the issue of federal versus state responsibilities has also played into the hands of organized crime. The Constitution does not allow federal involvement in the affairs of states, and regulation of interstate commerce has come about only gradually and only in specific areas. For many years, the federal government simply lacked the authority to take action against organized crime. The presidentially appointed Wickersham Commission recognized the dimensions of organized crime as early as 1931 and called for an "immediate, comprehensive, and scientific nationwide inquiry into organized crime."[46] Yet most of the laws designed to control organized crime were passed 40 years later. Even today, many of these laws have not yet been put to conclusive court tests.[47]

Given these problems, it is easy to understand the cautious approach of federal legislation against organized crime. Before 1934, racketeering was handled by a subcommittee of the Committee on Commerce. However, this group failed to clarify the nature of racketeering; and there was much confusion over whether racketeering was a federal, state, or local crime. Taking a stronger approach, the 1934 Anti-Racketeering Act defined racketeering as (1) the interference with trade and commerce by violence or threats, (2) the obtaining of another's property with that person's consent but induced by wrongful use of force, and (3) the obstruction or delay of commerce. It allowed for a $10,000 fine, not more than 20 years' imprisonment, or both. The Hobbs Act of 1946 pushed federal legislation into the areas of labor extortion and obstruction of movement of persons across state lines for the purpose of marketing goods; it also underwent subsequent expansion, both substantive and jurisdictional. However, local considerations are often involved in prosecutions under the Hobbs Act; and some recent commentators have argued that the act has suffered from vagueness.[48]

Politics of organized crime

In the absence of legislation on organized crime, there did develop what might be called a "politics of organized crime," one that was both subtle and complex. On the one hand, there has been the continued involvement of organized crime figures in legitimate politics. Indeed, it has been repeatedly reported that some high-echelon crime figures are very "close" to prominent public officials.[49] (E.g., see Box 15.) One estimate is that the "underworld" contributes 15 percent of the costs of local and state political campaigns.[50] On the other hand, organized crime is a good political issue, one that has been effectively used by ambitious politicians. In the 1940s Thomas Dewey, then an assistant district attorney, launched his career (he eventually attained the governorship of New York State and subsequently a presidential candidacy) on the basis of prosecutions of organized crime figures, especially Lucky Luciano. On the national level, the politically ambitious Estes Kefauver, a United States senator, gained much exposure through his hearings on organized crime in the early 1950s. Kefauver took a "conspiracy" approach to organized crime that was to set the direction for public policy for more than a generation.[51]

Another aspect of the politics of organized crime was the denial of its existence by the Federal Bureau of Investigation (FBI). This denial lasted nearly 30 years and is generally attributed to bureaucratic considerations. Founded in 1930, the FBI needed some good cases to establish its reputation and a rationale for its existence. As William Howard Moore argues, solving spectacular bank robbery and kidnapping cases made more sense than attempting to track down racketeers:

> While J. Edgar Hoover, director of the Federal Bureau of Investigation, launched a dramatic, publicity-laden campaign against isolated midwestern bank robbers and kidnappers, federal officials contented themselves with leaving the more perplexing fight against organized crime and racketeering to state and local authorities.[52]

Box 15: An Organized Crime "Lifestyle"

Consider the former way of life of Frank Costello, a man who has repeatedly been called a leader of organized crime. He lived in an expensive apartment on the corner of 72d Street and Central Park West in New York. He was often seen dining in well-known restaurants in the company of judges, public officials, and prominent businessmen. Every morning he was shaved in the barbershop of the Waldorf Astoria Hotel. On many weekends he played golf at a country club on the fashionable North Shore of Long Island. In short, though his reputation was common knowledge, he moved around New York conspicuously and un-ashamedly, perhaps ostracized by some people but more often accepted, greeted by journalists, recognized by children, accorded all the freedoms of a prosperous and successful man. On a society that treats such a man in such a manner, organized crime has had an impact.

SOURCE

President's Commission on Law Enforcement and Administration of Justice, *The Challenge of Crime in a Free Society*, Government Printing Office, Washington, D.C., February 1967, p. 439.

Later, in the 1950s, the FBI turned its attention to "communist infiltration" in American society; curiously, it gave much less attention to the findings that were emerging from Kefauver's investigations. The fight against organized crime was left to a more specialized agency created in 1954, the Organized Crime and Racketeering Section of the Department of Justice.

Recent legislation

It was not until the 1960s that legislative changes made possible a significant effort to deal with organized crime. In 1961, legislative statutes established federal jurisdiction in gambling cases, thereby authorizing the FBI to strike at sources of revenue for the criminal syndicates. In 1968 the Omnibus Crime Control and Safe Streets Act established the Law Enforcement Assistance Administration (LEAA), which gave support to the organization, education, and training of special law enforcement units to combat organized crime. In 1970 the Organized Crime Control Act provided the most significant justification for federal efforts in the area. Its stated purpose was

> to seek the eradication of organized crime in the United States by strengthening the legal tools in the evidence-gathering process, by establishing new penal prohibitions, and by providing enhanced sanctions and new remedies to deal with unlawful activities of those engaged in organized crime.[53]

Title IX of the Organized Crime Control Act has been described as "the most sweeping criminal statute ever passed by Congress." Incorporating 24 types of federal crimes and 8 types of state felonies, it stated that a person who committed two of these offenses would be guilty of "racketeering activity." It also provided for fines up to $25,000 and for penalties more severe than those for the individual offenses.[54]

The stronger legislation aimed at organized crime has by no means been translated directly into prosecutions of organized crime figures. Despite the federal legislation against gambling, one study found that more than 60 percent of the convictions for organized crime recorded between 1961 and July 1965 were the result of federal tax violations.[55] Deportation has also played a continuing role in prosecutions. The stronger statutes aimed specifically at organized crime have not been applied extensively, nor have they resulted in many convictions. According to the Attorney General's annual report, between 1968 and 1971 there were 5243 indictments of organized crime figures, only 39 percent of which resulted in convictions.[56] One overview of the national effort against organized crime reported that the average number of federal agents involved ranged between 112 and 165 in the early 1970s, and that the number of convictions ranged from a low of 418 in 1970 to a high of 1616 in 1973 and down again to 1004 in 1975.[57]

One study of 2967 indictments of the Organized Crime Strike Force illustrates vividly some of the problems in fighting organized crime. Among the indictments for which a disposition had been made, only 56 percent resulted in convictions after trial or after pleas of guilty or no contest. Of those convicted, only 48 percent received prison sentences, the majority of which were for two years or less. Nor were the results much different for convictions of high-echelon figures. As the report concluded, "Light sentences could preclude . . . efforts [of strike forces] to disrupt organized crime to any extent."[58] Another aspect of law enforcement efforts, the potentially strong Title IX of the Organized Crime Control Act of 1970, also suffers from underenforcement. Starting from zero in 1970 and 1971, the number of "racketeer-influenced" and "corrupt organization" cases filed under the act rose to 14 by 1977, the increase coming about mainly from the publicizing efforts of the attorney in charge of the Department of Justice Strike Force.[59]

The difficulties in developing and applying laws against organized crime show once again the complexities of the problem. Functioning in part in gray areas of the law, organized crime has thrived. Demand-oriented illegal enterprises flourish. Extortion, highjacking, smuggling, and other crimes appear to be carried on with impunity. Profits from illegitimate sources are pumped into legitimate business to keep income flowing in. In its totality, organized crime remains a thriving enterprise. Although no one knows for sure how large it is, or whether it is on the ascendency or on the wane, the fact remains that it is a definite part of the American scene. Moreover, laws do not seem to make much difference. Although those passed since 1970 are far more stringent, their actual enforcement, while enhanced by the support of organized crime strike forces, leaves much to be desired.

It seems that the structure of organized crime is of more importance than the laws which are promulgated against it. And understanding this structure seems to require a position midway between Cressey's "conspiracy" view and Ianni's "family business" view. In its totality, organized crime may indeed be extensive; but much depends on what is meant by the term "organized." Indeed, most recently Anderson found a crime family she studied in detail to be not as complex as a large corporation but more defined and formal than a family business.[60] As we have seen, some recent researchers also advance the view that organized crime in today's society is a decentralized operation with many groups involved. In some instances, which have been documented, control has passed from Italian to black, Puerto Rican, and Cuban groups, which operate in a rather different manner. To the extent that control has shifted, ethnic succession—which had once moved from the Germans, Jews, and Irish to the Italians—is now moving away from the Italians. As this has happened, organized crime has become more decentralized. Ethnic succession is an important theme that we need to pursue further as we turn to an analysis of the typical organized criminal offender.

ORGANIZED CRIMINAL OFFENDERS

Organized criminal offenders are unique in that for them crime is a primary source of income, a career, and even a lifestyle. Since criminal activity is pursued as a career, organized crime involves both young adults and older people. Advancement is presumably based on merit or ability; but there is also a continual need for trust, which leads some to favor family members and others to favor neighborhood gangs or childhood acquaintances. Because of its emphasis on income, career, and lifestyle, organized crime is heavily male-oriented; as a result, few females have been identified as organized crime figures. The organized crime career path tends to be followed by people of lower-class social origins who, consciously or unconsciously, see it as a means of escape from poverty.

Ethnicity

Important though the factors of career orientation, sex (male), and social origin (lower-class) may be, the key to understanding the organized criminal offender is again ethnicity. The successful gangster of the 1920s carved out a role remarkably similar to that of the successful business and professional people of the day. This role has been very influential for subsequent generations of organized crime figures. Take, for example, the description of Frank Costello presented in Box 15. Such a lifestyle reflects the conspicuous consumption practiced by an earlier generation of American capitalists. Today, some Italian organized crime leaders follow a more subdued or suburban lifestyle, living privately and orienting themselves to family and friends—again much like many successful business executives.

Like their Italian counterparts, the newly emergent black and Puerto Rican crime figures are also creatures of their culture who have their own lifestyle and enjoy the respect of those in the community. Ianni describes three types in his book *Black Mafia*. The first is a pimp, "Reginald Martin" of central Harlem, who is also into conspicuous consumption. He displays his wealth, cultivates an image, and has everything done for him. "Thomas Irwin," a fence, by contrast, styles himself as a successful entrepreneur. Finally, "James Mitchell" can be seen as a successful drug hustler seeking to improve his social status by investing his yearly income of $200,000 in boutiques. There is a prevalent image of lower-class people who experience social mobility by moving up the ladder of organized crime; but "Martin" and "Irwin" were not brought up as "street persons"—they became involved in crime when comparable opportunities for career development were not readily available to them.[61]

It must be noted that the criminal lifestyle is by no means universally condemned in American society. Whether Italian, black, or Puerto Rican, successful gangsters, pimps, fences, and hustlers are very often admired, especially by those of their own community or ethnic group. After all, they have "made it"—at least in terms of money—in a society which can be very impersonal or outright discriminatory to people of certain backgrounds. As was noted earlier, famous criminals such as Al Capone, and even the predatory gangs of the western frontier, have received much sympathy, support, and social recognition from the larger community.

Distance between Offender and Act

One factor which serves to increase the social acceptability of the organized criminal is the remoteness of the offender from the criminal act. Indeed, one hallmark of continuing success in organized crime is the placement of the criminal further and further away from the crime.

As one writer has put it:

> . . . Crime today has geared itself to a new era. The major criminals are far removed from direct conflict with the law. Narcotics worth thousands of dollars can be smuggled in by a pathetic refugee who is many levels away from contact with the head of a criminal syndicate. Industry rarely complains of labor abuses whose impact is oblique and can be passed on to the consumer, with economic gains accruing to all, so that management and unions often join in defending those who prey on them. The outright bribe is considered gauche. Matters are "fixed" through associations, connections, and political contributions.[62]

This "remoteness" or "untouchability" is practiced by successful criminals regardless of ethnic background. For offenders, it achieves a double purpose: (1) it enables them to use their money to gain social support without incurring the stigma of how it was earned; and (2) it insulates them from the risk of prosecution for criminal activity.

Socialization

In discussing organized criminal offenders, a word must be given to socialization—the process by which people become involved in organized crime. Here too the key variable is ethnicity. For the Italian Mafia family, the process is basically an informal one which, as described by Frederick Sondern, operates as follows:

> A mafioso selects one or more of his sons, perhaps a favorite nephew, trains and guides him in the traditional philosophy and methods, introduces him to the right people and another mafioso is gradually created.[63]

However, for blacks, Puerto Ricans, and other groups involved in organized crime, the routes into involvement are completely different. Ianni sees three: childhood friends, neighborhood gangs, and prison acquaintances. In each route, there is the necessity of knowing and being "recognized" by someone already involved in organized crime and a process of working one's way through the ranks or up the ladder.[64] In a well-ordered operation there is little room for an addict or petty crook who cannot submit to discipline.

Ethnic Succession

Finally, an examination of the characteristics of offenders shows once again the process of ethnic succession in organized crime. As was mentioned earlier, the Italian domination may be changing somewhat. With each generation of Italians, fewer members are recruited into the "family business." The median age of those remaining is on the increase. In moving further and further away from crime, successful mobsters may have relinquished some control of their rackets to newer ethnic groups, in particular to blacks and Puerto Ricans. As has been indicated, these newer groups have different forms of crime organization, although it can be argued that they too are using organized crime as a "queer ladder of social mobility."[65] If so, it is predictable that they will also be victims of their own success. On the one hand, they will achieve money and status through crime. On the other hand, they will insulate themselves from it, and their insulation will mean an eventual loss of control. Newer groups will then be ready to take over. In short, though the form may change, the process of ethnic succession reflects vividly the sense in which crime is "a Coney Island mirror, caricaturing the morals and manners of a society."[66]

VICTIMS OF ORGANIZED CRIME

Having discussed the offender involved in organized criminal activity, we now need to consider an elusive question: Who are the victims of organized crime?

In examining ethnic succession and exploring the rapidly changing forms of organized crime, it is easy to lose sight of the victim. In fact, victims of organized crime have generally suffered from lack of visibility. Fearing reprisals, many victims probably do not report crimes to law enforcement authorities. Social scientists do not include organized crime in their victimization surveys. Aside from journalistic accounts of organized criminal activity—often confined to sensational mob murders—little is said publicly about those who are the victims of organized crime.

Although not always visible, victimization from organized crime is quite extensive. It can take several forms, some direct and others indirect. One type of direct victimization involves literally all of us at one time or another; most often this has to do with businesses that have been penetrated by the mob. Because of such penetration, we eat adulterated meat and cheese. Because of the mob's hiring practices, illegal aliens work at substandard wages so that profits can be increased. Because of its threats, store owners pay for protection. Because of its influence in the trucking industry, the price of nearly everything "includes a heavy Mafia tax." Because of cigarette smuggling, millions of tax dollars are lost. Because of hijacking, inventory losses are incurred. In short, to the extent that all Mafia businesses are fixed, we pay for organized crime in one way or another.[67]

The problem is that the victims of fixed Mafia businesses, like the victims of corporate crime, are scattered over diverse areas and among diverse groups of people and may not even be aware of their victimization. It may well be that organized crime is in part responsible for the inflation of prices and deterioration of quality that many think have marked American products in recent years. The problem is how to judge the extent of victimization. Without data, estimates can only be speculative.

Another form of direct victimization involves willing participants in demand-oriented illegal enterprises. This form involves considerations similar to those we encounter with social-order crimes (discussed in Chapter 13). Although willing, the gambler who places a bet, the customer who visits a prostitute, and the person who goes to a mob-connected loan shark are victims of organized crime. Indeed, in many instances their victimization may also involve threats or actual use of violence. Direct victimization involving willing participants may also be seen in mob-related murders. Bugsy Siegel may have claimed, "We only kill each other," but the fact is that murder is the ultimate form of victimization, regardless of how it occurs.[68]

Aside from direct victimization, there is also indirect victimization. The indirect victim is the institutional structure of American society. This may sound

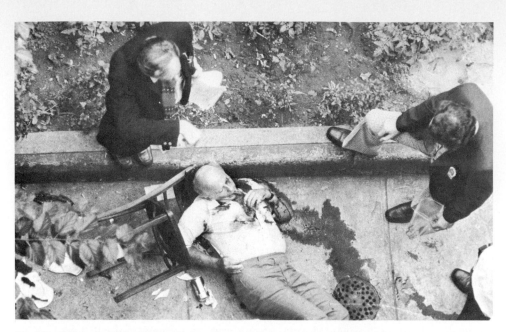

The bloodied body of the Mafia chieftan Carmine Galante, gunned down in the
backyard garden of a Brooklyn, New York, restaurant on July 12, 1979.
(WIDE WORLD PHOTOS)

abstract; but it was given recognition in the Organized Crime Control Act of 1970,
which begins as follows:

> Organized crime in the United States is a highly sophisticated, diversified, and
> widespread activity that annually drains billions of dollars from America's economy
> by unlawful conduct and illegal use of force, fraud, and corruption; organized crime
> derives a major portion of its power through money obtained from such illegal
> endeavors as syndicated gambling, loan sharking, . . . and other forms of social
> exploitation; this money and power are increasingly used to infiltrate and corrupt our
> democratic processes; organized crime activities in the United States weaken the
> stability of the Nation's economic system, harm innocent investors and competing
> organizations, interfere with free competition, seriously burden interstate and foreign
> commerce, threaten the domestic security and undermine the general welfare of the
> nation and its citizens.

The crux of indirect victimization is the rather intangible corruption of the
democratic process and the weakening of the stability of our economic system. If
organized crime has made everyone corrupt, or if it enables us to casually tolerate
corruption, or if it has become developed to such an extent that there is little or no
distinction between legitimate and illegitimate business, then it can truly be said
that indirect victimization has been substantial.

SOCIAL CONTEXT: ORGANIZED CRIME AND AMERICAN SOCIETY

In addition to criminal acts, offenders, and victims, we must also take a close look
at the social context of organized crime. In examining its social context, we

become aware of the great extent to which organized crime, harmful though it may be, is part and parcel of American society.

As the "Coney Island mirror caricaturing the morals and manners" of American society, organized crime is an integral part of its own social context. Its continuing existence means that part of American society is organized explicitly for crime. Indeed, crime and business may now be so intertwined that it is all but impossible to separate the two. We must bear in mind that organized crime is in a sense useful or, in the terminology of the sociologist, "functional." For one thing, it provides us with goods and services which we may say we don't want but really do want. For another, it provides a path of upward mobility to some members of ethnic or racial groups who are otherwise excluded from full participation in American life.

One problem of organized crime in American society is that it is supported and facilitated by many of the same cultural values that underlie legitimate pursuits. It also provides structure to a society that in some respects is very weak and decentralized. In other words, certain American cultural values and certain aspects of its political system are most conducive to organized crime. Let's take a look at some ways in which American society supports the continued existence of organized crime; we'll begin with cultural values and go on to the political system.

Cultural Values

Cultural values—which have to do with things that are socially desirable—cover a wide range of preferences. There are four sets of American values that contribute, generally in unintended ways, to the continuance of organized crime.

Probably the most important of these values is the attempt to enforce public morals. As Daniel Bell has noted, Americans have an extraordinary talent for compromise in politics and extremism in morality:

> . . . In no other country have there been such spectacular attempts to curb human appetites and brand them as illicit, and nowhere else such glaring failures. From the start America was at one and the same time a frontier community where "everything goes," and the fair country of the Blue Laws. . . . Crime as a growing business was fed by the revenues from prostitution, liquor, and gambling that a wide-open urban society encouraged and that a middle-class Protestant ethos tried to suppress with a ferocity unmatched in any other civilized country.[69]

In short, as has already been noted, organized crime is a creation of American values. A widespread public demand for illegal goods and services makes it both possible and profitable. To put it another way, were this demand to disappear suddenly, or were the goods and services to be legalized, organized crime as we now know it would be sharply curtailed or would assume a substantially different form.

The second set of values supporting organized crime are those that stem from our democratic heritage. Here too—as noted earlier—values related to invasion of privacy, self-incrimination, and arbitrary powers of government have all found their way into American law. Important though these laws may be for the preservation of individual liberty, they make it difficult for authorities to arrest and sustain prosecutions against organized criminals.

The situation is similar for business values, our third set. Impersonality in particular enables business and banking interests to carry on large commercial transactions without identifying the parties at each stage of the transaction. The boon to organized crime is tremendous. Indeed, it was not until recently that banks began requiring identification of parties when they accepted deposits in excess of $10,000 cash. Internationally, Swiss bank accounts have been utilized most effectively by organized crime figures. Money gets to Swiss banks in three ways: (1) American banks transfer it, preserving secrecy as they do so; (2) Swiss banks, sworn to secrecy as part of their normal operating procedure, have American branches; and (3) couriers take large sums of money out of the country. (The legal limit on cash that can be taken out of the country is $5000; but the disclosure of how much cash is carried is not checked, statements about it are voluntary, and misstatements carry no criminal penalty.)[70] Impersonality, useful for all business and investment in a large, complex commercial society, is of enormous importance to organized crime, which is faced with a constant need to dispose of or utilize the cash flow generated from its gambling operations.

Fourth and finally, there are the all-important values connected with success—which have often been referred to in this text. Organized criminals want some of the same things that are culturally approved and desired by many other Americans: money, status, and power. The rackets are, to use Bell's term, a "queer ladder of mobility,"[71] although one that is highly competitive. In "rationalizing" the rackets to make them a source of continuing profit, organized crime was doing in the 1930s what American business had done in the 1890s. At the same time, its major entrepreneurs adopted increasingly respectable life-styles—just as the crude, self-made capitalists had been transformed into respectable citizens.

In moving up the "queer ladder of mobility," organized crime figures can in a sense be seen as comparable to the early American capitalists. As was noted in Chapter 2, many American fortunes are based on sharp business practices or on outright crimes. Bell's comments capture the essence of the issue:

> The jungle quality of the American business community, particularly at the turn of the century, was reflected in the mode of "business" practiced by the coarse gangster elements, most of them from new immigrant families, who were "getting ahead," just as Horatio Alger had urged.[72]

From a sociological point of view, the legacy of the early capitalists is the enormous amount of crime in which corporations are involved. The legacy of the early gangsters is an efficiently run system of rackets, the profits of which are often invested in other business enterprises. Today, corporate and organized crimes are very subtle, hidden as it were under a cloak of respectability. For the corporate criminal there is the luxury of a noncriminal self-image. For the organized criminal there is a continual attempt to increase the social distance between the actor and the criminal act.

Political System

The decentralized American political system, with its ever-changing power blocs, has also proved an unwitting but effective aid to organized crime. In a sense, the social significance of organized crime is that it provides a shadow government or an "informal parallel system of internal policing" in a society where government is weak.[73] Historically, it fulfilled this social function in Italy and later in the American slums.

Organized crime as a shadow government

To function as a shadow government, organized crime needs the complicity of those in the legitimate power structure. This complicity is secured through "corruption," a phenomenon which will be discussed more fully in Chapter 15. Operating in a variety of ways, corruption in American society is facilitated by a decentralized government in which lines of responsibility are often unclearly drawn. The erratic attempts to develop and enforce laws against organized crime, as well as the intricate, subtle relationships between organized crime and politics, have already been noted. The decline of urban political machines dominated by corrupt bosses has meant a shifting configuration for organized crime. On the one hand, it is now more decentralized than it was previously; on the other hand, it allegedly operates as a shadow government at the federal level.[74]

If organized crime represents a part of American society that is organized for criminality and operates as a shadow government, even at the federal level, then we are dealing with a phenomenon that is far more subtle than the misdeeds of selected gangsters, many of whom are becoming respectable anyway. In this sense, the full dimensions of organized crime are evident in what Charles E. Silberman refers to as a deep-rooted cynicism of many Americans about their government, their businesses, and their society. As he puts it:

> Organized crime's biggest impact is indirect. . . . The fact that the rest of society looks down on organized-crime figures as criminals serves to solidify the community's sense of ethnic solidarity and intensify its sense of being victimized by a hypocritical, as well as corrupt society. Why pick on a numbers runner, bootlegger, or fence, the reasoning goes, when the *real* criminals—bribe-taking police, corrupt government officials, slumlords who fail to maintain their buildings, merchants who "rip off" the poor, congressmen who keep their mistresses on the Congressional payroll, corporate executives who offer bribes, a vice president of the United States who takes bribes, and a president who cheats on his income tax—all seem to go scot free?[75]

In such a cynical, hypocritical, or corrupt society, organized crime clearly holds the upper hand. If it is impossible to tell the difference between legitimate and criminal routes to success, between business and criminal enterprise, between wealth honestly earned and bribes received corruptly, then we must acknowledge organization for crime as an integral part of American society. Its continuing existence is part of an underlying social malaise.

Dealing with organized crime

One implication of this view of organized crime is that a solution to it does not lie along the lines of prosecuting particular organized criminals. As we have already seen, despite the increased "teeth" in the law, convictions are few in relation to the total volume of criminal activity. Instead, the "solution" requires us to deal with the social conditions that make organized crime possible. At least three different approaches have been suggested: (1) decriminalize the illicit goods and services offered by organized crime, thereby taking the profit out of it;[76] (2) regulate or restructure its markets or business conditions (e.g., use other regulatory agencies to deal with organized criminal offenses such as restraint of trade, tax evasion, illegal labor practices, and marketing of dangerous drugs)[77]; (3) work out a peace treaty with organized crime that might involve appeasement and accommodation but would enable the government to become aware of it and set limits to its activities.[78] The third approach and (to a lesser extent) the second approach involve tacitly recognizing organized crime, something that the government has been reluctant to do. However, many state governments are proposing to follow the first approach to the extent of decriminalizing some of the gambling activities which have traditionally proven lucrative to organized crime.

SUMMARY

The subject of considerable comment and discussion, organized crime has proven difficult to understand. Some investigators, such as Cressey, would compare it to national corporations; others, such as Ianni, would see it as an extended network of family, ethnic, and political relationships. Organized criminal activity may embrace a variety of criminal acts, including predatory crimes, demand-oriented illegal acts, and penetration of legitimate businesses. It can be defined in Schelling's terms as a monopoly which uses criminal means, including extortion by threat or use of violence, to establish and maintain itself.

Although criminal gangs have long been part of the American scene, the late 1920s and the 1930s saw intense rivalry, open warfare, and eventually consolidation into organized crime "families." Cressey has argued that these families are local groups controlled by the Mafia, a secret criminal society with roots in Sicily; whereas Ianni sees organized crime as essentially localized networks of individuals involved in racketeering activities. In any event, the present-day scope of organized crime is difficult to assess. While some would stress its expanding involvement in gambling and other demand-oriented illegal enterprises, its penetration into labor unions and legitimate business, and its having become a power in its own right, others have claimed that organized crime businesses are relatively unsophisticated and that the power of the Italian crime families is presently on the wane.

Laws designed to control organized crime have been fraught with difficulties. Some forms of organized crime fall into the category of social-order crimes, in which victims are willing participants. Some methods of dealing with organized crime conflict with constitutional guarantees of individual rights; and some involve conflicts between federal and state power. Given these ambiguities—and politics which have at times emphasized organized crime and at others denied its existence—significant legislation has been late in coming. The 1960s saw several key statutes, and the Organized Crime Control Act of 1970 provides the greatest justification for federal efforts. Yet only about half of the arrests made under this act have resulted in prison sentences, and many of those prison sentences have been relatively short.

The organized criminal is typically a mature male of lower-class social origins who uses organized crime as a career path which provides an escape from poverty. Recent years have seen (1) some distancing between organized criminals and the acts they perpetrate; (2) recruitment through childhood friendships, neighborhood groups, and prison acquaintanceships rather than family connections; and (3) some changes in the pattern of Italian domination.

Victimization by organized crime may be direct, in that literally everyone pays for the Mafia businesses that are fixed and in that some people who are willing participants also suffer. It may also be indirect, in that the institutional structure of American society is undermined.

In a larger sense, organized crime is appropriately seen as a creation of American society. It is inadvertently supported through the attempt to enforce public morals; through values that support individual liberty; through the impersonality that proves so useful to business; and through the idea of success, which places a premium on upward mobility regardless of how it is achieved. Moreover, the decentralized political system of the United States allows for corruption and permits a shadow government to operate. Given the deep entrenchment of organized crime in American society, a solution requires dealing with the social conditions which make it possible rather than simply attempting to prosecute particular organized crime figures.

NOTES

[1] Vincent Teresa with Thomas C. Renner, *Vinnie Teresa's Mafia*, Doubleday, Garden City, N. Y., 1975.

[2] For the former approach, see: Donald R. Cressey, *Theft of a Nation: The Structure and Operations of Organized Crime in America*, Harper and Row, New York, 1969. For the latter, see: Francis A. J. Ianni with Elizabeth Ruess-Ianni, *A Family Business: Kinship and Social Control in Organized Crime*, Russell Sage Foundation, New York, 1972.

[3] Cressey, *Theft of a Nation*, p. 319.

[4] Francis A. J. Ianni, *Black Mafia: Ethnic Succession in Organized Crime*, Simon and Schuster, New York, 1974, p. 15.

[5] On the types of organized crime, see: Ivan Light, "The Ethnic Vice Industry, 1880–1944," *American Sociological Review*, vol. 42, 1977, p. 464.

[6] For a justification of the former term, see: Joseph L. Albini, *The American Mafia: Genesis of a Legend*, Appleton-Century Crofts, New York, 1971, chap. 2. On the latter, see: Alan A. Block, "History and Study of Organized Crime," *Urban Life*, vol. 6, no. 4, January 1978, pp. 455–474.

[7] Thomas C. Schelling, "Economic Analysis and Organized Crime," In *Task Force Report on Organized Crime*, President's Commission on Law Enforcement and Administration of Justice, Government Printing Office, Washington, D. C., 1967.

[8] Michael D. Maltz, "On Defining 'Organized' Crime: The Development of a Definition and a Typology," *Crime and Delinquency*, vol. 22, no. 3, July 1976, pp. 338–346.

[9] See: James A. Inciardi, *Reflections on Crime: An Introduction to Criminology and Criminal Justice*, Holt, Rinehart and Winston, New York, 1978, pp. 32–41. See

also: Albini, *The American Mafia*, chap. 5; and Light, "The Ethnic Vice Industry, 1880–1944."

[10] Inciardi, *Reflections on Crime*, pp. 42–49.

[11] The issue as put by: Francis J. Ianni and Elizabeth Reuss-Ianni, *The Crime Society: Organized Crime and Corruption in America*, New American Library, New York, 1976, p. xiii.

[12] Frederick Sondern, Jr., *Brotherhood of Evil: The Mafia*, Farrar, Straus and Cudahy, New York, 1959, chap. 4.

[13] See: Albini, *The American Mafia*, chap. 5: and Dwight C. Smith, Jr., *The Mafia Mystique*, Basic Books, New York, 1975, part I.

[14] Sondern, *Brotherhood of Evil*, chap. 4.

[15] David Leon Chandler, *Brothers in Blood: The Rise of The Criminal Brotherhoods*, Dutton, New York, 1975, book 1.

[16] Burton B. Turkus and Sid Feder, *Murder, Inc.: The Story of "the Syndicate,"* Farrar, Straus and Young, New York, 1951. See also: Ianni and Reuss-Ianni, *A Family Business*, pp. 24f.

[17] Ianni and Reuss-Ianni, *A Family Business*.

[18] Chandler, *Brothers in Blood*, book 2.

[19] Daniel Bell, "Crime as an American Way of Life: A Queer Ladder of Social Mobility," in *The End of Ideology: On the Exhaustion of Political Ideas in the Fifties*, Collier, New York, 1961, pp. 127–150. See also: Chapter 11 of the present text.

[20] Smith, *The Mafia Mystique*.

[21] Cressey, *Theft of a Nation*, p. 35.

[22] Ibid., chap. 2.

[23] Ibid., chap. 6.

[24] See: *Task Force Report on Organized Crime*, pp. 1–10.

[25] Turkus and Feder, *Murder, Inc.*; quotation from p. xi.

26 Ianni and Reuss-Ianni, *A Family Business*, p. 108.
27 Albini, *The American Mafia*; and Smith, *The Mafia Mystique*.
28 Alan A. Block, "The Snowman Cometh: Coke in Progressive New York," *Criminology*, vol. 17, no. 1, May 1979, pp. 75–99; and Peter Reuter and Jonathan B. Rubinstein, "Fact, Fancy, and Organized Crime," *Public Interest*, vol. 53, Fall 1978, pp. 45–67.
29 Block, "History and the Study of Organized Crime."
30 President's Commission on Law Enforcement and Administration of Justice, *The Challenge of Crime in a Free Society*, Government Printing Office, Washington, D.C., February 1967, p. 441.
31 E.g., see: August Bequai, *Organized Crime: The Fifth Estate*, Heath, Lexington, Mass., 1979.
32 E.g., see: Jonathan Kwitny, *Vicious Circles: The Mafia in the Marketplace*, Norton, New York, 1979.
33 Bequai, *Organized Crime*, p. 231.
34 Cressey, *Theft of a Nation*, p. xi.
35 Michael Gartner, ed., *Crime and Business: What You Should Know about the Infiltration of Crime into Business–and of Business into Crime*, Dow Jones Books, Princeton, N. J., 1971.
36 U.S. Department of Justice, National Institute of Law Enforcement and Criminal Justice, "The Penetration of Legitimate Business by Organized Crime—An Analysis," monograph prepared by Melvin K. Bess, April 1970.
37 E.g.: Thomas Plate, *Crime Pays*, Simon and Schuster, New York, 1975.
38 U.S. Department of Justice, "The Penetration of Legitimate Business by Organized Crime," p. 13.
39 Harold D. Lasswell and Jeremiah B. McKenna, "The Impact of Organized Crime on an Inner City Community," monograph, Policy Sciences Center, New York, September 1972.
40 President's Commission on Law Enforcement and Administration of Justice, *The Challenge of Crime in a Free Society*, p. 446.
41 Ianni, *Black Mafia*.
42 Annelise Graebner Anderson, *The Business of Organized Crime: A Cosa Nostra Family*, Hoover Institute Press, Stanford, Calif., 1979.
43 James A. Inciardi, *Careers in Crime*, Rand McNally, Chicago; Ill., 1975, epilogue.
44 Reuter and Rubinstein, "Fact, Fancy, and Organized Crime."
45 Denny F. Pace and Jimmy C. Styles, *Organized Crime: Concepts and Control*, Prentice-Hall, Englewood Cliffs, N.J., 1975, p. 13.
46 National Advisory Committee on Criminal Justice Standards and Goals, *Organized Crime: Report of the Task Force on Organized Crime*, Law Enforcement Assistance Administration (LEAA), Washington, D.C., 1976, p. 15.
47 Ibid., p. 17.
48 "Prosecution under the Hobbes Act and the Expansion of Federal Criminal Jurisdiction," *Journal of Criminal Law and Criminology*, vol. 66, no. 3, 1975, pp. 306–324.
49 Ralph Salerno and John S. Tompkins, *The Crime Confederation*, Doubleday, Garden City, N. Y., 1969, especially pp. 243–256.
50 Cressey, *Theft of a Nation*, p. 253.
51 William Howard Moore, *The Kefauver Committee and the Politics of Crime, 1950–1952*, University of Missouri Press, Columbia, 1974.
52 Ibid., p. 16.
53 National Advisory Committee on Criminal Justice Standards and Goals, "Organized Crime," pp. 17–18.
54 Jeff Atkinson, "'Racketeer Influenced and Corrupt Organizations,' 18 U.S.C.: 1961–1968: Broadest of the Federal Criminal Statutes," *Journal of Criminal Law and Criminology*, vol. 69, no. 1, 1978, pp. 1–18.
55 National Advisory Committee on Criminal Justice Standards and Goals, "Organized Crime," p. 18.
56 Quoted by Pace and Styles, *Organized Crime*, p. 12.
57 *Report of the National Conference on Organized Crime, October 1–4, 1975*, U.S. Department of Justice, Law Enforcement Association Administration (LEAA), Washington, D. C., 1975.
58 Department of Justice, *War on Organized Crime Faltering—Federal Strike Forces Not Getting the Job Done*, microfiche, National Council on Crime and Delinquency, May 1977.
59 Atkinson, "'Racketeer Influenced and Corrupt Organizations.'"
60 Anderson, *The Business of Organized Crime*.
61 Ianni, *Black Mafia*, chap. 1.
62 Gerard L. Goettel, "Why the Crime Syndicate Can't Be Touched," *Harper's Magazine*, November 1960.
63 Sondern, *Brotherhood of Evil*, chap. 1.
64 Ianni, *Black Mafia*, chap. 6.
65 Bell, "Crime as an American Way of Life."
66 Ibid., p. 128.
67 Kwitney, *Vicious Circles*.
68 Dean S. Jennings, *We Only Kill Each Other: The Life and Bad Times of Bugsy Siegel*, Prentice-Hall, Englewood Cliffs, N. J., 1967.
69 Bell, "Crime as an American Way of Life," p. 128.
70 Matthew William Raffa, "The Utilization of the Numbered Swiss Account by Organized Crime," M.A. thesis, John Jay College of Criminal Justice (CUNY), September 1974.
71 Bell, "Crime as an American Way of Life."
72 Ibid., p. 128.
73 Ianni and Reuss-Ianni, *A Family Business*.
74 Bequai, *Organized Crime*; and Frank Pearce, *Crimes of the Powerful: Marxism, Crime, and Deviance*, Pluto, London, 1976.
75 Charles E. Silberman, *Criminal Violence, Criminal Justice*, Random House, New York, 1978, p. 108.
76 E.g., see: Edwin M. Schur and Hugo Adam Bedau, *Victimless Crimes: Two Sides of a Controversy*, Prentice-Hall, Englewood Cliffs, N. J., 1974, p. 22.
77 Schelling, "Economic Analysis and Organized Crime."
78 Cressey, *Theft of a Nation*, p. 319.

15

Political Crime

Understanding political crime—the last of our major types of crime—demands that we consider how crime is related to power in society. This consideration throws us into a serious criminological debate. On the one hand, virtually all the crimes discussed in Chapters 9 through 14 are political in that they challenge the existing power structure. On the other hand, only a small number are specifically defined as political crimes in penal codes.

To say that all crimes are political is to recognize that any crime is a threat to the established interests and rights of those who make, interpret, or enforce the law. In this sense, political crime is "nondestructible, . . . perhaps the oldest of all crime types."[1] In a democratic society the political nature of crime is seen in the facts that legislatures (elected by the people) define acts as criminal, courts (in which judges are elected or appointed by political authorities) decide whether criminal acts were committed, and police (whose law enforcement policies are controlled by politically appointed commissioners) carry out the punitive mandates of the courts. Conflict-oriented criminologists have pushed the idea that all crimes are political one step further, to argue that crime and criminality are inevitably defined so as to enable established groups to maintain their social advantages.[2] The discussions of corporate crime (Chapter 11) and social-order crime (Chapter 13) also revealed that political struggles among competing interest groups can be most critical in the definition and interpretation of criminal acts.

However, it is misleading to claim that all crimes are political. Many crimes are committed out of greed, vengeance, or some other motive that is not expressly political. There is a commonsense distinction between political assassination and other murder, between political kidnapping and kidnapping for ransom, between abuse of government office and taking a payoff on a business contract, and between corruption and embezzlement. To put it another way, some crimes but by no means all are political. We can define political crime in the following manner:

> Any violation of law which is *motivated* by political aims—by the intent, that is, of bringing about (or preventing) a change in the political system, in the distribution of political power, or in the structure of the political-governmental bodies.[3]

In political crime the symbolic meaning of the criminal act is more important than the act itself. Former president Richard Nixon's characterization of the Watergate break-in as a "third-rate burglary" was true except for a most important fact: that it was committed on behalf of the Committee to Reelect the President. When Father Philip Berrigan poured bull's blood on draft records, it was a minor inconvenience for those who had to clean up the mess but a major statement against the draft. As we shall see, political offenders are often imprisoned for comparatively minor offenses. It is the symbolic nature of their actions that constitutes a threat to society.

Since meaning is more important than act in the definition of political crime, assessing its scope and social importance can be most difficult and at times arbitrary. In his classical work on political crime, published originally in 1898, Louis Proal wrote the following:

> Ordinary evil-doers who are judged by the courts are only guilty of killing or robbing some few individuals; the number of their victims is restricted. Political malefactors,

on the contrary, count their victims by the thousand; they corrupt and ruin entire nations.[4]

In contrast to Proal, some criminologists, following Émile Durkheim, have asserted that political crime is useful, even necessary, for society because it leads to social change. For this reason, enforcement has often been left vague unless it is seen as necessary "to secure the polity against radical changes." Considerations of legality are secondary, and issues of individual innocence or guilt are of less importance than the possibility of deterring threats to the social order.[5] Taking still another approach, Eric Hobsbaum has noted that social banditry, seen in the gangs of the western frontier, has often arisen in periods of widespread social change and is actually a form of "prepolitical" consciousness.[6] Today, some stealing and shoplifting by politically conscious young people intent on "ripping off" the system might also be seen as the "revolutionary reappropriation of goods and services."[7]

To appreciate political crime, we need to examine its forms and focus in the United States, political offenders, victims of political crimes, and the context of power in which political crimes occur.

POLITICAL OFFENSES IN THE UNITED STATES

In the United States political crime has had a unique, almost curious history. American law—and for that matter English law—contains nothing resembling the continental European doctrine of political offenses.[8] When it came to their own government, the American colonists were most eager to avoid the arbitrary exercise of governmental power. Particularly suspect were institutions such as the Star Chamber, an English court which stood outside the common law and tried offenses that were a threat to the crown, i.e., the political crimes of the day. The Bill of Rights, the first 10 amendments to the Constitution of the United States (1) guaranteed Americans certain rights of dissent against their government: free speech, free press, free assembly, and petition for redress of grievances (First Amendment); and (2) restricted the arbitrary power of government by guaranteeing rights against unreasonable search (Fourth Amendment), for presentment or indictment of a grand jury (Fifth Amendment), to a speedy trial held in public with direct confrontation of charges, witnesses, and evidence (Sixth Amendment), to trial by jury (Seventh Amendment), and, finally, against excessive bail, fines, and cruel and unusual punishment (Eighth Amendment). In allowing citizens to dissent and in restricting the power of government, the Constitution points to a curtailed role both for political crime and for the politicalization of crime in American society.

Treason

Somewhat of an exception to the depoliticalization of crime implied in the Bill of Rights is treason, perhaps the most serious political crime. In fact, treason is the only crime specifically defined in the Constitution (Article III, Section 3). Yet treason is narrowly defined as levying war against the United States or giving aid and comfort to its enemies. Furthermore, two witnesses are needed to prove treason unless there is a confession in an open court. The history of enforcement

The first Americans executed for treason, Julius and Ethel Rosenberg are seen going to jail after their conviction in March 1951. (WIDE WORLD PHOTOS)

of Article III is quite interesting. Treason has been found in every great crisis in American history—Benedict Arnold, Aaron Burr, the Copperhead movement, the "fifth column," and Alger Hiss all played a part in the history of treason. Yet until the Rosenbergs in the mid-1950s, no American was ever executed for treason. Only a handful have died as traitors. Until World War II, every convicted traitor, including those who deserted the army during time of war, received a presidential pardon.[9]

However, to claim that crime is depoliticized in the United States and that treason has been narrowly defined and casually enforced is not to argue that political crime is nonexistent. Quite the opposite is true. There are political crimes. There have been many political trials. There are political prisoners in American jails and prisons today. In order to examine political crime further, let us take a look at two more general types: (1) dissent and (2) abuse of office.

Dissent

Despite the First Amendment guarantees to rights of dissent, the amount of dissent to be tolerated has never been made completely clear. In his review of the history of dissent in America, Charles E. Goodell found that there is an "uncomfortable blurring of the line between dissent and crime" and that lawbreaking has accompanied virtually every political change and reform.[10] In contrast to the constitutional guarantees of individual rights, the history of political crime in the United States shows that, for example, criminal laws were used to repress Tory sentiments in the colonial era; Quakers were accused of treason because they were opposed to the draft; First Amendment guarantees were suspended in the Alien and Sedition Acts, which were used against members of Congress; habeas corpus was suspended during the Civil War; there was judicial harassment of the women's rights advocate Susan B. Anthony; there was a politicized capital trial of two immigrant radicals, Sacco and Vanzetti; and there was systematic prosecution of workers involved in organizing unions.[11]

Let us now examine three significant aspects of dissent as a political crime: (1) relevant statutes, (2) "show trials," and (3) the era of the 1960s.

Statutes

The history of political dissent as it overlaps into crime also shows that the legal system of the United States contains many statutes designed to curb dissent of one form or another. Despite the First Amendment, more than 300 state statutes have been directed against subversive acts or speech. Federal legislation has seen the Espionage Act (1917), the Sedition Act (1918), the Smith Act (1940), the National Security Act (1947), the Immigration and Nationality Act (1952), and the Communist Control Act (1954).[12] The 1960s saw the passage and strengthening of conspiracy laws, which now require the government only to show that the defendants have communicated in some way, not that they necessarily committed overt criminal acts; and antiriot laws, which make it a felony to travel in interstate commerce with the intent to riot or participate in a riot.

Show trials

Very often, political dissent interpreted as crime has been dealt with by widely publicized "show trials" designed to serve as an example or warning to others not to engage in such behavior. In these trials the government can take unusually repressive measures:

> Chroniclers of such cases are appalled at the intimidation and harassment of defense lawyers, the high bail set—tantamount to preventive detention—the presumption of guilt, and the meretricious cooperation between prosecutors and judges, involving behavior that violates the basic canons of judicial ethics.[13]

Repressive measures such as these, as well as an increased level of dissent during the late 1960s, led to new strategies on the part of defendants. They were not docile or respectful of the court's authority. They tried to restructure the situation so that the judge, the prosecutors, and some of the witnesses should be the ones on trial. Spectators participated vocally and at times physically in the trial. Dissidents planned to use such trials to educate a wider public to dissent and frustrate the proselytizing efforts of the state.[14]

The effectiveness of the government's use of "show trials" is open to question. Legally, show trials have resulted in few clear-cut convictions; and many convictions have been reversed on appeal. (See Box 16.) On the other hand, conspiracy and antiriot laws have been used for political harassment: those who

Box 16: Three Cases of Political Crime

The Boston Five[a]

In 1968 Dr. Benjamin Spock, noted pediatrician and author of the renowned work *Baby and Child Care*—a work so widely read and acted upon that a whole generation of children were reared by it—was indicted along with four others for hindering administration of the draft. The federal government charged that Spock and the others (one of whom was William Sloane Coffin, Jr., chaplain of Yale University) had counseled, aided, and abetted others to violate the Selective Service Act and otherwise obstruct the draft. Supposedly all had "conspired" together, but in fact the five hardly knew one another. They were united only in their opposition to the Vietman War and to the draft. Spock and three others of the accused were convicted, fined, and sentenced to two years in prison. Their convictions were subsequently reversed, but the government had achieved its objective in suppressing dissent by subjecting them to a long, expensive trial and a good deal of psychic pain and emotional stress.

The Harrisburg Seven[b]

In 1972 Father Philip Berrigan and six others (the so-called Harrisburg Seven) were indicted and tried on charges of conspiring to kidnap the secretary of state, bomb the heating systems of public buildings in Washington, D.C., and vandalize draft offices. The government's case rested largely on a paid F.B.I. informer, who was the only person in the "conspiracy" (which became known as the "East Coast Conspiracy") who possessed any of the skills necessary to achieve its goals. After a three-month trial, the jury could not agree but found Father Berrigan and a nun, sister Elizabeth McAlister, guilty of participating in the smuggling of mail in and out of Lewisburg Penitentiary, where Father Berrigan had been confined. Ironically, it was the F.B.I. informer, Boyd F. Douglas, Jr., who had actually carried the letters in and out of the prison. However, after spending $1.5 million in prosecuting the Harrisburg Seven case, the government reluctantly dropped the charges rather than have a retrial. A further irony was that the case was initiated by J. Edgar Hoover, F.B.I. director. In one of his flamboyant appearances before a Senate appropriations subcommittee, Hoover—attempting to boost his organization's need for increased funding—referred to a "plot" to kidnap the secretary of state, who was to be held hostage until the bombing of Southeast Asia was halted. The only factual aspect of any of the accusations against these defendants that was ever

---

threaten the system can be detained for long periods of time at great personal expense. As one writer has argued, the real purpose of the Chicago conspiracy trial and the various Panther trials was to tie up the political activity of the defendants.[15] In show trials and the manner in which they are utilized, we can see one of the important themes of political crime: to law enforcement officials, the meaning of the act—i.e., its implied threat to the social order—is far more important than the act itself. Similarly, the show of the trial is of more importance than the innocence or guilt of the particular defendant or defendants.

The 1960s

During the 1960s, politics and crime were more intertwined than at any previous period of American history. One aspect of this situation was race. The civil rights dissent of the 1960s is sometimes thought to have begun in Montgomery, Alabama, when Rosa Parks, a black woman, refused to give up her seat on a bus to a white man and was arrested, jailed, convicted, and fined for violating Montgomery's segregation ordinance. The ensuing bus boycotts by black citizens showed the strength of their resistance to unjust social conditions. As is typical with political "crime," Martin Luther King and other blacks awaiting car pool

established was their individual and collective opposition to the war in Vietnam.

The Wilmington Ten[c]

The case of the Wilmington Ten grew out of a classic failure to enforce the law, which sparked outrage, protest and its own form of lawlessness. In 1966, a Federal court ordered the desegregation of the Wilmington high schools. The order was not implemented until late in 1970, when, in the midst of the school term, the one black high school became a junior high and its former students were divided between the two white high schools. Claims of discrimination by the high school administrators and teachers soon began to be heard from the black students. They complained about discrimination in grades, athletics, transportation and teacher hiring. Attempts at organization to protest their rights were met with counter threats and action by the Ku Klux Klan and a local militant group, Rights of White People (ROWP). There then followed a series of events which included meetings, protests, a fire, one death and the intervention of the National Guard. . . .

That is the log of events that led to the trial of the Wilmington Ten. Well over a year passed before the judicial system of North Carolina produced grand jury indictments. Early in the morning of March 15, 1972, police raided the homes of Mr. Chavis, Anne Sheppard (later Ann Sheppard Turner), a local VISTA poverty worker, and 14 former high school students who were allegedly involved in the Wilmington riots. The ten of these that were eventually brought to trial were charged on several counts: conspiracy to burn and burning with an incendiary device; conspiracy to assault and assault of emergency personnel; conspiracy to commit murder, and accessory before the fact to a crime. Sixteen defendants (six of whom have still not been tried) were arrested March 15, 1972. By that time, a number of people involved in the case had left Wilmington. Mr. Chavis was working in Raleigh.

SOURCES

[a] Abraham S. Blumberg, "Typologies of Criminal Behavior," in *Current Perspectives on Criminal Behavior: Essays on Criminology*, 2d ed., Knopf, New York, 1981, pp. 43–44.
[b] Ibid., p. 45.
[c] Everett C. Parker, "The Scandal of the Wilmington Ten," *Crisis*, vol. 84, no. 1, January 1977, pp. 29–32.

rides were arrested on charges of vagrancy and illegal hitchhiking. Another important aspect of dissent in the 1960s was resistance to the Vietnamese war. There were many famous cases of political crime during this period. Among the famous show trials beginning in the 1960s and continuing into the 1970s were those of the "Oakland Seven," the "Boston Five," the "Chicago Eight," the "Panther Thirteen," Angela Davis, the "Harrisburg Seven," the "Harrisburg Eight," Daniel Ellsberg, and Anthony Russo.[16]

Although the 1960s will undoubtedly be recorded as a decade of much political crime, it is impossible to state, even in a general way, how much occurred then—or for that matter how much occurs today. No clear statistics are kept. In the FBI's Uniform Crime Reports, conspiracy (which is not necessarily political) is included in the category "all other offenses." Moreover, as has already been stated, persons who dissent are often arrested on unrelated technical charges— vagrancy, illegal hitchhiking, parading without a permit, obstruction of government property, etc. Most of these are locally enforced ordinances. The result is that it is literally impossible to obtain a nationwide overview of the extent of political crime. "Show trial" cases exemplify critical issues, ones which arouse deep feelings. Some people are more involved in such issues than others. Out of political conviction, some commit actions which express their beliefs. Those in

Following his arrest on a charge of loitering, the Reverend Martin Luther King, Jr., is taken to a cell at police headquarters in Montgomery, Alabama. (WIDE WORLD PHOTOS)

power feel threatened and react with measures designed to reinforce what they feel is the integrity of the social order. But how often this occurs cannot be stated.

The decade of the 1960s also saw the emergence of a more violent form of political crime, political terrorism. Political terrorism is defined as:

> Violent, criminal behavior designed primarily to generate fear in the community, or a substantial segment of it, for political purposes.[17]

Such terrorism not only combines violence and politics but also tends to involve acts that are meant to convey fear to the larger community or perhaps to attract attention to a cause. Specifically, these acts may include murder, kidnapping, extortion, bombing, hijacking, and sabotage. In contrast to that of earlier periods, the political terrorism which emerged in the 1960s (1) has involved violence aimed at the state rather than action by one group of citizens against another, and (2) has in a number of cases involved crimes made possible by "high technology," e.g., airplane hijacking and takeovers of nuclear power facilities.

According to one estimate, during the 1960s the United States experienced 5 "terrorist episodes" and 14 terrorist campaigns.[18] Political terrorism was seen in the activities of radical white groups such as the Students for a Democratic Society and black groups such as the Black Panther party and the Symbionese

Liberation Army. While the radical whites may have employed terrorism in part as a response to personal identity crises, the blacks tended to employ it as a response to the despair of the black ghettos. Rather than develop systematic ideologies, both white and black groups tended to borrow concepts ecclectically, some from Marxism-Leninism and others from anarchism. Their overriding principle was "primacy of action." In retrospect, one can say that many of the political terrorist groups were relatively short-lived and that political terrorism appeared to subside during the 1970s in the United States.[19] However, active political terrorism is seen in many countries around the world, and the terrorist movement has international ramifications.[20]

Abuse of Office

The other side of political crime involves government breaking its own laws. This can be done in two ways: (1) the power of an agency or office can be used against citizens or against the public interest; and (2) the holder of an office can use it for personal gain. Again, the range of acts is as wide as crime in general. Violence, theft, deceit, violation of civil rights, and even sexual abuse may be involved. Although governmental lawbreaking has occurred for centuries, only in the past decade has it become a focus for sustained criminological attention. Indeed, the public exposure of Watergate and subsequent revelations of lawlessness by governmental agencies have meant that everyone is aware of this form of political crime. Governmental "overprosecution" of dissent, discussed in the preceding section, could also be interpreted as abuse of office.

Abuses against citizens or the public interest

In recent years the sheer number of individual citizens about whom intelligence has been gathered by governmental agencies is tremendous. In its review, the Senate Select Committee on Intelligence found that

> More than 500,000 domestic intelligence files were kept at FBI headquarters, plus more at their field offices. Between 1953 and 1973, nearly one-quarter million first class letters were opened and photographed.
>
> Millions of private telegrams were opened by the National Security Agency, which worked collusively with three American telegraph companies between 1947 and 1975.
>
> 100,000 intelligence files were maintained by U.S. Army Intelligence between the mid-1960s and 1971.
>
> 11,000 intelligence files were created by the Internal Revenue Service between 1969 and 1973.
>
> 26,000 persons were catalogued by the FBI to be rounded up in the event of a national emergency.[21]

The report concluded:

> Too many people have been spied upon by too many government agencies and too much information has been collected.[22]

Again, we have a situation in which technology—in this case, the computer—has made it possible to collect and maintain far more information than could ever have been accumulated previously. However, it is perhaps worth noting that few prosecutions and even fewer convictions ever resulted from all this surveillance.

Aside from accumulation of information, there is a pattern of instances in which government officials have committed criminal acts against American citizens and against the public interest. The most strikingly visible of these instances were the crimes related to Watergate which led to the resignation of former president Richard Nixon. The theft of Daniel Ellsberg's psychiatric files, the break-in at the Democratic party's national offices in the Watergate building, the attempts to suppress the investigation of Watergate, and the efforts to conceal and destroy legal evidence related to the Watergate cover-up constituted the "high crimes and misdemeanors" which were the basis for the impeachment proceedings begun against Nixon. While it can be argued that the Watergate crimes involved no violence, no harm or injury to any person, and no loss of money, they did raise fundamental questions concerning the way power was centralized in the presidency; the ways that centralized power was used; and, more generally, the nature of political legitimacy in modern American society.[23]

Some criminologists have attempted to link the abuse of power evident in the Watergate affair to other political crime, and in general to organized crime in American society. Thus, Richard Quinney writes:

> Inquiries into Watergate and the subsequent coverup disclosed many other alliances and related criminal operations, connecting the United States government, organized crime, and clandestine intelligence networks. Not the least of these discoveries is the possible connection of some of the Watergate figures, agencies, and operations to past political assassinations: John Kennedy, Martin Luther King, Robert Kennedy, and the attempted assassination of George Wallace were conspiratorial plots to maintain control over the established political and economic system in the United States by those groups, persons, and forces which arranged Watergate. From the assassination of John Kennedy in Dallas to the Watergate burglary in Washington, a single path appeared to be traceable.[24]

Another observer has argued that the ethical atmosphere of government which produced Watergate "largely reflects unwritten 'insider' norms accepted by politicians themselves."[25] Finally, after a detailed analysis of the Watergate tapes, Sherri Cavan concluded that it would be a mistake to call Nixon "crazy":

> If the backstage talk in the Oval Office reveals an administration with a Mafia mentality, it is not because the President is crazy. It is because the culture in which that position of leadership is embedded is organized in such a way that what was once considered criminal is now common practice.[26]

Although more certain proof is needed before firm conclusions can be drawn, the possibility of a link between political crime, as seen in the abuse of the powers of office, and organized crime is one that needs to be explored further.

While Watergate involved no violence, other abuses of office have involved violence. Government involvement in the death of private citizens can be seen in the killings of 4 Kent State University students (March 1970) and 39 inmates of the

Appearing on nationwide television on August 7, 1974, Richard Nixon announced his resignation from the Presidency. (WIDE WORLD PHOTOS)

prison at Attica (September 1971); what happened at Attica has been called "the bloodiest one-day encounter between Americans since the Civil War."[27] An even more sensitive area, which involves larger numbers of incidents, is abuse of citizens by the police. Although some of the more blatant abuses of earlier eras (such as station-house beatings) may have declined, there has been a definite escalation in the killing of civilians by police, and vice versa.[28]

Abuses for personal gain

The second type of abuse of office involves situations in which the holder of an office uses it for personal gain. Commonly called "corruption," this type of abuse has been the subject of comment ever since people have held positions of power. Curiously, it has long been studied by political scientists but only recently by criminologists. Perhaps this is because of a split among criminologists about how the crime of corruption should be perceived. While some would give corruption an important place in the study of political crime, others would prefer to see it "as a species of property offense rather than as political crimes committed with a political objective transcending individual aggrandizement."[29] This text takes the former view; corruption is included here as a political crime involving abuse of power. It is true that corruption involves individual aggrandizement, but the point is that the thefts and other crimes involved in corruption are possible only because of the political office that is held.[30]

It should be recognized that corruption is a very general concept which can be most difficult to apply in a particular case. The Oxford English dictionary defines corruption in political contexts as:

> Perversion or destruction of integrity in the discharge of public duties by bribery or favour; the use or existence of corrupt practices, especially in a state, public corporation, etc.

Noting this, one political scientist argues that corruption may be seen in terms of (1) duties related to public office; (2) concepts of demand, supply, and exchange derived from economic theory; and (3) the concept of the public trust.[31] Among sociologists, one widely followed definition of corruption comes closer to the commonsense use of the term:

> A public official is corrupt if he accepts money or money's worth for doing something that he is under duty to do anyway, that he is under a duty not to do, or to exercise a legitimate discretion for improper reasons.[32]

Whatever the definition, it is apparent that judgment of an act as corrupt involves not only a legal but also an ethical stance against the use of public office for private benefit.

Historical perspective on abuse of office

On one level it is impossible to estimate the total amount of corruption that has characterized American life and history. For long periods, corruption was simply "business as usual."

In the nineteenth century, American politics was greatly influenced by "land grabs," especially as the railroads and big business became established. As one historian writes of this period:

> For the entrepreneurs always had to pay, even for the fulfillment of the normal formalities, even if only *one* company applied for the right of way to one particular railroad franchise. If several railroad companies were trying to outdo one another, they had to compete in the size of the "bribes." Yet these were not real bribes because from the beginning it was understood that a concession could not be obtained without such special payments. Only the size of the payments differed, depending on whether and how many entrepreneurs and civil servants were in competition with one another.[33]

In the same period, there were numerous calls for reform, especially in the civil service—calls which were often self-serving on the part of reformers, since they may have exposed more corruption than actually existed.[34]

Walter Lippmann, perhaps the most analytical of American commentators, put the situation as follows:

> It would be impossible for an historian to write a history of political corruption in America. What he could write is the history of the exposure of corruption. Such a history would show, I think, that almost every American community governs itself by fits and starts of unsuspecting complacency and violent suspicion. There will be long periods when practically nobody except the professional reformers can be induced to pay attention to the business of government; then rather suddenly there will come a period when every act of the administration in power is suspect, when every agency of investigation is prodded into activity, and the civil conscience begins to boil.[35]

In short, "corruption" may mark the underlying reality; its exposure, the occasional interruption.

Abuse of office in the present day

The modern story of corruption appears to be but a variation on the well-developed historical theme. On the federal level, it is the United States Congress that has received most publicity. Perhaps the most blatant part of corruption today is the routine acceptance of conflict of interest—that is, of the fact that members of Congress pass legislation in areas where they have personal financial involvements and maintain private legal practices.[36] Another aspect of congressional corruption involves illegal behavior of members of Congress; this may range from violations of rules for campaign financing to mail fraud. It is worth noting that between 1941 and 1971, there were a total of 15 criminal prosecutions against members of Congress. Between 1972 and 1978, there were 21 prosecutions, or 3 per year—a fivefold increase. The number of prosecutions is remarkable, since there are a wide range of crimes for which members of Congress enjoy virtual immunity from arrest.[37]

To say that corruption in Congress has received the most publicity is not to say that the executive and judicial branches of the federal government are free of corruption. Although the Watergate scandal can best be seen in terms of a more general governmental abuse of power, it also involved questionable campaign contributions, laundering of funds, and suitcases full of $100 bills—all designed to ensure Richard Nixon's reelection, whether or not it was in the public interest. Lyndon Johnson reportedly was willing to pay Bobby Baker 1 million dollars to conceal crimes for which he thought he might have to go to prison.[38] Jimmy Carter was repeatedly the subject of allegations that he had received "sweetheart loans" to finance his gubernatorial and presidential campaigns.[39]

On the state and local levels, corruption appears to be even more common than on the federal level. It is here that political machines have thrived. One investigation into Massachusetts politics brought indictments against no fewer than 53 persons and 15 corporations:

> About two dozen of the individuals were (or had been) state officials, and they included the former Speaker of the House, a former governor, the public safety director, two present and two former members of the Governor's Council, the chairman of the state housing board, and several former state representatives.[40]

As the writer goes on to note, "One can be reasonably confident that much the same results could be produced by similar commissions in many other states."[41]

Investigations into local political corruption have found that much gambling and vice (especially prostitution) are associated with corruption as evidenced in official malfeasance, misfeasance, and nonfeasance of duties.[42] In two local communities examined in depth, corruption was found to be quite subtle in that not everyone in the system could be characterized as corrupt. Rather, the corruption was controlled by certain crime networks in which the people involved changed and roles fluctuated, but the system tended to perpetuate itself.[43] In Seattle, the group found by William J. Chambliss to manage and profit from organized crime

> was like crime networks everywhere in that it was composed of some of the city's and state's leading citizens. Working for, and with, this group of respectable community members was a staff to coordinate the daily activities of prostitution, card games, lottery, bookmaking, pinball machines, the sale and distribution of drugs, usury, pornography, and even systematic robbery and burglary. Representatives from each of the groups engaged in organized crime made up the political and economic power centers of the community, met regularly to distribute profits, discussed problems, and made the necessary organization and policy decisions essential to the maintenance of a profitable, trouble-free business.[44]

In Wincanton, campaign contributions, regular payments to higher officials, kickbacks on city purchases, and holiday and birthday gifts were the basis of a system used by the gambling interests to buy protection from the law:

> Just as the officials, being in control of the instruments of law enforcement, were able to facilitate Stern's gambling enterprises, so Stern, in control of a newtork of men operating outside the law, was able to facilitate the officials' corrupt enterprises. . . . Many local officials were not satisfied with their legal salaries from the city and their illegal salaries from Stern and decided to demand payments from prostitutes, kickbacks from salesmen, etc. Stern, while seldom receiving any money from these transactions, became a broker; bringing politicians into contact with salesmen, merchants, and lawyers willing to offer bribes to get city business; setting up middlemen who could handle the money without jeopardizing the officials' reputations; and providing enforcers who could bring delinquents into line.[45]

In other words, here too there was a network which was very effective, although limited in numbers of people. It probably involved no more than 10 of the 155 members of the police force, although as many as half may have accepted small Christmas presents from the Stern gambling interests. In other offices there were also a few people who could be identified either with Stern or with some form of free-lance corruption.[46]

In big cities, corruption has been more open and has taken a rather different form. Cities have long had political machines which (among other things) reward precinct captains with easy, often "no show," jobs when they get out the vote. To their constituents, the captains in turn provided "service and favors":

> In earlier days, the captain could do much more. The immigrant family looked to him as more than a link with a new and strange government: he was the government. He could tell them how to fill out their papers, how to pay their taxes, how to get a license. He was the welfare agency, with a basket of food and some coal when things got tough, an entree to the crowded charity hospital. He could take care of it when one of the kids got in trouble with the police. Social welfare agencies and better times took away many of his functions, but later there were still the traffic tickets to fix, the real estate tax assessments he might lower. When a downtown office didn't provide service, he was a direct link to government, somebody to cut through the bureaucracy.[47]

Today, at least one author would see public employee unions—with their lucrative jobs and pension programs—as part of a new, middle-class, welfare-state political machine which provides considerable rewards, especially in terms of lavish pension benefits, "to buy or encourage political support."[48] To the extent that this is true, we can see a subtle form of corruption being practiced on a truly grand scale.

In many areas of political life, corruption is so well established that the people involved in it do not even see their behavior as corrupt. One architect who had given gifts to members of government saw himself as a victim of hypocrisy when subsequently accused of corruption.[49] Police routinely distinguish between "clean" and "dirty" graft: clean graft comes from gambling, prostitution, or liquor; dirty graft comes from narcotics pushers, burglars, or robbers.[50] In one study of a medium-sized police department, there was no corrupt act that would be reported "every time" it was noticed by other police officers. Acts involving "corruption of authority"—e.g., free meals, services, or discounts on liquor—were particularly unlikely to be reported by other police officers (see Table 21). In New York City, the Knapp Commission distinguished "meat eaters," who aggressively misused police power for personal gain, from "grass eaters," who simply accepted the payoffs that came their way. The commission also argued that

TABLE 21. Question: In your opinion, how often do you think policemen in your department would report another policeman for the following acts?

	Responses (N = 43)			
Corrupt patterns	*Every time*	*Sometimes*	*Rarely*	*Never*
1. Corruption of authority				
a. Free meals	1 (2%)	9 (21%)	14 (33%)	19 (44%)
b. Services or discounts	4 (9%)	12 (30%)	13 (30%)	13 (30%)
c. Liquor	8 (19%)	13 (30%)	16 (37%)	6 (14%)
2. Kickbacks				
a. Money	19 (44%)	11 (26%)	8 (19%)	5 (12%)
b. Goods and services	11 (26%)	14 (33%)	11 (26%)	7 (16%)
3. Opportunistic thefts				
a. Victims	33 (77%)	7 (16%)	——	3 (7%)
b. Burglary or unlocked buildings	25 (58%)	11 (26%)	4 (9%)	3 (7%)
4. Shakedowns				
a. Criminals	30 (70%)	10 (23%)	1 (2%)	2 (5%)
5. Protection of illegal activities				
a. Vice operators	32 (74%)	6 (14%)	1 (2%)	4 (9%)
b. Businessmen	34 (79%)	5 (12%)	1 (2%)	3 (7%)
6. Traffic fix	32 (74%)	6 (14%)	1 (2%)	4 (9%)
7. Misdemeanor fix	21 (49%)	11 (26%)	6 (14%)	5 (12%)
8. Felony fix	37 (86%)	1 (2%)	1 (2%)	4 (9%)
9. Direct criminal activities				
a. Burglary	34 (79%)	5 (12%)	1 (2%)	3 (7%)
b. Robbery	38 (88%)	1 (2%)	——	4 (9%)
10. Internal payoffs				
a. Off days, etc.	18 (42%)	13 (30%)	7 (16%)	5 (12%)
b. Work assignments	20 (47%)	9 (21%)	9 (21%)	5 (12%)

SOURCE: Thomas Barker, "Peer Group Support for Police Occupational Deviance," *Criminology*, vol. 15, no. 3, November 1977, pp. 353–366.

the meat eaters, while they might grab the headlines, were only a "small percentage" of all corrupt police officers—although it went on to note that the grass eaters tended to make corruption acceptable.[51]

As it turns out, the acceptance of corruption may well extend beyond the intimate occupational groups of those directly involved in it. As the author of the Wincanton study notes, corruption is a definite part of politics in Wincanton:

> The questions of official corruption and policy toward vice and gambling, it seems, have been paramount issues in Wincanton elections since the days of Prohibition. Any mayor who is known to be controlled by the gambling syndicates will lose office, but so will any mayor who tries completely to clean up the city. The people of Wincanton apparently want both easily accessible gambling and freedom from racket domination.[52]

The deep-rooted nature of corruption has led Harold A. Larrabee to comment:

> The source of corruption is in the minds of the people. So rank and extensively seated is that corruption that no political reform can ever have any effect in removing it.[53]

Furthermore, by giving the word "corruption" an indeterminate sense

> a man affords himself a double gratification. He gratifies his own anti-social pride and insolence; and he affords his argument a promise of effectiveness by feeding the same appetites in the breasts of his auditors, whom he sees to be bound to him by a common sinister interest.[54]

In short, corruption—whether in the form of malfeasance, misfeasance, or nonfeasance; whether revolving around gambling, prostitution, alcohol, or drugs; whether involving a few people or a machine of vast proportions—appears to be an integral part of the body politic. The forms may change, but the underlying reality continues. It may well be that in corruption we find a type of crime which people like to complain about but which they also enjoy and benefit from. Perhaps this is why there have been so many reforms, both proposed and enacted, and so few real changes. The use of public office for private benefit appears to be a well-established part of the system by which power is exercised in society.

One may ask which of the forms of abuse of office is more critical. Sociologists such as Jack D. Douglas and John M. Johnson would argue that corruption, while more common, is probably secondary in importance to situations in which the power of an agency or office is used against citizens or against the public interest. Abuses against citizens or the public interest endanger basic institutions of our society and basic rights which are guaranteed by the Constitution. Where there is governmental violence outside the law, constitutional democracy cannot function.[55] However, it is difficult to generalize; and there are some forms of corruption that can be most destructive of social order. As with dissent, it may well be that in abuse of office the meaning of an act is of more importance than the act itself. How abuse is defined differs greatly with time and place. Very often, whether or not there is abuse is itself subject to the interpretation of acts and of the motives of those committing them.

POLITICAL CRIMINAL OFFENDERS

The problems in interpreting the nature and extent of political crime are also reflected in describing political criminals. However, some generalizations have been put forth, and it is important for us to take a look at them.

In one review of the literature on dissent, the characteristics of the offender were found to depend on the type of political dissent. Dissent in the form of disobedience typically involved offenders of higher social class; dissent in the form of evasion was more characteristically lower-class. There were also two types of violent political offenders. Spontaneous and unorganized violence was typically committed by lower-class people; planned and tactical violence was quite likely to be committed by "organized, politically sophisticated higher-class resisters."[56] Several other points should also be noted. As is true of other forms of crime, many political offenders were male—although there was also a history of political dissent by females. Age was not as outstanding a factor as in person-to-person crime; however, many offenders, especially draft resisters, were probably younger adults.

The picture changes if we consider the political criminal who abuses an office: holding political office in the United States almost always means being male, middle-aged or older, white, and middle- or upper-class. Hence, those who abuse their offices would also tend to have these social characteristics.

Focusing more specifically on the dissenter, some writers suggest that there is an attitudinal factor that sets these political criminals apart from other people. Stephen Schafer would call them "convictional" criminals, people who commit crimes for altruistic and communal motives rather than egoistic ones and are convinced of the truth and justification of their own beliefs.[57] Terrorists may be thought of as carrying this to an extreme. The following portrait of a true terrorist is by Serge Nechayev, a protégé of the revolutionary anarchist Mikhail Bakunin:

> The revolutionary is a dedicated man. He has no personal inclinations, no business affairs, no emotions, no attachments, no property, and no name. Everything in him is subordinated towards a single exclusive attachment, a single thought, and a single passion—the revolution. . . . He has torn himself away from the bonds which tie him to the social order and to the cultivated world, with all its laws, moralities, and customs. . . . The revolutionary despises public opinion. . . . Morality is everything which contributes to the triumph of revolution. Immoral and criminal is everything that stands in his way. . . . Night and day he must have but one thought, one aim—merciless destruction. . . . And he must be ready to destroy himself and destroy with his own hands everyone who stands in his way.[58]

One can only speculate as to the number of people in a society who would have this degree of dedication.

Another approach to studying the political criminal and the importance of political crime is to look at political prisoners. Here again the numbers are difficult to estimate or assess. One criminologist estimated in 1971 that one-third of all inmates of federal correctional facilities—about 10,000 prisoners—were serving sentences for ideological violations of law.[59] This high number probably reflects the large amount of political activity of the 1960s, especially protests against the Vietnamese war. A more recent estimate, in 1978, found that the number of political prisoners was "very small."[60] Moreover, state penitentiaries, where most felony offenders serve time, have only a few political prisoners.

In line with their view that all crime is political, radical criminologists have argued that there are many more political prisoners than there might appear to be at first sight. Barry Krisberg, for example, identifies four groups:

1. Those who are prisoners because of their political views and activities or are specifically victimized on the basis of class, racial, or national oppression. E.g., Angela Davis, Huey Newton, Bobby Seale, and Ericka Huggins.
2. Those who as a result of their political activities are found guilty of technical violations of law. E.g., Martin Luther King, Jr., the Berrigan brothers, and Cesar Chavez.
3. Those who have committed a variety of offenses but, lacking adequate representation or political redress, are imprisoned for long terms under inhumane conditions.
4. Those who may have committed a variety of offenses but became conscious of social injustices, i.e., politicized, while in prison. E.g., George Jackson, Eldridge Cleaver, the Soledad Brothers, and Ruchell Magee.[61]

Groups 3 and 4 add a new dimension to political crime in that their politicalization is related to prison experiences. Although no one knows how many have been politicalized, there are some indications of political consciousness among American prisoners.[62]

VICTIMS OF POLITICAL CRIME

Having characterized political criminal offenders, we now need to give some thought to the victims of political crime.

It is very difficult to assess the role of the victim in political crime. Generally, there are few individual victims. Those who do become individual victims are often "innocent bystanders" or "accidental bystanders" who happen to be in the wrong place at the wrong time—for example, passengers killed by a terrorist bombing of an airplane. On the other hand, it could be claimed that those who are punished for their dissent, often unjustly, are the real victims of political crime.

It seems most appropriate to take a "system" view of political crime. Such a view would go beyond particular offenders and victims to recognize that

> The labeling of political criminality is itself a tactical move in conflicts between those who are committed to preserving a political structure and those committed to its subversion. When the authorities wish to emphasize the subversion threat in order to rally popular support, they are quick to designate even limited civil disobedience as political crime. If the public is not considered sufficiently loyal, the threat may be ideologically minimized by denying the politicality of even major challenges by

stressing the irrationality and ordinary criminality of challengers. . . . Serious political challengers play the same game. Confronted by efficient repression and a populace unhelpful because of "false consciousness," resisters tend to prefer a low profile and encourage the perception of them as ordinary lawbreakers or, best of all, conventional political contenders or lobbyists.[63]

In other words, there is no absolute right or wrong about political crime. What an act means, or can be interpreted to mean, is of more importance than what it is. As is implied by its definition as crime motivated by political aims, political crime revolves around the issue of how groups and individuals should use power. The purpose of political policing is to secure the political structure of society against radical change. On the other hand, it may also be used against those who would seek to prevent change from occurring. Political crime seems to exist in all organized societies, especially those which are undergoing rapid social change.

THE CONTEXT OF POWER

Now that we have examined political crimes in the United States and considered political criminals and the complex issue of victims of political crime, we need to round out our study by dealing with the social context in which political crime takes place.

Like other forms of crime, political crime does not occur in a vacuum. It too is immensely influenced by its social context—in this case, the institutionalized process by which power is exercised. As it turns out, the nature and extent of political crime in a society are determined by the interplay of two factors: (1) how power is actually exercised, and (2) how people think it ought to be exercised. In recent years, American society has seen dramatic changes related to both of these factors.

In its actual exercise, the institutionalization of power in American society has historically been weak. First of all, to prevent any official from gaining too much, power was divided and separated by function (executive, legislative, and judicial) and by level (federal, state, and local). Second, terms of office were limited, so that officials were faced continually with the need of running for reelection. The Constitution even went so far as to provide for removal from office "on impeachment for, and conviction of treason, bribery, or other high crimes and misdemeanors" for the president, the vice-president, and all civil officers.[64] Finally, as was discussed earlier, the Bill of Rights served to set limits to various forms of power that would otherwise have been exercised by the government.

Although it may have averted tyranny, from the earliest period weakly institutionalized power has been associated with "corruption." Although not "permitted" by the Constitution, political parties soon arose to fill a need for coordination of power among the three branches and the three levels of government. To put it another way, the political boss emerged to fill a new function:

> To organize, centralize and maintain in good working condition "the scattered fragments of power" which are at present dispersed through our political organizations. By this centralized organization of political power, the boss and his apparatus can satisfy the need of diverse subgroups in the larger community which are not adequately satisfied by legally devised and culturally approved social structures.[65]

In other words, the political boss operating a ''machine'' was merely filling a need brought about by constitutional limits on power. Political machines provided services, both supporting and being supported by ''legitimate'' and ''illegitimate'' businesses (the latter including vice, crime, and the rackets). At times, such machines were regarded as efficient providers of goods and services. At others, they were seen as corrupt and in need of ''reform.''

In the modern, post-World War II, period the political institution of the state has vastly changed its scope and size. Americans have seen the emergence of a warfare state, with enormous resources devoted to the buildup of military power; and a welfare state, with enormous resources devoted to a wide range of programs designed to improve the situation of the aged, the sick, the poor, and a variety of other groups in American society. These developments have meant increases in governmental control of material wealth, in transfer payments, in rules and regulations, and in numbers of government employees. Government is simply much larger today than it was 30 or 40 years ago.[66]

Curiously, the increase in scope and size of government has not been accompanied by a proportionate increase in governmental deviance and political crime. This is so because the manner in which people expect power to be exercised has also changed. Dating back to the latter part of the nineteenth century, there have been numerous reform movements which attempted to clear up or eliminate the traditional forms of machine corruption. This has meant that the general public has become more rigorous in its standards of what to expect of government officials as they exercise power. Although the implications of ''middle classification'' are not completely understood, it may well be that officials have become less corrupt at all levels of government but that standards for expected behavior have escalated even more rapidly.[67]

In the long run, however, the trend toward increased scope and size of government and the trend toward increased public sensitivity about how power is to be exercised will conflict with each other. As Douglas has expressed it:

> The primary reason why the public is so outraged is precisely because we do have higher standards for government officials. Each act of deviance which has been transferred from the private sphere to the government by the Welfare State Revolution has increased our degree of moral outrage over that one deviant act. The result is that our overall sense of moral outrage, or of alienation and revolt, increases by the very fact of shifting deviance from the private to the public sphere.[68]

He goes on to argue that the greatly broadened scope of government has (1) led to an enormous increase in ''honest graft,'' situations where government officials are so interlocked with the private individuals they are supposed to regulate that they cannot do it ''honestly''; (2) enormously increased the possibilities for corruption and violation of rules and; (3) undermined the legitimation of the state to the point where the state's size and power are themselves deviant.[69] Given this situation, one can only expect more official deviance and more public protest.

Should these trends continue, we can expect political crime to play an increased role in criminological thought. Already, there are books, such as Jethro K. Lieberman's *How the Government Breaks the Law* and Morton H. Halperin's *Lawless State*, showing how governments violate their own laws.[70] Radical criminologists such as Quinney have repeatedly called attention to crimes against citizens' rights or human rights.[71] Political crime is hardly new. However, we can expect it to take on new dimensions and to become considerably more extensive as government plays an increasingly greater role in society and public definitions of honesty imply "higher," more stringent standards of conduct for government officials.

SUMMARY

Although all crimes are political in that they are a threat to the existing power structure, political crime is defined as a violation of law which is motivated by political aims. As a type of crime, political crime is unique in that the symbolic meaning of the act is often more important than the act itself. Moreover, considerations of legality are secondary; the possibility of deterring threats to the social order is primary. While some have stressed the extensive victimization possible in political crime, others have asserted its usefulness for social change.

United States law, as seen in the Bill of Rights, implies a limited role for political crime in American society. Indeed, the only specifically political crime defined in the Constitution is treason. However, the line between dissent and crime has been uncomfortably blurred; lawbreaking has accompanied virtually every political change and reform. Many statutes have been designed to curb dissent; and in show trials the government has taken some unusually repressive measures. Politics and crime became particularly intertwined in the decade of the 1960s; political terrorism also emerged in this period.

The other side of political crime is violation by the government of its own laws. This has also been prevalent in the United States. Government agencies have gathered enormous amounts of intelligence about citizens. The Watergate episode revealed documented abuses of governmental power. The use of office for personal gain has also been extensive in American political life. In the nineteenth century, corruption was "business as usual." Today, conflicts of interest for members of Congress are routine; and members of Congress appear to be involved in a variety of illegal behaviors. Recent presidents have also been the target of allegations of corruption. The interlocking of criminal networks and political power structures characterizes political corruption on both the state and the local level. The use of public office for private benefit appears to be well established.

Political criminal offenders are hard to identify. However, the political offender who is lower-class is likely to practice evasive dissent; one who is upper-class is likely to practice disobedience. Similarly, the lower-class dissenter is likely to engage in spontaneous and unorganized violence, whereas the upper-class dissenter is likely to engage in violence that is organized and politically sophisticated. Generally, dissenters are likely to be male, although many females could also be included among them. They come from a variety of age groups. The typical abuser of political office, however, is almost always male, middle-aged or older, white, and middle- or upper-class. Psychologically, political criminal offenders can be seen as "convictional criminals" who have enormous dedication to the ends they seek. The number of political criminals is very difficult to assess and may vary from time to time. However, some criminologists would argue that many offenders develop political consciousness while in prison.

Political crime usually has few individual victims. However, victimization, if seen in systemic terms, can be most extensive. Depending on how victimization is viewed, victims may be those who are unjustly persecuted for dissent, those whose politicality is denied, or the political and social system itself. If power is corrupt, victimization can be very extensive because the system will change without the approval of those subject to it.

In the end, political crime involves power. In the nineteenth century, weakly institutionalized power was part and parcel of corruption in the United States. The political party, symbolized by the political boss, is the creature of a system of constitutional limits on power. Beginning in the twentieth century, reform movements meant more rigorous expectations for government officials. However, the broadened scope of government has led to increases in "honest graft" and in possibilities for corruption, and to an undermining of the legitimacy of the state. Given these factors, political crime promises to be a continuing concern for criminologists and, indeed, for everyone.

NOTES

[1] Stephen Schafer, *The Political Criminal: The Problem of Morality and Crime*, Free Press, New York, 1974, p. 1.

[2] Barry Krisberg, *Crime and Privilege: Toward a New Criminology*, Prentice-Hall, Englewood Cliffs, N. J., 1975, especially chap. 2; and Julian Roebuck and Stanley C. Weeber, *Political Crime in the United States: Analyzing Crime by and against the Government*, Praeger, New York, 1978. See also: Chapter 4 of the present text.

[3] Edward Sagarin, "Introduction to the Reprint Edition," in Louis Proal, *Political Crime*, Patterson Smith, New York, 1973, p. viii.

[4] Ibid., pp. xxv–xxvi.

[5] Austin T. Turk, "Analyzing Official Deviance: For Nonpartisan Conflict Analyses in Criminology," *Criminology*, vol. 16, no. 4, February 1979, pp. 459–476.

[6] Eric J. Hobsbaum, *Primitive Rebels*, Norton, New York, 1959. See also: references to Karl Marx in Chapter 6 of the present text.

[7] Robert J. Kelly, "New Political Crimes and the Emergence of Revolutionary Nationalist Ideologies," in R. Serge Denisoff and Charles H. McCaghy, eds., *Deviance, Conflict, and Criminality*, Rand McNally, Chicago, Ill., 1973, p. 236.

[8] Frances A. Allen, *The Crimes of Politics: Political Dimensions of Criminal Justice*, Harvard University Press, Cambridge, Mass., 1974, especially p. 30.

[9] Nathaniel Weyl, *Treason: The Story of Disloyalty and Betrayal in American History*, Public Affairs Press, Washington, D.C., 1950.

[10] Charles E. Goodell, *Political Prisoners in America*, Random House, New York, 1973; quotation on p. 7.

[11] Ibid.

[12] William B. Prendergast, "Do State Antisubversive Efforts Threaten Civil Rights?" *Annals of the American Academy of Political and Social Science*, vol. 275, 1951, pp. 124–131; and Marshall B. Clinard and Richard Quinney, *Criminal Behavior Systems*, Holt, Rinehart and Winston, New York, 1973, chap. 16, especially pp. 156–157.

[13] Abraham S. Blumberg, "Typologies of Criminal Behavior," in Abraham S. Blumberg, ed., *Current Perspectives on Criminal Behavior: Essays on Criminology*, 2d ed., Knopf, New York, 1981, p. 45.

[14] David Sternberg, "New Radical Criminal Trials," *Science and Society*, vol. 36, Fall 1972, pp. 274–301.

[15] Paul Goodman, "The Disputed Trials: A Question of Allegiance," *Village Voice*, March 9, 1970, pp. 5–9.

[16] Goodell, *Political Prisoners in America*, chap. 8 and 9.

[17] National Advisory Committee on Criminal Justice Standards and Goals, *Report of the Task Force on Disorders and Terrorism*, Government Printing Office, Washington, D.C., 1976, p.3.

[18] Ted Robert Gurr, "Some Characteristics of Political Terrorism in the 1960s," in Michael Stohl, ed., *The Politics of Terrorism*, Dekker, New York, 1979, pp. 23–49.

[19] Walter Laquer, *Terrorism: A Study of National and International Political Violence*, Little, Brown, Boston, Mass., 1977, especially pp. 208–213.

[20] See: Stohl, *The Politics of Terrorism*, especially part II; and Ronald D. Crelinsten, Danielle Laberge-Altmejd, and Denis Szabo, *Terrorism and Criminal Justice: An International Perspective*, Heath (Lexington Books), Lexington, Mass., 1978.

[21] See: "Report of the Senate Select Committee on Intelligence," in M. David Ermann and Richard J. Lundman, eds., *Corporate and Government Deviance: Problems of Organizational Behavior in Contemporary Society*, Oxford University Press, New York, 1978, pp. 151–173.

[22] Ibid., p. 155.

[23] Arthur J. Vidich, "Political Legitimacy in Bureaucratic Society: An Analysis of Watergate," in Jack D. Douglas and John M. Johnson, eds., *Official Deviance: Readings in Malfeasance, Misfeasance, and Other Forms of Corruption*, Lippincott, Philadelphia, Pa., 1977, pp. 145–169.

[24] Richard Quinney, *Criminology: Analysis and Critique of*

Crime in America, Little, Brown, Boston, Mass., 1975, p. 171.

25 A. James Reichley, "Getting at the Roots of Watergate," in Erman and Lundman, *Corporate and Governmental Deviance*, pp. 186–197. For a discussion of parallels between heroin addicts and the Nixon political circle, see: Talcott Parsons and Dean R. Geistein, "Two Cases of Social Deviance: Addiction to Heroin, Addiction to Power," in Edward Sagarin, ed., *Deviance and Social Change*, Sage, Beverly Hills, Calif., 1977, pp. 19–57.

26 Sherri Cavan, "Gangster Talk in the Oval Office: Sociolinguistic Similarities between Law Makers and Law Breakers," paper presented at the 75th annual meeting of the American Sociological Association, August 1980, New York, p. 13.

27 Douglas and Johnson, *Official Deviance*, pp. 171–172.

28 Arthur L. Kobler, "Police Homicide in a Democracy," in Ermann and Lundman, *Corporate and Governmental Deviance*, pp. 198–217; see also: discussion in Chapter 16 of the present text.

29 Gresham M. Sykes, *Criminology*, Harcourt, Brace, Jovanovich, New York, 1978, p. 224.

30 Although there is little systematic sociological work on corruption, a good beginning has been made in: Douglas and Johnson, *Official Deviance*, especially parts VII and VIII. This is the basis of much of the discussion which follows.

31 Arnold J. Heidenheimer, *Political Corruption: Readings in Comparative Analysis*, Transaction Books, New Brunswick, N. J., 1978, p. 4.

32 M. McMullan, "A Theory of Corruption," *Sociological Review*, vol. 9, 1961, pp. 181–201.

33 Jacob van Klavern, "Corruption: The Special Case of the United States," in Heidenheimer, *Political Corruption*, p. 274.

34 Ari Hoogenboom, "Spoilsmen and Reformers: Civil Service Reform and Public Morality," in Heidenheimer, *Political Corruption*, pp. 276–283.

35 Walter Lippmann, "A Theory about Corruption," in Heidenheimer, *Political Corruption*, p. 294.

36 Mark Green with Michael Calabrese et al., *Who Runs Congress?* 3d. ed., Viking, New York, 1979, pp. 163–168.

37 Ibid., pp. 157–163.

38 William J. Chambliss, *On the Take: From Petty Crooks to Presidents*, Indiana University Press, Bloomington, 1978, pp. 172–175.

39 See: William Safire's columns, e.g., *New York Times*, May 12, 1980, p. A19.

40 James Q. Wilson, "Corruption: The Shame of the States," in Douglas and Johnson, *Official Deviance*, pp. 385–386.

41 Ibid., p. 386.

42 See: John A. Gardiner, "Wincanton: The Politics of Corruption," in Douglas and Johnson, *Official Deviance*, pp. 50–69; Chambliss, *On the Take*; and William J. Chambliss, "Vice, Corruption, Bureaucracy, and Power," *Wisconsin Law Review*, December 1971, pp. 1150–1173.

43 Chambliss, "Vice, Corruption, Bureaucracy, and Power."

44 Chambliss, *On the Take*, pp. 9–10.

45 Gardiner, "Wincanton: The Politics of Corruption," p. 61.

46 Ibid.

47 Mike Royko, "Daley's Machine in Chicago," in Douglas and Johnson, *Official Deviance*, pp. 70–78; quotation on p. 73.

48 Jack D. Douglas, "New York's Fiscal Crisis and the New Welfare-State Political Machine," in Douglas and Johnson, *Official Deviance*, pp. 90–105.

49 Steven Chibnall and Peter Saunders, "Worlds Apart: Notes on the Social Reality of Corruption," *British Journal of Sociology*, vol. 28, no. 2, June 1977, pp. 138–154.

50 Thomas Barker, "Social Definitions of Police Corruption: The Case of South City," *Criminal Justice Review*, vol. 2, no. 2, Fall 1977, pp. 101–110.

51 Knapp Commission, "Police Corruption in New York City," in Douglas and Johnson, *Official Deviance*, pp. 270–283. On police corruption, see also: Antony E. Simpson, *The Literature of Police Corruption*, vol. I, *A Guide to Bibliography and Theory*, John Jay Press and McGraw-Hill, New York, 1977.

52 Gardiner, "Wincanton: The Politics of Corruption," pp. 50–51.

53 Harold A. Larrabee, *Bentham's Handbook of Political Fallacies*, Johns Hopkins Press, Baltimore, Md., 1952, p. 183.

54 Ibid., p. 186.

55 "Introduction," in Douglas and Johnson, *Official Deviance*, pp. 1–9.

56 Austin T. Turk, "Analyzing Official Deviance," especially pp. 471–472. N.B.: Turk includes dissenters but not office abusers in his definition of political offenders.

57 Schaefer, *The Political Criminal*, chap. 5.

58 Quoted in: David C. Rapoport, *Assassination and Terrorism*, Canadian Broadcasting Corporation, Toronto, 1971, p. 79.

59 Sagarin, "Introduction to the Reprint Edition," in Proal, *Political Crime*.

60 Edith Flynn, "Political Prisoners and Terrorists in American Correctional Institutions," in Crelinsten et al., *Terrorism and Criminal Justice*, pp. 87–92.

61 Krisberg, *Crime and Privilege*, pp. 81–83.

62 See: Krisberg, *Crime and Privilege*, chap. 3; and Jessica Mitford, *Kind and Usual Punishment: The Prison Business*, Random House (Vintage), New York, 1973, chap. 13.

63 Turk, "Analyzing Official Deviance," p. 469.

64 Article II, Section 4.

65 Robert K. Merton, "Manifest and Latent Functions," in *Social Theory and Social Structure*, enlarged ed., Free Press, New York, and Collier Macmillan, London, 1968, p. 126.

66 On the increase in government in the welfare state, see: Jack D. Douglas, "A Sociological Theory of Official Deviance and Public Concerns with Official Deviance," in Douglas and Johnson, *Official Deviance*, pp. 395–410.

67 Ibid.

68 Ibid., p. 403; emphasis omitted.

69 Ibid., pp. 403–408.

70 Jethro K. Lieberman, *How the Government Breaks the Law*, Stern and Day, Briarcliff Manor, N. Y., 1972; and Morton H. Halperin, *The Lawless State: The Crimes of the U.S. Intelligence Agencies*, Penguin, New York, 1976.

71 Quinney, *Criminology*, chap. 5.

Review and Preview...
PART THREE AND PART FOUR

In our examination of crime in the United States we have seen that criminal acts can range from murder to vagrancy, from a corporation's earning millions of dollars through marketing defective products to an employee's theft of paper and pencils, from an abuse of elected office to a voluntary homosexual act. This diversity was organized by categorizing criminal acts into seven major types: (1) person-to-person violent crime, (2) person-to-person property crime, (3) corporate crime, (4) crime against organizations, (5) social-order crime, (6) organized crime, and (7) political crime.

For each of these seven major types of crime, we have examined (1) the criminal acts involved, especially how they are defined in the law; (2) the criminal offenders' social characteristics; (3) the nature of the typical victim; and (4) the social context within which the crime typically occurs. We have found great differences between types of crime on each of these points. Yet in the final analysis, crime touches every major group in American society, either as offenders or as victims. Laws are made to apply to all groups, even though they may not be equally enforced. In many ways, crime is supported or even encouraged by social factors which form part of its social context.

Table 22 (pages 382–383) summarizes the seven types of crime in terms of our four major topics. The acts listed in the left-hand column are the major forms of crime in American society. The laws by which these acts have been made crimes evolved over the centuries. Person-to-person violent crimes and burglary emerged in the thirteenth century; property-oriented crimes of theft in the eighteenth century; and the more sophisticated corporate and organized crimes in the late nineteenth and twentieth centuries, respectively. Social-order crimes have had the most erratic history, and today many people are arguing for their decriminalization. Political crime, which many would regard as the basis of all crime, is not a recognized category of crime under American law. However, a number of specific laws have been used to react to perceived threats to power, whether they come from the power of those in office or from those who choose to dissent.

One might try to compare the seven types of criminal acts with respect to their seriousness. Such a comparison is difficult, since it depends upon what is meant by ''seriousness.'' If one means violence, the four person-to-person violent crimes—murder, assault, rape, and robbery—are the ones which are likely to come first to mind. However, as we saw in Chapter 11, corporate negligence often involves injuries or even fatalities. In fact, corporate violation of safety regulations leads to more deaths than person-to-person murders. It might also be argued that organized crime is especially pernicious in that its violence involves deliberate murder or injury, often for pay. Finally, although it is most often aimed at social symbols, political crime can at times have considerable violence associated with it. Abuse of power is a prime case in point.

If we examine seriousness in terms of the dollar value involved in the various forms of crime, we come out with an entirely different ordering. Corporate crime is then most ''serious,'' at an estimated annual cost of about $200 billion. Crimes against organizations would be second, at about $30 billion to $40 billion a year. Although estimates are vague, the total value of illegal goods and services involved in social-order crime (a considerable part of which may overlap with organized crime) is several billions a year, which would probably place social-order crime third. Person-to-person property crime involves a smaller dollar value, about $5 billion a year. The dollar costs of violent, organized, and political crime—although probably considerable—are all but impossible to estimate.

The systematic overview of the major forms of crime demonstrated vividly that there is no one type of criminal offender in our society. The common assumption that crime is perpetrated by the disadvantaged—i.e., the young, the poor, or minorities—is erroneous. Although the assumption may be a fair characterization of those who are arrested for person-to-person violent and property crimes, it is certainly inaccurate for the other major types. Corporate crimes— and, some would say, organized crimes— are committed by offenders who are middle-aged, upper- or upper-middle-class, and white. Political crime involves a fair number of discontented middle-class intellectuals. Organized crime has distinctly ethnic offenders. Crimes against organizations and social-order crimes are committed by offenders from a cross section of American society.

That offenders come from all groups in American society is a dramatic sign that crime is as much linked to power and wealth as it is to powerlessness and poverty. Some situations—such as social-order crimes and fencing of stolen goods—even allow for significant interaction between people of vastly different social backgrounds. Virtually the only safe generalization one can make concerning offenders is that they are predominantly male for nearly every type of crime. Shoplifting and prostitution are the most notable exceptions. Yet even this is changing. Crime rates of females may increase somewhat as women move beyond their traditional roles in the home.

Of all the actors in the crime drama, the victim is most problematic; and the victim has traditionally been the forgotten person. Victim surveys have discovered that for person-to-person violent and property crimes (with the exception of larceny), victims display social characteristics remarkably similar to those of offenders. In other words, the poor, minorities, the young, and males are

TABLE 22. Summary Table: Types of Crime in American Society in Terms of Four Major Criminological Topics

Types of crime	Criminal acts	Criminal offenders	Victims	Social contexts
Person-to-person violent crime	Homicide Assault Rape Robbery Significant legislation: thirteenth century Overall cost: unknown	Arrestees are more likely to be: Male Young Nonwhite Of lower socioeconomic status	Much interaction with offender; some victim-precipitation Much nonreporting Victims more likely to be: Male Young Nonwhite Of lower socioeconomic status	Subcultures of violence Availability of guns City Shift of routine activities away from home Increase in urban and youthful populations
Person-to-person property crime	Burglary Larceny Motor vehicle theft Significant legislation: thirteenth, eighteenth, and twentieth centuries Overall cost: $5 billion per year (estimated)	Arrestees are more likely to be: Male (but increasingly female) Young Nonwhite Of lower socioeconomic status Some professionalization	Businesses Victimization more likely for households headed by: Younger persons Nonwhites (except larceny) Much nonreporting	Casual attitude toward property Increase in movable property Property recycling systems City Shift of routine activities away from home Increase in urban and youthful populations
Corporate crime	Monopoly and antitrust Unfair labor relations Environmental pollution Consumer harm Significant legislation: late nineteenth century Overall cost: $200 billion per year (estimated); death; injury	Juristic person Natural person is almost always: Male Middle-aged White Of upper or middle socioeconomic status Noncriminal self-image	Minimal interaction with offender Scattered Unorganized Sustaining large losses collectively Voiceless	Individualism Profit-orientation Competition Regulatory agencies coopted by corporations
Crimes against organizations	Theft by employees Shoplifting Computer theft Significant legislation: eighteenth century	Cross section, but offenders are somewhat more likely to be: Male (but female for shoplifting) Young	Organization: large more likely than small	Rip-off mentality Theft as wages Work groups' acceptance

Types of crime	Criminal acts	Criminal offenders	Victims	Social contexts
Crimes against organizations (continued)	Overall cost: $30 billion to $40 billion per year (estimated)	In a position with opportunity for theft Noncriminal self-image	Losses passed on to consumer or government as tax write-off	Minimal interaction between customers and salesclerks
Social-order crime	Illegal sex Drug use Gambling Laws are erratic and arbitrary Movement toward decriminalization Significant legislation: various countries Overall cost: several billions of dollars per year (estimated)	Primary deviant: cross section of public Secondary deviant (occupation or career): Sex-typed roles Young Socialized through peer group	Often willing participants Blend with offenders	Deviant subcultures: Street life Homosexual ''tearooms'' After-hours clubs Organizational networks: Localized for prostitutes Centralized for narcotics Variation by social class and ethnicity Politics of deviance
Organized crime	Predatory Demand-oriented illegal enterprises Penetration of legitimate businesses Significant legislation: mid-twentieth century Overall cost: unknown	Secondary deviant (occupation or career): Male Cross section of adult ages Socialized through family, acquaintances, or peer group Organized into ''families'' Striving for social respectability Ethnic succession	Some are willing participants Scattered Unorganized Consumers Institutional structure of American society through ''corruption''	Indirect support by certain cultural values: Enforcement of public morality Democracy Impersonality in business Success Weak, decentralized government ''Queer ladder of mobility''
Political crime	Dissent Abuse of office: Against citizens For personal gain Significant legislation: federal acts beginning in early twentieth century Overall cost: unknown	Cross section, but offenders are usually: Male Dissenters are of higher social class Abusers of office are middle-aged, white, upper- or middle-class ''Convictional criminals''	A few innocent bystanders Political institutions of American society	Weak, democratic government Broadened scope of government Increasing public sensitivity to ''corruption''

disproportionately the victims of person-to-person crimes.

For types of crime other than person-to-person, victimization assumes rather different dimensions, some of which are immensely subtle. For the organizational crimes—corporate crime, crime against organizations, and organized crime—there may be such social distance between offenders and victims that the latter are not even aware of being victimized. For social-order crimes, the supposed victim is in many cases a willing participant. For political, organized, and corporate crimes, the victim can also be seen as the more abstract political or social order. Indeed, in a highly organized, modern society such as ours, victimization is a complex matter. Its full dimensions and its extent are only beginning to be appreciated.

Finally, there is the social context. Crime does not occur in a vacuum. Although the absence of good, reliable data makes it impossible to specify the causes of crime, we have seen two important relationships. (1) Some complexes of cultural values and norms tend to lend encouragement or support to crime. Examples include violent subcultures; casual attitudes toward property; economic individualism and competition; expectations by management that employees will steal; public acceptance of many forms of sexual deviance; substance abuse and gambling; privacy, individual rights, and impersonality in business transactions; and the right to dissent. (2) A number of social factors are related in one way or another to the amount or rate of particular forms of crime. Examples here include urbanization; increases in the youthful population; availability of handguns; a shift of routine activities away from the home; increases in movable property; the nature of regulatory agencies; displays of consumer products; a weak, decentralized political system; and the greatly broadened scope of government.

Analyzing crime in terms of its major types shows that it is not a one-dimensional phenomenon. Rather, there are many types of crime—or, one might say, many problems of crime. Certainly crime is most visible in the form of person-to-person crimes which involve the young, the poor, and minorities. But, as we have stressed, it is equally if not more prevalent in the less visible forms of corporate, organized, and political crime among the middle-aged, the wealthy, and whites. Other forms involve a cross section of the public. Questions concerning types of crime and their relative importance are critical in considering works of criminologists who attempt to explain and theorize about the problem of crime, and in establishing priorities for the criminal justice system.

We also need to ask how, if at all, the different types of crime are interrelated. Does the perception that top management is involved in corporate crime make employees more ready to steal from the organization, so that they can get what they see as their share? Does tolerance of many forms of social-order crime lead to the condoning or even promoting of organized crime? Should we not agree with Robert Morgenthau, District Attorney of New York County (Manhattan)? Morgenthau has said:

> If the affluent flagrantly disregard the law, the poor and the deprived will follow their leadership. If the indigent

who is brought into the police station rightly believes that the affluent are going unpunished for their crimes, then we have not only failed to achieve our goal of equal justice, but we have also created the conditions that breed further disrespect for the law.[1]

In short, even if linked only by perceptions, does not one part of a society have an influence upon the others? Although speculative, these questions cannot be overlooked as we move on to examine the criminal justice system.

The criminal justice system is the fifth major topic addressed by criminologists. While the first four topics—acts, offenders, victims, and social contexts—are directly related to crime, the criminal justice system is more appropriately seen as the key part of our response to crime. It has been reserved for Part Four of this text because it raises a host of organizational questions concerning the manner in which criminal justice agencies operate. Moreover, it is a topic to which criminologists of the 1970s and 1980s have been and are devoting a great deal of attention.

To appreciate the criminological work analyzing the criminal justice system, we shall deal with the three major components of the system: the police, the criminal courts, and corrections. For each component, we need to examine its history and present form, a number of present-day concerns, and alternative forms of organization that are being proposed. For the police, we shall also look at the relationship between police work and crime. In the discussion of each component, three major theoretical perspectives will be presented, which have been taken as ways of interpreting its structure and operation.

Finally, in Chapter 19 we shall look generally at alternative societal responses to crime. Here the attempt will be to draw upon what we have learned in order to suggest other possible ways for the United States to deal with crime. The suggested alternatives have been organized along now-familiar lines: those that deal with restructuring criminal acts, those that deal with rehabilitating criminal offenders, those that deal with compensating or helping victims, and those that deal with restructuring social contexts. In this way, Chapter 19 will serve to show how the theories and analyses presented earlier can be applied to improve the practice of criminal justice in the United States today.

NOTES

[1] Quoted by: Gilbert Geis, "Avocational Crime," in Daniel Glaser, ed., *Handbook of Criminology*, Rand McNally, Chicago, Ill., 1974, p. 279.

PART FOUR

The Criminal Justice System

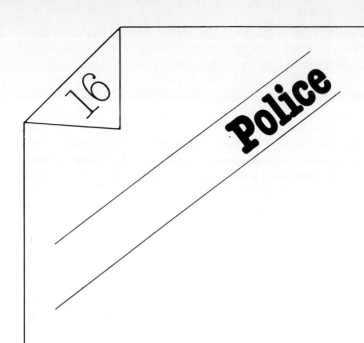

16

Police

The societal response to crime begins with the police. It is through its police that a society discovers and investigates criminal acts and apprehends criminal offenders. Were it not for the police, many, if not most, criminal incidents would go undetected or be handled as if they were private matters between the parties involved.

The policing of crime can assume a variety of forms in today's society. The most common form is the response of uniformed police officers to citizens' complaints. However, policing may also take the form of investigations by plainclothes detectives; attempts by vice squad detectives to control various forms of illicit sex, substance abuse, and gambling; and attempts by secret police to uncover political subversion. Many police, especially those employed by nongovernmental agencies, act as guardians of property. Finally, citizens function as police when they "blow the whistle," that is, report crimes of which they become aware.

Although crime can be policed in different ways, it can also be said that responding to crime is only a small part of what is commonly known as "police work." Indeed, as will be noted below, the full-time, professional, uniformed police officer appeared in the nineteenth century more out of the need to maintain order in cities than to fight crime. In fact, fighting crime is a distinctly twentieth-century addition to police work. Police have also taken on a variety of service roles in areas as diverse as controlling motor vehicle traffic, handling family disputes, curbing public nuisances such as dogs and noise, locating missing persons, dealing with drunks, handling licenses, and guarding foreign embassies and consulates.

The variety of roles comprised by police work has led observers such as Egon Bittner to argue that the uniqueness of police work is not so much what police do as what police are: "nothing else than a mechanism for the distribution of situationally justified force in society."[1] Or, as David Bayley has recently put it, "Police are a group authorized in the name of territorial communities to utilize force within the community to handle whatever needs doing."[2] This authorization to utilize force has put police in the center of an intense debate over the type and amount of force that is appropriate in a democratic society.

This chapter deals with policing in today's society. We shall begin by considering three major perspectives on the police. Following that, our attention will turn to the history of police work and present-day issues related to policing: the police role, discretion, corruption, and conflict with the community. Then we shall make an assessment of how the major forms of crime discussed in Chapters 9 through 15 are policed. Finally, we shall look at some recent suggestions about "depolicing" our society.

THREE MAJOR PERSPECTIVES

Important as the police are, it is only in recent years that they have been seriously studied by criminologists. Although some of the writers of the classical school of criminology were influential in the call for establishment of police agencies, the preoccupation of the positivist school with offenders' pathology as the cause of crime served to downplay questions concerning how the law was administered. Neither school attempted to study what police actually do.

It remained for sociological and critical criminologists to raise questions concerning the social purpose of police. For some, the police are a necessary evil, a group that is needed to enforce the norms necessary to maintain social order in a free society.[3] For others, especially the critical criminologists, police are oppressors who represent the interests of the dominant groups in the United States.[4] Finally, there are those who would take a "dramaturgical view" and see police as symbol manipulators.[5] Since these perspectives lead to different interpretations of police work, they will be stated briefly here and then expanded in the discussions of various aspects of policing.

Police as Norm Enforcers

Seeing the police as norm enforcers is a perspective that is frequently taken by sociologically oriented criminologists. For many of these writers, the problem is how the demands of policing are to be made compatible with the demands of a democratic social order. As expressed by Jerome Skolnick in the mid-1960s, the problem is this:

> Are the police to be principally an agency of social control, with their chief value the efficient enforcement of the prohibitive norms of substantive criminal law? Or are the police to be an institution falling under the hegemony of the legal system, with a basic commitment to the rule of law, even if this obligation may result in a reduction of social order?[6]

In calling attention to the problems of policing in a democratic society, Skolnick was responding to studies conducted by himself and others which had shown (1) that discretion played an enormous role in police decision making, (2) that community relations programs were notoriously problematic, and (3) that peace-keeping made up the bulk of police work. Moreover, as we shall see in this chapter, since the mid-1960s there have been a number of fundamental changes in the way sociologists conceptualize the police role.[7]

Police as Oppressors

The second of our major perspectives on the police—often assumed by critical criminologists—would see them as oppressors. From this point of view

> the police have *primarily* served to enforce the class, racial, sexual and cultural oppression that has been an integral part of the development of capitalism in the U.S.[8]

In short, on this estimate, police are enforcing a system of law created in the interests of those who benefit from private profit. Selective enforcement operates to show leniency toward white-collar and corporate offenders and harshness

Police can play the role of oppressor. This confrontation occurred in
Washington, D.C., during an anti-Nixon rally.   (H. KUBOTA/MAGNUM)

against the poor and the minorities.[9] Critical criminologists have seen policing as
"fundamentally bourgeois and anti–working class from its inception."[10]

Police as Symbol Manipulators

Perhaps the most subtle of the perspectives on police has been advanced by Peter
Manning, who argues for a "dramaturgical view of policing." This view also
stems from critical criminology, but it is more in tune with labeling or symbolic-
interaction theory. For Manning, the most significant product of policing is
symbolic: the police ritualize and create in everyday life an appearance of
consensual, constraining moral order.[11] According to Manning, police are incapable of control; but they have to create the appearance of control—i.e., develop a
"police myth," as it were. Such a myth is seen in presentational strategies, such
as the use of the rhetoric of professionalism or scientific management; and in
operational strategies, such as saturation patrol, undercover work, and special
juvenile officers.[12]

As it turns out, all three of the major perspectives are useful in shedding light on
various aspects of policing. However, rather than consider them generally, it will
be more useful to see how they have been employed to understand the history of
police work and to shed light on some present-day issues in policing. Let's
examine the history of policing first.

The English Experience

Before the nineteenth century, crime was controlled by local groups of private citizens pledged to maintain law and order in their communities. Families were grouped into ten-unit associations called "tithings." Tithings in turn were grouped into "hundreds," which in turn were grouped into "shires." Shires were supervised by "reevers," who were officials appointed by the crown. This system placed the responsibility for crime in the hands of the private citizen:

> Every man was responsible not only for his own actions but also for those of his neighbors. It was each citizen's duty to raise the "hue and cry" when a crime was committed, to collect his neighbors and to pursue a criminal who had fled from the district. If such a group failed to apprehend a law-breaker, all were fined by the crown.[13]

In short, the citizen was expected both to make crime publicly known and to apprehend lawbreakers so that they could be brought to justice.

The control of crime by the private citizenry was found to be less than effective when industrialization and urbanization brought massive social changes to London in the late 1700s. To be sure, there were early attempts to have citizens undertake watch duties comparable to those of night constables. There were also scattered and fragmentary attempts at establishing a professionalized police force. Two groups for whom provision was made were the Thames river police and the Bow Street foot and horse patrols, the former designed to combat crime on the waterfront and the latter to patrol the main roads out of London.[14]

London of the late 1700s saw an extensive debate about the desirability of a professionalized police force. On one side were reformers, such as Patrick Colquhoun and Jeremy Bentham, who saw in the police an agency for the "prevention and detection of crimes" and one which would be involved in "internal regulations for the well order and comfort of civil society."[15] On the other side were parliamentary groups who saw the police as incompatible with British liberty and viewed them with mistrust, suspicion, and hostility. The opponents of the police particularly distrusted the French system of policing, in which soldiers were used as police, police agents roved among citizens in plain clothes, and administrative intervention in communal and individual life was common.[16]

The intense debate over the police in England delayed the establishment of a professionalized police until 1829. It was in that year that Robert Peel, home secretary in the Duke of Wellington's administration, introduced his "Bill for Improving the Police in and near the Metropolis" and convinced Parliament that the time for a professionalized police force had arrived. With the passage of this act, the London police—soon nicknamed the "bobbies" after Sir Robert—came into existence.

The debate about the police did influence their major characteristics. To make them visible, the new police were a uniformed force employed for preventive patrol; there was no detective branch. The officers were "constables," an ancient English public office that was incompatible with any military rank. They were paid low wages, since hard times made labor available and Peel was determined to keep political patronage out of the police. Promotion was to be upward so that channels of advancement would not be blocked by outsiders in supervisory positions. So as not to constitute a threat to society, the police were disarmed. Finally, there were checks upon the police; for example, commissioners invited members of the public suffering from police abuse to come to their offices, bring an action in court, or hold an impartial inquiry.[17]

Police in the United States

As with many other aspects of its social life, law enforcement in the United States followed along the lines of the English model. In colonial America there were sheriffs for the counties and daytime constables and nighttime watchmen for the cities and towns. However, between the 1830s and 1850s American cities experienced what historians have called a "riot era," marked by large-scale rioting and increasing urban disorder. These decades saw the development of a modern urban police system. In 1844, New York City created the first unified day and night municipal police force, modeled on that of London. Soon after, Chicago, New Orleans, Cincinnati, Philadelphia, and Boston also created their own police forces.[18]

In the United States the advent of municipal police forces must be seen in the context of a society experiencing tremendous social changes. James Richardson has described how New York of the early nineteenth century experienced rapid population growth with sharp increases in immigration; heightened distinctions between class, ethnic, and religious groups; and a dizzying economic cycle of boom and bust.[19] Similarly, Roger Lane has demonstrated how the more conservative city of Boston found its traditional system unable to meet the challenges posed by riots, increasing crime, and disorderly behavior related to drunkenness.[20] By the 1840s both cities lacked the broad consensus on laws that had made them comparatively easier to govern in earlier eras. It should also be said that both cities were concerned as much with the social-order crimes related to alcohol, prostitution, and gambling—crimes having to do with the habits of different ethnic groups—as with person-to-person violent and property crimes. In fact, Lane estimates that two-thirds of the criminal convictions in Boston were for common drunkenness, vagabondage, assault and battery, and lewd and lascivious behavior.[21]

Although the new police in the United States were like the English police in that they were uniformed constables who were paid relatively low wages and promoted from within, they differed in certain key respects from their English counterparts. To begin with, they were locally rather than nationally organized. Other, more problematic, differences reflected the conflicting pressures often placed on police departments and police officers. With the absence of community consensus, especially regarding the social-order crimes, law came to be enforced selectively, instances of brutality went unchecked, corruption was common, and politicians were allowed to interfere in the work of police commanders and individual members of the police force.[22]

Policing also took other forms in the second half of the nineteenth century. One was the private police employed by numerous detective agencies such as Pinkerton's.[23] Many industrial corporations also set up their own private police forces. Other, often unofficial, American forms of policing were the vigilantes and lynch mobs in which citizens assumed police, judicial, and correctional roles and administered punishment without due process of law.[24]

In the twentieth century, policing underwent significant changes in the 1920s and 1960s. The 1920s saw increasingly adversarial contacts between police and public, as well as increased opportunities for corruption, as police enforced the immensely unpopular Prohibition laws.[25] The 1920s also saw efforts to professionalize police work; the development of the notion that a professionalized police should measure, explain, and attempt to reduce crime rates; and increased use of technology.[26] The 1960s saw police confronted by a crisis of legitimacy. During the 1960s, it became apparent that there was an immense conflict between the police and those they policed, especially minorities and the poor.[27] There were also what one observer later called "police riots," in which the police engaged in collective violence against all who happened to be in their way. One case in point is the Democratic National Convention of 1968, held in Chicago, at which innocent bystanders were beaten, the McCarthy campaign headquarters was smashed, and scores of campaign staff and accredited journalists were roughed up.[28]

Today, professional police in the United States constitute a large and powerful agency of social control, still locally organized. There are approximately 20,000 police departments employing nearly 700,000 persons and costing more than $13 billion per year. Among the criminal justice agencies, police are the largest. They employ 57 percent of the personnel and receive 54 percent of all criminal justice expenditures.[29]

The somewhat less visible private police can also be seen as part of the present-day policing system. Although there is less publicly available information about this group, one estimate is that private police number between 350,000 and 800,000 (as of 1971) and that as many as two out of every three police officers may be on private payrolls. Four big firms dominate the private policing field: Pinkerton's, Burns, Walter Kidde and Company, and Wackenhut. Their revenues tripled between 1963 and 1969 and then nearly doubled again between 1970 and 1974.[30]

It is in interpreting the history of police work outlined above that we can begin to appreciate the importance of the major criminological perspectives on the police. The historical approach developed here would accord with the perspective of the police as norm enforcers. Policing is seen as evolving in response to the growing complexity of society. It appears in urban areas as a means of maintaining social order.

Other criminologists would put a very different interpretation upon the history of policing. Consider, for example, how the history of police work has been interpreted by certain critical criminologists. To begin with, the earliest form of police were not the urban police departments in New York City and other cities but the southern plantation slave patrols designed to control slaves; these patrols appeared around 1800. Second, the bureaucratic organization of police forces arose not because of popular demand for improved policing but as part of an effort by the ruling class to continue and extend control over a docile working class. Third, vigilantism was a movement of the wealthiest and best-educated segments of the community, one closely linked to private police and one which worked in conjunction with police power. Finally, the movement to professionalize police was a further attempt to use police organizations in the service of class interests.[31]

SOME PRESENT-DAY CONCERNS

The controversy over the interpretation of the history of police work is also reflected in debates over various aspects of policing today. In many instances these debates have been illuminated by empirical studies conducted by sociologically oriented and critical criminologists. To appreciate the complexities of policing, let's take a look at some present-day concerns—in particular; the police role; discretion in arrest and use of violence; corruption; and conflict with the community. As we review these concerns, we shall again note the major perspectives on policing outlined earlier.

The Police Role

Analyzing the role of police officer is difficult, since police work has few unique characteristics other than the authorization to utilize force. It is commonly believed that the job of the police is to enforce the law; but the historical reality is that police arose out of a perceived need to maintain order in urban communities. Over the years police have also undertaken traffic regulation; licensing of various activities; and a variety of service roles that may involve them in activities such as accidents, ambulance calls, escorting drunks, catching runaway dogs, and asking people to turn down radios or televisions.

Studies of calls made upon police departments suggest that law enforcement is a comparatively small part of police work. James Q. Wilson's study of calls to the Syracuse police department found that only 10 percent were related to law enforcement. Of the remaining, 22 percent were for information, 38 percent for service, and 30 percent for maintenance of order. In fact, only 7 percent of the calls to which police officers responded led to an arrest.[32] Similarly, Albert J. Reiss found that about eight out of every ten incidents handled by the Chicago police department were regarded by the police as noncriminal matters.[33] Finally, in a recent study of 26,000 telephone calls to police in 21 jurisdictions in three metropolitan areas, George Antunes and Eric J. Scott found that only about 20 percent involved predatory crime of any type.[34]

One can also assess what police do by looking at arrests. In the aggregate, police make what appear to be a large number of arrests—more than 10,000 per year—for other than traffic violations. Nationally, this would average out to about 14 arrests per police officer. However, as was noted previously, many of these arrests are for social-order crimes (see Chapter 13). In fact, only about one arrest in five is for an index crime. It would appear that most felony arrests are made by plainclothes police; and that most arrests, especially arrests that hold through prosecution and court processing, are made by a relatively small percentage of police officers.[35]

The unstructured nature of the police role is revealed in the different forms

Traffic regulation consumes a great deal of police effort. (BRUCE ANSPACH/EPA NEWSPHOTO)

that police work can assume. In his examination of eight police departments, Wilson identified three major styles of policing. One was the "watchman" style, in which maintanance of order was seen as the principal function. Minor violations—especially traffic violations, juvenile offenses, and "private" disputes or assaults among family or friends—were treated informally or ignored wherever possible. A second style was the "legalistic" style, which emphasized law enforcement rather than maintenance of order. Legalistically oriented departments valued technical efficiency and tended to issue traffic tickets at a high rate, arrest a high proportion of juvenile offenders, act vigorously against illegal enterprises, and make many misdemeanor arrests. In some cases, departments had switched from the "watchman" style to the "legalistic" style following some scandal. The third style was the "service" style. In this style, police take seriously all requests for either law enforcement or maintenance of order but are less likely to arrest or impose legal sanctions upon members of the community they serve. Often found in homogeneous middle-class communities, the "service" style uses law enforcement primarily against outsiders. Moreover, agreement among citizens on social-order crimes leaves police freer to concentrate on managing traffic, regulating juveniles, and—as the name implies—providing services.[36]

   It is in seeking to answer the question *why* police have assumed so many different roles that the major perspectives on policing again become apparent. Policing can, on the one hand, be seen as an agency of last resort, one to which people can turn for relief after other public and private agencies have failed them.

After all, it can be argued, someone has to deal with family quarrels, minor nuisances, and disruptive juveniles. On the other hand, radical criminologists have argued that the service work of the police constitutes a "velvet glove" which makes their repressive "iron fist" acceptable to the communities they serve.[37] If the police are seen as symbol manipulators, in a pluralistic society they can best be seen as coping with the uncertainty of their role by maintaining multiple definitions of what they do. Thus, they are able to respond to different audiences in different ways.[38]

Discretion

Having looked at what police do, we now need to examine how they do their work. To begin with, police are given a great deal of authority:

> The specific form of their authority—to arrest, to search, to detail, and to use force—is awesome in the degree to which it can be disruptive of freedom, invasive of privacy, and sudden and direct in its impact upon the individual.[39]

At the same time, they are given comparatively little guidance on how to use their authority; guidelines and manuals more often list things officers should *not* do than things they *should* do.[40] This means that police officers are required—often within a matter of seconds or minutes—to make decisions on their own. Compared with other organizations, police departments are unusual in that the need to make critical decisions increases as one goes *down* the hierarchy; the lower-ranking officer on the street usually has to make the most important decisions.[41]

To ask how police should use their authority is to raise the complex issue of discretion—a subject of much debate in recent years. "Discretion" can assume at least three different meanings, the first two of which may at times be inconsistent. They are: (1) uncontrolled delegation of power in which the law leaves police officers and other officials free to fight crime and otherwise do their work; (2) exceeding the restrictions which define the limits of police power; (3) the "faculty of discerning judgment, to be discrete, prudent, sagacious, circumspect, to be capable of wise, sound judgment."[42] The third definition often gets lost in public debate; but it emphasizes the positive role of discretion and the necessity of discretion in the application of the abstract, written law to the concrete events of everyday life. To consider police authority and discretion further, we need to examine two key areas of police work—arrest and use of force—and the issue of offenders' rights.

Arrest

Arrest is the focal point of police authority. The power of arrest is probably greater than is commonly realized. As Abraham Blumberg puts it:

> In a simple situation involving a defendant of modest means, arrest may cause a loss of job, a period of detention, the indignities of being fingerprinted and photographed, immeasurable psychological pain, at least several court appearances, and the expenditure of hundreds, even thousands of dollars for bail bond and a lawyer. Arrest can be a powerful weapon—indeed, a form of summary punishment.[43]

Despite the power inherent in the authority to arrest, the decision to arrest is delegated to the individual police officer, who in most instances is able to act without prior review and control.[44]

How police use their authority to arrest or not to arrest has been the subject of several studies of the police. Looking at police practices in the eight communities he studied, Wilson argued that "the normal tendency of the police is to underenforce the law"—i.e., that police make substantially fewer arrests than citizens' observed behavior would warrant.[45] More specifically, Reiss found that in 43 percent of the felony cases and 52 percent of the misdemeanor cases he examined, police did not arrest even though they had probable cause to do so. As he went on to argue, before they arrest police often need to have a moral belief that the law should be enforced. By the same token, once having made an arrest, they become enraged at prosecutors who drop charges or judges who give light or suspended sentences.[46]

The situations in which police are more likely to arrest, and the types of people that police are more likely to arrest, have been neatly summarized by Donald Black:

1. Most arrest situations arise through citizen rather than police initiative.
2. Arrest practices sharply reflect the preferences of citizen complainants, especially in the desire for leniency.
3. Police use routine arrest power far less than written law would allow.
4. Evidence is an important factor in arrest.
5. Probability of arrest is higher in legally serious than in relatively minor crime situations.
6. The greater the relational distance between complainant and suspect, the greater the likelihood of arrest.
7. Probability of arrest increases when a suspect is disrespectful toward the police.
8. No evidence exists to show that the police discriminate on the basis of race.[47]

While many of these conclusions have also been drawn by other investigators, it is the last one that has been the object of most thought and debate.

As was noted in the analysis of person-to-person violent and property crimes, blacks account for a far larger percentage of arrests than their percentage in the population (see Chapters 9 and 10). This raises the question whether the police discriminate against blacks. Although there is no doubt that the relationship between police and the black community is tense, the evidence that police systematically discriminate against blacks has been inconsistent.[48] Some studies have indicated that racial differences disappear when other variables are taken into account. For instance, Donald Black observed that racial differences disappeared when the variable "respect" was considered: i.e., police are more likely to arrest those who are disrespectful of their authority, and blacks are more likely to be disrespectful.[49] Edward Green, who examined racial differences in arrests in Ypsilanti, Michigan, concluded that bias is more a matter of social class than of race. In particular, migrant whites showed higher arrest rates than Michigan-born blacks at each occupational level.[50]

On the other hand, more recent studies have found that police do discriminate against blacks, especially in minor criminal matters. Richard Lundman has shown that police are more likely to give traffic tickets to blacks.[51] John Hepburn found that police are more likely to arrest blacks under conditions later viewed as inadequate to justify prosecution.[52] Other studies have found that police are more likely to use force against blacks (see below). In considering the issue of race and arrest, it might also be noted that race of complainant and race of police officer should be taken into account. In many cases, offender and complainant are of the same race. Concerning police, one study found that black police officers are more likely than white officers to arrest blacks and to write official reports in response to complaints of blacks.[53]

In thinking about arrests and the larger issue of police discretion, it must be recognized that arrests cannot always be taken at face value. Suspects may be picked up on minor charges in order to give police an opportunity to interrogate them. Also, police may "overcharge" suspects, perhaps with the intention of plea-bargaining at a later point.[54] Arrest clearance rates may become ends in themselves in that they are taken as measures of police efficiency.[55] On skid row, police are more likely to use arrest to handle situations than to enforce the law.[56] Whatever the reasons, the use of arrests for purposes other than those for which they were intended is an abuse of discretion that may undermine

> not only . . . due process of law, but also the basic standard of justice—that those equally culpable shall be given equal punishment.[57]

Use of force

The use of force is the other major area in which police exercise discretion. As with arrest, police are given the authority to use force but are more often told what *not* to do than *what* to do. Over the years, police have used a variety of types of force, often called "brutality" or "abuse" by those subjected to them. (See Box 17.) The crisis of confidence experienced by the police in the 1960s opened up for public discussion a number of questions related to the legitimate nature of force and the proper limits to police behavior.

Box 17: Police Abuse in the Black Community

Police abuse is a fact of life in every black community—none of us is immune. NCBL (National Conference of Black Lawyers) member, attorney John Walker was beaten mercilessly in a bar in Mississippi by the police on New Year's Day 1977 and then charged with aggravated assault and battery on a police officer. During the summer of 1975, three black men sitting in a parked car in the Washington Heights section of Manhattan found themselves in a rain of police fire in a case of what the police called "mistaken identity." A young black child of 15, shot and killed by a New York officer in the Brownsville section of Brooklyn, was in a basement preparing for a birthday party, when the police charged in on a false burglary tip. One social scientist views the problem in this way: "police have one trigger finger for whites and another for blacks."

SOURCE

Lennox S. Hinds, "The Police Use of Excessive and Deadly Force: Racial Implications," in Robert N. Brenner and Marjorie Kravitz, comps. *A Community Concern: Police Use of Deadly Force*, U.S. Department of Justice, Washington, D.C., January 1979, p. 8.

The use of force is a key form of police discretion. Here, Missouri police officers aim their guns at an office where a gunman has taken two hostages. (UPI)

The proper limits for use of force by the police have never been clearly defined in American society. Several traditional police practices—forced confessions, beatings, ordering people to "move on," etc.—were, as late as 1930, found by the National Commission on Law Observance and Enforcement (the Wickersham Commission) to be "shocking in . . . character and extent."[58] Although the forms may have changed somewhat, one can still readily find examples of police abuse, especially in the black community (Box 17). Moreover, as was mentioned earlier, there is also a disturbing pattern of "police riots," in which force has been used in an arbitrary and discriminatory manner.

In a systematic study of police brutality in the late 1960s, Reiss found that the meanings attached by citizens to police brutality covered the "full range of police activities":

The use of profane and abusive language
Commands to "move on" or "get home"
Stopping and questioning people on the street or searching them and their automobiles
Threats to use force if not obeyed
Prodding with a nightstick or approaching with a pistol
The actual use of physical force or violence itself

In this study, in which observers accompanied police officers on patrol, Reiss found police brutality—in particular, the excessive use of force—to be "far from rare.'' Reflecting traditional police behavior, it was most likely to be directed against lower-class citizens. Furthermore, police brutalized citizens even though observers were present.[59]

Looking at the use of force from another perspective, the National Center for Health Statistics has reported that 3082 citizens died between 1968 and 1976 (342 per year) as a result of ''legal intervention'' at the hands of law enforcement officers.[60] The majority of these deaths were attributable to discharge of firearms by police officers. Moreover, the number of civilian fatalities appears to be on the increase. Between 1960 and 1969, an average of 284 were killed each year. Between 1952 and 1959, the figure was 236 per year.[61] The use of force also shows racial selectivity: 49 percent of those killed between 1960 and 1969 were non-white.[62]

It must also be pointed out that police officers suffer from deadly violence inflicted upon them in the line of duty. The 558 killings of police officers between 1974 and 1978 would average out to 112 per year (about one officer for every three civilians). Although the figure 112 represents an increase over earlier years, there has also been an increase in the number of police officers, so that the rate of fatalities among officers has remained about the same. At the same time, the rate of civilian fatalities has increased considerably, as is shown by the figures in the preceding paragraph.[63] Moreover, in evaluating police fatalities, it is interesting to note that the rate is actually lower than that of some civilian occupations, such as nursing, agriculture, contract construction, and transportation.[64]

Studies of the confrontations between police and civilians which result in fatalities have come to contrasting conclusions. After examining more than 900 incidents, Arthur Kobler concluded that many of them were unjustifiable. His data showed that 30 percent of the civilian victims were not involved in any criminal activity or misdemeanor. One-fourth of the victims had no weapon; half had a firearm; 15 percent had a knife or sharp instrument. One-fourth of them were shot in the back, and one-third in the head.[65]

Kobler's conclusions have been questioned in a study conducted by Catherine H. Milton and her associates. Examining 320 shooting incidents from seven police departments in 1973–1974, they found that many shootings are difficult to categorize after the fact as justified or unjustified. Generally, they attempted to show that police in the 1970s were far more likely than those in the 1960s to ''rely on negotiation and patience rather than on snap decisions and arbitrary commands to establish and preserve order.''[66] Although Milton et al. did acknowledge that the proportion of blacks and other minorities shot by police is greater than their proportion in the population, they argued that it is ''not inconsistent with the number of blacks arrested for serious criminal offenses (Index crimes).''[67]

The problems of defining the proper use of police force are evident if we consider public attitudes and police attitudes about its use. The public, it would appear, is quite accepting of police violence. In one survey, 32 percent of a random nationwide sample of 1374 American males felt that police should ''almost always'' or ''sometimes'' shoot to kill when dealing with gang troubles. Thirty percent felt they should do so during social disturbances. When asked separately whether the police should shoot but not to kill, 64 percent replied ''almost always'' or ''sometimes'' for dealing with gang troubles, and 61 percent for racial disturbances.[68] A commission on violence found considerable support for the following statements:

> 78 percent agreed: "Some people don't understand anything but force."
>
> 56 percent agreed: "Any man who insults a policeman has no complaint if he gets roughed up in return."
>
> 51 percent agreed: "Justice may have been a little rough-and-ready in the days of the Old West, but things worked better than they do today with all the legal red tape."
>
> 45 percent agreed: "The police are right to beat up unarmed protestors, especially when these people are rude and call them names."[69]

Concerning police attitudes toward the use of force, studies beginning with the classic research of William Westley in the 1930s and 1940s have found violence to be a normal part of confrontations with civilians in which respect for the police is an issue.[70] Brutality can also be explained in terms of promotion possibilities and occupational stress. Violence may be used to effect an arrest for which a citation or promotion is later awarded. Occupational stress for police officers can include administrative red tape, lack of administrative backing, conflicting expectations on the job, and shift work. When stressses become great, police officers are predictably more likely to brutalize suspects.[71]

Offenders' rights

This discussion of police authority also needs to take into account the attempt on the part of the Supreme Court, under Chief Justice Earl Warren, to curtail some of the discretion formerly allowed to police officers. A number of famous cases have been decided. The *Mapp* decision (1961) declared that evidence illegally seized could not be used at a subsequent trail. The *Escobedo* (1960) and *Miranda* (1966) decisions placed substantial restrictions on police interrogation practices: suspected offenders must be warned of their rights to remain silent, to consult a lawyer, to have a lawyer present during interrogation, and if indigent to have a lawyer appointed to the case.[72]

However far-reaching the Supreme Court decisions may be, their impact upon police practices is less than completely clear. It is interesting to note that the Supreme Court under Chief Justice Warren Burger, far more conservative in orientation, has chipped away at but not struck down these basic decisions.[73] At the same time, it must also be recognized that

> police power and authority is derived from law. So much residual power has been granted to the police in achieving their formal statutory responsibilities that they have carved out a large, amorphous, de facto area of informal power and authority; and the courts have sustained this control.[74]

Whether we are speaking of arrests or use of force, the proper role of discretion is an issue which goes to the heart of police work. Police are given more authority with fewer controls than virtually any other occupational group in American society. All three major perspectives on policing are critical of the discretion presently allowed to police officers. As we have seen, sociologically oriented criminologists are concerned with the manner in which improper discretion can subvert democratic values. Critical criminologists have been concerned with the use of discretion to harass and control working-class and minority populations. Those who see police as symbol manipulators would argue that the law serves not as a prospective guide to police action but "as a mystification device or canopy to cover selectively, legitimate, and rationalize police conduct."[75]

Corruption

Having examined the critical area of discretion, let us continue our discussion of present-day concerns about policing by looking at police corruption. Once again, we have a long-standing problem that has changed its form somewhat but continues to plague police work.

In police corruption we see a paradox of criminal justice: the involvement in criminal activity of those sworn to uphold the law. The law itself contains no separate category for police corruption but subsumes it under the various state crimes that apply to public officers in general. John Meyer has recently offered the following conceptual definition:

> . . . An accommodation through which the effect and force of a law is neutralized in violation of the lawful exercise of police authority for personal gain by one or more parties to the act[76]

As we shall see, personal gain can take a number of forms.

The forms of corruption range from what appear to be relatively minor acts such as mooching, chiseling, favoritism, and prejudice to major ones such as extortion, bribery, shakedown, and premeditated theft. (See Box 18.) The Knapp Commission made a distinction between "meat-eaters" who aggressively sought out opportunities for personal gain and "grass-eaters" who accepted the opportunities that came their way.[77] Lawrence Sherman has suggested a classification that would run along organizational lines. It has three types: (1) "rotten apples and rotten pockets," in which only a few police officers accept bribes; (2) "pervasive unorganized corruption," in which corruption is widespread but not organized; (3) "pervasive organized corruption," in which corruption is highly organized and may range beyond the police department to include other groups such as politicians and even the media.[78]

In that corrupt activities are naturally kept secret, it is nearly impossible to estimate their extent. However, investigations into police corruption have turned up many instances of it. Systematic studies such as that of the Knapp Commission, which examined police corruption in New York City in 1970–1971, have found corruption to be widespread—although the Knapp Commission did say that most police did *not* engage in corrupt behavior.[79] An investigation of the Chicago police force, after nearly a decade under a "reformer" police superintendent, led to Chicago's largest police scandal; the investigation found that police were actually aligned with organized crime.[80] Similarly, Reiss's study, cited earlier,

Box 18: An Informal "Code" of Police Deviance

Mooching: An act of receiving free coffee, cigarettes, meals, liquor, groceries, or other items either as a consequence of being in an underpaid, undercompensated profession *or* for the possible future acts of favoritism which might be received by the donor.

Chiseling: An activity involving police demands for free admission to entertainment whether connected to police duty or not, price discounts, etc.

Favoritism: The practice of using license tabs, window stickers or courtesy cards to gain immunity from traffic arrest or citation (sometimes extended to wives, families and friends of recipient).

Prejudice: Situations in which minority groups receive less than impartial, neutral, objective attention, especially those who are less likely to have "influence" in City Hall to cause the arresting officer trouble.

Shopping: The practice of picking up small items such as candy bars, gum, or cigarettes at a store where the door has been accidently unlocked after business hours.

Extortion: The demands made for advertisements in police magazines or purchase of tickets to police functions, or the "street courts" where minor traffic tickets can be avoided by the payment of cash bail to the arresting officer with no receipt required.

Bribery: The payments of cash or "gifts" for past or future assistance to avoid prosecution; such reciprocity might be made in terms of being unable to make a positive identification of a criminal, or being in the wrong place at a given time when a crime is to occur, both of which might be excused as carelessness but no proof as to deliberate miscarriage of justice. Differs from mooching in the higher value of a gift and in the mutual *understanding* regarding services to be performed upon the acceptance of the gift.

Shakedown: The practice of appropriating expensive items for personal use and attributing it to criminal activity when investigating a break in, burglary, or an unlocked door. Differs from shopping in the cost of the items and the ease by which former ownership of items can be determined if the officer is "caught" in the act of procurement.

Perjury: The sanction of the "code" which demands that fellow officers lie to provide an alibi for fellow officers apprehended in unlawful activity covered by the "code."

Premeditated theft: Planned burglary, involving use of tools, keys, etc., to gain forced entry or a prearranged plan of unlawful acquisition of property which cannot be explained as a "spur of the moment" theft. Differs from shakedown only in the previous arrangements surrounding the theft, not in the value of the items taken.

SOURCE

Ellwyn Stoddard, "The Informal 'Code' of Police Deviancy: A Group Approach to 'Blue-Coat' Crime," *Journal of Criminal Law, Criminology, and Police Science*, vol. 59, 1968, pp. 201–213.

found that 20 percent of the police officers observed by the teams of researchers were in violation of criminal laws. The violations included taking money and property from defendants, stealing merchandise from previously burglarized stores, taking bribes instead of issuing traffic citations, and accepting money to alter testimony.[81]

One theory would see systematic corruption as related to (1) the environment within which police do their work (for example, the organization of vice in a community); (2) the organizational capacity of the department (for example, the ability of police organizations to change leadership following a scandal); and (3) changes in policy, which are often related to factors 1 and 2. If we take an environmental approach, control of police corruption can assume a variety of forms. For one thing, departments can mount arrest campaigns against bribery, instructing officers to press charges rather than to spurn offered bribes. For another, some discretionary situations that are corrupting can be controlled; e.g., unpopular laws such as sabbath violations and certain types of gambling can be enforced only upon request. Still another approach would utilize investigative techniques such as spying. In any event, there are controls for police corruption; the key appears to lie in changes in the environment within which the police work and changes in policy which are influenced by the capacity of police organizations.[82]

Each of our major perspectives on policing would see corruption as a problem inherent in police work, and one with consequences that can be severe:

> In whatever form, it reduces police morale, undercuts administrative control, induces policemen and the public to share a mutual perception of each other as hypocrites, and increases public cynicism (especially if scandal is involved). More importantly, it denigrates the social order represented by the police.[83]

Yet if we take the viewpoint of the police as oppressors, we could argue that they are more repressive when they are *not* corrupt and incompetent. From this point of view, the movement to professionalize police by eliminating or reducing problems such as these only paves the way for more efficient repression of the working class.[84]

Conflict with the Community

Given the historical development of police—and the police role, discretion, and corruption—it is almost inevitable that police are thrown into conflict with part or all of the communities they are designated to serve. In the late 1800s, there were clashes between police and workers. During the 1920s, police found themselves attempting to enforce the unpopular Prohibition laws. During the 1960s, police clashed with middle-class students. Today, there remains tension between police and black and other minority communities.

The tension between police and minority communities has been both long-standing and bitter. We have already seen the disproportionate use of police discretion to arrest and use force against blacks. Box 17 provided some vivid examples. Consider also the following comments of Lennox X. Hinds, former national director of the National Conference of Black Lawyers:

> We at the National Conference of Black Lawyers do not need scholarly journals to tell us that police lawlessness is widespread and particularly targets black citizens in big cities and small—for beatings, illegal surveillance and searches, for harassment, and for murder on the street. Each day letters and petitions come to my desk describing in gross and horrifying detail the experience of blacks in every walk of life at the hands of the police.[85]

Indeed, one spokesperson for the black community would attribute every major riot in the United States to "some precipitating police action."[86]

Two important phenomena need to be seen in the context of the conflict between the police and the community. One is the police subculture, which is in part a response to the conflict. The other is the attempts that have been made to give communities control over police work.

Police subculture

The police subculture is seen in the development of moral standards which differ from those of the community. For one thing, police tend to consider themselves "failures," "dirty workers," and minorities without honor.[87] For another, they are cynical, especially as they mature in police work;[88] and they become distrustful of people in general.[89] Outside groups, such as minorities, are particularly suspect.

Bill Sommerville has argued that the influence of the police subculture is so great that the police share many self-concepts with minorities:

> Both suffer from a lack of respect; both see the larger community as an enemy which does not understand them, both are aggressive in their response to those not in their community, both stay within their own group, and both see the other as a threat and strike out at the other.[90]

Another observer has gone even further, to argue that there is a "patrol" subculture separate and distinct from the general police subculture. Among other things, such a subculture helps patrol officers to cope with being at the bottom of the police ladder, supports them in the use of discretion, and serves as a source of recognition of accomplishments.[91]

The development of police subcultures is the result of a number of historical and social factors and is reinforced by the nature of police work as an occupation. Law enforcement is never totally popular; some elements of the community do not want various laws enforced, especially against themselves. As a result, police distance themselves and are also distanced from the communities they are supposed to serve. They may live away from the place where they work. Shift work may preclude regular social contact with "outsiders." Thus peer groups become a powerful source of support for police work.

Community control over police work

The conflict between police and the community is especially evident in disputes over how policing can be controlled. To put it another way: How should the community control police abuses of arrest and use of force? The conventional answer to this question has been to tighten civilian control over police operations. Two approaches have been taken. One is to make the police administratively accountable to political figures such as the president, the governor, the mayor, or an elected council. Another is to have prosecutors and judges review the substantive aspects of police work by making decisions on whether and how to prosecute the persons arrested by police officers.

Both conventional methods of police control have led to problems. Accountability to political figures has left the police subject to political influences and generated resentment on the part of police officers. Review by the courts has provided a check upon the police; as we shall see in Chapter 17, over half of those arrested by the police are subsequently dismissed by prosecutors, and many other cases are prosecuted on reduced charges. At the same time, there has developed an immense rivalry—accompanied by "deals"—among police, prosecutors, and judges.[92]

As a way to avoid the limitations of conventional controls, the early 1970s saw the establishment of a number of community relations units designed to open up communication between police departments and communities, especially minority communities.[93] However, so deep-seated are the differences between police departments and communities that these units have largely failed to achieve their aims. Many police officers have remained unsympathetic to the programs; some have openly sabotaged them. Nevertheless, several reforms have emerged: (1) some command and control responsibilities were decentralized; (2) the importance of peacekeeping, as distinct from law enforcement, was recognized; (3) police services were linked to community needs through study and consultation with local community organizations; and (4) the idea of measuring the effectiveness of the programs with social science research techniques lent seriousness and importance to an activity that had not formerly rated official attention.[94]

Despite their accomplishments, community relations programs have been the object of criticism by many criminologists. Radical criminologists who see the police as oppressors have been particularly critical, and they are pessimistic about the possibility of resolving conflicts between police and community. In their estimate, the "new community pacification strategies" (as they would call them) involve no real transfer of control from police to the communities, nor do they deal with the underlying social conditions which cause crime.[95]

In taking a symbolic approach to policing, Manning too sees the police in an adversarial relationship with the public. However, he argues that the police develop a myth to reconcile the divergent perspectives:

> To the middle classes, the police wish to symbolize crime control (of the lower classes), while their actions toward the middle classes are in accord with the middle classes' general moral and social position (that is, they maintain good police/community relations). On the other hand, to the lower classes, the police wish to symbolize . . . police/community relations, while their conduct is in actuality crime-repression oriented.[96]

In a field study of police, William K. Muir, Jr., makes specific the symbolic nature of police work by seeing the police officer as a "streetcorner politician" or as an "oppressor [who] must instinctively anticipate resistance from the oppressed."[97] He finds police officers to be continually confronted by four "paradoxes of coercive power": the paradox of dispossession ("The less one has, the less one has to lose"); the paradox of detachment ("The less the victim cares about preserving something, the less the victimizer cares about taking it hostage"); the paradox of face ("The nastier one's reputation, the less nasty one has to be"); and the paradox of irrationality ("The more delirious the threatener, the more serious the threat; the more delirious the victim, the less serious the threat"). Furthermore, Muir argues, so complex is the social and moral reality of the police role—often requiring rapid decision making in immensely complex situations—that the officer is always tempted to simplify moral choices; to be self-defensive, detached, remorseless, and irrational; and to segregate police life from personal life.[98]

We have explored the history of police work and examined several present-day concerns about policing. In the next section, we need to tie our understanding of policing into what we have learned about crime in American society. How, we need to ask, does our system of policing relate to the types of crime that are prevalent today?

POLICE AND CRIME

Examining police in relation to crime in today's society demands that we confront a paradox. On the one hand, police deal directly with a relatively small part of crime. On the other hand, much police work is focused upon matters that few people regard as criminal. The paradox is of practical significance because the police are expected to do something about crime; indeed, as we have seen, their "success" is often evaluated in terms of reductions in crime rates. Let's explore the paradox further by looking at major types of crime, unrealistic expectations, and the social-class implications of police work.

Major Types of Crime

The paradox of police work in relation to crime becomes apparent if we take a systematic look at policing in relation to the types of crime discussed in Chapters 9 through 15: person-to-person, violent; person-to-person, property; corporate; crimes against organizations; social-order; organized; and political.

Person-to-person crimes

It is the major types of person-to-person crimes—i.e., violent and property—for which police have generally assumed responsibility. These major forms are highlighted in the police statistics found in the Uniform Crime Reports. For the index crimes, police keep records both of crimes reported to them and of arrests they make. Their records have been supplemented by the LEAA victim surveys (see Chapter 3), which include most of the index crimes. As a result, the person-to-person index crimes provide us with the most extensive information upon which to base a tentative assessment of how the police relate to crime.

The most striking fact is that police have direct contact with only a small percentage of the crimes that are committed. For index crimes as a whole, only 21 percent of those reported to police are cleared by arrest—about one in five. The remainder elude official action. Clearance rates run from a high of 76 percent for murder to a low of 15 percent for motor vehicle theft. Violent crimes have higher clearance rates than property crimes, although only 26 percent of robberies are cleared by arrest. Moreover, the percentage of crimes cleared by arrest declines sharply if one relates arrests to estimates formulated on the basis of data from victim surveys. Although different methods are used to calculate the survey

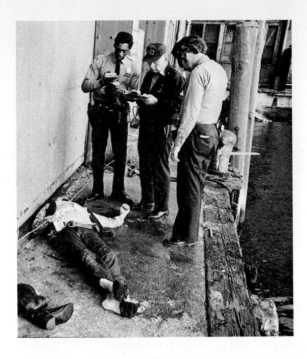

Police check the body of a young man found floating in the Hudson River. Investigating seemingly accidental deaths and identifying the victims are common tasks for metropolitan police forces. (LEONARD FREED/MAGNUM)

estimates, a rough calculation (dividing the number of arrests by the number of crimes as estimated in victim surveys) shows that the clearance rate drops markedly. For index crimes as a whole—with the exception of murder, which would not affect the overall clearance rate—the rate drops from 21 percent to 11 percent. (See Table 23.)

TABLE 23. Number of Crimes Reported and Percent Cleared by Arrest; and Number of Crimes Estimated by Victim Survey and Percent Cleared by Arrest

Index crime	Crimes reported	Percent cleared	Crimes estimated by victim survey	Estimated percent cleared
Murder	22,520	72	N.A.[a]	N.A.
Aggravated assault	643,720	58	1,768,683	21
Rape	81,540	48	191,739	20
Robbery	574,130	24	1,115,870	12
Burglary	3,739,800	14	6,684,018	8
Larceny	7,154,500	19	10,631,289	13
Motor vehicle theft	1,074,000	14	1,392,837	11
Total index offenses	13,290,210	19	21,784,436	12

[a] N.A. = not applicable.

SOURCES: Data for "crimes reported" and "percent cleared" from: Federal Bureau of Investigation (FBI), *Uniform Crime Reports–1981*, Government Printing Office, Washington, D.C., 1981, pp. 36 and 152. Data for "crimes estimated by victim survey" from: Timothy J. Flanagan, David J. von Alstyne, and Michael R. Gottfredson, eds., *Sourcebook of Criminal Justice Statistics—1981*, Government Printing Office, Washington, D.C., 1982, p. 232. Totals include personal and household victimizations.

The relationship between policing and the other types of crime is even more tenuous. Corporate crime, by some estimates the most costly of all forms of crime—is untouched by conventional policing methods. Although there are a host of federal and state regulatory agencies concerned with corporate crime, theirs is more often a judicial role than a policing role. In one study of antitrust violations, the most established area of corporate crime, it was found that between 80 and 90 percent of matters coming to antitrust lawyers at the U.S. Department of Justice are turned down. Antitrust enforcement is hindered by the ambiguity of antitrust law, by changes in interpretation, by the length of time required for prosecution, and by the large amounts of information that are required in most cases. The result is that the number of indictments is minimal compared with the dollar volume of corporate crime.[99]

Crimes against organizations, which also incur costs that exceed those of person-to-person property crime, are policed in a still different manner. Here there is a heavy reliance on private police (see Chapter 12). There is no way of measuring the proportion of crimes against organizations with which private police deal. Nevertheless, it appears that the number of private police is substantial and on the increase. At the same time, the dollar volume of goods stolen from organizations is high.

Social-order crimes are the most problematic area for law enforcement. They have long been a focus of attention for uniformed, professional police officers. Indeed, as we have seen, the attempt to control activities such as gambling, prostitution, and certain aspects of alcohol use was part of the rationale for developing policing in the 1800s. Today, after a decade of attempts to decriminalize some of these offenses, there are still more arrests for social-order crimes than for person-to-person crimes. In fact, 31 percent of all arrests are for the social-order crimes, as compared with 22 percent for person-to-person crimes. Although there is also an enforcement effort on the federal level, through the Drug Enforcement Agency, despite all the policing efforts, gambling, prostitution, and narcotics and alcohol abuse appear to be quite extensive.

There are several other ways in which social-order crimes are problematic for law enforcement. As we have seen, the possibilities for corruption are great. Moreover, absence of a complaining victim means that police have to take unusual measures to police these crimes; for example, they must rely on paid informers and assume plainclothes roles. Finally, social-order crimes pose problems in the use of police discretion, such as whether or not to arrest petty offenders.[100]

Since organized crime is so closely related to social-order crime, many of the policing problems mentioned above also apply to it. Policing is especially difficult where part or most of the political power structure of the community is controlled by organized crime (e.g., "Wincanton" and Seattle; see Chapter 15). Perhaps the most effective form of policing organized crime is the work of the "organized crime task force." However, there is no way of judging whether the several thousand arrests made during the 1970s have brought about an appreciable difference in organized crime activities.

Finally, there is political crime. When it comes to dissent, the police have, as we saw in Chapter 15, been quite active in their policing efforts, many of which are controversial. Police have used a variety of trespass, rioting, and public-order laws as the basis for taking action against dissenters. On the other hand, abuse of political office has been virtually ignored as a law enforcement problem for the police.

In short, much crime of all types seems to elude police efforts. About four out of five of the serious index offenses reported to the police remain uncleared by arrest. Police rarely come into contact with the corporate criminal, the organized criminal, or the political criminal. They do make many arrests for social-order crimes; but these arrests appear to have relatively little impact on the prevalence of these crimes.

Unrealistic Expectations

The tenuous relationship between police work and crime would not present a problem were it not for the assumption that police *can* or *should* do something about crime. The police themselves have fostered this assumption. As Manning notes, in the 1930s, with the publication of the Uniform Crime Reports,

> the police began to tie their own fate to changes in the crime rates as measured by these published figures. The crime rate became the responsibility of the police both in the sense of measuring, explaining, and accounting for it, and for substantially reducing it.[101]

Even on the federal level, the assumption that the government can and should do something about crime, combined with an unclear vision of what it should do, has frustrated the development of the Safe Streets Act and subsequent attempts to establish a viable Law Enforcement Assistance Administration to administer it.[102]

There are two problems with expecting the police to do something about crime. One is that police priorities may be unclear, in that police are also expected to do something about many other problems. Indeed, as we have noted, 80 percent of requests made of police agencies do not involve criminal matters. The other is that whether or not the police can do something about crime remains an open question. If crime is the result of social conditions, there may be limits to what the police can do about it. To put it simply, arresting people, while it may prevent and deter some individual criminals, does not change social conditions. In the words of the former police commissioner of Boston, Robert Di Grazia:

> Most of us are not telling the public that there is relatively little the police can do about crime. We are not letting the public in on our era's dirty little secret: that those who commit the crime which worries citizens most—violent street crime—are, for the most part, the products of poverty, unemployment, broken homes, rotten education, drug addiction and alcoholism, and other social and economic ills about which the police can do little, if anything.[103]

In other words, we may need to revise our expectations of policing by recognizing the social context within which the police work.

The third part of the "police paradox" is that the structure of police work raises serious questions about inequality in American society: Whose crimes are policed, and whose crimes should be policed? In particular, leaving corporate crime relatively unpoliced and crimes against organizations to be policed privately means that the uniformed police spend a great deal of time dealing with offenses which—while some are very serious—may be of comparatively less social importance (the minor property crimes are an example).

The question whose crime should be policed is one with serious ramifications. To rigorously police corporate crime and crimes against organizations would require a considerable expansion of policing efforts which are now handled at the state and federal rather than the municipal level. New techniques would have to be developed; for example, open publication of data from the Internal Revenue Service, more rigorous attention to air and water quality, and new levels of accountability for professionals such as doctors and lawyers. In these situations it is the auditor, accountant, or data-processing officer responsible for fraud who would become the policing agent. In short, if one is to police upper- and middle-class crime in a highly technological society, policing can no longer be left to the uniformed police officer. In fact, certain crimes elude routine police efforts to the extent that they can be policed only by "whistle-blowers," coworkers who do not fear the consequences of revealing crimes of which they are aware.[104]

In other words, to balance the scales of social justice requires some hard choices. One route would be to expand the policing of middle- and upper-class crimes, so that they too would incur social penalties. Another would be to reduce the policing of person-to-person and social-order crimes, especially minor ones, so that the lower classes are not disproportionately subject to policing. Whatever the choice, it is clear that the present system—which polices person-to-person and social-order crimes, some of which are comparatively minor, while leaving corporate crimes, crimes against organizations, and other middle- and upper-level crimes comparatively unpoliced—is manifestly unfair.

POLICING ALTERNATIVES

The serious questions raised by police work—discretion, corruption, conflict with the community, and the tenuous relationship between police and crime—lead us to wonder about alternatives or solutions. As it turns out, there are many possibilities. Three are suggested by the major perspectives we have considered. Others would go beyond these to picture a police state at one extreme and a "depoliced" society at the other.

The solutions advanced by proponents of the major perspectives outlined earlier are probably quite clear by this point. The sociologists who see police as norm enforcers would seek to make them clearly accountable to the rule of law, although they would also note that the ultimate responsibility for the rule of law lies in the hands of the citizenry.[105] Critical criminologists who see the police as oppressors have called upon working-class and third world community groups to organize against police repression and to create neighborhood and block associations to provide police-type community services.[106] Finally, understanding the police as symbol manipulators demands, among other things, new ways of measuring police accountability in matters of public concern.[107]

Two alternatives that would go substantially beyond the possibilities suggested by the three major perspectives are polar opposites. One is the police state, in which the police have the upper hand in the entire administrative apparatus of the state. In a police state—i.e., a totalitarian society—the police can act secretly with virtually unchecked power.[108] The other, a far more optimistic possibility, would be a "depolicing" of society. This utopian alternative has been argued most eloquently by Donald Black, who gives the following scenario:

> If police protection were reduced, . . . the volume and intensity of self-help would be expected to rise correspondingly, reversing the trend toward ever greater dependence upon law.[109]

This idea is also supported by the innovative approach of Harold Pepinsky, who would see an increased commitment to ongoing, supportive relationships that would circumvent both the reporting of crime and the need for police services.[110] While "depolicing" is far from realization, it does imply that a reduction in policing efforts may at some point be a desirable direction for public policy.

SUMMARY

The police—seen as a group authorized in the name of territorial communities to handle whatever needs doing—have been the focus of much criminological attention in recent years. Three major perspectives on policing have emerged: police as norm enforcers, police as oppressors, and police as symbol manipulators. Each perspective has generated considerable study.

Police work emerged in nineteenth-century England under Sir Robert Peel. The English "bobbies" were constables who were paid low wages, given the possibility of advancement, disarmed, and subject to a number of checks. American police followed somewhat along the lines of the English bobbies; but they were organized locally rather than nationally, armed, subject to conflicting community pressures, allowed to enforce laws selectively, permitted to use brutality, and likely to be corrupt. Private police and vigilantes were also part of the American scene.

Over the years policing has undergone significant changes. The 1930s saw a movement towards professionalization. The 1960s saw a crisis of legitimacy. Today, police are a large, powerful agency of social control. Law enforcement, which includes the police, is the largest of the criminal justice agencies, employing more than 700,000 people and expending over $13 billion per year. While less visible, private policing appears to be nearly as extensive.

There are a number of present-day concerns about police work. (1) As an agency of last resort, police have assumed a variety of roles, so that law enforcement has become only a small part of what police do. (2) Police are given an immense amount of authority and considerable discretion to arrest and to use force. Some studies of arrest suggest that police officers discriminate against blacks in minor criminal matters. Studies of police "brutality"—although that term is subject to various definitions—have found it to be quite extensive. Court guarantees of offenders' rights have attempted, with mixed success, to curtail certain forms of police discretion. (3) Corruption is a continuing problem, especially in a highly structured, "pervasive organized" form. Although statistics are unavailable, corruption is felt to be far from unusual. Control of corruption could come through changing the environments within which the police work. (4) Police have seen active conflict with some of the communities they are designated to serve. In response, they have developed a police subculture. Attempts of the past decade to create new forms of effective community controls over police work have been less than completely successful but have led to certain modifications of policing practices.

Perhaps the major paradox of policing is that police deal directly with a relatively small part of crime. Even for the index crimes for which police keep records of crimes reported, arrests, and crimes cleared by arrest, clearance rates are low. About four out of five crimes are never cleared by arrest. Some major types of crime remain unpoliced by traditional uniformed personnel and traditional methods of police work—especially corporate crime, crimes against organizations, and organized crime. Police do deal extensively with social-order crime, but it remains prevalent despite their efforts.

Part of the paradox of police work is that it is assumed, often by the police themselves, that police can do something about crime. However, this assumption is not tenable if crime is caused by social conditions. Another part of the paradox is that policing has enormous social-class implications. Balancing the scales of social justice requires either new forms of policing, to expand police work to upper- and middle-class crimes; or reducing the policing of person-to-person and social-order crimes, especially minor ones, so that the lower classes are not disproportionately subject to police power.

There are many possible alternatives to the present policing system. Sociologists who see police as norm enforcers would make them more accountable to the rule of law. Critical criminologists who see police as oppressors encourage people to organize against police repression and to develop block associations to provide community services. Criminologists who see police as symbol manipulators would establish new ways of measuring police accountability. Beyond these basic perspectives, sociologists interested in the police have also presented the pessimistic possibility of a police state and the optimistic one of self-reliant, supportive relationships among people which would reduce the need for police services.

NOTES

[1] Egon Bittner, *The Functions of the Police in Modern Society*, Government Printing Office, Washington, D.C., 1970, p. 39.

[2] David H. Bayley, "Police Function, Structure, and Control in Western Europe and North America: Comparative and Historical Studies," in Norval Morris and Michael Tonry, eds., *Crime and Justice: An Annual Review of Research*, University of Chicago Press, Chicago, Ill., 1979, p. 113.

[3] Herman Goldstein, *Policing a Free Society*, Ballinger, Cambridge, Mass., 1977.

[4] Center for Research on Criminal Justice, *The Iron Fist and the Velvet Glove: An Analysis of the U. S. Police*, 2d ed., Center for Research on Criminal Justice, Berkeley, Calif., 1977.

[5] Peter K. Manning, *Police Work: The Social Organization of Policing*, MIT Press, Cambridge, Mass., 1977.

[6] Jerome H. Skolnick, *Justice without Trial: Law Enforcement in Democratic Society*, 2d ed., Wiley, New York, 1975, p. 1.

[7] See: Ruben G. Rumbaut and Egon Bittner, "Changing

Conceptions of the Police Role: A Sociological Review,'' in Morris and Tonry, *Crime and Justice*, pp. 239–288.

[8] Center for Research on Criminal Justice, *The Iron Fist and the Velvet Glove*, p. 11.

[9] Ibid. See also: Richard Quinney, *Critique of Legal Order: Crime Control in Capitalist Society*, Little, Brown, Boston, Mass., 1974.

[10] Sidney L. Harring, "Policing in a Class Society: The Expansion of the Urban Police in the Late Nineteenth and Early Twentieth Centuries,'' in David F. Greenberg, ed., *Crime and Capitalism: Readings in Marxist Criminology*, Mayfield, Palo Alto, Calif., 1981, pp. 292–313.

[11] Peter K. Manning, "Dramatic Aspects of Policing,'' *Sociology and Social Research*, vol. 59, no. 1, 1974, pp. 21–29.

[12] Manning, *Police Work*, pp. 34–35.

[13] President's Commission on Law Enforcement and Administration of Justice, *Task Force Report: The Police*, Government Printing Office, Washington, D.C., 1967, p. 3.

[14] T. A. Critchley, *A History of Police in England and Wales*, 2d ed., Patterson Smith Series in Criminology, Montclair, N.J., 1972, pp. 42–45.

[15] Ibid., p. 39.

[16] Philip John Stead, "The New Police,'' in David H. Bayley, ed., *Police and Society*, Sage, Beverly Hills, Calif., 1977, pp. 73–84.

[17] Ibid.

[18] Charles P. McDowell, *Police in the Community*, Anderson, Cincinnati, Ohio, 1975, pp. 10–12.

[19] James F. Richardson, *The New York Police: Colonial Times to 1901*, Oxford University Press, New York, 1970.

[20] Roger Lane, *Policing the City——Boston, 1822-1885*, Harvard University Press, Cambridge, Mass., 1967.

[21] Ibid., p. 6.

[22] Wickersham Commission (National Commission on Law Observance and Enforcement), *Report on Lawlessness in Law Enforcement*, Government Printing Office, Washington, D.C., 1931.

[23] Milton Lipson, *On Guard: The Business of Private Security*, Quadrangle (New York Times), New York, 1975.

[24] Richard Maxwell Brown, "Historical Patterns of American Violence,'' in Hugh Davis Graham and Ted Robert Gurr, eds., *Violence in America: Historical and Comparative Perspectives*, rev. ed., Sage, Beverly Hills, Calif., 1979, pp. 19–48.

[25] James Q. Wilson, "What Makes a Better Policeman?'' *Atlantic*, vol. 223, March 1969, pp. 129–235.

[26] Manning, *Police Work*, pp. 97–98. See also: Gene E. Carte and Elaine H. Carte, *Police Reform in the United States: The Era of August Vollmer, 1905–1932*, University of California Press, Berkeley, 1975.

[27] E.g., see: David H. Bayley and Harold Mendelsohn, *Minorities and the Police*, Free Press, New York, 1969.

[28] Rodney Stark, *Police Riots*, Wadsworth, San Francisco, Calif., 1971.

[29] Michael J. Hindelang et al., eds., *Sourcebook of Criminal Justice Statistics—1980*, U.S. Department of Justice, Criminal Justice Research Center, Washington, D.C., 1981, pp. 7 and 21.

[30] Steven Spitzer and Andrew T. Scull, "Privitization and Capitalist Development: The Case of the Private Police,'' *Social Problems*, vol. 25, October 1977, pp. 18–29.

[31] Center for Research on Criminal Justice, *The Iron Fist and the Velvet Glove*, part II. See also: Harring, "Policing in a Class Society.''

[32] James Q. Wilson, *Varieties of Police Behavior: The Management of Law and Order in Eight Communities*, Harvard University Press, Cambridge, Mass., 1968, p. 18.

[33] Albert J. Reiss, Jr., *The Police and the Public*, Yale University Press, New Haven, Conn., 1971, p. 71.

[34] George Antunes and Eric J. Scott, "Calling the Cops: Police Telephone Operators and Citizen Calls for Service,'' *Journal of Criminal Justice*, vol. 9, 1981, pp. 165–179.

[35] PROMIS Research Project, *What Happens After Arrest? A Court Perspective of Police Operations in the District of Columbia*, National Institute of Law Enforcement and Criminal Justice, Law Enforcement Assistance Administration, U.S. Department of Justice, May 1978, pp. 48–49.

[36] Wilson, *Varieties of Police Behavior*.

[37] Center for Research on Criminal Justice, *The Iron Fist and the Velvet Glove*, part V.

[38] Manning, *Police Work*, pp. 317–19.

[39] Goldstein, *Policing a Free Society* p. 1.

[40] Wilson, *Varieties of Police Behavior*, p. 279.

[41] Ibid., p. 7f.

[42] Arthur Rosett, "Connotations of Discretion,'' in Sheldon L. Messinger and Egon Bittner, eds., *Criminology Review Yearbook*, vol. I, Sage, Beverly Hills, Calif., 1979 pp. 377–401.

[43] Abraham S. Blumberg, *Criminal Justice: Issues and Ironies*, 2d ed., New Viewpoints (Franklin Watts), New York, 1979, p. 54.

[44] Goldstein, *Policing a Free Society*, p. 1.

[45] Wilson, *Varieties of Police Behavior*, p. 49. (Emphasis omitted.)

[46] Reiss, *The Police and the Public*, pp. 134–38.

[47] Donald Black, "The Social Organization of Arrest,'' *Stanford Law Review*, vol. 23, June 1971, pp. 1087–1111.

[48] This discussion draws on: Donald Black, *The Manners and Customs of the Police*, Academic Press, New York, 1980, especially pp. 107–108.

[49] Ibid.; and see: Donald J. Black and Albert J. Reiss, "Police Control of Juveniles'' *American Sociological Review*, vol. 35, no. 1, February 1970, pp. 63–77.

[50] Edward Green, "Race, Social Status, and Criminal Arrest,'' *American Sociological Review*, vol. 35, no. 3, June 1970, pp. 476–490.

[51] Richard J. Lundman, "Organizational Norms and Police Discretion: An Observational Study of Police Work with Traffic Law Violators,'' *Criminology*, vol. 17, August 1979, pp. 159–171.

[52] John R. Hepburn, "Race and the Decision to Arrest: An Analysis of Warrants Issued,'' *Journal of Research in Crime and Delinquency*, vol. 15, January 1978, pp. 54–73.

[53] Robert James Friedrich, "The Impact of Organizational, Individual, and Situational Factors on Police Behavior,''

unpublished doctoral dissertation, Department of Political Science, University of Michigan, Ann Arbor, 1977, pp. 308–313.

54 For case studies of arrest abuses, see: Paul Chevigny, *Police Power: Police Abuses in New York City*, Pantheon, New York, 1969.

55 Skolnick, *Justice without Trial*, chap. 8.

56 Egon Bittner, "The Police on Skid-Row: A Study of Peace Keeping," *American Sociological Review*, vol. 32, no. 5, October 1967, pp. 699–715.

57 Skolnick, *Justice without Trial*, p. 181.

58 Wickersham Commission, *Report on Lawlessness in Law Enforcement*, no. 11, Patterson Smith, Montclair, N.J., 1968, p. 5; originally published by Government Printing Office, Washington, D.C., 1931.

59 Albert J. Reiss, Jr., "Police Brutality—Answers to Key Questions," *Transaction*, vol. 5, no. 8, July-August 1968, p. 10–19.

60 As reported in: Cynthia G. Sulton and Phillip Cooper, "Summary of Research on the Police Use of Deadly Force," in Robert N. Brenner and Marjoria Kravitz, comps., *A Community Concern: Police Use of Deadly Force*, U.S. Department of Justice, Law Enforcement Assistance Administration, 1979, p. 70.

61 Arthur L. Kobler, "Police Homicide in a Democracy," *Journal of Social Issues*, vol. 31, no. 1, Winter 1975, pp. 163–184.

62 Arthur L. Kobler, "Figures (and Perhaps Some Facts) on Police Killings of Civilians in the United States, 1965–1969," *Journal of Social Issues*, vol. 31, no. 1, Winter 1975, pp. 185–191, especially p. 187.

63 For a discussion from the perspective of the radicals, see: Paul Takagi, "A Garrison State in a 'Democratic' Society," *Crime and Social Justice*, vol. 1, Spring-Summer 1974, pp. 27–33.

64 Sulton and Cooper, "Summary of Research on the Police use of Deadly Force," p. 71.

65 Kobler, "Figures (and Perhaps Some Facts) on Police Killings of Civilians in the United States, 1965–1969."

66 Catherine H. Milton et al., *Police Use of Deadly Force*, Police Foundation, 1977; quotation from p. iii.

67 Ibid., p. 11.

68 Robert L. Kahn, "Violent Man," *Psychology Today*, vol. 6, June 1972, pp. 47, 48, 82–84. See also: Robert L. Kahn, "The Justification of Violence: Social Problems and Social Solutions," *Journal of Social Issues*, vol. 28, no. 1, 1972, pp. 155–175.

69 Campbell Report, *Law and Order Reconsidered*, Bantam, New York, 1975, especially p. 339.

70 See: Hans Toch, *Police, Prisons, and the Problem of Violence*, Government Printing Office, Washington, D.C., 1977, chap. 2.

71 William H. Kroes, *Society's Victim—The Policeman: An Analysis of Job Stress in Policing*, Thomas, Springfield, Ill., 1976.

72 Alexander B. Smith and Harriet Pollack, *Criminal Justice: An Overview*, Holt, Rinehart and Winston, New York, chap. 8.

73 Ibid., p. 181.

74 Blumberg, *Criminal Justice*, p. 104. (Emphasis omitted.)

75 Manning, *Police Work*, p. 101. (Emphasis omitted.)

76 John C. Meyer, Jr., "The Nature and Investigation of Police Offenses in the New York City Police Department," Ph.D. dissertation, State University of New York at Albany, 1976, p. 8.

77 *The Knapp Commission Report on Police Corruption*, Braziller, New York, 1972.

78 Lawrence W. Sherman, "Toward a Sociological Theory of Police Corruption," in Lawrence W. Sherman, ed., *Police Corruption: A Sociological Perspective*, Anchor (Doubleday), Garden City, N.Y., 1974, pp. 7–8.

79 *The Knapp Commission Report on Police Corruption.*

80 Herbert Beigel and Allan Beigel, *Beneath the Badge: A Story of Police Corruption*, Harper and Row, New York, 1977.

81 Reiss, *The Police and the Public.*

82 Lawrence W. Sherman, "Police Corruption Control: Environmental Context versus Organizational Policy," in Bayley, *Police and Society*, pp. 107–126.

83 Manning, *Police Work*, p. 355.

84 Center for Research on Criminal Justice, *The Iron Fist and the Velvet Glove*, pp. 32–42.

85 Lennox S. Hinds, "The Police Use of Excessive and Deadly Force: Racial Implications," in Brenner and Kravitz, *A Community Concern*, p. 8.

86 Charles E. Owens, "Looking Back Black," in Charles E. Owens and Jimmy Bell, eds., *Blacks and Criminal Justice*, Heath (Lexington Books), Lexington, Mass., 1977, pp. 11f.

87 Manning, "Dramatic Aspects of Policing."

88 Arthur Niederhoffer, *Behind the Shield: The Police in Urban Society*, Anchor (Doubleday), Garden City, N.Y., 1967.

89 Stark, *Police Riots*, especially chap. 3.

90 Bill Sommerville, "Double Standards in Law Enforcement with Regard to Minority Status," *Issues in Criminology*, vol. 4, Fall 1968, p. 39.

91 Thomas A. Johnson, "Police Resistance to Police Community Relations: The Emergence of the Patrolman Subculture," *Journal of Forensic Sciences*, vol. 17, no. 3, 1972, pp. 464–488.

92 For a discussion of these issues, see: David H. Bayley, "The Limits of Police Reform," in Bayley, *Police and Society*, pp. 219–236. See also: Chapter 17 of the present text.

93 D. P. Geary, ed., *Community Relations and the Administration of Justice*, Wiley, New York, 1975.

94 These reforms are outlined by: Rumbaut and Bittner, "Changing Conceptions of the Police Role," pp. 248ff.

95 Center for Research on Criminal Justice, *The Iron Fist and the Velvet Glove*, pp. 126–131.

96 Manning, *Police Work*, p. 360.

97 William K. Muir, Jr., *Police: Streetcorner Politicians*, University of Chicago Press, Chicago, Ill., 1977, p. 44.

98 Ibid., pp. 211–213.

99 Suzanne Weaver, *Decision to Prosecute: Organization and Public Policy in the Antitrust Division*, MIT Press, Cambridge, Mass., 1977.

100 Skolnick, *Justice without Trial*, chap. 7.

101 Manning, *Police Work*, pp. 97–98.

102 Malcolm M. Feeley and Austin D. Sarat, *The Policy Dilemma: Federal Crime Policy and the Law Enforcement Assistance Administration, 1968–1978*, Univeristy of Minnesota Press, Minneapolis, 1980.

103 Robert F. DiGrazia, "Intelligence Report," *Parade Magazine, San Diego Union*, August 22, 1976.

[104] Charles Peters and Taylor Branch, eds., *Blowing the Whistle: Dissent in the Public Interest*, Praeger, New York, 1972.
[105] Skolnick, *Justice without Trial*, chap. 11.
[106] Center for Research on Criminal Justice, *The Iron Fist and the Velvet Glove*, pp. 194–197.
[107] Manning, *Police Work*, pp. 356–375.
[108] Blumberg, *Criminal Justice*, pp. 63–65.
[109] Black, *The Manners and Customs of the Police*, p. 197.
[110] Harold E. Pepinsky, *Crime Control Strategies: An Introduction to the Study of Crime*, Oxford Univeristy Press, New York, 1980, chap. 5.

Criminal Court

After arrest and booking by police, suspected offenders are put into the criminal court system. It is in this system that they are (1) found guilty or not guilty; and (2) if found guilty, sentenced. Being found guilty or not guilty involves a complex series of steps. Depending on how a case proceeds, a suspect may be taken before a magistrate to have the arrest recorded, investigated by a prosecutor, indicted by a grand jury, and brought before a judge for arraignment. Finally, the suspect may plead guilty or not guilty. A suspect who pleads guilty will be sentenced. A suspect who pleads not guilty will be tried before a judge or a jury. A defendant found not guilty will be let free; a defendant found guilty will be sentenced.

There is a social paradox in the day-to-day operation of the criminal court. On the one hand, the courts profess some of the noblest ideals of American society: equal justice for all; adversarial proceedings to determine truth; and constitutionally guaranteed rights of offenders, such as the right to a speedy and public trial, the right not to have excessive bail imposed, and the right not to have cruel and unusual punishments inflicted. On the other hand, as we shall see, the operation of the courts belies these ideals. Very few offenders use their right to a public trial; justice is far more often the result of bargaining among prosecutors, defense attorneys, and judges. There is much evidence to suggest that social variables such as the class and race of the offender are very important when it comes to justice, especially the sentence received by the offender. Moreover, the considerable discretion allowed to prosecutors and judges suggests that our criminal court system is (in the traditional phrase) a "rule of men" rather than a "rule of law."

As with the police, it is only in recent years that criminologists have turned their attention to the operation of the criminal court. The early writers of the classical school of criminology were more concerned with how legislatures formulated criminal law than with how criminal courts worked in practice. Writers in the positive tradition of criminology were far more interested in pathology of offenders than in their processing through the criminal court system. The lack of criminological emphasis on the courts had its counterpart in the court system itself: many court officials maintained a "purple curtain" of secrecy about how the courts actually worked. Research on the courts has rarely been encouraged.[1]

Since the late 1960s, criminology has made a distinct turnabout. Researchers have gone into the courtroom and gained access to case records. Sociologically oriented criminologists have become intrigued by the organizational processes and accommodations underlying the supposedly objective operation of the courts. Critical criminologists have become preoccupied with injustices perpetrated by the courts. Many criminologists have concluded or implied that conviction for criminal behavior—i.e., designation of criminal status—often has more to do with how the offender is processed through the criminal court than with his or her actual behavior. Sentencing of offenders is especially problematic and in many cases is influenced by social variables which hardly demonstrate a commitment to equal justice for all.

In this chapter we shall concern ourselves with how criminal courts operate in today's society. We shall begin by examining three major perspectives taken by criminologists in their studies of the courts. Then we shall look at the history of the criminal court and three present-day issues related to the functioning of the court: case attrition, plea bargaining, and current sentencing practices. Finally, we shall look at some recent suggestions for limiting the scope of criminal courts in our society.

THREE MAJOR PERSPECTIVES

Courts as Due Process

In thinking about the criminal courts, it is perhaps best to use as our first perspective a statement of how they should operate. Americans pay much lip service to the rule of law, and it is often held up as the standard for the courts to follow. The key is the Constitution, especially the Bill of Rights. Taken in their entirety, these documents articulate what Herbert L. Packer has called a "due process model," one designed to serve the needs and rights of individual defendants and limit the arbitrary use of governmental power.[2] Under this model, the defendant has certain guaranteed rights: to trial by jury, confrontation of accusers and witnesses in public trials, assistance of counsel, and indictment by grand jury; and not to be subject to illegal search and seizure, self-incrimination, excessive bail, and cruel and unusual punishments. Moreover, the Fifth and Fourteenth Amendments to the Constitution also include general omnibus due process clauses which have been interpreted to mean that the government must be fair in its proceedings against individuals. In recent years, a host of Supreme Court decisions have attempted to guarantee constitutional rights in criminal cases tried in state courts.

Criminologists have taken two major lines of criticism that call the "due process model" sharply into question. One line has argued that the courts are bureaucracies serving their own internal needs rather than guarding the rights of citizens who come into contact with them. The second sees the courts as perpetrators of the social injustices which characterize American society. It calls attention to the manner in which race and social class of offenders influence the quality of justice dispensed by the criminal courts.

Courts as Bureaucracies

Seeing the courts as bureaucracies has been an important part of the sociologically oriented literature since Donald J. Newman noted that avoidance of trial had become the primary objective of both the state and the accused in the criminal court process.[3] It has also been a central concern of Abraham S. Blumberg:

> In fact, the rational-instrumental goals of the court organization, in its urgent demand for guilty pleas, have produced a bargain-counter, assembly-line system of criminal justice which is incompatible with traditional due process.[4]

Finally, there have been more recent studies such as those of Roberta Rovner-Pieczenik and Boyd Littrell. As a result of these studies, it can be said that parties more often than not seek to avoid criminal trials; that a "shadow code" of informal collaboration among judges, prosecutors, and defense attorneys guides everyday court operations; and that disposition of cases may have less to do with legal evidence than with the personal style of the attorneys involved.[5] It can also be said that the bureaucratic organization of the courts has allowed detective bureaus of police departments and prosecutors to select cases, to develop evidence, and generally to take "the dominant positions in the organization of prosecution."[6]

Courts as Perpetrators of Injustice

The view of the courts as perpetrators of injustice has been a concern of both sociologically oriented and critical criminologies. There are numerous inequities in the administration of justice. Racial bias in imposition of the death penalty has been studied by writers such as Thorsten Sellin since the 1930s.[7] It has also been an important part of several studies of sentencing which will be reviewed below.

In its general form the argument that the courts dispense unequal justice has been most cogently stated by William J. Chambliss and Robert J. Seidman:

> The probability of a group's having *its* particular normative system embodied in law is *not* distributed equally among the social groups but, rather, is closely related to the group's political and economic position. . . . The higher a group's political or economic position, the greater is the probability that its views will be reflected in the laws.[8]

They go on to say, "Given this twist in the content of the law, we are not surprised that the poor should be criminal more often than the nonpoor."[9] In their book, Chambliss and Seidman present numerous data to support these propositions.

Some of the new criminologists have linked unequal justice to the development of monopolistic capitalism. As Richard Quinney put it:

> Justice is grounded not in some alternative idea of the social good or natural order, but in the survival needs of the capitalist system. Judgment is now in the hands of legal agencies of the capitalist state.[10]

Quinney sees criminal justice in the United States today as little more than an attempt on the part of the state to rationalize its mechanism of social control. Applying Quinney's approach to public defenders—lawyers who represent indigent clients—Gregg Barak finds that they undermine the position of the poor because their role assumes that the poor need the benevolence of the state to represent them.[11]

As we found in our examination of police work, each of the major perspectives is useful in explaining the role of the criminal courts in our society. Let's turn first to the history of the courts and then to some of the present-day issues confronting them.

CRIMINAL COURT: HISTORICAL DEVELOPMENT AND OVERVIEW

The English Experience

The English legal system is the product of centuries of experience. In its earliest form, at the time of the Norman conquest in 1066, justice was locally administered. England was divided into "tithings," a number of which made up the "hundred"; a number of hundreds made up a "shire." Criminal cases were heard in the hundred court or in the shire court.[12]

In criminal cases in early England, twelve "freemen" would serve as accusers, presenting under oath the names of those they believed to have committed crimes. Guilt or innocence would be determined either by compurgation or by the ordeal. To be cleared by compurgation, a defendant would be required to get oath takers who would assert that he or she had told the truth. Ordeal was based on the belief that God would intervene in the administration of justice. Ordeal could be by fire, water, or dry bread. In ordeal by fire, the defendant had to hold a hot iron and walk about 9 feet; then the hand that had held the iron would be bound, and three days later it would be examined by a priest. A foul wound was taken to indicate guilt; a clean wound, innocence. In one form of ordeal by water, the accused had to plunge an arm into a pot of boiling water to retrieve a stone; the condition of the burn on the arm would indicate the verdict. In ordeal by dry bread, the accused was required to eat dry bread; choking on it was considered proof of guilt.

Subsequent centuries saw a slow but substantial evolution of English legal institutions and the criminal court system. For one thing, the king extended the "peace" by assuming jurisdiction over increasing numbers of criminal cases. Also, certain basic institutions appeared, including the grand jury, which was responsible for examining evidence against and presenting indictments to those suspected of crimes; and the petty (petit) jury, which was responsible for determining guilt or innocence after hearing evidence from both sides. These centuries also saw the development of habeas corpus—which meant that persons could not be held in prison without a trial—as a cornerstone of English law.

American Criminal Courts

Unique characteristics

The basic English legal institutions of the grand jury, the petit jury, and habeas corpus are all included in the Constitution of the United States. Moreover, English legal experience is also reflected in our adversarial or accusatory type of legal system. In this system there are two opposing lawyers, one for the state and one for the defense; each presents facts favorable to his or her side to an impartial judge or jury. The function of the judge or jury is to listen passively and then make critical decisions. A judge makes decisions on the basis of precedent, which means that any given decision is to be based upon earlier decisions of the same court. The use of precedent is designed to ensure consistency in legal decision making.[13]

Although imported from England, the American criminal courts have developed a structure that differs in some respects from the English model. Suspicious of the highly centralized judicial system dominated by the English royal governors of the colonial period, the colonists after the Revolution set up a decentralized judicial system in which each court was relatively autonomous. Moreover, courts were organized by states; today there are 51 court systems—50 state and 1 federal. Judges were selected on a political basis, usually through election. At the same time, law was made by the legislature and there was a deemphasis of judge-made law. There was also a further check on the authority of judges in the form of a multiple appeal system under which cases, in a variety of circumstances, might be appealed from inferior courts to general trial jurisdictions and finally to appellate courts.

Today, it is the trial judge who handles most of the cases that pass through the courts. As presiding officer in the criminal trial, the judge oversees the fairness of the trial proceedings. In particular, judges decide whether evidence and testimony should be sustained or overruled. They present cases to the jury with a charge which instructs the jury how to reach a verdict. After the jury has reached a verdict, judges set sentences for offenders who are convicted. Judges' power to set sentences enables them to play a key role in plea bargaining.

Another important part of the American court structure is the prosecutor. Rather than allowing the police to prosecute, as is the case in the English system, Americans created the public office of prosecutor (who in some jurisdictions is called the "district attorney," "solicitor," "state's attorney," "county attorney," or "city attorney"). After the Jacksonian reforms of the 1830s, prosecutors were most often elected. Prosecutors are technically responsible for seeking justice. The prosecutor has great discretionary power in the American system because it is he or she who decides whether or not there is sufficient evidence to prosecute a case; where the evidence is insufficient, the prosecutor recommends the release of the accused person. Moreover, most of the prosecutor's decisions are nonreviewable.[14]

Robert Hanna, accused of stabbing two of his daughters to death, stands trial in Paterson, New Jersey, January 1980. (ROBERT BRUSH/THE RECORD, N.J.)

The third major role in the American courts is that of the defense attorney. His or her task is to protect the legal rights of the accused. As a result of several Supreme Court decisions, all accused persons have a right to legal representation. In many criminal cases, the defense attorneys are public defenders who are paid from public funds to represent accused persons too poor to afford their own attorneys.[15] The adversarial system of American justice pits defense attorneys against prosecutors in the attempt to arrive at the truth in criminal cases.

In addition to judges, prosecutors, and defense attorneys, there are also other important elements in American criminal courts. One is the grand jury, before which prosecutors in some (but not all) jurisdictions must appear in order to request an indictment or "true bill" which requires the accused to be brought before the court. Composed of between 16 and 23 citizens, grand juries meet at periodic intervals.[16] Another element of the courts is the petit jury, normally composed of 12 persons (but sometimes of fewer), whose role is to decide whether the defendant is guilty or not guilty. The petit jury is expected to hear testimony from witnesses, from experts, and possibly from the accused, and then to reach its own independent decision about the facts of the case.[17] Finally, there are probation officers who are responsible for preparing reports to assist judges in sentencing offenders. Probation officers sometimes argue for treatment of the offender. One study of superior courts in a western county of the United States showed that judges concurred with these reports in 93 percent of the cases.[18]

Case processing in American criminal courts

Today, criminal courts process offenders through a complex series of steps from initial appearance to sentencing. (See Figure 10, pages 426–427; and Box 19, page 428.) Each step allows for charges to be dropped or cases to be dismissed. Many of the stages, especially the later ones, allow for judges, prosecutors, and defense attorneys to enter into negotiations over the charge or the sentence.[19]

As with the police (described in Chapter 16), it is in the interpretation of the history and present-day function of criminal courts that the differences among the major perspectives become apparent. A "due process" view of the courts calls attention to the constitutional guarantees of offenders' rights. From this perspective, the extension of constitutional rights to offenders in state criminal cases represents a most positive development. Cases such as *Gideon v. Wainright*, which established the right to counsel in criminal cases; *Mapp v. Ohio*, which declared unconstitutional the use of illegally seized evidence in state courts; and *Escobedo v. Illinois*, which served to protect defendants' right against self-incrimination, can be cited as hallmarks of a trend toward fairness and equity in criminal court procedure.[20]

On the other hand, the other two perspectives sharply question the appropriateness of the "due process" model. Those who see courts as bureaucracies claim that the adversary system is in its twilight and that

> . . . the concern for better and more extensive rules has served as a facade of moral philosophy to divert our gaze from the more significant development of the emergence of "bureaucratic due process," a non-adversary system of justice by negotiation.[21]

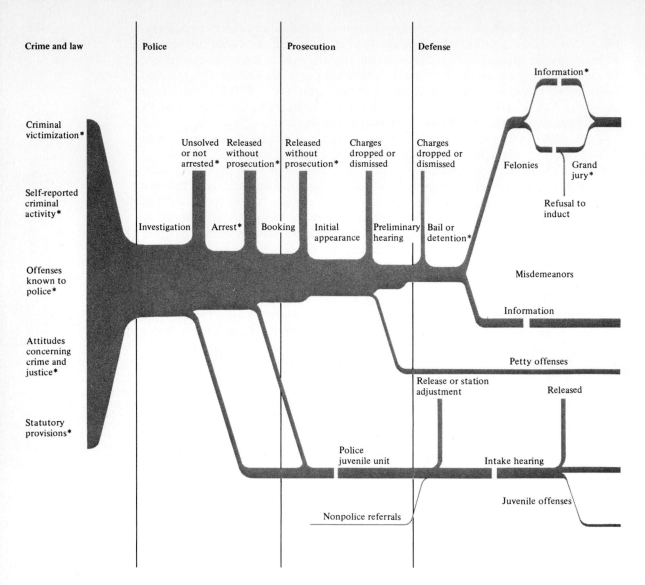

Crime and law **Police** **Prosecution** **Defense**

Criminal victimization*

Self-reported criminal activity*

Offenses known to police*

Attitudes concerning crime and justice*

Statutory provisions*

Investigation Arrest* Booking Initial appearance Preliminary hearing Bail or detention*

Unsolved or not arrested* Released without prosecution* Released without prosecution* Charges dropped or dismissed Charges dropped or dismissed

Information*

Felonies Grand jury*

Refusal to induct

Misdemeanors

Information

Petty offenses

Release or station adjustment Released

Police juvenile unit Intake hearing

Nonpolice referrals Juvenile offenses

FIGURE 10.
Overview of the criminal justice system as given in *Sourcebook of Criminal Justice Statistics—1978*. Asterisks indicate areas in the criminal justice system for which data are included in the *Sourcebook*. (SOURCE: President's Commission on Law Enforcement and Administration of Justice, *The Challenge of Crime in a Free Society*, Government Printing Office, Washington, D. C., pp. 8, 9.)

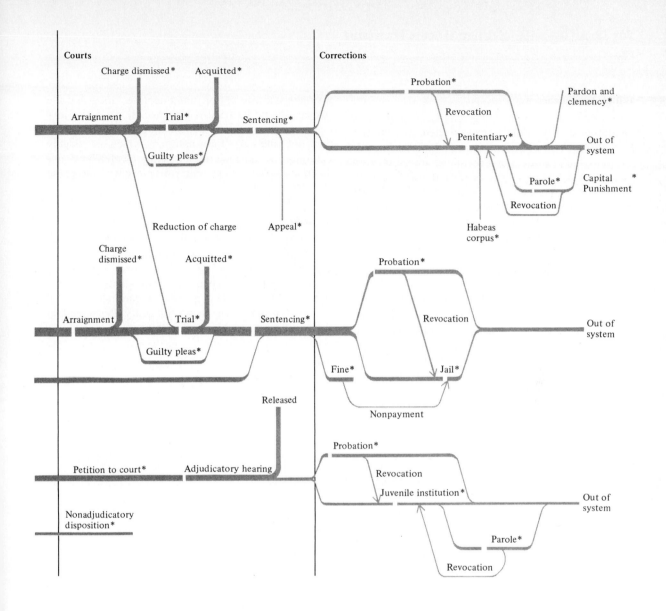

Some critical criminologists who see the courts as perpetrators of injustice would go one step further to argue that the courts are instruments of the ruling class and that legal reformers have "utilized the rhetoric of 'due process' to incorporate state control over the adjudication of the lower classes."[22]

Bearing the historical development and overview of the criminal courts in mind, let us turn now to consider some of the present-day concerns facing the courts.

Box 19: An Overview of Criminal Court Processing

Initial Appearance

After arrest, a suspect is fingerprinted, photographed, and advised of the right to remain silent and the right to counsel. He or she is then brought before a judge for an "initial appearance." At the initial appearance, the judge decides whether the complaint that led to the suspect's arrest is sufficient to charge the suspect with a crime and whether the court has jurisdiction in the particular case. Evidence is not evaluated; testimony is not taken. Few complaints are dismissed. The accused is notified of the charge by an oral reading of the complaint that led to the arrest.

Preliminary Hearing

After the initial appearance, the accused is given a "preliminary hearing," which is a judicial examination to determine "probable cause" for belief that a crime has been committed. In the presence of the judge, the defense attorney, and the accused, the prosecutor begins to detail the probable cause for his or her claim that a crime has occurred. The complaint becomes a charge. The police officer places the accused at the scene of the crime. Using discovery motions, the prosecutor reveals evidence concerning the guilt of the accused.

Bail or Detention

Also after the initial appearance, the accused is taken before a judicial authority for a bail hearing. Since the charges may remain pending for a period of time, the purpose of the bail hearing is to decide whether the accused should be released on bail, released on his or her own recognizance (i.e., without bail), or detained until the trial date.

Grand Jury Indictment

In this stage, the grand jury hears the evidence developed by the prosecutor. If it agrees that prosecution is warranted, a true bill or indictment declaring that the suspect should be tried is returned. If the grand jury does not agree—i.e., refuses to indict—the prosecutor may still file an "information," which is roughly equivalent to an indictment. Neither defendants nor defense attorneys nor judges are present at the grand jury proceedings.

Arraignment

At the arraignment, the indicted suspect appears before a judge. After hearing the charges, the suspect may plead guilty or not guilty. Once the plea is entered, the suspect becomes a defendant. If the plea is guilty, the defendant is held or continued on bail until sentencing. If the plea is not guilty, the defendant is given the choice of a trial with or without a jury.

Trial

In the trial, evidence is presented and challenged both by the prosecution and by the defense. On the basis of the evidence, a verdict of guilty or not guilty is reached. If found guilty, the convicted defendant may be held for sentencing, or released or continued on bail until sentencing. If found not guilty, the defendant is released unconditionally.

If the trial is before a judge, the judge decides on both matters of law and matters of fact. If the trial is before a jury, the judge decides on matters of law, and the jury on matters of fact.

Sentencing

At a separate hearing, the convicted defendant is sentenced. In sentencing, a number of alternatives are available to the court, based on the statutes in a given state. These generally include probation, incarceration, fine, and suspended sentence. Some states also provide for restitution to the victim and for community service.

Although the courts today face many problems, let us consider three which have attracted a great deal of criminological attention: case attrition, plea bargaining, and sentencing practices. As we shall see, each of these problems throws the "due process" model into question. Case dismissals and "bargain justice" have been special concerns of those who see courts as bureaucracies. Inequity in sentencing has been the subject of much attention from criminologists who see courts as purveyors of injustice.

To appreciate the first two concerns—case dismissals and plea bargaining—it is useful to note the enormous discrepancy between the number of felony arrests made by police and the number of offenders who serve time in prisons. Although there is much variation around the country, a rough estimate is that fewer than 5 of every 100 felony arrests result in a prison sentence. One reason is that many cases are dismissed at one point or another before they come to trial; another is that many cases are plea-bargained or sentence-bargained to a point where prison time is no longer an option. Let's examine case dismissal first, and then bargaining.

Case Attrition

There are many reasons why cases are dismissed before they ever get to trial. Two major studies have undertaken to follow groups of cases as they wind their way through the criminal court system. One tracked 17,534 arrests brought by Washington, D.C., police to superior court in 1974; the other tracked 100,739 felony arrests made by New York City police in 1971. The Washington study was conducted by the Institute for Law and Social Research (INSLAW); the New York City study was conducted by the Vera Institute of Justice (VERA). Although both studies document the enormous attrition of cases after arrest, they analyze that attrition from rather different perspectives.[23]

Both studies found the amount of attrition to be extremely high. The findings of the INSLAW study can be summarized as follows:

> More than half of the 17,534 adult arrests for felonies and misdemeanors brought to the Superior Court in 1974 were rejected or dismissed by the prosecutor. Judges dismissed another 8 percent of the arrests; 6 percent were not adjudicated because the defendants violated their obligation to return to the court; and 1 percent left the court due to grand jury rejection. The remaining cases either went to trial (4 percent of all the arrests went to trial as felonies, 6 percent as misdemeanors), or were disposed of as guilty pleas (13 percent as misdemeanors and 10 percent as felonies).[24]

In the VERA study, which took a different analytical approach, 56 percent of felony arrests resulted in convictions for some offense. Only 15 percent of the arrests resulted in conviction for a felony. Of all those arrested for felonies, only 5 percent were given prison sentences of more than the one year prescribed for all felonies.[25]

In analyzing the reasons behind case attrition, the INSLAW study focused on the nature of the arrest. There were surprisingly few differences in percentage of arrests leading to conviction for the major groups of crimes. The study did find that four factors led to a higher percentage of convictions: (1) tangible evidence was recovered; (2) two or more lay witnesses testified; (3) the crime involved strangers; (4) there was less time lapse between offense and arrest. These factors operated for each of the major groups of crime. In robbery, for instance, recovery of tangible evidence increased the proportion of convictions from 25 to 40 percent of cases; the testimony of two or more lay witnesses increased convictions from 27 to 38 percent; and the involvement of strangers increased convictions from 30 to 34 percent. Time lapse from offense to arrest also made a dramatic difference. Where it was less than 5 minutes, 43 percent of the arrests led to conviction. Where it was more than 24 hours, only 23 percent led to convictions.[26]

The INSLAW study also documented the key role of the prosecutor in processing cases through the court system. As noted above, more than half of the felony arrests were rejected or dismissed by the prosecutor. Further analysis shows that there are two points at which such rejection or dismissal can occur: (1) at the preliminary hearing stage and (2) after arraignment. Of the 17,534 cases, 21 percent were rejected at the preliminary hearing and 29 percent after arraignment. The reasons differed somewhat. For initial rejections, the findings parallel those for arrests; i.e., they are often due to problems with evidence or witnesses. However, the reasons for rejection or dismissal after arraignment were more varied: in 32 percent of these cases no reason was given; in 28 percent the offender completed a successful diversion program; in 13 percent there were problems with witnesses; and the remaining 27 percent involved a range of other problems. There is also a curious contradiction. A review of case loads over several years suggests that the prosecutor's office appeared to be moving in the direction of rejecting a slightly lower percentage of cases at the preliminary hearing stage but increasing rejection after arraignment. It would appear that seemingly technical policy changes made rather substantial differences in the manner in which defendants were being processed.[27]

Two other findings from the INSLAW study are also worthy of note. One is that a relatively small proportion of police officers—15 percent—produced over half of all the arrests that led to conviction; i.e., some officers appeared able to make "arrests that stuck." Another is that a small percentage of defendants accounted for a relatively large number of arrests, prosecutions, and convictions. Taking a five-year perspective on recidivism, the study found that

> 7 percent of the defendants accounted for almost one quarter of all arrests; 12 percent of those prosecuted for 32 percent of all prosecutions; and 5 percent of those convicted, for 15 percent of all convictions.[28]

In other words, there was a substantial minority of recidivist offenders. At the same time, it can be said that the majority of those who were arrested, prosecuted, and convicted were processed only once during the five-year period.

In contrast to the INSLAW study, the VERA study focused upon relationship between offender and victim as an explanation of case attrition. In order to do this, the VERA researchers interviewed police officers, prosecutors, defense attorneys, and judges who were concerned with the cases in their sample. They found the courts to be flooded with criminal cases resulting from conduct that could be seen as

> the explosive spillover from ruptured personal relations among neighbors, friends and former spouses. Cases in which the victim and defendant were known to each other constituted 83 percent of rape arrests, 69 percent of assault arrests, 36 percent of robbery arrests, and 39 percent of burglary arrests.[29]

They went on to observe that reluctance of the complainants to pursue prosecution, whether because of reconciliation with the defendants or because of fear, "accounted for a larger proportion of the high rate of dismissal than any other factor."[30] It is also interesting to note that while the penal laws make no mention of relationship between offender and victim, judges, prosecutors, and some police officers apparently take it into account on a regular basis.

As it turned out, there was a second factor in the VERA study which was important in both conviction and sentencing: the defendant's previous record. Defendants with heavier criminal histories were more likely to be convicted and, if convicted, to receive heavier sentences than those with lighter or clean histories.[31]

In short, both the INSLAW and the VERA studies documented the enormous number of cases which leave the criminal justice system for one reason or another. However, in accounting for the attrition, the two studies employed different approaches. The INSLAW study drew attention to the importance of the prosecutor and factors related to tangible evidence, witnesses, relationship between parties, and time lapse between offense and arrest. The VERA study found the relationship between offender and victim to be very important, although the defendant's previous criminal record was also a strong factor.

Plea Bargaining

We have seen that many cases are dropped by prosecutors. Of the remainder—those which do go to court—the majority are plea-bargained. Basically, a "plea bargain" is "the defendant's agreement to plead guilty to a criminal charge with the reasonable expectation of receiving some consideration from the state."[32] Five major types of plea bargains have been distinguished: (1) judicial participation and indication of the sentence; (2) modification of charges by the prosecutor; (3) prosecutorial agreement to make sentencing recommendations; (4) type 2 and type 3 combined; (5) type 1 and type 2 combined.[33]

Considered in terms of the charge, the plea bargain may involve "horizontal charge reduction," in which a defendant picks one, two, or three out of many similar charges and pleads guilty only to those; or "vertical charge reduction," in which a defendant pleads guilty to a less serious charge. Concerning the latter, it is important to note that a given criminal incident often involves multiple charges, some of which are more serious than others. For example, an armed person burglarizing an apartment would be committing four crimes: breaking and entering, theft, criminal trespass, and possession of a dangerous weapon. In such a case, plea bargaining could consolidate the four and than reduce the one charge to criminal trespass, a lesser crime.

Since much plea bargaining occurs within the judicial system and remains hidden from public view, it is difficult to quantify the cases falling into each type of bargaining. However, there is little doubt that plea bargaining is far more common than trials are in virtually all jurisdictions of the United States. One study conducted by Herbert S. Miller and his associates found that guilty pleas ran from 65.6 to 93.5 percent of cases in various jurisdictions with populations of more than 500,000 in 20 selected states. They were correspondingly high in smaller jurisdictions, where the proportion varied from 67.3 percent to 96.2 percent of cases.[34]

Looking at a metropolitan criminal court between 1950 and 1974, Blumberg found that between 86 and 95 percent of cases were decided by guilty pleas while 5 percent or less were disposed of by trial.[35]

Perhaps the most definitive study of plea bargaining was conducted by David A. Jones. Looking at 21 states and the District of Columbia, he too found that the rate of guilty pleas varied from 67 to 97 percent. However, he went on to note that guilty pleas were used much less often in violent crimes than in nonviolent crimes. Property crimes such as forgery, burglary, and theft were especially likely to be plea-bargained. Jones also listed ten national trends in plea bargaining: (1) Single charges are reduced at least one grade (e.g., from class C to class D felony or from felony to misdemeanor). (2) Multiple charges are reduced to no more than two. (3) Even though permissible by law, consecutive sentences are rarely imposed. (4) All pending charges are incorporated into one plea. (5) Use of a weapon rarely adds to a sentence, even where that is allowed by law. (6) Where public defenders engage in trade-offs between offenders they regard as "good" and "bad," they usually make things easier for those seen as "good." (7) There is some evidence of "batch processing," in which prosecutors make comprehensive deals for a group of cases. (8) Public defender agencies sometimes engage in "court busting" tactics by threatening to bring too many cases to trial. (9) Delayed payment of legal fees fosters plea bargaining because lawyers are under financial pressure. (10) Fee ceilings discourage lawyers from bringing cases to trial.[36]

To explain the dynamics of plea bargaining, Pamela J. Utz suggests three models. One is the "administrative model," in which plea bargaining grows out of the need to handle large case loads. It stems from the statutory threat of severe sanctions and is encouraged by indeterminate-sentencing laws in states such as California. The second is the "adversary bargaining" model, in which the prosecutor's office denies favorable early deals in order to build a tight case against defendants. The third is the "embrace of negotiation" model, in which the prosecutor's office actively facilitates the negotiation process by "undercharging" and accepting the participation of judges and public defenders in court negotiations. Utz's study of California found that counties such as San Diego approximated the "adversary bargaining" model while counties such as Alameda were closer to the "embrace of negotiation" model.[37]

It is interesting to note that plea bargaining is by no means a recent phenomenon. In a historical study of criminal cases in Connecticut going back to 1880, Milton Heumann has observed that the proportion of cases going to trial was not really higher in earlier years than it is at present.[38] Albert W. Alschuler found plea bargaining to be reported in surveys conducted during the 1920s. Its beginnings, he argues, can be traced to the early 1900s, when relatively simple criminal procedures were replaced by lengthy criminal codes which invited challenge and negotiation. Moreover, its use increased as the "due process" movement made the criminal trial a far more elaborate affair than it had been in earlier times.[39]

Nevertheless, despite its prevalence and historical basis, bargaining justice continues to be regarded with suspicion. Certainly, bargaining justice is contrary to the notion of due process; the constitutional right to a fair trial is given up. In one recent public opinion survey of respondents in the state of Washington, the

Despite its historical basis and its widespread use, bargaining justice continues to outrage many citizens.   (CHARLES GATEWOOD)

courts were generally seen as too lenient and 82 percent of those polled were against charge reduction or plea bargaining.[40] Perhaps even more cogent is a statement made in 1973 by the National Advisory Commission on Criminal Justice Standards and Goals, which found (among other things) that plea bargaining encouraged offenders to give up their constitutional right to a fair trial, that its use left many statutes unenforced, and that it gave judges too much power. The commission went so far as to advocate the prohibition of plea bargaining by 1978, a goal that has, of course, proved elusive.[41]

The negative aspects of plea bargaining should not be allowed to obscure its positive functions, which perhaps explain why it continues despite strong disapproval in practice and principle. There are three major positive functions.

For one, many cases processed by criminal courts are matters of interpersonal disputes, such as barroom brawls, neighborhood squabbles, and disputes between spouses.[42] In such cases bargaining is useful in that it allows courts to consider factors such as strength of case, seriousness of offense in terms of its impact on the victim, offender's previous record, reputation of the offender, reputation of defense counsel, how police reported the incident, applicable sentencing provisions, victim's account of the incident, previous relationship between offender and victim, and the offender's attitude toward the victim.[43] In short, it allows courts to individualize the process of dispensing justice.

Second, bargain justice is reportedly favored by defendants. As Judge Milton Mollen commented:

> A defendant who pleads guilty receives mercy; a defendant who is convicted after trial receives justice.[44]

From a statistical viewpoint, the proclivity of defendants to bargain appears quite reasonable. With conviction rates in trials running over 75 percent, once caught up in the system a defendant has little chance of escaping conviction. This means that it makes sense for defendants to plead guilty to a lesser charge and thereby receive a lesser penalty.[45]

Third—and most important to criminologists who see the courts as bureaucracies—bargain justice represents the full bureaucratization of justice. It functions in a society in which jails are crowded, court dockets are long, and due process has become so elaborate that guilt is sometimes difficult to establish. Immensely practical, it saves the time and money incurred in trials and gives prosecutors leverage in cases where evidence is weak. It also gives prosecutors the opportunity to increase conviction rates, an opportunity which can often be turned to political advantage. In this sense, bargain justice is part of a historical trend which has made the prosecutor rather than the judge the key person in the judicial system.[46]

Case attrition and plea bargaining are two critical issues facing criminal courts. It remains now to examine sentencing, our third major issue. Although sentencing can also be seen as a part of bargain justice, its background is so complex that it merits a separate discussion.

Current Sentencing Practices

Sentencing of offenders who are found guilty is the second major function of criminal courts. To understand sentencing, we must first examine the rationale of sentencing, noting the considerable amount of discretion allowed to judges. Then we must review the substantial body of research which has examined racial and social-class discrimination in sentencing.

The rationale of sentencing

The sentences received by convicted offenders represent the cutting edge of criminal justice policy. According to Judge Marvin E. Frankel, the imposition of sentence is "probably the most critical point in our system of administering criminal justice."[47] Yet even a casual overview of sentencing reveals enormous disparities and a system which allows judges great discretion.

A number of people concerned with the criminal courts have commented on the great variation in sentences received by convicted offenders. Senator Edward Kennedy has called sentencing a "national scandal." Judge Frankel writes that there is

> compelling evidence that widely shared unequal sentences are imposed every day in great numbers for crimes and criminals not essentially distinguishable from each other.[48]

> Sentenced prisoners are being released prematurely from drastically overcrowded prisons; white-collar felons who have stolen hundreds of thousands of dollars are sentenced to give lectures on the evils of crime but are not required to disgorge their ill-gotten gains; poor street criminals are sentenced to long terms of imprisonment and on release promptly commit more crimes; and the victims of crime are totally ignored by the criminal justice system.[49]

If we take a systematic approach, we can distinguish disparity in sentencing between judges, between people who have committed the same offense, between offenders, between geographical areas, and between federal and state systems.[50]

Disparities in sentencing are reinforced by a legal system which allows judges great freedom in sentencing and fails to hold them accountable for the sentences they render. Box 20 demonstrates the extremes to which sentencing can go. One might also cite the case of Lynette Fromme, who attempted to assassinate President Ford. Under federal law her sentence could have involved nearly any term of years in prison. Under the applicable California statute it could have involved six months to life in prison, less then a year in a county jail, a fine not exceeding $5000, or probation. At the same time that judges are allowed such great freedom regarding choice of sentence, they receive virtually no training in sentencing, are given few guidelines, are subject to very little accountability or review, and engage in little consultation or interaction with other judges on the same bench concerning case disposition.[51]

Underlying the disparity among sentences are flexible sentencing policies. Legislatures have promulgated indeterminate sentences that allow decisions to be made by judges and parole boards in terms of individual offenders rather than in terms of individual acts. Such policies, which have been pursued since the latter part of the nineteenth century, reflect a shift from the thinking of the classical school (which emphasized the act) to that of the positivist school (which emphasized the offender). Once considered important reforms, positivist policies have in the past several years been subjected to much criticism. Let's take a look at the rationale behind flexible sentences geared toward the offender and then at present-day criticisms.

There are a number of reasons for flexible, indeterminate sentences.[52] To begin with, flexible sentences allow for individual needs and unique circumstances in which offenders may find themselves. Second, the lack of a universally accepted theory of crime causation has meant that sentencing policy has been subject to both classical and positivist influences. Third, one might argue that an area as large and as geographically and culturally heterogeneous as the United States should have sentencing policies that allow for local variation: for example, robbery may be far more serious to the community in a small town than in a big city. Fourth, judges' own temperaments and personalities differ, so that personal variables come to influence the decision-making process.[53] Finally, flexibility in sentencing may be necessary to deal with the pressures created in the day-to-day. operations of criminal courts.

One problem of the flexible, indeterminate sentence is—as was mentioned earlier—that it allows for so much variation that consistency is out of the question. It is reported that inmates of prisons are disturbed when they see fellow

Box 20: An Extreme Example of Sentencing

November 28, 4579

Circuit Judge Richard Samuels of Markham, Ill., imposed a sentence last week that risks making him look either like the harshest judge alive or the silliest. What looks harsh is sentencing a convicted murderer to a maximum of 2,600 years in prison. In theory, the prisoner might have to serve until Nov. 28, 4579, a date more appropriate to the log of the Starship Enterprise. What looks silly, or sillier, is that the defendant will be eligible for parole in 11 years and 3 months.

In truth, Judge Samuels is neither harsh nor silly. The problem does not lie with him but with the way many states still approach the issues of sentencing and parole. In this case, the judge knew that no matter what sentence he imposed, the murderer would be automatically considered for parole in 1991. The purpose of the exaggerated sentence was to send the then-parole board a reverberating message: This prisoner is truly dangerous.

Illinois has reformed its sentencing law since the case began, but many states still make themselves look harsh and silly by their sentencing systems. Judges are given wide discretion in the terms they mete out, including no set term at all. One frequent result is injustice; prisoners guilty of the same crime receive vastly disparate sentences. Bitterness smolders, and sometimes erupts.

Another result is political vulnerability. When the public becomes concerned about crime, the natural reaction of public officials is to throw the book at criminals. That is often hypocritical, given their knowledge that parole boards are likely to undo harsh sentences. It can also be self-defeating; recall New York's experience with the harsh Rockefeller drug law that was repealed last year. Life sentences for pushers did not deter pushers—only juries, which thought such a penalty too drastic for small operators.

There is a still more poisonous result of subjective sentencing: public cynicism. Word of a 2,600-year sentence, whatever its technical purpose, feeds the suspicion that no severe sentence means much, that "they all get off on parole."

As it happens, a solution to these problems is now making its way through Congress. Senator Kennedy has developed and nurtured extensive sentencing reform as part of his proposed new Federal criminal code. The proposal has just sailed through the Senate Judiciary Committee with bipartisan support and a parallel bill is being studied by a House committee.

The broad principles of the proposed system—already urged as a model for New York and other states—are sound and simple: no more parole and no more open-ended sentencing. Judges would mete out fixed terms according to guidelines. There would be time off for good behavior according to a set schedule. And to guard against either "crime-coddling" or hanging judges, either prosecution or defense could appeal against a sentence it thought unjust. At last, prisoners would know exactly and credibly how long they would have to serve—and so would the public.

SOURCE

New York Times, December 7, 1979, editorial page.

---

prisoners sentenced to much shorter sentences or other offenders, not in prison, receiving probation for crimes comparable to those they committed. In addition, critics of the effectiveness of rehabilitation have argued that sentences should be based not upon the offender's potential for rehabilitation but rather upon protection of the community, revenge, or "just deserts."[54] Finally, flexible indeterminate sentences—especially when unchecked—give public officials immense power that is subject to potential abuse.

In thinking about indeterminate sentences, it should also be noted that such sentences enable legislatures to pass their responsibility for setting sentencing guidelines on to judges or to parole boards. For instance, in the extreme case cited in Box 20, the judge had a wide choice of sentences from which he could choose. With such a wide choice, it might well be said that the judge was making law rather than applying law made by legislatures. His decision was further complicated by automatic eligibility for parole, which could make the effective sentence 11 years and 3 months rather than 2600 years. In cases such as these, the critical decision is passed beyond the judge to the parole board, an agency accountable neither to the legislature nor to the judge but to the state governor. Which agency—legislature, judge, or parole board—should make the sentencing decision is a question that lies at the heart of the current debate over sentencing.

Critics of the indeterminate sentence have offered three alternatives: flat-time sentences, presumptive sentences, and mandatory minimum sentences.[55] *Flat-time sentences* provide specific, relatively short-term punishments for all offenders, recidivists, or certain offenders in special circumstances. They are relatively simple, allow for "just deserts," and place authority for sentencing policy squarely in the hands of the legislature.[56] Andrew von Hirsch and Kathleen J. Hanrahan, proponents of flat-time sentences, were also two early avocates of abolishing parole.[57] The second alternative, *presumptive sentences*, would require legislatures to fix punishment for an average or typical offense in a given category rather than attempt to imagine a variety of circumstances and assign a correspondingly wide range of punishments. Sentencing judges could then vary the presumptive sentence to allow for aggravating or mitigating circumstances. The third alternative is a variation of the second: legislatures would assign *mandatory minimum sentences* which judges could increase but not decrease. It should be noted that all three alternatives would decrease the authority of parole boards, and to a lesser extent of judges, and increase the role of legislatures in determining sentencing policy.

Another approach to sentencing has been advanced by Leslie Wilkins and his associates, who have analyzed records of probation departments to find which factors are actually related to offenders and to the offense. As it turned out, only age and previous criminal records of offenders and aggravating and mitigating factors of offenses were related to sentencing decisions. Using these variables, they developed sentence models which stated in tabular form the sentence actually given in over 85 percent of the cases processed in the five-year sample period. Models such as these would provide judges with a set of sentencing guidelines that reflect actual rather than hypothetical possibilities.[58]

Despite the alternatives proposed for sentencing, flexible indeterminate sentencing continues to have its defenders and indeed its advocates. Probably its main attraction is that it holds out the possibility of individualized justice in a system that has become bureaucratic and, it follows, deindividualized:

It's said that like crimes should be treated with like sentences. . . . Yet I must, I will, I still cling to the ideal of individualized justice. . . . In abandoning individualization here we make it progressively easier to abandon it elsewhere. I fear that if we shift from concern with the individual to mechanical principles of fairness, we may cease trying to learn as much as possible about the circumstances of life that may have brought the particular offender to the bar of justice.[59]

Even Judge Forer, who sharply criticizes the disparities in present-day sentencing policies, would also allow for individualization:

> Rehabilitation of offenders is a worthy aim for a humane, democratic government. Despite the difficulties it poses and the past failures, it should not be wholly abandoned in pursuit of another indefinable mirage—just desert.[60]

In the end, the future course of sentencing is a matter of degree. There is no panacea for the ills of sentencing, no automatic solution that works for all cases. Each case is unique. As was noted earlier, an enormous proportion of cases involve some sort of previous relationship between the accused and the victim. In the spirit of repairing these troubled relationships, some exceptions to rigid rules may well be in order. At the same time, there is also a need for much greater certainty and consistency in sentencing if fairness is to be achieved:

> . . . Under presumptive sentencing a far greater number of serious criminals would be imprisoned but . . . the median duration of such imprisonment would be reduced. . . . Discretion and disparity will not be eliminated: Policemen will still decide whom to arrest; prosecutors will still engage in plea-bargaining and Presidents and Governors will still pardon and commute. But a major source of discontent and unfairness will be regulated.[61]

In other words, we need to recognize that classical and positivist thinking are inconsistent and find some compromise which avoids both the excessive rigidity of the classical school and the excessive flexibility of the positivist school.[62]

Racial and social-class discrimination in sentencing

The second aspect of current sentencing practice (rationale having been the first) is the way in which social variables, especially race, play a part in sentencing decisions. To the extent that social variables do influence sentencing, the American norm of equal justice for all has been violated.

The study of discrimination in sentencing is extensive and complex. One recent review of racial discrimination in adult criminal sentences covered 60 empirical studies.[63] Complicating the picture are the different offenses studied, the different methodologies used, and the different perspectives taken by researchers. Some of the studies have looked at socioeconomic status, which is often related to race. Perhaps it is no wonder that the findings have been less than consistent. Recognizing that we cannot reach a definitive conclusion, let's take a look at studies finding discrimination, studies not finding it, and attempts to explain the inconsistent findings.

Studies finding discrimination Some studies, especially earlier ones, have shown clear-cut racial bias in sentencing, especially in the imposition of the death sentence.[64] Studying reports of the attorney general of South Carolina for the years 1920–1926, H. C. Brearly stated in 1930 that "of the persons accused of homicide, the whites were found guilty in only 31.7 percent of the cases, while the Negroes were in 64.1 of the verdicts."[65] Studying both defendants and victims in 423 capital murder cases in North Carolina between 1930 and 1940, Harold

Garfinkel found that race of the victim made a critical difference. Of the blacks who murdered blacks, 5 percent received the death sentence. Of the whites who murdered whites, 15 percent received the death sentence. However, of the blacks who murdered whites, 43 percent received the death sentence. Finally, none of the whites who murdered blacks received the death sentence.[66] In a study which examined whether or not death sentences were executed in North Carolina between 1933 and 1939, Guy B. Johnson found that the proportion of death sentences commuted was about the same for blacks and whites, one in three; but if the offender was black and the victim white, the chance of receiving a commutation was only one in five.[67]

A number of more recent studies have also reported racial bias in sentencing. Concerning the administration of capital punishment, William J. Bowers argues that the lower mean age at execution of nonwhites compared with whites, as well as the lower percentage of cases appealed by nonwhites, is evidence of discrimination.[68] Similarly, Bowers and Glenn L. Pierce find that arbitrariness and discrimination in capital punishment continued after the *Furman* and *Gregg* decisions of the Supreme Court, which were designed to correct them.[69] Perhaps the sharpest pattern of racial discrimination occurs for black defendants who raped whites; in fact, in some states the death penalty for rape has been used mostly for blacks who had raped whites.[70] In a study which followed rape cases

One outcome of inequities in sentencing is that state prison populations are disproportionately male, poor, young, and minority-group members. (BRUNO BARBEY/MAGNUM)

through the courts, Garry D. LaFree found that even though they were no more likely to be arrested or found guilty, black men who assaulted white women received more serious charges and longer sentences. Moreover, the black men were more likely to have their cases filed as felonies, to have their sentences executed, and to be incarcerated in the state penitentiary.[71]

Some sentencing studies dealing with noncapital punishment and lesser offenses have also found evidence of racial discrimination. For example, Theodore G. Chiricos and his associates found that the Florida courts were more likely to impose the status of "convicted felon" on defendants who were older, black, and poorly educated, and who had a previous record.[72] In a work examining individual judges in a Georgia superior court (rather than the court as a whole), James L. Gibson found that three of eleven judges treated blacks more severely than whites while another three treated whites more severely than blacks.[73] Finally, Alan J. Lizotte found in a sample of Chicago court cases "gross inequality in sentencing . . . due to race and occupation and their indirect effects through not making bail."[74]

Studies failing to find discrimination   Challenging the studies which have uncovered patterns of racial or class bias in sentencing is another line of research which either has failed to show discrimination or has shown only mixed results. In this vein, one can cite a study by Chiricos and Gordon P. Waldo which—unlike the study by Chiricos et al. noted above—concluded that "socioeconomic status of convicted offenders is unrelated to the severity of the state's official sanction"; this study was based on an analysis of data on 10,488 inmates sentenced for 17 criminal offenses in North Carolina, South Carolina, and Florida.[75] Another study, by Michael J. Hindelang, compared arrest rates of whites and blacks in the Uniform Crime Reports, in National Crime Panel victimization surveys, and in self-report surveys; Hindelang also concluded that the high crime rates of blacks are accurate indicators of criminal behavior rather than a result of bias in the courts.[76]

In a comprehensive overview of nearly 60 articles on racial discrimination in sentencing for criminal offenses, Gary Kleck found much inconsistency in the reported findings. As Table 24 shows, more than half of the studies found no discrimination or a mixed pattern, whether for capital or noncapital sentencing. A pattern of discrimination was more apparent in capital than noncapital sentencing; in fact, in capital sentencing involving rape, four of five studies showed racial discrimination. In noncapital sentencing, severity of the defendant's previous record played a major role. When this factor was taken into account, patterns of discrimination were much less apparent.[77]

The studies of racial discrimination have also been challenged in another way: several recent studies have found that the courts are more strict in sentencing white defendants than black defendants. In their study of all males arraigned in a city in New York State, Ilene Nagel Bernstein and her associates found that white defendants, as well as those employed for longer periods of time, were "more severely sentenced."[78] Calculating executions of blacks and whites throughout the nation for murder, and relating those executions to homicide rates for blacks and whites from 1930 through 1967, Kleck concluded that "blacks were subject to a lower execution risk than whites."[79] Kleck also calls attention to the studies of H. A. Bullock and Martin A. Levin. Bullock found that significantly

TABLE 24. Summary of Research Findings on Racial Discrimination in Sentencing (Figures Are Numbers of Studies)

	Yes	*Mixed*	*No*	*Total*
Capital sentencing				
All studies	7	4	6	17
Murder	3	4	5	12
Rape	4	0	1	5
Noncapital sentencing				
All studies	8	12	20	40
Control for prior record	2	8	13	23
No control for prior record	6	4	7	17

SOURCE: Gary Kleck, "Racial Discrimination in Criminal Sentencing: A Critical Evaluation of the Evidence with Additional Evidence on the Death Penalty," *American Sociological Review*, vol. 46, December 1981, pp. 783–805.

shorter prison sentences were given to blacks convicted of murder;[80] Levin found that blacks received more lenient dispositions than whites in eight out of nine categories of offenses.[81] Finally, Randall J. Thomson and Matthew T. Zingraff discerned a consistent and substantial increase in both number and proportion of prison inmates who are white, who have not been imprisoned before, and whose present sentence is based on a single offense.[82]

Explaining the inconsistent findings A number of writers have attempted to explain the diverse findings of sentencing studies. Thomson and Zingraff noted that sentencing could be expected to vary because of changes over time and differences in jurisdictions, individual judges, and types of decisions. Hence, it may well be that the historical racial inequities in capital sentencing have diminished in the southern states since 1950 and, in any case, were never characteristic of the remainder of the United States.[83]

Another explanation is that the real discrimination in sentencing is not a matter of bias against blacks as offenders but rather a matter of devaluation of blacks as victims. As we saw in Chapter 9, most violent offenses involve members of the same race. To the extent that blacks are sentenced more leniently—as some of the recent literature noted above indicates—it is very possible that this bias reflects an assumption that black victims are less of a loss to the community than white victims.[84] Studies which have used victims' characteristics to account for sentencing patterns have found them to be most important. We have already considered La Free's finding that black men who assault white women receive more serious charges and longer sentences. In a study of 20 Florida counties in 1976 and 1977, Michael L. Radelet reported:

> . . . Those accused of murdering whites have a significantly higher probability of being placed in jeopardy of receiving the death penalty by being indicted for first degree murder than those accused of murdering blacks.[85]

However, once the indictment is made, racial differences disappear.

Radelet's finding that indictment is the critical variable points up the need for examining racial and class inequities not simply in sentencing decisions, but in the larger court system. This line of inquiry has been incisively pursued by Victoria Lynn Swigert and Ronald A. Farrell, who examined how a criminal court in a large urban jurisdiction in the northeastern United States used a court-affiliated diagnostic and evaluation center. They found that the court seemed to operate on the basis of a stereotype of a "normal primitive" person, often lower-class or black, who was supposedly prone to the spontaneous expression of violence. Defendants regarded as "normal primitive" received a certain pattern of processing: i.e., public counsel, denial of bail, and waiver of trial by jury. In effect, they were "denied the presumption of innocence constitutionally guaranteed to all." Blacks and those in low-prestige occupations were far more likely to be designated as "normal primitives"; and "normal primitives" fared poorly at all stages of the legal process.[86] Steven Burnet Boris has given support to Swigert and Farrell's model; he has found that the factors Swigert and Farrell cited as contributing to the "normal primitive" designation operate in the initial decision to prosecute cases.[87]

In thinking about inequities in sentencing, two additional points need to be borne in mind. First, there may be so little regularity in sentencing procedures that the nature of bias is difficult to determine. Lack of regularity is a result of indeterminate sentencing policies, which provide judges with an immense amount of latitude in sentencing offenders.[88] Moreover, sentencing is the end product of a "loosely coupled" criminal justice system in which organizational needs may override objectivity in decision making.[89]

Second, since most defendants in state criminal courts are poor, marginally employed, and of minority status, differences among them may not be sharply pronounced. Differential justice does not become fully apparent until one examines other types of jurisdictions and prosecution for other types of offenses.[90] To date, few studies have done this. One study, by John Hagan and his associates, examined white-collar offenders in ten federal district courts. This study found that these offenders do receive lenient sentences for white-collar crimes. However, because of the small number of cases, this disparity was noticeable in only one district, where the prosecution of white-collar crime was sufficiently aggressive to generate a large volume of cases.[91] In other words, one might say that the real disparity is that few white-collar cases or white-collar offenders are ever tried in court.[92]

In short, while there may be some clear examples of racial and social-class discrimination in sentencing, it is difficult to prove systematic bias on the part of the criminal court system itself. Some studies, especially those conducted in southern states in the early decades of the twentieth century, have found patterns of discrimination in sentencing; but others have not. A few have found "reverse discrimination" in that black offenders receive less severe sentences than white offenders.

The lack of clear-cut findings from studies of racial and class discrimination in sentencing has led researchers into more complex lines of questioning. There may be changes in sentencing patterns over time and in different places. Blacks may be devalued as crime victims, with the result that black offenders may be punished more leniently. Stereotypes such as the "normal primitive" may play a dramatic role in court decisions before sentencing. Sentencing procedures may be so flexible that bias attributable to offenders' race and class is not apparent. Last, white-collar offenses—and hence white-collar people—may receive far more lenient sentences, in part because they are processed through federal rather than state legal systems.

These more complex lines of questioning can also be seen as an attempt to refine the critical criminological perspective on the courts as perpetrators of injustice. The test of that perspective lies in its ability to locate the social sources of disparity in sentencing. If decisions before sentencing are the key, they need to be examined more fully. If indeterminate sentencing policies lead to such varied outcomes that sentencing is unpredictable, these policies need to be reviewed. If there are different court systems which process offenders of different racial and class backgrounds differentially, these systems need to be studied. At present, the numerous studies of racial and class discrimination do show that in some respects the courts have been and are perpetrators of injustice. Although the particulars remain to be developed, it is clear that the general perspective has already influenced much useful research on the criminal courts. Furthermore, there is little doubt that this perspective will continue to influence much future research in this area.

ALTERNATIVES FOR CRIMINAL COURTS

The problems posed by case attrition, plea bargaining, and sentencing practices have led some criminologists to advocate fundamental changes in the operation of the criminal court. One line of proposed change would be to have victims play a more active role in court proceedings. Another would be to intentionally divert more cases from court processing. A third would be to create a fundamentally different form of criminal court.

Involvement of Victims

In the past, criminal courts have emphasized prosecution of offenders to the point that victims have been almost totally ignored. Victims rarely receive compensation for injury or damage suffered; in some cases, they have to sue offenders in civil actions to recover property lost through crime. Victims also have to make the difficult decision whether or not to press charges against offenders. As witnesses, they are often required to make numerous court appearances.

However, the plight of the victim has been increasingly recognized in recent years. Many states now provide for restitution to victims who have lost property. Some states allow victims to be compensated for injuries or damages suffered, the compensation coming from a state fund amassed through fines.[93] Another step is to involve victims in court proceedings—in particular, in sentencing and plea-bargaining decisions.[94] Finally, women who are victims of rape are now interviewed by female police officers and given greater protection from public humiliation while testifying as witnesses.[95] Each of these provisions has merit; but none is universal or even widespread.

Diversion of Offenders

The second form of change advocated by criminologists is diversion of offenders from the court system. "Diversion" has many different meanings; but in general its purpose is to avoid processing offenders through the criminal court system.

Diversion can occur at any number of points. The police may refer arrested persons to treatment agencies. In the courts, there may be diversion from pretrial detention or diversion by the prosecutor. Diversion has even been tried after conviction. In each instance the emphasis is on returning the offender to the community, often to some form of community treatment.[96]

There are several rationales for diversion. One is that it avoids labeling a person as "criminal"—a label which makes it difficult for convicted offenders to return to society. Another is that offenders can be given appropriate treatment rather than punishment. Still another is that diversion relieves court congestion and saves the court costs of processing offenders. Given these advantages, it is hardly surprising that diversion became increasingly popular during the 1970s. There have been literally hundreds of diversion programs, frequently funded by the Law Enforcement Assistance Administration. Diversion has been especially popular for juvenile offenders, alcoholics, and narcotics addicts.[97]

However, despite their promise and widespread use, diversion programs have experienced a number of difficulties. In a recent review of diversion programs for juvenile offenders, Malcolm W. Klein listed no fewer than five categories of impediments to proper implementation of diversion programs: (1) insufficiently developed rationales; (2) inappropriately selected groups of clients; (3) insufficiently and narrowly conceived social services and treatment strategies; (4) professional resistance to attempts at reform; (5) inappropriate settings for programs. Furthermore, Klein reported, diversion programs have had unintended consequences such as "alternative encapsulation" (inserting children into a social service network that is as pervasive as the court network), relabeling of juvenile justice clients, and increases in number of clients drawn into the justice system.[98] This suggests that major problems need to be worked out before diversion programs can be successful.

Fundamental Changes in Court Structure

Some criminologists have argued for more fundamental changes of court structure than are implied by involvement of victims or diversion of offenders. They propose that the courts should assume dramatically new forms. Harold Pepinsky, for one, has argued for seeing criminal justice as one aspect of disputes and dispute management. From this viewpoint, the role of the courts would switch from deciding on blame or guilt according to law to attempting to resolve disputes, perhaps with the aid of third parties, in order to facilitate amiable, cooperative future relationships.[99] "Community moots," or centers for mediation and resolution of conflicts, which have been established in many urban neighborhoods, are models of this general idea.[100]

In attempting to conceptualize new forms of court structures, Larry L. Tifft has expressed doubt that the principal of legality "can satisfactorily resolve conflicts, settle disputes or meet needs." Hence, Tifft argues, we need to move to a "retrospective needs based justice," which would make the settlement of disputes a direct, face-to-face, collective process.[101] William L. F. Felstiner has contrasted two models of society—the technologically simple poor society and the technologically complex rich society—linking the former to resolution of disputes and the latter to adjudication or avoidance. Felstiner argues that in the United

States—a technologically complex rich society—quarrels involving different segments of heterogeneous communities are best resolved by avoidance or "lumping it" where practicable and by "adjudication where continued contact is inescapable."[102]

The proposals for fundamental changes in the operation of the criminal courts in American society take us somewhat beyond the major perspectives used by criminologists to study the criminal courts. Those seeing the courts in terms of the "due process" model have been more concerned with making them live up to their stated ideals than with basic changes in their structure. Those seeing the courts as bureaucracies, while chiefly concerned with criticizing the operation of courts, would also seek to eliminate some of the evils of overbureaucratization. The more radical possibilities presented here represent an attempt to conceptualize new forms of courts and new standards of justice that would begin to address some of the inequities perpetrated by the courts.

SUMMARY

Responsible for determining guilt or innocence and sentencing offenders, the courts are caught in a social paradox. On the one hand, they express some of the highest ideals in American society. On the other, their operation often falls far short of these high ideals. Since the late 1960s, criminologists have focused increased attention on the courts. Three major perspectives have emerged: courts as models of due process, courts as bureaucracies, and courts as perpetrators of injustice.

The present form of our criminal courts is the product of centuries of experience. Early England had locally administered justice in which guilt or innocence was determined by compurgation or ordeal. Over the centuries the king assumed jurisdiction over increasing numbers of criminal cases; and basic institutions—such as the grand jury, the petit jury, and habeas corpus—took shape. These institutions, as well as the adversarial and precedent-based structure of the English courts, were transplanted to the United States during the colonial period.

Although modeled on the English courts, American criminal courts after the Revolution assumed somewhat different forms. Decentralization, political selection of judges (often through elections), deemphasis of judge-made law, and a multiple appeal system are all used to check the power of judges. Moreover, the basic decision to prosecute cases is left in the hands of the prosecutor—a public official, usually elected. In later years, probation officers and public defense attorneys have also become recognized criminal court officials. Today, processing of cases through criminal court has a number of steps, each of which involves a unique form of decision making: initial appearance, preliminary hearing, bail or detention, grand jury indictment, arraignment, trial, and sentencing.

Three present-day concerns about criminal court have been the object of much criminological attention: (1) case attrition, (2) plea bargaining, and (3) sentencing. Negotiation and bargaining between and among offenders, defense attorneys, prosecutors, and judges appear to be the rule rather than the exception. An enormous proportion of cases, well over half, are dismissed. Of those cases which are prosecuted, a considerable number are plea-bargained; i.e., the defendant agrees to plead guilty in exchange for some consideration from the state. The net result is that very few offenders, probably less than 5 percent, ever receive their "day in court." Although strongly disapproved in principle and practice, bargain justice continues. For one thing, it allows courts to consider mitigating factors in cases. For another, it is favored by defendants. It also represents the triumph of bureaucratized justice in that it serves the interests of prosecutors, judges, and other court professionals concerned with processing cases.

Along with attrition and bargaining, the third present-day concern about criminal court is sentencing practices. Despite the immense importance of sentencing in the administration of criminal justice, sentences meted out by judges reveal enormous disparity and inconsistency. One reason is the lack of account-ability of judges for sentencing decisions. Another is indeterminate sentencing policies, which allow judges enormous latitude in sentencing. Although there are some justifications for latitude in sentencing, indeterminate sentencing policies have been much criticized in recent years. Critics have offered three alternatives; flat-time sentences, presumptive sentences, and mandatory minimum sentences. Each of these represents an attempt to decrease disparity in sentencing.

Sentencing practices have also been examined to assess the role of social variables, particularly race and social class. Although the studies are extensive, the findings are less than consistent. Some studies have shown clear-cut racial bias in sentencing, especially in the imposition of the death sentence; and others have shown some racial or class bias in noncapital sentencing. On the other hand, another line of research has found little or no racial or class bias in criminal court processing. In fact, several recent studies have claimed that blacks are subject to less severe penalties than whites, a form of "reverse discrimination."

There are a number of possible explanations for the inconsistent results of studies of racial and class bias in sentencing. One possibility is that there may be differences in sentencing over time and among jurisdictions, judges, and types of decisions. Another is that apparent discrimination in favor of black offenders may actually be a result of devaluation of black victims. A third possibility is that race and social class play a dramatic role in court processing before sentencing. A fourth is that there may be so little regularity in court processing that bias may be difficult to determine. Finally, since most defendants in state criminal courts are poor, marginally employed, and of minority status, differences among them may not be sharply pronounced. The real inequity in court processing may be based on type of offense. According to one study, white-collar offenders receive more lenient sentences for white-collar crimes in federal courts. Corporate crimes, if prosecuted at all, are often handled by regulatory agencies which dispense a totally different form of justice.

Responding to problems such as those posed by bargaining justice and sentencing practices, a few criminologists have advocated changes in the criminal courts. Three possibilities are foremost: involving the victim in the activities of the court, diverting offenders from court processing, and making fundamental changes in the structure of the court. One basic change would be to shift the function of the courts away from determination of blame or guilt toward facilitation of amiable, cooperative future relationships. Another basic change would be retrospective, "needs-based" justice or increased avoidance of court processing. Finally, certain recommendations for change are implicit in the three major analytical perspectives: have the courts live up to their stated ideals, eliminate the more pernicious aspects of bureaucracy, and establish standards of justice that would reduce the inequities perpetrated by the courts.

NOTES

1 For a discussion of the issues in the mid-1960s, see: Theodore L. Becker, "Surveys and Judiciaries; Or, Who's Afraid of the Purple Curtain," *Law and Society Review*, vol. 1, no. 1, November 1, 1966, pp. 133–143.

2 Herbert L. Packer, "Two Models of the Criminal Process," *University of Pennsylvania Law Review*, vol. 113, November 1964, pp. 1–68.

3 Donald J. Newman, "Role and Process in the Criminal Court," in Daniel Glaser, ed., *Handbook of Criminology*, Rand McNally, Chicago, Ill., 1974, pp. 593–620.

4 Abraham S. Blumberg, *Criminal Justice: Issues and Ironies*, 2d ed., New Viewpoints (Franklin Watts), New York, 1979, p. 146.

5 Roberta Rovner-Pieczenik, *The Criminal Court: How It Works*, Heath (Lexington Books), Lexington, Mass., 1978.

6 W. Boyd Littrell, *Bureaucratic Justice: Police, Prosecutors, and Plea Bargaining*, Sage, Beverly Hills, Calif., 1979.

7 Thorsten Sellin, *The Penalty of Death*, Sage, Beverly Hills, Calif., 1980, chap. 3.

8 William J. Chambliss and Robert J. Seidman, *Law, Order, and Power*, Addison-Wesley, Reading, Mass., 1971, p. 474.

9 Ibid.

10 Richard Quinney, *Class, State, and Crime: On the Theory and Practice of Criminal Justice*, McKay, New York, 1977, p. 4.

11 Gregg Barak, *In Defense of Whom? A Critique of Criminal Justice Reform*, Anderson, Cincinnati, Ohio, 1980.

12 This discussion of English legal institutions follows: C. Gordon Post, *An Introduction to the Law*, Prentice-Hall, Englewood Cliffs, N.J., chap. II.

13 On the American legal system, see: Lewis Mayers, *The American Legal System*, Harper, New York, 1955; James Willard Hurst, *The Growth of American Law*, Little, Brown, Boston, Mass., 1950, especially pp. 85–195; and Laurence M. Friedman, *A History of American Law*, Simon and Schuster, New York, 1973. It should be noted that the discussion in the present text is geared toward the adult criminal courts rather than the juvenile courts. The latter evolved in a different manner and operate under different legal assumptions. For an account of juvenile courts, see: Sheldon Glueck, *The Problem of Delinquency*, Houghton Mifflin, Boston, Mass., 1959; for a critical criminological perspective, see: Anthony M. Platt, *The Child Saver: The Invention of Delinquency*, 2d ed., University of Chicago Press, Chicago, Ill., 1977.

14 On the prosecutor, see: Joan E. Jacoby, *The American Prosecutor: A Search for Identity*, Heath (Lexington Books), Lexington, Mass., 1980; and Herman Schwartz

and Bruce Jackson, "Prosecutor as Public Enemy," *Harper's Magazine*, February 1976.

15 Barak, *In Defense of Whom?*

16 On the grand jury, see: Marvin E. Frankel and Gary P. Naftalis, *The Grand Jury: An Institution on Trial*, Hill and Wang, New York, 1977.

17 For a review of jury studies conducted by sociologists, see: Harry Kalven and Hans Ziesel, *The American Jury*, Little, Brown, Boston, Mass., 1966.

18 Rodney Kingsworth and Louis Rizzo, "Decision-Making in the Criminal Courts: Continuities and Discontinuities," *Criminology*, vol. 17, no. 1, May 1979, pp. 3–14.

19 David A. Jones, *Crime without Punishment*, Heath (Lexington Books), Lexington, Mass., chap. 6.

20 Alexander B. Smith and Harriet Pollack, *Criminal Justice: An Overview*, 2d ed., Holt, Rinehart and Winston, New York, 1980, chap. 8.

21 Blumberg, *Criminal Justice*, p. 159; and James Eisenstein and Herbert Jacob, *Felony Justice: An Organizational Analysis of Criminal Courts*, Little, Brown, Boston, Mass., 1977.

22 Barak, *In Defense of Whom?* p. 99 and chap. 4.

23 On the VERA study, see: Vera Institute of Justice (VERA), *Felony Arrests: Their Prosecution and Disposition in New York City's Courts*, rev. ed., Longman and Vera Institute of Justice, New York, 1981. The original study was conducted in 1971. On the INSLAW study, see: Prosecutor's Management Information System (PROMIS) Research Project, *Highlights of Interim Findings and Implications*, National Institute of Law Enforcement and Criminal Justice, Law Enforcement Assistance Administration, U.S. Department of Justice, September 1977; and PROMIS, *What Happens after Arrest? A Court Perspective of Police Operations in the District of Columbia*, National Institute of Law Enforcement and Criminal Justice, Law Enforcement Assistance Administration, U.S. Department of Justice, May, 1978.

24 PROMIS, *What Happens after Arrest?* p. xiii.

25 VERA, *Felony Arrests*, pp. 1–2.

26 PROMIS, *What Happens after Arrest?* chap. 3

27 Ibid., chap. 5. For another analysis of issues related to prosecution, see: Jan M. Chaiken, Peter W. Greenwood, and Joan Petersilia, "The Criminal Investigation Process: A Summary Report," *Policy Analysis*, vol. 3, no. 2, Spring 1977, pp. 187–217.

28 PROMIS, *Highlights of Interim Findings and Implications*, p. 4.

29 VERA, *Felony Arrests*, p. 135.

30 Ibid., p. 135.

31 Ibid., p. 20.

32 Herbert S. Miller, William F. McDonald, and James A. Cramer, *Plea Bargaining in the United States*, U.S.

Department of Justice, Law Enforcement Assistance Administration, National Institute of Law Enforcement and Criminal Justice, September 1978, p. xii.

[33] Ibid., p. xiv.

[34] Ibid., pp. 16–24.

[35] Blumberg, *Criminal Justice*, pp. 171–172.

[36] Jones, *Crime without Punishment*, pp. 117–124.

[37] Pamela J. Utz, *Settling the Facts: Discretion and Negotiation in Criminal Court* Heath (Lexington Books), Lexington, Mass., 1978.

[38] Milton Heumann, "A Note on Plea Bargaining and Case Pressure," *Law and Society Review*, vol. 9, no. 3, Spring 1975, pp. 515–528.

[39] Albert W. Alschuler, "Plea Bargaining and Its History," *Law and Society*, vol. 13, no. 2, Winter 1979, pp. 211–245.

[40] Ronald W. Fagan, "Public Support for the Courts: An Examination of Alternative Explanations," *Journal of Criminal Justice*, vol. 9, no. 6, 1981, pp. 403–417; figure reported on p. 407.

[41] National Advisory Commission on Criminal Justice Standards and Goals, Task Force on Courts, *Report on Courts*, Government Printing Office, Washington, D.C., 1973.

[42] E.g., see: Malcolm M. Feeley, *The Process Is the Punishment: Handling Cases in a Lower Criminal Court*, Russell Sage Foundation, New York, 1979.

[43] Miller, McDonald, and Cramer, *Plea Bargaining in the United States*, p. xvi.

[44] Quoted by: Jones, *Crime without Punishment*, p. 42.

[45] Blumberg, *Criminal Justice*, pp. 173–174.

[46] Littrell, *Bureaucratic Justice*.

[47] Marvin E. Frankel, *Criminal Sentences: Law without Order*, Hill and Wang, New York, 1972, 1973, p. vii.

[48] Ibid., p. 8.

[49] Lois G. Forer, *Criminals and Victims: A Trial Judge Reflects on Crime and Punishment*, Norton, New York, 1980, p. 304.

[50] Charles Bahn, "Sentence Disparity and Civil Rights," pamphlet submitted to the U.S. Commission on Civil Rights, 1977. It should be noted that not all studies agree with these statements about sentencing disparity. See, for example: Paul L. Sutton, *Variation in Federal Criminal Sentencing: A Statistical Assessment at the National Level*, U.S. Department of Justice, Utilization of Civil Justice Statistics Project, Analytic Report 17, 1978.

[51] Frankel, *Criminal Sentences*. On discretion and accountability, see also: Michael R. Gottfredson and Don M. Gottfredson, *Decisionmaking in Criminal Justice: Toward the Rational Exercise of Discretion*, Ballinger, Cambridge, Mass., 1980; and Albert J. Reiss, "Discretionary Justice," in Glasser, *Handbook of Criminology*, pp. 679–699.

[52] This dicussion follows: Smith and Pollack, *Criminal Justice*, pp. 211–219.

[53] Alexander B. Smith and Abraham Blumberg, "The Problems of Objectivity in Judicial Decision-Making," *Social Forces*, vol. 46, no. 1, September 1967, pp. 96–105.

[54] E.g., see: David Fogel, *We Are the Living Proof: The Justice Model for Corrections*, Anderson, Cincinnati, Ohio, 1975. On the critique of interdeterminate sentencing, see: Report of the Twentieth Century Fund

Task Force on Criminal Sentencing, *Fair and Certain Punishment*, McGraw-Hill, New York, 1976; and Jessica Mitford, *Kind and Usual Punishment: The Prison Business*, Vintage (Random House), New York, 1973.

[55] See: Alan Dershowitz, "Let the Punishment Fit the Crime," *New York Times Magazine*, December 28, 1975.

[56] Andrew von Hirsch, *Doing Justice: The Choice of Punishments—Report of the Committee for the Study of Incarceration,* Hill and Wang, New York, 1976.

[57] Andrew von Hirsch and Kathleen J. Hanrahan, *The Question of Parole: Retention, Reform, or Abolition?* Ballinger (Harper and Row), Cambridge, Mass., 1979.

[58] Leslie T. Wilkins, Jack M. Kress, Don M. Gottfredson, Joseph C. Calpin, and Arthur M. Gelman, *Sentencing Guidelines: Structuring Judicial Discretion*, National Institute of Law Enforcement and Criminal Justice, Law Enforcement Assistance Administration, Washington, D.C., 1978.

[59] Judge David Bazelon, quoted by: Albert W. Alschuler, "Sentencing Reform and Prosecutorial Power: A Critique of Recent Proposals for 'Fixed' and 'Presumptive' Sentencing," in Sheldon L. Messinger and Egon Bittner, eds., *Criminology Review Yearbook*, vol. 1, Sage, Beverly Hills, Calif., 1979, p. 435.

[60] Forer, *Criminals and Victims*, p. 96.

[61] Dershowitz, "Let the Punishment Fit the Crime," p. 27.

[62] On the problems of implementing sentencing reform, see: Alschuler, "Sentencing Reform and Prosecutorial Power," pp. 416–445; and David Brewer, Gerold E. Beckett, and Norman Holt, "Determinate Sentencing in California," *Journal of Research in Crime and Delinquency*, vol. 18, July 1981, pp. 200–231.

[63] Gary Kleck, "Racial Discrimination in Criminal Sentencing: A Critical Evaluation of the Evidence with Additional Evidence on the Death Penalty," *American Sociological Review*, vol. 46, December 1981, pp. 783–805.

[64] The studies quoted in this paragraph are cited in: Sellin, *The Penalty of Death*, chap. 3.

[65] H.C. Brearly, "The Negro and Homicide," *Social Forces*, vol. 9, 1930, p. 252.

[66] Harold Garfinkel, "Inter- and Intra-Racial Homicides," in Marvin E. Wolfgang, ed., *Studies in Homicide*, Harper and Row, New York, 1967, pp. 46–65.

[67] Guy E. Johnson, "The Negro and Crime," *Annals of the American Academy of Political and Social Science*, vol. 217, 1941, p. 100.

[68] William J. Bowers, *Executions in America*, Heath, Lexington, Mass., 1974, pp. 81–107.

[69] William J. Bowers and Glenn L. Pierce, "Arbitrariness and Discrimination under Post-Furman Capital Statutes," *Crime and Delinquency*, vol. 25, no. 4, October 1980, pp. 563–635.

[70] E.g.: Oakley C. Johnson, "Is the Punishment of Rape Equally Administered to Negroes and Whites in the State of Louisiana?" in William L. Patterson, ed., *We Charge Genocide*, International Publishers, New York, 1970, pp. 216–228. See also: Marvin E. Wolfgang and Marc Riedel, "Rape, Race, and the Death Penalty in Georgia," *American Journal of Orthopsychiatry*, vol. 45, 1975, pp. 658–668. In 1977, the Supreme Court ruled

448

that the death penalty for rape constitutes cruel and unusual punishment (*Coker v. Georgia*).

71 Gary D. LaFree, "The Effect of Sexual Stratification by Race on Official Reactions to Rape," *American Sociological Review*, vol. 45, October 1980, pp. 842–854.

72 Theodore G. Chiricos, Phillip D. Jackson, and Gordon P. Waldo, "Inequality in the Impositon of a Criminal Label" *Social Problems*, vol. 19, no. 4, Spring 1972, pp. 553–572.

73 James L. Gibson, "Race as a Determinant of Criminal Sentences: A Methodological Critique and a Case Study," *Law and Society Review*, vol. 12, 1978, pp. 455–478.

74 Alan J. Lizotte, "Extra-Legal Factors in Chicago's Criminal Courts: Testing the Conflict Model of Criminal Justice," *Social Problems*, vol. 25, 1978, pp. 464–480. Ethnic bias in sentencing has also been studied by: Peter L. Sissons. "The Hispanic Experience of Criminal Justice," monograph no. 3, Hispanic Research Center, Bronx, New York, 1979. Sissons found a disproportionate increase in numbers of hispanics in the criminal justice system; for any given offense, hispanic offenders were more likely to be sent to prison or, if placed on probation, more likely to serve longer sentences.

75 Theodore G. Chiricos and Gordon P. Waldo, "Socioeconomic Status and Criminal Sentencing: An Empirical Assessment of a Conflict Proposition," *American Sociological Review*, vol. 40, 1975, pp. 753–772.

76 Michael J. Hindelang, "Race and Involvement in Crimes," *American Sociological Review*, vol. 43, 1978, pp. 93–109.

77 Kleck, "Racial Discrimination in Criminal Sentencing."

78 Ilene Nagel Bernstein, William R. Kelly, and Patricia A. Doyle, "Social Reaction to Deviants: The Case of Criminal Defendants," *American Sociological Review*, vol 42, 1977, pp. 743–755.

79 Kleck, "Racial Discrimination in Criminal Sentencing," p. 794.

80 H.A. Bullock, "Significance of the Racial Factor in the Length of Prison Sentences," *Journal of Criminal Law, Criminology, and Police Science*, vol. 52, 1961, pp. 411–417.

81 Martin A. Levin, "Urban Politics and Judicial Behavior," *Journal of Legal Studies*, vol. 1, 1972, pp. 220–221.

82 Randall J. Thomson and Matthew T. Zingraff, "Detecting Sentencing Disparity: Some Problems and Evidence," *American Journal of Sociology*, vol. 86, no. 4, January 1981, pp. 869–890.

83 Ibid.

84 This argument is advanced by: Kleck, "Racial Discrimination in Criminal Sentencing," p. 800.

85 Michael L. Radelet, "Racial Characteristics and the Death Penalty," *American Sociological Review*, vol. 46, December 1981, pp. 918–927.

86 Victoria Lynn Swigert and Ronald A. Farrell, *Murder, Inequality, and the Law: Differential Treatment in the Legal Process*, Lexington Books, Lexington, Mass., 1976.

87 Steven Burnet Boris, "Stereotypes and Dispositions for Criminal Homicide," *Criminology*, vol. 17, no. 2, August 1979, pp. 139–158.

88 See: Lizotte, "Extra-Legal Factors in Chicago's Criminal Courts"; and Gibson, "Race as a Determinant of Criminal Sentences."

89 See: John Hagan, John D. Hewitt, and Duana F. Alwin, "Ceremonial Justice: Crime and Punishment in a Loosely Coupled System," *Social Forces*, vol. 58, no. 2, December 1979, pp. 506–527.

90 For a discussion of this issue, see comments on Chiricos and Waldo in: *American Sociological Review*, vol. 42, no. 1, February 1977, pp. 174–185.

91 John Hagan, Ilene H. Nagel (Bernstein), and Celesta Albonetti, "The Differential Sentencing of White-Collar Offenders in Ten Federal District Courts," *American Sociological Review*, vol. 45, October 1980, pp. 802–820.

92 On the conditions necessary for indictment in white-collar cases, see: Donald I. Baker, "To Indict or Not to Indict: Prosecutorial Discretion in Sherman Act Enforcement," in Messinger and Bittner, *Criminology Review Yearbook*, pp. 402–415.

93 Stephen Schaefer, "The Proper Role of a Victim-Compensation System," *Crime and Delinquency*, vol. 21, no. 1, January 1975, pp. 45–49.

94 Anne M. Heinz and Wayna A. Kerstetter, "Victim Participation in Plea Bargaining: A Field Experiment," in William F. McDonald and James A. Cramer, eds., *Plea Bargaining*, Lexington Books, Lexington, Mass., 1980, pp. 167–177.

95 "Note: Recent Developments in the Definition of Forcible Rape," *Virginia Law Review*, vol. 61, June 1975, pp. 1500–1543.

96 Elizabeth W. Vorenberg and James Vorenberg, "Early Diversion from the Criminal Justice System: Practice in Search of a Theory," in Lloyd E. Ohlin, ed., *Prisoners in America*, Prentice-Hall, Englewood Cliffs, N.J., 1973, pp. 151–183.

97 On diversion, see: Raymond T. Nimmer, *Diverson: The Search for Alternative Forms of Prosecution*, American Bar Foundation, Chicago, Ill., 1974. On juvenile diversion, see: Robert M. Carter and Malcolm W. Klein, *Back on the Street: The Division of Juvenile Offenders*, Prentice Hall, Englewood Cliffs, N.J., 1976.

98 Malcolm W. Klein, "Deinstitutionalization and Diversion of Juvenile Offenders: A Litany of Impediments," in Norval Morris and Michael Tonry, eds., *Crime and Justice: An Annual Review of Research*, vol. 1, University of Chicago Press, Chicago, Ill., 1979, pp. 145–201.

99 Harold E. Pepinsky, "A Radical Alternative to 'Radical' Criminology," in James A. Inciardi, ed., *Radical Criminology: The Coming Crisis*, Sage, Beverly Hills, Calif., 1980, pp. 299–315.

100 Richard Danzig and Michael J. Lowy, "Everyday Disputes and Mediation in the United States: A Reply to Professor Felstiner," *Law and Society Review*, vol. 9, Summer 1975, pp. 675–694.

101 Larry L. Tifft, "The Coming Redefinitions of Crime: An Anarchist Perspective," *Social Problems*, vol. 26, no. 4, April 1979, pp. 392–402; quotations from p. 397.

102 William L. F. Felstiner, "Influences of Social Organization on Dispute Processing," *Law and Society Review*, vol. 9, Fall 1974, pp. 63–94; and "Avoidance as Dispute Processing: An Elaboration," *Law and Society Review*, vol. 9, Summer 1974, pp. 695–706.

Corrections

18

After being arrested, booked, found guilty, and sentenced, offenders are put into the correctional system. It is in corrections that something is done *to* them or *for* them, or both. This "correcting" may take place in secure facilities such as prisons or jails, may involve supervision in the community in the form of probation or parole, and may involve participation in one of many community correctional programs. Moreover, correction may be intended as punishment for wrongs committed or as treatment designed to alter the offender's subsequent behavior.

The field of correction is beset by controversy and conflicting philosophies. The major purpose of corrections has remained less than completely clear. For one thing, the correctional system has been saddled with conflicting goals: e.g., punishment, deterrence, reform, rehabilitation, and incapacitation. For another, probation and parole operate under quite different assumptions from imprisonment, even though all three are part of the same system. Finally, the lack of clarity or agreement on the purpose of corrections has become especially apparent with the demise of the "treatment ideology" which pervaded correctional practice during the 1950s and 1960s.

As a field of study, corrections has moved increasingly to the center of criminological attention. As with the police and the courts, the new criminology has often placed more emphasis on how society responds to offenders than on how offenders behave. It has been especially sensitive to the close relationship between social structure and punishment. In this connection, there has also been much concern with racial and class inequalities in the administration of corrections.

This chapter on corrections will open by examining the three major perspectives which dominate the field today. Then it examines the history of corrections, especially in the United States. Following that, we shall look at several present-day concerns: the internal workings of the prison, the inequity of punishment, and the chaotic state of correctional philosophies. In the last section, we shall take a look at some of the correctional alternatives currently being proposed.

THREE MAJOR PERSPECTIVES

During the 1950s and 1960s, corrections was dominated by the belief that offenders were sick people whose illnesses could be diagnosed and then treated. Such a "therapeutic attitude" was perhaps best expressed in the work of Karl Menninger, who put it as follows:

> Do I believe there is effective treatment for offenders and that they *can* be changed? *Most certainly and definitely I do.* Not all cases, to be sure. . . . But I believe the majority of them would prove to be curable.[1]

Working under this ideology, prisons expanded their staffs to include psychologists, psychiatrists, social workers, counselors, and educators. Probation and parole practices also came to reflect a "social work" orientation.

Beginning in the late 1960s, the treatment model became the object of extensive critical inquiry. Perhaps the sharpest criticism came from Douglas

Lipton, Robert Martinson, and Judith Wilks, who examined 231 evaluative studies of treatment of criminal and juvenile offenders conducted between 1945 and 1967, only to conclude that there is "no treatment that holds a promise of easily and effectively impacting the recidivism of all offenders."[2] Moreover, a well-controlled study by Gene Kassebaum, David Ward, and Daniel Wilner of the California prison system, long a leader in treatment for inmates, also found no significant relationships "directly or indirectly involving treatment as a variable."[3] The pessimistic findings of these studies led many to the conclusion that "nothing works."[4]

The individualized treatment model also came under attack from other quarters. Civil libertarians argued that indeterminacy of parole (i.e., waiting until a prison inmate was "ready") led to secret procedures, unreviewable decision making, and unwillingness to formulate sensible rules or social policy.[5] Jessica Mitford argued that the indeterminate sentence was tantamount to harsher punishment in that it ensured longer sentences for most offenders.[6] Thomas S. Szasz led virtually a one-man crusade against involuntary psychiatric hospitalization of criminally insane offenders, which he regarded as "the most severe penalty our legal system can inflict on a human being; namely, loss of liberty."[7]

With the decline of the individualized treatment model and the corresponding perception that "nothing works," three major perspectives have come to influence thinking about corrections and studies of corrections: (1) corrections as sanctions, (2) corrections as treatment, and (3) corrections as class control. Let's consider these three perspectives now; they will be employed again later in this chapter.

Corrections as Sanctions

Those who see the legitimate purpose of corrections as sanctions would argue that correction is retributive punishment, in which society inflicts suffering as revenge for wrongs committed. Graeme Newman, for one, has argued that society must punish and that punishment must (1) involve pain or unpleasant consequences, (2) be for an offense against a rule, (3) be for an actual or supposed offender, (4) be intentionally administered by human beings other than the offender, and (5) be imposed and administered by authority constituted by a legal system.[8]

Beyond Newman's general perspective, there are at least two viewpoints on retributive punishment. On the one hand, James Q. Wilson and Ernest van den Haag have claimed that our present system has been excessively lenient and has therefore promoted rather than deterred crime.[9] On the other hand, Andrew von Hirsch and David Fogel have argued for a "just deserts" model, in which offenders are punished by relatively short, uniform, definite sentences based on the offenses they have committed.[10] Proponents of the "just deserts" model would keep punishment as the central focus of the corrections system but would attempt to ensure that it was administered with justice and with certainty.[11]

Corrections as Treatment

Even though the "treatment ideology" no longer dominates corrections, there are still those who believe that offenders can be treated. To begin with, Lipton, Martinson, and Wilks's argument (see above) was overstated; even their own data showed that a few treatment methods did produce results.[12] Moreover, in another paper Wilks and Martinson found that those placed on probation, which some would see as a form of treatment, "perform better relative to recidivism than do those of similar background and criminal history who are placed in prison."[13] A positive view of treatment programs in corrections has also been conveyed by research studies such as those of Charles A. Murray and Louis A. Cox, Jr., which found substantial reductions in the recidivism rate of participants in a variety of correctional programs;[14] and by community correctional advocates, such as Kevin N. Wright, who want offenders to receive treatment from noncorrectional agencies in the community.[15]

Corrections as Class Control

Whereas the first two perspectives—corrections as sanctions and corrections as treatment—are expressions of what corrections *should* be, the third perspective provides an analysis of the *actual* social function of corrections. This third view has been advanced by certain critical criminologists; it argues that corrections generally is a form of control by elites over the lower classes. Among the early advocates of this viewpoint were Georg Rusche and Otto Kircheimer, who open their classic work by stating:

> Every system of production tends to discover punishments which correspond to its productive relationships.[16]

They go on to observe that convict labor coincided with the decline of corporal punishment as modern industrial society emerged in the seventeenth century.

Modern writers who see corrections as class control have argued that the real purpose of corrections, especially prison, is to remove unemployed workers from the labor market and provide slave labor for prison industries. This position is suggested in the arguments of Charles E. Reasons and Russell L. Kaplan[17] as well as in the empirical research of Matthew G. Yeager and Ivan Jankovic.[18] Broadly, those who see corrections as class control hold that the correctional system is not a response to criminal activity but a highly political process by which sanctions are applied to those who threaten the capitalist state and its class interests.

This section has only sketched an outline of the three major perspectives on corrections. In later sections of this chapter, we shall find these perspectives to be most useful in interpreting the complex trends and issues in corrections today.

HISTORY AND OVERVIEW OF CORRECTIONS

The variety of techniques that have been used to punish, treat, or otherwise correct offenders has been enormous. The death penalty, physical torture, banishment, exile, public humiliation, involuntary slavery, and fines have their origin in the ancient world. Imprisonment, probation, parole, and community corrections have a distinctly modern flavor. Indeed, when it comes to corrections, there are few possibilities that have not been tried in one form or another.

Fortunately, there is some order in the variety of correctional techniques.

Certain historical periods are characterized by particular correctional practices. Basic shifts in the structure of society are reflected in changes in ways offenders are punished, treated, or otherwise corrected. Moreover, the right to administer corrections is an important form of power exercised by the state. Its control over the lives of citizens is evidenced in the types of punishment and treatment it is permitted to impose.

In the following historical overview of correctional practices, we shall find it useful to look at the English experience, especially early England and the 1700s; and then to examine the American experience, focusing on the colonial period, the 1820s, the later 1800s, the 1960s and 1970s, and the present. Each of these periods represents a distinct shift in correctional practices and correctional philosophy.

The English Experience

Early England

Before the Norman conquest in 1066, England—for the most part a country of small, independent villages—left the responsibility for reacting to crime to the private citizen. The vendetta, or blood feud, required that the victim seek revenge by inflicting a similar injury on the offender or on a member of the offender's kinship group. Private vengeance proved so disruptive to society that gradually a system of monetary fines came to replace it. Generally, monetary fines involved payment of "wergild" ("man money") to the victim or his or her kin, the amount being dependent on the type of injury and the social status of the victim. In cases where the act involved malice, a "wite"—an additional fine—had to be paid to the king. It is interesting to note that early Anglo-Saxon laws contained detailed listings of the worth attached to every part of the body; e.g., from 50 shillings for an eye or foot to sixpence for a toenail. Injuries interfering with the ability to work or fight brought higher rates of compensation.[19]

The following centuries saw large-scale social changes. The development of the feudal system meant that some previously free private citizens sought the protection of local lords. Others became landless and joined outlaw bands roaming the countryside.[20] To those in power—the nobility and the king—crime presented a serious problem. Crime was defined as a wrong against the state, and during this period various laws covering a variety of acts were passed in the attempt to control criminals. The landless workers were a special target of these lawmaking efforts.[21] Increasingly harsh punishments were developed. Capital punishment, mutilation and branding, whipping, and use of the pillory and stocks all became common. This period also saw class differentiation in punishment, with fines and exile most often reserved for the rich and corporal punishment for the poor.[22]

England of the 1700s

The 1700s saw social changes on an even greater scale than earlier centuries. The enclosure movements—which combined small farms into large farms, first for sheep raising and subsequently for large-scale agriculture, uprooted large segments of the population from the countryside. These landless people represented a continual oversupply of labor; they went, propertyless, to the cities or joined outlaw bands in rural areas.

Capital punishment in the eighteenth century. (BETTMANN ARCHIVE)

Along with the social changes of the 1700s, there were corresponding changes in punishments administered by the state. England came to rely heavily on capital punishment. By 1780, the number of crimes carrying the death penalty was 350.[23] Executions were common; moreover, they were held in public, and criminals were often tortured before death and their bodies mutilated after death so that others would be deterred from committing similar crimes.

Aside from the death penalty, the most characteristic punishment of the 1700s was transportation to the colonies. With the opening up of new lands, it became possible simply to ship criminals away from England. In 1717 an act of Parliament authorized the courts to put convicted offenders under the custody of private contractors who would then sell their services as indentured servants in the colonies. An estimated 50,000 to 100,000 convicts were sent to America; the practice was ended only with the American Revolution. (Thereafter, England turned to Australia as a dumping ground for convicts; transportation to Australia continued well into the 1800s.[24])

At this point, it is appropriate to continue the discussion of corrections by shifting attention to the United States. Although the American legal system resembled the British one in its overall structure, practices of punishment were somewhat different. Moreover, as we shall see, correctional practices and philosophies were to undergo substantial changes in the American experience.

Corrections in America

Colonial period

The criminal codes of the colonial period in America were quite inclusive in that they provided for fines, whippings, banishment, the gallows, and mechanisms of shame such as the stocks, the pillory, the public cage, and the scarlet letter.[25] The two most common penalties were the fine and the whip. Fines were employed for those with property; the whip was used for those unable or unwilling to pay fines. For minor crimes, the stocks were often prescribed as an alternative to fines. It is interesting to note that jails were used mainly for persons waiting to be tried or sentenced or for people unable to pay their debts, rather than as instruments of punishment in their own right.[26]

Compared with England, the American colonies relied more heavily on corporal than on capital punishment and more on the mechanisms of public shame than on transportation. However, a significant exception was the nonresident offender—the wandering or strolling vagrant who was not considered a member of the small, close-knit colonial community. The typical penalty for the nonresident offender was whipping and expulsion. Yet expulsion was problematic. With each town expelling nonresident offenders, a migratory criminal group was created. Communities were faced with the persistent problem of setting up mechanisms to scrutinize strangers.[27]

The 1820s

The early 1800s saw a significant shift in the practice and philosophy of punishment. As has been noted by a French philosopher, Michel Foucault, the target of penal repression changed from the body to the soul, the scene from public spectacle to private penitance or forced labor, the personnel from the executioner to technicians who administered correctional institutions, and the mode from the festival to the school.[28] In this shift, placing convicted offenders in institutions became the "preferred solution" to the problem of crime. In the new institutions—"penitentiaries," as they came to be called—the hope was that isolation of the offender, combined with a disciplined routine, would provide a cure for vice, idleness, and a life of crime.[29]

The 1820s proved to be the decade of the prison. Two important new models appeared; each was applied in prisons which had been built earlier. In the Auburn model, first established at the Auburn state prison in New York between 1819 and 1823, prisoners slept alone in their cells at night and labored together in workshops during the day. The Pennsylvania model, reflecting a Quaker influence, began in 1826 in Pittsburgh and 1829 in Philadelphia. It isolated convicts for the entire period of their confinement, required them to maintain silence, and made them work alone in their cells. Although there were intense debates between advocates of the two models, both were dependent upon isolation of prisoners from the community and establishment of a disciplined routine. Regimentation became the standard mode of prison life.[30]

This change in the dominant mode of corrections—from corporal punishment or the mechanisms of shame to imprisonment—is so fundamental that a more complete explanation is in order. Taking a historical viewpoint, David Rothman observes that social changes in the early 1800s were so great that Americans of that period were forced to rethink the methods of social control that had been passed on to them. Population increase, movement to the cities, rapid upward and downward social mobility, and the demise of local self-policing communities led many to believe that criminals would roam out of control and that a drastically new approach was necessary to contain them.[31] Taking an economic viewpoint, other writers have linked the birth of the prison to industrialization. The prison provided a new, more oppressive means of punishment designed to impose discipline upon those who were marginal to industrial society. Furthermore, the products of prison labor were useful and profitable. This economic view has been developed by those who see corrections as a form of class control.[32]

The late 1800s

Despite the optimism of their founders, prisons experienced problems literally from the outset. A well-ordered, regimented environment had been envisioned; but wardens became preoccupied with preventing riots and escapes. Many prisons were overcrowded. Silence proved impossible to enforce. Use of prison labor was a continual problem; leasing of prison laborers to outside contractors was corrupt, and efforts to establish manufacturing enterprises in prisons created internal difficulties and the threat of competition with outside enterprises. Finally, there were many reported instances of cruel punishments (one New York State investigation found inmates being hanged by their thumbs), leading some to question whether the prison was as humane as it had originally been portrayed by its advocates.[33]

The most problematic aspect of the prison was its harmful effect upon those who were subjected to it. As early as 1852, the New York Prison Commission, the first of many such commissions, argued that

> protracted incarceration destroys the better faculties of the soul. . . . Most men who have been confined for long terms are distinguished by a stupor of both the moral and intellectual facilities. . . . Reformation is then out of the question.[34]

Early on, the prisons experienced high rates of recidivism. Furthermore, because prisoners were required to complete predetermined, unalterable sentences, they knew that they would be released regardless of their behavior or how well reformed they appeared.

The prison became, and remains to this day, paradoxical. On the one hand, it is still seen by many people as the core of the American corrections system. On the other hand, the problems it has posed and the harmful effects it has had upon prisoners have stimulated a continual search for alternatives. Some reform efforts came from within the prison system. Others, such as probation and parole, reflected attempts to handle offenders in dramatically different ways.

Prison reform   Within the system, prison reform dates back to the middle 1800s. Perhaps the most famous pioneer of penal reform was Alexander Maconochie, the superintendent of Norfolk Island, one of the places to which English convicts were transported, between 1840 and 1844. Recognizing the debasing nature of brutal punishments, Maconochie claimed that the purpose of imprisonment should be to reform offenders so that they would leave prison "capable of useful citizenship." To do this, Maconochie proposed substituting task sentences for time sentences and a mark system by which a prisoner's labor and improvement in conduct were measured. Prisoners were to work in groups of six or seven, and the whole group would be answerable for the conduct and labor of each member. In the final stage of imprisonment, prisoners were to be given a proprietary interest in their own labor.[35]

Maconochie put his ideas into practice in 1840, when he assumed command of Norfolk Island. The process worked as follows. Prisoners would be transported to Norfolk Island in British prison vessels. There they would engage in public employment. After some time, they would be granted a "ticket of leave"; this in effect was a rudimentary parole system. If their conduct was satisfactory, they would receive a conditional pardon followed by penal settlement in some type of civilian communal setting. The final stage was retransportation to England and restoration of the prisoner's status as a free person.[36] The process worked. In fact, Maconochie's accomplishments were so impressive that they stimulated American prison reformers, such as Thomas Mott Osborne and Howard B. Gill, who also attempted to develop the self-respect and integrity of prison inmates by involving them in meaningful participatory government of prisons.[37]

Prison reform took a somewhat different course with the establishment of the Elmira Reformatory under the leadership of Zebulon R. Brockway in 1876. In this reformatory, prisoners whose age ranged from 16 to 30 were graded into four categories. A prisoner would begin in the second category and then either remain there, progress to the first category, or be demoted to the third or fourth category. A prisoner who reached the highest classification would become eligible for parole. Progress was judged by how hard the offenders worked; by how well they kept out of trouble; and by the interest they showed in institutional programs, which included vocational, religious, academic, and physical training.[38]

Part and parcel of the reformatory movement was the adoption of the indeterminate sentence. This form of sentence, in which judges removed defendants to prison and let parole boards fix dates for their release, was advocated with much enthusiasm at the 1870 Prison Congress, held in Cincinnati. As one speaker of the day put it:

> The supreme aim of prison discipline is reestablishing moral harmony in the soul of the criminal himself, and effecting, as far as possible, his regeneration. . . . Reformation is the work of time; and a benevolent regard to the good of the criminal himself, as well as to the protection of society, requires that his sentence be long enough for reformatory processes to take effect.[39]

During the late 1800s, state after state established reformatories and developed indeterminate sentencing policies. This period also marked the beginning of efforts at "treatment," which involved psychiatrists, psychologists, physicians, educators, chaplains, and social workers working in prison settings.

The various efforts at prison reform should not, however, mislead one into thinking that prisons were significantly changed. The very positive experiment of Maconochie at Norfolk Island was abruptly terminated, four years after it began, for reasons that were by no means clear.[40] Plagued by problems such as overcrowding, deterioration of facilities, and inadequate staffing, the reformatories soon came to look much like adult prisons. The indeterminate sentence, about which hopes were so high, resulted in prison sentences which were on the average much longer than they had been earlier. These sentences have also proved nearly impossible to administer with equity or fairness.[41]

Probation and parole The other alternatives to the prison were far more radical in that they aimed to get convicted offenders out of the prison system. Both probation and parole involve keeping the convicted offender in the community under the supervision or custody of the state and with conditions that permit incarceration in the event of misbehavior. In short, both are forms of restrained liberty. The difference between the two is that probation is used in lieu of a prison sentence, whereas parole is used after a convicted offender has served part of a sentence in prison.[42]

Although precedents for probation date back to the Middle Ages, the modern probation system can be traced to the efforts of one man, John Augustus.[43] In 1841, Augustus—a prosperous, middle-aged Bostonian bootmaker who was an avid follower of the temperance movement—persuaded the court to release an offender, charged with being a common drunkard, into his custody. Augustus took the man home, fed him, and found him a job. Saved from prison, the man signed a temperance pledge and became sober. Three weeks later, Augustus brought the man back to the courtroom, obviously much improved; and the judge fined him 1 cent instead of sending him to prison. For Augustus, this began an 18-year career during which he bailed out on probation nearly 2000 offenders from the police and municipal courts of Boston. Of this number, reportedly only ten absconded before their term of probation expired.

Over the years probation has retained the characteristic feature established by Augustus: personal service from a probation officer who sees work with offenders as assistance rather than punishment. However, by the 1930s probation had come to be quite bureaucratic; and probation offices had become part of the court or executive branch, either centralized in the state or diffused in local administrations. One function assumed by probation was presentence investigation, designed to assist courts in determining the proper sentence for an offender. Another was supervision, in which the probationer remains under the jurisdiction of the court subject to certain specified conditions and regular reporting to a probation officer.

Today, probation is appropriately seen as a process that provides links between the courts, the offender, and the offender's community:

> The process includes the offenders' *reporting* regularly to their probation officers; the *servicing* of their needs through treatment, counseling, and so on; and the officer's *supervision* of probationers to ensure that the rules of the probation order are observed.[44]

The handling of offenders' needs is very varied and may include provision for employment, education, training and recreation, methadone maintenance, and counseling.

Probation has also been the subject of much controversy. For one thing, case loads have often been so large that effective supervision is all but impossible. There are also other problems. Local administration has often meant underfinanced, fragmented, and overlapping services. Combination of the investigatory and supervisory roles in one officer compromises the quality of assistance that officers can render. Criteria for probation have often remained unclear; and heavy case loads have prevented the development of detailed, intensive presentence reports.[45]

Despite its problems, supervised probation has emerged in the twentieth century as the most common sentence for offenders. The extensive use of probation reflects the belief held by many professionals that time served in prison harms rather than helps offenders. Moreover, some studies have found probation to have a relatively low failure rate.[46] Yet the popularity of probation also has something to do with cost; the estimate is that the cost of maintaining offenders on supervised probation is one-tenth that of maintaining them in prison.[47]

Parole resembles probation in that it too provides for personal services designed to assist offenders in the community. However, parole differs from probation (as was noted earlier) in that it comes after a prison sentence has been served. Conditional pardons and tickets of leave for criminals who agreed to be transported from England in lieu of execution are sometimes considered the antecedents of parole. However, parole is best traced to the innovative tickets of leave used by Maconochie. His ideas were further developed by Sir William Crofton during the 1880s, in the so-called Irish system, under which prisoners earned marks for good conduct and achievement in prison and could be discharged early on tickets of leave. These tickets were given after provision for employment and police supervision had been worked out. Like probation, the Irish system of parole had conditions and required reporting, in this case to the police. In Ireland and England the supervision of those released on parole came to be handled by prisoners' aid societies, funded in part privately and in part by government. In the United States, fear of police surveillance led to the development of professional parole officers to whom parolees had to report. In many jurisdictions supervision of parolees is handled by the same person or persons as supervision of probationers.[48]

Parole came to be administered by the executive branch of government, whether in the person of the governor or in the form of a politically appointed parole board. Parole boards visit institutions and respond to requests from prisoners and recommendations from staff for early release. These boards have come to be much criticized for lack of clear criteria in decision making, for too much conservatism in their estimates of whether communities will be able to accept offenders, and for failure to coordinate their decision making with prison personnel.

In thinking about parole, it is useful to bear in mind that only a comparatively small proportion of convicted offenders are ever placed on parole. Over 90 percent of misdemeanants sentenced to jail are simply released after serving their sentence. For imprisoned felons, a smaller group to begin with, the figures are different: in the United States as a whole, 60 percent are released on parole; however, there is great variation from state to state. One survey found that the proportion of felons released on parole varied from 9 percent of all state prisoners in South Carolina to 98 percent in New Hampshire and Washington.[49]

Parole is part and parcel of the indeterminate sentencing system. As we saw, Crofton tied parole directly to the mark system. It could also be argued that parole was made necessary by the excessively long prison sentences allowed by indeterminate sentencing. Parole gave the executive branch of government a way of controlling prison populations and, for that matter, a means of controlling judicial excesses in individual cases. However, there was a considerable cost; decision making turned out to be conducted by small groups, secretive, subject to few checks, and therefore often arbitrary. For reasons such as these, parole has come under attack, especially by those who would advocate linking punishment to the criminal act rather than to the offender.[50]

The 1960s and 1970s

The most recent shift in correctional policy and practice began in the late 1960s, in the form of community corrections programs. Such programs were developed in response to the lack of effectiveness of treatment in prisons and to demands for stricter custody than is afforded by probation or parole. The intent of community corrections programs is to give prisoners who have served time a bridge back to the free community. Their rationale is "reintegration" of the offender. Community corrections received official endorsement when it was recommended in 1967 by the President's Commission on Law Enforcement and Administration of Justice.[51]

At the heart of early community corrections were two programs, work release and residence in a halfway house. Work release provides for selected prisoners to be released during working hours, usually to private employers, to family or home (in the case of women), to academic or vocational training programs, or to voluntary community service. Earnings are used to pay the costs of the prisoners' board, to cover their personal expenses, to support their dependents, to save money to be used upon their release, and to help defray maintenance charges. Halfway houses provide for residence in the community; they avoid the security, regimentation, and size of prisons and at the same time afford a greater degree of supervision and security than probation and parole. They can take a variety of forms. Some are private, some are religious, and some are operated by ex-offenders. Some offer only food and shelter; others provide counseling services; and still others are therapeutic communities.[52]

In the 1970s, community corrections moved beyond work release and halfway houses. At least one writer characterized the decade as one of "bureaucratic expansion," including work-furlough programs, work-release centers, volunteers in probation, intensive probation, group therapy, community corrections, halfway houses, and aftercare.[53] The 1970s also saw considerable expansion of diversion programs, under which alleged offenders were diverted from court processing and offered services.[54] Although the success of the community corrections model has yet to be demonstrated, it can be said that the proliferation of alternatives in the 1970s represents dissatisfaction with the large-scale prison. It is also interesting to note that the community corrections movement has kept alive the ideal of rehabilitation.[55]

Corrections today

The present-day correctional system is an amalgam of agencies which have their origins in the various historical periods discussed above. We can gain an overview of corrections today by looking at the numbers of people under various forms of correctional supervision.

Table 25 shows that an enormous number of Americans are subject to some form of correctional supervision on a given day. The grand total of over 2 million

TABLE 25.   Persons under Correctional Supervision, 1980

Type	Adults	Juveniles	Total
State and local facilities			
Prison	287,635	46,980 (public)*	361,905
		27,290 (private)*	
Jail	158,394	1 611*	160,005
Probation	923,064*	328,854*	1,251,918
Parole	156,194*	53.347*	209,541
Totals	1,525,287	458,082	1,983,369
Federal system			
Prison			26,371
Probation			64,450
Overall total			2,074,190

SOURCE: Timothy J. Flanagan, David J. Van Alstyne, and Michael R. Gottfredson, eds., *Sourcebook of Criminal Justice Statistics—1981*, U.S. Department of Justice, Bureau of Justice Statistics, Government Printing Office, Washington, D.C., 1982, sec. 6. Figures marked with an asterisk are from earlier editions.

means that about 9 out of every 1000 Americans are under the umbrella of the correctional system at any time. About three-fourths are adults; the remainder are juveniles. More age-specific calculations would show that 16 out of every 1000 adults between ages 20 and 60 and 22 out of every 1000 juveniles between ages 15 and 19 are under correctional supervision.

Table 25 also shows the considerable reliance upon probation. It is by far the category in which the largest numbers of adults or juveniles under correctional supervision fall: 62 percent of the adults and 72 percent of the juveniles in the correctional system are subject to probation. It is also worth noting that statistics from state and local facilities show that for every 100 adults in prison, there are 66 out on parole. Similarly, for every 100 juveniles in prison or secure facilities, there are 72 out on parole. Compared with prison and probation, relatively few of those under correctional supervision are held in jail. This is because jails are used mainly for holding offenders before trial in cases where bail is not or cannot be posted, or for offenders serving sentences of less than one year.[56]

Although probation is the dominant form of correctional supervision, populations of state and federal prisons are on the upswing. Changes in sentencing practices have led to a dramatic increase in state prison populations since about 1970. Between 1971 and 1975, the population grew 14 percent: from 177,113 to 201,420. Between 1975 and 1981, it grew nearly 50 percent: to 299,134. This increase is especially significant when it is realized that the United States has an imprisonment rate far in excess of nearly all other nations in the world.[57]

To summarize briefly this history and overview of corrections, virtually all correctional possibilities have been tried at one time or another. Different historical periods are characterized by different types of punishment; and corrections today reflects a mix of practices originating in the nineteenth century. The most common is probation; but in the 1970s the prison population began to swell,

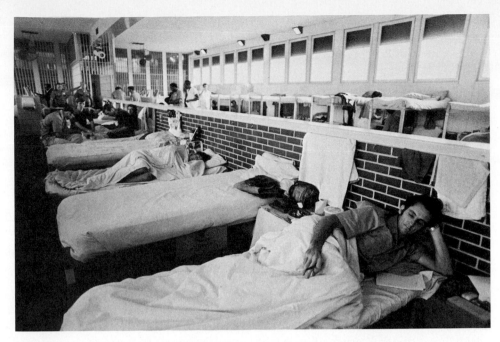

Some correctional institutions are so overcrowded that halls have been turned into dormitories.   (ALEX WEBB/MAGNUM)

so that the United States today has one of the highest rates of imprisonment in the world. At the same time, during the 1970s community correctional programs grew apace.

The three perspectives developed at the outset of the chapter shed some light on the diversity of correctional practices. Those who see the purpose of corrections as sanctions would generally advocate the use of imprisonment, but with short, uniform, definite sentences. Those who see corrections as treatment would generally encourage rehabilitation in prisons, use of probation, or community correctional programs. Those who see corrections as class control have argued that type of punishment is directly related to the needs of a society. In their estimate, high imprisonment rates are associated with high unemployment because the real purpose of imprisonment is to control those who are a potential threat to the state.

At this point, we need to shift our focus away from a general history and overview of corrections to present-day concerns.

SOME PRESENT-DAY CONCERNS

Although there are many issues currently confronting the corrections field, it will be useful to focus on three: (1) the internal dynamics of prisons, (2) the inequality of imprisonment, and (3) the purpose of corrections. Each of these issues is a modern problem with historical roots in situations we have already examined; and each continues to generate considerable interest among criminologists.

Internal Dynamics of Prisons

Prisons are complex social organizations. They are closed communities, generally unisexual and relatively homogeneous in terms of age, that attempt to maintain total social control over every aspect of the prisoner's life. Theoretically, such total control would be possible if inmates were willing to submit to it—or if every prisoner remained locked in a cell, gagged and straitjacketed. In practice, prisoners, who have little to lose, are unwilling to submit easily, and prison administrators are unwilling or unable to impose such stringent measures. Moreover, since prisoners outnumber guards, the two groups strike a bargain concerning what behaviors will be tolerated. In other words, prisons are run only with the tacit consent of inmates. Power is shared rather than absolute. Discretion rather than rigid adherence to rules characterizes the operation of virtually all prisons.[58]

Early sociological research on prison life saw the bargain between inmates and guards in terms of an inmate subculture which led to corruption of authority within the prison.[59] In his study of a maximum security prison, Gresham M. Sykes found three reasons why guards were unable to use the total power they are given: (1) It is difficult to maintain social distance from prisoners when there is close and intimate contact throughout the working day. (2) Guards need to engage in "deals" or "trades," especially since they are evaluated in terms of the conduct of the prisoners under their supervision. (3) As trusted prisoners are allowed to engage in minor chores (e.g., making out reports and checking cells), the dominance of the guards is undermined. In short, "only by tolerating violations of 'minor' rules and regulations can the guard secure compliance in the 'major' areas of the custodial regime."[60]

More current research suggests that the inmate subculture of today's prison is "generally less conforming, more fractionalized, and often enraged."[61] One observer sees "less willingness on the part of prisoners to exercise controlling effects over other inmates" and "increased tolerance of the use of violence on the part of fellow inmates." She attributes these changes to (1) an increase in the number of offenders being sent to prison; (2) a continued increase in the number of blacks, Puerto Ricans, and other hispanics in prisons; (3) increased politicalization and militancy of prisoners; and (4) fusion of prison militants and radical movements outside the prison.[62]

Another characteristic of prisons today is the emphasis on prisoners' rights. Emerging out of a new militancy among prisoners, the prisoners' rights movement has brought a veritable legal assault on the courts. Writs by "jailhouse lawyers" have increased markedly since the 1960s. The number of lawyers concerned with litigation by prisoners is also on a sharp upswing. Substantial victories have been won in a number of areas: proscription of cruel and unusual punishment, especially limitations on solitary confinement; prisoners' right of access to courts, counsel, and legal materials; freedom of religion; and freedom from censorship of mail or of communication with the outside world, especially the media. In addition, courts are dealing with issues such as due process in disciplinary proceedings, grooming and attire, administrative investigation and interrogation, inmates' safety, facilities, medical treatment, administrative liability, rehabilitation, classification and work assignments, transfers, and detainers.[63]

The greatest problem of prison life today is the violence that seems to be so much a part of it. Violence in the prison is multifaceted. It takes the form of prison riots and minor disturbances; and it can be seen in the treatment of inmates by staff members, in inmates' reaction to staff, in violence of inmates toward other inmates, and in self-inflicted violence among inmates in the form of suicide. Violence may emanate from racial conflict, may pit gangs against each other, or may simply be interpersonal. Flare-ups of violence are often quite unpredictable. Let's take a look at some of its forms.

Large-scale violence appears in the riots and disturbances which periodically arise in correctional institutions. Historically, 1929 and 1952 were years that witnessed waves of prison riots. One series of 25 riots began in 1952 in Jackson, Michigan, and continued until 1953 in other institutions around the country. A series of 10 riots began in Walla Walla, Washington, in 1955. From 1955 to about 1968, the number of riots declined; but since 1969, violence and injuries in prisons have increased in severity each year. In 1970, major insurrections occurred at Folsom, Rahway, and the Men's House of Detention in New York City. The infamous Attica riot, which touched off 12 other riots, took place in 1971. Since Attica, collective violence in prisons has cost the lives of 150 inmates, corrections officers, and state troopers in more than 21 states. A riot in the New Mexico State Penitentiary in 1980 caused the deaths of 36 inmates, setting a new record.[64]

Another form of prison violence can be seen in the rapes, assaults, homicides, and suicides which characterize prison life in the United States today. Rape is a vivid case in point. Although estimates of its extent are difficult to make, the following studies are indicative. In 1968, Alan J. Davis found that of 60,000 prison inmates in Philadelphia, 2000 had been subject to sexual assault in a 26-month period. He went on to note, "Virtually every slightly built young man committed by the courts is sexually approached within hours after his admission to prison."[65] A report on the Federal Correctional Institution at Tallahassee in the early 1970s found that three of every ten released prisoners said they had been propositioned for sexual activity.[66] A study of the Tennessee State Penitentiary found that three-fourths of the prisoners recalled at least one rape per month; 30 percent reported rapes occurring more than once each week.[67] Finally, of prisoners interviewed in New York State institutions, 28 percent reported that they had been targets of sexual aggressors at least once while in institutional custody.[68]

Assaults, homicides, and suicides are also a part of violence in prisons. Although it is again difficult to make accurate estimates, rates of assault for the correctional institutions or systems which have been studied are far greater for prison inmates than for the general population. This is especially true when the rates are calculated on the basis of interviews with prisoners rather than official data.[69] However, one national study found that the rate of homicides in prison is about the same as that in the general population, and that the general death rate in prisons is lower than that in comparable noninstitutional populations. But suicide rates of prison inmates are double those of the general population.[70]

The problem of violence in prisons is particularly striking when we consider prison guards. Brutality by guards appears to be an integral part of the prison situation. There are numerous instances, both in former times and today, in which prisoners have been harassed (e.g., forced to stand in the sun), tortured, and even killed. Prisoners also have been victimized psychologically, economically, and socially.[71]

One writer holds that violence inflicted by guards is rationalized by a subculture which favors using violence against prisoners.[72] Others have attributed such violence to undereducation, poor training, and low pay. However, an experiment by Philip G. Zimbardo suggests that a representative group of predominantly middle-class college students may hardly fare better at restraining brutalizing tendencies or attempting to beat the system. (See Box 21.) Zimbardo's experiment took place in a simulated situation which is not the same as a maximum security prison. However, to the extent that his experiment accurately reproduced reality as it exists in prisons, it can be asserted that the proclivity to

Box 21: The Zimbardo Experiment

In an attempt to understand just what it means psychologically to be a prisoner or a prison guard, Craig Haney, Curt Banks, Dave Jaffe and I created our own prison. We carefully screened over 70 volunteers who answered an ad in a Palo Alto city newspaper and ended up with about two dozen young men who were selected to be part of this study. They were mature, emotionally stable, normal, intelligent college students from middle-class homes throughout the United States and Canada. They appeared to represent the cream of the crop of this generation. None had any criminal record and all were relatively homogeneous on many dimensions initially.

Half were arbitrarily designated as prisoners by a flip of a coin, the others as guards. These were the roles they were to play in our simulated prison. The guards were made aware of the potential seriousness and danger of the situation and their own vulnerability. They made up their own formal rules for maintaining law, order and respect, and were generally free to improvise new ones during their eight-hour, three-man shifts. The prisoners were unexpectedly picked up at their homes by a city policeman in a squad car, searched, handcuffed, fingerprinted, booked at the Palo Alto station house and taken blindfolded to our jail. There they were stripped, deloused, put into a uniform, given a number and put into a cell with two other prisoners where they expected to live for the next two weeks. The pay was good ($15 a day) and their motivation was to make money.

We observed and recorded on videotape the events that occurred in the prison, and we interviewed and tested the prisoners and guards at various points throughout the study. Some of the videotapes of the actual encounters between the prisoners and guards were seen on the NBC News feature "Chronolog" on November 26, 1971.

At the end of only six days we had to close down our mock prison because what we saw was frightening. It was no longer apparent to most of the subjects (or to us) where reality ended and their roles began. The majority had indeed become prisoners or guards, no longer able to clearly differentiate between role playing and self. There were dramatic changes in virtually every aspect of their behavior, thinking and feeling. In less than a week the experience of imprisonment undid (temporarily) a lifetime of learning; human values were suspended, self-concepts were challenged and the ugliest, most base, pathological side of human nature surfaced. We were horrified because we saw some boys (guards) treat others as if they were despicable animals, taking pleasure in cruelty, while other boys (prisoners) became servile, dehumanized robots who thought only of escape, of their own individual survival and of their mounting hatred for the guards.

We had to release three prisoners in the first four days because they had such acute situational traumatic reactions as hysterical crying, confusion in thinking and severe depression. Others begged to be paroled, and all but three were willing to forfeit all the money they had earned if they could be paroled. By then (the fifth day) they had been so programmed to think of themselves as prisoners that when their request for parole was denied, they returned docilely to their violence on the part of guards—and for that matter inmates—is an outgrowth of the attempt to exert power over people who are reluctant to be controlled.

Adding to the inherently tense relationships between guards and inmates is the demise of treatment as an ideal. The problems associated with this ideal have already been noted; it must also be noted that nothing has replaced it. Edith Elisabeth Flynn has said:

> Corrections today is characterized by a philosophical vacuum and a profession without a guiding rationale. The cumulative effect of dismantling the rehabilitative ideal has impacted the prison more than any other component in corrections. The result of this development has been a serious demoralization of prison staff and increasing stress, strain, and resentment between staff and inmates.[73]

cells. Now, had they been thinking as college students acting in an oppressive experiment, they would have quit once they no longer wanted the $15 a day we used as our only incentive. However, the reality was not quitting an experiment but "being paroled by the parole board from the Stanford County Jail." By the last days, the earlier solidarity among the prisoners (systematically broken by the guards) dissolved into "each man for himself." Finally, when one of their fellows was put in solitary confinement (a small closet) for refusing to eat, the prisoners were given a choice by one of the guards: give up their blankets and the incorrigible prisoner would be let out, or keep their blankets and he would be kept in all night. They voted to keep their blankets and to abandon their brother.

About a third of the guards became tyrannical in their arbitrary use of power, in enjoying their control over other people. They were corrupted by the power of their roles and became quite inventive in their techniques of breaking the spirit of the prisoners and making them feel they were worthless. Some of the guards merely did their jobs as tough but fair correctional officers, and several were good guards from the prisoners' point of view since they did them small favors and were friendly. However, no good guard ever interfered with a command by any of the bad guards; they never intervened on the side of the prisoners, they never told the others to ease off because it was only an experiment, and they never even came to me as prison superintendent or experimentor in charge to complain. In part, they were good because the others were bad; they needed the others to help establish their own egos in a positive light. In a sense, the good guards perpetuated the prison more than the other guards because their own needs to be liked prevented them from disobeying or violating the implicit guards' code. At the same time, the act of befriending the prisoners created a social reality which made the prisoners less likely to rebel.

By the end of the week the experiment had become a reality, as if it were a Pirandello play directed by Kafka that just keeps going after the audience has left. The consultant for our prison, Carlo Prescott, an ex-convict with 16 years of imprisonment in California's jails, would get so depressed and furious each time he visited our prison, because of its psychological similarity to his experiences, that he would have to leave. A Catholic priest who was a former prison chaplain in Washington, D. C., talked to our prisoners after four days and said they were just like the other first-timers he had seen.

But in the end, I called off the experiment not because of the horror I saw out there in the prison yard, but because of the horror of realizing that I could have easily traded places with the most brutal guard or become the weakest prisoner full of hatred at being so powerless that I could not eat, sleep or go to the toilet without permission of the authorities. I could have become Calley at My Lai, George Jackson at San Quentin, [or] one of the men at Attica. . . .

SOURCE

Excerpt from Philip G. Zimbardo, "Pathology of Imprisonment," *Society*, vol. 9, April 1972, pp. 4–8.

In other words, without the rehabilitation ideal or some other humane purpose, corrections can only revert to custody. Experience has shown that when custody becomes the major goal, violence emerges—on the one side from a staff reacting to perceived threats from inmates and on the other from retaliatory behavior on the part of inmates.[74]

In short, prisons are organizations whose internal dynamics are fraught with tension. Prisoners' subcultures are fractionalized, nonconforming, and frequently enraged. Violence of various types keeps prisons from functioning effectively as an instrument of either rehabilitation or punishment. How can the inmate who is brutalized by staff members or by fellow inmates ever regain a sense of self-worth and become rehabilitated? How can victimized inmates understand the punishment they are receiving—the prison sentence—when its most brutal aspects are carried out illegally by correctional officers or by fellow inmates who have been given a free rein? In other words, in the context of a prison whose internal dynamics produce violence, neither treatment nor punishment makes any sense.

The Inequality of Imprisonment

In the American correctional system, the prison is the most punitive institution. As was mentioned earlier, corporal punishment is very much on the decline even if not completely extinct. The death penalty affects very few offenders. Probation, parole, and community corrections may set restraints and controls on an offender's behavior, but they do not entail the isolation from the community that characterizes prisons.

Since prison is the most punitive of the correctional institutions, the question who is sent to it is a most important one. It is in the answer to this question that social inequalities are dramatically apparent. As was shown in Part Three, crime is committed by people in all walks of life. However, many of those who commit crimes are never arrested. Many of those who are arrested are dismissed in subsequent court processing; others engage in plea bargaining or sentence bargaining. Discretion is exercised at all stages of the criminal justice system. As a result, relatively few offenders are given prison sentences, compared with the total amount of crime committed.

The social inequality of imprisonment lies in the fact that the few who are punished by imprisonment are disproportionately young, male, from racial or ethnic minorities, and of lower-class social origins. A quick rundown of the demographic characteristics of state prison inmates in 1979 is indicative: 63 percent are under 30 (compared with 19 percent of the general population); 96 percent are male; 48 percent are black (compared with 11 percent of the general population); 25 percent report an income of $10,000 or more in the year before their incarceration (compared with 35 percent of unrelated individuals generally); and 30 percent were unemployed (compared with 6 percent of the general population).[75] One writer has described the population of death row—obviously the most extreme form of imprisonment—as consisting of victims and losers, mostly poor, illiterate, and from ethnic minorities.[76] Prisons have also been characterized as "the one institution in American society which blacks 'control' "[77] and as centers of class-consciousness.[78]

In short, it would appear that serving time in prison is a function not only of guilt but also of poverty and powerlessness in American society. Middle- and upper-class people who are not members of minorities may commit crimes, but not the type for which they would be sent to a state prison. Moreover, middle- and upper-class offenders may benefit from flexible sentencing procedures, more favorable conditions of court processing, or correctional "alternatives." (See Chapter 19.) Whatever the factors are, the result is aptly captured in the title of a book by Jeffrey Reiman: *The Rich Get Richer and the Poor Get Prison.*[79]

The Purpose of Corrections

Corrections today is a field caught up in conflict. Now that the "treatment ideology" no longer dominates, the questions are (1) whether the purpose of corrections should be sanctions (i.e., punishment) or treatment, and (2) whether the real purpose of corrections is social (or class) control. Prisons are at the heart of this debate. Despite their immense problems—which have been sketched above—there is great reluctance to dispense with them. This reluctance has inhibited the development of workable alternatives. In this section we shall consider the philosophical elements of the conflict as they apply to prisons. First, we shall look again at punishment versus treatment; then we shall look at the issue of social-class control.

Punishment or treatment

The diverse, often conflicting, purposes of corrections are immediately apparent in the several goals which prison administrators are charged with implementing. As Thomas O. Murton observes:

> The warden is charged with the responsibility of concurrently instituting the philosophies of punishment, deterrence, retribution, incapacitation, and rehabilitation.[80]

In other words, prisons are expected to punish offenders so that they will commit no further crimes, to represent a threat to others who have not yet offended, to be the vehicle by which society wreaks vengeance, to keep offenders isolated from the community, and at the same time to modify offenders' future conduct.

It may be that conflicting expectations stem from the dual function of the criminal law, which is caught between the retributive position that we need to seek revenge and inflict punishment and the utilitarian position that the purpose of penal sanctions is to prevent antisocial behavior by modifying the future behavior of the criminal.[81] To make the prison system responsible for implementing these incompatible philosophies is simply unrealistic. George Herbert Mead recognized this in 1918, when he wrote that control of crime through the hostile procedure of the law is incompatible with control of crime through comprehension of social and psychological conditions.[82] More recently, Goldfarb and Singer put it as follows:

> The very notion that the way to prepare an asocial person to be a responsible citizen is to isolate him from his natural community and opportunities and normal life and keep him for prolonged periods, either alone or with others with similar or worse problems, defies credibility; yet, it is the basic plan.[83]

At times, rehabilitation bears no relationship to punishment or treatment.
Convicted of murder when he was a young man, James Lee Walton escaped
from prison and lived many years as a "straight" citizen. Then, in an effort to
clear his name, he gave himself up. Walton is seen in prison awaiting a
reexamination of his case. (ARTHUR SIRDOFSKY/EDITORIAL PHOTOCOLOR
ARCHIVES)

The incompatibility of punishment and treatment underlies the failure of the
treatment model. As many people have argued, it is unjustifiable to attempt to
conduct treatment in the setting of the prison.[84] Some would claim that the
demands of custody are so great that treatment is never given a chance.[85]
However, others see treatment itself as a crime when it is combined with coercion
under any conditions:

> Mixing treatment with coercion in the penal system not only lengthens sentences and
> increases the suffering and the sense of injustice, it also vitiates the treatment
> programs that are its justification.[86]

Somewhat more moderately, Norval Morris has argued that the rehabilitative
ideal can be saved, but only if facilitated change is substituted for coerced cure.
From this viewpoint, rehabilitation programs need to recognize the offender's

right to choose to be treated or not treated, and such programs should not be related to time served in prison or to conditions of incarceration.[87]

Social control

The second aspect of the debate over corrections is the real purpose of the prison. As we have seen, the record of prisons is one of failure on many counts. Internally, violence and brutality are an integral part of prison life. In the broader picture, there is inequity when one looks at who is and who is not sent to prison. Finally, prisons are saddled with so many goals operating at cross-purposes that none appear to be achievable. Given all these problems, why is it that Michel Foucault is able to assert, with a touch of irony:

> So successful has the prison been that, after a century and a half of "failures," the prison still exists, producing the same results, and there is the greatest reluctance to dispense with it.[88]

Why, we might go on to ask, is it not merely that prisons continue to exist but that the number of inmates continues to increase?

Many social scientists would follow the lead of Émile Durkheim and George Herbert Mead in explaining the continued existence of prisons despite their record of failure. Durkheim saw crime as normal—indeed functional—in society because it stimulates negative sentiments and the response of punishment.[89] Mead put it in slightly different words when he wrote, " . . . The attitude of hostility toward the law breaker has the unique advantage of uniting all members of the community in the emotional solidarity of aggression."[90]

Criminologists who see corrections as class control have gone beyond Durkheim and Mead to argue that the attainment of increased social solidarity has distinct class implications. We have already noted the disproportionate numbers of lower-class people who are incarcerated. From this viewpoint, prisons function to maintain the systems of social inequality and social class. As Rusche and Kircheimer put it for punishment generally:

> . . . So long as society is unable to solve its social problems, repression, the easy way out, will always be accepted. It provides the illusion of security by covering the symptoms of social disease with a system of legal and moral value judgments.[91]

More recently, Reasons and Kaplan have applied a critical perspective to prisons and delineated what they see as latent or not immediately obvious functions of corrections (see Box 22).

In short, the view of prisons as instruments of social control clashes with the view of prisons as sanctions or treatment with regard to what prisons should be and what they are. Unclear resolution of the question whether prisons should punish or treat offenders has rendered them ineffective on both counts. Many sociologists have argued that prisons survive because they enhance social solidarity. More pointedly, they can also be seen to serve as a means of control over the lower classes, who bear the brunt of penal sanctions in general and imprisonment in particular.

1. The prison system establishes an atmosphere in which values supportive of criminal behavior are reinforced and additional criminal behavior is learned.
2. Prison provides the opportunity for politicalization of the "dangerous classes."
3. The prison enhances the inmates' self-esteem and prestige (through the inmates' social system).
4. Prisons provide employment to 70,000 persons, many of whom would find it difficult to procure jobs elsewhere.
5. Some prisons provide psychic satisfaction for authoritarian employees who have a need for domination.
6. Some prisons provide slave labor for the prison industries.
7. Prisons function to reduce the level of unemployment rates.
8. Prisons provide subjects for scientific research, especially on drug testing.
9. Prisons give volunteers and civic organizations an opportunity to discharge their humanitarian impulses at little economic cost.
10. Prisons provide a safety valve for racial tensions; tensions in our society are reduced as we incarcerate the minorities and the poor.
11. Imprisonment serves to lower the birthrate for the "undesirables" in prison.

SOURCE

Adapted from Charles E. Reasons and Russell L. Kaplan, "Tear Down the Walls? Some Functions of Prisons," *Crime and Delinquency*, vol. 21, 1975, pp. 365–372.

This discussion of present-day concerns in corrections has followed the literature of the field and focused mainly on prisons. Prisons pose many critical issues for corrections. Their internal dynamics are characterized by immense tension. They are bastions of social inequality in that their populations are disproportionately young, male, from racial or ethnic minorities, and of lower social class. Finally, their manifest purposes are in conflict in that they are expected to punish, deter, seek retribution, and incapacitate and rehabilitate offenders all at the same time. Observing this situation, many social scientists would claim that there are latent purposes which undercut the manifest ones. For one, crime stimulates punishment, thereby enhancing social solidarity. For another, prisons help maintain social inequality. Perhaps it is for these latent reasons that the number of prison inmates is on the upswing even though the problems associated with incarceration are well known.

As with the police and the courts, it is necessary to look beyond the present correctional system to discuss possible alternatives. We now need to ask whether or not there are better or more appropriate ways of punishing criminal behavior and treating criminal offenders.

CORRECTIONAL ALTERNATIVES

In discussing correctional alternatives, it must be recognized that a certain amount of caution is in order. The history of corrections is full of alternatives, some of which have created problems as intractable as the ones they were designed to alleviate. Prisons are a prime case in point; they were originally advanced as a humane alternative to corporal and capital punishment, but problems such as internal tension, social inequality, and incompatible philoso-phies continue to plague their operations. Treatment is another case; also advanced as humane, it has often turned out to be both punitive and ineffective, especially when administered in a prison setting. One can only hold up the standard that alternatives being proposed today—"tearing down prison walls" and other plans for community corrections—are not mere label switching but an actual improvement over the present system.

Tearing Down Prison Walls

The crux of alternatives to the present correctional system is "tearing down prison walls." Its most radical form is the total abolition of prisons, a proposal that has been advocated since the late 1800s.[92] A more moderate form is the proposal that prisons should play a much reduced role in the overall correctional system.[93] Clearly, such ideas are easier to propose than to implement. The most notable instance of "tearing down walls" is the closing of juvenile institutions in Massachusetts under the leadership of Jerome Miller. One subsequent analysis of this experiment found that although recidivism did not decrease, there was also no "explosive youth crime wave." Moreover, further community efforts would have helped to foster reintegration of offenders.[94]

Other Community Correctional Alternatives

Once the walls of the prison are torn down, the locus of corrections would move into the community. On one level, the rationale of community corrections is clear. In the words of Dennis Sullivan, community corrections means opting for the healing power of self-determining and autonomous communities.[95] In the words of Calvin R. Dodge, community corrections means following the maxim: "The optional punishment for a civilized society is that which departs least from the normal conduct of life in all its characteristics."[96] Others have proposed "reinte-gration" and "development of self-esteem" as rationales for community correc-tions.[97]

However, clear and positive though the philosophy of community correc-tions may be, the programmatic possibilities are enormous and difficult to assess comprehensively. Work release, residence in a halfway house, and a variety of other community correctional programs have already been mentioned. To these possibilities might also be added some ideas that are far more innovative but largely untried: fines based on gravity of the offense and income of the offender; community service orders involving work or other service to the community; and creative reconciliation of offenders and victims through mutual restitution.[98]

Community corrections could also take other turns. It could be tied into the probation system, so that professional probation officers would serve as links between offenders and community services.[99] In his argument for treatment, Menninger proposes "community safety centers" in which offenders would be treated as if they were outpatients.[100] Perhaps the most extreme form of this proposal is to have offenders monitored in the community through the use of various electronic devices. Offenders would wear personal transmitters that would send continual signals of their location; male sex offenders would be monitored by "transducers" that would measure penile changes and record them in an electronic locator system.[101]

This section has presented only the bare outlines of community correctional alternatives. Obviously, such alternatives need to be debated, analyzed, and more fully understood. Although the current trend in corrections appears to be toward increased use of prison, it may well be that for all the reasons previously discussed, prisons will be an increasingly less viable form of social organization. Community programs will then demand far more serious attention than they have received to date.

SUMMARY

Corrections involves doing something *to* or *for* offenders. Increasingly at the center of criminological attention, corrections is a field beset by controversy and conflicting philosophies. In the 1950s, it was dominated by the belief that offenders were sick people whose illnesses could be diagnosed and subsequently treated. However, after being subjected to much criticism, this belief no longer dominates the field. Rather, three major perspectives have emerged. Two of them, corrections as sanctions and corrections as treatment, are expressions of what corrections should be. The third, corrections as class control, provides a perspective on the social function of corrections.

Like the courts, corrections evolved over the centuries. Early England, before 1066, had a system of private vengeance that came to be replaced by monetary fines. In the following centuries, as England moved into feudalism, more crimes became defined and increasingly harsh punishments were developed. Capital punishment, mutilation and branding, whipping, and use of pillory and the stocks all became quite common, especially for the poor. In the 1700s, England experienced enormous social changes associated with industrialization; capital punishment and transportation both became common during that period.

Punishments in America reflected a harshness comparable to that of England. However, Americans of the colonial period tended to rely more on corporal than on capital punishment and more on the mechanisms of public shame than on transportation. Community nonresidents received different punishments from residents. They were whipped and expelled, a system which eventually created a migratory criminal group.

Perhaps the most distinctive period of corrections was the 1820s, when prisons emerged. In these newly developed institutions, offenders were to be isolated and subjected to a disciplined routine. Serving time in prison was to replace capital punishment, corporal punishment, and the mechanisms of public shame as the primary mode of corrections in the United States. This drastic shift in corrections has been linked by writers such as Rothman to the immense social changes in the early decades of the 1800s, and by others such as Rusche and Kircheimer to the industrialization of American society.

Plagued by problems literally from the outset, the prison has been the object of attempts at reform that date back to the mid-1800s. One of the most problematic reforms was the indeterminate sentence, in which judges sent defendants to prison and let parole boards fix dates for their release. Indeterminate sentences paved the way for treatment and the introduction of psychiatrists, psychologists, and other professionals into the prison. Other reforms, such as probation and parole, aimed to get convicted offenders out of the prison system. Probation, which can be traced to the work of John Augustus in the 1840s, involves offering personal services to the offender in the community in lieu of incarceration. Parole dates back to the 1880s and also involves personal services to the offender in the community, the difference being that it is used after a period of incarceration. The most recent correctional reforms occurred in the 1960s and 1970s, when community corrections came into existence. Arguing that reintegration of the offender was the principal aim of corrections, advocates of community corrections sponsored work release, halfway houses, and a variety of other community-based programs.

Today, the American correctional system is an amalgamation of agencies that reflect various stages of historical experience. On any given day, about 9 out of every 1000 Americans are under its umbrella. Most are on probation, although the number on parole is also significant, especially when compared with the number in prison. However, recent years have seen dramatic increases in state prison populations—14 percent between 1971 and 1975 and 50 percent between 1975 and 1981. Now at an all-time peak, the imprisonment rate of the United States is far higher than that of most other countries.

The focus of much present-day concern in corrections is the prison. Three issues are of particular importance: (1) The internal dynamics of prisons are problematic. Attempting to maintain total social control over every aspect of the prisoner's life, prisons represent a bargain between guards and inmates. In recent years, this bargain has become more tenuous, and violence of various forms has come to characterize prison life. (2) Prisons are an indicator of social inequality in American society in that prison populations are disproportionately young, male, minority, and of lower-class social origin. (3) Prisons are caught up in conflicting correctional goals. On a manifest level, punishment clashes with treatment. On a latent level, the real purpose of the prison may be seen as enhancing community solidarity and control of the lower classes.

The most radical alternative to the present-day correctional system is "tearing down prison walls," partly or totally. After this first step has been taken, the locus of corrections would move away from isolation and toward meaningful involvement of the offender in the community. The possibilities for corrections in the community are considerable and were only partly developed in the programs of the 1960s and 1970s. Fines, community service orders, reconciliation of offenders and victims through mutual restitution, more creative use of probation officers, community safety centers, and (a rather extreme proposal) monitoring offenders with electronic devices are all possibilities. Given the limitations and problems of the prison system, it is important that these possibilities be thoroughly examined and their implications fully understood.

NOTES

[1] Karl Menninger, *The Crime of Punishment*, Viking, New York, 1966, 1968, p. 261.

[2] Douglas Lipton, Robert Martinson, and Judith Wilks, *The Effectiveness of Correctional Treatment: A Survey of Treatment Evaluation Studies*, Praeger, New York, 1975; quotation on p. 560.

[3] Gene Kassebaum, David Ward, and Daniel Wilner, *Prison Treatment and Parole Survival: An Empirical Assessment*, Wiley, New York, 1971.

[4] E.g., see: Robert Martinson, "What Works? Questions and Answers about Prison Reform," *Public Interest*, vol. 35, Spring 1974, pp. 22–54.

⁵ American Friends Service Committee, *Struggle for Justice*, Hill and Wang, New York 1971, especially chap. 3.

⁶ Jessica Mitford, *Kind and Usual Punishment: The Prison Business*, Vintage (Random House), New York, 1973, chaps. 6 and 7.

⁷ Thomas S. Szasz, "Crime, Punishment, and Psychiatry," in Abraham S. Blumberg, ed., *Current Perspectives on Criminal Behavior: Essays on Criminology*, 2d ed., Knopf, New York, 1981, pp. 342–363; quotation on p. 346.

⁸ Graeme Newman, *The Punishment Response*, Lippincott, Philadelphia, Pa., 1978, pp. 7f.

⁹ James Q. Wilson, *Thinking about Crime*, Basic Books, New York, 1975, especially chap. 8; and Ernest van den Haag, *Punishing Criminals: Concerning a Very Old and Painful Question*, Basic Books, New York, 1975.

¹⁰ Andrew von Hirsch, *Doing Justice: The Choice of Punishments—Report of the Committee for the Study of Incarceration*, Hill and Wang, New York, 1976; and David Fogel, *We Are the Living Proof: The Justice Model for Corrections*, Anderson, Cincinnati, Ohio, 1975.

¹¹ Fogel, *We Are the Living Proof*.

¹² Ted Palmer, "Martinson Revisited," *Journal of Research in Crime and Delinquency*, July 1976, pp. 133–152.

¹³ Judith Wilks and Robert Martinson, "Is the Treatment of Criminal Offenders Really Necessary?" *Federal Probation*, vol. 40, no. 1, 1976, pp. 3–9.

¹⁴ Charles A. Murray and Louis A. Cox, Jr., *Beyond Probation: Juvenile Corrections and the Chronic Delinquent*, Sage, Beverly Hills, Calif., 1979.

¹⁵ Kevin N. Wright, "A Re-Examination of Correctional Alternatives," *International Journal of Offender Therapy and Comparative Criminology*, vol. 24, no. 2, 1980, pp. 179–192.

¹⁶ Georg Rusche and Otto Kircheimer, *Punishment and Social Structure*, Russell and Russell, New York, 1939, 1967, 1968, p. 5.

¹⁷ Charles E. Reasons and Russell L. Kaplan, "Tear Down the Walls? Some Functions of Prisons," *Crime and Delinquency*, vol. 21, 1975, pp. 360–372.

¹⁸ Matthew G. Yeager, "Unemployment and Imprisonment," *Journal of Criminal Law and Criminology*, vol. 70, Winter 1979, pp. 586–588; and Ivan Jankovic, "Labor Market and Imprisonment," *Crime and Social Justice*, vol. 8, Fall-Winter 1977, pp. 17–31.

¹⁹ Christopher Hibbert, *The Roots of Evil: A Social History of Crime and Punishment*, Little, Brown, Boston, Mass., 1963.

²⁰ Alan Harding, *A Social History of the English Law*, Penguin, Baltimore, Md., 1966, chap. 3.

²¹ William J. Chambliss, "A Sociological Analysis of the Law of Vagrancy," *Social Problems*, vol. 12, 1964, pp. 45–69.

²² Rusche and Kircheimer, *Punishment and Social Structure*, chap. 2.

²³ Frank E. Hartung, "Trends in the Use of Capital Punishment," *Annals of the American Academy of Political and Social Science*, vol. 284, November 1952, pp. 8–19.

²⁴ Harry Elmer Barnes and Negley K. Teeters, *New Horizons in Criminology*, 3d ed., Prentice-Hall, Englewood Cliffs, N.J., 1959, chap. 19.

²⁵ The following discussion of corrections in early America is much indebted to: David J. Rothman, *The Discovery of the Asylum: Social Order and Disorder in the New Republic*, Little, Brown, Boston, Mass., 1971.

²⁶ Ibid., chap. 2.

²⁷ Ibid.

²⁸ Michel Foucault, *Discipline and Punish: The Birth of the Prison*, Vintage (Random House), New York, 1977.

²⁹ Rothman, *The Discovery of the Asylum*, chap. 4.

³⁰ Ibid.

³¹ Ibid., chap. 3.

³² See: Rusche and Kircheimer, *Punishment and Social Structure*; Foucault, *Discipline and Punish*; and Michael Ignatieff, *A Just Measure of Pain: The Penitentiary in the Industrial Revolution, 1750–1850*, Pantheon, New York, 1978.

³³ Rothman, *The Discovery of the Asylum*, chap. 10.

³⁴ George Underwood et al., "Report of the Committee Appointed to the Several State Prisons," *New York Assembly Documents*, no. 20, 1852, pp. 40–41, 55; quoted by: Rothman, *The Discovery of the Asylum*, p. 244.

³⁵ John Vincent Barry, "Alexander Maconochie, 1787–1860," in Hermann Mannheim, ed., *Pioneers in Criminology*, Patterson Smith, Montclair, N.J., 1972, pp. 84–106.

³⁶ See: Thomas O. Murton, *The Dilemma of Prison Reform*, Holt, Rinehart and Winston, New York, 1976, pp. 15–16.

³⁷ Ibid., chap. 9. In his efforts to turn the Tucker Prison Farm in Arkansas into a humane institution, Murton himself followed the pattern set forth by the earlier reformers.

³⁸ Barnes and Teeters, *New Horizons in Criminology*, pp. 425–439.

³⁹ Quoted by: Mitford, *Kind and Usual Punishment*, pp. 91–92.

⁴⁰ Murton, *The Dilemma of Prison Reform*, p. 200.

⁴¹ See: Mitford, *Kind and Usual Punishment*, chap. 6.

⁴² See: George C. Killinger and Paul F. Cromwell, Jr., eds., *Corrections in the Community: Selected Readings*, West, St. Paul, Minn., 1974, especially chaps. 3 and 4.

⁴³ The following discussion of probation and parole is much indebted to: Ronald L. Goldfarb and Linda R. Singer, *After Conviction*, Simon and Schuster, New York, 1973, chaps. 4 and 5.

⁴⁴ Harry E. Allen and Clifford E. Simonsen, *Corrections in America: An Introduction*, 2d ed., Glencoe, Encino, Calif., 1978, p. 162.

⁴⁵ Ibid., chap. 4. See also: Eric W. Carlson and Evalyn C. Parks, *Critical Issues in Adult Probation: Issues in Probation Management*, U.S. Department of Justice, Government Printing Office, Washington, D.C., September 1979.

⁴⁶ E.g.: Robert L. Smith, *A Quiet Revolution*, U.S. Department of Health, Education, and Welfare, Washington, D.C., 1972, pp. 51f.

⁴⁷ On probation, see also: Mona McCormick, *Probation: What the Literature Reveals*, Western Behavioral Sciences Institute, La Jolla, Calif., 1973.

⁴⁸ On parole, see: Goldfarb and Singer, *After Conviction*, chap. 5.

476

[49] President's Commission on Law Enforcement and the Administration of Justice, *Task Force Report: Corrections*, vol. 60, Government Printing Office, Washington, D.C., 1967.

[50] E.g.: Andrew von Hirsch and Kathleen J. Hanrahan, *The Question of Parole: Retention, Reform, or Abolition?* Ballinger (Harper and Row), Cambridge, Mass., 1979.

[51] President's Commission on Law Enforcement and the Administration of Justice, *Task Force Report: Corrections*, p. 7.

[52] Goldfarb and Singer, *After Conviction*, chap. 8. See also: Richard Kwartler, ed., *Behind Bars: Prisons in America*, Vintage (Random House), New York, 1977, especially chap. 4, "Community Programs for Offenders."

[53] Robert G. Culbertson, "Corrections: The State of the Art," *Journal of Criminal Justice*, vol. 5, 1977, pp. 39–46.

[54] See: Killinger and Cromwell, *Corrections in the Community*, especially chap. 1.

[55] Benjamin Frank, "The American Prison: The End of an Era," *Federal Probation*, vol. 43, September 1979, pp. 3–9.

[56] On jails, see: Ronald Goldfarb, *Jails: The Ultimate Ghetto*, Anchor (Doubleday), Garden City, N.Y., 1975.

[57] Eugene Doleschal, "Rate and Length of Imprisonment: How Does the United States Compare with the Netherlands, Denmark, and Sweden?" *Crime and Delinquency*, vol. 23, no. 1, January 1977, pp. 51–56.

[58] Hans W. Mattick, "The Prosaic Sources of Prison Violence," in Anthony L. Guenther, ed., *Criminal Behavior and Social Systems: Contributions of American Sociology*, 2d ed., Rand McNally, Chicago, Ill., 1976, pp. 529–540; and Gresham M. Sykes, "The Corruption of Authority and Rehabilitation," *Social Forces*, vol. 34, March 1956, pp. 257–272.

[59] Gresham M. Sykes and Sheldon L. Messinger, "The Inmate Social System," in Richard A. Cloward et al., eds., *Theoretical Studies in the Social Organization of the Prison*, Social Science Research Council, New York, 1960, pp. 5–19.

[60] Gresham M. Sykes, *The Society of Captives: A Study of a Maximum Security Prison*, Atheneum, New York, 1965, chap. 3; quotation on p. 58.

[61] John Irwin, *Prisons in Turmoil*, Little, Brown, Boston, Mass., 1980, chap. 7; quotation from: John Irwin, "The Changing Social Structure of the Men's Prison," in David Greenberg, ed., *Corrections and Punishment*, Sage, Beverly Hills, Calif., 1977, p. 21.

[62] Edith Elisabeth Flynn, "From Conflict Theory to Conflict Resolution; Controlling Collective Violence in Prison," *American Behavioral Scientist*, vol. 23, no. 5, May-June 1980, p. 752f. See also: Ronald Berkman, *Opening the Gates: The Rise of the Prisoner's Movement*, Lexington Books, Lexington, Mass., 1979.

[63] Jessica Mitford, *Kind and Usual Punishment*, chap. 14; and South Carolina Department of Corrections, *The Emerging Rights of the Confined*, monograph, 1972.

[64] Flynn, "From Conflict Theory to Conflict Resolution."

[65] Alan J. Davis, "Sexual Assaults in the Philadelphia Prison System and Sheriff's Vans," *Trans-Action*, vol. 6, December 1968, pp. 8–16.

[66] Peter L. Nacci, "Sexual Assault in Prisons," *American Journal of Corrections*, vol. 40, January-February 1978, pp. 30–31.

[67] David A. Jones, *The Health Risks of Imprisonment*, Heath, Lexington, Mass., 1976.

[68] Daniel Lockwood, *Prison Sexual Violence*, Oxford and Elsevier, New York, 1980.

[69] For a review, see: Lee H. Bowker, *Prison Victimization*, Oxford and Elsevier, New York, 1980, pp. 21–27.

[70] Sawyer F. Sylvester, John H. Reed, and David O. Nelson, *Prison Homicide*, Spectrum, New York, 1977. See also: W. T. Austin and Charles M. Unkovic, "Prison Suicide," *Criminal Justice Review*, vol. 2, no. 1, Spring 1977, pp. 103–106.

[71] See: Thomas O. Murton, *The Dilemma of Prison Reform*, Holt, Rinehart and Winston, New York, 1976, chap. 2; Thomas Murton and Joe Hyams, *Inside Prison, U.S.A.*, Grove, New York, 1969; and Bowker, *Prison Victimization*, chap. 7.

[72] Hans Toch, *Police, Prisons, and the Problem of Violence*, Government Printing Office, Washington, D.C., 1977, especially pp. 65–67.

[73] Flynn, "From Conflict Theory to Conflict Resolution," p. 757.

[74] Ibid. See also: Murton, *The Dilemma of Prison Reform*, chap. 2.

[75] Timothy J. Flanagan, David J. van Alstyne, and Michael R. Gottfredson, eds., *Sourcebook of Criminal Justice Statistics—1981*, U.S. Department of Justice, Bureau of Justice Statistics, Government Printing Office, Washington, D.C., 1982, p. 485.

[76] Robert Johnson, "Warehousing for Death: Observations on the Human Environment of Death Row," *Crime and Delinquency*, vol. 25, October 1980, pp. 545–562.

[77] James B. Jacobs, "Race Relations and the Prisoner Subculture," in Norval Morris and Michael Tonry, eds., *Crime and Justice: An Annual Review of Research*, University of Chicago Press, Chicago, Ill., 1979, p. 24.

[78] Berkman, *Opening the Gates*.

[79] Jeffrey H. Reiman, *The Rich Get Richer and the Poor Get Prison: Ideology, Class, and Criminal Justice*, Wiley, New York, 1979.

[80] Murton, *The Dilemma of Prison Reform*, p. xi.

[81] Herbert L. Packer, *The Limits of the Criminal Sanction*, Stanford University Press, Stanford, Calif., 1968.

[82] George Herbert Mead, "The Psychology of Punitive Justice," *American Journal of Sociology*, vol. 23, 1918, pp. 586–592.

[83] Goldfarb and Singer, *After Conviction*, p. 11.

[84] E.g., see: Dennis Sullivan, *The Mask of Love—Corrections in America: Toward a Mutual Aid Alternative*, Kennikot, Port Washington, N.Y., 1980.

[85] Newman, *The Punishment Response*, chap. 13.

[86] American Friends Service Committee, *Struggle for Justice*, p. 97.

[87] Norval Morris, *The Future of Imprisonment*, University of Chicago Press, Chicago, Ill., 1974.

[88] Foucault, *Discipline and Punish*, p. 277.

[89] Émile Durkheim, *The Rules of Sociological Method*, Free Press, New York, 1974.

[90] Mead, "The Psychology of Punitive Justice."

[91] Rusche and Kircheimer, *Punishment and Social Structure*, p. 207.

[92] For a brief account, see: Mitford, *Kind and Usual Punishment*, pp. 297–298.

[93] Morris, *The Future of Imprisonment*; American Friends Service Committee, *Struggle for Justice*; and Calvert R. Dodge, ed., *A Nation without Prisons*, Heath (Lexington Books), Lexington, Mass., 1975.

[94] Robert B. Coates, Alder D. Miller, and Floyd E. Ohlin, *Diversity in a Youth Correctional System: Handling Delinquents in Massachusetts*, Ballinger, Cambridge, Mass., 1978.

[95] Sullivan, *The Mask of Love*, pp. 21–22.

[96] Dodge, p. xvi; quotation from the foreword by Milton G. Rector.

[97] On reintegration, see: Wright, "A Re-Examination of Correctional Alternatives." On self-esteem, see: Lawrence A. Bennett, "Corrections Adrift—New Objectives Needed," *Corrections Today*, vol. 42, July 1980, pp. 96–97, 102.

[98] See: Dodge, *A Nation without Prisons*. On the possibilities of reconciliation, see: Richard Korn, "Of Crime, Criminal Justice, and Corrections," *University of San Francisco Law Review*, vol. 6, October 1971, especially pp. 38–47 and 74.

[99] Goldfarb and Singer, *After Conviction*, chap. 4.

[100] Menninger, *The Crime of Punishment*, chap. 10.

[101] Ralph K. Schwitzgebel, *Development and Legal Regulation of Coercive Behavior Modification Techniques with Offenders*, National Institute of Mental Health, Center for Studies of Crime and Delinquency, Rockville, Md., 1971.

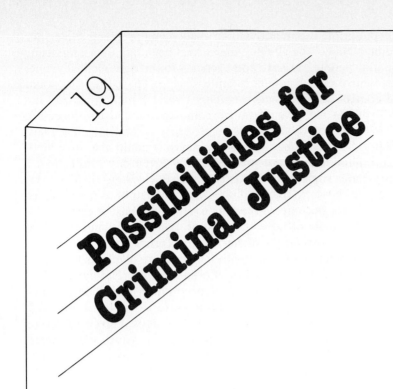

19

Possibilities for Criminal Justice

What to do about crime is one of the most challenging problems facing our society today. Since the 1960s, there has been an ever-increasing commitment of people, money, and agencies to the fight against crime. The resultant crime-control establishment is quite sizable. There are now about 56,000 public crime-control agencies which employ over 1.2 million people and spend more than $25 billion per year to police communities and to prosecute, defend, sentence, and correct those accused of being offenders.[1] To these numbers, the 350,000 to 800,000 police on private payrolls could also be added. Each year, about 10 million arrests are made. On any given day, more than 2 million Americans are under some form of correctional supervision—nearly 1 out of every 100. Yet despite these extensive efforts, the problem of crime remains. Many would argue that it has become worse than ever. In the past several years, rates of reported crime, rates of arrest, rates of conviction, and rates of incarceration have all been substantially higher than in earlier years.

To contrast the phenomenon of crime with the structure of efforts to control it demonstrates just how difficult the problem of crime can be. The most costly, the most violent, and the most subtle crimes—corporate crime, crime against corporations, organized crime, and political crime—are often left unnoticed, uncounted, and untouched by the crime-control establishment. Person-to-person crimes involving violence and property receive the most intensive crime-control efforts. The attention given to social-order crimes is most erratic; enforcement may be marked by all-out crusades, by highly discretionary practices, or by complete neglect.

The shortcomings of efforts to control person-to-person crime are apparent when we examine the data on major index crimes. According to the victim surveys, there are about 21.7 million incidents of personal and household victimization in a year. About 13.3 million are reported to police. The police clear about 2.5 million by arrest. Following arrest, there is much attrition of cases. If we apply the percentages of the VERA study to that 2.5 million (see Chapter 17), there would be 1.4 million convictions and 675,000 prison or jail sentences, of which 125,000 would be for "felony time." Obviously only a small percentage of those who commit crimes are ever arrested and incarcerated for them. The disparity is especially sharp in light of self-report crime surveys which suggest that a substantial proportion (if not a majority) of the population have at some time in their lives committed a crime for which they could have been jailed or imprisoned. (See Chapter 10.)

The attrition of criminal cases reflects some important questions about crime control. Should we encourage people, especially victims, to report crimes of all types, so that more crimes are known to the police? Should we beef up police forces, so that they can clear more crimes by arrest? Should we give prosecutors more latitude, so that they can obtain more convictions? Should we incarcerate or put on probation those who are convicted? Should incarceration or probation be punishment-oriented or treatment-oriented? Finally, there are questions related to justice. What allowances should we make for violence related to police work or violence in prisons? What allowances should we make for rights of offenders?

Unfortunately, criminology offers no simple answers to such questions. There is some evidence that some crimes can be deterred, but no evidence that increased efforts at control are an effective deterrent for all crime—especially in a criminal justice system that is as "loosely coupled" as ours. There is some evidence that a few types of treatment work for a few types of offenders; but a treatment program that works for all offenders is simply not to be found. Preventing crime by fighting its "root causes"—poverty, unemployment, and discrimination—makes sense but seems too indirect to make an impact in the short term. Finally, the decriminalization, diversion, and deinstitutionalization suggested by the new criminology are most suggestive but have yet to be fully put into practice.

The uncertainties of criminology mean that there is no one preferred solution to the problems of criminal justice and crime control. These uncertainties also reflect the multidimensionality of crime and its relationship to a variety of social factors. Indeed, in our examination of the seven major types of crime in Part Three, we found relationships between crime and numerous social factors such as age, sex, race, class, mobility, social relationships, and cultural values. In short, crime is a problem that may well have neither a single cause nor a single solution.

However, to say this is not to despair. There are numerous possibilities for improving criminal justice and improving crime control. To explore these possibilities, we will return to the framework in which we analyze crime in terms of the criminal act, the offender, the victim, and the social context. The criminological perspectives are also important, since some of the possibilities lie along the lines of the classical, positivist, sociological, and critical approaches we examined in Part Two. A few possibilities extend beyond these perspectives, and it will be useful to examine them also.

THE CRIMINAL ACT: TOWARD REDEFINITION

One starting point for a consideration of possibilities for criminal justice is the criminal act itself. As we have seen, the criminal act has been a central concern both of the classical school, which attempted to create a rational scheme in which punishments would be proportional to crime; and of the new criminology, which has argued for decriminalization, particularly of social-order crimes. The general question posed by both schools is: Which types of behavior and how much behavior should society attempt to control through the criminal law?

To gain a perspective on the control of behavior through criminal law, it is useful to begin with Donald Black's historical observation that the use of law has increased along with the amount of crime; with the appropriation by some people of other people's property; and with social inequality, as evidenced in greater hierarchy, differentiation, and relational distance.[2] This tendency to criminalize more and more areas of conduct in modern society can be seen in social-order crime and corporate crime; in the practice of calling on the police, even for comparatively minor incidents; and in the spillover of personal and family disputes into the criminal justice system.

Against the strong historical trend to criminalize more areas of conduct, one might posit a utopian vision in which crime and "creeping legality . . . will all diminish, . . . and in their place will be a continuous process of anarchy and justice." This vision would include a concept of "needs-based" rather than "rights-based" or "deserts-based" justice.[3] A somewhat related approach would be to raise the level of deviance that can be tolerated and "as a result of such tolerance experience less deviance,'' because fewer people are stigmatized as deviants for comparatively minor offenses.[4] Raising the level of tolerance is a possibility that is usually advanced in connection with decriminalization of various social-order crimes. (See Chapter 13.) But Milton Friedman and Rose Friedman and other politically conservative economists would also seek to deregulate and decriminalize many business-related offenses.[5]

Decriminalization or legalization is not necessarily a clear-cut straightforward process:

> In fact, we find ourselves shifting from the relative conceptual simplicity of criminal prohibition to the subtlety and complexity of administrative regulation. Agencies of decriminalization are devised by law making bodies to replace earlier models of morality enforcement.[6]

Several models of decriminalization are possible:

1. *Nullification*; the law withdraws entirely (e.g., all forms of sexual relations between consenting adults are allowed).
2. *Commodity model* (e.g., ''over-the-counter'' sales of tobacco or alcohol).
3. *Commercial service* (e.g., legal prostitution with controls for health).
4. *Vice* (e.g., in prostitution, the seller is held liable but the customer is absolved of guilt).
5. *Medical* (e.g., drugs sold under a doctor's prescription).
6. *Licensing* (a variety of forms).[7]

In reflecting on these possibilities, it should be noted that the politics of decriminalization often dictate a compromise between, or a mixture of, one or more models. Moreover, in all the models except nullification some form of social control is maintained. However, administrative control along the lines of models 2 through 6 is generally less costly, easier to put into practice, and less arbitrary than control through the criminal justice system.

It would also be possible to decriminalize or legalize some but not all aspects of certain offensive behaviors. There are wide limits for legal use of pornography, alcohol, and tobacco, except when minors under age 16 or age 18 are involved. With regard to alcohol consumption, gambling, and many of the sex crimes, enforcement could concentrate on the public rather than private aspects of the behavior. Thus, drunken driving can be criminalized without making the consumption of alcohol a crime. Such selective criminalization dramatically narrows the numbers of people and situations that need to be policed. Selective criminalization is a policy that might be pursued for other social-order crimes as well as for certain business crimes. One possible model for selective criminalization was advanced over a century ago by John Stuart Mill, when he stated:

> . . . The only purpose for which power can be rightfully exercised over any member of a civilized community, against his will, is to prevent harm to others.[8]

Another possibility for a criminal justice system oriented toward acts would be to use relatively short determinate sentences in the name of punishment rather than long indeterminate ones in the name of treatment. (See Chapter 17.) This would capture the spirit of Beccaria's certainty in sentencing, increase predictability, and allow comparable sentencing for similar offenses. Thus, it holds out the prospect of a criminal justice system that is both more equitable and more effective as a deterrent.

Finally, in contrast to decriminalization, the criminal justice system can be seen as a tool for moral education. From this viewpoint, criminal law is

> a tool of moral learning by the society at large. If the system of criminal justice is properly arranged, the punished behavior becomes widely perceived as intrinsically wrong and is avoided owing to an intense feeling of its immorality. This is a powerful motivation, much stronger than the fear of sanction.[9]

However, developing this moral, educative function of the law is not easy. It assumes a "moral referendum" which provides the foundation for criminal codes. Moreover, it means reform of the legal system so that (1) the proper forms of behavior are selected for punishment, (2) the law is administered with consistency, and (3) discretion and leniency are curtailed while constitutional rights are observed. Nevertheless, the vision is that

> the overwhelming majority of potential lawbreakers will, following the just and certain punishment of the "first generation," forgo the criminal way and avoid the misery. [We will see a] . . . general improvement of the social fabric and, by making men better, contribute to the moral progress of our society.[10]

This vision has long been the hope of criminal law, and it continues to provide a rationale for future efforts.

To summarize briefly, to question the criminal act is to ask about the type and amount of behavior that ought to be criminalized. To suggest new possibilities is to buck the historical trend toward increased use of criminal law. One may advance the utopian vision of needs-based rather than rights- or deserts-based justice. One may advocate decriminalization of specific crimes, usually social-order or business offenses, recognizing that decriminalization is a subtle matter with several options. One may call for shorter determinate sentences that would tend to ensure both equity and deterrence. Finally, one could see the criminal justice system as a means of moral education. Whichever route we take, there is an implicit recognition that the criminal justice system is overloaded and that it needs to back away from criminalizing as much behavior as it has criminalized in the past. In taking the act as the key to reform of criminal justice, we are asking which behavior and how much behavior we want to attempt to control through the criminal law.

THE OFFENDER: TOWARD WORKABLE TREATMENT

Many proposed solutions to problems of criminal justice involve doing something about or something to the offender. The offender was, indeed, the main concern of the positivist school which so strongly influenced mainstream criminology and the practice of criminal justice. The offender has also been a concern of the sociological school. Out of this interest in offenders has come a considerable variety of treatment programs.

For all the attention given to offenders, there is surprisingly little knowledge about workable treatment strategies. A considerable number of people are subject to correctional supervision. Yet recidivism remains high; no treatment program has had a dramatic impact on recidivism rates. In fact, many evaluations have shown little difference in recidivism between people subjected to treatment and comparable control groups not receiving treatment. (On the debates about treatment, see Chapter 18.)

However, against the general despair about treatment and rehabilitation, it can be argued that the conventional approaches to treatment have been neither sufficiently distinctive nor sufficiently far-reaching. The untried possibilities for treatment run along several lines, each of which has had success in at least one specific setting:

1. Guided group interaction
2. Use of ex-offenders to rehabilitate offenders
3. Reform of prisons
4. Income maintenance for ex-offenders
5. Community corrections

Let's take a look at each of these.

A few treatment programs have reported success with *guided group interaction*, an approach which uses group processes to undermine delinquent attitudes and develop self-concepts favorable to rehabilitation. At Highfields—an experiment in guided group interaction for rehabilitation of delinquents in the mid-1950s—emphasis was placed on helping the boys to be like everyone else. Four methods were used: (1) Family members and friends of the boys were encouraged to visit them at Highfields. (2) An effort was made to educate the surrounding community to accept the boys. (3) The boys did useful work and received pay for it. (4) A boy's stay at Highfields was limited to a maximum of four months.[11] The Highfields approach was successfully replicated in Provo, Utah, and has subsequently been widely used for adult probationers and parolees.[12]

One model, which according to its participants has achieved success, involves *use of ex-offenders to rehabilitate offenders*. Based on the methods of Alcoholics Anonymous, this approach may rely on therapeutic communities and leaves professionals completely out of the picture. [13] One study found ex-offenders working as aides to be as effective as parole officers; in particular, they were highly rated both by the supervisors in whose units they worked and by the parolees who were being supervised.[14]

Some would argue that treatment and rehabilitation of individuals in prison can only be accomplished by *reform of the prison itself*. For one thing, prisons need to be small organizational units. For another, to rehabilitate prisoners, they must be given freedom to make decisions and to accept the responsibility for those decisions. In several historically significant prison reforms,

> . . . the common view was that the inmate is a human being with certain rights that should not be violated. Further, all believed that reformation cannot be imposed from

the top but must emanate from within. The individual must come to have self-respect, confidence, and belief in his own worth. To this end, the iron hand of the prison dictatorship's discipline was rejected and replaced with an environment conducive to the development of responsibility.[15]

Other reforms, somewhat less ambitious in design, would reject rehabilitation as the purpose of imprisonment but allow for expansion of treatment programs in prison and outside of prison so that those who want them can receive services. In other words, they would make treatment available but would not force it on offenders.[16]

A recently developed approach—one which has been subjected to careful evaluation—would use *income maintenance* (on the model of severance pay—e.g., $200 upon release from prison and 10 weekly payments of $60 each) to reduce recidivism among ex-offenders. The formulators of this approach note:

> It is cheaper to provide payments of between $800 and $1200 to 100 released prisoners than to process about five additional persons through the criminal justice system and provide prison places for them for periods of two to three years, not to mention the costs averted through reduced welfare payments for dependents and other costs of imprisonment.[17]

Finally, there has been a movement toward *community corrections* that has followed recommendations originally set forth in the mid-1960s by the President's Commission on Law Enforcement and Administration of Justice. The term "community corrections" has taken on many meanings: furloughs from prison, work release from prison, probation, parole, halfway houses, and proposals for community penal institutions located near urban centers. If the goal is treatment, this approach makes sense because the various programs bring the offender back into contact with the community of which he or she will eventually become a part. However, the community corrections movement has encountered many difficulties: quite a few offenders come from communities which may not be "desirable" to begin with; local residents often protest or resist community correctional programs; rates of absconding for some programs are quite high; and some programs have used practices as inhumane as those of large prisons. Although there can be no significant rehabilitation until an offender is accepted back into a community, community corrections needs some refinement before it can be advanced as an answer to the treatment of offenders.[18]

Each of these approaches is of interest; but none has received widespread acceptance or use as a solution to the problems of dealing with offenders. The prison system has been amazing in its defiance of reforms. Even those states which have attempted to rewrite laws in the spirit of definite and certain sentences have often set longer instead of shorter sentences.[19] The result is that recent years have seen more use of prisons, with increases in prison populations. A corresponding deemphasis of rehabilitation has left prisons with little more than custody as their rationale.

Since prisons seem to be here to stay, one can argue for a prison system in which punishment is "fair" and "humane." Such a rationale accepts imprisonment itself as a punishment but does not see prison as a place where corporal or other punishment ought to be administered. A fair and humane punishment system is one in which offenders receive comparable sentences for comparable crimes. A fair and humane prison system is one which respects offenders' rights, as defined by law, and one which recognizes both the right to treatment and the right not to be treated. In such a system, the offender is clear about the terms and conditions of his or her incarceration.[20]

A realistic correctional policy must also deal with the question whether we can learn to tolerate the offender at the same time that we denounce the crime. Because virtually all offenders are released back into society, the treatment or lack of treatment and the punishment or lack of punishment they receive in prison may well be an important factor in how they behave upon release.

THE VICTIM: TOWARD INVOLVEMENT

Long the forgotten person in the criminal justice picture, the victim cannot be ignored in our consideration of possibilities for criminal justice. At a minimum, one might suggest that the victim be compensated somehow for his or her loss. Certain victims—e.g., victims of rape—also need counseling and understanding that go beyond monetary compensation. Some criminologists have argued for systems of justice in which offenders and victims achieve some form of reconciliation with one another. Such systems would return justice from the hands of impersonal third parties to the parties actually involved in criminal incidents.

Compensation of victims is an idea whose time has come.

> The right question is whether victim compensation programs are worth what they cost—not how much they cost. These are programs to compensate *innocent* victims of crime, selected to bear the burden of society's failures. The foreseeable costs seem plainly justified.[21]

Victim-compensation programs were first developed in New Zealand in 1963 and in Great Britain in 1964; they have since been introduced in California, New York, Hawaii, Maryland, Massachusetts, New Jersey, Illinois, Alaska, Wisconsin, and Delaware, among other states. Although the details differ from state to state, all the programs are based on shifting responsibility for crime from the offender to the state. Their logic has two premises: (1) that since the state has failed to protect its individual members, it is obliged to recover damages for them; and (2) that compensation and restitution may soften the effects of the wrong done to the victim and, at the same time, begin the process of reforming the offender.[22] Despite the clarity of their logic, it should be recognized that victim-compensation programs are only in their initial stages. Many programs remain virtually unknown to the general public.[23]

Another rather different possibility would be to attempt some reconciliation of offenders and victims. This approach is seen in the community or neighborhood justice centers that have been established in a considerable number of cities across the country. These centers do not act as courts in which there is an adversarial proceeding to prove an offender's guilt and subsequent punishment as retribution. Rather, they use mediation, arbitration, and restitution in an effort to restore relationships between conflicting parties. Professional judges are replaced by lay "dispute resolvers" who are part of the community. The potential for such centers is great. They have already proved useful for the large numbers of disputes that occur between neighbors, between tenants and landlords, and between schools and students.[24] Their significance must also be seen in terms of the considerable numbers of essentially interpersonal conflicts that appear in courts in the form of major crimes such as assault, rape, and even robbery, burglary, and larceny.

Compensation of victims and reconciliation of victims and offenders are two interesting possibilities for a criminal justice system that would involve victims in dramatically new ways. Making the victim an important concern of the criminal justice system is a revolutionary proposal in that it would orient the system away from its disproportionate emphasis on the offender. It would also pave the way for a community-based system of criminal justice rather than the present system, in which professional, third-party outsiders are responsible for resolving problems. Its spirit was perhaps best expressed by a Japanese police officer interviewed by David Bayley: "People establish peace, not the police."[25]

In any event, we ought to pose questions about victims similar to those previously posed about offenders. What is a fair and humane policy for victims? How would such a policy be put into practice? In addition, we might also ask: Are people willing to forgo punishment in order to help offenders and restore relationships between offenders and victims?

THE SOCIAL CONTEXT: TOWARD CHANGING CONDITIONS OF CRIME

In examining the major types of crime in American society, we have consistently dealt with the social factors that are related to crime rates. We saw, for example, that changes in lifestyles are associated with increases in violent crime; that an abundance of movable property underlies the high rate of person-to-person property crime; and that corporate crimes, as well as crimes against corporations, stem from the organizational revolution that has characterized American society since the late 1800s. The various social factors have been grouped together as the "social context" of crime. Social context was the central point of concern for the sociological school of criminology, and some of that concern has been carried over to the new criminologies.

We now need to ask how profitable it would be to pursue criminal justice by attempting to alter the social context in which crime occurs. Although such an approach is indirect, it does offer a way of dealing with criminal justice that does not seek to do something for or to the offender. In the following presentation, possibilities for changes in social context are organized under four categories: (1) the community; (2) population and demographic factors; (3) targets, opportunities, and other conditions; and (4) quality of social relationships. Again, most of the possibilities to be discussed here are at the level of suggestions. Few have been put into widespread practice. Hardly any have been systematically evaluated or assessed.

Community

Changing the community has been one of the most popular approaches of those looking for new possibilities for criminal justice. Indeed, we have already looked at community corrections and community or neighborhood justice centers, both of which attempt to take criminal justice functions away from impersonal third parties and place them in the hands of community agencies. In terms of general social context, the community can have an even broader role: it can prevent crime from occurring in the first place. As Oscar Newman would have it, rather than relying on paid, third-party protectors, the solution to crime is creating a community in which each citizen feels responsible for aiding in policing.[26]

Using community influences as an antidote to crime is not in and of itself a new idea. As early as 1840, Alexis de Tocqueville noted that American communities had a spontaneous system of justice which restrained crime and offenders without the need to rely on magistrates or other public officials. To this, one might add the American tradition of vigilantism, an indigenous community movement that has been constructive at some times although very destructive at others.[27] However, the historically powerful neighborhood community entered a long

Job programs can be used in the battle against crime. These young men, who were unemployed and unskilled, are at work in Washington state's Youth Development and Conservation Corps planting trees in a state park.   (WIDE WORLD PHOTOS)

period of decline in the late 1800s, as populations migrated to cities, as large-scale corporations emerged, and as industrialization changed the pace of American life.

Today, the attempt to pursue criminal justice through the community works on two levels: rebuilding some communities and having other communities mobilize to take action against crime. The notion of rebuilding communities in order to fight crime has grown out of attempts to put the concepts of the sociological school into practice. Indeed, it is noteworthy that this idea has survived the disappointing results of the antipoverty program. It is seen, for instance, in the words of John Conyers, Jr., chairman of the House Subcommittee on Crime:

> After all, crime is not primarily caused by criminals, outlandish though that may sound. Crime in the aggregate is more fundamentally the product of desperation brought on by joblessness, poverty and community disintegration. Criminal acts multiply when a neighborhood or a city—even a nation—has so degenerated in its ability to provide for the well-being of people that individuals feel that stealing, mugging or selling dope is an acceptable means of survival. In short, crime is the economic and political consequence of a system rooted in indifference toward, and exploitation of, marginal and disadvantaged people.
>
> When a community begins to be starved of jobs, public institutions and social services, it needs to survive (once a neighborhood is defined as a high-crime area, services disappear at an alarming rate), and when its members are so desperate they must fend for themselves—that's when a community loses the chance to flex enough political muscle to fight for the larger social goals necessary to effect a turnabout.[28]

One interesting account of a community effort that reportedly worked is La Playa (Center for Orientation and Services) in Puerto Rico. This project had a corps of 10 full-time advocates who built personal relationships linking people with a civic center and those who could provide help. It attempted to change adults' attitudes in order to alter juveniles' behavior. In a period of about seven years, the number of "adjudicated" delinquents (those processed through the courts) dropped 85 percent.[29]

Community mobilization in the fight against crime has assumed diverse forms. For one, there is a new vigilantism by citizens responding to what they see as ineffectiveness on the part of the police. In Newark, New Jersey, for example, there are 425 members of Anthony Imperiale's North Ward Citizens' Committee who patrol the streets in radio-equipped cars.[30] In New York City, there are the Guardian Angels, who patrol the subways in an attempt to deter crime. A second form of mobilization is volunteers who devote time and effort to criminal justice agencies, especially to court-sponsored programs offering services to probationers and parolees. One estimate is that there are now more than 200,000 volunteers in about 2000 court systems throughout the United States.[31]

In its most general sense, organizing communities to fight against crime can be an important part of neighborhood redevelopment. Concern about crime may well be an important factor in the new citizens' movement which has led to the formation of a variety of community and neighborhood groups.[32] At the same time, there is plausibility in the statement of Carol Bellamy, president of New York's City Council:

> Crime prevention is not having a police officer in front of everyone's door. It's having an alert, informed citizen in each house and apartment.[33]

A Guardian Angel, on patrol, answers a subway rider's question. (UPI)

In short, neighborhood redevelopment and citizens' awareness of crime may well go hand in hand.

Population and Demographic Factors

In considering the social context of crime, we saw that a number of population and demographic factors are related to patterns of crime. Person-to-person violent crimes are disproportionately committed by those 18 to 21 years old, and person-to-person property crimes by those between ages 14 and 17. Both forms of person-to-person crime also are considerably higher in urban than in rural areas. Larceny is more likely than the other index crimes to be committed by females. Corporate crimes are related to organizational difficulties in meeting profit goals. Crimes against organizations tend to be greater for firms with more employees. Finally, organized crime stands out as a natural arena for new immigrant groups as they try to move upward rapidly in American society.

In that patterns of crime are associated with these factors, crime rates can be expected to increase or decrease as the factors change. Indeed, in examining these factors, we saw that increases in person-to-person crimes are related to increases in youthful and urban populations; that larceny increases as more females become part of the labor force; that corporate crimes increase as large, impersonal corporations, competitively pursuing profits, play a leading role in the economy; that crimes against corporations increase as the numbers of employees increases; and that organized crime has thrived with the continual influx of new immigrant groups.

In considering the possibilities for criminal justice today, the questions are (1) how far these trends can be projected into the future and (2) whether any of them can be controlled.

Concerning the first question, it seems possible that larceny will continue to increase for the forseeable future as female roles continue to change; but, at the same time, that urbanization is levelling off (if only because so many people are already living in cities) and that the youthful population will show substantial declines in the mid-1980s (in particular, the age group 14–24 should decline by about 3 million between 1977 and 1984). A few sociologists—such as Jackson Toby—have made this projection the basis of the optimistic claim that the crime rate in 1984 will "almost certainly be lower than it is today."[34]

It is provocative to examine the possibilities of attempting to control some of the trends that are related to crime. Comparing the Japanese experience and the American experience, Pepinsky is led to the conclusion that rates of reported crime could be reduced if citizens could learn how to restrain themselves from changing families, jobs, and residences; in short, if people would substantially reduce their mobility rates. To facilitate this, the government should become involved:

> . . . Measures that encourage people to stay together in the same families, jobs, and neighborhoods might be encouraged while measures that facilitate mobility might be abandoned.[35]

Such measures could be expected to create "an increased commitment to ongoing, supportive relationships."[36] Hence, more people would play roles that tend to prevent crime.

Another possibility would be to use immigration policy to control crime by restricting or containing the flow of new immigrant groups into American society. Such policies are followed by European societies, such as Germany and Switzerland, which admit foreign workers but sharply define their alien status in the society. Many of these workers are simply forced to leave when their work permits expire or when their services are no longer needed. The United States, by contrast, has a comparatively open immigration policy with weak control over the entry of illegal aliens.

In projecting trends and assessing the possibilities of controlling them through deliberate governmental policy, a few cautions are in order. One is that any single trend is not the only factor which operates to influence crime. Indeed, if we look at only the trends mentioned above, we can see that crime rates may be pushed upward by the changing role of women at the same time as they are pushed downward by the drop in numbers of teenagers and young adults. Moreover, the trends mentioned here may not coincide with other changes on the social scene— for example, changes in community awareness of crime. A second caution is that the governmental policies discussed here involve trade-offs with other social values. Encouraging people to stay together may violate traditional freedoms or liberties valued by many Americans. Curtailing immigration would mark the end of the United States as one of the world's distinctly open societies. In other words, to fight crime in this manner, choices have to be made. The question is whether the urgency of the problem should lead us to sacrifice deeply held values.

Targets, Opportunities, and Other Conditions

Making targets of crime more secure, reducing opportunities for crime, and changing conditions under which crime can occur are perhaps the most immediate and direct approaches to dealing with crime. Such approaches emphasize prevention rather than deterrence or treatment; they attempt to reform the environment rather than people. These approaches have been advanced by thinkers from a variety of disciplines such as biological engineering, physiological and environmental psychology, urban design and planning, operations research, and systems analysis.[37]

Part of the emphasis here is on anticrime devices: locks, alarms, security systems, etc. But there is also emphasis on redesigning urban environments to make them more crime-free; on repackaging products to make them more difficult to steal; on limiting the availability of handguns to make violent crime more difficult to commit; and on restructuring markets to deal with organized crime. In all this, "target hardening" is a key term; and the notion that certain situations are crime-producing is an important concept. Let's take a look at some of the specifics.

Officers of Atlanta's Crime Prevention Bureau travel to city neighborhoods to demonstrate and explain anticrime devices and tactics. (TONY O'BRIEN/ TRICORN)

The importance of "hardware"—anticrime devices—has been stressed by official government sources. As the National Advisory Commission on Criminal Justice Standards and Goals commented:

> Of all the things a citizen or a community can do to reduce crime, the most immediate and most direct approach is to eliminate obvious opportunities for criminals. Locked cars, well-lighted streets, alarm systems, and properly designed and secure housing make crime, particularly acquisitive crimes such as larceny, burglary, auto theft, and robbery, more difficult to commit.[38]

Indeed, the possibilities of anticrime "hardware" are endless. One might go on to cite house telephones and closed-circuit televisions for apartment buildings; electronic sensors and alarm systems tied into police stations for buildings and homes; television scanners and electronic listening devices for stores and shopping centers; and burglar alarms on automobiles.[39] Anticrime gadgetry appears more than able to keep up with the pace of technological development. All this can be regarded as "target hardening," i.e., making targets less readily accessible to would-be offenders.

Changing the conditions for crime could focus on the interplay between physical sites and social behavior. Development of community feeling is fostered or hindered by architectural design. As Jane Jacobs noted in her classic work on American cities, safe city streets are possible only when they clearly separate public and private space and when they are full of people who have watchful eyes. When deserted, they become scenes for crime; the back alley is the classic image.[40]

Newman continues in the spirit of Jacobs when he outlines his prescription for an architectural design that would inhibit crimes:

> By grouping dwelling units to reinforce associations of mutual benefit; by delineating paths of movement; by defining areas of activity for particular users through their juxtaposition with internal living areas; and by providing for natural opportunities for visual surveillance, architects can create a clear understanding of the function of a space, and who its users are and ought to be. This, in turn, can lead residents of all income levels to adopt extremely potent territorial attitudes and policing measures, which act as strong deterrents to potential criminals.[41]

It has been shown that ignoring Newman's prescription can be perilous. One case in point is the Pruitt-Igoe public housing project in St. Louis, Missouri. Pruitt-Igoe was built in 1955. It had over 2700 apartments in 33 buildings, 11 stories tall. Its high-rise elevator apartments fostered isolation and led to constant vandalism, high vacancy rates, and discontent about living in the project. So great were these problems that the project was demolished in 1973.[42]

One evaluation of a field application of Jacobs's and Newman's principles reported extremely positive results. The field application took place in the Asylum Hill neighborhood of Hartford, Connecticut, a once choice area that was beginning to show signs of decline and was plagued by crime, especially burglary and robbery. The field application involved: (1) Data collection. (2) Crime-prevention efforts by an existing citizens' organization and two newly founded groups (including block watch parties, cleanup activities, and an Operation Identification program to mark residents' valuables). (3) Community redesign that included closing off some streets to reduce through traffic and rerouting traffic to perimeter roads; encouraging residents to increase their use of yards, sidewalks, and parks; and restoring the residential character of the neighborhood. Among the findings of the evaluation were the following:

Burglary rates dropped 42 percent from 1976 to 1977.

Street robbery and purse snatching dropped 27.5 percent.

Victimization surveys also showed similar reductions in residents' fears of burglary and robbery.

No evidence of displacement of burglaries from North Asylum Hill to adjacent areas was found, but some displacement of robberies may have occurred.

A significant number of residents said they walked more frequently in the neighborhood in 1977 than in 1976. Their daily walks increased above 15 percent.[43]

Making targets more secure, reducing opportunities, and changing the conditions for crime are also applicable to types of crime other than those associated with neighborhoods. Anticrime gadgetry has become an important part of retail merchandising today. The easily stolen cassette tape has been packaged in a cardboard container that is three times its size. Bolts are put into articles of clothing so that they cannot be slipped on and taken out of stores. Floor samples of furniture and electronics goods are chained down. The widespread use of such devices reflects the assumption that anticrime gadgetry reduces the opportunity for shoplifting at less cost than prosecuting offenders, even though the shopping public may be somewhat inconvenienced.

Motor vehicle theft also provides an interesting example of a costly crime for which targets can be "hardened" and opportunities for theft reduced. It appears that design can make a difference. In 1957, when the Chevrolet division of General Motors discontinued stamping identification numbers on engines, police sources noted a surprising jump in thefts of Chevrolets. When the stamping was resumed, the rate of thefts declined. Open-position ignitions, in which automobiles could be left running without keys, made automobiles especially vulnerable to theft. Rates of theft declined when these types of ignitions were discontinued. More recently, when the Ford Motor Company upgraded ignition column locks, there was a 25 percent drop in the rate of thefts of Ford passenger cars between 1975 and 1977. Given such experiences, Andrew Karmen would put the onus for vehicle theft on corporations and would require

criminal penalties and stiff fines for companies and their officers who knowingly market cars that are easy to steal; and recalls to correct security defects at the companies' expense. It is much more practical to seek to control the actions of a small number of top executives . . . than to try to curb the activities of thousands of thieves and fences, and millions of sometimes careless, usually cautious motorists.[44]

Another approach to reducing the opportunity for violent crime would be to control handguns. Given the number of murders in which guns are involved and the high rate of murders committed with guns in the United States in comparison

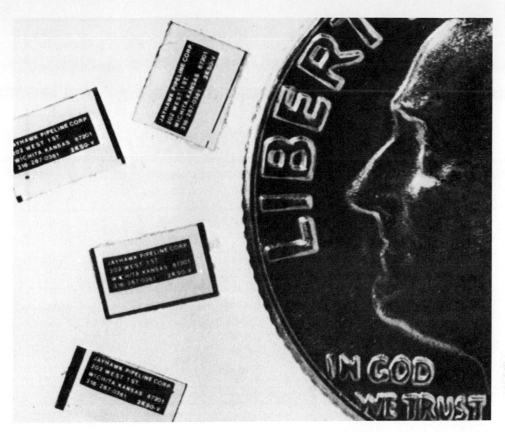

A novel approach to securing property; microdots far smaller than a dime are
placed by the thousands in crude oil in an effort to catch oil thieves. (WIDE
WORLD PHOTOS)

with other countries, it seems reasonable to propose some type of restriction on
firearms or accountability concerning firearms, especially handguns. This idea
was advanced by the National Commission on the Causes and Prevention of
Violence and is often advocated by journalists. (E.g., see Box 23, pages 497–498.)
However, many people believe that gun control flies in the face of the constitutional right of citizens to bear arms; and it is opposed by many organized interest
groups. Some scholars have also raised serious questions concerning the validity
of the arguments for gun control.[45]

An entirely different application of the general idea of changing the conditions under which crime operates is Thomas C. Schelling's approach to organized
crime. Schelling argues that the national policy of indicting and trying organized
crime figures might better be changed to a policy of regulating, accommodating,
and restructuring markets and business conditions. Recognizing that crime
syndicates are extortionate monopolies, Schelling concludes that we should deal
with organized crime through "legal arrangements that make it a punishable
offense to pay tribute" or in some cases through "the deliberate stimulation of
competing enterprises."[46]

Officer: "I hate to see kids play with guns." (JILL FREEDMAN/ARCHIVE)

Preventing crime through changes in environmental design sounds far more reasonable than the uncertain course of deterring crime through law or changing offenders through rehabilitation. However, it must be remembered that there is no cure-all for crime, and that—as we saw with population and demographic approaches—other factors also influence crime. It should also be added that an approach based on targets, opportunities, and conditions of crime is most appropriate for the occasional or amateur offender, who is more likely to be influenced by the situation; the dedicated, professional offender may well find ways of committing crime regardless of "crime-free" environmental design. While the Hartford study raises expectations, follow-up studies and further evaluative assessments are necessary before this avenue can become a dominant approach to the problem of crime.

Making potential targets less vulnerable, reducing opportunities for crime, and changing conditions of crime will also be problematic if crime is caused or fostered by uniquely American values and lifestyles. Social relationships are less tangible than targets, opportunities, and conditions; but no attempt to reform criminal justice can ignore the quality of social relationships. Let us now turn to this final aspect of the social context. After we have considered it, we will be able to undertake a general assessment of all the possibilities for improving criminal justice.

You, Me and Handguns

By Tom Wicker

On the night of Dec. 8, in New York City, John Lennon was killed by four shots fired from a .38-caliber concealable handgun legally purchased in Hawaii for $169.

That was three nights after Dr. Michael Halberstam was killed in Washington, D.C., by two shots in the chest from a .32-caliber handgun.

Police have charged an apparently mentally disturbed young man with shooting Mr. Lennon. A skilled professional thief, interrupted during a burglary of Dr. Halberstam's house, has been charged with his shooting.

Mr. Lennon was a musician of world renown. Dr. Halberstam was well known in Washington medical and literary circles. Thus, their deaths caused much comment in the press.

Except for that, nothing about either murder was unusual. Such violent and unexpected deaths happen all the time. They are almost always caused by handguns, sometimes in the hands of the unstable, sometimes in the hands of the criminal, sometimes in the hands of people like you and me.

Someone is murdered with a handgun in the United States every 50 minutes; it could be you or me, or someone we love, or know. Look at your watch; by 24 hours from the time indicated, 29 persons will have been killed with handguns.

By the end of October, the toll of dead this year from handgun bullets had risen to 6,660. In 1979, handgun fire caused 10,728 American deaths.

This is not a new problem, although the casualties may have increased. During the seven peak years of the war in Vietnam, for example, 40,000 Americans were killed in action; during the same years, 50,000 Americans were killed with handguns in the nation's streets, barrooms, households and public places.

But death is just the most grievous consequence of handgun use. Next year, about 250,000 Americans will be victimized in some way—robbed, raped, injured as well as murdered—by other Americans wielding handguns. That's as if everyone in a city the size of Sacramento, Calif., were to become a handgun victim.

In 1978, in New York City alone, 23,000 robberies were committed at the point of a handgun. Handgun killings in the city totaled 882. Police that year confiscated 9,100 handguns—a useful effort but a minuscule result.

Minuscule, because no one should be in doubt about what causes this record of carnage, violence and crime. The reason is that, for anyone who wants one, too many handguns are too easy to obtain—a fact which no amount of sophistry and self-delusion and gun-lobby propaganda can refute.

When Peter L. Zimroth, chief assistant district attorney for Manhattan, was asked by Edward A. Gargan of The New York Times how two boys who had been arrested had obtained handguns, he made the essential point:

"If you take seriously the estimate that there are one to two million guns in the city, the question is how a kid can't get a gun."

That estimate is to be taken seriously indeed. It may be conservative. Nationally, 55 million handguns are believed to be in circulation. Every year, about 2.5 million more join the total—nearly 2 million manufactured in this country, several hundred thousand imported. Handgun Control of Washington, D.C., estimates 100 million handguns will be in circulation in the U.S. by the end of the century.

Many of these handguns are easily obtainable through the 175,000 dealers now licensed by the Federal Government. In many states, notably in the South, no more than a driver's license is required for identification of the buyer, and the license need not even be checked for authenticity.

Other handguns by the thousands are little more difficult to acquire through the illegal traffic that flourishes in every city. Thousands of guns are also stolen every year, obviously not by persons with a legitimate need. There are few such people anyway; only 28,000 have ever obtained a handgun license from the New York City police.

John Lennon and Michael Halberstam are dead primarily because of the easy availability of handguns. So are thousands of other Americans this year, last year, every year. And those statements cannot be refuted by the mere argument that some would still have died if handguns were tightly controlled, or that some would have been killed even if all handguns were confiscated. Of course some would have been; but

Continued on next page.

most who were killed by handguns would be alive if Americans were willing to see these weapons adequately controlled or confiscated.

But the least disputable truth of American politics is that neither of those things is going to be done. Even though the man who buys a handgun "to protect my family" is demonstrably more likely to shoot his wife, or the newspaper delivery boy, or a barroom buddy, or himself in the foot, than a burglar or a rapist; even though the "legitimate" demand of the American people for handguns makes it impossible to shut off the illegal supply to criminals and madmen; even so, the truth is that that perverted demand from you and me is so great that politicians cannot stand against it.

Nor will they ever, while we persist in it.

SOURCE:

New York Times, December 12, 1980.

Quality of Social Relationships: Values and Lifestyles

The discussions of the major types of crime in American society repeatedly pointed to the social values which underlie various aspects of crime. In particular, we looked at subcultures of violence; casual attitudes toward property; individualism; maximization of profits; competition; the "rip-off" mentality; widespread public acceptance of many forms of gambling, sexual deviance, and substance abuse; individual rights; impersonality in business; the American emphasis on success; and public sensibility concerning corruption. We also took a look at considerations having to do with lifestyle: the shift of routine activities away from the home; minimization of interaction between customers and salesclerks and between employers and employees; acceptance of deviant subcultures; crime as an avenue of mobility; and the broadened scope of governmental activity. In dealing with values and lifestyle, we were in effect dealing with the quality of social relationships in American society.

In thinking about the quality of social relationships, a few words of caution are in order. First of all, clear-cut recommendations are difficult to formulate. Much criminological analysis has been oriented toward describing, analyzing, and criticizing things as they *are* rather than developing models of what they *could be*. Second, some of the approaches developed out of the sociological school have met with modest success. However, since we are now looking for new possibilities for criminal justice, it is important to examine relationships between people and groups in American society. Such an examination can of course take several directions; of these, two seem to stand out as particularly important for future efforts: (1) developing personal intimacy and (2) moving toward a just and fair society.

Developing personal intimacy

Thinking about the quality of social relationships in relation to crime in American society, one must begin with the increase in impersonality and the decrease in intimacy that typify the times in which we live. We have seen the decline of community in the shift of routine activities away from the home—a shift which has helped to create the environment of the two major forms of person-to-person crimes. We have also seen the social distancing between offenders and victims that facilitates corporate crime as well as crimes against corporations. Finally, we have seen how organized crime exploits scattered, unorganized consumers and how it too thrives on the impersonal nature of business transactions.

With regard to criminal justice, increased impersonality and decreased intimacy are seen in the kinds of expectations that people hold for the criminal justice system. As was noted in Chapter 16, people expect the police to deal with relatively minor matters involving their families and their neighbors. At the level of the courts, the VERA study found courtrooms flooded with cases best described as "the explosive spillover from ruptured personal relations among neighbors, friends and former spouses."[47] (See Chapter 17.)

From this perspective, the possibilities for a new criminal justice would revolve around learning how to work constructively with relationships that may be problematic at times.

> Progress in crime control implies that people who regularly live and work together wrong one another less and help and support one another more. It implies that family, neighbors, and co-workers are more successful in preventing and defending against attack and predation by outsiders.[48]

Desirable though all this may sound, if criminal justice were to develop along these lines, it would also mean less geographical and social mobility, some restrictions of "freedoms" such as the right to divorce, less privacy among intimates, and greater anonymity among strangers.[49]

Moving toward a just and fair society

We can also pursue criminal justice through social justice. To do this, the criminal law must be applied equally to all people—rich and poor, majority and minority. In part, this is a matter of social definition: crimes committed by the upper and middle classes need to be specified as sharply as crimes of the poor. In part, it is also a matter of administration of the law: money, power, and influence should be equally available to all who need to defend themselves against legal charges. No longer can we afford a criminal justice system in which the poor, the minorities, and the underprivileged find themselves in prison while the wealthier and more privileged members of society go completely free, even though they commit crimes of equal or greater magnitude.

The issue of social injustice is particularly apparent when we consider corporate crime and crimes against organizations. As we saw in Chapter 11, corporate criminal acts involve great injury and cost. As we saw in Chapter 12, thefts committed by employees against organizations involve far greater amounts of money than person-to-person thefts. Both of these types of crime are likely to involve offenders who are middle-age, white, and middle- or upper-class; and neither type receives as much official attention as person-to-person property crimes. Applying the criminal law equally to all people would entail far more systematic efforts to police, to convict, and to punish those who are guilty of corporate crime and crimes against corporations.

More fundamentally, true or complete criminal justice is impossible without social justice. However, social justice—an equality of condition among people—is a concept which can be defined in several ways. Marx's vision of a just society in which the state with its extensive control apparatus would "wither away" has dominated much social thought. Later Marxist-oriented criminologists have envisioned a socialistic society in which criminal justice is replaced by popular justice.[50] E. F. Schumacher proposes to achieve social justice by creating small, decentralized, modestly capitalized technologies which will permit people to become directly involved in their work—thus avoiding or reducing alienation, excessive concentration of wealth, greed, and envy and enhancing values and human creativity.[51] Friedman and Friedman have a conservative vision of social justice in terms of greater freedom for the individual and more limited government.[52]

At first sight, the attempt to achieve criminal justice through social justice may appear impractical, perhaps even utopian. If we consider it further, however, we are confronted with the persistent question whether criminal justice is possible in a society without social justice. The particular form of social justice may not make much difference; but when there is no social justice, there is no criminal justice. If conditions are unjust—if people do not feel that they have a fair chance—there is less incentive to obey the law or to accept punishment for disobedience as legitimate.

SUMMARY

This chapter has explored a variety of possibilities for dealing with the problems of criminal justice. We can redefine criminal acts. We can attempt to find workable methods of treatment for offenders who are processed through the criminal justice system. We can seek to involve the victim. Finally, we can endeavor to change the social context of crime through community action; through control over population and demographic trends; through "hardening" targets, reducing opportunities, or changing conditions of crime; and through improving the quality of social relationships, whether by developing personal intimacy or by moving toward a just and fair society. There is no shortage of possibilities.

It is true that some possibilities would be more difficult to implement than others. Some involve greater cost. Some would invoke public opposition. Some, such as manipulating population and demographic factors and developing personal intimacy, involve the ambitious attempt to alter long-standing social trends. Then too, it should be said that there is no single possibility that can be expected to produce clear, instantaneous results; criminological theory and practice do not permit such dogmatism. Many more systematic studies and evaluative assessments of the various alternatives are needed. Finally, it should be mentioned that some of the possibilities—e.g., bringing communities together and moving toward a just and fair society—may well be worthwhile social goals regardless of their implications for criminal justice.

Nevertheless, the possibilities presented here show that there are approaches to criminal justice which could substantially reduce not only the size of the criminal justice establishment and its cost ($25 billion per year), but also the millions of victimizations (both reported and unreported), the millions of people who are arrested, the million or so court cases that are processed, and the hundreds of thousands of prison or jail sentences that are served each year. For the future, let us hope that the constructive ingenuity of Americans can be applied to finding ways to reduce rather than increase these numbers. Let us hope that an honest appraisal of the considerable costs and human failures of present criminal justice policies will persuade Americans that new approaches to our complex and subtle problem of crime need to be developed, implemented, and assessed. The future of criminal justice is in our hands.

NOTES

[1] Timothy J. Flanagan, David J. van Alstyne, and Michael R. Gottfredson, eds., *Sourcebook of Criminal Justice Statistics—1981*, U.S. Department of Justice, Bureau of Justice Statistics, Government Printing Office, Washington, D.C., 1982, sec. 1.

[2] Donald Black, *The Behavior of Law*, Academic Press, New York, 1976.

[3] Larry L. Tifft, "The Coming Redefinitions of Crime: An Anarchist Perspective," *Social Problems*, vol. 26, no. 4, April 1979, pp. 392–402.

[4] Leslie T. Wilkins, *Social Deviance*, Prentice-Hall, Englewood Cliffs, N.J., 1965, pp. 87–94.

[5] Milton Friedman and Rose Friedman, *Free to Choose: A Personal Statement*, Harcourt Brace Jovanovich, New York, 1980.

[6] Jerome H. Skolnick and John Dombrink, "The Legalization of Deviance," *Criminology*, vol. 16, no. 2, 1978, pp. 193–208; quotation on p. 194.

[7] Ibid.

[8] John Stuart Mill, *On Liberty*; reprinted in Mary Warnock, *John Stuart Mill: Utilitarianism, Liberty, Essay on Bentham*, World, Cleveland, Ohio, 1962, p. 135. For a contemporary discussion, see: Edwin M. Schur and Hugo A. Bedau, *Victimless Crimes: Two Sides of a Controversy*, Prentice-Hall, Englewood Cliffs, N.J., 1974, especially pp. 76–87.

[9] Jan Gorecki, *A Theory of Criminal Justice*, Columbia University Press, New York, 1979, p. xiii.

[10] Ibid., p. 133.

[11] F. Lovell Bixby and Lloyd W. McCorkle, "Guided Group Interaction in Correctional Work," *American Sociological Review*, vol. 16, August 1951, pp. 45–59. See also: Howard E. Freeman and H. Ashley Weeks, "Analysis of a Treatment Program of Delinquent Boys," *American Journal of Sociology*, vol. 62, July 1956, pp. 56–61.

[12] For an evaluation of the Provo experiment, see: LaMar T. Empey and Jerome Rabow, "The Provo Experiment in Delinquency Rehabilitation," *American Sociological Review*, vol. 26, October 1961, pp. 679–696.

[13] For a personal account, see: William Overend, "Ex-Con a Success as Rehabilitator," in Barry J. Wishart and Louis C. Reichman, eds., *Modern Sociological Issues*, 2d ed., Macmillan, New York, 1979, pp. 158–166.

[14] Joseph E. Scott, *Ex-Offenders as Parole Officers: The Parole Officer Aide Program in Ohio*, Heath, Lexington, Mass., 1975.

[15] Thomas O. Murton, *The Dilemma of Prison Reform*, Holt, Rinehart and Winston, New York, 1976, p. 221.

[16] Norval Morris, *The Future of Imprisonment*, University of Chicago Press, Chicago, Ill., 1974.

[17] See: Peter H. Rossi, Richard A. Berk, and Kenneth J. Lenihan, *Money, Work, and Crime: Experimental Evidence*, Academic Press, New York, 1980; quotation on p. 19. See also: Richard A. Berk, Kenneth J. Lenihan, and Peter H. Rossi, "Crime and Poverty: Some Experimental Evidence From Ex-Offenders," *American Sociological Review*, vol. 45, October 1980, pp. 766–786.

[18] For a review of community corrections, see: John Irwin, *Prisons in Turmoil*, Little, Brown, Boston, Mass., 1980, chap. 6; Mary A. Toborg et al., *The Transition from Prison to Employment: An Assessment of Community-Based Assistance Programs*, National Institute of Law Enforcement and Criminal Justice, Law Enforcement Assistance Administration, Washington, D.C., 1978; and Hassim M. Solomon, *Community Corrections*, Holbrook, Boston, Mass., 1976.

[19] See: Irwin, *Prisons in Turmoil*, pp. 223–230.

[20] Morris, *The Future of Imprisonment*.

[21] Herbert Edelhertz and Gilbert Geis, *Public Compensation to Victims of Crime*, Praeger, New York, 1974, p. 290.

[22] Stephen Schafer, "The Proper Role of a Victim-Compensation System," *Crime and Delinquency*, vol. 21, no. 1, January 1975, pp. 45–49.

[23] See: James Brooks, "How Well Are Criminal Injury Compensation Programs Performing," *Crime and Delinquency*, vol. 21, no. 1, January 1975, pp. 50–56. See also: Roger E. Meiners, *Victim Compensation: Economic, Legal, and Political Aspects*, Lexington Books, Lexington, Mass., 1978.

[24] Benedict S. Alper and Lawrence T. Nichols, *Doing Justice by the Community*, Heath (Lexington Books), Lexington, Mass., 1981.

[25] On the Japanese system, see: David H. Bayley, *Forces of Order: Police Behavior in Japan and the United States*, University of California Press, Berkeley, 1976.

[26] Oscar Newman, *Defensible Space*, Collier, New York, 1973.

[27] Richard Maxwell Brown, "The American Vigilante Tradition," in Hugh Davis Graham and Ted Robert Gurr, eds., *Violence in America: Historical and Comparative Perspectives*, rev. ed., Sage, Beverly Hills, Calif., 1979, pp. 153–185.

[28] John Conyers, Jr., "Our Sickly Efforts to Cut the Crime Rate," *Los Angeles Times*, January 5, 1977.

[29] Charles E. Silberman, *Criminal Violence, Criminal Justice*, Random House, New York, 1978, chap. 11.

[30] Laurin A. Wollan, Jr., "Coping with Crime in Tomorrow's Society," *Futurist*, June 1976.

[31] Thomas J. Cook and Frank P. Scioli, Jr., "Public Participation in the Criminal Justice System: Volunteers in Police, Courts, and Correctional Agencies," in John A. Gardiner and Michael A. Mulkey, eds., *Crime and Criminal Justice: Issues in Policy Analysis,* Heath, Lexington, Mass., 1975, pp. 107–112.

[32] See: Harry C. Boyte, *The Backyard Revolution: Understanding the New Citizen Movement*, Temple University Press, Philadelphia, Pa., 1980; and Anthony Sorrentino, *Organizing against Crime: Redeveloping the Neighborhood*, Human Sciences Press, New York, 1977.

[33] Quoted in: *Family Circle*, September 22, 1981.

[34] Jackson Toby, "A Prospect of Less Crime in the 1980s," *New York Times*, October 26, 1977.

[35] Harold E. Pepinsky, *Crime Control Strategies: An Introduction to the Study of Crime*, Oxford University Press, New York, 1980, p. 106.

[36] Ibid., p. 106.

[37] Clarence Ray Jeffery, "The Historical Development of Criminology," in Hermann Mannheim, ed., *Pioneers in Criminology*, 2d ed., Patterson Smith, Montclair, N.J., 1972, especially pp. 497–498.

[38] National Advisory Commission on Criminal Justice Standards and Goals, *A National Strategy to Reduce Crime*, Avon, New York, 1975, p. xiii.

[39] Wollan, "Coping with Crime in Tomorrow's Society."

[40] Jane Jacobs, *The Death and Life of Great American Cities*, Random House, New York, 1961.

[41] Newman, *Defensible Space*, pp. 3–4.

[42] Lee Rainwater, "Fear and the House-as-Haven in the Lower Class," *Journal of the American Institute of Planners*, vol. 32, January 1966, pp. 23–37.

[43] On the field application and its evaluation, see: National Institute of Law Enforcement and Criminal Justice, Law Enforcement Assistance Administration, *Research Bulletin,* June 1979.

[44] Andrew A. Karmen, "Auto Theft and Corporate Irresponsibility," *Contemporary Crises*, vol. 5, 1981, pp. 63–81; quotation on p. 77. See also: Andrew A. Karmen, "Victim Facilitation: The Case of Automobile Theft," *Victimology*, vol. 4, 1979, 361–370.

[45] James D. Wright, "The Recent Weapons Trend and the Putative 'Need' For Gun Control," paper read at American Sociological Association meetings, 1980; used by permission.

[46] Thomas C. Schelling, "Economic Analysis and Organized Crime," in *Task Force Report on Organized Crime*, President's Commission on Law Enforcement and Administration of Justice, Government Printing Office, Washington, D.C., 1967.

[47] Vera Institute of Justice (VERA), *Felony Arrests: Their Prosecution and Disposition in New York City's Courts*, rev. ed., Longman and Vera Institute of Justice, 1981, p. 135.

[48] Pepinsky, *Crime Control Strategies*, p. 153.

[49] For a complete discussion, see: ibid., pp. 153f.

[50] Richard Quinney, *Class, State, and Crime: On the Theory and Practice of Criminal Justice*, McKay, New York, 1977.

[51] E. F. Schumacher, *Small Is Beautiful: Economics As If People Mattered*, Harper and Row, New York, 1973.

[52] Friedman and Friedman, *Free to Choose.*

Acknowledgments

THE BUSINESS OF ORGANIZED CRIME: A COSA NOSTRA FAMILY, by Annelise Graebner Anderson, with the permission of the publishers, Hoover Institution Press. Copyright 1979 by the Board of Trustees of the Leland Stanford Junior University.

"Gambling," by Linda Bailey and Elaine Knapp, *State Government News*, 20 (September 1977).

"Peer Group Support for Police Occupational Deviance," by Thomas Barker, *Criminology*, vol. 15, with permission of Sage Publications Inc.

"Typologies of Criminal Behavior," by Abraham S. Blumberg, in CURRENT PERSPECTIVES ON CRIMINAL BEHAVIOR, 2d ed., edited by Abraham S. Blumberg (New York: Alfred A. Knopf, 1981).

"One Piece at a Time," recorded by Johnny Cash and the Tennessee 3. Copyright 1976 Tree Publishing Co., Inc., 8 Music Square, West, Nashville, TN. International Copyright Secured. All Rights Reserved. Used by permission of the Publisher.

"Criminology: Criminal Statistics in the United States," by Roland Chilton, *The Journal of Criminal Law and Criminology*, 71, 1 (1980). Permission granted by Northwestern University.

"Our Sickly Efforts to Cut the Crime Rate," by John Conyers, Jr., *Los Angeles Times*, January 5, 1977.

CRIMINAL VIOLENCE, by Lynn A. Curtis (Lexington, Mass.: Lexington Books, D.C. Heath and Co.). Copyright 1974, D.C. Heath and Company.

DELINQUENCY AND DROPOUT, by Delbert S. Elliott and Harwin L. Voss (Lexington, Mass.: Lexington Books, D.C. Heath and Co.). Copyright 1974, D.C. Heath and Co.

Feiffer cartoon: *Village Voice*, April 6, 1972. Reprinted with permission from Universal Press Syndicate.

MANAGEMENT'S ROLE IN LOSS PREVENTION, by Charles Hemphill. Copyright 1976 by AMACOM, a division of American Management Associations, New York. All rights reserved.

CAUSES OF DELINQUENCY, by Travis Hirschi (Berkeley and Los Angeles: University of California Press, 1969). Reprinted by permission of the University of California Press.

THE AMERICAN CRIMINAL: AN ANTHROPOLOGICAL STUDY—THE NATIVE WHITE CRIMINAL OF NATIVE PARENTAGE, by Ernest Albert Hooton. Harvard University Press, 1939.

BLUE-COLLAR THEFT: CONCEPTIONS OF PROPERTY, ATTITUDES TOWARD PILFERING, AND WORK GROUP NORMS IN A MODERN INDUSTRIAL PLANT, by Donald N.M. Horning,

Indexes

Name Index

Adelson, Daniel, 47n.
Adler, Alfred, 112
Adler, Freda, 242n., 287, 298n.
Adler, Patricia A., 298n.
Adler, Peter, 298n.
Ageton, Suzanne, 228, 243n.
Air Transportation Association, 265
Akers, Ronald L., 147n.
Albini, Joseph I., 338, 355n., 356n.
Albonetti, Celesta, 449n.
Alix, Ernest Kahlar, 215n.
Allen, Francis A., 119, 378n.
Allen, Harry E., 121n., 476n.
Alper, Benedict S., 501n.
Alschuler, Albert W., 432, 448n.
Altheide, David L., 298n., 299n.
Altheide, Duane A., 298n.
Alwin, Duana F., 449n.
American Friends Service Committee, 85, 95n.,
    476n., 477n.
American Law Institute, 306
American Management Association, 271,
    272n.
American Psychiatric Association, 116, 120n.
Amir, Menachem, 207, 215n.
Anderson, Annelise Graebner, 342, 346, 356n.
Antunes, George, 396, 416n.
Arbaleda-Florez, J., 298n.
Archer, Dane, 211, 217n.
Astor, Saul D., 297n., 298n., 299n.
Athens, Lonnie H., 142, 148n.
Atkinson, Jeff, 356n.
Auger, Michael, 329n.
Austin, W. T., 477n.

Bachman, Jerald G., 310n., 328n.
Bahn, Charles, 448n.
Bahr, Howard M., 328n.
Bailey, Linda, 313n.

Bailey, William C., 94n.
Baker, Donald I., 449n.
Bakunin, Mikhail, 373
Baldwin, John, 172, 176n., 177n.
Ball, John C., 328n.
Barak, Gregg, 422, 447n.
Bard, Morton, 47n.
Barker, Thomas, 371n., 379n.
Barnes, Harry Elmer, 72, 93, 476n.
Barnett, Harold, 177n.
Barry, John Vincent, 476n.
Bayley, David H., 328n., 390, 415n., 416n., 417n., 487,
    501n.
Bazelon, Judge David, 448n.
Beattie, Ronald, 64n.
Beccaria, Cesare, 72–75, 92, 94n., 101, 483
Bechdolt, Burley V., Jr., 94n.
Becker, Howard S., 19n., 82, 88, 95n., 139–140,
    147n., 320, 329n.
Becker, Theodore L., 447n.
Beckett, Gerold I., 448n.
Bedau, Hugo Adam, 155, 157n., 306, 327n., 356n.,
    501n.
Beirne, Piers, 96n., 181n.
Bell, Daniel, 30, 46n., 47n., 351, 352, 355n., 356n.
Bell, Jimmy, 417n.
Bellamy, Carol, 489
Bendix, Reinhard, 146n.
Bennett, Lawrence A., 478n.
Bensman, Joseph, 297n., 299n.
Bentham, Jeremy, 50, 72–75, 92, 94n., 393
Bequai, August, 340, 356n.
Berk, Richard E., 47n., 88, 95n., 96n., 146n., 162,
    176n., 242n., 243n., 501n.
Berkman, Ronald, 477n.
Berle, Adolph A., 268n.
Berman, Daniel M., 267n.
Bernard, Thomas J., 95n., 119n., 176n.
Bernstein, Ilene Nagel, 440, 449n.
Biderman, Albert D., 64n.

Weber, Max, 27, 29, 47*n*.
Weeber, Stanley C., 378*n*.
Weeks, H. Ashley, 501*n*.
Weinreb, Lloyd L., 19*n*., 242*n*.
Weis, Joseph G., 65*n*., 215*n*.
Weissman, Harold H., 147*n*.
Wellford, Charles, 96*n*., 148*n*.
Westley, William, 403
Weyl, Nathaniel, 378*n*.
Wheeler, Stanton, 327*n*.
Whiteside, Thomas, 297*n*., 298*n*.
Wiatrowski, Michael D., 137, 147*n*.
Wicker, Tom, 497
Wickersham Commission, 343, 400, 416*n*., 417*n*.
Wilkins, Leslie T., 95*n*., 437, 448*n*., 502*n*.
Wilks, Judith, 452, 453, 475*n*., 476*n*.
Williams, Jay R., 47*n*., 65*n*.
Williams, Kristen M., 157*n*.
Wilner, Daniel, 452, 475*n*.
Wilson, James Q., 94*n*., 379*n*., 396, 399, 416*n*., 452, 476*n*.
Winick, Charles, 304, 327*n*., 328*n*.
Winslow, Robert W., 328*n*.
Winslow, Virginia, 328*n*.
Wishart, Barry J., 501*n*.

Witkin, Herman A., 110, 120*n*.
Wolfe, Nancy, 157*n*.
Wolfgang, Marvin E., 47*n*., 67*n*., 119*n*., 131, 145, 147*n*., 151, 155, 156, 157*n*., 189*n*., 198, 199, 207, 210, 215*n*., 216*n*., 227–229, 232, 233, 242*n*., 243*n*., 269*n*., 311, 328*n*.
Wollan, Laurin A., 502*n*.
Women's Christian Temperance Union, 88
Wright, James D., 217*n*., 502*n*.
Wright, Kevin N., 453, 476*n*.
Wyle, J. C., 65*n*., 242*n*.

Yeager, Matthew G., 171, 177*n*., 453, 476*n*.
Yeager, Peter C., 249, 268*n*., 269*n*.
Young, Jock, 77, 148*n*.

Zeisel, Hans, 447*n*.
Zeitlin, Laurence R., 298*n*., 299*n*.
Zeitlin, Maurice, 268*n*.
Zimbardo, Philip G., 466, 467*n*.
Zimring, Franklin E., 78
Zingraff, Matthew T., 441, 449*n*.

Durham rule, 8
Durkheim, Émile, 160–162

Ecological approach, 172
Ecological fallacy, 159, 172
Economic approaches, 166–168
Economy of deviance, 320
Ectomorph, 107
Electrodermal recovery rate, 110
Ellsberg, Daniel, 366
Embezzlement, 249, 271, 273, 280, 284, 287, 288, 293, 358
Emotional disturbance, 111
Employees, theft by, 271, 273–278, 283, 285–286, 292–295
Enclosure laws, 88, 125
Endomorph, 107
Environmental Protection Agency, 256
Escalation, 170
Espionage Act, 361
Ethnic succession, 348–349
Evolution, 101
Ex-offenders, rehabilitation by, 484
Extortion, 229, 346, 364

Fair Labor Standards Act, 263
Family feuds, 26, 37
Family offenses, 196
Family violence, 195
Fear of crime, 1
Federal Trade Commission, 252, 256
Feeblemindedness, 111
Felony murders, 188
Fencing of stolen property, 172, 221, 224, 226, 230, 238, 280, 281, 340, 381
Ferri, Enrico, 102–103
Flat-time sentences, 437
Food, Drug, and Cosmetic Act, 264
Food and Drug Administration, 256
Forcible rape (see Rape)
Forgery, 219, 224, 226, 229, 287
Fornication, 302, 305
Fraud, 271, 274–275, 277, 280, 282, 284, 287
Fraudulent securities, 255–256
Free will, 72, 76, 77, 102, 138, 139
Freud, Sigmund, 112

Gambling, 5, 23, 31, 90, 301, 302, 312–315, 317–318, 320, 323–324, 332, 339, 343, 345, 372
Gangs, 22, 133, 260, 333–334
Gangsters, 23, 42, 347, 353
Garofalo, Rafaele, 103–104
Genetic factors, 109
Genocide, 150
Goring, Charles, 104–105
Graffiti, 5

Graft, 371–372
Group interaction and struggle, 84–85
Guided group interaction, 484

Habitual antisocial deviant, 116
Handguns, 173, 211–212, 497–498
Harrisberg Seven, 352
Harrison Act, 72
Hatfield-Coy feud, 26
Healy, William, 112–113
Hijacking, 80, 346, 364
Historical approaches, 168–169
Homicide, 21, 26, 30, 38–39, 42, 54, 90, 151, 171, 186–190, 194, 196, 197, 203, 204, 205–208, 211, 214, 358, 364
Homosexuality, 302–305, 316–318
Hooton, Earnest, 106–107
Hoover, J. Edgar, 344
Horizontal mergers, 252
Human rights violations, 86

Illegal financial manipulations, 255
Illegal kickbacks, 247
Illegal price manipulations, 248, 264
Immigration, 23–24
Immigration and Nationality Act, 361
Imperialism, 86, 90
Incest, 90
Income maintenance, 485
Income tax violators, 80
Indeterminate sentence, 435–437, 452, 460
Index crime (See Person-to-person property crime; Person-to-person violent crime)
Industrial sabotage, 276, 278
Inequality of imprisonment, 468–469
Informal social controls, 80, 211, 294
Inherited criminal tendencies, 101
Inmate subculture, 464
Insanity, 99
Institute for Law and Social Research (INSLAW) study, 429–431
Intelligence, 113, 117–118
Intention, 7
Internal dynamics of prisons, 464–468
International Business Machines, 253–254
Interstitial areas, 163
Inventory shrinkage, 271

James, Jesse, 22
Johnson, Lyndon, 369
Jukes family, 108
Juristic person, 256–257
Justification by law, 7
Juvenile delinquency, 118
Juvenile justice, 170